AQUA EXPEDITIONS

A Global Travel Guide
For The
Scuba Diver and Snorkeler

Wendy Canning Church

Aqua Expeditions: Copyright © 1995, ISBN 0-9643711-0-3
All rights reserved.
No part of this book may be reproduced or used in any manner whatever, stored in a retrieval system, or transmitted in any form by means of electronic, mechanical, photocopyoing, recording, or in other ways, without written permission from the publisher except in the case of brief quotations embodied in critical articles and reviews.

Printed in Lewiston, Maine by Penmor Lithographers.
Cover design and inside world map by Joyce Huber.
Cover photo of Editor, Wendy Canning Church,
   Los Roques, Venezuela, by Humberto Nahim.
Back cover photo of Wendy Canning Church by Jim Kozmik.

All information in this book is subject to change without notice. We strongly recommend that you send a fax to Divers Exchange International at 617-227-8145 in advance to verify the information in this book before making final plans. The authors and publisher cannot be responsible for inaccurate or out of date information.

Dedication

With warm thanks I dedicate Aqua Expeditions, Volume I to each writer and photographer who gave so generously and freely of their time and talents to create this book.

All writers are members of Divers Exchange International (DEI) and have chosen a favorite destination to share.

When I decided to compile a Global Guide I sent out letters to members worldwide asking if they would like to join with me on this project. The only two requisites for their articles were that any facility they wrote about must uphold high safety standards and the lodging at that destination, whether five star or simple, must deliver what was promised.

We have not left destinations out intentionally, but rather this is the first in the series of guide books, Aqua Expeditions, Volume I.

I will continue to travel and bring my adventures to you. I invite other DEI members to contribute.

Aqua Expeditions was my idea but you would never hold this gift in your hand today unless it was for others. For this book is truly a gift, DEI members have shared their awe of the sea, its wonderment, enjoyment and adventure.

The sea gave unconditionally to them and they in turn have given unconditionally to you.

This is the truest meaning of friendship.

Wendy Canning Church

FORWARD

Both Divers Exchange International, Inc. and Aqua Expeditions, Inc. were founded on the principals of quality and safety. This cornerstone philosophy has gained us a worldwide reputation for integrity.

Our aim has always been to supply our members with the most recent and reliable diving and snorkeling information on their domestic or international destination. Our files are constantly being updated from both our members and our own traveling. This information is now available worldwide through Aqua Expeditions Vol. I, the first in a series.

Rather than write the entire guide myself, I decided to call upon our members throughout the world to contribute their thoughts and experiences on favorite dive or snorkel locations. The guide has been compiled from these articles, and those that I have written.

It is difficult for anyone to be familiar with every destination. We have covered not only the "hot spots" such as Grand Cayman, Bonaire and Australia, but also the "hideaways" with virgin diving, such as Minado and Mauritius. Also included is information on countries, for example, Scotland, Italy, Greece and Turkey, that offer a variety of diving and snorkeling experiences.

Because of its global coverage, we feel that Aqua Expeditions Vol. I will appeal not only to the traveling sport diver and snorkeler in North America, but to those who participate worldwide in perhaps this last frontier.

TABLE OF CONTENTS

Dedication iii
Forward iv

AFRICA AND OFF ISLANDS 1
Kenya East 1
Kenya West 5
Mozambique 7
   Pemba and Ibo Island 7
South Africa 12
   Aliwal Shoal 12
   Sodwana 19

INDIAN OCEAN 25
Maldives 25
Inhaca 28
Mauritius 32
   Reunion Island 37
   Rodrigues Island 41
Seychelles 47

AUSTRIA AND BAVARIA 52

AUSTRALIA 53

BAHAMAS 59
Nassau 59
Turks & Caicos 64

BERMUDA 69

CANADA 79
San Juan and Canadian Gulf Islands 79

CARIBBEAN 83
Anguilla 83
Antigua and Barbuda 87
Aruba 90
Barbados 92
Belize 97
Bequia 99
Bonaire 101

BRITISH VIRGIN ISLANDS 108
Tortola 111
Cayman Islands 116
   Grand Cayman 117
   Cayman Brac 123
   Little Cayman 126
Costa Rica 126
   Cocos Island 126
Curacao 129
Dominica 136
Honduras 138
   Roatan In The Bay Islands 138
Martinique 141

Saba	143
St. Lucia	146
U.S. Virgin Islands	149
St. Croix	149
St. John	151
St. Thomas	156
CARIBBEAN LIVEABOARDS	**161**
Caribbean Explorer	161
Saba	162
St. Kitts	164
Star Flyer	169
CYPRUS	**173**
GREECE	**179**
Corfu	179
Crete	186
Mykonos	187
HONG KONG	**189**
INDONESIA	**193**
Bali	193
Manado	197
Tropical Princess Live-Aboard	201
IRELAND	**203**
JORDAN	**207**
MEXICO	**211**
Akumal	211
Cancun	215
Cozumel	218
MICRONESIA	**221**
Palau, Caroline Islands	221
NEW GUINEA	**225**
Papua	225
NEW ZEALAND	**229**
PHILIPPINES	**233**
Elegre, Northern Cebu	238
RED SEA	**241**
RUSSIA	**244**
SAUDI ARABIA	**247**
SCOTLAND	**251**
SOUTH AMERICA	**259**
Brazil	259
Colombia	276
Venezuela	281
THAILAND	**291**
Bangkok	292
Phuket	292

TONGA	**295**
TURKEY	**299**
UNITED STATES	**311**
Alaska	311
California	313
Los Angeles	313
San Diego	317
Florida	321
Crystal Springs	321
Florida Keys	322
Palm Beach	330
Hawaii	334
Kona Aggressor Live aboard	334
SEVEN UNDERWATER WONDERS OF THE WORLD	**345**
Blue Hole, Belize	345
Truk Lagoon, Caroline Islands	347
Stingray City, Grand Cayman	349
Ultimate Wall Dive, Grand Cayman	351
Portofino, Italy	353
Aliwal Shoal, South Africa	354
Uluburun, Turkey	356
HONEYMOON AND ANNIVERSARY SECTION	**365**
Ocean Club, Nassau, Bahamas	365
Sandy Lane, Barbados	367
Lantana Club, Bermuda	369
Pirates Point, Little Cayman, Cayman Islands	370
Vista Palace Hotel, Cote d'Azur, France	374
Corfu Hilton, Corfu, Greece	375
Kona Village, Kona, Hawaii	376
The Kahala Hilton, Oahu	379
S.S. Constitution, Hawaiian Islands	383
Maui	388
Hilo, Kona	392
Star Clipper, Italian Islands, Italy	393
Swept Away, Negril, Jamaica	400
Caneel Bay, St. John, U.S. Virgin Islands	406
APPENDIX	**411**
Environment - Divers and Reefs	412
Safe Snorkelling	416
How to Choose an Instructor	420
First Aid	422
How to Choose a Dive/Snorkel Charter	425
Tips for Travelers	428
Camps for Kids - Camp Marchand	430

"Nature is the living, visible garment of God." -Goethe

Africa and Off Islands

Kenya East

Steve Curtis arrived in Kenya, from Zimbabwe 11 years ago. Having dived a great deal with the Military in Rhodesia, Steve decided to make his deep love of the water into a career by pursuing the sport of Scuba Diving.

After a diving bit in Kenya, Steve went to Florida in order to attain his P.A.D.I. Instructors rating. That was in 1983. He then returned to Kenya to run a dive centre for a Swiss company, later moving on to open his own base. Having dived much of Kenya, Steve decided Watamu was the optimum dive spot and therefore ideal for his base. With over 6,000 accident free dives to his credit, Steve runs Aqua Ventures with safety, but fun, in mind.

Steve's thorough briefings are legendary, as is his caring attitude to both new and experienced divers. Where the boats go each day depends on an assessment of the conditions, with good visibility and no currents a top priority. Customers' requests for specific dive sites are honored when possible.

One of Steve's pet projects is the conservation of the reefs. He voluntarily trained members of the Kenya Wildlife Service (a Government organization set up to control and protect the Parks and Reserves in Kenya) to P.A.D.I. Open Water Diver Status in order that they may "police" and protect the reefs more effectively.

Kenya, located on the East Coast of Africa and divided by the equator, is a land of great diversity and friendly people. North and Northeast Kenya are hot and arid, while the Highland areas of the South are cool and lush, with Mount Kenya, Africa's second highest mountain towering over the fertile land of central Kenya.

> The coastline ... 300 kms of white, palm fringed beaches, dotted with small islands, some seemingly held back in time, with donkeys the only transport amongst the ancient Arab buildings.

Lion Fish by Steve Curtis

The National Parks of Kenya are great tracts of rich savannas, arid deserts, lakes, forests and towering rock formations and hills, set aside for the preservation of the unique flora and fauna of the country.

Aqua Venture, a P.A.D.I. training facility, is situated halfway up the coastline at the friendly Ocean Sports Hotel on Watamu Beach (100 kms north of the main port of Mombassa). Here you can experience Kenya's underwater world at it's finest.

You will be dazzled by the variety of colorful and interesting fish, as well as the beautiful and extensive coral "gardens". Truly a photographer's paradise and all under the protection of the Marine Parks of Kenya.

A dive on one of our many buoyed dive sites (about 13) in the heart of the Marine National Reserve involves a briefing at the base, followed by a short and easy boat ride to the dive site. There, at their own pace and with the help of the Aqua Ventures staff, the divers kit up and drop into the calm blue waters of the Indian Ocean. Descending, perhaps onto the aptly named "Canyon" dive site, the diver first notices the reef top, at about 30 feet, layered with an amazing variety of soft and hard corals. Beautiful butterfly and angel fish dance over the formations, whilst the occasional turtle glides by. Not far off lies the drop off, its edges decorated with orange, purple and white soft corals, the prominent walls home to a colorful variety of fish. Swimming over the edge, one immediately notices a large arch filled with shoals of iridescent glass fish, whilst up squadrons of jacks can often be seen patrolling the drop

Crossing over the narrow, sandy "gully (at about 80 feet) that separates two reefs, the diver can observe snapper, sweet lips, various rock cod, and schools of fusiliers and banner fish, all the time keeping an eye out for the lurking shapes of the reef and whale shark that frequent these waters.

At the end of the dive, it is worth spending some time near the buoy line studying the small or more camouflaged treasures of the reef such as the gently swaying anemones and their companions the "clown fish" and the vividly colored nudibranch or the strange looking crocodile fish.

On your return boat journey you may be lucky enough to encounter the playful dolphins and we do not mind stopping whilst you don mask, snorkel and fins to enable you to jump in the water and watch these beautiful creatures more closely.

You can fit in two dives a day in order to experience all the Indian Ocean has to offer a diver, whether exploring our nearby wreck - not very old, but already home to an impressive variety of corals and marine life - or visiting our underwater caves, or exploring more of the reef.

Though Watamu cannot boast of the immense drop-offs and permanent gin clear waters of the Red Sea and The Great Barrier Reef, we can show divers unspoiled dive sites with abundant and varied coral and marine life which divers return to explore time and time again.

Our professionally trained diving staff is headed by Steve Curtis, diver and operator of Aqua Ventures, who has been diving in these waters for 10 years.

Aqua Ventures, under Steve Curtis, has grown steadily and gained reputation for high safety standards and happy customers.

S.C.U.B.A. Diving with "Aqua Ventures"

Situated at Ocean Sports Hotel - a 2 minute, walk from Hemingways, Aqua Ventures is able to cater for all those interested in the sport of Scuba Diving, from those wishing to learn how to dive, to the more experienced who wish to renew their acquaintance with the underwater world.

DIVE SITES

Watamu Marine Park boasts some of the finest diving off the coast of Kenya. The diving grounds which lie in the Marine Reserve are unspoiled with a wide variety of both soft and hard corals as well as many varieties of fish.

There are 17 dive sites, all of which are no more than a 20 minute boat ride away. The sites are all buoyed in order to prevent any coral damage due to anchors being thrown. The sites are generally 30 feet, dropping off to about 80 feet in depth with visibility sometimes exceeding 100 feet. There is also the possibility to dive on a nearby ship wreck or some caves where one might be lucky enough to see the giant rock cod.

BRAIN CORAL
At the end of one of the reefs stands a piece of rose coral approximately 3 metres high by 4 metres diameter. This large piece of coral is often a favorite spot for large rock cod and at the right time of year, manta rays.

One side of the coral slopes directly to the sand in which the diver often finds blue spotted rays resting. There is also a resident, very striking clown trigger fish. The other side of the coral is joined to the top of the reef which is covered in a large variety of corals and home to a plentiful cross-section of the Indian Ocean marine life.

MORAY REEF
Buoyed slightly back from the drop off, this dive site means a short swim to visit the star of the show who lives halfway down the drop off "George, the tame Moray!" George is a large brown moray (about 4 feet long) who is willing to be touched and has endless patience in posing for the photographer, often leaving his hole for a closer look at all the activity. The diver may be lucky enough to also spot what must be George's grandfather, as he is at least twice the size of George!

CANYON, SOUTH CANYON
(See article). A favorite area of the reef where it is often possible to spot white tip reef sharks and dolphins have occasionally been spotted.

MIDA WRECK AND CAVES
These dive sites are a slightly longer boat ride (30 minutes) and can only be scheduled at certain tides. The wreck is approximately 5 years old and is an old steel hull shrimp boat (about 60 meters in length). It is home to many an octopus, moray, crocodile fish and rock cod, while keeping a close eye on the divers are large schools of batfish! The Caves are only in 6 meters of water and house some very large rock cod and are also teeming with sweet lips and red snappers. White tip shark and barracuda are often spotted cruising by the caves.

If you bring your own equipment, you must have a buoyancy control device with auto inflator, a regulator with alternate air source, depth and pressure gauge. Wet suits are advised although the water is very warm.

We recognize any diving qualification, i.e., PADI, NAUI, BSAC, VDST, VIT , VDTL, SAA.

The use of spear guns is absolutely forbidden.

There is to be no collecting of or molesting of marine life whatsoever.

Apart from charges at the various dive centers, there is a Marine Park fee.

SCUBA AND SNORKELING FACILITIES QUESTIONNAIRE

NAME **Steve Curtis**
ADDRESS **P.O. Box 275 Watamu**
Kenya, East Africa
CONTACT **As above**
TITLE
TELEPHONE **(122) 32420/32008**   FAX **(0122) 32266/32256**

CAPITAL: **Nairobi**   GOVERNMENT: **Corrupt**
POPULATION: **25 million**   LANGUAGE: **English/Swahili**
CURRENCY: **Kenya Shillings**   ELECTRICITY: **220v**
AIRLINES: **Kenya Airways**   DEPARTURE TAX? **US $20**
NEED VISA/PASSPORT? YES **x**   NO   PROOF OF CITIZENSHIP?   YES   NO **x**

YOUR FACILITY IS CLASSIFIED AS: SCUBA CENTER **x**   RESORT
BUSINESS HOURS: **0700 - 1700**
CERTIFYING AGENCIES: **PADI, BSAC, CMAS**
LOG BOOK REQUIRED?   YES **x**   NO
EQUIPMENT: SALES **x**   RENTALS **x**   AIR FILLS **x**
PRIMARY LINE OF EQUIPMENT: **Spirotechnique**
PHOTOGRAPHIC EQUIPMENT: SALES **x**   RENTALS **x**   LAB **x**

CHARTER/DIVE BOAT AVAILABLE? YES **x** NO   DIVER CAPACITY   **10-15-20**
COAST GUARD APPROVED?   YES **x** NO   CAPTAIN LICENSED? YES **x**   NO
SHIP TO SHORE? YES **x** NO   LORAN? YES   NO **x**   RADAR? YES **x**   **Furuno AGPS**
DIVE MASTER/INSTRUCTOR ABOARD? YES   NO   BOTH **x**

DIVING & SNORKELING: SALT **x**   FRESH
TYPE OF DIVING/SNORKELING IN AREA: WALL **x**   BEACH   WRECK **x**   REEF   CAVE **x**   ICE
DIVING/SNORKELING IN YOUR AREA IS BEST SUITED FOR
    BEGINNER **x**   INTERMEDIATE **x**   ADVANCED **x**
BEST TIME OF YEAR FOR DIVING/SNORKELING: **Oct. - April**
TEMPERATURE: **NOV-APRIL 84 F**   **MAY-OCT: 84 F**
VISIBILITY   **DIVING: 80 FT**   **SNORKELING: 80 FT**

PACKAGES AVAILABLE: DIVE **x**   DIVE STAY **x**   SNORKEL **x**   SNORKEL-STAY **x**
ACCOMMODATIONS NEARBY: HOTEL **x**   MOTEL   HOME RENTALS **x**
ACCOMMODATION RATES: EXPENSIVE   MODERATE **x** INEXPENSIVE
RESTAURANTS NEARBY: EXPENSIVE   MODERATE   INEXPENSIVE **x**
YOUR AREA IS: REMOTE   QUIET WITH ACTIVITIES **x**   LIVELY
LOCAL ACTIVITY/NIGHTLIFE: **Nearby casino and nightclub**
CAR NEEDED TO EXPLORE AREA? YES **x**   NO
DUTY FREE SHOPPING?   YES **x**   **At airport**

LOCAL EMERGENCY SERVICES   NEAREST HYPERBARIC TREATMENT FACILITY
COASTGUARD: **Kenya Navy, Mombasa**   AUTHORITY: **Kenya Navy**
TELEPHONE: **011-3448**   LOCATION: **Mombasa**
CALLSIGNS: TELEPHONE: **011-3468-3498**

LOCAL DIVING DOCTOR:
NAME: **Dr. Bakara**
LOCATION: **Kenya Navy, Mombasa Harbor**
TELEPHONE: **011-451201**

Kenya West

Safari in Masai Mara, West Kenya, Before Sailing the Seychelles
Wendy Canning Church

Opting to take the Safari in Masai Mara, West Kenya before our sailing through the Seychelles Islands, we flew directly into Nairobi, Kenya. When we landed early in the morning, we were met by Raymond Mwachange of Micato Tours. He greeted us with the warmest of smiles which we found ever pleasant on our four day Safari. Raymond took care of even the smallest detail, handling any problem that occurred, spoiling us outrageously. We were definitely "happy campers" throughout the trip.

We overnighted at the Hilton because of an overflow at the Safari Club where we stayed when we returned from Safari. Our choice of hotels in Nairobi would have been the Norfolk Hotel or the Windsor Golf and Country Club.

We flew out of Nairobi the next morning via Kenya Airways and landed in the Mara Masai Reserve. The Reserve encompasses 750 square miles and borders South West Tanzania. Our home for the next four days was the lovely Mara Sopa Lodge, tucked

Masai Mara National Reserve by Wendy Canning Church

high in the lush green hills of the Reserve. The Lodge has all the comforts of a first class hotel and the true blessing of no telephone, television or radio, in the guest rooms. The Lodge can accommodate 200 guests in small bungalows that have a spacious bedroom and bath. The public rooms are large and there is a pool and a boutique on the premises.

After unpacking and lunch, we embarked on our first game run. Game runs are scheduled for early in the morning and late in the afternoon, because the animals take shelter from the heat at midday. The Reserve allows no vans out after 6:00 pm to give the animals privacy. We set out, donned in our safari hats (a gift from Micato Tours), anxious to spot the "big five": elephant, lion, rhino, leopard, and water buffalo.

Peter Irungu was our guide and our driver: definitely request him! His warm manner, sense of humor, patience and eagle eyes made our Safari a very special one. The vans that Micato Tours use carry a maximum of six people and a guide. This way everyone is assured a window seat for spotting game. Binoculars are provided to each guest and Peter makes sure that the cooler in the van is always filled with cold soft drinks to quench the thirst from the heat and dust. The roof shelters the passengers from the sun, but there is an opening so one can stand up to take photographs. No request for a photo shot was ever denied. Peter would wait as long as it took for each of the photographers to get their shot. He always positioned the van so that the sun was in back of us to help us get the best possible picture - not always an easy feat.

We saw herds of buffalo, grazing lazily before our eyes. Elephants moved gracefully, despite their size, out of the bush and into the morning's haze. Families of lions played and ate together, while rhinos romped in the river. On our last day we saw the remains of an impala, which a leopard had killed and carried high into a tree so that no other predators could move in on his catch.

The myriad of animal life that we saw was breathtaking. Families of zebra, giraffe, water buck, cheetah, dik-dik impala, marabou stalk, jackal, ostrich, monkey, brown llama, vulture, crocodile and even wart hog. The wart hogs mate at the Reserve and then go across the border to Tanzania from February until April to have their babies. In August and September when they return you will see thousands of them in the Reserve.

The vegetation at the Reserve is sparse as it is the main staple of the animals, each elephant alone eats up to 250 kilograms a day and the hippo eats another 125 kilograms each day. The topography consists of flat plains that run up into the hilly terrain and into the mountains beyond. One finds sausage trees, candelabra trees and palm trees within the grounds. The baby lion cubs especially favor the shade of the palm trees.

The days slipped by quickly with so much to see and delight the eye. Early mornings were spent on game runs, followed by lunch, then a dip in the pool or a siesta. In the afternoons we set off again on another game run.

There are two optional tours that one may also take: the hot balloon trip and a visit to the Masai village. The hot air balloon drifts high above the Reserve so that one can see and photograph the animals in the bush and roaming the plains. The ride is followed by a champagne breakfast.

The Masai tribe lives just outside the Reserve. The tribe is one of the 42 that dwell in Kenya. Each tribe speaks its own language, but they all speak Kiswahili as well so all the tribes are able to communicate. The Masai are a nomadic tribe, moving every two years in search of grazing pasture and water, but they never move more than ten miles from their existing village.

They dwell in huts that are made of groups of sticks tied together and then the groupings are stuck together with mud. There is one large room in the hut with a small partition off the bedroom to house the husband when he comes to visit. As you enter the house there is a small alcove where the animals are kept. A small fire burns throughout the day and night for cooking. The tribe spends most of its day outdoors.

The clothing that they wear during the day serves as their blankets at night. Their diet consists of meat and milk mixed with animal blood. There is a school nearby, but most of the children do not attend for their parents fear they will run away.

The boys are considered to be more important than the girls, as they can carry on the family line. Young men go out of the village to find their brides at the age of 18. The bride will be 14. The men live a polygamous life, taking as many wives as they can afford, usually having to pay 10 cows for each bride. If the wife is unable to produce children, he is free to divorce her. Each wife has her own hut. Husbands who wish to visit a wife send a stool to the house with a boy child signaling that he will be having dinner at her hut and spending the night. A man who wishes to spend the night with another man's wife, whose husband is within the same age group as the prospective visitor, merely needs to put a sword in front of the hut. This is interpreted as a "do not disturb" sign. There is no jealousy as this has been the custom for generations.

The Masai tribe values its cows highly, both for dowry purposes, and because they sacrifice them to their God, Engai. If there are heavy rains, they will rejoice by sacrificing a cow. Their spiritual leader, Laibon, communicates with Engai if there are problems. Duties are delegated and are different for the male and the female. The wives build the huts, make jewelry, fetch water and firewood, and milk the cows. After circumcision at the age of 14, the men are called Moran and they then take care of the village and graze the cows. At age 25 the men become Junior Elders. At age 40 they are Senior Elders and become part of the Counsel of Elders that resolves disputes. They are also responsible for seeking out new areas to live when it is time to move.

The average age at death is 50 for the males and 55 for the females. Healthcare is a problem. There are no inoculations in the village, so the village can suffer yellow fever, cholera and malaria.

Nevertheless, the Masai are a happy lot. A visit to their village is truly educational and an important step in the understanding of Kenya and its culture. There is a small fee to enter the village. They will let you photograph the village and its people. You can also purchase their crafts which include lovely colorful jewelry, masks and spears.

How can one describe all this - adventurous? Perhaps, "truly mystical." To see animals in their natural habitat, roaming free, caring for their young, quenching their thirst at the watering holes, sleeping peacefully under the shade of a tree, and yes, witnessing them kill is fascinating. One is reminded of the laws of the jungle and the ways of survival.

At the end of the day, the path is lit by millions of stars for both the Southern and Northern constellations are visible at the same time. You slip into your bed and discover the hot water bottle tucked under the covers to help ward off the cool night air. The aroma of the many beautiful plantings is carried on the breeze and fills your room. The sound of no sound and the thoughts of tomorrow's adventure lull you to sleep in this perfect unspoiled environment.

Editor's Note: I flew British Airways to London and then on to Nairobi. As a world traveler, I find that they not only have excellent connecting routes, but also continue to uphold the highest standard of service.

Mozambique

Pemba and Ibo Island

By Al J. Venter

A DISTANT CORNER OF TROPICAL AFRICA

Northern Mozambique, next door to Tanzania, is likely to be one of the great diving destinations of the future. It is still a fairly unspoiled, unpolluted little backwater and the northern region is about as big as Switzerland and speckled with more than twenty tropical islands.

This is a corner of Africa that until recently was very rarely visited by foreigners. Parts of it, known as Cabo Delgado, are so inaccessible and have remained isolated from alien influences for so long that inhabitants, many of them speaking their native East African Kiswahili dialects, call all those who are not of dark brown negroid colour or the lighter olive brown of the Arabs "muzungu". But when you visit those parts of this country adjoining the Tanzanian border, you soon understand the reserve of the people toward strangers.

This is a society that experienced centuries of Portuguese colonial rule. Its people had observed the brutalities of the German imperialists to the north, who came much later and, until the war of Kaiser Bill, ruled what was then Tanganyika with tongue, whips and rifle.

On their own soil they lived through a bitter colonial war against the Portuguese, then the warlike Makonde tribe wearing their new East German uniforms that went well with Russian Kalashnikov carbines slung over their shoulders - came across from Tanzania and created the kind of havoc that modern insurgents are all too capable of.

They were successful, too. After fifteen years of war in Mozambique, the Portuguese trussed up their weapons, packed their kit bags and left abruptly for home and most of them never returned.

Fisherman by Wendy Canning Church

But five hundred years of colonial rule had clearly left its mark; in the language, a Roman Catholic church that still retained a nervous following under the newly independent socialist government, and in some of its place-names, many more characteristic of the Algarve or Oporto than of Africa.

Santa Isabel, a town of about twenty thousand people, half of them refugees from the bush - on the beautiful isthmus jutting into the entrance to Pemba — is one of these; although the new Maputo government these days prefers to call it simply Pemba.

It must have been one of the most coveted posting in the Portuguese colonial service. Nowadays, many of the buildings are covered with moss and are in a poor state. But it is possible to recapture some of the graceful images that are so distinctively Lusitanian.

The open-air cafe (there is only one); the once splendidly Iberian-tiled esplanade along the bay; the house of the regional commander (today used by the chief political commissar of the region, although he calls himself something else now, after the advent of free elections) and the cheap Doura vinho tinto that many of the locals prefer to imported South African beer or palm wine.

> **The sea is, of course, the main attraction for anyone who comes to Pemba; brilliant aquamarine as far as the eye can see and quite breathtaking as the brand new Boeing 767 of Linhas Aereas de Mozambique banks towards finals on the hilltop runway.**

For much of the year this part of the Indian Ocean is as tranquil as a lake.

> **On either side of the peninsula coral reefs suddenly give way to the deep azure and the kind of drop-offs that one usually associates with the Caribbean, the pattern broken now and again by the off-white triangular sails of an Arab dhow leaving or entering harbour.**

There are a few big ships in Pemba although the tidal area is littered with wrecks. For, too long the country has been at war and as a result there are no prospects for the kind of tropical cargoes that form the main business of other ports along this stretch of coast; Dar as Salaam to the north and Maputo a thousand kilometres to the south.

It is surprising that there are many eager and expectant youthful white faces on the aircraft with you, and it is only after once again presenting your passport and clearing customs that you become aware that a fairly large proportion of the "muzungu" are foreign aid personnel. Pemba is the first choice of aid workers in East Africa. They come from all over the world; Scandinavia, Germany, America, Britain, Spain, Canada, France, Portugal, Italy and elsewhere.

Nearly all have a pair of flippers, a mask and a snorkel. It is that kind of place.

Diving in the vicinity of Pemba can be an unusual experience; but you must be careful about where your dive master takes you.

Much of the Mozambique coast is used as a supplementary source of food by the local tribesmen; small fish caught daily in hundreds of nets, mussels and other marine creatures such as the occasional octopus or crayfish, are all grist to the mill for people who have known starvation for years.

The result is that near more populous regions the inshore parts of the north have been badly fished out. That is certainly true round Pemba. So it is necessary for boats to get further afield; but it is well worth the time and effort.

While much of the diving is within a kilometer or two of the Complexo Nautica at Wimbe Beach, where we stayed, was poor, it took us only ten minutes by boat across the bay to reach some of the best inshore diving along the East African coast.

The farther north or south we went, the better it became.

At the time of writing, much of this region had never been dived before, with the result that the coral and marine life we discovered was often spectacular. Near Pemba we found most fish species to be wary of undersea intruders, largely because so many of the local people have acquired their own, often primitive, dive gear, some of it made locally out of discarded rubber inner-tubes. Although they lack the kind of formal training that we are accustomed to, these native fishermen are adept; they often stay down while freediving with spear guns for three minutes or more. As a result, most of the shallow water reefs in the Pemba area have been cleaned of fish.

Some really outstanding dives are to be found among a score of offshore islands to the north of Pemba. These stretch for several hundred kilometres, almost to the Tanzanian border. The first of these, that we came to while flying on the daily run to Ibo Island - which lies about half an hour by small aircraft from Pemba - can be seen north of the bay soon after takeoff. Having crossed a number of low coastal plains speckled with palms, tidal flats and mangrove swamps, you suddenly spot the islands lying ahead along a barrier reef spread out as far as your vision will reach. It was hardly visited by tourists until the early nineties, but this stretch of coast compares with any other group or coral atolls in the Indian Ocean. In places it is like the Great Barrier Reef. The diving here is outstanding; Much of the water is shallow. It is crystalline and skates, rays, porpoises, moray eels and game fish are plentiful.

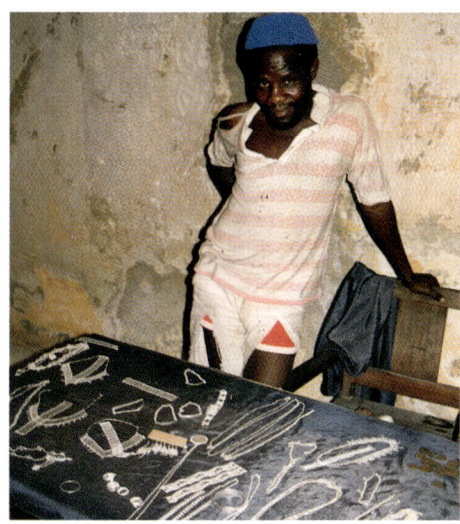

Once you reach deeper water, with numerous drop-offs reminiscent of the Red Sea, things become spectacular. For several months of the year large schools of whale, marlin, tunny, black and white tip reef sharks and swordfish can be seen on every dive.

Whale sharks gather here in crowds during the southern summer. It is thought that they migrate all the way across the Indian Ocean from Australia.

A large boat is necessary, preferably one with a compressor. If deep diving

Silver filigree jeweler inside Ibo Castle by Wendy Canning Church

is desired, a portable decompression chamber of the type made by Drager would be suitable. Although there are few current and no rip tides, like those off the Comores, which lie not far to the east, you must watch your depth and decompression times, perhaps cutting the tables each dive by five minutes for safety. The nearest decompression chamber is in South Africa, more than a thousand kilometres and who knows how many bureaucratic bungles, away!

The area is growing steadily in popularity, and already there is talk by Steve and Linleigh Anderson, the diving concession holders at Pemba, to bring in a portable chamber. Let us hope so, since accidents have a way of happening when least expected.

At Pemba all roads lead to the Anderson facility, The Coral Bay Diving and Fishing Club, which forms part of the Complexo Nautica on the seaward side of the isthmus. It is a mere ten minute drive through the old town which was originally settled from Lisbon three hundred years ago, and the presence of the Mozambique military in large numbers and two or three roadblocks make little difference to the breezy welcome. Even for a complete stranger, there are always smiles and and greetings all round.

One of the most interesting places along the entire stretch of Indian Ocean coast is Ibo Island, at the end of the air shuttle from Pemba. If you like ancient Portuguese castles mildewed 17th and 18th century mosques and cathedrals, palaces and colonial buildings all mold-ering to ruin, you will love the island.

It is basic, though. Many of the buildings need much attention and there is only one vehicle on the island, a tractor. On arrival over Ibo the pilot usually circles the administration block to warn the officials that he intends to land. They then send the tractor (usually hauling rubbish is its normal duty), with a trailer fitted with two loose wooden benches to fetch the passengers. If the tractor is immobilized, visitors have to walk but it is only about ten or so minutes to the airstrip; though in the heat and humidity even that can be exhausting.

Apart from the harbour, which warms with Arab dhows and other sailing craft at the turn of the tide - many from anzania - the most interesting thing on Ibo Island is the castle, dating from 17th century. Until a year or two ago it was used as a high-security prison for political prisoners; the inmates were usually bundled off into the jungle in chains when visitors or representatives of the International Red Cross arrived.

Ibo castle is now the centre of a burgeoning industry in silver filigree jewelry; real bargains can be had at very little cost.

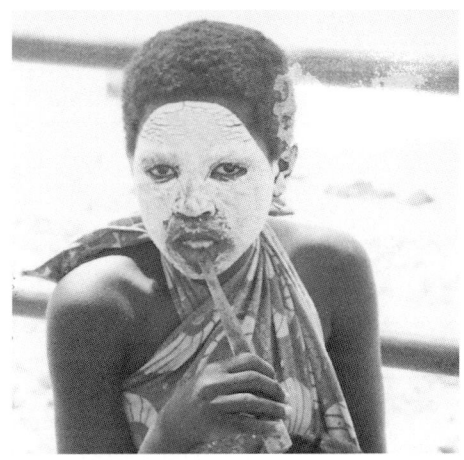
Young Lady at Ibo by Wendy Canning Church

The silver used in this most delicate craft comes from melted-down Maria Theresa dollars taken from an unidentified old East Indian man that went down on this shore two or three hundred years ago. No one will reveal the true position of the wreck; it still yields coin on occasion.

Many of these fine pieces of jewelry used to find their way to Zanzibar, but since the Marxist revolution in Tanzania in the sixties that trade has stopped. In socialist Mozambique, western money has always been more acceptable than Russian rubles or Chinese renminbi.

As is to be expected, the island reflects a way of life that probably has not changed for centuries. There is an air service to the island and radio communications but little else. The water is slightly brackish, but safe to drink; it is drawn from the local well. Palm wine in this mostly Islamic society is the only alcoholic drink that is tolerated, and the island hierarchy, apart from the commissar, is still structured on tribal custom; women are worth little more than cattle, and their sole purpose in life appears to be cooking, tilling the soil and procreating. The Portuguese succeeded to some extent, by fair means or foul, in making some impact on this mediaeval system. They ruled with an iron hand. But as soon as they were gone the natives returned to the ancient ways, even after several centuries of alien pressure.

Ibo is a beautiful island, unique in all East Africa. Its atmosphere is heady with a chiaroscuro lattice of tropical light and shade that produces an almost surreal effect.

The sunsets over nearby Africa are awe inspiring. Just before the sun rises over the ocean to the east as the world comes slowly to life, the light is even more crystalline.

lbo island, although somewhat shabby for want of attention in recent years, is still almost wholly intact as a society. The roofs of some houses have fallen in; others have been abandoned and occupied by families of the ubiquitous East African goats.

It would not cost much to make these buildings habitable and restore the former colonial imprint; only its comely facade, however; the old imperial authority is gone for good. It would be nice to make lbo island into an attraction for foreign tourists. There is an opening for such a place on East African coast.

Some foreign interests have recognized this potential and have tried to prevent further deterioration. On Ibo there are now half-a-dozen agents of economic aid, mostly French, who are supplying some of the local needs; teachers, agricultural experts, medical personnel and so on. They have moved into some of the finer old colonial houses on the outskirts of the town and, from my own personal observation, appear to have readily accepted the lackadaisical and soporific manner of life. Nothing is done in a hurry, and nothing with Prussian thoroughness.

But no one starves, and everyone on Ibo is spared the vicissitudes of mainland politics and civil war. The sea is still crystal clear and full of life. What more could any body wish for?

It is the sort of island that Paul Theroux, might have gravitated to if he had heard about it earlier.

For the serious diver there are as yet no scuba facilities whatever. But that is hardly necessary when you only need to snorkel out from any beach to find all sorts of exciting marine life.

Moray eels slither on the top of the coral outcrops that stand out above the surface at night when the moon is full. If you have a torch and the will, you can see dozens of them lying out of the water.

There is vast potential in this entire region; of the thirty-odd islands, nearly half are now being being developed for tourism.

There is also great interest in big-game fishing, which is estimated to be among the best in the Indian Ocean. In Northern Mozambique, one of the results of thirty years of guerrilla conflict is that few of the choicest fishing or diving spots have been made known, far less exploited.

Considering that the waters off Tanzania including the Zanzibar and Pemba Channels, hold a dozen or more world records for game-fish, Mozambique promises to be a most desirable region

Wendy Church and natives by Al J. Venter

Editor's Note:. The Andersons no longer run facilities in this area but there is a liveaboard. For more information contact DEI, telephone 617-723-7134.

11

South Africa

Aliwal Shoal Natal
By Andy Cobb

The coast of southern Africa supports thousands of different types of plants and animals from virtually every major marine group. Although some of these species occur all around the coast, many are restricted to particular regions. Three distinct coastal regions are recognized in southern Africa. The east coast, incorporating Natal and Tanskei, is bathed by the warm, southerly flowing Agulhas current. Although this region lies well outside the tropics, it is colonized mainly by warm water species of tropical origin. By contrast, the cold, northerly flowing waters of the Benguela system on the west coast from Cape Point northwards, are occupied by a quite distinct group of cold water species which only give way to more tropical forms near the Angolan border. Along the Cape south coast is an intermediate temperate zone which, because of its isolation from other temperate regions of the world, contains a high proportion of species that are unique to southern Africa.

The Aliwal Shoal is four miles off shore and 48 miles south of Durban, the harbour city of Natal.

The Aliwal Shoal is a fossilized sand dune formed 80,000 years ago. It is half a mile wide and one and a half miles long.

The sandstone has eroded over the years to form caves, overhangs and gullies. The caves, overhangs and gullies form an ideal habitat for the Spotted Ragged Toothed Shark to rest in during the day. Most of their feeding activity is at night. The Shoal itself has a mixture of warm water reef fish and cold water reef fish and the water temperatures vary from 60 degrees F to 80 degrees F in summer. The colder water brings a lot of activity to the reef. We have Whales coming through, notably the Humpback Whale and the Small Toothed Whales. We also have three species of Dolphins and three species of Turtle. The reef has some exceptionally hard corals on it, plus a variety of Bryzoan lace corals. The soft corals and sponges are notable.

Tiger, Blacktip and Hammerhead Shark apart from the Spotted Ragged Toothed Shark come through in large number.

The launch site is from a coastal town called Umkomaas. This is a Zulu word and the area was named by the Zulu king Shaka and means the "Place of Whales".

DIVE SITES

The Pinnacles
The Pinnacles are best dived when there is no to very slight surge and the current is not too strong. There are many caves, overhangs, holes, craters, tunnels and gullies to explore.

Manta Point
The eastern shoulder of the Southern Pinnacle is a point at 16 meters with overhangs on the southern edge and a cave and a blow hole on the northern edge.

North Sands
This large overhang with a back door is on the southeast of North Sands and has its own residents and a rest house for Raggies when they are passing through. Hound Sharks have plenty of refuge in the area but are very shy.

Strike I
The first strike can be found at the back of the cave by the Outer Anvil Rock. This cave has a back door which can be dived through if there is no swell. The hole in that area and the Raggy Cave are good for Angler/Frog fish. You have to be very observant.

Strike II
The Aimee Lykes on her maiden voyage struck the Shoal twice. Evidence of this can be seen by giant pieces of swarf lying nearby to the Pinnacle cave. The amount of metal removed was amazing, but apparently only from the outer skin. The Aimee Lykes returned to Durban for repairs.

Lion Fish Hole
This is a crater in the Southern Pinnacle, which for the last 8 years that I know it, has always had a Lion Fish residing there.

Anvil Rock Outer
This rock looks like an anvil, looking from the eastern side. This is a collecting point for Raggie, when they are around, and a good pointer for Raggie Cave.

Raggie Cave & Shark Alley
From July to December this area is in demand to see the Raggies, but is also an excellent area for all flora and fauna.

South Sands
A good area for the Giant Guitar fish, Stingrays, and Skates.

Tiger Cove
Very different to the outside edge, but with some large tunnels and caves. This area was a Tiger Cowrie colony.

Cathedral
28 metre dive to an outer edge reef hole. Large Stingrays, Moray Eel and Sharks.

LOCAL FLORA AND FAUNA
Whales
Whales seen most often are the Humpback whales; however, Sperm whales, Pygmy Sperm whales and Minke whales do pass through.

Dolphins (Baby Whales)
The most noticeable are the Indian Ocean Bottle Nose, Common and Spinner Dolphins. No porpoises off S.A. on its Indian Ocean coastline.

Aliwal Shoal Shark by Andy Cobb

Rays
The most commonly seen are: Manta, Short Tail, Honeycombe, Devil, Marbled Electric and Butterfly Rays, also the Blue Spotted and Round Ribbontail Rays.

Shark
The most seen and enjoyed are the Ragged Toothed Shark. Those commonly seen are the Hammerhead, Zambezi, Black Tip, Spinner and Hound Shark. Others seen are the Thrasher, Blue Pointer,, Tiger and Bronze Whaler Sharks.

Fish
The Shoal and the Produce have the Harlequin Goldie which is peculiar to the area. There are many of the Coral fish. A haven for Dagga Salmon, Gerrick, Barracuda (all seasonal) and the resident shoals of Slinger and Tassle fish. The largest fish in the ocean,

13

again seasonal, the Whale Shark is a magic experience to see and ride. Anemone fish are scarce but "Clive" the Potato Bass, is well evident when in his territory. The wrecks will host the Brindle Bass.

Crustacea
Several are evident: The Spiney Lobster of which there is the Red Rock lobster and Blue Mozambique lobster, Little Squill fish, Crabs, Hermit crabs, Cleaner shrimp and Mantis shrimp.

Nudibranch
A wide selection of Nudibrancs are to be seen.

CURRENT
The main ocean current that affects Aliwal Shoal is the Agulhas, which brings down the warmer water of the Mozambique current. The strength of the Agulhas current can reach 7 knots and this will encourage some of the smaller freighters to steam inshore, between the Aliwal Shoal and the shore. The M.V. Produce made a serious error and the Aimee Lykes' evidence of a near miss to that of the Produce wreck.

The wind has the most effect on the diving and launch conditions.

NE wind will make the wave stand up or create a chop and create a Southerly current.

SE wind will flatten the waves and create a Northerly current.

If there is no current for too long, the coastal polluted water will affect the visibility on the Shoal and wrecks. A Northerly current keeps the wrecks clear, whereas a Southerly current will cover the wreck with effluent.

Swells: Sometimes the Coastal conditions are perfect, yet there is a large swell. This condition is the remaining effect of a storm out at sea. A strong coastal wind can create an obvious surge with the consequent surf. To determine whether it is safe to launch or not depends on many factors such as:

A long swell will give the boat time to run between the waves for a long break. Hence the size of the wave is not the determining factor.

A short break requires a limit to the size of a wave should the skipper need to punch a wave, as the skipper has no time to run before a wave with a short set.

The sand bank on the route out to the sea requires enough water over it for the boat to clear. Medium to large waves breaking on the sand bank will prevent a launch.

The overall factor is SAFETY:

No. 1 the divers.

No. 2 the boat.

> **RULE: Never push a skipper to take you diving if he is going to launch out of his comfort zone. This is exactly when an accident happens.**

SURGE
There are other factors about surge that should be considered:

To move against surge to reach a drop off or similar refuge, bottom crawling will reduce the air and effort used. Care must be taken to select rocky hand holes so as not to damage the reef.

Swimming deep or below the edge of a drop off will reduce the effect of the surface surge.

Nobody enjoys a dive with a heavy surge due to the pendulum effect and accompanying debris.

HAZARDS
Surge will reduce visibility and create problems:

Avoid gullies, as surge can transport a diver down a gully like an express train.

Avoid caves, as a cave might have a back door and a diver could end up like a cork in a bottle.

Avoid blow holes, as a diver can be seriously hurt by being cut, stuck or drowned.

Avoid breaks in the reef edge if diving below the edge, as surge can push a diver through the gap at high speed or spin the diver to the surface.

SEASONAL VARIATIONS
Temperature
The water temperature can drop from 26 -22 degrees C in summer, by 8 - 10 degrees C in winter. However, there can be similar drops in summer with some very cold thermoclines.

Weather
The weather is a very changeable factor and with a strong front will occasionally require a dive to be terminated early so that the return journey is safe.

Visibility
The summer rains bring down Natal's top soil and colors the sea to look like weak tea. The Umkomaas River used to be 6 meters deep at the old South Coast Bridge and Zambezi sharks were seen easily from the bridge as they went up river to feed off the river fish. Earlier times, the river was navigable for small coastal freighters to seek shelter or off load cargo.

Effluent enters the sea at +60 degrees C, with high solids content, plus reject dyes from the "rag trade"

HAZARDOUS ANIMALS
Blue bottles, jellyfish and some stinging plankton can be considered hazardous, as an encounter is not planned.

Sea urchins, scorpion fish and the infamous stonefish are not a problem on Aliwal if you are neutrally buoyant, the exception is bottom crawling and on those occasions, gloves are essential and each hand hold carefully-selected so as not to damage the reef flora and fauna.

Sharks are to be respected and avoid:

Diving in a sardine run.
Diving in low visibility water where the shark cannot see you clearly.
Diving when injured and bleeding.
Do not splash and make noise on the surface.
Do not react but stay calm and in a group.

Sharks are hazardous when not respected or basic rules not followed.

GET OUT OF THE WATER IF SHARKS ARE DISTURBED.

There are many creatures with teeth and one of the most intelligent is the moray eel and they can be enjoyed, but at all times with respect. Stingrays are gentle creatures and can inflict a poisonous wound if interfered with or trodden on.

Electric rays will attack if interfered with and know exactly what their power packs are for and how to use them.

DANGEROUS ANIMAL
Man is the most dangerous species and can even destroy himself and the world. The marine FLORA & FAUNA is very vulnerable to man's incursion.

WRECKS
The Nebo
This was a small coastal steam freighter that was carrying bridge structures and was pooped and sunk on the 20th of May, 1884. The wreck has collapsed, apart from a section, that hosts a large brindle bass. The NEBO lies at an average depth of 24 meters and at the prop, 26 meters.

The Produce
This was a molasses freighter which hit the Shoal and the skipper tried to beach the ship. However, it sunk 3 kms off shore. The wreck is badly broken up and very dangerous to enter. The marine life is well established.

SCUBA INFORMATION RELATED TO NATAL: SOUTH AFRICA

For all Open Water Dives every diver must wear a Buoyancy Compensator. Life jackets not B.C.'s to be worn for surf exits by boats.

Certification from recognized diving bodies is needed to dive or have cylinders filled for all, in South Africa.

Spear Fishing prohibited while on Scuba. License required to spear fish without Scuba from the Natal Parks Board.

Natal Parks Board licenses required for fishing - quota's for species given plus certain species have a closed season. Likewise for Crayfish - Spiny Lobsters - Crabs - Cuttlefish - Octopus and Squids. All Shell fish require a license and have a quota. No licenses given for collecting Shells.

There are no licenses or fees for Scuba sports diving for tourists or military personnel assigned to South Africa.

"Clive" The Potato Bass
By Andy Cobb

Clive The Potato Bass by Andy Cobb

Aliwal Shoal is a large reef and the first time I swam into "Raggie Cave" was without a mask an as my diving buddy, Chris Lacey, tried to stop me entering as he saw the cave was full of shark. I swam on unaffected, by the loss of the mask, as I knew my mask would be returned sometime. When it was and I cleared the mask I saw the sharks. I stayed and observed them and that was the start of 10 years of magic with the Ragged Toothed Shark, and the story of the encounter was the origin of the name "Raggie Cave".

March, 1994, Raggie Cave was where I first saw "Clive" as he used to live in an ante chamber to Raggie Cave.

The next 9 months I got to know all Clive's caves and would make a point of looking for him and to try and get closer each time before he fled.

After 9 months I was able to get close enough to touch him. Once I had fed him with a Spiny Lobster tail that seemed to seal a friendship pact.

I already knew Potato Bass were partial to trigger fish as "Archie", a very gentle Potato Bass at Sodwana Bay, though well gorged on sardines was addicted to trigger fish.

Potato Bass are very territorial and Archie was illegally fished out of two mile reef, which is a sanctuary. The fisherman concerned was nearly lynched by the divers and had to be escorted off the beach.

SCUBA AND SNORKELING FACILITIES QUESTIONNAIRE

NAME **Andy Cobb Eco Diving**
ADDRESS **10 Marion Rd. St. Winifreds, P.O. Box 386, Winklespruit, 4126**
South Africa
CONTACT **Andy Cobb**
TITLE **NAUI Instructor**
TELEPHONE **(031)964239** FAX **(031) 962308**

CAPITAL: **Durban** GOVERNMENT: **South African**
POPULATION: **(1991) 720,000** LANGUAGE: **English**
CURRENCY: **Randss** ELECTRICITY: **Yes**
AIRLINES: **South African Airways** DEPARTURE TAX? **No**
NEED VISA/PASSPORT? YES x   NO   PROOF OF CITIZENSHIP? YES x   NO

YOUR FACILITY IS CLASSIFIED AS: **SCUBA SCHOOL AND DIVE TOUR OPERATOR**
BUSINESS HOURS: **07H00 - 17H00**
CERTIFYING AGENCIES: **Umkomaas Aliwal Dive Tour Operators Association**
LOG BOOK REQUIRED? YES x   NO
EQUIPMENT: SALES x   RENTALS x   AIR FILLS x
PRIMARY LINE OF EQUIPMENT: **Buoyancy Compensators, Cylinders, Regulators w/weight belt, wetsuit**
PHOTOGRAPHIC EQUIPMENT: SALES   RENTALS   LAB x

CHARTER/DIVE BOAT AVAILABLE? YES x   NO   DIVER CAPACITY **Max. 10 divers**
DEPT. TRANSPORT APPROVED? YES x   NO   CAPTAIN LICENSED? YES x   NO
SHIP TO SHORE?   YES x   NO   LORAN? YES   NO x   RADAR? YES   NO x
DIVE MASTER/INSTRUCTOR ABOARD?   YES x   NO   BOTH x

DIVING & SNORKELING: SALT x   FRESH
TYPE OF DIVING/SNORKELING IN AREA: WALL   BEACH x   WRECK x   REEF   CAVE   ICE
DIVING/SNORKELING IN YOUR AREA IS BEST SUITED FOR: BEGINNER   INTERMEDIATE   ADVANCED
BEST TIME OF YEAR FOR DIVING/SNORKELING:
TEMPERATURE: NOV-APRIL   F   MAY-OCT: F
VISIBILITY: DIVING: FT   SNORKELING: FT

PACKAGES AVAILABLE: DIVE   DIVE STAY   SNORKEL   SNORKEL-STAY
ACCOMMODATIONS NEARBY: HOTEL   MOTEL   HOME RENTALS
ACCOMMODATION RATES: EXPENSIVE   MODERATE   INEXPENSIVE
RESTAURANTS NEARBY: EXPENSIVE   MODERATE   INEXPENSIVE
YOUR AREA IS: REMOTE   QUIET WITH ACTIVITIES   LIVELY
LOCAL ACTIVITY/NIGHTLIFE:
CAR NEEDED TO EXPLORE AREA? YES   NO
DUTY FREE SHOPPING?   YES

LOCAL EMERGENCY SERVICES   NEAREST HYPERBARIC TREATMENT FACILITY
COASTGUARD: AUTHORITY:
TELEPHONE: LOCATION:
CALLSIGNS: TELEPHONE:

LOCAL DIVING DOCTOR:
NAME:
LOCATION:
TELEPHONE:

There are people who know about Clive and who will deliberately go out of their way to try and hook him. This attitude is beyond my comprehension. Anybody who feeds Clive sardines is also likely to seal his fate. Clive's danger time seems to be Easter as the shoal is normally like a parking lot full of boats. However, the exceptionally warm water this Easter chased all the fish away and only a handful of boats were fishing on the shoal.

During Easter, 1985, I found Clive with two, two metre stainless steel traces hanging out of his mouth. By that time I could stroke Clive and he would nudge me in the ribs to tell me to go and catch a trigger fish for him to eat. I was therefore able to open his mouth and check the hooks. Fortunately none of the hooks were in his throat. Each time I touched a hook he would spit my hand out of his mouth. So the next dive I took some wire cutters down and removed the traces. The remaining hooks were not a problem as they would rot out in a couple of weeks.

During Easter, 1988, the same problem occured but with only one trace. Two weeks after Easter, 1991, the same occurred. I did not see it but only the result. Another diver cut the hook out of Clive's lip.

Trident started to take divers out to the shoal early in 1982 with three commercial fishermen, Clive Holme, Bob Janssen, and Cook Janssen and as Clive is a large man and Clive the fish, a large fish, I had a short naming ceremony at the Umkomaas River launch site.

Clive gives a lot of joy to all divers and may if they have not seen Clive, have "not had a dive".

I am not sure about the retentive memory of a Potato Bass and whether he recognizes me anymore as an individual diver - what I do know is that if I call him underwater, he will turn and come to me.

A moray eel and an octopus are very intelligent and have a good memory as they can remember, recognize and respond to individuals.

Clive's territory has expanded in the last year and he will even join a diving group in the Pinnacle area.

Clive is quite happy swimming amongst the ragged toothed shark, especially when the shark are feeding.

Clive will be there to pick up scraps. It is a different story when there is a great white shark around, as he is very shy and will not come out of his refuge, for a trigger fish or to a call!

Long may Clive survive but it is frightening to think what will happen to the shoal eco system, with another effluent outlet being planned at Park Rynie. As the development of the textile industry inland at Umzinto would more than likely use the local outlet, for their waste dyes and inks. The present outlet is already nicknamed purple death.

Aliwal Shoal is a unique place to dive anywhere in the world. The shoal should be protected from bottom fishing, spear and bottom fishers, as both kill the reef, by removing the inhabitants. A vibrant reef attracts the pelagic fish and the spear fishermen who harvest the pelagic fish would be well rewarded.

> *Al J. Venter has been diving for a quarter of a century from the South China Sea to the Caribbean, including the Indian Ocean, Red Sea, the Mediterranean and most of Africa and the Atlantic Islands (Cape Verde, Sao Tome, etc.).*
>
> *Al is an author, publisher, journalist, and documentary film maker. He has made 33 films on African and island states, and others on the wars in Afghanistan, El Salvador, Middle East (including Lebanon and Beirut), Israel, Biafran, Ethiopia, Portugal, Rhodesia, and Angola. He has also produced an underwater film entitled "The Witch Hunters".*
>
> *His main preoccupations include diving and writing and highlighting potential ecological disasters.*

Sodwana Bay: Zululand Seafari

In the mid 1970's, quite unexpectedly, the Portuguese withdrew from Mozambique and civil war broke out. South African deep sea anglers and scuba divers were cut off from a coast that they had come to regard as their own. That was when they discovered Sodwana. Nothing has ever been the same since.

"In the year after the closure of Mozambique to South Africans," says the former Warden of Sodwana Bay, Johan Korf, "We had to take out a government loan to build 23 ablution blocks at Sodwana. That's how sudden and great the increase in traffic was. We had no time to plan an orderly extension of the existing campsite; it was merely a question of carving several hundred more out of the bush as quickly as possible."

Zulu Dancers with Wendy Canning Church at Sodwana

At holiday weekends up to six thousand people flooded into Sodwana. It simply couldn't take that kind of pressure so now the Natal Parks Board has begun to plan more extensively. Campsites have been reduced in size, chalets have been built, and, in these few years, the number of divers has doubled. During 1992, 93,000 dives were conducted on the reefs at Sodwana. It is still increasing.

In the last ten years the influx has been sudden and there are fears that the ecological balance may be disturbed.

"That isn't so," says the Conservator of the Natal Parks Board, Billy Howells. "The ecology of the reefs has not noticeably changed under this pressure. Research by the Oceanographic Research Institute in Durban has shown that the reefs off Sodwana are resilient. So long as divers do not meddle unnecessarily with them, there should be no detrimental effects to the general ecological process that made them what they are."

The largest of the reefs, Two Mile Reef, is only dived on between 15 and 20 percent of its total surface area, on the southern tip. The farther a particular reef is from the launching pad, the less it is frequented by divers, so Two Mile Reef can confidently be used as an accurate gauge of damage.

Complaints of damage by divers to this stretch of reef have been received by the Natal Parks Board, but an investigation has shown no visible or measurable ill effects, says Howells.

Although the launching area is small, Sodwana is one of the safest launching beaches on the entire north coast of Natal.

Anyone familiar with this peculiarly South African form of boating might be forgiven for a certain apprehension as he helps to haul the inflatable dinghy to water's edge, seeing great walls of roaring water foaming and exploding over the reef.

From the beach it looks as though there can be no safe way through those breakers. Certainly there have been mishaps, usually caused through inexperience or mechanical failure going through the surf, but with an experienced skipper and reliable motors, launching from Sodwana looks more difficult than it really is. Yet accidents happen; the sea is always unpredictable.

The semi-rigid inflatables used by many of the diving schools operating from Sodwana are virtually unsinkable, but they can easily capsize; so it is regular procedure to lash down all diving gear before leaving the beach.

The vessel has to be taken out through the shallows and into a foaming trough between the waves, and that demands some skill.

This is the tricky part, for there are waves breaking on both sides of the boat and she must be kept in the calm water between them until the right moment is chosen to make a dash for the open sea. It is certainly exciting!

> **Suddenly there is a lull in a set of waves. The skipper sees his chance, guns the craft towards a wave just beginning to form, thrusts bow into it and flies off the crest before it begins to break.**

For a moment we are airborne, then the rubber duck slams down again and we are through the surf and accelerating over a smooth blue ocean. A few minutes later we are approaching the Natal Parks Board anchor buoys that mark Two Mile Reef.

Because no anchoring is permitted anywhere on the reefs, a top man is necessary every dive. Drift-diving, in which the unmanned boat is used as the surface marker for divers under water, is not allowed, and Billy Howells believes that that has greatly improved safety for all divers at Sodwana.

The old buoys demarcating the eastern edge of Two Mile Reef have been carried away by the sea, but they will in due course be replaced in deeper water to direct northbound ski-boat fishermen away from divers.

The five main diving areas at Sodwana, besides the deeper parts of Jesser Point itself, which is renowned as a gathering place for breeding ragged-tooth sharks during the summer months, are: Two Mile, Five Mile, Seven Mile and Nine Mile Reefs. All are fairly shallow dives, seldom exceeding 25 meters.

Two Mile Reef has mostly a flat bottom. Five Mile Reef has remarkable staghorn coral beds. Seven and Nine Mile are more broken, with large boulders and drop offs beginning at about 15 meters and falling to 25 meters. Sponge Reef next to Two Mile Reef is about 30 meters deep.

None of these dive locations is more than two kilometres from shore; the names signify the distance along the coast from Sodwana, not the distance out to sea. All the reefs are north of Sodwana, with the exception of the unattractively named Algae Reef ten kilometres south of Sodwana, which is seldom dived and is said to be rather uninteresting.

Three diving concessions operate from inside the Sodwana protected area, all with fixed camps in Natal Parks Board Property.

It is necessary to examine the geographical importance of Sodwana to appreciate its true value.

> **Sodwana is the southern limit in the Indian Ocean of the tropical coral beds, and the fish seen there include a wide range of coral species; parrotfish and various rock cods, angels and idols, surgeons and triggerfish. Game fish such as Spanish mackerel, barracuda and kingfish make occasional appearances, but sharks are seldom seen perhaps because the reefs are shallow.**

There has been a serious shark attack in shallow water near the launch pad, but it is believed to have been provoked.

It is also hot. By the time you have hoisted the heavy tank on to your back and strapped a weight belt round your waist you are sweating profusely inside the clinging neoprene wetsuit. The rubber boat is swaying at anchor as the waves sweep under it, and you are beginning to feel seasick. It is a relief to roll backwards off the boat and let the cool water enfold you.

The coral can be dimly seen through the green water beneath you, about twenty meters down. When all seven divers are ready, the touch on a press button releases air from your buoyancy compensator, and you sink silently beneath the surface. The light is bright, the water clear; the only sounds now are the gurgle of the regulators releasing spent air and the constant crackle of life on a coral reef, like a submarine bushfire.

Fish become visible as the bottom rises to meet you, revealing itself not as the flat landscape that it had appeared to be from the surface but as a broken terrain of coralline hills, valleys and tunnels populated by a great variety of marine life.

Green and pinktailed parrotfish nibble at the coral with their strange beaks; moorish idols float past; large eyed squirrel fish, all nail-varnish pink, pop in and out of caves.

The leader is just ahead of me when a movement to one side catches my eye. I turn my head for a better look. A large moray eel rises like a column of spotted muscle out of a cave in the reef; it might be a python, over two meters long and as thick as a man's leg. With its mouth slightly agape, revealing wicked fangs, it is now undulating straight towards us. This is a treat.

At the last moment our dive master turns to meet the fish. Man and giant eel get into a tangle of human limbs and snaky coils. Through it all I catch a glimpse of his face, and through the mask he is smiling like a man enjoying a romp on the lawn with the family dog.

I can now see that the way in which the huge eel is coiling round him, flowing through his arms and then doubling back again, is not at all aggressive. It is almost catlike. In fact, it displays what might be interpreted as affection for the man. These two are evidently old friends.

I look behind me to see Joe Barnett, Lee Reinecke, Marc Stock, Hans Graspointner and Alison Mauchen smiling at me through their face masks and I realize that I have been gently had. I have just met "Monty the Amazing Moray".

It as a love affair that began two years ago; love at first bite. Robbie Keene was leading a dive off Two Mile Reef when they saw a moray's head peering at them from a coral cave.

"Normally," says Robbie, "that's all you'll see of a moray, just its head sticking out of the reef and then withdrawing less you get too near. But this one didn't withdraw; it seemed to feel friendly towards us, and after we'd seen him in the same cave a few times I decided to try feeding him.

'Nobody had fed morays at that time. They were considered dangerous creatures, responsible for many attacks on divers. But Monty was quick to accept sardines from my fingers, and careful not to bite me. Only once he made a mistake, and his jaws closed on my hand. But he realized his mistake before he bit down, and immediately let go without harming me.

After the third or fourth feeding, Monty left his cave and swam freely among us. Now he joins us on every dive, and we usually bring a few sardines along for him. We know now that morays are not at all dangerous to human beings. They're actually shy creatures, and although some divers have been hurt by morays, it's almost certainly because they've stuck their hands into caves where they are living and got bitten because the morays were frightened."

From a two-litre plastic soft drink bottle tied to his wrist our dive master extracted a couple of sardines and offered them to Monty. He took them with the delicacy of a cat accepting scraps from the table. I moved nearer and put my hands out, feeling the great strength of the eel as it slid easily through my hands and then came back for more, obviously enjoying the caress as much as I did.

We swam on, with Monty undulating along beside us like a playful submarine lapdog, until we reached the invisible boundary that marked the edge of his territory. There he stopped, and slowly vanished in the distance as he went back towards his hole in the reef. Now we were in a part of the reef dominated by an even larger fish, and it was not long before we met him.

He appeared in the gloom ahead like a dark shadow hovering above the coral reef, and as we swam nearer he came to meet us. George Two is a potato bass, a huge member of the rock cod, or grouper, family, with gray and black spots. He probably weighs 120 kilograms; a squat, fleshy fish with a huge mouth and pugnaciously protruding lower jaw bristling with teeth.

It was obvious from the way in which he inspected each of us that George Two knew what was what. I felt like a guardsman on parade as his huge and startlingly blue eyes swiveled from diver to diver until he saw what he was looking for: the transparent plastic bottle with its sardines visible inside.

George Two was evidently no fish to waste time with formalities. He swam straight up to our dive master, opened his cavernous mouth and engulfed the plastic bottle. The "crunch" as his iron jaws clamped down on it was audible through the water; then he turned and swam away, dragging the instructor behind him.

Our dive master was not a small man. He had vast experience of encounters with large fish. Now his free fist thudded down hard on George Two's bony skull, right between those two eyes. Startled, he spat out the crumpled plastic bottle. Fragments of sardines floated from it; George Two quickly sucked them in as a host of small fish, colorful as butterflies, rushed up to join the feast.

Having devoured the last of the sardines, George Two moved from diver to diver, inspecting us closely to make sure that we weren't hiding any more food from him. I fluttered my fingers in front of my face mask, which brought him right up for an eyeball- to-eyeball confrontation. His gaping mouth, capable of doing to my head what it had done to the plastic bottle, was only inches away.

It is amazing what one notices at a glance. As he slowly backed away I was acutely conscious of two finger-length cleaner wrasse swimming in and out of his nostrils.

Like Monty, George Two followed us for a while, showing every sign of enjoying human company, but he left us when we passed beyond the boundary of his territory. Back on shore, our dive master apologized for George Two's deplorable table manners. George One, he said, was a gentleman; but George Two was a voracious boor.

What had happened to George One? Oh, he had been taken by fishermen.

It is forbidden to catch reef fish at Sodwana, but sometimes, either through ignorance or greed, anglers break the rules. The fishermen who had caught George One were obviously ignorant, because they had proudly displayed their catch back on the beach.

"There was almost a riot that day," Hans Graspointner told me. "Some of the fellows wanted to lynch then. They left the beach in rather a hurry."

The rule allowing anglers to fish only for the migratory openwater game fish at Sodwana is a good one, and John Korff, a former Warden of the Natal Parks Board at Sodwana, told me that the Oceanographic Research Institute at Durban has reported a remarkable recovery among populations of reef fish since the prohibition of bottom-fishing was imposed.

Sharks at Sodwana? Certainly, although they are seldom seen, and the chances of an attack on a Scuba diver along this stretch of coast are almost negligible; almost as negligible as the chances of a failure of modern diving equipment.

Editors' Note: DEI member, Al Venter,, arranged my trip to South Africa back in November-December 1992. In between our excursions, Al and his family hosted me in their home. I shall never forget their kindness and hospitality.

I also want to thank South African Airways and Satour, without which the journey would never have been so well planned and comfortable!

South African Airways' (SAA) motto is "We didn't invent flying, we just perfected it!" I flew to South Africa via SAA and the service was not only efficient and professional, but warm and personal was well. They offer such amenities as complimentary wines, spirits, headphones, and exceptional cuisine in all classes. It is no wonder that they are ranked as one of the top airlines in the world, in addition to being voted the best airline to Africa by leading international publications.

In 1990, SAA created the African Wildlife Heritage Trust, a foundation that helps preserve the wildlife of Southern Africa. A portion of the fare on every international SAA ticket iscontributed to the Trust.

North American Gateway: New York (JFK)
South American Gateway Rio de Janeiro
European Gateways: London and Manchester, Frankfurt, Zurich, Paris, Amsterdam, Lisbon, Brussels, Milan, Athens
Far East Gateways: Taipei and Hong Kong
Middle East Gateway: Tel Aviv
African Gateways: Johannesburg, Cape Town, Durban. and an extensive network throughout South Africa.
Other African gateways include: Abidjan, Ivory Coast, Moroni, Comores, Harare, Bulawayo and Victoria Falls, Zimbabwe, Lilongwe, Malawi, Lusaka, Zambia, Maputo, Mozambique, Nairobi, Kenya, Windhoek, Namibia, Poet Louis, Mauritius.

For reservations call 212-826-0995 or USA residents toll-free 1800-722-9675; Fax 212-418-3744. Cargo office toll-free 1-800722-3734; Fax 718-917-6716.

Satour, the South African Tourist Board, was responsible for planning our trip throughout the country. They are the people one should be in touch with if you want your trip to go smoothly, whether it's business or pleasure. They offer VIP treatment to each of their customers. They even contacted me along the way to make sure that all was going well on my journey.

For more information contact: Ana Paula C. Vaz, Head of Guest Programs, Satour, Private Bag, X164 Pretoria, 0001 The Republic of South Africa.

SCUBA AND SNORKELING FACILITIES QUESTIONNAIRE

NAME   **Sodwana Bay Lodge & Hotel Resort**
ADDRESS   **P.O. Box 5478, Durban 4000**

CONTACT   **Sue Van Onselen**
TITLE   **Marketing & Sales Manager**
TELEPHONE   **(031) 3045977**   FAX   **(031)3048817**

CAPITAL: GOVERNMENT: **National Party**
POPULATION: LANGUAGE: **English**
CURRENCY: ELECTRICITY: **Yes & Gas**
AIRLINES: DEPARTURE TAX? **Yes**
NEED VISA/PASSPORT? YES   NO   PROOF OF CITIZENSHIP? YES   NO **x**

YOUR FACILITY IS CLASSIFIED AS: SCUBA CENTER   RESORT **x**
BUSINESS HOURS:
CERTIFYING AGENCIES:
LOG BOOK REQUIRED?   YES   NO
EQUIPMENT: SALES   RENTALS   AIR FILLS **x**
PRIMARY LINE OF EQUIPMENT:
PHOTOGRAPHIC EQUIPMENT: SALES   RENTALS   LAB

CHARTER/DIVE BOAT AVAILABLE? YES **x**   NO   DIVER CAPACITY   **10-11 Divers**
COAST GUARD APPROVED?   YES **x**   NO   CAPTAIN LICENSED? YES **x**   NO
SHIP TO SHORE? YES   NO **x**   LORAN? YES   NO **x**
RADIO   YES **x**   NO
DIVE MASTER/INSTRUCTOR ABOARD? YES **x**   NO   BOTH **x Depends on #'s**

DIVING & SNORKELING: SALT **x**   FRESH
TYPE OF DIVING/SNORKELING IN AREA: WALL   BEACH **x**   WRECK   REEF **x**   CAVE **x**   ICE
DIVING/SNORKELING IN YOUR AREA IS BEST SUITED FOR: BEGINNER **x**   INTERMEDIATE **x**   ADVANCED **x**
BEST TIME OF YEAR FOR DIVING/SNORKELING: **Year round**
TEMPERATURE: **NOV-APRIL**   20-40C   **MAY-OCT: 19-21C**
VISIBILITY: **DIVING:**   **+50 FT**   **SNORKELING:**   **50 FT**

PACKAGES AVAILABLE: DIVE **x**   DIVE STAY **x**   SNORKEL   SNORKEL-STAY **x**
ACCOMMODATIONS NEARBY: HOTEL **x**   TENTED CAMPS **x**   HOME RENTALS **x**
ACCOMMODATION RATES: EXPENSIVE   MODERATE   INEXPENSIVE **x**
RESTAURANTS NEARBY: EXPENSIVE   MODERATE **x**   INEXPENSIVE
YOUR AREA IS: REMOTE **x**   QUIET WITH ACTIVITIES **x**   LIVELY
LOCAL ACTIVITY/NIGHTLIFE: **Quiet - Pool Bar**
CAR NEEDED TO EXPLORE AREA? YES **x**   NO **Excursions also available**
DUTY FREE SHOPPING?   YES   NO **x**

LOCAL EMERGENCY SERVICES   NEAREST HYPERBARIC TREATMENT FACILITY
COASTGUARD: N.R.S.I. - **Durban**   AUTHORITY: **Durban**
TELEPHONE: **031 372200 - Durban**   LOCATION:
CALLSIGNS: **Radio**   TELEPHONE:

LOCAL DIVING DOCTOR:
NAME: **M.R.I.**
LOCATION: **Natal Parks Board - Sodwana**
TELEPHONE: **035-571-0051**

INDIAN OCEAN

MALDIVES

A Garland of Emerald Islands
Al J. Ventor

Al Venter has been to the Maldives Several times. To him it is the ultimate diving experience in any ocean.

One or two of my diving friends who have spent a good deal of time in the Maldives say that you could have a different underwater experience on every single dive even if you were to go out every day of the year, and there are 1,200 islands to choose from.

They are so diverse that no one is entirely certain exactly how many islands there are. This is the most unusual atoll cluster nation in the world. Arithmetically, there is an island for every 140 people, through only 210 are inhabited.

> **Scattered across the equator, this long necklace of mostly deserted islands, none of which rises more than two meters above the sea, offers the ancient fantasy of a tropical paradise .**

The Maldives, stretching a distance of about a thousand kilometres from north to south, are totally different from, for example, the Seychelles group or Mauritius, or Reunion or Madagascar, because nearly every one of them is tropical, palm fringed, with sparkling white beaches and turquoise lagoons.

> **The islands also boast a range of coral reefs and marine life that is arguably better than anything to be found in any other comparable top-class diving region, such as the Australian Great Barrier Reef or the entire length of the Red Sea. The Maldives are unique.**

I spent a fortnight on the islands a few years ago when they were utterly unspoiled. I have been back since, and, apart from the cost (the Maldives are certainly not cheap), very little has changed.

Then there was a nudist colony at one of the resorts north of Male, the capital, but this has since been closed by the conservative and somewhat authoritarian Imams. Alcohol is totally prohibited, though the prohibition is not strictly enforced.

Then, as now, there is a shortage of fresh water, and the tourist capacity of each island is determined by the amount of effluent that is judged that would contaminate the natural supply on each island. This is a conservation issue and it is rigorously controlled. Pollution in the Maldives is as much an anathema as pork.

When I went there in 1978, it was in a cramped, antiquated, propeller-driven Air Lanka aircraft. The airstrip was still being lengthened, and there was no question of allowing jets, never mind 747s on the runway. Navigational aids were not entirely reliable. The day before I flew, one flight had spent hours circling dozens of islands looking for the Hulnule airstrip without finding it. The pilot had to take the plane and all its passengers back to Colomoo before its fuel ran out.

Today, all that is history, whatever way you choose, by sea or by air, you will still be as enchanted by the rare beauty of the Maldive Archipelago as the early seamen were by the spectacle that greeted them. The name, "Maldives", means in Sanskrit, "garland of islands".

Marco Polo called the archipelago the "flower of the Indies"; although he could not have seen more than a few of the islands on his voyage to the Far East.

> **Similarly, that venerable old Arab navigator and explorer, Ibo Batutta, declared the Maldives "the most agreeable place that he had ever seen;" "one of the wonders of the ancient world" and certainly he should have known, having sailed across much of the Indian Ocean.**

Whether the sun is taken as a deity, as in ancient time, or not, it certainly has a great power to attract worshippers from all parts of the globe to the Maldive Islands.

At any rate, these islands are probably one of the favorite haunts of divers. There are of course others: Palau, Sharm el Sheikn, Truk Lagoon, the Amirantes, Rodrigues and the outer islands of the Great Barrier reef, to name only a few. But none arouses such interest among the diving fraternity as the Maldives.

Bluestriped Snapper by Alan Marquardt

I remember coming ashore at Viligili from one of the island "choanis" that brought me from the airport in 1978, There was nothing particularly spectacular about the island itself, except that all the women were topless, and I could walk right round it in four or five minutes. The rooms were adequate, though spartan. It was pleasant, but nothing to write home about.

Having missed the afternoon dive, I was determined to have my first taste of it that same evening, even though it would be with mask, flippers and snorkel. It was probably providential that the first time that I stuck my head below the surface near the tiny breakwater, a full moon broke through the cloud and opened up the ocean floor below me as if it were day.

In over thirty years of diving, it was certainly the most memorable experience I have had underwater. There have been others; my first encounter with sharks, a dive off Banque Vaillon off the Comores, the deep-hole drop-off and underwater caves near Di Zahav in what was then still Israeli-occupied Sinai, and the unforgettable migration of hundreds of sharks over our heads at Aliwal Shoal, when every one was so transfixed by the experience that not one among us took a photograph.

All these experiences are imprinted on my mind. But none compares with that moonlit night of Viligili when every creature in the Indian Ocean seemed to come out to greet me.

There were rays, a couple of rock cod that escorted me along the length of the sea wall, moray eels flitting about from one gap in the seawall to another (something you rarely see during the day) and even a few small reef shark that were not even considered a threat.

And the smaller creatures of the reef: nudibranchs, more clownfish than I had ever seen before, a clutch of prawns - longlimbed and tentacled - and one or two spiny lobsters, the wariest of all the creatures that I encountered in the hour-long snorkel. And the family of rays that came into shallow water from outside and stayed a while and then left, as graceful as eagles in flight.

I never snorkeled at night in the Maldives again. It was "just not done", I was told by the instructor at one of the other resorts some years later, and since I was expected to "set an example to the younger members of the party" so it was.

That did not stop me from diving at night on several other occasions in the Maldives. As always after dark the experience gives an extra dimension to the sport, especially off these islands where you never really know what you are likely to encounter at the next coral bommie.

In 1978 the Maldive Islands hardly attracted more than forty thousand tourists, most of them to Male on the main Kaafu Atoll. Now the number of tourists annually tops 200,000 and they account for almost three-quarters of the country's foreign earnings.

The half-dozen resorts that I knew in the early days have burgeoned to seventy; most of them within a couple of hours of the airport by boat. No one, other than a Maldavian national or the Government may own any of these properties; outside investors lease the land and develop it for a certain period, usually reckoned in decades. Unfortunately, this system has not been free from abuse. Several property developers in the early eighties spent a great deal of money establishing extensive facilities for tourists, only to be given their marching orders on the flimsiest of pretexts. You need to know with whom you are dealing if you propose to invest money in the Indian Ocean. It happened in Mozambique as well.

The facilities offered to tourists by the Maldive Islands can be spectacular. Some of the resorts are distinctly five-star, though with ten-star prices.

They attract small numbers of very wealthy tourists, up to now mostly from Europe, but increasingly from Japan and other Far Eastern countries. Cocoa, for example, takes only eight or ten guests at a time. Only the very wealthy can afford it.

The most remote resort (at the time of writing) is Kunfunadhoo in Baa Atoll, northwest of Male. It takes two hours by fast boat to get there and it is a most delightful trip.

Prices on these atolls are generally far higher than what one would pay for anything comparable in the Caribbean, but then, compare the two: one totally unpolluted, decidedly under populated and (most important of all) isolated; the other trying desperately and against all odds to cope with hard times (Caribbean islanders are not flocking to the United States in great numbers without good reason).

In the Maldives, every one of the resorts caters to the sybaritic delights that most tourists expect. A few have additional amenities such as tennis or squash courts, snooker tables, jacuzzis, saunas and whatever other roguish thing imagination may suggest, but diving is still the main thing.

In spite of this accent on tourism, nothing about the Maldives is oversized. The longest stretch of road on the islands is between Gan and Hithadhoo in the southern extremity of the archipelago, only nine kilometres. There is only one international airport, and Male, the capital, is little more than a village; you can walk from one end to the other in half an hour; ten minutes if you jog. There are no factories, no slums and almost no beggars.

The harbour at Male cannot accommodate anything bigger than two hundred tons. Larger ships have to lie in the roadstead in order to off load on to lighters.

The official trapping of Government power are a sort of faint shadow of the pomp and circumstance that are now normal in so many "Third-World" countries. The Maldavian Parliament, or 48man Citizen's Majlis would not be too grand as a lecture room in an American university, while the Presidential "Palace" was built eighty years ago and looks quaint and colonial with its tin roof and facade decorated in blue pastel set off with fretted white wooden patterns over the gables. It is something out of a Somerset Maugham novel.

The most impressive building in the country - and its golden dome can be clearly seen from the air as you approach Hulhule Airport - is the Islamic Centre, which was opened in 1984. It was built to hold 5,000 worshippers.

I could not help feeling, on seeing the Maldives again recently, that Male appears to have had difficulty in coming to terms with some of the things that the late twentieth century takes for granted. It seemed to me that the people were not particularly friendly; they were certainly taciturn, and, although they are accustomed to being gaped at by tourists who come over for the day, many of the islanders do not care for it. They have heard plenty about the degenerate West, and genuinely do fear our influence.

Sadly, western popular music has supplanted the plaintive Arabic music that was usually heard when the British RAF ran the Gan Air Force Base to the south.

Dress, too, is much less formal that before; western garb is in fashion, and will remain so no matter what Islam has to say about it. There is very little fundamentalist zealotry here.

Another unfortunate change for the worse has been the arrival of the internal combustion engine, and its influence on the island life has been deplorable. On my last visit it was clear that pollution of the streets of Male was caused by the 2,500-odd trucks, scooters, motorcycles, taxis and cars that now throng the narrow lanes. Thank goodness this trend does not extend beyond the capital, although some of the larger towns in the atolls are slowly being engulfed by the inexorable advance of civilization.

For those who can't afford a car, a brand new Raleigh bicycle (made in Taiwan or Korea) is quite adequate; and there must be thousands of them, even though you can ride round the entire circumference of Male in less than an hour.

Social activities still centre on the family; you see father, mother and children of all ages strolling together after work or during the weekends, or older children jogging or cycling, emulating their American television heroes with the "keep fit" fetish. Jane Fonda's workout videos can be bought in the shops, no doubt pirated copies.

If there has been a revolution, it took place with the arrival of colour television in the Maldives in 1978.

Every house in Male has its own VCR. The most popular programs are four-hour long Hindu tearjerkers, reflecting an increasing Indian influence in the islands. Also, you may remember that when a group of western "soldiers of fortune" tried to overthrow the Male government a few years ago, it was the Indian Air Force and Navy that prevented a coup d'etat.

Some of the conspirators were arrested and banished to remote islands for their pains. There is no death penalty in the archipelago. Not a bad alternative to being shot.

Inhaca
A Hint of African Adventures Past
Al J. Venter

Mozambique is always a rather unusual experience, but perhaps even more now during this heady period of transformation in southern African relations when new forms of political dispensation are slowly taking shape.

Go in from South Africa by road from Swaziland, through numerous roadblocks, past the rusting, burnt-out hulks of hundreds of vehicles, across the line of fire of the Russian 54/55 tank on the hill near the border post (it rarely moves because there is no petrol) and you will encounter a new and sometimes disturbing aspect of travel overland in Africa. If you fly direct to Maputo, the experience is a little more sedate.

The uniforms are all there and the Kafkaesque bureaucracy has barely slackened.

Mozambique today is cheap (unless you are staying in five star accommodation), easily accessible and, as we always used to say in the old days, "you ain't gonna be disappointed".

Soon there will be Portuguese, Colonial-style Laurentina beer again. The prawns and chicken peri-peri are as they always have been: excellent; and, most important of all, 'the natives are friendly', although Maputo in 1993 is a far cry from the Lourenco Marques of old. Even the revolutionary fervor of the two decades has flagged. There are major thoroughfares named after the likes of Ho Chi Minh, Che Guevara, Lenin, Marx, Stalin, Tito, Mao Tse Tung and a host of others. Foreign visitors tend to gather along Julius Nyerere Avenue; the Polana Hotel is on it, so are many of the better restaurants and bars. The Pilli Pilli offers an excellent meal and they sometimes have draught beer.

Although there are likely to be snags in the immediate future, the roads to the north and south of Maputo are still patrolled by the Army, the Indian Ocean coast provides tourists with the kind of African quasi-Colonial experience that an older generation still speaks of with nostalgia.

Indeed, the variety of people and places improves the farther north into the tropics you travel and applies especially to Mozambique, though conditions will have to stabilize before totally unrestricted travel is allowed. You no longer need to travel in convoy from the border.

Spotted Moray Eel with diver by Al Venter

Right now there is a corner of that huge country that was once known as Portuguese East Africa, and is bigger than Texas and twice as interesting, that is immediately accessible and capable of giving visitors a memorable experience. That is Inhaca, the island with a coastline of about 100 kilometres at the entrance to Delagoa Bay.

Inhaca offers a week-long seafari that incorporates scuba diving, two or three days of overland hiking with beachside camps and big-game fishing with catches that may include marlin, shark, sailfish, tuna, dorado, kingfish and barracuda.

During our stay two large sailfish were hooked off the adjacent Portuguese island, barely a kilometre away and well within sight of where we were staying, the Inhaca Protea Hotel.

The most interesting experience for people keen on scuba-diving is the scatter of shipwrecks that lines the entrance to what was once one of Portugal's most important imperial possessions on the sea route to India. There are many of them dating from the 1939-45 war.

One of these, on the Bassas Denae - a large reef about 12 kilometres out to sea, offers a wealth of marine life. It was apparently torpedoed on its way out of Lourenco Marques harbor during World War II.

No one could tell me the name of the ship, but she lies on the reef, totally broken up and covering an area of about three or four football fields. Almost all that remains of the wreck that is identifiable are the boilers; we counted four of them, all sheltering a wide variety of fish: rock cod, grouper, the occasional shoal of barracuda, shark, morays, moorish idols and other reef fish. The visibility, so far out in the Mozambique current, was excellent.

On both mornings when we dived off Bassas Denae there were several shoals of whale with their calves frolicking off the deep-water drop-off a few hundred metres from where we entered the water. Every few minutes one of them would breech and fall back in a cascade of white water with clap of thunder that could be heard miles away. Divers have approached them in the past, though this is not recommended when they are with their young.

Several wrecks can be dived much closer inshore. One of these, discovered in the spring of 1992, has not yet been properly explored or identified.

There are other diving attractions, one of them quite startling. The 'airport' lies to the north of the island and is so named because of the number of ragged-tooth sharks that can be found lounging on the "runways" it is of course not to be confused with the airstrip that brings visitors to Inhaca in small aircraft from Maputo airport on the mainland.

This is always an exciting dive, better in certain respects than Aliwal Shoal.

> **Most of the local inhabitants are ragged-tooth sharks, but there are also zambezi tiger, and according to some reports, great white sharks to be found off Inhaca all year round.**

Other excellent dive sites are situated to the south off Cape Santa Maria, Ponte Torres, and, farther down the mainland coast all the way to the Natal border with South Africa.

While spear fishing is permitted on the offshore reefs as there is nothing the authorities can do about it, it is prohibited in the immediate vicinity of Inhaca, which has now been declared a national park. The parks staff are active and, by comparison with most African standards, dedicated to their task. While we were there two South Africans spear fishing in the area of the Reserve were arrested, escorted to Maputo and deported, sans gear.

Treasure from Mozambique Shipwreck by Al Venter

One of the greatest attractions of Inhaca is that conditions in the inshore areas are excellent for novices. While the visibility may not be as good as on the offshore reefs, marine life is plentiful. The best dives here take place at the turn of high tide. You can catch the tide on the way out and drift a kilometre along the reef.

To the south, near the Saco da Inhaca, there are coral gardens with more marine life than any other inshore reefs that I have seen. My thirteen-year old son, Luke, who was weaned on inshore reefs in Mauritius, the Comores, Natal and elsewhere, regards these reefs as the most abundant in varieties of fish and shells that he had ever seen.

Not even the historical archives in Lisbon provide a clue as to when Inhaca was first discovered by the Portuguese.

In 1502, however, there was in existence a map showing the Baie de Lagoa and its three rivers. That veteran navigator of the East, Vasco da Gama, is likely to have sheltered in the lee of the island on his voyage hugging the contours of the east coast, though the Arabs of Sofala, farther up the coast would certainly have told him about the place when he eventually reached them.

The explorer, Lourenco Marques (also Portuguese), after whom the port was named, was sent there in 1545 to survey the trading possibilities of the bay and he reported enormous quantities of ivory to be had. This was the beginning of a long period of Lisbon's sailors being commercially active there. What is today known as Portuguese Island was the official trading station; it was then, appropriately, known as Elephant Island.

In time, Inhaca also became a haven for shipwrecked Portuguese sailors who made their way northwards up the coast to places like the Transkei's Wild Coast. Among these were the survivors of the wrecks of the Sao Tome (1589) and the Sao Joao (1552) which went ashore in South Africa near the Umzimvubu River where Port St John's now stands. There were also the Sao Joao Baptista (1622), the Santissimo Sacramento and the Nossa Senhora de Atalaya do Pinheiro (both 1647).

In 1587 three English vessels arrived off Inhaca to trade, a year later, came the Dutch, onboard the Noord for the specific purpose of accurately charting Delagoa Bay. They established themselves in a fort near the present city of Maputo in 1721, but left nine years later declaring the region 'unprofitable'. Uninhabitable would have been more appropriate because of the mosquitoes and fever.

Before the Portuguese took control again, both the English and the Austrians had been active in and around Inhaca and, consequently, the area is steeped in the early history of European expansionism in Africa.

A series of two or three day hiking trails form an important adjunct to outdoor activities on Inhaca. Whether these are routed through Gone Fishin' Safaris or simply on your own, with tent, camping equipment and fishing gear on your back, all paths lead to and from the water.

A feature of hiking trails are the mangrove swamps which cover much of the interior, and provide a fascinating array of above-and-below water aquatic life. The tidal flats to the north and south are an experience; the shell-life alone will make the trip worthwhile. There are flamingoes, as well as a huge variety of African bird life at several locations and it is all quite safe for visitors.

Sand dunes provide another dimension. In keeping with African east coast topography, the seaward side of Inhaca consists of huge railing dunes abutting the sea with sand surfing a possibility. What is nice is that you are guaranteed not to have to dodge a single beach buggy or motorcycle.

The combinations on Inhaca are endless. The hotel has its own transport and they will take parties of up to eight to any location of your choice. Other activities include waterskiing, wind surfing, there are hobie cats, and less pleasant, there is a 20 per cent tourist charge on all facilities. It is as well that you know this beforehand.

A serious word of warning. Inhaca, as with the rest of East Africa, falls within the malaria belt a scourge which seems to be spreading southwards and into parts of South Africa that has not known the disease for generations.

This is a serious matter; people who have not taken a prophylactic have died of a particularly virulent strain of what is believed to have been imported from South East Asia during the revolutionary period. There have been thousands of Vietnamese and North Koreans in Mozambique since 1974.

It is essential that every member of party regularly take some or other of the antimalarial pills. Even if this does not provide adequate protection, your level of malarial infection will be greatly diminished and consequently much easier to treat if and when it happens. Also if you are not under air-conditioning, mosquito nets and a good insect repellent like Tabard or Peaceful Sleep as well as mosquito coils are important considerations.

What is vital is the need to recognize the earliest signs of malaria which are not unlike flu; headaches, coughing hot flushes and, eventually, fever. If you have not been taking a prophylactic, by then it might be too late!

For the rest, enjoy the island, a quite magnificent ocean experience, the people and sea-food dishes which have lost none of the old Lusitanian gastronomic appeal.

For those who cannot afford many of the facilities mentioned, pack a pup tent, gather together your fishing gear and diving equipment, take the ferry Maputo to Inhaca (its schedule is frustratingly erratic) and head for one of the quiet little coves on the south of the island.

> You can fish or snorkel for a week or year. 'The sea will provide most of your needs and you can always arrange for a passing canoe to bring you a few additional beers, or a carafe of cheap Portuguese vinho tinto, paraffin for your lamps, a basketful of camaroes or a clutch of those delightfully delicious white clams or mussels that so many of the island women spend their time in the mud flats at low tide searching for.

Make sure they are fresh though; use your nose for that litmus test.

Mauritius - A Must!
Wendy Canning Church

"God modeled Heaven After Mauritius"
Mark Twain

In November 1992, I flew from South Africa to Mauritius which lies 500 miles east of Madagascar in the Indian Ocean. While visiting, I stayed at La Pirogue Hotel and Casino.

La Pirogue takes its name from the local fishing boats - strong, yet elegant crafts with a single mast that still sail across the lazy lagoons. The three story main building billows from the tropical scenery like a pirogue sail.

It is incidentally a world acknowledged design to withstand the cyclones that occasionally roll across Mauritius. Under its domed, overhanging roof you will find the Terrace restaurant stretching languidly alongside the hotel's swimming pool. On other floors you will find comprehensive conference facilities, a spacious bar and the casino and slots area. The hotel has two boutiques, a gift shop, a hairdresser, and a masseuse on the premises. A doctor is also on call at any time and the hotel has a dispensary with a nurse and a comprehensive range of pharmaceuticals.

The accommodations are a comfortable blend of air-conditioned luxury and a seaside cottage. Take your choice of twin-bedded rooms, twin-bedded suites or interleading rooms. Each bungalow resembles an upturned pirogue basking on the beach. The highly peaked roofs are heavily thatched - to exclude both heat and noise - while the interiors, each with an informal lounge area, contain everything you need: private bath, piped-in music, telephone, individually controlled air-conditioning, electric razor plug (110/220v) and a secluded patio. The wonderful service helps to make this patio your own private hideaway, yours to enjoy with prompt and efficient bar service, scrumptious continental breakfasts and gentle trade winds breathing through cascades of bougainvillea.

> **Share your mornings with an inquisitive mynah bird, your sun soaked days with groves of sighing Casuarina trees and your evenings with the delicate fragrance of exotic midnight flowers that bloom, in lush profusion between bungalows.**

La Pirogue is one of the three Sun International resorts on Mauritius and is a perfect spot for the single diver, diving couple, family, or group of divers, as well as non-divers. Not only is there good diving nearby, but there are plenty of other activities at the hotel to keep everyone happy.

Each night, a different theme dinner is offered under the stars in the pleasant dining room that surrounds the pool. Luncheon is served at the beach bar or at the adjacent Paul and Virginie restaurant. The cuisine at each spot is excellent and the service is warm and friendly and highly professional. Andrew sets the standards of a five star hotel for La Pirogue and his staff.

Parents of young children will be delighted to note that La Piroque also has resident Children's Hostesses, experienced in the ways of junior guests. A complete program to entertain children has been organized and each child over the age of three years can become a member of the Young Pirates Club and will be given a T-shirt and a membership card. They can enjoy supervised swimming in the pool or in safe, shallow lagoon waters, as well as an endless variety of games and pastimes. Arrangements can be made for a babysitter, and children's meals are served between 18:OO and 19:OO.

TAKING IN THE SCENERY

It is tempting to never leave the grounds, but Mauritius has a variety of sights to investigate. White Sands Tours has a desk in the lobby at La Pirogue and can arrange for a private car or tour bus to take you to the open air markets and the downtown shops in Port Louis, to the spectacular Pamplemousses Gardens, the Aquarium, or to one of the many beautiful beaches to sun, snorkel or scuba dive.

Wendy Canning Church and dive buddies aboard Kevin's Yacht by Kevin Cock

The entire island should be seen and White Sand Tours can fulfill any request. With its 1,865 square kilometers, (160 of which are coastline, almost all of which are surrounded by coral reefs), the visitors to this wonderful paradise will never, and I mean never, be bored. If you do chose to take a private tour ask for Robert at White Sand Tours. He was my driver and his pleasant and friendly manner, in addition to his wealth-of knowledge of the island, will make your journey a delight.

Scuba divers and snorkelers will be delighted with the center and its personnel. The resort's diving center is the most modern and up-to-date on the island.

It is fully equipped with modern tanks, compressors, diving equipment, and a lecture room. The director of the dive operation is 29 year old Thierry De Chazal, who has been diving for eleven years. He has been an instructor at La Pirogue for seven years. Thierry is the only Mauritian qualified under the auspices of the American Professional Association of Diving Instructors to tutor and qualify divers for Open Water and Advanced Open Water certificates. His professionalism, warmth and sense of humor make the time before and after a dive a delight. Phillipe, his right hand man, is a tremendous asset. Not only is he a terrific underwater guide, but he is also extremely patient with all the newly certified divers. Both their love for the water and their zest for diving is infectious!

The waters off La Pirogue hold some of the best diving spots in the area. Corals, rock caves, submarine cliffs and, of course, an abundance of fish guarantee excitement with every dive.

The sites are only minutes away from the hotel which is a plus. Between dives you sit at the charming beach restaurant at the water's edge and have an espresso or cappuccino with Thierry, Phillipe and the other divers while you fill out your log books, identifying all the new fish you have just discovered and identifying the beautiful corals.

The dive center receives high praises for its professionalism, adherence to safety standards, and for making each dive an interesting and adventurous one. Thanks, Thierry and Phillipe, for a fantastic week!

DIVE TO EXPLORE

L'Eveille: Here the depth is 25m. The rock formation and drop off allows divers the opportunity to view a large variety of sea life including a garden of sea anemones, clam shells and black coral.

Aquarium: This is a shallow dive to a maximum of 15m. So called because of the abundance of fish of many varieties which are quite accustomed to terrestrial visitors. A moray nicknamed "Kong" is the star attraction having been trained to feed "mouth to mouth."

Cathedral: One of the most interesting underwater rock formations comprising two drop offs leading to a cave. The waters abound with crayfish, king fish, lion fish, and schools of soldier fish. A torch is recommended to explore the surrounding small crevices. The depth here reaches 28m and you have a bottom time of about 30 minutes.

Couline Bambou: Maximum depth is 30m. This dive takes you through a series of tunnels and caves. A torch is needed to see the variety of sea life and black coral. Good for close-up photography.

Lion Fish by Kevin Cock

Rempart-Suisse: One of the longest reefs in Mauritius, found at an average depth of 25m. Here you will find a good variety of fish and marine life, especially the balloon fish.

Canon: At 22m a 19th century wreck buried partially in the sand. An old canon can be seen and copper nails can be found in the sand. Exciting exploration.

Night Dives: The Aquarium, because of its abundance of fish is the ideal spot for a night dive. Depart from the hotel at sunset returning about 2 hours later in time for dinner.

DEEP-SEA FISHING

The resort is fast gaining a reputation as the world's premier center for big-game fishing. The coveted Sun International Marlin World Cup is presented annually at La Pirogue. Deep-sea fishing trips can be arranged by contacting the Fishing Office at the beach, and fully-equipped boats take day cruises out into the blue depths where fishermen will find marlin (the black and blue striped varieties), tunny, barracuda, bonito, kingfish, wahoo, sailfish and shark. The best time for fishing in Mauritian waters is October to March. Jackfish and barracuda, however, are caught close to the reefs between June and September. Andrew Slome, the General Manager, is an avid fisherman and orchestrates the fishing tournaments; he will share many a fish story with you.

Big-game fishing organizations operate from nearby Black River and guests from the hotel can get all the information they need from the Fishing Office at the beach.

TRIMARIN CRUISE

For those who wish the pleasure of a cruise without fishing, the hotels private Trimarin will take guests on a never-to-beforgotten trip up the reef and lagoon on the West Coast. The Trimarin excursion departs from Black River, only 15 minutes away, and includes a luncheon of smoked salmon and champagne. Snorkeling equipment is provided to explore Aladdin's cave of neon-colored fish and coral.

Editor's Notes

One day we ventured out to **Paradis Diving** and spent the day on Kevin Cock's beautiful yacht. She is a spectacular catamaran and well worth booking. However, do not forget your lunch and bring along your snorkeling gear.

SCUBA AND SNORKELING FACILITIES QUESTIONNAIRE

NAME **La Pirogue Diving School**
ADDRESS **Wolmar-Flic-En-Flac**
Mauritius
CONTACT **Thierry De Chazal**
TITLE **Diving Instructor**
TELEPHONE **203-4538449**   FAX **203-4538449**

CAPITAL: **Port Louis**   GOVERNMENT:
POPULATION: **1,000,000**   LANGUAGE: **French and English**
CURRENCY: **Rupee**   ELECTRICITY: **220v**
AIRLINES: **Air Mauritius**   DEPARTURE TAX? **RS 100**
NEED VISA/PASSPORT? YES **x**   NO   PROOF OF CITIZENSHIP? YES **x**   NO

YOUR FACILITY IS CLASSIFIED AS: SCUBA CENTER   RESORT **x**
BUSINESS HOURS: **Open at 8:30 a.m.**
CERTIFYING AGENCIES: **PADI and CMAS**
LOG BOOK REQUIRED?   YES **x**   NO
EQUIPMENT: SALES   RENTALS **x**   AIR FILLS **x**
PRIMARY LINE OF EQUIPMENT: **SPIRO and US DIVERS**
PHOTOGRAPHIC EQUIPMENT: SALES   RENTALS   LAB

CHARTER/DIVE BOAT AVAILABLE? YES **x** NO   DIVER CAPACITY **12**
COAST GUARD APPROVED?   YES **x** NO   CAPTAIN LICENSED? YES **x**   NO
SHIP TO SHORE? YES   NO   LORAN? YES   NO   RADAR? YES   NO
DIVE MASTER/INSTRUCTOR ABOARD? YES **x**   NO   BOTH

DIVING & SNORKELING: SALT **x**   FRESH
TYPE OF DIVING/SNORKELING IN AREA: WALL **x**   BEACH   WRECK **x**   REEF   CAVE   ICE
DIVING/SNORKELING IN YOUR AREA IS BEST SUITED FOR: BEGINNER   INTERMEDIATE **x**   ADVANCED **x**
BEST TIME OF YEAR FOR DIVING/SNORKELING: **All Year**
TEMPERATURE: **NOV-APRIL**   **27-28C**   **MAY-OCT: 20-25C**
VISIBILITY: **DIVING:**   **60 FT**   **SNORKELING: 60 FT**

PACKAGES AVAILABLE: DIVE **x**   DIVE STAY   SNORKEL   SNORKEL-STAY
ACCOMMODATIONS NEARBY: HOTEL **x**   MOTEL   HOME RENTALS
ACCOMMODATION RATES: EXPENSIVE   MODERATE **x**   INEXPENSIVE
RESTAURANTS NEARBY: EXPENSIVE   MODERATE   INEXPENSIVE **x**
YOUR AREA IS: REMOTE   QUIET WITH ACTIVITIES **x**   LIVELY
LOCAL ACTIVITY/NIGHTLIFE: **Bar, restaurant, discos**
CAR NEEDED TO EXPLORE AREA? YES **x**   NO
DUTY FREE SHOPPING?   YES **x**   NO

LOCAL EMERGENCY SERVICES   NEAREST HYPERBARIC TREATMENT FACILITY
COASTGUARD: AUTHORITY: **Special Mobile Force**
TELEPHONE: LOCATION: **Vacoas**
CALLSIGNS: TELEPHONE:
LOCAL DIVING DOCTOR:
NAME:
LOCATION:
TELEPHONE:

SCUBA AND SNORKELING FACILITIES QUESTIONNAIRE

NAME   **Paradise Diving**
ADDRESS   **Royal Road, Grand Bay**
                  Mauritius, Indian Ocean
CONTACT   **Kevin Cock**
TITLE   **Director & Instructor**
TELEPHONE   **230-2637220**   FAX **230-2368534**

CAPITAL: **Port Louis**   GOVERNMENT: **Democratic**
POPULATION: LANGUAGE: **English & French**
CURRENCY: **Mauritius Rupees**   ELECTRICITY: **220v**
AIRLINES: DEPARTURE TAX? **RS 100**
NEED VISA/PASSPORT?   YES x   NO
PROOF OF CITIZENSHIP?   YES x   NO

YOUR FACILITY IS CLASSIFIED AS: SCUBA CENTER x   RESORT x
BUSINESS HOURS: 8:30 a.m. to 5:30 p.m.
CERTIFYING AGENCIES: **NAUI**
LOG BOOK REQUIRED?   YES x   NO
EQUIPMENT:
SALES   RENTALS x   AIR FILLS x
PRIMARY LINE OF EQUIPMENT: **DACOR and SEAQUEST**
PHOTOGRAPHIC EQUIPMENT: SALES   RENTALS x   LAB x

CHARTER/DIVE BOAT AVAILABLE? YES x   NO   DIVER CAPACITY **15**
COAST GUARD APPROVED?   YES x   NO   CAPTAIN LICENSED? YES x   NO
SHIP TO SHORE? YES x NO   LORAN? YES   NO x   RADAR?   YES   NO x
DIVE MASTER/INSTRUCTOR ABOARD? YES   NO   BOTH

DIVING & SNORKELING: SALT x   FRESH
TYPE OF DIVING/SNORKELING IN AREA: WALL x   BEACH   WRECK x   REEF   CAVE   ICE
DIVING/SNORKELING IN YOUR AREA IS BEST SUITED FOR: BEGINNER x   INTERMEDIATE x   ADVANCED x
BEST TIME OF YEAR FOR DIVING/SNORKELING: **All Year**
TEMPERATURE: **NOV-APRIL**   30-34C   **MAY-OCT:**   28C
VISIBILITY: **DIVING:**   90 FT   **SNORKELING: 90 FT**

PACKAGES AVAILABLE: DIVE x   DIVE STAY x   SNORKEL   SNORKEL-STAY
ACCOMMODATIONS NEARBY: HOTEL x   MOTEL   HOME RENTALS x
ACCOMMODATION RATES: EXPENSIVE   MODERATE x   INEXPENSIVE
RESTAURANTS NEARBY: EXPENSIVE   MODERATE   INEXPENSIVE x
YOUR AREA IS: REMOTE   QUIET WITH ACTIVITIES x   LIVELY
LOCAL ACTIVITY/NIGHTLIFE: **Bar, restaurant, discos**
CAR NEEDED TO EXPLORE AREA? YES x   NO **Typical Indian Ocean tropical island, good hospitality,**
DUTY FREE SHOPPING?   YES x   NO **good diving, and watersport facilities.**

LOCAL EMERGENCY SERVICES   NEAREST HYPERBARIC TREATMENT FACILITY
COASTGUARD: **Grand Bay**   AUTHORITY: **(SMF) Special Mobile Force**
TELEPHONE: **2637220**   LOCATION: **Vacous**
CALLSIGNS: **16**
TELEPHONE:
LOCAL DIVING DOCTOR:
NAME:
LOCATION:
TELEPHONE:

Kevin has built a luxurious live aboard. We will bring you more news and information when we spend time aboard her. Many thanks to Kevin for a great day and for the underwater photos!

The beautiful and understated **Le Tousserak**, another Sun International Hotel, has undergone a complete renovation. We plan to return to bring you a story of its amenities. This property will surely be included in our Honeymoon chapter.

Be sure to visit the **Green Island Rum Factory** and bring some home to friends, even if you do not drink! It's more of a sipping rum, like brandy, and just as delicious.

We flew Air Mauritius to Mauritius and the service was first class in every class! I highly recommend flying them when possible. They have many worldwide routes. You will not be disappointed. I rate Air Mauritius as one of the best airlines I have ever flown! For booking information contact: (In the US) Air Mauritius, 560 Sylvan Avenue, Englewood Cliffs., NJ 07632. Telephone: 1-800-537-1172. Facsimile: 201-871-6983. (In Los Angeles) 213-893-7375; facsimile: 213-893-7374.

For more information on La Pirogue contact: La Pirogue Hotel and Casino, Wolmar, Flic en Flac, Mauritius. Telephone (230)4538441/2/3. Telex: 4255 IW. Fax: (203) 453-8449.

Reunion: An Unusual French Experience
Al J. Venter

There is an island in the Indian Ocean that is neither independent not yet a colony in the strict sense of the word. Administered directly from Paris, in the same way as Tahiti, Martinique, Guadeloupe and other members of the former French empire they are still members of metropolitan France. It offers some really excellent diving.

The gallicism of La Reunion includes the French language, several flights daily from Charles de Gaulle Airport, the presence of the French security forces and, to greet you on arrival at St. Denis Airport, French gendarmes on the tarmac in their distinctive khaki kepis. When you get out of the airport building you can board a bus into town and pay with French francs. In town you can drink "cafe au lait" or "pastis" just as in any French town. Yet, La Reunion is almost 12,000 kilometres from Paris.

The Francophonic Ile de Reunion "is" France. In spite of often violent protests by a very vocal and radical minority, the Elysee Palace clearly has no intention of changing the state of things, either now or in the future.

It has apparently all to do with extended international French interests that reach far beyond the Atlantic to the Indian and Pacific Oceans. That policy includes the concept of a greater territorial influence, access to such places as Djibouti in the Horn of Africa (which is, in fact, independent only in name), the Ivory Coast on the west coast of Africa and the French possessions in the Pacific. And, of course, the graceful old volcanic island of Reunion.

Some measure of the importance of Reunion can be gauged from the fact that there are sometimes as many as three or four Air France Boeing 747s parked on the apron at the airport at any time, This is all "domestic traffic"; and in the number of flights alone, it must consume a large proportion of the French budget for overseas development.

These aircraft bring in anything from yesterday's Paris newspapers, chilled Norman beef, fresh supplies of "pate de foie" and a small army of French civil servants who keep the administration and the mechanics of the island comfortable in trim.

Compared with other semi-tropical islands in the Indian Ocean, La Reunion is run like a provincial "department" on the European mainland. It has more in common with Corsica in the Mediterranean than Mauritius or the Seychelles in the Indian Ocean, apart from geographical location.

The Reunionnais public transport system is among the most efficient in all the Indian Ocean basin west of Australia; and much better than that of South Africa. Modern double-lane highways have been built round the entire circumference of the island. Like the French, the Reunionnais drive like maniacs, with an inordinate number of car accidents. To that extent they share a characteristic of what the moderan cant call the "Third World".

French domestic television is relayed by satellite live from Marseilles, Paris and Lyons (you can watch Five Nations Rugby live on Saturday afternoons during the Southern Hemisphere summer) and the schools follow the same curriculum as French schools, the lessons for each day being centrally determined on a nationwide basis.

Municipalities, hospitals, security, sewage, ports, the city hall, recreation, rubbish disposal and evening activities are exactly as the visitor would find them in a French provincial capital "chez nous".

Shark by Al Venter

Since it is theoretically an integral part of France, most of the expatriate functionaries on La Reunion tend to return "home" when their two or three year tours of duty are over. Anybody who thinks that the island is not a French colony is deluding himself.

Much of the infrastructure on La Reunion is distinctly advantageous to the enthusiast who proposes to use the island as a base for serious diving.

Although it is situated in an isolated corner of the Indian Ocean, Reunion is an half-an-hours' flight from Mauritius, which itself has direct links with the Far East, Europe, Africa and Australia. That makes it two interesting destinations for the price of one.

Since the climate is not so balmy as that of Mauritius, it has a rather different undersea marine life, topography, terrain and ecology. The ocean floor is of lava, and much of it is of fairly recent volcanic origin. In places it is "visually" almost like diving off the Cape Peninsula in South Africa, though the water is not nearly as cold.

Reunion is less tropical than Mauritius; there are more and larger fish (including sharks) which have presented serious problems to non-divers in the past few years; there have been several attacks on swimmers and sailboarders. There are also more wrecks, and the diving is generally deeper.

Although more expensive that either Mauritius or the Seychelles, La Reunion has some excellent small hotels and restaurants. You can also find accommodation at family-run pensions or "gites".

Avoid anything five-star; it will cost you 50 percent more than a comparable place in Paris. Beware of tourist traps in places like St. Gilles-les-Baines or St. Pierrre. Then your holiday will be a pleasure.

There are about two dozen diving operations in La Reunion, run with professional French competence. Safety controls are rigorously maintained.

There are also a dozen doctors trained in diving medicine emergency facilities with helicopters. All these provide a remarkable experience in an area that a few years ago offered only the bare essentials.

While on Reunion Island I have tended towards the two western towns of St. Gilles, my favorite, and St. Pierre, a little farther to the south. Much of the area round St. Gilles is sheltered by coral reef several hundred metres out, and the beach is good, with a shallow, white sanded lagoon. Many of the beaches on the rest of Reunion are of black coral sand, but the diving is none the worse for that.

The sea life is rich and varied.

St. Gilles in the mid-nineties is a "Cote d'Azur" in the Indian Ocean. Ten years ago it was a sleepy little backwater; now it is a swinging modern holiday centre where you can pay a lot of money for two cokes or coffees and croissants for breakfast in an unpretentious coffee bar.

Any diving of consequence is centred in the area of the harbour, where eight clubs operate at a very competent level. (There are five clubs in St. Denis and two more in St. Paul).

All the clubs have very good boats and equipment, and the dive masters are all French-qualified and sticklers for procedure. You won't get a dive if you cannot produce a recognized certificate. Nor will you get your bottles filled.

The dive masters check out all newcomers, even if they claim to be related to the Cousteaus.

Probably the most enterprising of the diving groups at St. Gilles is the "Groupe Exploration Ocean", known as GEO. The place was acquired not long ago by Thierry Donatien and he offers perhaps the most reasonable service for overseas visitors. A former French equestrian at national level in the metropolis, Thierry and his father know how to welcome strangers to their club. I and other friends who have been there since have been made very welcome indeed; Thierry had made the point that anyone from the English-speaking world would be well looked after, though he needs a little help with his broken English.

Thierry has an arrangement with a local small hotel that can accommodate two persons for less that US$50 "per room". There is a kitchen for self-catering. Normally GEO charges 160 Ffr per dive or 750 Ffr for six dives, but they suggested that anyone who proposes to come to the island should write first and arrange a package deal beforehand. Do that and you could save yourself a packet. Telephone Reunion 245603 or write to GEO, Enceinte Portuaire, 97434, Saint Gilles-les-Baines, La Reunion.

It matters little whether the diver has his own gear; the charge is standard. GEO has a seven-metre Zodiac rubber duck, among others, 28 tanks and a Bauer 28 compressor.

Diving is a very well-established sport. The thousand or so members of clubs and diving centres welcome visitors but again, it does not help if you cannot communicate in French. Very few islanders speak any English.

Diving takes place all year round on Reunion. There is a cyclone season between January and April but unlike Mauritius, you need to be unlucky to have your activities curtailed by the weather. If you cannot dive one side of the island, you can always try the other.

Even during cloudy weather, the visibility underwater is excellent largely because the level of pollution is low. The French are conscious of their pristine island ecology.

Thierry Donatien lists 17 dive locations within easy reach of St. Gilles. Nine of these are at 25 metres or less; four are between 30 and 36 metres and another four range in depth from 54 metres to 75 metres. According to Thierry only very experienced divers are allowed to participate in deep diving, and then with adequate back-up in the event of problems. Strong currents are sometimes a feature of this rugged coastline.

There have been several diving accidents off Reunion in spite of precautions; some of these have resulted in loss of life. As a consequence, all deep dives off Reunion are carried out with a 15-litre tank coupled to four octopus rigs strung on a line five or six metres below the surface.

The French, tend to decompress at shallow levels for as long as it takes to exhaust your entire air supply. Increasingly it is the view that "washing out" your system is the only answer to long-term problems that may manifest themselves years hence, and I concur.

These people also like to keep an oxygen bottle and rig onboard and are great believers in drinking large quantities of fruit juice and a little salt immediately on returning to the boat after a dive. Many French divers will then also take an aspirin tablet for better blood flow. If there are any "silent bubbles", it has been shown that the aspirin will reduce the possibility of clotting.

Troise Grottes
This takes place in an area offshore from St. Gilles-les-Baines at a depth ranging from about 20 to 24 metres. The reef is made up of strips of granite between 30 and 40 metres in length with connecting caves crisscrossing the reefs and interspersed here and there by connecting caves and passages. Very complicated, but interesting! But not for the overweight; you could get stuck in a tunnel.

The gorgonians on Trois Grottes are spectacular. Plenty of emperor and angelfish as well as a wide variety of butterflyfish.

Boucan Cannot
This reef is situated about 200 metres offshore from the village of Boucan and lies at depths ranging from about 10 and 20 metres. It is made up largely of cooled lava rock, again interspersed with cavities and caves. Because the reef acts as a break for incoming waves, there is sediment in the water and visibility is not what it is elsewhere along the coast, but still an interesting dive. There is usually a current running, so divers tend to drift along the reef. There are a great number of smaller reef fish, clownfish and lionfish.

Pierre aux Merous
At depths of about 30 metres there is a small reef about 15 metres in height, riddled with tunnels and caves and home to several large rock cod that are tame enough to be touched. During one dive, one of the grouper was trying, from behind, to get my head into his mouth in a moment of tomfoolery. Who says that fish don't have sense of humor?

There is also a large moray here that is said to be tame, though even Thierry was not prepared to embrace the creature.

Barque St, Paul
This barge measures 20 metres by 10 metres, is a metre-and-a-half high and sits in 26 metres of water. It was sunk as an artificial reef about five years ago and is alive with a huge variety of marine life including hard and soft corals and stonefish.

A 30 metre length of chain is attached to the wreck and this allows for some excellent macro-photography. One will see plenty of lionfish, honey-comb electric rays, skate, game-fish and the occasional moray. The barge is a marvelous experience and is not to be missed.

Epave Hai Staing
This is a deep dive to 56 metres, but it can be regarded as something of a milestone for anyone diving off Reunion.

The wreck, is a big one; roughly 10,000 tons and about 50 metres long. It was sunk in position off St. Gilles by the French navy in 1982. Visibility in this location is about 25 metres, even though the island is enveloped in thick cloud.

Roches Merveilleuses
This is a 52 metre dive. For decompression, Thierry hung a 15 metre bottle below the boat with four second stages.

On the reef we discovered the biggest "mother" of a moray we had ever encountered. It was truly a monster.

Much other sea life was encountered in the short time that we remained down. There was no current and no surge while on the dive, even when decompressing.

Clearly, diving in La Reunion is an unusual and very "different" experience. Diving in these French waters is not the kind of "resort" experience that one finds offered by Mauritian hotels, largely because dive operations on La Reunion are run as independent businesses and are dependent - not so much on novice holiday makers - as local residents, the majority of whom are CMAS qualified. To the French, NAUI and PADI qualifications are American and therefore "inferior" to European standards.

Certainly, these people take their diving seriously. They are aware that they are placed in a most unusual milieu and the few opportunities that are presented, they grab eagerly. It all makes for a very active scuba-oriented little community.

Thierry Donatien and his associates play a prominent role in maintaining adequate standards and offering the kind of services that you would have difficulty equating elsewhere in the Indian Ocean.

Rodrigues Island
Al J. Venter

"There are special places we speak of in whispers; those few unspoiled islands we hesitate to mention lest others discover, develop and ruin the dream forever. Rodrigues is such a place" says Marie Levine.

The instant the last wisp of cloud rushes past the Air Mauritius AR-42, turbo-prop you get the first glimpse of Rodrigues. This vast expanse of deep blue Indian Ocean is broken by a tiny land mass with what looks like a frothy skirt made by the swell breaking on the barrier reef surrounding it.

On final approach we pass over the outer reef and are enchanted by the beauty beneath. With every meter that we descend the great coral lagoon becomes more impressive. Fishermen's pirogues can be seen inside the protected passages of the lagoon

The smallest of the Mascarene islands, Rodrgues is barely eighteen kilometers long and eight wide.

It is not only small it is remote; Rodrigues lies in the Indian Ocean at 19 degrees south and 63 degrees east. To the north and south, the nearest land is thousands of kilometers away. Eastward there is nothing but ocean until the coast of western Australia is reached; Mauritius lies 653 kilometers to the west.

Although you can reach Mauritius without difficulty, unless you charter or sail your own yacht. There are only two carriers that can get you to Rodrigues: by boat, the M. V. Mauritius makes regular runs between Mauritius and Rodrigues. It usually takes 36 hours each way, or you can fly Air Mauritius which has two flights between Mauritius and Rodrgues each week. The flight takes ninety minutes. In short, it takes some planning even to reach the island.

There is only one hotel on Rodrigues, **Pointe Venus**. If you are the unusual kind of person who made the effort to reach Rodrigues in the first place, you will love it! Built for the Cable and Wireless Company in the 1930's, it seems preserved in the amber of time. With its teak floors, corrugated iron walls (a safe-guard on an island in the cyclone belt) and cast-iron pillars, it appears like the setting for a Joseph Conrad novel. All rooms open on to the wide verandah that surrounds the hotel. Here guests relax in the roomy rattan chairs to watch ships entering and leaving the harbor.

From the verandah you can see the hull of an old sailing ship. She sank long ago, but a cyclone tore her from the depths and left her spars to rot on the reef near the entrance to the channel.

The manager of Pointe Venus, Serge Rousetty, makes your stay feel too short; he is a living repository of island lore. Serge knows where to find anything and everyone on the island. If you want a long-out-of-print book on local history or a dive-master, just ask Serge.

If all fifteen rooms at Pointe Venus are booked, you will probably find lodgings at one of the three boarding houses in Port Mathurin. It would be unwise to arrive without reservations; at present the island can accommodate only a few tourists.

Topography
Rodrigues rose out of the sea about a million years ago from a branch of the Mid Indian Ocean Submarine Ridge that runs parallel to the Mascarene plateau. Lava oozed

from the fissures to create her rounded mountains. The highest peak, Mount Limon, in the center of the island, rises to a height of more than 400 meters. Rodrigues has a number of peaks and only four-wheel-drive vehicles can negotiate the steep roads and hairpin turns.

The island is fringed by a broad reef that on the south stretches five nautical miles beyond the island. Other than Port Mathurin, the only entries through the reef are narrow channels. Because Rodrigues was born at a different time than other islands in this corner of the Indian Ocean, different forms of life have developed here. This tiny island is unique and so are its inhabitants.

Tortoises

The earliest human inhabitant, Francois Leguat, lived on Rodrigues from 1691 to 1693. He described its fauna as the dugongs that used to live in the shallow waters of the island, the herds of two or three thousand giant tortoises.

At one time there were between 150,000 and 200,000 of them on Rodrigues. They were so abundant that they formed an important export to Mauritius. In the early 1760's thirty thousand tortoises were exported in four ships within an eighteen-month period, but by 1795 there were only a few left in inaccessible ravines.

The dugongs have vanished, and giant tortoises survive only in zoos... How sad.

Solitaire

Mauritius had its dodo, but Rodrigues had a counterpart. The now extinct, flightless bird called the solitaire (Pezophaps Solitarius) once inhabited the forests of the island. According to Leguat, this bird was so named because, although abundant, it was usually seen alone, never in a flock. It somewhat resembled a turkey, but rather more elegant, with longer legs and a stately neck; it weighed up to twenty-five kilograms.

Males were brownish-gray, while females were "the color of fair hair" with a white crop. They had no tail but had "a kind of rump like a horse's in shape", and their wings had a bony knob at the tip "about the size of a musket ball".

When the birds rattled their wings they "make a noise like thunder that could be heard a furlong away".

The birds lived in the forests eating leaves and the fruits of palms and lataniers. They mated for life, and each nest - constructed of palm leaves on open ground - contained a single egg, greenish-white and speckled with brown, about the size of a goose egg. Unfortunately, the fledglings were very tasty. Adults were also eaten; they were hunted, particularly from March to September, when they became fat. Although the birds could not fly they could run very fast, especially over rocky ground, and they had a sharp hooked beak that they used for defense.

Sadly the solitaire could not be domesticated; when caged it "shed tears without crying" and starved to death. They were hunted to extinction some time in the late eighteenth century.

Diving

Henri Munier is the man to approach for diving on Rodrigues. He was born and bred on the island, and he has been diving for twenty years. After ten years as a commercial diver in Mauritius he returned to Rodrigues. After your first dive in Rodrigues you will know what brought him back.

Look for Henri when you arrive; he also runs a taxi service, and he is the best tour guide on the island.

Bring all your own equipment, including cylinders.

Air is no problem; Henri can have your tanks filled. The water is warm; a lycra suit is sufficient to keep you from getting chilled, so you won't need to pack many weights.

DIVE SITES
Coral Gardens - Grand Pate

Just beyond the channel to Port Mathurin, you find corals of every conceivable color, even colors that do not exist on land.

Experts say there are 170 species of coral in this part of the Indian Ocean. Every one must be represented here.

There are branching corals, terraces of layered plate corals, coral towers rising to within a few meters of the surface and colonies of stinging corals. (These fan-shaped structures orient themselves at right-angles to the prevailing current and sting the unwary diver like nettles.)

Most magnificent of all are the blue corals. There are huge coral heads of vibrant cobalt blue. Some dead corals in the overhangs and deep gullies glow with an iridescent blue light.

According to Dr. Gary Williams of the South African Museum, this light that is emitted may be due to the presence of bioluminescent bacteria. An examination of some of these fragments (plate and finger coral) on the surface showed that they were coated with a gray slimy material.

Grand Bassin

You may find sharks swimming at the base of the coral pinnacles in this area. Most are whitetip reef sharks, but gray sharks and hammerheads have also been seen.

The Aux Sables and the Ile Cocos nearby, are two of the many islands that lie within the giant fringing reef. These islands can be visited only on a spring high tide. Shoals of black kingfish patrol the outer edges of the reefs, and large parrotfish feed among the corals. Look our for the huge plate corals in this area.

These two islands are breeding grounds of the noddy, the lesser noddy and the fairy tern. The fairy terns have a dazzling white plumage; they are among the tamest and most inquisitive of seabirds. They breed in summer and nest in unlikely places: lumps of coral, tree forks and, it is said, even on the arms of the cross in front of the chapel

Pointe Cotton

At depths of four to five meters divers will find huge parrotfish and see more of the spectacular coral reef. At most places dive sites are listed, but here on Rodrigues, the reef is unspoiled and pulsating with life.

You skim along the surface in the pirogue, conscious of the shadow of your boat on the reef below (yes, the water is as clear as that) and note the colors of the fish. When a particularly beautiful coral outcrop is seen, or when you find a fish you want to photograph, simply slip over the side of the boat and dive.

Port South East

This area can only be dived on the incoming tide; and no diver should miss it. You dive in a passage near the entrance to the barrier reef. A rock heaved over the side of our pirogue serves as an anchor and touches bottom eighteen meters below.

The base of the cliff is a sandy bottom, but the best diving is on the northern wall at a depth of four to seven meters.

As we slip below the surface shoals of garfish, like quicksilver, wheel overhead. Shoals of kingfish and black chub patrol the passage. The cliff wall is festooned with lavender soft corals and yellow sea-fans. Enormous tiger cowries move sedately among the corals, and the long black spines of sea-urchins wave from crevices. The cliff wall is pocked with caves and tunnels. Shafts of sunlight penetrate the overhangs and barely illuminate the caverns. Gigantic trumpetfish hang almost motionless inside, solemn eyed squirrelfish watch as we approach, and swirling clouds of glassy sweepers rush past us. In this sheltered channel our greatest fear was running out of film before the end of our dive, each cave was more spectacular than the last!

Shipwrecks

Rodrigues lies far from the busy shipping route. Most of the ships that have been lost on her reefs were island traders. Since they were uninsured, their loss went unrecorded in London and New York. However, a search in the holdings of the Mauritius Institute and the archives of the Marine Board of

Rodrigues reveals their secret. A few of them have been located, but most lie buried beneath the luxuriant coral.

At Booby Island, you can visit the wreck of the White Jacket. She was lost on May 23, 1871 and now lies broken apart in three meters of water.

On the south-western barrier reef you can visit the remains of the 1,250-ton Clytemnestra. On September 4, 1870 the six-year-old ship was bound from Rangoon for Queenstown with a cargo of rice and sundries when she was lost on the reef. She now lies in six meters of water.

Less than a year later, in 1871, the 292-ton Clare Sayers was lost on the south-southwest side of Rodrigues. She had sailed from the Newcastle, New South Wales to Mauritius, under the command of Captain George Middleton with a cargo of coal, but she never reached Port.

And in the following year, 1872, the Bella Maria also foundered off Rodrigues.

Before that about 1704 or 1706, pirates captured and destroyed a French ship at Rodrigues.

The French and British once competed for Rodrigues. One June morning early last century as the French vessel, *L'Oiseau* lay anchored in the creek, the English ship *Plassey* arrived, flying Dutch colors. (The *Plassey*, commanded by Captain Thomas Hague, carried sixteen guns. She also had 110 men on board, sixty-five of them soldiers). The *Plassey* captured the *Mignonne*, opened fire on the shore batteries and fired volleys at the *L'Oiseau*.

Captain Julienne beached the *L'Oiseau* to prevent her from falling into enemy hands. She was burnt, along with her cargo of about three metric tons of rice. The shore battery was set on fire and the troops looted the settlement. A fifty-ton French vessel, *L'Heureux* was also burned. She was anchored in the creek when she was seen by the British frigate Duncan.

Captain Sneeds sent a boarding party to capture the French boat, but the British found a keg of rum and got so drunk that their officers were left to set the vessel on fire.

We know only that the *Swift* was wrecked on 5 August 1827 on Rodrigues and that the *Victoria* was lost there 16 years later, in 1843. The ship *Oxford*, commanded by Captain Thomas Marshall, was bound for Liverpool from Calcutta with a cargo of silk shawls when, on September 1, 1843, she was wrecked on the Southwestern reefs of Rodrigues.

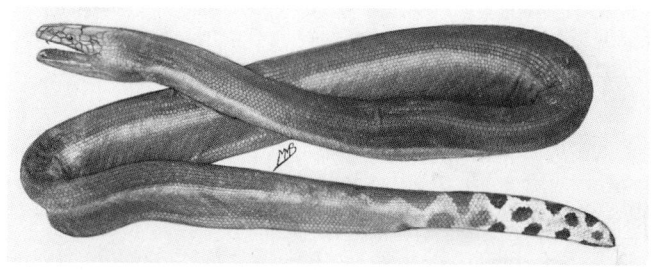

Probably the most dangerous creature in the sea is the sea snake. There is no known antidote against its venom. Artwork by J.L.B. Smith

The *Barque Trio*, under the command of Captain Smith, sailed from Calcutta on January 20, 1846 with a cargo of wheat and two passengers, a Mr. Gardyne and a Mr. Higgin. She was wrecked on the reefs of Rodrigues, but no lives were lost. Poor Higgin was sorely tried; the ship's boat capsized as he went ashore.

When it was learned that the *Barque* had been wrecked, the Mauritian government chartered a ship to retrieve the two passengers. Both Higgin and Gardyne were detained at Rodrigues for two months, during which time Higgin wrote an account of the island which was subsequently read before the Royal Geographical Society in 1848.

On November 15,1847, the *Samuel Smith*, bound from Penang to London, was wrecked at Rodrigues. She lies in six meters of water. The wreck of the *Nussur Sultan* also rests in six meters. She was bound from Calcutta with a cargo of grain worth seven thousand rupees -payable in Mauritius - when she was lost on one of the reefs of Rodrigues.

The *Masaniello* was lost on Rodrigues on March 30,1862, and in May 1863 the 150-ton Jemina was abandoned there. She arrived from Mauritius, under the command of Captain Jean Guenet.

The 918-ton *Salem* was twelve years old when she was lost on the reefs of Rodrigues. She was bound from Bassein for Falmouth via Mauritius laden with rice and under the command of Captain R. Mitchell.

The Hamburg schooner *Chin-Chin* was lost on the island on February 11, 1868. The 289-ton *Neptune* sailed from Singapore with a cargo of rice and planks under the command of Captain P.J. Buesnel, but she never reached port.

Divers will find - with Henri Munier's help - the remains of the 1,420-ton threemaster Traveler. The 85-meter vessel was wrecked on the reefs at Port Mathurin when she arrived in distress after losing her captain and thirteen of her crew from yellow fever.

The loss of this vessel apparently created quite a stir in London. She lies, broken apart in six meters of water.

Many old anchors can be seen in the shallow coral forests near Port Mathurin, and divers can visit the remains of other vessels at the edge of the channel to the harbor, though visibility in this area is often poor.

Henri took us to the wreck of an old wooden vessel resting in six meters. As we descended we saw scattered ballast stones and a large timber keel protruding from the sand. Other than a few ribs and planks, little was visible.

The cannon, which are displayed opposite the Custom House in Port Mathurin, are said to have come from this wreck.

Henri took us to another wreck. Her iron hull rises out of the sand at a depth of thirteen meters, and large metal fragments litter the sand. Large sedentary scorpionfish waited for an easy meal, while pairs of butterflyfish darted amid the twisted wreckage. A beautiful but venomous lionfish postured amid the remains of her deck.

Tiny stinging anemones are often found on metal wrecks in the Indian Ocean. I had forgotten to wear my gloves and my hands itched for days afterwards.

Hazard

Scorpionfish and the dreaded stonefish are dangers to avoid in these waters. The venom of scorpionfish and lionfish, produce painful stings; but an encounter with a stonefish, can be deadly. Black and white striped catfish, have a nasty sting. Be careful of the blackspined sea urchins with their sharp spines.

I wanted to photograph stonefish. After a stern lecture on the injuries inflicted by the creature, Serge directed me to the sand flats, just north of Port Mathurin. In the murky water every shapeless lump looked like a stonefish.

Although the water was barely a meter deep,, I stayed afloat remembering Serge's warning. I was afraid to put my feet on the bottom! Aggressive banded eels rose like cobras and unnerved me in the sinister half-light. Cheeky little moray eels peered inquisitively at me as I pawed overhead. Tentacle mouths, holothurians that look like tartan-patterned slinky toys, writhed along the sea bed, tentacles incessantly stuffing sand into their mouths. They are only two meters in length and twenty centimeters in diameter, these miniature versions of the sand-worms of Dune.

If the holothurian hadn't brushed against the stonefish I wouldn't have seen him. his camouflage was perfect, only the movement of his eyes betrayed him.

In Rodrigues over a score of people are stung by stonefish every year. All suffer intense pain, and some die. The fish isn't aggressive; injuries occur only when the swimmer or fisherman inadvertently treads on the fish. I took my photographs and swam back to shore and stood up only when my chin grounded on the beach.

If you want a break from diving, there are caves to visit but pack a picnic lunch -you will need a full day to explore them. You could go hiking and search for the bat that flies by day, or go down to the harbor and watch the cattle being loaded on board ship. There are also those who prefer to bask in the sun and do nothing at all. Time seems to have stopped in this place.

> **On Rodrigues there are no peddlers, no souvenir shops, no duty-free shops and you will have to search to buy even an old faded postcard of Rodrigues.**

Seychelles
Still a Coveted Destination
Al J. Venter

Unquestionably, the diving is still excellent but not great, in the tradition of the Red Sea or the Maldives.

Weave a pattern of orchidaceous tropical hues with an azure sea and dotted islands and you have happiness. Add to that the resplendent colors of a flaming sunset on the Indian Ocean and you enter a new realm.

This is the Seychelles; you will find a cordial welcome here.

Tucked away in a remote part of the vast Indian Ocean, 1,110 km from the northern tip of Madagascar and 1,600 km from the East African mainland, this variegated group of 92 islands was a legend for much of the twentieth century. Until the airport was completed on Mahe in 1971, the only way to reach Victoria, the capital, was by boat either from India or from Mombassa on the Kenya coast. Only the most determined travelers took the trouble, for so much time was needed for the passage that few people could spare it in those days.

Now, all that has changed. The island paradise is only hours away from anywhere in the world. Little more than 27 km long and between five and eight kilometers across, Mahe Island is a tapestry of sandy beaches and palm-fringed coves almost unequaled anywhere else. Granite peaks are interspersed with luxuriant forests; and the contrasts are great but inviting.

Victoria is the busy capital of the islands; a British version, say, of Papeete in the Pacific or Fort de France on the French island of Martinique in the Caribbean. The shops stock a fair array of goods, many of them duty free.

Town life provides cinemas, nightclubs, a public house and a hotchpotch of cultures that represent both East and West; Chines, French, Malaysian, Indians, Creoles, Africans and British mix easily and affably. There are several car hire firms that provide day-long safaris into the interior.

Or it is possible to take a late afternoon dip on Beau Vallon Beach and afterwards, drink in hand, to contemplate the beauty of an Indian Ocean sunset in an atmosphere and climate that demand little formality.

Almost 80 percent of the population of the Seychelles lives on Mahe. The rest are clustered on the nearby islands of La Digue, Praslin (pronounced Prahlin), the Farquhars and others. A small community lives on the Amirante islands, a beautiful group about 240 km southwest of the main island. There the diving is as good as the best in the world, with visibility often as much as 50 meters horizontally and vertically.

Scissortail Sergeants by Al Venter

Praslin is the second largest island in the archipelago, and there life goes on with a rhythm of its own. Unlike Mahe, there is no real "town" life as such. The simplicity charms most people who visit the place, for there are not enough vehicles to cope with the steady stream of visitors who come to visit the famous Vallee de Mai which General Gordon believed was the site of the Garden of Eden.

He may have been right, for the sheer unspoiled beauty and towering trees, many hundreds of years old, would seem to confirm the myth of a paradise lost. Huge green fronds hem the visitor in a green temple of silence and, if you are lucky, you may hear the call of the black parrot. Few visitors have seen the bird, but if you do you are said to be blessed with longevity.

The valley is the only place in the world where the coco de mer grows naturally. For centuries the fruit of this tall plant was reputed to have aphrodisiac qualities, particularly in the East.

Some visitors who stay for a while spend their time at the Cote d'Or Fishermen's Lodge beach overlooking the tiny island of St. Pierre. The diving there is good and the fish abundant.

The lore of centuries is embedded in the history of the Seychelles. The islands are believed to have been discovered by the Portuguese navigator Mascarenhas in 1505, nearly a century and a half before the first Dutch settled at the Cape of Good Hope.

At that time there was no sign of human life on any of the clusters. Captain Sharpleigh of the British East India Company arrived off Mahe in 1609.

The present indigenous are the descendants of early French settlers and slaves who came from the then French island of Mauritius in 1870. A number of freed African slaves were landed on the island from time to time by British men-of-war. Most of the islanders still speak French, or a Creole patois of French which is also spoken on some of the other Indian Ocean islands. Although British traditions go deep, most of the inhabitants are still Roman Catholics.

The islands were also the haunt of European privateers that scoured the Indian Ocean in search of prizes centuries ago. One was the notorious French pirate Olivier de Lasseur, who captured a Portuguese treasure ship in 1721. He paid for his crimes by being hanged ten years later, but not before he managed to dispose of his treasure, believed to be still buried somewhere on Mahe. It included gold and jeweled religious ornaments belonging to the Archbishop of Goa. There are still people searching for the treasure.

Relics of other wrecks are on display in Victoria. At the end of the old Long Pier stands a small, well-ordered museum that has a number of artifacts recovered from the sea, including an old bronze cannon recovered from a wreck off the outer island.

Above and below the water the Seychelles islands are rich in fauna and marine life. So far about 800 species of fish have been identified on the continental shelf.

About 85 percent of these species are wide-ranging forms that are found in the whole tropical area from Africa to the western and mid-Pacific.

Many of the islands in the group are renowned for their bird life. On the island of La Digue, for example, a special reserve has been created to protect the magnificent Paradise Flycatcher.

Because of the steady flow of tourists the government recognizes the prime need to protect the natural beauty and resources of the islands. Spearfishing has therefore been totally prohibited within the entire area. No guns for that purpose may be brought in; and these measures have had their reward.

POPULAR DIVING AND SNORKELING SITES
Mahe

There are many sites round the main island of Mahe that are easily accessible to divers and snorkelers.

St Anne Marine National Park

This park is based round the islands east of Victoria; all the travel agencies run boat trips out to the park from the Marine Charter Association. Since it is reached by a quite narrow channel directly outside the main commercial port, the park does suffer from silting, and much of the coral is in poor condition.

Snorkelers should head for reef patches to the north of Cerf Island and the fringing reef to the north and east of Moyenne Island. Here corals still flourish, and the shallow water species of fish can be observed at close range.

Divers should make for Beacon Island, its granite outcrops form interesting archways frequented by many fish.

North-West Bay

From L'Ilot Island to Sunset Beach Hotel the coast is of rugged granite which provides many crevices for fish to hide in and it is a good snorkeling area. L'Ilot is an interesting spot for diving, with lush soft coral formations in some places. There are other submerged granite outcrops off Petit Blanche Bay and Sunset Hotel.

A fringing reef extends from the Sunset Hotel to Beau Vallon Beach, and it is typical of this type of formation. The shallow inner reef of hard dead coral is covered by seaweed with only a few isolated coral colonies but many long-spined sea urchins. Snorkelers should concentrate on the reef front, and be careful to avoid areas of wave action that might drive them on to the coral. The top three or four meters of the front consists mainly of staghorn coral which shelters many timid fish; below that there is a zone of large coral heads interlaced with beds of leather corals. Larger fish and an occasional hawksbill turtle are seen in this slightly deeper zone.

Beau Vallon Beach itself is just sand. However, the local diving centers run trips out to the patchwork reef that extends across the bay from Sunset Hotel to Danzilles, which is very exposed during the northwest monsoon. The inner reef is mainly covered with soft leather corals; it then slopes away to the reef front which starts at a depth of about ten meters. The diving in this area is rewarding; there is a wide variety of coral species and some giant coral "bommies" that give shelter to a wealth of fish.

There are diving centers at several of the main hotels that arrange daily boat dives round the bay. Glass-bottomed boats are also available for trips round the bay and into the neighboring marine park. For the more adventurous there are also various boats to be hired for longer expeditions.

Baie Ternay and Port Launey Special Marine Reserve

The fringing reef at Baie Ternay is one of the best areas of live coral round the island; it is separated from the shore by a shallow lagoon up to 800 meters wide. The shallow inner reef is cut by many surge channels and it is a favorite spot for snorkelers and glass-bottomed boats, with a wide range of fish life.

The reef deepens to its edge, which starts at about 12 meters and extends to the rocky point of Cap Ternay right across the bay except for a hundred meter gap by the opposite shore. This is an area of large hard coral "bommies" interspersed with a multitude of smaller coral heads of different species; areas of dead coral are quickly overgrown by the subtly shaded mats of Alcyonarian soft leather corals. The deeper parts of the reef are home to a number of larger reef fish and are often visited by species from the deeper waters, especially rays.

Port Launay has narrow fringing reefs off the rocks at either end of the beach. They consist mainly of smaller coral heads and leather coral mats, but there are, however, some large coral "bommies" off the southern point.

OTHER SITES

The southern end of the island has some idyllic coves and beaches, however they are exposed to big surf and strong currents, and it is wise to seek local advice before snorkeling or diving. Petite Police Bay is well worth a visit; as is the reef next to Barbarons Hotel.

On the eastern coast the northern end of Anse Royale has some good coral formations and fish life, while the outer reef at Anse aux Pins is too far from shore for most snorkelers. Both of these reefs are exposed to large waves during the southeastern monsoon.

Trois Bancs

An amazing, almost sheer granite outcrop off the west coast of Mahe rises from the seabed at 23 meters to five meters from the surface. It is a natural focus for fish of all kinds, and it is frequented by the larger pelagic fish, predators and large shoals of eagle rays. Because of its exposed position it is possible to visit this site only on very calm days.

The Wreck of the Ennerdale

The *Ennerdale* was a Royal Fleet auxiliary tanker which struck an uncharted rock about 12 km off the northeastern point of Mahe in 1970. She was sunk by the Royal Navy as a hazard to shipping, and she now lies in 15 fathoms of water. She is in three sections, her bow still more or less intact, a tangled middle section and her stern. The stern section is dived most often, and the aft deck gear is easily accessible. The bridge has been blown off the deck and lies upside down on the sand next to the stern. Fish life is abundant round the wreck, which has given shelter to many large moray eels and some big groupers. Care must be taken because of the many-sharp steel edges round the wreck.

Brisarre Rocks

Also off the northeast of Mahe, these granite outcrops provide an amazing fish watching spectacle to both divers and snorkelers; snorkelers should attempt this site only if it is calm, as waves surge powerfully round the area. Giant Napoleon wrasse live here, also large bump-head parrotfish, snappers, groupers. Sweetlips and dense shoals of fusiliers; some large morays have also made their homes in the granite crevices and, whitetip sharks and sleeping sharks can often be found in the larger caves.

Silhouette

Silhouette, a beautiful granite island with towering palm-clad mountains, also has same good diving. While there is little coral, the granite rock outcrops are home to many large fish. Although the island is large, there is little boat traffic, so that pelagics are seen regularly in the shallow waters round the coast.

La Digue and Neighboring Islands

The west coast of La Digue is bordered by a well-developed fringing reef, with the exception of the harbor area at La Passe, which has been dredged to improve facilities for boats; although the reef top is shallow enough for snorkeling, the coral here is in poor condition because of silting.

North of La Passe, the fringing reef off Anse Severe is in better condition with colorful live coral colonies along the reef front. On the northern end there is a shallow zone of staghorn coral down to about five meters, below which is an area of larger boulder corals that extends to the sand seabed at 12 meters.

Ave Maria Rocks

This granite outcrop is a spectacular diving site with extensive coral formations covering the rock walls; it is visited regularly by the diving centers from both Praslin and La Digue. It tends to be exposed to currents, but there is almost always an area of calm sea. These waters are often visited by large offshore fish, and shoals of eagle rays are not uncommon.

Cocos Island and Albatross Rocks

This pretty granite island is crowned by a thicket of coconut palms and it has always bean popular with tourists. It is one of the best shallow water sites in the Seychelles, with an amazing profusion of fish life. The coral formations are mainly dead staghorn, although there are several flourishing banks of live staghorn. The encrustation of algae on both granite and dead coral is the main reason for the huge shoals of powder blue and convict surgeonfish. Access to this island has been restricted because of littering by visitors, so ask the hotels or tour operators what the present position is.

Frigate Island and Chimney Rocks

Chimney Rocks is another spectacular diving spot when the visibility is good; again the granite rocks bear good branching coral formations. Being further away from the main boat passages, the area tends to harbor an abundance of large fish and predators. Back fish are frequent visitors, and the various species of shark, large Napoleon wrasse, bump-headed parrotfish and groupers are all found round these rocks.

Frigate Island itself presents similar opportunities for fishwatching round the rocks to the right of the landing area. The fringing reef itself is unfortunately often too rough to dive or snorkel near.

The best months for diving are April-May and October-November when the seas are the calmest visibility can be over 30 meters on offshore sites, and the water can reach 29 degrees centigrade.

DIVING FACILITIES

Most facilities are situated at the beachside hotels. The Association of Professional Divers, Seychelles (APDS), sets strict standards of operation for its members and requires that all activities should be supervised by qualified staff. Dive operations which are members of the APDS are recommended by the Seychelles Tourist Board.

Austria and Bavaria

Dr. Phil Peter Jakob

The first things that come to many peoples, minds when they think of Bavaria or Austria are beer, Lederhosen, high mountains and yodeling.

Well, yodeling and Lederhosen are somewhat out of fashion these days, but the beer is still more than just good, and the Alps provide excellent diving in mountain lakes but, you will want to wear a thick wet suit, thick gloves and a hood, or better still, a drysuit!

Alpine lakes are very cold - even in August, the temperatures will range between 15 or 20 degrees C in many lakes. But what you experience is worth freezing - blue lakes surrounded by mountains and pine forests, trout and other fish, crayfish at high altitudes, sometimes visibility of more than twenty meters, "sunken forests" - these are some of the goodies in store for you.

Many places have dive operations, particularly in the Salzkammergut region of Austria, the capital of which is Salzburg, and which boasts many of the finest dive sites in Austria. Steep drop offs and sunken trees, preserved by the freezing water, form an exciting scenery.

Lake Contance, a few hours by car from Munich, offers a dive site with ruins of prehistoric lakeside villages, or you can take a cable car up the Zugspitze, Germany's highest mountain, in the morning, and plunge into the waters of the **Eisbee**, a beautiful lake at the bottom, in the afternoon.

Just a word on freshwater diving: this is not like diving in tropical seas! Make sure you are physically fit, and never dive these lakes without a local dive buddy or guide.

A ten hour car drive from Munich will take you to Italy's Riviera. Diving the Med will be a disappointment to those of you who are used to the Caribbean and such places, but you will still be rewarded by good visibility and lots of gorgonia coral if you dive below 20 meters.

AUSTRALIA

John Orr was born and raised in Australia. Although he is now an ex patriot living in Connecticut, USA, he visits his native, beloved country yearly.
Before my daughter and I took a 25 day trip through John's native land, he was kind enough to write a brief overview of the country and the "musts" we should do and see.

An Overview

Joanne and I discussed Wendy's trip over the weekend to make sure that she sees some of the "musts" while she's Down Under. From the schedule, she's going to see some of the really picturesque scenes of Australia. Cairns/Green Island is very tropical and, I'm told, extremely beautiful. She will see the coral of The Great Barrier Reef. Both of these things I have not seen! Surfers Paradise, which is about 40 miles South East of Brisbane (Broadbeach is part of Surfers) is a highly developed beach resort area. It's Australia's Gold Coast - much in the style of Miami, but much newer. I had invested heavily in a resort area about 100 miles north at a place called Noosa Heads (much smaller than Surfers and less commercialized) and lost everything when interest rates soared to the mid 20's. Oh well! But all along the coastline of Queensland the N.East state of Cairns and Surfers Paradise with Brisbane (pronounced Brizben) as the capital is studded with stunning beaches. One thing which may surprise them is the distances.

The academics still are not sure whether Australia is the largest island in the world or the smallest continent.

Cairns to Brisbane is about 22,500 miles. Brisbane to Sydney is another 600 miles. East-West is 3,000 miles. You're talking the same landmass as mainland USA. A population of 16 million, 85% of the population is on the coastal strip in about 5 cities. Sydney and Melbourne combined comprise about 45-50% of the total population. We are the most urbanized nation in the world. Big empty middle! Sydney is 3.5-4 million, and boasts one of the most beautiful harbors (it's really harbours) in the world. Life in Sydney revolves around the water, and combined with the temperature and climate, the lifestyle tends to be somewhat casual (similar to L.A.). At this time of year, however, it's the Fall and maybe a little cool. Certainly, they'll miss all the topless bathing on the beaches, and the harbour totally congested with sailboats of every shape, size, make, model, and colour careening in all directions under a stiff Nor'Easter. The city of Sydney (a sister city to San Francisco) is built on the water. The suburban homes line the harbor shores, all straining for water views above one

*Wendy Canning Church in Sydney
by Daphne Canning Church*

another on the hills of the peninsula strips surrounding this large water basin. Then there's the Pacific Ocean on the other side. Beaches everywhere. Reputed to be the best in the world where the surfs are real and not just ripples on a glassy pond. (Do you detect some longing nostalgia in this prose?) However, getting back to the itinerary. The northern sectors look pretty well organized. In Surfers, they can walk to most places. It's very concentrated, albeit sprawling with resort developments everywhere. I'm sure the local organizers will show them the major highlights.

In Sydney, there's a little time to see some extra places and to sample some of the culinary delights which we have to offer.

Restaurants are abundant everywhere and excellent. As I said, in a French restaurant, they'll be served by a Frenchman. Italians will serve them Italian. Greeks will serve Greek. Many, Asian restaurants, Japanese, Chinese, Singaporean, Malaysian, Indonesian - all over. Foods from every nationality. And the genuine fare! That's how the immigrants restarted in their new country.

But they must eat the seafood. The best in the world! Fresh and unpolluted!

While the country is still dominantly British, immigration has dramatically changed the cultural landscape. Sydney is a very cosmopolitan city. The honor still is uniquely Australian. And the accent is essentially Crocodile Dundee.

The schedule in Sydney will not allow the time for side trips (because of distances), although I see where they will see a sheep farm. Looking at the hotel, it suggests that they will be staying in "The Rocks" area around Circular Quay. Let me explain what that means.

Sydney was the first settlement in Australia, and the spot where the British started this settlement was called Sydney Cove (a cove of the harbor). This cove is now called Circular Quay where the city meets the harbor waters. The Quay, as it's called, is the main water terminal for all the harbor ferries transporting commuters and tourists to and from the suburbs and the city.

You may know, from your spartan history, that Australia began as a convict settlement. The first settlers were the convicts, the constabulary and the free settlers.

In Sydney Cove, they built a large stone jail which is now a converted complex of boutiques, restaurants, arts and crafts shops and touristy gift stores

This is called "The Rocks" area, and is to the side of the ferry wharves. It's a main tourist hub. In this concentrated area, there's also the Sydney Opera House. So there's lots to see and do in a small area. It's very, historical by our standards. I've touched on a number of things (in a rambling diatribe of memories), but let's now get to some specifics to slot into the itinerary!

RESTAURANTS

In the Rocks area, I'm sure there are many restaurants that I don't even know about very provincial and atmospheric. They won't be able to miss them. Highly recommended.

Additionally, there are two quite outstanding (and expensive restaurants); The Benelong located at the front of the Sydney Opera House atop the front steps to the concert halls (part of the Opera House complex). Large panoramic glass windows. Exquisite. The Waterfront located at The Rocks by the water. Has a tall ship's mast out front. Famous for its seafood, but quite pricey! Lobsters and jumbo shrimp are musts!

The itinerary mentions Doyle's Restaurant, which is mentioned as part of their own time. This cannot be missed! This is out of the city in the eastern suburbs. A cab ride will get them there without too much problem, and I hope, not too big a fare. One thing, you do not tip the cabbies. They will try to have you believe otherwise once they hear the American accents, but it's not done as it is here. There are a few Doyles restaurants around Sydney. The one they want is in Watsons Bay, but no other. This will take them through Vaucluse, suburb of Sydney where just about every home is $1 million. The waterfront homes reach as high as $13 million. Maybe even higher as that figure is now about 6 months old . This is my old stomping ground. Watsons Bay is just about at the mouth of Sydney Harbor at the end of a long peninsula (the harbor on the left and the ocean on the right). There's an old wharf when they get there at a turning circle. On the right, there's the Watsons Bay Hotel (a pub) with an outside beer garden overlooking the harbor. Walk along the promenade by the beach to the restaurant (next to the hotel). They don't take reservations, and they are unlicensed. Buy some wine at the hotel. They'll see a sign which says "Bottle Department". This is where they buy the wine. The restaurant will uncork it for them. If the weather permits, try to sit outside on the promenade. Looking back, they will see glimpses of the city and all the harbor. About half an hour before sunset is the best time as they will have a magnificent vista in reddened and golden hues. They will probably have to stand in line (in lieu of reservations). One holds the place while the other gets the wine. Doyles is a third or fourth generation seafood restauranteur family who have become famous worldwide for their seafood tradition. Oysters are great. Lobster is great. If they want to try some unique fish, I suggest Barramundi (pronounces as is) , John Dory (similar to Sole), or the Red Schnapper (rich and juicy).

Don't forget, French fries are called chips.

It will be a meal to remember.

Don Lanman is a PADI Rescue level diver with over 27 years of diving experience. He has logged hundreds of dives around the world including: Hong Kong,, Truk Lagoon, Honolulu,, Maui, Kona, Bahamas, Netherlands Antilles, Bimini, Cabo San Lucas,, Puerto Vallarta, Cozumel, Grand Cayman, Australia, Florida, Nevada, Ohio, Arizona, New Mexico, Texas and California. Don owns a Direct Response Advertising Agency in Sausalito, California with a focus on the travel industry.

Dive the Reef - Australia

I had taken a powerful sleeping tablet just before getting on the aircraft. The drug placed me in a wonderful coma which allowed me to miss the several movies, three meals, two snacks and the screaming infant two rows behind during the 17 hour trek to Sydney.

Despite the wonderful effort by the flight attendants to make this long trip comfortable, it's simply too much time to be doing the same thing...unless, of course, you're diving!

The additional 2 and a half hours from Sydney to Townsville, however, was somewhat more bearable given the 17 hours of sleep and my growing anticipation of diving the most famous reef system in the world.

My teenage son, older brother and I had been planning this dive vacation for

Clownfish in Anemones by Lynn Funkhouser

over a year. Each of us had different goals in mind for making the long journey. My brother wanted to dive the incredible reefs, I was seeking the wreck of the mighty "SS Yongala" and my son was interested in meeting Aussie girls.

You know you're getting older when you prefer diving to women...or is that wiser?

As the small plane circled the small town of Townsville, I was reminded of an old West frontier town. Located along a barren coast between Sydney and Cairns, it's perfectly situated as an embarkation point for diving the Great Barrier Reef.

Townsville turned out to be a friendly city of about 100,000 people. There had been no rain for six years which gave the place its barren appearance. As it turned out, however, the city was very interesting with several good restaurants, museums, aquarium and a 5 star PADI dive center called Mike Balls Dive Expeditions.

We rented some mopeds and made our way to the dive center for check in. The local representatives checked our C-cards and log books while getting an idea of our level of experience.

Having satisfied them of our diving qualifications, we toured the town and counted the hours until we could go aboard the 70' steel catamaran that would be our home and diving platform for the next 14 days.

We were the first divers aboard the "WaterSport", arriving 30 minutes before the scheduled boarding time. The crew was very friendly showing us to our cabins and providing a brief tour of our new home.

The crew consisted of one dive master and several assistant dive masters, however, it was interesting to learn that everyone aboard, even the engineer, were certified divers.

Jack, our dive master, was a pleasant, knowledgeable, serious man of about 33. He made it very clear that he was there for both fun and safety. With an initial safety briefing, he provided clear instructions that it would be several hours from a hyperbaric chamber in the event of a diving accident.

The message was clear "mind your dive tables and the sign in/out log at all times." A careless dive accident, here in the middle of the Coral Sea, could ruin the trip for everyone.

Finally, we were underway and the destination was the wreck of the mighty SS Yongala. The Yongala was a 350' cargo/passenger ship that disappeared in 1911 with her crew and 120 passengers.

She wasn't discovered until 1958 by the Royal Navy and immediately designated a national wildlife refuge. The cause of her sinking is unknown, it's speculated that she fell victim to cyclones which occur in this part of the Coral Sea.

The wreck itself lies at a 45 degree angle on her starboard side in about 80' to 90' of water. Despite her 82 years in water, the ship plus her cargo of bricks, tires and glass objects are remarkably intact.

Owing to her status as a wildlife refuge this wreck has produced the most exciting aquarium like ecosystem I have ever experienced. Turtles, Barracuda, Batfish, Stripers, Rays, Cobia, Sea Snakes, Flowery Cod, Coral Trout and the mighty Queensland Groupers greet divers as they descend to the wreck.

Following the detailed dive briefing, we made several dives to the Yongala over the next two days. The water temperature varied from 78 to 85 degrees Fahrenheit with visibility consistently over 150 feet. In addition to the fish life, the wreck itself was alive with flowing sea fans, soft and hard coral. It was like diving in a giant aquarium.

"Now I can die a happy man," was brother's reflection following our first dive on this wreck. Even my 16 year old son was impressed.

The onboard dive procedures required long surface intervals following each dive, regardless of what your dive computers registered. In fact, all divers were required to note their repetitive dive group following each dive.

My, son, as it turned out, had been somewhat casual about this requirement and when the dive master requested his status, his humorous reply was, "I'm little fuzzy on how to use dive tables." The dive master solved this problem by conducting a special two hour class just for my son.

He never forgot to log in his dive group again, funny?

We moved from reef to reef starting each day with a dive at 6:30 and ending at 7:30 pm with a night dive. With over 2,600 individual reefs making up the Great Barrier, it would take a lifetime to dive them all.

Shark Reef stands out as one of the many great dive locations. Apart from the remarkable 200 pound giant clams, we had an opportunity to meet and feed the beautiful White Tip Reef Shark.

These incredible animals roam the deep with no enemies save man were eating bait from the hands of the dive masters as we watched in awe. Each shark would move in with remarkable determination to take the morsels of food. Truly an exciting experience.

Chromodora Nudibranch by Lynn Funkhouser

Life on board the WaterSport was wonderful; diving, wind surfing, swimming, relaxing, reading a book or seeing the Southern Cross for the first time. However, all good things, they say, must end and so ended our trip to the Reef.

The Reef holds over 350 species of coral, 1,500 species of fish and is visible from outer space. We only scratched the surface of this remarkable dive location and look forward to our next visit. I recommend that all divers do themselves a favor and Dive the Reef.

SCUBA AND SNORKELING FACILITIES QUESTIONNAIRE

NAME **Mike Rall Dive Expeditions**
ADDRESS **252 Walker Street**
Townsville, Australiaan
CONTACT **Mike Rall**
TITLE **Owner**
TELEPHONE **077-723022**   FAX **077-212152**

CAPITAL:	GOVERNMENT:
POPULATION:	LANGUAGE: **English**
CURRENCY:	ELECTRICITY:
AIRLINES:	DEPARTURE TAX?
NEED VISA/PASSPORT? YES **x** NO	PROOF OF CITIZENSHIP? YES NO

YOUR FACILITY IS CLASSIFIED AS: SCUBA CENTER **x**   RESORT
BUSINESS HOURS: **8:30 a.m. to 5:30 p.m.**
CERTIFYING AGENCIES: **PADI**
LOG BOOK REQUIRED?   YES   NO
EQUIPMENT: SALES **x**   RENTALS **x**   AIR FILLS **x**
PRIMARY LINE OF EQUIPMENT: **All major brands**
PHOTOGRAPHIC EQUIPMENT: SALES **x**   RENTALS **x**   LAB **x**

CHARTER/DIVE BOAT AVAILABLE?   YES **x** (3)   NO   DIVER CAPACITY   **22 to 28**
COAST GUARD APPROVED?   YES **x**   NO   CAPTAIN LICENSED?   YES **x**   NO
SHIP TO SHORE?   YES **x**   NO   LORAN?   YES **x**   NO   RADAR?   YES **x**   NO
DIVE MASTER/INSTRUCTOR ABOARD?   YES **x**   NO   BOTH

DIVING & SNORKELING: SALT **x**   FRESH
TYPE OF DIVING/SNORKELING IN AREA: WALL **x**   BEACH   WRECK **x**   REEF **x**   CAVE   ICE
DIVING/SNORKELING IN YOUR AREA IS BEST SUITED FOR: BEGINNER **x**   INTERMEDIATE **x**   ADVANCED **x**
BEST TIME OF YEAR FOR DIVING/SNORKELING: **July - December**
TEMPERATURE: NOV-APRIL   MAY-OCT:
VISIBILITY: DIVING: SNORKELING:

PACKAGES AVAILABLE: DIVE   DIVE STAY **x**   SNORKEL   SNORKEL-STAY
ACCOMMODATIONS NEARBY
ACCOMMODATION RATES:
RESTAURANTS NEARBY:
YOUR AREA IS: REMOTE **x**   QUIET WITH ACTIVITIES   LIVELY
LOCAL ACTIVITY/NIGHTLIFE:
CAR NEEDED TO EXPLORE AREA?
DUTY FREE SHOPPING?

LOCAL EMERGENCY SERVICES   NEAREST HYPERBARIC TREATMENT FACILITY
COASTGUARD: **Flinder Street East**   AUTHORITY:
TELEPHONE: **714831**   LOCATION: **Townsville General Hospital**
CALLSIGNS: TELEPHONE:

LOCAL DIVING DOCTOR:
NAME:
LOCATION: **Townsville General Hospital**
TELEPHONE: **819211**

THE BAHAMAS

Nassau

Wendy Canning Church

This archipelago comprising 700 islands and islets intermittently dispersed over 100,000 square miles of open sea was first discovered by Christopher Columbus in 1492. The Spanish followed in his footsteps naming the islands "Baja Mar," meaning low sea or shallows.

It was not until the English arrived in 1629 and renamed the islands the "Bahamas," that permanent settlements were established. Since that time, the English have retained a stronghold and have had a great influence on the island's wealth and culture.

In 1953, Lyndon Pindling, a barrister educated in London, was elected to parliament, in 1956 he led his Progressive Party (PLP) to power, and for six uninterrupted terms he led the government, until he was unseated by Hubert Ingraham in August 1992.

Independence from Britain was gained in 1973. The Bahamas still remain part of the Commonwealth of Nations. They recognize Elizabeth II as sovereign and she appoints the Governor General, who resides in a pink palace in Nassau. Political power is shared by the Prime Minister and the "Front Street Boys," the major businessmen in Nassau.

Because of its semi-tropical climate, (except for the Fall when there is always the danger of hurricanes), the Bahamas were earmarked early on as a vacation playground.

I had not visited the Bahamas in fourteen years and was curious to see the changes both above and below the water.

We booked Bottom Time II, a live-aboard that plies the waters of Florida and the Bahamas. We chose this trip because it takes you to the outer islands of the Exuma chain.

Before and after our charter, we would spend time in Nassau, the Bahamian capital.

Since Bottom Time II was docked at the Nassau Harbour Club near Paradise Island, we chose to overnight at **Britannia Towers**, which is part of the immense hotel complex owned by Merv Griffin on Paradise Island. The resort is just over the bridge and is only five minutes from Nassau Harbour. It is by far the largest resort on the island, comprised of four very different hotels.

The Britannia Towers is one of the most up-market resorts on the island. The 10th, llth and 12th floors are VIP with concierge service, with the Presidential Suite being the utmost in luxury. All of the rooms face the ocean and have balconies. Each of the rooms is quite spacious, with a lovely bath, and decorated in Bahamian pastels.

For those who are looking for an all inclusive package, the **Paradise Island Resort and Casino** is a good take. The Paradise Hotel is a cheerful, small hotel situated in the middle of the complex. Rooms are decorated in pale pastels, with nice baths and a view of either the lagoon or ocean.

The third hotel in the complex is the **Paradise Towers**, sitting to the right of the others and facing the ocean. This hotel is less expensive than the others, but offers the same amenities. It has charming rooms and is tastefully decorated throughout. It appears to be quieter, since it is set apart from the others and the action that permeates them.

The fourth property on the compound is the understated **Ocean Club**. This resort is set apart from the others and is quite elegant We made a reservation at this property for when we returned from our cruise aboard the Bottom Time II. (Please see our Honeymoon chapter for information on **The Ocean Club**.)

Whichever of these four you choose, you cannot go wrong, especially if you enjoy gambling. There are ten restaurants and the hotels have a "dine around" program, so you can take advantage of the variety of the cuisine. The is also a full shopping arcade that offers a variety for the shopper as well. **For more information on any of these resorts call (809) 363-3000 or (800) 321-3000.**

BOTTOM TIME II

I had seen photos of Bottom Time II, but was not prepared for the grace and beauty of this vessel.

Commissioned in October 1986 and designed by International Catamaran of Australia, she was built in Fort Lauderdale according to U.S. Coast Guard specifications, and makes an ideal live-aboard.

She is 86' x 30' and has 7000 square feet of interior space for guests and storage. Fifteen staterooms accommodate 30 divers. The staterooms have either queen size beds or bunk beds. Each stateroom has a sink, but the heads and the showers are communal.

Air-conditioned throughout, her Rolls-Royce engines give her trans-Atlantic range and a top speed of 30 knots. 3600 gallons of fresh water are made daily from salt water.

Bottom Time II yacht by Lloyd Orr

When we first saw the Bottom Time II, she sat at her berth quiet and seemingly content, with an aura of adventurous beauty. We disturbed this calm, as we and the other guests arrived simultaneously. The crew were there to greet us: Ron, the Captain, Chip, the Steward, Mike and Clay. We quickly stowed our luggage in our cabin and stored our dive gear on the stern, where each diver has an individual locker with tanks awaiting the first dive.

We gathered topside in the spacious and cheerful dining room for our first meeting. The tables are arranged so that the divers can mingle in groups or couples. Lunch consisted of guinea hens, wild rice, mixed vegetables and non-alcoholic beverages. I immediately put aside any reservations I had regarding quality of food. It was excellent well-balanced and plentiful throughout the trip. (Snacks are also available throughout the day and after each dive). Captain Ron introduced the crew, checked our C-cards, and had us complete the standard medical forms and releases.

PINNACLE POINT

We headed out of Nassau Harbour toward the Exumas and our first dive destination. Stopping thirty-five minutes out of Nassau, Captain Ron gave us the dive plan. This dive was to be a shallow one at 25 feet, (I suspect to get divers re-oriented with ocean waters and give the crew an idea of the passengers individual diving skills). After this dive, there were only a few occasions where the crew members dove with us. My buddy and I were on our own and this was fine for us, but one should check carefully before booking if they feel hesitant about this and prefer to dive with a guide or instructor.

Our entry point was a giant stride off one of the two large dive platforms at the stern. We descended to a sandy bottom at 20 feet. I have never seen so many sand dollars! Even though tempted to bring back a souvenir, the Bahaman government does not allow taking anything from the sea.

We swam further on and my buddy came across a 12 foot sleeping nurse shark. We left it at peace. The reef was blanketed by a wide variety of sponges and coral. Queen angelfish swam along the floor of the ocean and up and down the reef. I never cease to wonder at their grace and beauty. They always remind me of ladies sashaying back and forth in party dresses. We also came across black durgeons, schools of bar-jack, a gray sole, yellow jack, spotlight parrotfish, a school of blue hamlet and gray angelfish. My buddy even came upon a small manta ray taking a siesta.

Bottom time up, we swam slowly back to the boat along the reef, enjoying the various sponges, coral and sea fans.

It was a perfect way to begin the trip. Snacks were waiting upon our return.

STAGHORN REEF

We changed tanks, pulled anchor and headed deeper into the Exumas for our second dive of the day. Our second dive was at Staghorn Reef, another shallow dive.

We dropped down and swam north of the boat. There were all varieties of reef fish, but the dive's beauty was really due to the topography. Slowly we moved along amidst its splendor and beauty, careful not to disturb the elk horn coral. We came, upon the largest formation of flower coral I had ever seen. Although the scene was monochromatic, this only gave strength to the drama.

> **As we ascended, dusk was on the horizon. Hot showers and a delicious dinner, accompanied by a good bottle of red wine, were waiting for us when we returned.**

A night dive is available after dinner every evening, but no alcohol can be consumed during the day by a diver who chooses to take advantage of these nighttime adventures. However, in addition to the spectacular scenic rewards of night diving, the night dives are also followed by a wonderful reward of a homemade dessert created by Mike!

For the early risers coffee is available at six o'clock, and a full breakfast is served at eight.

HIGHBORNE PINNACLE

Our first dive on our second day was at the Highborne Pinnacle. The top of the reef sits between 50 and 60 feet and the wall drops down to 400 feet. We swam towards the top of the reef and then descended to 100 feet. On our descent we saw numerous small reef fish, deeper, a school of large yellow-jack, a number of barracuda, a pair of hog fish, a Nassau grouper and a 14 foot nurse shark. The wall was covered with every type of coral and sponge imaginable. The barrel coral came in all sizes, along with the beautiful lavender colored vase coral. Giant mustard colored tube sponges were also in abundance. The dive profile had to be monitored carefully. One was tempted to descend deeper

Giant openings separate the reef, with tunnels running through them. Again on this dive, it was not the fish life that made the dive memorable, but the reef and the surrounding topography.

Ascending, we made a safety stop. This is now recommended for all dives. It is such a simple procedure that once you get in the habit, you would no more think of skipping this step than you would decide to dive without a mask.

Another plus of diving with Bottom Time II is that they use steel tanks allowing divers to dive without a weight belt, even when wearing a wet suit. The feeling of freedom is fantastic!

Interval time having passed, we suited up for our second dive at Highborne Pinnacle. This time we chose to swim further towards shore. Our reward was a large spotted eagle ray and to our sheer amazement, the largest spotlight parrotfish my buddy and I had ever seen. It was three and a half to four feet in length and weighed at least ten pounds. While stopped at the line for a safety stop, four silvery, shimmering, slick barracuda stopped to watch.

> **Moving deeper into the Exumas, we dropped anchor off Leaf Island, part of the Allens. This tiny little island is sanctioned by the Bahaman government as a wildlife reserve for the Iguana.**

There were many boats moored about and we were given the choice to snorkel or take the Zodiac to the island.

The island is inundated with iguana and it is clearly their territory. They crawl and scamper here and there while hosts of yachters watch in delight.

We reboarded and motored towards **Dragon Reef**. The Captain had timed our arrival so that we could dive the reef at slack tide. There are cuts that run between all of the islands, therefore, one must dive them at slack tide since the currents ordinarily run at 3 to 4 knots.

> **Entering the water, we were greeted by a school of at least 50 barracuda. The dive was a shallow one, only 30 feet, and as we swam along the reef, we had the feeling of being in an aquarium.**

Two baby sting ray, schools of yellow-jack, spot-fin butterfish, four-eyed butterfish, spotlight parrotfish, rock beauty, queen and french angelfish, marble grouper and sea cucumber were just a sampling of our new found friends.

Apart from these beautiful reef fish was the interesting way in which each time the tide changed and the current became stronger, a different variety of fish appeared.

The current really picked up, and we made our way back to the boat, which was not an easy task, and could have been even more difficult if not timed correctly.

Pulling anchor we cruised to the north side of **Highborn Cay**.

CRAB MOUNTAIN

We awoke plagued by high seas and swells. We were tempted to skip the dive. Assured that it was a beautiful wall dive and carefully briefed on our entry and exit, we decided to join in. A giant stride quickly brought us underwater and out of the turbulence and into clear aquamarine water. The sun shone through as we made our way along sandy highways flanked on each side by corals. We reached the wall and began to descend further.

> **Realizing we had reached 100 feet, we knew our time to investigate the sponges, tunnels, crevices and coral formations would be short. Ascending, we made our way back while being totally ignored by a 6 foot sting ray and by what appeared to be its tiny offspring.**

Getting back onboard was very tricky, for the seas had grown higher with 10 foot swells. I was amazed to see each crew member at the ladder dressed in foul weather gear.

Was it worth it? The answer is yes! However, novice divers, or those faint of heart, should have sat this one out.

LOBSTER KEY

We pulled anchor and found shelter inside the reef. Captain Ron set up his video gear and Mike, the first mate, got out his camera and joined us in the water.

This was a "mellow" dive. We stayed around 30 feet. The parade of reef fish was wonderful. The sunlight gave both the photographers and the divers a completely different experience then our early morning foray.

Four Atlantic spade fish swam by in unison. A school of barjack, a very large queen trigger fish, a squirrel fish, redband parrotfish, juvenile angelfish, a pair of banded butterfly fish and a juvenile yellowtail damsel fish were a wondrous spectacle as they swam by. On our way back we saw an enormous lobster..tempted...but remembered we were out of season for taking lobster.

We docked at Highborn Cay for the evening. Highborn Cay consists of a small town with a general store and a great bar, with ornately decorated doors. There would be no night dive tonight since a Rum Party was planned. The rum flowed and the reggae music played and the laughter continued into the night and the cold New England weather was nothing but a fleeting memory.

The next morning (while we were recovering from all the festivities) the crew washed down the boat, made new lines, and checked all boat gear. We stopped just outside of Highborn Cay for a planned drift dive at **Highborn Bite**.

Chip guided the group through the waters and we drifted lazily along with the current. Our first sighting of the day was a southern sting ray sleeping on the bottom. This was a shallow dive at 25 feet, so we had plenty of light to see the myriad of fish below. A sandy bottom was interspersed with sponges and corals of all colors and varieties. I have never been on a dive where so many reef fish traveled either in pairs or in schools.

Cheap Charlies by Wendy Canning Church

> **The purple sea fans, colorful barrel sponges, Venus sea fans, sea rod, corky sea fungus, and gorgonia were a splendid background for the profusion of reef fish that swam along with us and the current. Even those addicted to the night dives agreed that this was the best dive of the trip.**

Barracuda Reef off **Rock Key** was the next site. Nudibranches, puffer-fish, shrimp with blue eyes and sea cucumber were just a few of the fish sighted.

DOG ROCKS

Dog Rocks was a wall dive and serves as a shelter for all manner of sea life.

We again encountered surges and swells, but deep beneath the surface all was calm. We swam towards the wall and found that it dropped off sharply. Along the wall was a profusion of soft black coral trees and purple coralene. There were caverns to investigate with tiny sea creatures hiding from intruders and different colored hard and soft corals clinging to the walls.

As we swam back, we found blue cromia, file fish, trumpet fish and lobster.

BLUE HOLE

On our last day diving from the Bottom Time II, we anchored just north of Nassau, off Paradise Beach. Seas were growing stronger, but we made a short dive at Blue Hole to investigate the hidden habitats and sand shoots, as well as the coralene coral.

The first of two dives at this spot was on three wrecks that had teen sunk to make an artificial reef. The deepest was 100 feet. They are known as the ABC Wrecks. The newest wreck was put down in the past year. The Avalis has been down the longest and the third, a Texaco trader, was sunk three years ago. These three freighters are beginning to attract reef life and growths of sponges and coral. Our payoff for this dive was spotting a large ray.

The second dive was on the De La Salle, north of Nassau. She is 160 feet long, her maximum depth is 55 feet and 10 feet at the top. The De La Salle was a confiscated drug boat sunk in 1986, again to make an artificial reef.

NOTE: *We commend the Bottom Time II for its high safety standards. The food was excellent, the quantity certainly adequate. And the crew? Well they were the best and friendliest you will find anywhere. Please check first however, to see if they we be able to provide guides for you, if you are a single diver, or the least apprehensive about ocean diving. I would rate the diving intermediate to advanced. Bottom Time II travels the Florida coast and other destinations in the Bahamas. They also offer bicycle and kayak tours. These all are well worth looking into.*

For information and brochures contact. Divers Exchange International, 37 West Cedar Street, Boston, 02114, or call (617) 723-7134.

Raymond Elman is an artist and writer living in Truro, Massachusetts on Cape Cod, and Lexington, MA near Boston. He has written travel pieces for various newspapers and magazines and is the author of A Critical Guide to Cross Country Ski Areas, published by Viking/Penguin. He has also published and edited several art magazines.

Mr. Elman's paintings, prints, and drawings have been widely exhibited, beginning with his first exhibit in Provincetown in 1971. His work hangs in many U.S. embassies around the world, and in several museums.

He is also deeply involved with computer graphics and multi-media mediums, and currently serves as Director of Creative Services for Coopers & Lybrand.

Providenciales
Turks & Caicos, British West Indies

How many times must I hear someone, say, "You should have been here 10 years ago, it used to be great." Well, the answer is Providenciales, because right now is Provo's golden era.

Provo is on the cusp of major recognition and development but it hasn't fallen over the edge yet. What that means is that beaches are still sugar white and empty; waters are crystal clear (up to 250 feet visibility) and unpolluted; coral reefs, walls, and marine life are abundant and not fully explored; the native population is still friendly; and creature comforts and infrastructure are in place.

HISTORY

It's difficult to find a colonial bed in New England that George Washington didn't sleep in, and it's equally difficult to find a Caribbean island that Columbus didn't step upon. He stepped on Grand Turk almost five centuries ago, Lucayan Indians are believed to have been the first people to actually reside on the islands.

In the 16th and 17th centuries the islands provided "cover" for a motley assortment of pirates. Western civilization and slavery arrived in 1678 when Bermudian salt rakers claimed the islands. From 1700 to the late 1800s, Turks & Caicos was claimed by a succession of colonial adventurers — Spain, France, England, and eventually Jamaica annexed the islands. In 1972, ten years after Jamaica became independent, the Queen of England appointed a governor for Turks & Caicos, and they remain an independent crown colony.

Today Turks & Caicos is the proverbial melting pot of nationalities. There are so many Canadians residing on the islands that there have been several efforts launched in the Canadian parliament to make Turks & Caicos a Canadian protectorate.

The Turks & Caicos Islands are 575 miles southeast of Miami. The Bahamas are 30 miles to the northwest, and the Dominican Republic is 100 miles southeast.

The nine major islands of Turks & Caicos are clustered in two groups separated by a 22 mile wide channel.

The eastern group is the Turks: Grand Turk and ten cays, including Salt City. The western group is the Caicos: North, Middle, East, South, and West Caicos, Providenciales, and 10 cays, including Pine Cay. Encircling the group of islands is a reef that extends for more than 200 miles.

There are international airports on Grand Turk, Providenciales, and South Caicos, and domestic airports on all the inhabited islands.

Air service to Turks & Caicos has fluctuated with the recent rise and fall in the fortune of various airlines. The islands used to be serviced by Pan Am. Today, regular scheduled service from Miami is provided by Cayman Airways, American Airlines and Turks & Caicos Airways.

Unquestionably, the best way to get there is by charter flight. We flew GWV charter from Boston (door to door in 3 1/2 hours) for less than $500 round-trip.

WHERE TO SLEEP

Most of the hotels and condominium establishments are located on or overlooking Grace Bay, a gorgeous 13 mile stretch of white sand and turquoise waters. At first most of the hostelries were small in size and quaint. However, now it is not unusual to find large chains. For example, the Ramada Turquoise Reef Resort and Casino opened to launch the nineties. Construction on a large Sheraton was temporarily halted, but is scheduled to resume in June.

The following hotels either have diving centers on the premises or are located within a snorkel throw of a dive shop:

Ramada Turquoise Reef Resort & Casino
(809) 946-5555

Erebus Inn
(809) 946-4240

Le Deck Beach Club
(809) 946-5547

Ocean Club Condominium Resort
(809) 946-5880

Turtle Cove Yacht & Tennis Resort
(809) 946-4203

However, the best way to experience Provo is to rent one of the available houses or villas.

We rented Villa Camilla, a fantastically well conceived main house and guest house compound right on Grace Bay Beach.

For more information contact Diver's Exchange, International, 37 West Cedar Street, Boston, MA 02114 (617) 723-7134 or Fax (617) 227-8145.

Villa Camilia offers a three bedroom main house with an adjacent two-unit guest house. Every bedroom has its own deck facing the water and custom bathroom. We rented the main house with two other couples and had all the privacy we needed. In addition, the main house has a large, comfortable, vaulted ceiling living area on the second floor, flowing around an open atrium, between the kitchen and the dinning area, There are two more decks on the second floor, one facing the sunrise, the other facing the sunset.

During the week we stayed at Villa Camilla there was never an uninvited sole sitting on our beach, and just to the south of our beach was a reef, teeming with marine life, that started in five feet of water and descended to a depth of thirty feet – perfect for both snorkeling and diving.

In fact, one beautiful full-moon-lit night, we finished our dinner, grabbed our diving gear, and climaxed a wonderful evening with a night dive on our "private" reef.

Surprisingly, a week's stay at Villa Camilla costs less than a room for two at the Ramada.

WHERE TO EAT

Dining out on Provo is okay - you can pick your way through most menus and develop a good meal - but you're better off suspending your critical culinary instincts.

Because we had a fully equipped contemporary kitchen at Villa Camilla (and almost everyone, in our party was capable of preparing an elegant meal), we opted to eat most breakfasts and lunches at home, and went out to dinner every other night.

The restaurants we enjoyed the most were inexpensive and unpretentious. The only places we returned to for more than one experience were the following:

Banana Boat Restaurant

A full Caribbean bar & grill overlooking the water on Turtle Cove. We especially enjoyed all of the conch dishes, though everything we ate was well prepared.

Hey Jose Cantina

Located in The Centre on Leeward Highway, Hey Jose (tel: 64812) serves (surprise) Mexican dishes and California pizza (again no surprise because the proprietors are from California).

Tasty Temptation

Despite the cutesy name, Tasty Temptations, located near the downtown area (tel: 64049), is a serious French bakery and coffee house, managed by French Canadian expatriates. They offer the same quality croissants, breads, pastries, espresso, and capuccino that you'll find in Montreal.

DIVE OPERATORS

The three best dive operators on Provo

Flamingo Divers

P.O. Box 322, Providenciales
Turks & Caicos Islands, B.W.I.
Phone/Fax: (809) 946-4193

Provo Turtle Divers

Turtle Cove Marina, Providenciales
Phone,: (809) 946-4232/4585
Fax: (809) 946-4326/5296

Dive Provo

Ramada Turquoise Reef Resort, Providenciales
Phone: (809) 946-5029/5040
Fax: (809) 946-5936
In the USA 1-800 234-7768

Art Pickering, proprietor of Provo Turtle Divers, is commonly regarded as the Godfather of Provo diving, having pioneered SCUBA diving in these waters, he rightfully bills himself as the oldest and most experienced diving operation in the Turks & Caicos Islands. Nevertheless, during our one-week stay on Provo, we placed a higher value on friendliness and flexibility than on experience, and we, found that with Flamingo Divers.

We told Jim and Linda Richardson, the Canadian (did I mention that my wife was from Canada) proprietors of Flamingo Divers, that we wanted to customize our dive package so that we could keep all of their gear at our Villa to enable us to make beach dives on the days that we didn't go out with them on one of their boats. No problem, and the rates they charged were very reasonable.

They were, extremely friendly and dependable. They allowed their patrons to help choose the dive sites for the week and were not married to a tight time schedule. Some of their gear was a little worn but all was serviceable.

DIVE SITES

The best known (though by no means fully explored) dive spot in the Turks & Caicos is the WEST WALL or NORTHWEST POINT, which is really hundreds of dive sites along a vertical edge of the Continental Shelf. It's about a 45 minute boat ride to the wall. Some of the named dive sites are:

Black Coral Forest, which starts at 45 foot and descends to about 130 feet, where red gorgonians, elephant ear sponges, and black coral trees abound.

Eagle rays and sharks have been seen cruising this site.

The Crack, a steep crevice which drops from 50 feet to 100 feet. We met large friendly groupers at this spot that swam right up to our mask and stared us in the eye.

The Plateau, a home for eagle rays, sharks and manta rays in about 60 feet of water.

Closer to where you are likely to be staying on the North Shore, or Grace Bay, are several shallower dive sites, some which can be reached from shore and double as excellent snorkeling spots.

The Aquarium, located right in front of Villa Camilla, features a crescent shaped coral head that begins in about 5 feet of water and gently descends to about 25 feet. The reef hosts a plethora of reef fish, and is frequently visited by schools of barracuda. This is an excellent dive for beginners and snorkelers, and also a good spot for a night dive.

Another dive spot close to shore is SMITH'S REEFS which is just beyond the cut that leads to Turtle Cove. This coral head also varies in depth from 5 to 25 feet. It is home to eagle rays, turtles, and an occasional grouper, which makes it one of Provo's most popular snorkeling spots.

Pinnacles, which is roughly in front of the Ramada, is an interesting series of coral ridges varying in depth from 35 to 60 feet. At Pinnacles you may find grouper, turtles, eels, and reef fish.

Southwind is an 80 foot long cargo ship resting at 60 feet which sank in 1985. It's visitors include Nassau groupers and schools of horse-eyed jacks.

OTHER ACTIVITIES

There are tennis courts at several of the hotels (Ramada, Ocean Club, Turtle Cove, Erebus). The courts at Erebus are open to the public, and if you know the right people guest privileges at Turtle Cove can be arranged.

The first golf course on Provo opened in late 1992.

Bill fishing and bone fishing in and around Turks & Caicos is among the best in the world.

Anything that can be done with a sail on warm water can be done here: windsurfing, para-sailing, and sailing.

Two wildlife events not to be missed are feeding iguanas on the uninhabited cays near Provo, and swimming with Jo Jo the dolphin when he makes one of his frequent excursions inside the barrier reef.

Right now is Providenciales golden moment. It has the comforts of the present, while still retaining the charms of the past, and the diving is at the top end of the spectrum.

67

SCUBA AND SNORKELING FACILITIES QUESTIONNAIRE

NAME **Flamingo Divers**
ADDRESS **P.O. Box 322**
Providenciales, Turks & Caicos, BWI
CONTACT **Jim Richardson, Larry McCain**
TITLE **Owners**
TELEPHONE **809-946-4193**   FAX **809-946-4193**

CAPITAL: **Grand Turk**   GOVERNMENT: **Democratic British**
POPULATION: **7,000**   LANGUAGE: **English**
CURRENCY: **U.S. $**   ELECTRICITY: **110v**
AIRLINES: **American/Cayman Air**   DEPARTURE TAX? **$10.00**
NEED VISA/PASSPORT?   YES   NO **x**   PROOF OF CITIZENSHIP?   YES **x**   NO

YOUR FACILITY IS CLASSIFIED AS: SCUBA CENTER **x**   RESORT
BUSINESS HOURS: **8:00 a.m. to 4:30 p.m.**
CERTIFYING AGENCIES: **NAUI, YMCA**
LOG BOOK REQUIRED?   YES   NO **x**
EQUIPMENT: SALES **x**   RENTALS **x**   AIR FILLS **x**
PRIMARY LINE OF EQUIPMENT: **Sherwood**
PHOTOGRAPHIC EQUIPMENT: SALES   RENTALS   LAB **x**

CHARTER/DIVE BOAT AVAILABLE?   YES **x**   NO   DIVER CAPACITY **2 boats, 24 divers max.**
COAST GUARD APPROVED?   YES **x**   NO   CAPTAIN LICENSED?   YES   NO **x**
SHIP TO SHORE?   YES **x**   NO   LORAN?   YES   NO   RADAR?   YES   NO
DIVE MASTER/INSTRUCTOR ABOARD?   YES   NO   BOTH **x**

DIVING & SNORKELING: SALT **x**   FRESH
TYPE OF DIVING/SNORKELING IN AREA: WALL **x**   BEACH **x**   WRECK **x**   REEF   CAVE   ICE
DIVING/SNORKELING IN YOUR AREA IS BEST SUITED FOR: BEGINNER **x**   INTERMEDIATE **x**   ADVANCED **x**
BEST TIME OF YEAR FOR DIVING/SNORKELING: **Summer**
TEMPERATURE: **NOV-APRIL: 80 F**   **MAY-OCT: 90 F**
VISIBILITY: **DIVING: 100 FT**   **SNORKELING: 100 FT**

PACKAGES AVAILABLE: DIVE **x**   DIVE STAY **x**   SNORKEL   SNORKEL-STAY
ACCOMMODATIONS NEARBY: HOTEL **x**   MOTEL   HOME RENTALS **x**
ACCOMMODATION RATES: EXPENSIVE   MODERATE **x**   INEXPENSIVE
RESTAURANTS NEARBY: EXPENSIVE   MODERATE **x**   INEXPENSIVE
YOUR AREA IS: REMOTE   QUIET WITH ACTIVITIES **x**   LIVELY
LOCAL ACTIVITY/NIGHTLIFE: Ramada Inn Gambling Casino, Golf Course, 2 night clubs
CAR NEEDED TO EXPLORE AREA?   YES   NO **x**
DUTY FREE SHOPPING?   YES   NO **x**

LOCAL EMERGENCY SERVICES   NEAREST HYPERBARIC TREATMENT FACILITY
COASTGUARD: AUTHORITY: **Ewan Menzies Medical Clinic**
TELEPHONE: LOCATION: **Leeward Highway, 1 mile from our shop**
CALLSIGNS: TELEPHONE: **809-946-4242**

LOCAL DIVING DOCTOR:
NAME: **Ewan Menzies**
LOCATION: **Leeward Highway, 1 mile from our shop**
TELEPHONE: **809-946-4242**

BERMUDA

"Isles of the Devils"
Wendy Canning Church

My remembrance of Bermuda was of a picture perfect island of pastel-colored manor houses stretching to the sea, crystal clear waters in different hues of aquamarine and a pace reminiscent of an early 19th century English novel. On this, my third return, little had changed.

> **One cannot speak of Bermuda's 378 years of history without discussing her hundreds of shipwrecks. Although a Spanish mariner, Juan de Bermudez, discovered Bermuda in 1513, it was a shipwreck that led to the first permanent settlement by the English in 1609.**

> **Bermuda is not one island. It is actually some 140 large and small islands connected by bridges that sit on a submerged volcano.**

The Royal Navy referred to Bermuda as the "Isles of Devils" because of its network of uncharted and treacherous reefs that surround these islands. It is these reefs, along with a history of countless hurricanes, storms,, strong currents, piracy and privateers, that has left a legacy of excitement and adventure for both the scuba diver and snorkeler to explore.

Today it is believed that only a handful of the total number of wrecks have been uncovered and that countless numbers sleep silently beneath the shifting sands. Sailors refer to Bermuda as a ship trap, since the separate islands are fraught with reefs and shoals as well as shifting sands, with only one deep water channel running through the maze. Sailors beware! Charts must be followed with exact precision or your yacht may become the next artificial reef.

We traveled to Bermuda in August when visibility ranges from 80 to 100 feet. Some say that this is the best month to dive as it is the period right before the plankton blooms. However, the season for diving spans from March to November.

Glencoe Harbor Club was our first retreat during our stay in Bermuda. This charming manor house perched at the water's edge in Salt Kettle, Paget contains both guest and public rooms. Another house has been added to the property, which is a stone's throw away. One has the sense of a rambling waterfront estate rather than a hotel.

The original house was home to a 17th century sea captain engaged in the salt trade. Today it is a favorite of yachtsmen and to guests who prefer an intimate, warm and friendly atmosphere with true Bermudian flair.

The rooms are decorated with English chintz and are air-conditioned. Some suites have working fireplaces. The rooms face either the bay, garden or pool Closet space is ample, and the large baths are replete with English soaps and sundries. Twice a day maid service is supplied and a "goodnight chocolate" on your pillow is only one example of the perfect service.

Dining is on the waterfront terrace, weather permitting, with different entertainment provided each evening. Dinner is especially delightful. One is reminded of Venice as you dine by candlelight overlooking Salt Kettle Bay with the waves gently lapping against century old well-worn steps that lead down to the water's edge.

There is no question that Glencoe has one of the best kitchens on the island and is a favorite of the locals. Guests who stay at any of the Bermuda Collection hotels participate in the Carousel Dining Program. This allows guests of Glencoe, Cambridge Beaches, Newstead, Lantana, The Reefs, Stonington and the Pompano Beach Club to take dinner at any of the other member hotels.

Glencoe refers to its beach as the "Sandbox" and aptly so, for it is man-made and quite small. However, as with all other details at Glencoe, Reggie Cooper, the owner has provided guests with access to one of the most beautiful beaches on the island at the Elbow Beach Hotel. A shuttle service runs from May to October. Ask the kitchen to pack you one of their sumptuous box lunches to take along!

Tennis, golf, and watersports are all available either at Glencoe or nearby. Horseback riding can also be arranged. Glencoe's sailboats, kayaks and windsurfers are available to guests free of charge.

A real advantage for those staying at Glencoe is that it is only a short ferry ride to Hamilton. The array of beautiful, duty-free international goods will tempt the most parsimonious.

Glencoe Harbour Club, PO Box PG 297, Paget PGBX Bermuda. Tel. 1800 468-1500 direct from USA or 1800 268-0424 from Canada. Fax. 1809 236-9108.

Horizons and Cottages is under the direction of the very qualified and affable General Manager, Wilhelm Sack.

Approaching the compound, thirteen pink cottages come into view. They sit atop the hillside, nestled among lush greenery and flowering vegetation. The main house, where the public rooms are found, also accommodates guests in an additional nine rooms. This graceful structure is one of Bermuda's oldest and most charming mansions dating back nearly four centuries. It is fashioned in true Bermudian architectural style, with a white-washed keystone center and knee-high fireplaces and tray ceilings.

The evening we dined at Horizons, a buffet was served on the lower terrace after the Manager's cocktail party (a weekly event). The buffet was varied and perfectly prepared. The entire staff possesses an equally perfect manner, warm, charming and highly professional. We sat with newly made friends, dining by candlelight, in a setting high on a hillside, with views of the pool and ocean beyond.

Because of the ambiance and service at Horizons and Cottages, it will continue to be assured of its favored standing in the Relais Chateaux Hotel family.

NOTE: *There is no beach, but guests are extended private access to the Coral Beach Club, which Horizons overlooks.*

Horizons & Cottages, PO Box PG 198, Paget PGBX, Bermuda, Tel, 1809 236-0048 or 1800 468-0022 direct from USA. Fax. 1809 236-1981.

We booked our first four days of diving with the Nautilus Dive Center, located at the Southampton Princess Beach Hotel. Charles Green, the owner of Nautilus, picked us up on the first morning and delivered us to the dive center. There are no rental cars allowed on Bermuda. You can rent mopeds or take taxis, or if you are going to the right place the ferry service is inexpensive and excellent. The brave at heart rent mopeds, others pay through the nose for taxis which are very expensive. Each day we had to pay $20 round-trip for the short trip to the dive center at the Southampton Princess.

Mark Adams is the skipper of the Nautilus dive boat, the Crackling Rose, as well as instructor and dive guide extraordinaire. The Crackling Rose is a comfortable dive boat with a permanent canopy and enough room for both gear and divers.

The Bermuda climate is sub tropical, 85 degrees Fahrenheit in summer, 65 degrees Fahrenheit in winter. This makes March to November the ideal time to dive. Our first dive was the Marie Celeste. She was a Confederate side paddle wheeler that sank on the September 26, 1864 while carrying a cargo of corned beef and rifles bound for Savannah, Georgia.

The wreck lies in 60 feet of water. The storms and the passage of time have done great damage to her, many only the paddle wheel is still intact. After inspecting the wreck you can explore the reef nearby. Mark led us up and down the reef and through tunnels that were frosted with both coral and sponges in a variety of colors.

Our second dive was at South West Reef. Situated at the breakwater, this is a shallow dive, but due to the topography, it is an interesting one and the depth gives you plenty of time to explore. There is a bit of a current, and it is best just to drift along with it and view the brain, lettuce and star corals, as well as the giant basket and tube sponges as you go by. Spotlight parrotfish, durgeons, jack and wrasse dance by in numbers as the small reef fish nibble at their food.

Our reward for the morning was a school of over one hundred barracuda, the largest that I have ever seen. We kept a conservative distance and watched them for some time.

Cambridge Beaches

That evening we took a taxi to the western side of the island to dine at Cambridge Beaches. Uniquely Bermudian, this idyllic cottage colony sits on a 25 acre peninsula. Guests stay in one of 78 cottages that are dotted along the hillside and run down to the sea. Each cottage is decorated differently, and guests have the feeling of being in a home rather than a hotel. Your maid prepares breakfast at your cottage each morning.

We dined by candlelight, buffet style, on the terrace that overlooks an enchanting bay. The buffet was delicious and beautifully presented. The service was quick and friendly. A quartet provided island music intermingled with Gershwin and Porter tunes.

Tennis, boat rentals, water skiing and mopeds are available. A spa will be completed by the time this book goes to press. Scuba diving is available through Dive Bermuda.

Cambridge Beaches has been ranked one of the top 10 resorts of the world. Their motto is "Cambridge Beaches, for the Romantic of any age"-We agree!

Cambridge Beaches, Somerset, MA02 Bermuda. Telephone: (809) 234-0331 or (800) 468-7300 direct from the USA. Facsimile: (809) 234-3352.

Diving with Nautilus-Day Two

Our first dive of the day was on the Minnie Bresslauer, an English steamer situated in one of the many wreck areas protected by the Bermuda Government She was wrecked on her maiden voyage on January 1, 1873, with Captain Peter Corket at the helm on his way from Lisbon to New York with a cargo of lead, dried fruit and cork. Lying in 70 feet of water, she has been badly broken up through the years due to the battering of storms, but she is still an interesting one to investigate.

The next dive was at Hang Over Reef. This is a spectacular reef with a myriad of beautiful crevices and caves to be investigated. Two years ago, fish traps were banned in Bermuda and since then scuba divers and snorkelers have begun to notice a resurgence of fish life.

Waterloo House

We dined that evening at **Waterloo House** in Hamilton. This charming hotel, a short walk from the ferry, is in an ideal location for the vacationer who wants to stay in the heart of Hamilton. The handsome, original building was constructed in 1920. Both public rooms and guest rooms are beautifully appointed. They are decorated in chintz, antiques and porcelains. There are lovely small gardens interspersed throughout the grounds. All rooms face Hamilton Harbor or the gardens. Waterloo House has one of the best dining rooms on the island. In good weather, one dines on the terrace overlooking the harbor amid lush green plantings and flowering shrubbery.

NOTE: They are part of a dine around program with Horizons, Cottages, and Newstead. Guests have beach privileges at the Coral Beach Club.

Waterloo House, PO Box HM333, Hamilton, HNBX Bermuda. Telephone: (809) 290-4480. Facsimile: (809) 295-2585.

Diving with Nautilus-Day Three

Our next day of diving started with a deep dive south of Horsehorse Beach. We descended the mooring line to a ledge at 70 feet, from there you drop off and descend down to 100+ feet and glide along with the current. To our amazement, there was fantastic visibility that enables you to view the many types of hard and soft coral, but we saw only a few fish other than a school of large jack. The overhangs were breathtaking. As we went along we searched the reefs and gullies for what might be hidden there.

Our next dive profile was 40 feet for 40 minutes, so this gave us enough time to cover a good part of the reef whose beautiful topography was comprised of the common sea fan, the venus sea fan and deep water gorgonia. Large spotlight parrotfish, gray angelfish, smooth trunkfish, rock beauty, spotted drum, black cap bass, and squirrel fish were all in great abundance.

After the dive we dined again at Glencoe where the service and cuisine remained impeccable.

Whenever one stays on Bermuda, lunch or dinner at Glencoe is a must!

Diving with Nautilus-Day Four

Our last day with Nautilus was spent diving the wreck of the **Hermes**, sunk on May 16, 1986, by Nautilus Dive Shops in conjunction with the Bermuda Dive Association in order to create an artificial reef and to give divers a wreck that is completely intact and can be partially penetrated. It is 165 feet long and has a 35 foot beam. She sits in 80 feet of water. The engine room and cargo area can be penetrated without any difficulty.

We commend Nautilus on their safety standards and genuine warmth and the time they take with each diver, novice or experienced. Mark, our skipper and our guide for all our dives can make any ho-hum dive a great adventure. This, as divers know, is no easy task. His knowledge of sea life and where to find all the critters is such a plus. He will take you through caves and tunnels that at first seem hair-raising, but his manner and safety measures put you at ease.

A special thank you to Mark and the entire crew at Nautilus.

Two's Company by Alan Marquardt

NOTE: *All your gear is set up, broken down and rinsed for you. I never refuse this welcomed service. Most dive sites are minutes from the center.*

Nautilus Dive Center, Southampton Princess Beach Hotel, telephone: (809) 238-2332 or 238-8000 ext. 6073; facsimile (809) 236-4284.

Our next destination was the Sonesta Beach Hotel and Spa located in Southampton Parish. Rising up from the reefs on the ocean's edge, the Sonesta is a modern luxury hotel with majestic views of 25 acres of picturesque landscaped grounds that surround three natural bays.

A very different home from Glencoe, the Sonesta is a complete resort within itself offering 400 guest rooms. Its size does not in any way deter from the high degree of professionalism and warmth conveyed by the entire staff. The Sonesta is in every way a full service resort, offering tennis, outdoor and indoor pools, three beaches, scuba diving, snorkeling, sailboats, fishing from shore and moped rentals. They have croquet and miniature golf on the grounds. Golf can be arranged at the Port Royal Course (10 minutes), Belmont Golf Course (15 minutes) or Riddler Bay (10 minutes). The lobby has branches of Hamilton's finer stores. There is also a health club and spa on the premises. A children's program is offered from June 15th until Labor Day with supervised activities.

MAP guests can choose from the many restaurants: La Sirina serves Italian food, the Boat Bay Club has American cuisine, the Sea Grape Bar, overlooking the pool, serves barbecue, The Cafe is deli style and casual and Lillians is their gourmet restaurant. All the restaurants are very good, but I must confess that my favorite was Lillians.

The ambiance and excellent service at Lillians brings diners from all over the island. Begin with the hot duck appetizer or the fresh spinach and endive salad topped with goat cheese. The entrees are expertly prepared and the presentation is splendid. The wine list is extensive. Dessert is a must, followed by international coffee. Not to worry, scuba diving allows you to shed those calories.

Each room has a terrace facing the ocean or the pool. It is a perfect place to sun or to begin your day with breakfast, or just to inhale the intoxicating fresh ocean breeze. Looking out to sea, a diver cannot help but ponder what awaits them on the 9 am dive.

NOTE: *At the Sonesta, be sure and stop by guest services and introduce yourself to Tori Sheppard. She is not only a delightful lady but very knowledgeable about the goings on in the hotel and throughout Bermuda.*

Sonesta Beach Hotel and Spa, P.O. Box HM1070, Hamilton, HMEX, Bermuda. Telephone (809) 238-8122 or (800) 343-7170.

Tucked away at the far end of the beach is South Side Scuba and Watersports, run by the very competent and friendly Alan Marquardt and his staff Terry, Tony, John and Nancy. South Side ranks up there with the most safety conscious operations. Alan and his staff don't just follow the rules because it is required, they follow them because each staff member truly cares that the diver has both a safe and enjoyable experience.

Certification cards are a requirement. Those without them have a checkout in the pool, as do those who have been "out of the water for awhile".

Our first dive was on a shallow reef and was geared to novices and open water checkouts, but we were happy to join. Never turn down a shallow reef dive in Bermuda, you get plenty of bottom time, great visibility, and interesting light and fishlife.

Their boat, *Calypso*, is 36 feet long, licensed for divers, Coast Guard approved and equipped with VHF radio, oxygen and first aid. The entire crew is very environmentally conscious and adheres to the policy "take home memories not shells or artifacts from wrecks."

Our gear was set up and we were off to Southwest Breakers. This was our second trip to this site (actually my third for I had done it on a previous trip to Bermuda). A few days later we even came back for a night dive. The beauty of this dive is that it is never the same. Being at the breakwater with the sea conditions constantly changing, each dive reveals new and interesting sea life.

We descended 25 feet to the sandy bottom and began to investigate the crevices and caves about the reef. This was a perfect day and a perfect dive, a cameraman's dream. The sun gleamed through the clear water like a spotlight. Fish an infinite varieties swam by dressed in colorful costumes for the performance and the photographers went wild.

We went up and down gullies and through caves with a backdrop of sea fans and coral. There used to be a great barracuda that lived among the corals, but our companions on this dive were only three feet long. A good guide will educate you about sea life. When we later talked about barracuda, Tony told us that you should never eat a barracuda longer than your arm as those of longer length are poisonous. As we approached the breakwater, we swam just above the sea floor watching in wonderment as the thundering waters crashed with a vengeance above us.

The next morning we were off to the wreck of the Tug Boat King. It seems that Gary Tamb, a native Bermudan used the tug for treasure hunting. The tug is now treasure for the diver with the coral formations that have begun to take hold. South Side Scuba intentionally sank the tug on the January 17, 1984 in order to form an artificial reef. She is situated in the National Park waters. The tug is in 60 feet of water, so we had 40 minutes to explore her and the reef beyond. She lies on her side and some divers have experienced vertigo because of the positioning. She is completely intact, but penetration is limited to the bridge. There is also compressor on the back and an L-shaped mailbox similar to the one Mel Fisher used after finding the Atocha to vacuum up the mother lode.

Wreck Dive by Alan Marquardt

After viewing the wreck we went on to the reef where we came upon gracefully elongated trumpetfish, goat fish, black durgeons, brain and lettuce coral as well as other sea fans.

The second dive of the morning was at Middle Breaker. This is also a shallow dive. There was a great myriad of reef fish, but the most interesting aspect of the dive was the different size arches one could swim through.

That night we went back to Southwest Breakers for our night dive. We entered the water around nine under a bright full moon which offered excellent visibility. As our eyes became accustomed to the dark the lights became brighter, we were able to discover a far different group of sea life than we had seen during our day dives.

We caught sight of a large lobster and later in the dive we would see two more, a spiny and a guinea chick lobster. There was also a very large speckled Moray eel winding itself in and out of the coral. Alan came upon a gobe pufferfish. These amazing creatures are small, delicate, and beautiful, but will defend themselves from predators by continually swallowing water and making themselves many times larger so the predator cannot get their mouths around them.

Another in the group found a sleeping terminal parrotfish. You can identify them by the curled fin and yellow spot on the pectoral fin. There are thirteen different types of parrotfish, and each type has a male, a juvenile, and adult female gender within it. With the princess parrotfish for example, there is an interim period between the male and the female. The male changes sex to female and becomes a dominate female for the remainder of its life.

Night dives are spectacular in Bermuda. The coral changes color, the fish that are active during the day are found sleeping and the critters that hide in the daytime come out at night.

Alan, an experienced and published underwater photographer and videographer was our guide and a superb one at that. Thanks to Alan, our night dive was a very special one.

NOTE: *All dive sites are minutes away from the shop at Sonesta. All gear is set up and broken down.*

South Side Scuba - 3 Locations - Sonesta Beach, Marriott's Castle Harbour Resort and Grotto Bay Beach Hotel. Telephone (809) 293-2915.

Our last and only dive on the western side of the island was with *Dive Bermuda*, which is owned by John Slaughter, who until recently operated a "six pack". He has now teamed up with Submarine Enterprise. John takes his divers on a large launch that accompanies the submarine excursion. Both leave from the Royal Navy Dockyard in Somerset.

The *Submarine Enterprise* has been certified to the standards of the Bermudian Bureau of Shipping. She carries 44 passengers in air-conditioned comfort with a narration that informs them throughout the cruise about what they are viewing through the portholes.

The launch and the submarine reach the wreck of the *Larrington* in about 25 minutes. The Larrington went down in 1878 and lies amongst magnificent corals on a sandy bottom in about 40 feet of water. The depth allows for plenty of bottom time.

When we descended down to the wreck, John penetrated a small portion of it and motioned for me to follow. I thought this was a dead end and hesitated.

He reached down and pulled me up into the wreck. Shocked, I could hear him speaking to me. We were in an air pocket and both started to laugh.

We meandered along the wreck and onto the reef. The submarine had descended to the sandy bottom and sat silently. John took out food and schools of reef fish appeared. Black durgeons, sergeant major, and yellow tail swarmed around us. We circled the submarine, fish in tow, waving to those inside the submarine.

This is truly an unusual dive and a new experience for us. I recommend it highly and because of the depth it is a good dive for novices as well as the experienced. John warns divers to keep clear of the submarine jets which could act as a vacuum cleaner. Just follow John and you will have nothing to worry about.

Dive Bermuda before 9 a.m. (809) 234-0225; after 9a.m. 234-3547.

Editor's Note: Unfortunately Dive Bermuda does only this one dive trip. For a variety of diving we suggest South Side Scuba who will also store your gear for the duration of your stay.

We returned to the *Dockyard* which is a fascinating spot unto itself. The Maritime Museum and other historical monuments and buildings are plentiful. A tour of the Dockyard makes for a full informative and enjoyable day. There are a number of pub style restaurants and duty-free shops. We had lunch at the Frog and the Onion. It is as British as any London pub. The food was quite good and they carry a wide range of beer and ale.

Our final destination on Bermuda was the beautiful, and elegantly understated, *Lantana Colony Club*. (Please see Honeymoon Section for additional information.)

We spent two weeks on Bermuda and feel well informed about her sights, both above and below the water. Bermuda is most famous as a golf destination and the courses are indeed up to high standards.

We feel very comfortable recommending Bermuda as a dive destination for those who are seeking a beautiful, crime free, clean island with warm and friendly natives and an elegant international flavor.

There is a wide range of guest accommodations that fit every need and every pocket book. There is excellent duty-free shopping and many interesting historical sights.

The best snorkeling on the South Shore is at Church Bay. The reef goes straight out. Take Middle Road to Church Bay Park.

Three scuba centers are available to show you the reefs and the wrecks. The visibility by most standards is unlimited, the fish life is colorful and abundant, the guides take you through tunnels, arches, Bermuda's many subaqueous caves, and show a genuine warmth and interest in each diver's safety. The BSAC (British Sub Aqua Club) may permit limited access to experienced and qualified cave divers. Telephone: 1809-293-9531.

Who knows you might be the one to uncover one of the long hidden wrecks and like Peter Benchley, write your novel or cash in on a mother lode that allows you to stay on Bermuda forever. Believe me that would not be hard duty.

SCUBA AND SNORKELING FACILITIES QUESTIONNAIRE

NAME **Nautilus Diving Ltd**
ADDRESS **P.O. Box HM 237**
Hamilton, Bermuda
CONTACT **Mike Bacon**
TITLE **Course Director**
TELEPHONE **809-238-9332**   FAX **809-236-4284**

CAPITAL: **Hamilton**   GOVERNMENT:
POPULATION: **54,000**   LANGUAGE: **English**
CURRENCY: **U.S. $**   ELECTRICITY: **120v**
AIRLINES: **Various**   DEPARTURE TAX? **$15.00**
NEED VISA/PASSPORT?   YES **x**   NO   PROOF OF CITIZENSHIP?   YES **x**   NO

YOUR FACILITY IS CLASSIFIED AS: SCUBA CENTER **x**   RESORT
BUSINESS HOURS: **8:00 a.m. to 6:00 p.m.**
CERTIFYING AGENCIES: **SSI, PADI, BSAC**
LOG BOOK REQUIRED?   YES **x**   NO
EQUIPMENT: SALES **x**   RENTALS **x**   AIR FILLS **x**
PRIMARY LINE OF EQUIPMENT: **Sherwood, Scubapro**
PHOTOGRAPHIC EQUIPMENT: SALES   RENTALS **x**   LAB

CHARTER/DIVE BOAT AVAILABLE?   YES **x**   NO   DIVER CAPACITY **30**
COAST GUARD APPROVED?   YES   NO **x**   CAPTAIN LICENSED?   YES **x**   NO
SHIP TO SHORE?   YES **x**   NO   LORAN?   YES **x**   NO   RADAR?   YES **x**   NO
DIVE MASTER/INSTRUCTOR ABOARD?   YES   NO   BOTH **x**

DIVING & SNORKELING: SALT **x**   FRESH **x**
TYPE OF DIVING/SNORKELING IN AREA: WALL   BEACH **x**   WRECK **x**   REEF   CAVE **x**   ICE
DIVING/SNORKELING IN YOUR AREA IS BEST SUITED FOR: BEGINNER **x**   INTERMEDIATE **x**   ADVANCED **x**
BEST TIME OF YEAR FOR DIVING/SNORKELING: **March until November**
TEMPERATURE: **NOV-APRIL: 65 F**   **MAY-OCT: 70-86 F**
VISIBILITY: **DIVING: 100 FT**   **SNORKELING: 80 FT**

PACKAGES AVAILABLE: DIVE **x**   DIVE STAY   SNORKEL **x**   SNORKEL-STAY
ACCOMMODATIONS NEARBY: HOTEL **x**   MOTEL   HOME RENTALS
ACCOMMODATION RATES: EXPENSIVE **x**   MODERATE   INEXPENSIVE
RESTAURANTS NEARBY: EXPENSIVE   MODERATE **x**   INEXPENSIVE
YOUR AREA IS: REMOTE   QUIET WITH ACTIVITIES **x**   LIVELY
LOCAL ACTIVITY/NIGHTLIFE: **Lots**
CAR NEEDED TO EXPLORE AREA?   YES   NO **x**
DUTY FREE SHOPPING?   YES **x**   NO

LOCAL EMERGENCY SERVICES   NEAREST HYPERBARIC TREATMENT FACILITY
COASTGUARD: **Harbour Radio & Marine Police**   AUTHORITY: **Bermuda**
TELEPHONE: LOCATION: **Hospital**
CALLSIGNS: TELEPHONE:

LOCAL DIVING DOCTOR:
NAME: **Lots**
LOCATION: **Hospital**
TELEPHONE:

SCUBA AND SNORKELING FACILITIES QUESTIONNAIRE

NAME **South Side Scuba**
ADDRESS **Sonesta Beach Hotel & Spa**
Hamilton, Bermuda
CONTACT **Alan Marquardt**
TITLE **Owner**
TELEPHONE **809-293-2915** FAX **809-286-0394**

CAPITAL: **Hamilton** GOVERNMENT: **British Parliament**
POPULATION: **65,000** LANGUAGE: **English**
CURRENCY: **Bermuda & US $** ELECTRICITY: **110AC**
AIRLINES: **CO, Delta, AA, US Air, NW, BA** DEPARTURE TAX? **$15.00**
NEED VISA/PASSPORT? YES x   NO PROOF OF CITIZENSHIP? YES x   NO

YOUR FACILITY IS CLASSIFIED AS: SCUBA CENTER x   RESORT
BUSINESS HOURS: **8:00 a.m. to 5:00 p.m.**
CERTIFYING AGENCIES: **PADI, NAUI**
LOG BOOK REQUIRED? YES   NO x
EQUIPMENT: SALES   RENTALS x   AIR FILLS x
PRIMARY LINE OF EQUIPMENT: **Sherwood, Dacor**
PHOTOGRAPHIC EQUIPMENT: SALES   RENTALS x   LAB

CHARTER/DIVE BOAT AVAILABLE? YES x (3)   NO   DIVER CAPACITY **68 total**
COAST GUARD APPROVED? YES x   NO   CAPTAIN LICENSED? YES x   NO
SHIP TO SHORE? YES x   NO   LORAN? YES   NO x   RADAR? YES   NO x
DIVE MASTER/INSTRUCTOR ABOARD? YES   NO   BOTH x

DIVING & SNORKELING: SALT x   FRESH
TYPE OF DIVING/SNORKELING IN AREA: WALL   BEACH   WRECK x   REEF x   CAVE x   ICE
DIVING/SNORKELING IN YOUR AREA IS BEST SUITED FOR: BEGINNER x   INTERMEDIATE x   ADVANCED
BEST TIME OF YEAR FOR DIVING/SNORKELING:
TEMPERATURE: **NOV-APRIL: 65-75 F** **MAY-OCT: 75-85 F**
VISIBILITY: **DIVING: 80-100 FT** **SNORKELING: 80-100 FT**

PACKAGES AVAILABLE: DIVE x   DIVE STAY x   SNORKEL x   SNORKEL-STAY
ACCOMMODATIONS NEARBY: HOTEL x   MOTEL   HOME RENTALS x
ACCOMMODATION RATES: EXPENSIVE x   MODERATE x   INEXPENSIVE
RESTAURANTS NEARBY: EXPENSIVE x   MODERATE x   INEXPENSIVE x
YOUR AREA IS: REMOTE   QUIET WITH ACTIVITIES x   LIVELY
LOCAL ACTIVITY/NIGHTLIFE:
CAR NEEDED TO EXPLORE AREA? YES   NO x   Use Mopeds
DUTY FREE SHOPPING? YES x   NO

LOCAL EMERGENCY SERVICES   NEAREST HYPERBARIC TREATMENT FACILITY
COASTGUARD: **Bermuda Harbour Radio**   AUTHORITY: **Bermuda Recompression Chamber**
TELEPHONE: **809-297-1010**   LOCATION: **King Edward VII Memorial Hospital**
CALLSIGNS: **2000 Bravo Mike**   TELEPHONE:

LOCAL DIVING DOCTOR:
NAME: **Dr. Carol Ferris**
LOCATION: **King Edward VII Memorial Hospital**
TELEPHONE: **809-286-2345**

CANADA

San Juan and Canadian Gulf Islands

Molly Andrews–Smith, John C. Smith, Dan Fehrenbacher, Eric Peterson

Our group of sixteen, chartered three boats; a 34 foot Hunter sailboat, "Windlust", a 39 foot Jeneau sailboat, "Tsa-la-gi", and a 42 foot Grandbanks yacht, "Schwendi".

First Day (Saturday) - The group assembled at Anacortes. After finding each other in the channel we headed toward the north end of the San Juan Islands. We anchored deep within protected waters of the main channel of Sucia (Susha) Island and discussed over cocktails what our course would be for the next day. Sucia Island is a state park and provides a variety of terrains, ranging from evergreen forest to beaches with bizarre rock formations. There are hiking trails and campsites, and fresh water is available.

Second Day (Sunday) - To start things off, the divers boarded the yacht, Schwendi, and headed toward Lawson Bluff on the north/northwest section of Sucia. This dive site is only accessible by boat. With the depth sounder bouncing off the 300 foot floor, Captain Mark motored us within 30 feet of the wall before we jumped overboard. Descending, we were greeted with 15 feet visibility, and a blackness below that emphasized the steepness of this colorless wall.

> **As we continued down, the visibility cleared to about 30 feet, at a depth of seventy. Drifting with the one knot current, we found the home of a giant octopus. His home was identified by broken crab and clam shells at the opening. He was hiding behind flowering mouths of giant sea anemones. We attempted to entice him out with a small rock crab but the oversized mollusk pushed the offering away with it's tentacle and retreated further into his hole. We found a small quantity of rock and free swimming scallops along the many ledges of the wall. The scallop hunt would provide a few tasty appetizers to compliment the evening's sea bass entree.**

After diving, we sailed and motored to West Beach Resort on Orcas Island to refill our scuba tanks and buy ice, For divers, the resort only supplies air fills and some miscellaneous dive gear (lead weights and dive belts, etc.). Ensure your tanks are current with the visual inspection, or they may refuse to fill them. The general store has various other supplies for fishing and regular grocery items.

By mid-afternoon, under clear skies at six knots, we were making our way to Bedwell Harbor, Prevost Island, Canada, to clear customs. We used passports, but a valid driver's license works as well. Familiarize yourself with liquor limits etc., in case of a physical inspection. The marina offers water services, groceries and a restaurant/bar.

At end of day we tied up in Ellen Bay, Prevost Island, Canada. Would not recommend rafting with other boats in this bay, given the amount of ferry traffic that crosses the area.

Third Day (Monday) - At breakfast we were greeted by B.C, Ferry wake, so we pulled anchor and headed to our second dive site, Obstruction Rock, one quarter mile from the south end of Salt Spring Island. It's indicated by a marker on top of the reef. The south end of the reef is fairly desolate, with limited sea life and a sandy bottom. We were somewhat disappointed with the beginning of the dive.

Upon cresting the reef and heading toward the north end, we dropped over a wall with no bottom, containing numerous crevices and caverns and an abundance of sea life. Unfortunately, the two divers that were spear fishing only had 1,000 PSI of air left, so few fish were speared before ascent was required.

The other divers that were gathering had greater success and provided enough crab for the whole troop.

After the dive, we went under sail and found plenty of mid-afternoon wind,

That night we tied up in the natural inlet between Kuper and Theitus Islands, known as Clam Bay, Given the B.C. Ferry incident at breakfast, each boat opted to test their own anchoring expertise at a distance from the other boats.

Fourth Day (Tuesday) - At daybreak, the crew rowed ashore and collected oysters and clams. The tide was minus a few feet and made the expedition very easy. After pulling up anchor, we headed into Ganges Harbor for sundries and supplies (ice). Dock space is limited and some areas of the marina are shallow for sailboats. We recommend staying clear of the section closest to land. There is also a second marina area on the other side of the harbor that provides easier access.

We headed toward Sydney Harbor, Vancouver Island. As the sun was beginning to set, we decided on Portland Island, as it was closer and we were losing daylight. Upon arrival, we set our anchor with a four to one scope in the bay. We determined the swing would be too great and cause for an unexpected cocktail hour with the other boats in the harbor. Given gentle prodding from the others anchored there, we pulled up anchor and headed toward Sydney. We had to pass through John's Passage which requires extreme expertise due to shallowness and rocks. The passage is between Coal Island and an unnamed island.

Sydney Harbor greeted us with one of the most beautiful sunsets we had seen the entire trip. The harbor is protected and provided calm waters for the overnight stay. Sydney Harbor has a marina with groceries, ice and diesel. The highlight was a real shower. $2.00 bought you unlimited time and it was well worth the investment.

Fifth Day (Wednesday) - From Sydney Harbor our last dive was targeted off the northeast end of Coal Island with plans to dive the kelp bed. (Before entering the water ensure all divers are ready, as the current can pull you from the wall before descent if divers are waiting in the water.) As we submerged, the current was pulling to the west, so we decided to drift with the current. We found ourselves surrounded by large boulders, crevices, and caves housing numerous varieties of sea life, An easy dive at 45 feet allowed us to investigate the topography below the water. There was not an abundance of sea life, but a fair amount of smaller sea bass and greenling. Along with the fish, our collection of sea life included sea cucumber and rock crabs.

Sea cucumber is an interesting delicacy. We grilled it, and the consistency was similar to squid.

Sixth Day (Thursday) - Heading towards Friday Harbor winds carried the Windlust up to 6 knots from Canadian into U.S. waters. Entering Friday Harbor, we cleared customs by telephone and rejoined Tsa-la-gi and Schwendi for a final night of partying before returning to Anacortes. Friday Harbor has an abundance of restaurants and pubs that are an easy walk from the marina. Plenty of gift shops and general service stores are also available.

Seventh Day (Friday) - We left Friday morning and motored the remaining distance to Anacortes. The trip takes about four hours. All in all, it was a great time.

SNORKELING

Given the water temperature of Puget Sound and the Canadian Gulf Waters (approximately 50 degrees), snorkeling is not a good option.

BOAT CHARTERS
PENMAR MARINA, Anacortes, Washington, (206) 293-4839

LOCAL ACCOMMODATIONS
FRIDAY HARBOR, San Juan Island
San Juan Inn, 50 spring Street, Friday Harbor
(206) 378-2070, Moderate, VISA/MasterCard

TUCKER HOUSE, 260 B Street, Friday Harbor (206) 378-2783, moderate, VISA/MasterCard.

CARIBBEAN

Anguilla

Martha Watkins Gilkes is a free lance photo journalist, an underwater photographer, and a professional underwater model based on Antigua. She has been scuba diving for 18 years and has been a scuba diving Instructor through the Professional Association of Diving Instructors for 13 years. She owns and operates her own scuba diving business, Fanta-Sea Island Divers, on Antigua and also Fanta-Sea Island Excursions, a dive travel company specializing in exclusive dive travel to remote dive destinations. Although an American, she has lived in the Caribbean for 15 years and has dived throughout the entire region. She is married to Barbadian Captain Tony Gilkes who flies for LIAT. Martha is a frequent contributor to regional and international publications specializing in the subject of scuba diving and is presently producing a book for MACMILLIAN/London on Eastern Caribbean diving. She has served as the President of the Barbados based Eastern Caribbean Safe Diving Association for the past 8 years and also serves as the Diving Liaison Officer for the Historical and Archeological Society of Antigua.

Anguilla, one of the few really unspoiled Caribbean islands left, is truly the adventuresome diver's paradise! There are few divers with only one dive shop but it is only a matter of time until she becomes discovered.

Meanwhile, for those who are lucky enough to explore Anguilla while she is still unknown, there is the added excitement of diving places few divers have been.

Certainly one will not encounter the development of diving found on many of the islands, where there are large dive boats with 20 or 30 divers crowding aboard to dash to the same spot dived 364 days previously.

Anguilla, located in the Eastern Caribbean, is the most northerly of the Leeward Islands. Her nearest neighbor is the island of St. Maarten, which is half Dutch and half French.

Anguilla is a long flat coral island that is fringed with around thirty magnificent white sand beaches. They are said to be among the best beaches in the Caribbean. Indeed, if privacy is what one is seeking, be assured of finding an uninhabited beach on Anguilla. The fact that Anguilla is all coral makes for excellent reef diving around the island. However, there are also other choices for the diver than the reef.

In the summer of 1990, the Government of Anguilla, along with a U.S. based commercial salvage company, sank four ships around the island. There were already two wreck diving sites so this added to the choices for the avid wreck diver.

The M.V. Sarah, a freighter, the largest of ships, at 222 feet, lies totally intact in 80 feet of water. The shallowest part is in 30 feet and can be clearly seen from the surface.

The Sarah was built in the Grangemouth Dockyard Company, Ltd., located on the Firth of Forth on the east coast of Scotland. She was completed on March 9, 1956 and began her life as the GANNET as a general purpose dry cargo vessel. She was renamed SARAH by her second owner, in honor of his mother, and moved to Newfoundland. In 1983 she was moved to the Caribbean where she was purchased by the Anguilla Marine Transportation Company, Ltd. On November 7, 1984 she was hit by Hurricane Klaus while at anchor in Road Bay, Anguilla, where she partially sank. On June 29, 1990 as most of the island's population looked on, SARAH was lifted out of the water and relocated to the Eastern end of the Sail Reef system.

Martha Gilkes & Friend by Alice Bag Shaw

Tamariain Water Sports has a detailed history of SARAH. Common marine life around her includes rays, barracudas and schools of jacks and the superstructure left intact makes an excellent backdrop for avid underwater photographers.

The M.V. Commerce, a 137 foot freighter, built in Holland in 1955 lies in 45 to 80 feet of water off Flat Cap Point. She was intentionally sunk as a dive site in 1986 and sits intact and upright on a sloping bottom. The structure is very open and allows for divers to swim through her in complete safety. Having been down for some years there is a large variety of fish life on the wreck and occasionally large sting rays are spotted.

The *M.V. Ida Maria*, a 110 foot freighter, built around World War I, also intentionally sunk in 1985, sits upright, semi-intact, in 60 feet of water. She started her life as a general cargo vessel on European trade routes until she was sold and brought to the Caribbean by Mr. Clement Daniels. He donated her to be sunk as a diving attraction. Penetration of this wreck is not allowed as it is not safe. This site affords the diver a unique interaction with marine life as the dive masters have hand fed the marine creatures at the wreck and they are most approachable. The marine life includes large French angel fish, schools of Atlantic spade fish, rock beauties and exceptionally large spotted drums. Lobsters have also made this site home. Truly for abundant marine life, and good photographic material, this site is super.

Other wrecks which were part of the 1990 summer sinking program include the *M.V. Oosterdiep*, lying in 80 feet off Barnes Bay, the *M.V. Meppel* and the *M.V. Lady Vie*, also lying in 80 feet. All three sites are upright and intact. Marine life is slowly being attracted to all sites with such marine creatures as turtles, spadefish, angelfish, sting rays and grunts being regularly seen.

The reef dives around Anguilla are also to be enjoyed as marine life abounds. Some of the sites include Sandy Island, Sandy Deep, Paintcan Reef, and Prickly Pear, there nurse sharks are often seen resting on the sandy bottom. There are numerous other sites dived by the dive operations, each with added excitement and generally excellent visibility.

Prickley Pear ranges from 30 to 70 feet and is a suitable dive for the novice or the experienced. Two reefs are separated by a white sand channel which provides coral overhangs, ledges and small caves in between the reef systems. Varied invertebrate and marine life abound under these colorful ledges, such as coral banded shrimp and arrow crab. Occasional nurse sharks are tucked under the ledges and sting rays are sometimes seen lying on the sandy bottom.

Sandy Deep off of Sandy Island provides a mini wall dive dropping from 15 to 60 feet with an abundance of hard and soft corals and a large variety of reef fish.

Little Bay Cove is a very shallow dive (10-30 feet) but one is usually guaranteed to see shoals of literally thousands of tiny silver sides swaying in the water. The site is an excellent second dive of the day.

Grouper Bowl, 25 to 50 feet, is part of Sail Reef system and has some of the most spectacular and beautiful hard coral formations around the island. Turtles and lobsters are usually found.

Authors Deep, in 110 feet, is the deepest site normally dived. Black coral, not still found on many islands is abundant, although no taking is allowed. Large pelagic fish like sharks and eagle rays are sometimes spotted.

When one tires of diving, beach combing is a must on Anguilla, as this island has some of the most beautiful beaches found in the Caribbean.

One advantage of double dives is visiting a few beaches only reached by boat, in between dives. Other beaches that can be reached by rental car (or taxi) are Rendezvous Bay, Cove Bay, Maundays and Shoal Bay. Here, sparkling white sand beaches stretch for longer than one can walk. On the opposite end of the island is Captains Bay, where breakers roll in, if a bit of surf is desired. This bay is very isolated and rather difficult to reach, but worth the journey for the adventuresome. The one dive shop on the island, Tamariain Water Sports, is run by Iain Grummitt, a transplanted Scotsman and his partner. Thomas Peabody, an American. They offer friendly, personal service and will only take a maximum of 20 divers at a time, although there are rarely that many divers at once on the island. They operate 7 days a week. All dives are done an the leeward side of the island from a boat. Their 38 foot dive boat (with two 125 hp. outboards) gets one to the dive site in a mere 10-15 minutes.

Iain and Thomas are especially safety minded and very careful to stick to the rules with diving! No decompression diving is required, although decompression computers are allowed.

SCUBA AND SNORKELING FACILITIES QUESTIONNAIRE

NAME **Tamariain Watersports Ltd.**
ADDRESS **P.O. Box 247**
The Valley, Anguilla, BWI
CONTACT **Thomas L C Peabody/Iain I. Grummit**
TITLE **Owners/Managers**
TELEPHONE **809-497-2020**   FAX **809-497-5125**

CAPITAL:	**The Valley**	GOVERNMENT:	**British Dependent Territory**
POPULATION:	**8,000**	LANGUAGE:	**English**
CURRENCY:	**EC Dollar, US $**	ELECTRICITY:	**110**
AIRLINES:	**American/Winair/Charter**	DEPARTURE TAX?	Yes
NEED VISA/PASSPORT?	YES NO	PROOF OF CITIZENSHIP?	YES **x** NO

YOUR FACILITY IS CLASSIFIED AS: SCUBA CENTER **x**   RESORT
BUSINESS HOURS: **8:00 a.m. to 4:00 p.m.**
CERTIFYING AGENCIES: **PADI**
LOG BOOK REQUIRED?   YES   NO **x**
EQUIPMENT: SALES **x**   RENTALS **x**   AIR FILLS **x**
PRIMARY LINE OF EQUIPMENT: **Sherwood, Dacor, Amico**
PHOTOGRAPHIC EQUIPMENT: SALES   RENTALS   LAB **x**

CHARTER/DIVE BOAT AVAILABLE?   YES   NO   DIVER CAPACITY
COAST GUARD APPROVED?   YES **x** NO   CAPTAIN LICENSED? YES   NO **x**
SHIP TO SHORE?   YES **x**   NO   LORAN? YES NO **x**   RADAR? YES NO **x**
DIVE MASTER/INSTRUCTOR ABOARD?   YES   NO   BOTH **x**

DIVING & SNORKELING: SALT **x**   FRESH
TYPE OF DIVING/SNORKELING IN AREA: WALL   BEACH **x**   WRECK **x**   REEF   CAVE   ICE
DIVING/SNORKELING IN YOUR AREA IS BEST SUITED FOR: BEGINNER **x**   INTERMEDIATE **x**   ADVANCED
BEST TIME OF YEAR FOR DIVING/SNORKELING: **May - November**
TEMPERATURE: **NOV-APRIL: 79-81 F**   **MAY-OCT: 81-84 F**
VISIBILITY: **DIVING: 60-100 FT**   **SNORKELING: 60-100 FT**

PACKAGES AVAILABLE: DIVE **x**   DIVE STAY **x**   SNORKEL   SNORKEL-STAY
ACCOMMODATIONS NEARBY: HOTEL **x**   MOTEL   HOME RENTALS **x**
ACCOMMODATION RATES: EXPENSIVE **x**   MODERATE **x**   INEXPENSIVE **x**
RESTAURANTS NEARBY: EXPENSIVE   MODERATE **x**   INEXPENSIVE **x**
YOUR AREA IS: REMOTE   QUIET WITH ACTIVITIES **x**   LIVELY
LOCAL ACTIVITY/NIGHTLIFE: **Local clubs with live music, hotels**
CAR NEEDED TO EXPLORE AREA?   YES **x**   NO
DUTY FREE SHOPPING?   YES **x 15 minute ferry boat ride to St. Maarten (Duty Free)**

LOCAL EMERGENCY SERVICES   NEAREST HYPERBARIC TREATMENT FACILITY
COASTGUARD: AUTHORITY:
TELEPHONE: LOCATION:
CALLSIGNS: TELEPHONE:

LOCAL DIVING DOCTOR:
NAME:
LOCATION:
TELEPHONE:

Antigua and Barbuda
The Sister Islands
Martha Watkins Gilkes

Around much of Antigua the surf breaks on barrier reefs, alive with colorful tropical fish. This makes for mostly shallow diving (above 60 feet) and one has to seek out deep diving depths. The underwater terrain of Antigua tends to match the topside, as Antigua is a coral island, which makes the majority of the island very flat.

It is said that there are 1,000 square miles of coral reef surrounding Antigua and Barbuda.

One of the better dive sites for diving is Cades Reef, a 2 1/2 mile reef running along the leeward coast of the island. This reef is still virginal. Part of it has been established as an underwater park. It will therefore, hopefully, remain a top notch diving site for years to come. Diving on Cades Reef often affords the diver 80 to 100 foot visibility (and sometimes up to 150 feet) which is certainly what one expects in the clear, warm Caribbean waters. Most of the dive shops will schedule dives to Cades Reef. Each dive shop has its own list of names and dive sites on Cades Reef, but as the reef is so extensive, there are unlimited diving sites available. Fish life abounds on the reef, with parrotfish providing a rainbow of colors amidst the staghorn coral that readily grows on the shallow reefs. Schools of blue tang and masses of small harmless barracuda are readily seen. Some of the dive sites on Cades Reef include Eel Run, Snapper Ledge, Big Sponge and The Chimney, with the reason for the names being obvious.

Sandy Island Reef, a short 15 minute boat ride from the nearest dive shop on the leeward coast, is a favorite dive choice for two of the shops nearby. The reef is covered in a variety of types of coral and gorgonias. A diver can explore the reef in shallow water, only 30 feet, or swim along the edge of the reef, fringed by a white sand bottom, in 50 feet of water.

There are known wrecks which have been dived for some time by the local diving shops, although names are not known for all of the sites.

Six wrecks are the "ANDES" in Deep Bay, lying in only 20 feet of water, the "HARBOR OF ST. JOHNS", a 90 foot steel tug. She originally sank in St. Johns Harbor while the water pump was being repaired. This same water pump is still held in the vice in 40 feet of water where she now rests in Deep Bay. About 60 feet behind the "HARBOR OF ST. JOHNS" and 20 feet to the left one can find the remains of an old barge, known locally as "THE UNKNOWN BARGE." Although nothing is known about her past, her present provides a home for schools of small reef fish. The steamship "JETTIAS" lies in shallow water (about 25 feet) just off Diamond Bank, and the "WARRIOR GERRIANT" is just off Maiden Island. The wreck of the "H.M.S. WAYMUND", for which the reef off Sandy Island is named, was carrying missionaries to South America in the 1700's and went aground. The ship's carpenter insisted they abandon ship, but the missionaries maintained they would not sink. Thus, all but the carpenter remained and perished.

There are 3 or 4 other wrecks around Waymund Reef and Sandy Island and anchors and cannon can be spotted in various locations. The wrecks of Antigua vary in the size, depth and growth of marine life, so a choice can be made as to what type of wreck one wishes to dive!

For a deep dive, Sunken Rock is spectacular, with a maximum depth of 122 feet (very unusual for Antigua diving)! This dive is for more experienced divers, however. Along the drop off of the rock ledge one may see magnificent open water fish (sting rays, large barracuda and maybe even a dolphin or two.) The rock formations forms a cleft allowing divers to swim through. This gives the sensation of a cave dive, as one glides along under a few coral overhangs, between the cleft of the large coral forma-

Boat at Rest by Wendy Canning Church

tions, but one is not subjected to the dangers of cave diving as the diver is always in open water and can easily surface. The main danger is depth, which must be monitored to stay within safe decompression time. Once the sandy bottom is reached, a gentle ascent can be made along the outside of the coral formation, until one is on a typical tropical coral reef, in 40 feet of water, with an abundance of colorful reef fish. Blue and brown chromis, and sergeant majors protecting their territory and lots of colorful parrotfish are always seen in residence.

Other sites include Horseshoe Reef (so named for its shape), Barracuda Alley (named for the barracuda often seen in this area, though not guaranteed) and Little Bird Island. These sites provide the typical tropical reef scenes of the Caribbean, with a host of small colorful reef fish. Divers are sometimes fortunate to experience more unusual marine life like a school of graceful eagle rays gliding by, which are often seen off Little Bird Island. Unlike many of the islands, lobster can be more readily spotted in Antigua waters. On a recent dive off Little Bird Island, 14 were counted under the sprawling branch of elk horn coral. Lobsters are protected by law, with it being illegal to take small lobsters. Hopefully, this will allow divers to continue to experience the thrill of sighting a mass of lobsters in their natural environment. For the underwater photographer this is a real treat.

Shirley Heights is also a spectacular dive, and affords up to 110 feet for those seeking deeper dives. There are coral overhangs providing homes for an abundance of small reef fish and colorful sponges.

In addition, one often sees rays, turtles, tiger groupers, and even sharks gliding by.

Schools of spadefish are also spotted around this dive site.

A newly discovered diving site off Antigua has brought much excitement of the diving community and shops. Ariadna Shoal is located 11 nautical miles off Antigua and although a long boat ride, taking nearly an hour, once on the site the diver has something very exciting to look forward to. This site, until recently, has been virtually unexplored and the marine life is prolific!

Barbuda, mentioned earlier, is the lovely "little sister island" of Antigua, and the waters surrounding this tiny gem of an island are totally unexplored.

However, the facilities are greatly limited unless one is on a boat with gear and a compressor (which are not readily available) diving Barbuda can be difficult. Barbuda waters, like Antigua, are very shallow, so one can easily enjoy lovely snorkeling.

SCUBA AND SNORKELING FACILITIES QUESTIONNAIRE

NAME **Fanta Sea Island Divers**
ADDRESS **c/o Captain David Gilkes**
LIAT, V.C. Bird International Airport, Antigua, West Indies
CONTACT **Martha Watkins Gilkes**
TITLE **Owner/Instructor**
TELEPHONE **Not available (very limited on island)** FAX **By letter or telegram (allow at least 3 days)**

CAPITAL:	GOVERNMENT:
POPULATION:	LANGUAGE:
CURRENCY:	ELECTRICITY:
AIRLINES:	DEPARTURE TAX?
NEED VISA/PASSPORT? YES NO x	PROOF OF CITIZENSHIP? YES x NO

YOUR FACILITY IS CLASSIFIED AS: SCUBA CENTER   RESORT
BUSINESS HOURS: **Varies - By appointment only**
CERTIFYING AGENCIES: **PADI Instructor**
LOG BOOK REQUIRED?   YES   NO
EQUIPMENT: SALES   RENTALS x   AIR FILLS x
PRIMARY LINE OF EQUIPMENT: **Dacor - some very limited equipment for sale**
PHOTOGRAPHIC EQUIPMENT: SALES   RENTALS   LAB

CHARTER/DIVE BOAT AVAILABLE?   YES x   NO   DIVER CAPACITY
COAST GUARD APPROVED?   YES   NO   CAPTAIN LICENSED?   YES   NO x
SHIP TO SHORE?   VHF x   NO   LORAN?   YES   NO x   RADAR?   YES   NO x
DIVE MASTER/INSTRUCTOR ABOARD?   YES x   NO   BOTH

DIVING & SNORKELING: SALT x   FRESH
TYPE OF DIVING/SNORKELING IN AREA: WALL   BEACH x   WRECK x   REEF x   CAVE   ICE
DIVING/SNORKELING IN YOUR AREA IS BEST SUITED FOR: BEGINNER x   INTERMEDIATE x   ADVANCED
BEST TIME OF YEAR FOR DIVING/SNORKELING: **All year**
TEMPERATURE: NOV-APRIL: F   MAY-OCT: F
VISIBILITY: DIVING: FT   SNORKELING: FT

PACKAGES AVAILABLE: DIVE   DIVE STAY   SNORKEL   SNORKEL-STAY
ACCOMMODATIONS NEARBY: HOTEL x   MOTEL   HOME RENTALS
ACCOMMODATION RATES: EXPENSIVE   MODERATE   INEXPENSIVE
RESTAURANTS NEARBY: EXPENSIVE   MODERATE   INEXPENSIVE
YOUR AREA IS: REMOTE   QUIET WITH ACTIVITIES x   LIVELY
LOCAL ACTIVITY/NIGHTLIFE: **All types of water activities, sightseeing of island**
CAR NEEDED TO EXPLORE AREA?   YES   NO
DUTY FREE SHOPPING?   YES   NO

LOCAL EMERGENCY SERVICES   NEAREST HYPERBARIC TREATMENT FACILITY
COASTGUARD: AUTHORITY: **St. Thomas**   (809) 427-8819
TELEPHONE: LOCATION: **Barbados**
CALLSIGNS: TELEPHONE: **(809) 776-2686**

LOCAL DIVING DOCTOR:
NAME: **Dr. Kelvin Charles**
LOCATION: **St. Johns, Antigua**
TELEPHONE:

Aruba

Liz O'Connor is a novice diver certified 1987 in St. Croix, USVI (20+ dives). She is also a Registered Nurse at Boston's Brigham & Women's Hospital.

My dive log is longing for an entry and after years this novice diver is quite anxious to add more dives to the 20 or so already under my belt. My desire to dive runs deep, and I often find myself dreaming about being underwater, swimming with fascinating sea life all around me.

In January, 1991, I came close to living those dreams when I took a five day winter trip to Aruba. A last minute charter, promoting the newly built Sonesta Hotel and Resort was our destination. Although my traveling companion is a non-diver, I was most hopeful to get some diving in. After all, my last dives were in 1989 in Bonaire, when every waking moment you have you could spend diving if you wanted to. An earlier inner ear inflammation had been acting up giving me bouts of lightheadedness, and some dizziness. My doctor said diving could actually aggravate it. Just knowing that I was going to the Caribbean and would not be able to dive was disappointing, to say the least. Somehow, being able to only sail upon the turquoise waters and not descending below its surface, left a very important dimension of the trip missing as any diver can understand.

It was the captain of the sailboat we ventured out on one afternoon who took us to snorkeling spots and the dive sites who helped somewhat to satisfy my desire and allowed me to experience some of Aruba's sea life from my snorkeling position above.

Having departed from the beachfront of the Aruba Palm Beach Hotel and Casino, we sailed north along the bright turquoise waters of Eagle Beach to its northernmost end. This end, often known as Arashi Beach, even north of Malmok where all the surfers go, is where we did some snorkeling.

We also sailed further out after lunch to the German freighter, Antilla, that was sunk by forces stationed on Aruba during World War II, when it was found to be supplying German subs in the area. Its bow is still lapped by waves at the surface. Lying in about 80 feet of water, it is a popular dive for many of Scuba Aruba's dive boats, whose divers explore its hull numerous times each day.

Another wreck in the same area, the Peder Nales, lies in only 25 feet, and is located just south of Antilla, but closer to the beach. Scuba Aruba also offers a south side shore dive which has been recommended, but has a very tricky beach entry and unpredictable current. A definite, "take someone who knows the dive spot well," kind of dive.

The day of our sail on this 30 foot sloop was the only day we had showers which raced along the beach bringing a ten minute downpour only to be followed quickly by bright sunshine. Of course, every day is filled with warm sunshine in Aruba.

The island, being in a hurricane belt, which usually affects most Caribbean islands in September/October, offers much sun, a dry climate, and makes it fairly mosquito-free.

And the beaches ... you decide if you have ever seen better.

As we pulled up to our mooring of Aruba Palm Beach Hotel, the sun reappeared as bright as before, and seemed to illuminate the turquoise waters once again as we climbed aboard the Zodiac for the late afternoon skip over the water to the beach. Once ashore, we marvelled at the scene. The steam was rising from the walkways about the pool area just having been sprinkled with rain that preceded our arrival. Even at this late afternoon time, it was still warm enough to make a slip into the water off the beach for an irresistibly refreshing dip. As we were the Sonesta's guests, we had free reign of their private island, a five minute boat ride from the inner harbor. This little island boasts two beaches, one with a waterfront restaurant and water sports facility, and the other one for those desiring a few less tan lines upon their mid-winter return to Boston.

It is also from this vantage point that on a clear day, as you leave your beach chair and strawberry daiquiri for a cool swim, some of Venezuela's highest peaks can be seen on the horizon.

For diving enthusiasts who are also novices, there are two sunken planes just off of Sonesta Island. They don't have much coral growth, but are a relatively easy dive being in only about 20 feet of water.

I know people always wish for their room to open up onto the beach, and this is possible from many of the low rise and high rise hotels on Palm Beach, the largest and most beautiful beach on the island, but being right downtown is also quite enjoyable. You are convenient to many of the island's favorite restaurants and night spots, and after a few hours in the sun, and a cool swim in the pool, we were always ready to treat ourselves to an early evening walk through downtown streets to one of the popular restaurants. Shopkeepers tend to close shop early and then open up after dinner for a few hours. We found many people out strolling, mostly tourists, on their way to dinner, or another of the Casinos located in the area.

One restaurant we especially liked was El Gaucho. It specializes in Argintinean cooked beef and seafood, and is done in a Conquistador motif. It reminded me of a scene out of those old Zorro episodes. A little closer to our hotel, and on the waterfront, we frequented the Seaside Restaurant, famous for their charbroiled red snapper or grouper. Sitting on their patio under the awning whose fringe blew freely in the balmy evening breezes was most relaxing.

After dinner it was time to head out to catch some of the night life on Aruba, which includes not only dinner and dancing at resort hotels, but your choice of five different casinos.

The Crystal Casino, a part of the Sonesta Hotel's Complex, is smaller but one of the fanciest, reminiscent of the Casino at Monte Carlo in Europe, with its dark mahogany woodwork, and crystal chandeliers.

A couple of evenings we ventured out to the Alhambra on Palm Beach in the low rise section of hotels. A ten minute bus ride from town brought us door to door. Even though it was after 9 pm the sun had not yet set, and we were treated to views of the island's beaches, resorts, and evening activity.

I always find traveling by public transportation one of the best ways to feel a part of the life and culture of the place one is visiting. Whether residents are on their way home from work, the market, or just out to visit friends, they can be very helpful and pleasant to talk to. These interactions have always added a different dimension to my travel.

Our last day included a morning stroll down Naussaustraat Street, which boasts many-international shops where one can purchase duty-free French perfumes, Colombian emeralds, or gold Swiss watches while enjoying Dutch-inspired architecture. Besides Naussaustraat Street, there are also shops within the Sonesta Complex, offering many different gifts to bring to the folks back home who were not lucky enough to escape the latest New England winter.

After shopping, we had to take one last dip in the ocean. A few extra rays certainly would not hurt, especially since the use of various sun blocks all week had, prevented any major sun burns.

We departed at 2 pm for the airport, taking with us memories of the island and its people who were such gracious hosts for our 5 day visit.

I will especially remember the international diversity of the island with visitors from both South America and Europe, who met and mingled in the sun and fun ambiance of Aruba.

If one dives, sails, wants to practice some windsurfing, or just soak up the rays and the Casino atmosphere by night, there is something for everyone. It is a place that one promises to return someday.

Barbados, "The Rock"

Wendy Canning Church

Barbados, the most easterly and one of the more developed of the Caribbean islands is referred to fondly by its population of 231,000 (the Bajans) as "The Rock," perhaps this is because it is set atop a volcano.

The island is 21 miles long and up to 14 miles wide. The calm, serene waters of the Caribbean are found on its leeward side and the thunderous, tumultuous Atlantic waters on its windward side. At one point within eight miles or one half-hour by car of each other.

The climate is a moderate one. There is no land mass for approximately 3,000 miles between Barbados and Africa. Thus Barbados is assured fresh breezes and clean waters year round.

June through November brings the rainy season, but not to worry, these showers disappear as suddenly as they appear. Visitors can quickly return to water sports and tanning.

According to the history of Barbados, the first settlers were the Arawak Indians from South America, but recent archaeological digs have begun to disprove this. It is now thought that the earliest visitors to the island could have been the Egyptians or the Phoenicians who took advantage of the calm currents to make the crossing in their boats of reeds and wood.

Divers on Beach by Peter Smith

The Arawak Indians, a gentle and loving tribe, settled on Barbados approximately 300 years before Christ. They were eventually obliterated by the Carib Indians who captured, tortured, raped and even practiced cannibalism on their victims.

The Portuguese landed in 1536 naming the island, Los Barbados (the Bearded Ones) after the fig trees whose roots resemble beards. The Spanish landed afterwards, but neither of these visitors ever established a permanent settlement

British Captain John Powell landed in Holetown in 1625 claiming this 166 square mile island in the name of James I, King of England, unaware that he was deceased. He returned to Barbados on February 17, 1627 with 80 settlers and slaves, establishing a permanent settlement near Holetown and laying a cornerstone for prosperity by the planting of cotton, tobacco and yams.

In 1637, a Dutchman, Peter Blower brought the first sugar cane plants to Barbados. Sugar was in high demand in Europe and remained Barbados main crop for 300 years leading to its lucrative rum industry.

In 1639, the first legislature was established, the oldest in the Caribbean.

Slaves were needed to till the fields and by the 1600's slaves outnumbered the white settlers by 3 to 1. This created great unrest and the landowners went to great lengths in order to keep them under control.

Slavery was finally abolished in 1838, but was it was not until the depression and the riots of 1937 that Barbados' black leaders emerged and began to rule the island with the white landowners.

In 1966, Barbados became a fully independent nation within the British Commonwealth.

The greatest legacy of the English settlers is the school system, which to this day is the finest in the Caribbean.

This was my fourth trip to Barbados, and so as our plane approached this beautiful island, flying over its lush green hills and valleys of sugar cane, I wondered what changes I would encounter.

I booked five days at the Sandy Lane Hotel and Golf Club for a number of reasons. For thirty years Sandy Lane has been a haven for the world's most discriminating travelers. The hotel is situated on the Caribbean side of the island which offers calmer seas and therefore all the watersports. Thirty years after it opened on February 1, 1961 a decision was made to completely shut down the hotel for six months of renovations, and I was eager to see the transformation.

Disembarking, I spotted a petite lady with a warm smile and a sign saying "Sandy Lane." Marjorie introduced herself and escorted me through immigration and retrieved my luggage. After wishing me a pleasant journey, she put me in the capable hands of William, Sandy Lane's chauffeur. Shutting the door behind me, I was a captive of the luxury of a cream colored Rolls Royce limousine.

As we glided along familiar roads I could feel the slower, calmer way of the islands.

For more information on the truly luxurious and beautiful Sandy Lane Hotel and Golf Club, please see our Honeymoon Section.

Awaking to a sunshine filled morning, I could see from my terrace that the conditions were perfect for a morning dive.

Most of the diving in Barbados, other than that on the wrecks, is drift diving.

The majority of the reefs are either named after a restaurant or cove that is directly off the site. The reef dives do not compare to the "hot spot" dive sites of Belize, Australia or Mauritius, but they do offer an interesting array of fish life.

I think divers will be most intrigued by the number of wrecks.

JOHNSON'S REEF

We chose this spot for our first dive. We slipped down into the silent underwater world and drifted along with the

Underwater Barbados courtesy of Tourist Department

current. To our left a hawksbill turtle glided through the water. The visibility was good as we drifted along viewing this coral garden. We were at 80 feet, but the light still shown through, illuminating the barrel and fan coral. A school of barjack swam above us and I caught sight of my first yellowtail trumpet fish. We were spotted by an interested barracuda who decided to follow us for the rest of the dive.

A myriad of brilliantly colored reef fish provided us with a backdrop for our accent from a great first dive.

DOTTIN'S REEF

Richard Silva, an instructor and excellent underwater photographer, joined us for our second dive at Dottin's Reef. He proved to be a delightful addition to the group, for he knew not only where to find all sorts of critters, but also was knowledgeable as to their habits, and shared this information with us after our dive.

With Richard as our guide we were able to spot a beautiful puffer fish. Please do not torment the puffer fish by picking it up and intentionally making it "puff up." Divers should be aware that this species grows larger by swallowing many times its weight in water as a protective defense against predators trying to swallow it, not to serve as an amusement to divers.

While in the British Virgin Islands, I had seen many spotted drum, but never anything like the pair of juveniles we saw that day. They were so small and delicate that they seemed more like tiny jewels than fish.

Our keen eyed guide noticed a moray eel poking its head very cautiously and curiously out a crevice. Mustard colored sponges, finger coral, along with an abundance of plate coral decorated the surface of the reef. Beware, there is also a great deal of fire coral at this site!

COBBLERS COVE HOTEL

A perfect day of diving ended with a perfect evening spent at Cobblers Cove Hotel in the parish of St Peter. It is located 20 minutes from Sandy Lane.

The hotel has a Manager's cocktail party each week, and that evening I had the pleasure of meeting Hamish Watson, the General Manager. This evening the party was held in the Camelot Suite.

The Camelot Suite, created in 1989, is located in the main building of the hotel. It is designed and furnished to the highest standards giving maximum comfort. The bedroom is 23' x 16' and has a king size four poster bed and sitting area complete with sofa, armchairs and a writing desk. The 18' x 8' bathroom has a whirlpool bath, two basins, bidet, lavatory and 'his and her' showers. English soaps, toweling robes and fresh flowers add the finishing touches.

The roof top terrace is accessed by a coral stone spiral staircase, leading from the suite below. This partially covered area affords total privacy to the sun worshipper. To cool off there is a pool and another wet bar.

The entire area has been decorated in the English style by Prue Lane Fox, who has combined marble floors with beautifully colored fabrics to achieve a cool, deluxe atmosphere.

As one sits in the main salon of the hotel itself, sipping a glass of wine before dinner, you have a sense that you are in an English drawing room and that Hamish is your host at a private gathering. Dinner is served on the terrace overlooking the hotel and its beach.

Cobblers Cove is one of only three hotels and restaurants in the Caribbean to be invited to be a member of the prestigious Relais and Chateaux organization. It has been awarded the Barbados Gold Award five times. Its cuisine is prepared by French chefs and special meals may be ordered in advance. The wine selection is extensive and excellent.

Many thanks to Hamish, his wife and daughter, (who at the time was in the process of getting certified), for sharing their "gem" with me.

The next day we had more sunshine and fantastic visibility allowing us to take advantage of wreck diving off Barbados.

S.S. Stavronikita was our first wreck dive of the day. She lies in 130 feet of water off the west coast. Unlike most wrecks, the S.S. Stavronikita is intact and can be penetrated.

She is also well marked by a buoy.

A Greek cargo ship 356 feet long that was on its way from Ireland to Barbados carrying cement. She caught fire on August 26, 1976 in the open sea. An attempt was made to tow her remains closer to the shores of Barbados but while she was in transit the lines broke due to the weight of 101,000 bags of cement.

She lay at bay for two years until 1978 when the Barbados government purchased her with the intent to sink her closer to shore in order to clear the shipping lane and establish an underwater park. Hence, the *S.S. Stavronikita* is now under the auspices of the Barbados Marine Reserve. As a result, the ship and the marine life that inhabits her are protected by strict laws.

We descended her buoy line and at 80 feet we had reached the top deck. From here we investigated the large cargo hold. To our delight, George, "the dancing barracuda," was aboard that day.

Goerge has been living there since she was sunk in 1978. When spotted, George sits upright and sways back and forth, hence his nickname. He continually stares at his reflection in the bubbles of the divers. Many people believe that his mate has been lost, and with his eyes and his heart he thinks he sees her in the bubbles. If you do meet George on your dive here, do not approach or crowd him. The passage way is very small and he has been known to act unfavorably.

George is a delight and a perfect adjunct to the colorful sponges and corals which have grown in abundance over the hull and the many passageways. There is also an abundance of fish life that has chosen to make the *S.S. Stavronikita* their home, making this a great dive for photographers!

NOTE: *This is a deep dive and should only be attempted by an experienced diver. Bottom time and air consumption should be monitored regularly.*

We pulled anchor, and headed for Carlisle Bay, 20 minutes away, where the next three wrecks awaited us.

After a suitable interval time, we were given the next dive plan. We would be diving all three wrecks in one dive since are in close proximity of each other and lay in shallow water.

The Bermend is 50 feet in length and was a French Navy tug that sunk in 1919. Her top deck lies in 10 feet of water and her bottom is at 25 feet. Time and the tides have taken their toll on her hull, but it is a delightful dive due to the colorful and plentiful species of fish that call her home, such as the parrotfish, blue tang butterfly fish and the red tipped blenny. She makes a good dive for the beginner or the snorkeler and she can be accessed by shore or by boat.

Located just to the north of the Bermend, the Mariam Bell Wolfe sank in a hurricane in September of 1955. She is a wooden boat which has been largely broken up. Similar to the Bermend, the interesting thing about this dive is the abundance of fish that flock to her remains.

The Granny lies north of the Mariam Bell Wolf in 45 feet of water. Turtles frequent Carlisle Bay and the Granny seems to attract them. Therefore, she is sometimes referred to as the "Turtle Wreck." Like the Mariam Bell Wolf, there is very little left of her structure, but a myriad of fish can still be found swimming about.

That evening I ventured out to visit the Royal Pavilion Hotel. Barbados offers a range of hotels and villas from the modest to the luxurious, and the Royal Pavilion is definitely amongst the latter. It is a member of the Pemberton Hotel Group and was built in 1987. The pastel pink hotel is nestled amongst lush and beautifully landscaped grounds.

Just as I believe that there should never be a bad or inferior table in a restaurant, I feel that there should never be a bad or inferior hotel room. Royal Pavilion did not disappoint me —each of its 75 suites faces the ocean! They are tastefully decorated and include the special amenities that make one feel at home. They have incorporated the practical with the luxurious. The air-conditioned rooms each have direct dial telephones, mini bars, seersucker robes, a selection of bathrooms toiletries, international and local newspapers and maid service twice a day. There are 200 staff members that serve the guests of these 75 suites — that says it all!

After my tour I dined with Peter Bowling, the General Manager. Peter brings a wealth of knowledge from his former post as General Manager at the exquisite Jumby Bay in Antigua, West Indies. I have always considered Antigua a truly international island, and I feel that his experience there is his greatest gift to the Royal Pavilion. He seems to have an intrinsic sense of what the worldwide traveler not only desires, but expects. Peter's wife runs the boutique at the hotel.

Barbados is fortunate to have this young and gracious couple who bring a fresh approach to the art of hotel management.

My fourth day on Barbados was much like the others preceding it -full of sunshine!

Our first dive of the morning was at Little Sandy Lane. We rolled over the side of the boat and descended to 80 feet. As we drifted along behind the boat, at least fifteen different types of reef fish scurried by in schools of 20 to 300! It was truly unbelievable!

Among the schools of fish, a marble grouper and a jewfish were playing, and four-eyed and banded butterfish darted to and fro. Bluehead wrasse swam in schools between them as juvenile blue tang circled below. A spotlight parrotfish however, chose to swim along with us, and leave the others behind. Together, we came upon a spotted moray eel totally preoccupied with the entire event as the trumpetfish swam around him.

FISHERMAN'S REEF

Our next dive, Fisherman's Reef, is located off the Bamboo Bar. The intrigue of this dive are the finger reefs that make up its topography. This dive took us on a dream like journey through a mountainous terrain. We swam up and down through the peaks and valleys.

We discovered a large barrel coral that was housing one of the largest lobsters I have ever seen.

Coral gardens were all about us along with a profusion of sponges in every color, including the most perfect purple and the spiciest mustard color.

As we drifted along, schools of angelfish swam along with us. A large hawksbill turtle was spotted to the right as we continued on. Our guide even found an octopus on this dive, and we all gathered around until it caught site of us, changed color, and darted off. Following this lead, the yellow trumpetfish nose dived into the caverns as well.

No diver could ever complain about this dive.

I am asked quite often about the diving in Barbados, and how I would rate it. My answer is if you are looking for Belize, Australia, Indonesia or Cocos Island diving Barbados is not for you. Yet, because of its underwater topography, its coral reefs, the unusual banking reefs and finger reefs you get to do some very interesting and fun diving — especially in the summer when the visibility can reach 180 feet When you couple this with the array of wreck dives available, I would say that Barbados makes a very good dive destination!

POINTS OF INTEREST

First of all rent a Moke, motor scooter or bicycle from Fun Seekers to get around and really see this beautiful island. You will need to procure a temporary driver's license ($10 U.S.) and you can do this when you arrive at the airport, at the car company, or at the police station.

The Barbados Wildlife Reserve, St Peter. Telephone (809) 499-8826 for more information.

The Mount Gay Rum Distillery, St. Andrews.

Folkstone Marine Museum and Underwater Park, St James. There is a snorkeling trail in the reef.

The Atlantis Submarine — a one hour underwater adventure. telephone (809) 436-8929 for more information.

The Jolly Roger, a replica of an old pirate ship, cruises along the west coast with both day and evening cruises. Chose from steak, chicken or flying fish for lunch. Each is served with cold salads. Calypso music plays throughout the cruise and there is even a dance floor on the top deck. Rum punch is free so watch out! After lunch they pull into a cove where you can enjoy water-skis, jet-skis, walk the plank or go ashore for tanning and snorkeling. This is truly an adventure for the entire family. We have gone each time we go back to Barbados and it never ceases to be a great time. For more information call (809) 436-6424.

Barbados Museum, the showplace of Barbadian natural history and artifacts is located at Garrison, St Michael.

Flower Forest, a 50 acre site 850 feet above sea level and located at Richmond Plantation, is being developed into a unique garden interspersed with a wide variety of fruit trees and banana groves. It is near the western edge of Scotland District, the most picturesque and scenic area of Barbados; a photographer's paradise.

George Washington House, a modest house at the junction of Bay Street and Chelsea Road, once housed the first president of the United States. At the time he was visiting Barbados with his brother, and suffered an attack of small pox while on the island. It is thought that Barbados is the only place outside of the United States ever visited by Washington.

The Chase Vault, is famous because of the unsolved moving coffins mystery. Situated in the cemetery of Christ Church Parish Church on the cliff above Oistins visitors can still see the vault, where during the 19th Century, coffins were discovered to have moved from the positions in which they were placed.

Harrison's Cave, is acclaimed as of the most unique Caves System in the Western world. The Cave has large chambers, stalagmites and stalactites, lakes, streams and waterfalls. The Cave was officially opened in 1981 and has proven to be of great educational and scientific interest, as well as a major tourist attraction.

Belize is the New Bonaire!

Douglas Triggs has been a scuba diver since 1977 with experience diving in the Caribbean.

Lives there a diver unfamiliar with Bonaire, that diving jewel of the Caribbean? Accessible with agreeable accommodations; modern with magnificent diving; and Dutch with a dollar economy.

> **"Scuba spoken here" (in English) on every shopkeeper's lips.**

Tuly, Bonaire has it all for the discriminating diver.

> **Move over Bonaire. Behold Belize, the emerging emerald of the Caribbean!**

Not that Belize was unknown in the past. After all, this coastal country just south of Mexico has always had its incomparable barrier reef, and neither divers nor dive operators were strangers to its shores. Until recently, however, a vacation to Belize was an Indiana Jones adventure into an uncertain infrastructure and an unorganized economy.

Tunicates by Carol Boone

Nowhere was that more apparent than the Belize airport. Five years ago our group, the Buff Divers, flew into Belize and stepped off the airplane into an airport terminal whose halcyon days must have been early in the British Colonial period. Those woeful wooden buildings pluckishly signed "Belize International Airport" served to remind us that this was an "anything could happen" vacation.

Two years ago, Belize's new and modern airport terminal was completed. Now Belize not only has the diving, but is well on its way to achieving the reliable transportation connections that are the sine qua non for many of our fellow scuba divers.

> **The attraction of Belize to divers is the Belize Barrier Reef, 250 kilometers of multi-colored coral. In addition, Belize has three of the Caribbean's four atolls—Turneffe Island Atoll, Lighthouse Reef Atoll, and Glovers Reef, and a Blue Hole as well.**

Belize diving is from offshore islands or live-aboards. That means you are either flying out again from Belize International Airport by small plane to your island, or you are headed to Belize City (a few miles from the airport via a multitude of taxis) to find your live-aboard or boat for the transit to the caye (island) of your choice. Or, perhaps you have planned to stay in Belize City for a few days. Picture Belize City as a small city in the American West in the 1930's, and that will adequately convey the very muted rumble of everyday life there.

Island accommodations and dive resorts in Belize vary from relatively developed Ambergris Caye at the northern end of the country to primitive Glovers Reef Atoll Resort on Long Caye toward the southern end. Whatever type of dive resort you want you can find it in Belize, barring only Holiday Inn type high density resorts and their associated cattle-boat dives.

Our group, the Buff Divers, has dived annually with Manta Resort. Manta Resort is on a small and very picturesque l2 acre caye just at the edge of Glovers Reef, four long hours by boat from Belize City. There is no air strip on or available to Manta Resort, so arrival is only by boat. Since our group is comprised of nudist divers and snorkeler's, the welcome isolation of Manta Resort more than offset the long transit time.

The resort itself has 12 sturdy two person guest cabins and a staff lodging house interspersed among the palm trees, and the bar/restaurant/dive shop built to overlook the lagoon. The caye curves into a near half-moon shape, and the concave side of the caye is a delightful lagoon with easy snorkeling. This lagoon, no more than eight feet deep has resident octopi and frequent manta ray visitors.

Diving at Manta Resort was nearly as effortless as being on a five-aboard. The closest dive sites are 5 minutes away from the dock and the others generally no more than a half hour away. Since Manta is at the edge of the atoll, dives could be planned for the shallow reef gardens or the plunging atoll walls, depending on our wishes. The classic Manta vacation pattern was a morning wall dive, followed by lunch, an hour in one of the hammocks strung between the palm trees, an afternoon reef dive, with the remainder of the afternoon for snorkeling, shore diving, outlandish fish stories, or simply relaxing. There were no wrecks or caves in the area.

Water temperature for diving is quite warm, and we dove with shortie wet suits, lycra suits, or no suits, depending on the preferences of the individuals. Water visibility was consistently very good, except for one day following a storm.

The staff at Manta Resort was friendly and the dive operation was efficient, safety conscious, and fun. The dives were planned taking the slight currents into account, and the boats were right there to pick us up at the end of the dives, day or night. The dive boats themselves were outboard powered open boats with tank racks down the middle. and well served every purpose except for shelter from the sporatic rain. The Manta staff washed all gear after each dive and set up the gear for the following dive.

Our Buff Diver group included newly certified divers and veteran divers. The dive guides at Manta provided follow-along underwater guiding, but also allowed experienced divers to dive with buddies separately from the group.

Non-diving individuals were accommodated by snorkeling in the lagoon, at the nearby- offshore reef, or through special snorkeling boats that went out as requested to other coral gardens.

As you would expect, non-diving activities at Manta were minimal. The Belize government has a small lighthouse on this caye, but the structure is neither imposing nor picturesque. Video movies, card games and conversation served to while away the hours between the evening meal and sleep. As always, you are likely to have more fun at a small resort such as Manta if you are traveling with friends or a compatible group.

Isolation has an associated disadvantage for Manta Resort. The nearest decompression chamber is quite a distance north, at San Pedro, on Ambergris Caye. Contact with the chamber is through DAN at (919) 684-8111. Many in our group combined a week at Manta with additional days in the jungle and towns of the Belize mainland. Specialties on the mainland include Maya ruins, jaguar and baboon sanctuaries, various festivals, and birdwatching.

ON THE COUNTRY OF BELIZE:

Belize Tourist Board, 405 Seventh Avenue (18th floor), New York, NY 10001; phone (212) 268-8798, fax (212) 695-3018. One of the better travel guides is Mallan, *Belize Handbook*, from Moon Publications, Inc. Great Trips is a tour operator that has been promoting diving in Belize and travel to Belize since 1982. They were part of a small group that were the early pioneers in this venture.

Judy Quam is Great Trips, sales manager. She is well known for making sure that every one of our great trips is both personalized and customized to give the traveler and sportsperson what is expected, and even more. For further information about Great Trips, please call 1-800-552-3419 or 218-847-4441; fax: 218-847-4442.

Bequia

Joan Iaconetti is a freelance writer/photographer based in Manhattan and in the Caribbean during the winter months. Her diving/travel articles have appeared in Travel & Leisure, Caribbean Travel & Life, and New Woman, and she covers the Caymans and the Grenadines for Fodor's Caribbean Guidebooks.

For decades my brother was the diver in the family: he got NAUI-certified when he was 16 and I was 14, in an era when it was unthinkable for pre-womens-liberation teenage girls to try anything as "macho" and "dangerous" as scuba diving.

But 25 years later, quite by accident, I got my chance. I was on an assignment to promote a resort in St. Vincent and the Grenadines, and the PR woman said, "Why not learn to dive, and write about that angle for Cosmopolitan Magazine?" Gee, that sounds like fun, I thought ... always wanted to see what my brother was so gaga about. Her off-hand suggestion changed my life.

It took me 5 minutes to fall in love with diving, and three days to fall so in love with St. Vincent and the Grenadines that I decided to live in Bequia (part-time at least). Since that resort course in 1987, I've made over 100 dives on 25 Caribbean islands, plus Florida, the Indian Ocean, Hawaii, and the Great Barrier Reef. Over the years, I admit to visiting more colorful and dramatic sites and wrecks that Bequia has to offer, but while the Little Cayman and the GBR may be richer in aquatic life, Bequia makes up for it with professionally-run safe diving that is truly uncrowded (dive motorboats hold no more than 6 to 8 divers), and many unspoiled sites, sometimes literally just-discovered.

Compared to scrubby Caymans and Bonaire, the Grenadines are mini-Tahitis, everybody's fantasy of what a lush-green-tropical-paradise should be. The fact that the Grenadines are still undeveloped – no hotel bigger than two dozen rooms, very few tourists – is a major draw for the seasoned diver/traveler.

No matter where you stay on Bequia, you can dive with any operator. The Bequia Beach Club is somewhat isolated from the main drag in beachside Port Elizabeth, but the German management specializes in divers and diving. Full equipment is available here, but note that their tanks have European fittings, and at last visit did not fit USA regulators. However, in a pinch, US tanks can probably be rented from other dive shops.

Visibility varies, but is never less than 50 feet, and often up to 100 on a clear, calm day.

During the summer, water temperatures can be up to 82 F; in winter, it's consistently 78 or 80 F. Even on cooler days, I never wear more than a t-shirt under my BC. There's just no necessity for wetsuit or even diveskin here, unless you're supersensitive to chills.

DEVIL'S TABLE

It doesn't look like much – a shallow dive, barely 40 feet, a "beginner's" dive, close by in Admiralty Bay near the Fort, but it's one of the richest and most accessible sites on Bequia. Arrow crabs, giant schools of damselfish and sergeant majors, an occasional spiny lobster (most of them are seen on your dinner plate during season), brain and soft corals, nudibranchs, and most every fish seen on that laminated plastic card that's sold in every dive shop. Finally, when you've shown the instructor you can handle it, you'll be taken to visit an 8-foot green moray eel who lives in a sunken tugboat at 90 feet.

WEST CAY, "THE WALL"

Relatively big water makes for a sometimes heart-thumping entry, as you position yourself so that the surge can propel you through a notch in the reef ... a reef that is very near the surface.

Often surrounded by swarms of needlefish, you navigate the cut and find yourself in 90 feet of water. You sink slowly along the cay, past all manner of coral hard and soft. The dive is actually a gradual circular ascent around the wall of the cay (a tiny islet, pronounced "key") that is home to numerous species of fish and marine life.

> **Eagle rays, single and mating octopi, nurse sharks, small seahorses, baby squid, and the more usual suspects (trumpetfish, angelfish, big-eyed reds, squirrelfish, morays, tile and trunk fish of all sizes) have been spotted regularly on this dive**

Because entry is a bit tricky, West Cay is only available in good weather and after you've already completed 2 or 3 dives with any Bequia operator. Water is a bit cooler (maybe 75-77 F.) than on calmer dives and even on overcast days visibility is still more than acceptable. Getting back aboard a small dive boat ladder can be a bit challenging in big waves, but assistance is always available if you prefer to remove tank and BC before climbing aboard.

THE BOULDERS, MOONHOLE

> **Moonhole is a unique, private community of people who live on the south end of Bequia in stone houses with no electricity and no glass in the windows. Despite the fact you cannot explore this area without an invitation from a resident, the community does welcome snorkelers and divers who come via boat to the bay just east of Shipstern, Bequia's whale-shaped headland.**

The water is that impossibly beautiful turquoise, with brain and staghorn coral visIble from the surface at 20-30 feet. All the usual Caribbean fish life noted above is present, and the site is ideal for travel companions who snorkel but don't dive. In fact, snorkelers need only hire a water taxi and arrange to be picked up an hour or two later; it's not necessary to book a dive boat to come here.

Unlike most snorkel sites, Moonhole is also a good dive site because of the calmness and clarity of the water. Nearby to the east is a site called The Boulders (40-60 feet), so named for the giant underwater rocks you can swim among. Here you're diving on Bequia's underwater ledge, and instructors know where to look to show you hiding lobsters, morays, arrow crabs, and spiky pufferfish.

THE BULLET

Often inaccessible because of rough seas or weather, The Bullet is a beachless cay that juts almost straight up, just off Bequia's northeast point. The circular dive takes half an hour to reach by speedboat, but is worth the trip: nurse sharks have been spotted, along with the occasional eagle ray (one lucky boatload even heard whale songs, but this is rare). Abundant coral of all kinds is seen on both the wall of the cay and on the sea floor, and large schools of fish are common.

NON-DIVING ACTIVITIES

All of the, restaurants along Admiralty Bay are acceptable, with the best food at Mac's Pizzeria and Bake Shop. The Porthole is the place to meet yachties and hard-core sailors from every country imaginable, as is the bar at the Frangipani. For quieter atmosphere and good local food try Theresa's Restaurant and Dawn's Creole both on the far end of Lower Bay.

Jump-ups (barbecue/dances) constitute island nightlife: at the Frangi on Thursday, the Plantation House on Tuesday, and Friendship Bay Resort on Saturday.

Hike over to the La Pompe area to see Bequia's famous "two-bow" boats, being constructed by eye without plan. These are still used for fishing and even whaling. Bequia is one of the only areas where limited whaling, by hand-held harpoon, has Greenpeace's okay.

BEQUIA LODGING

The Frangipani Hotel. The Frangi, a Caribbean institution, has five units surrounded by trees and bushes, built of stone with private verandahs and bath. Four simple rooms are in the main house, only one with private bath. Dive packages available, breakfast included. 11 rooms. Phone (809) 45-83255. Sunsports dive shop, next door, is affiliated with the hotel, and offers packages, snorkeling, and instruction.

Resting Sails by John Tipper

Plantation House Hotel. Formerly the Sunny Caribbee, this upscale property is lovely, with its own tiny beach, but too pricey for most divers. However, anyone can book dives with Dive Bequia, the on-property scuba shop that offers full instruction, boat dives, snorkeling. 17 cottages, five rooms in the main house. Phone 809-45-83425.

Friendship Bay Hotel. A main house on the hill (large terraces, sweeping views) and rooms built of coral stone closer to the beautiful, long, quiet beach. Has its own tiny dive facility: 27 rooms. Phone 800-223-6764; locally, (809) 45-83222. AE, MC, V.

Bequia Beach Club. Looking for all the world like a little ski chalet on a tropical beach, the BBC is run by Germans for a mainly German clientele, but welcome others for full-service diving. Phone (809) 45-83248. 10 units.

Keegan's Guest House. For those truly on a budget, Keegan's offers family-style West Indian meals, no hot water, and Salvation Army furnishings. But it's on gorgeous Lower Bay Beach, about a mile stroll from Dive Bequia. Phone (809) 45-83530.

Isola and Julie's Guest House. In Port Elizabeth on the main beachfront drag, this simple (no amenities) inn has a good restaurant and some rooms have hot water. 25 rooms, phone (809)-45-83304, -83323, -83220.

Bonaire
James E. Lydon

Diving the Northeast United States and the Caribbean since 1963

The Author is the Executive Director of the Boston Fenway Program, a not for profit 50IC3 corporation that was founded by area institutions to provide for the regions interests. Contributions may be made to the Boston Fenway Program, 236 Huntington Ave., Boston, MA 02115

Participating Institutions: Berkiee College of Music, Boston Symphony Orchestra, Boston University, First Church of Christ, Scientist, Forsyth Dental, Isabella Stewart Gardiner Museum, Harvard School of Public Health, Museum of Fine Arts, New England Conservatory of Music, Northeastern University, Wentworth Institute of Technology, Wheelock College, Greater Boston YMCA

M'a Perde Ariba (I have overslept, Papiamentu).

BRRRMMMM!!!!! The morning dive boat was a hundred yards off the Sand Dollar dock and heading out to a dive spot called Ol' Blue as my dive buddies Sandy, Bill and

I arrived with our dive gear. Perhaps it was the sensuous breezes of the warm Caribbean night that had caused my wife and I to stay up too late the night before or maybe it was the Parrot Smash at the Green Parrot Bar. But there we were on the dock with no boat.

Disaster? Not in Bonaire. My dive buddy Bill asked me if I wanted one tank or two as we loaded up the car. Topped off with gas and dive gear, we headed north and out of town. No buildings just sandstone cliffs, cactus, divi divi trees and the beautiful Caribbean aquamarine twenty five feet below us. We drove for a couple of miles along a primitive road shared with iguanas, parrots and those funny little Bonaire lizards with the swatch of the Caribbean blue on their back. As we pulled in at a little turn-off, there was our dive boat 75' off shore.

Who would take a dive charter boat to a dive destination just a few miles down the road? Well, the only way I can explain it is that you can not believe how lazy you can get after ten days of diving in Bonaire.

Located south of the hurricane belt and somewhat north of Venezuela, Bonaire resembles a piece of arid Arizona desert misplaced in a tropical sea of crystal clear aquamarine.

Shaped as a boomerang with its back arched to the trades and the buffeting of the waves, one side of Bonaire provides a perfect lee shore with absolutely calm conditions. Klein Bonaire, a smaller uninhabited island a few miles off-shore, also benefits from this lee.

Being a Northern diver, accustomed to my face squished by my hood, twenty to thirty pounds of lead about my waist, ten feet of visibility and that cold rush of water whenever I turn my head the wrong way; what a treat it is to enter the water at OL' Blue with water temperature at 76F, a skimpy wet suit, no hood and 8 lbs. of weight, this does not seem like the same sport. Bill, Sandy and I continue out to about waist deep water twenty five feet from shore and don our fins and inflate our BC's and begin to swim seaward. About fifty feet from shore and against a backdrop of increasingly lush background of fire coral and finger coral, a large lavishly painted queen angel fish swims to within four inches of my mask, apparently looking for breakfast. Fortunately, I've brought a hot dog and the queen begins to nibble from my fingers.

Not realizing that I've just won over a new companion for the rest of the dive and seventy five feet from shore, I deflate my BC and slowly descend to thirty feet and the awaiting pillar coral above the drop off zone. Beautiful and dramatic fish are everywhere but onward beyond the drop off is a school of blue chromis. Thousands in numbers, I inch slowly forward and I am enveloped by the school. Floating in the midst of a living, blue cylinder that is swirling about me; twenty feet below my toes, Bill is working his way to the deeper and dramatic climes.

Exhale. A rush of bubbles and I float downward out of my beautiful blue castle. My descent is halted at the sight of a big Nassau grouper who is standing stationary with his mouth open amidst some dramatic growths of mountainous star coral. This is a cleaning station, the "car washes" of the reef and a tremendous reminder of our interdependence with others and our environment. Cleaning symbiosis occurs at regular fixed points along the face of the reef and is marked by certain shrimp and smaller fishes relieving larger fishes of parasites. As I watch this large grouper with his huge mouth agape, tiny neon gobies trustingly dart in and out picking at parasites in the groupers mouth. As I get a little too close, the grouper closes its mouth expelling the gobies and leisurely swims away. He is clean and the gobies are fed.

With the wall of coral becoming increasingly steep, we continue our descent to a hundred or so feet, and close to the limit of our fragile sport divers existence. The volume and variety of fish life has diminished but their sizes increase. Twenty feet away a large dramatic ocean going trigger fish watches us with a detached indifference.
From this depth, the views of the wall draped in its endless rows of sheet coral interspersed with stands of black coral beckon us to stay, but alas the dive computer reminds us of our fragility and another existence.

From a hundred feet we can hear and see on the silvery underside of the ocean's surface, the Sand Dollar dive boat leaving it's mooring allowing us the full tranquillity of the ocean's depth. The ascent is slow, allowing us special glimpses of the reef. Banded coral shrimp, the unusual shovel nose lobster, a smoking purple tube sponge disgorging its spores and back near the drop-off, our friendly queen angel are all part of our morning. Bill and I dawdle in the shallower depths relieving ourselves of pent up nitrogen and enjoying the sunlight we had briefly left. I play with the tiny gobie whose match tip size head protrudes from a large growth of brain coral. His ever alert eyes seemingly moving in all directions at once catch sight of my finger and he darts for cover. As if attached by strings, my finger and the gobie play at our game.

Bill and Sandy are twenty feet away but I feel a tapping on my leg. Turning I discover the most ferocious fish of the sea, a two inch damsel fish.

*With the courage of ten lions
and less the size of a mouse,
this fish reminds me
I'm too close to its house.*

Through the surface hand, head, shoulders and back to the beach we swim. There is the hiss of compressed air and that salt taste on the lips. Up to the car we stagger and doff our dripping gear.

It's the start of another day on Bonaire.

As recently as the early eighties, a stay in Bonaire meant some roughing it. A stay at Captain Don's Habitat provided accommodations in a tin roofed Caribbean stucco hut with no air conditioning, no hot water, no water at all between 9:00 pm and 5:00 am and the best means of transportation a four wheel drive vehicle, but the best diving in the world. Things have changed and have been modernized. While I look back at the old days, I have a tendency to romanticize and miss the primitive nature of the island but as I stand in the warm shower of my Sand Dollar Condo after my night dive recognizing that in the old days not only would I have no hot water, but at 9:30 pm, I would have no water at all, I recognize that some things are for the best.

The Sand Dollar Condominium and Beach Club, is a medium sized resort. It offers a low rise elegance on the waters edge and beautiful water view units facing north to the mountains or southwest to Klein. Only a few years old, the facility contains a full service dive shop with morning and afternoon dive boats. While the facility is new most of the dive guides have been diving on Bonaire for years.

"There goes a cattle boat"! For most of the experienced Bonaire divers, diving is a personal pleasure and not a group or team sport. As a result, whenever one of the three larger hotels sends out one of its boats with thirty or more divers aboard the "cattle boat" cry is heard.

Sand Dollar offers much more personalized diving service with its boats headed off to the moored dive sites with about six divers aboard.

As many of the dive locations are accessible by automobile, those wishing a more private time can simply drive the coast road and pull over and park on the side at the dive locations marked by the small yellow cairns.

In general, we split our days between the boat and the car. In my opinion some of the more spectacular dive sights such as Rappel, La Dania's and those of Klein can only be reached by boat. But the auto can also get you to some great dives and the car affords you some interesting views of the island above water.

The Coast road north of Captain Don's is one way resulting in a round the island tour when diving in this region. Some good dive sites in this region are the previously mentioned OL' Blue, A Thousand Steps and Karparta.

Bring a cooler, because it can get very dry and when returning to Kralendijk, the capital city, try both routes and you will be rewarded with spectacular views. The right hand turn at Karpata will take you into the hills above the city of Rincon. Here you will see lizards darting across the road and an occasional iguana soaking up the sun's rays. As you reach the crest of the hill and begin to descend into the valley you will be rewarded with a breathtaking view of Rincon, the oldest town on the island. Originally developed by the Spanish to avoid coastal raiders, Rincon became the home of the slaves that were brought to the island to work in the salt pans of the south and later the plantations of the north.

Make sure to stop, at the end of the day at Rincon's Amstel Bar for refreshments. The people of Rincon are always quick to smile and usually wave as you pass through town.

The longer route (go strait at Karpata) will treat you to some spectacular views of Goto Meer, the Flamingo sanctuary. Bonaire is one of the few remaining places in the Caribbean where this truly amazing bird breeds in the wild.

Goats are everywhere. Big, small, brown, and white; there is a goat to fit every description and I can not tell how the owners tell them apart.

French Angelfish by Carol Boone

A drive to the south is no less spectacular. This end of the island is flat and originally developed by the Europeans as salt pans, whose operation continues until today. Though underwater visibility at the dive sites in the south tends to be a bit less than that of the north, there are some very nice dives. Salt City, the double reef complex of the Invisibles or even a trip to the recently sunk Hilma Hooker are all worth doing and can be very easily reached from shore. After the dive, drive into the salt works. These mountains of snow white salt appear as incongruous hills of snow in torrid temperatures.

While in this region keep watching the salt pans for flamingos. As the seawater becomes salt it changes hues and it is from this coloration that the flamingo derives its vivid color. Also in the south are the slave huts. History tells us that the slaves were marched from Rincon on Monday to work the salt pans. These poor, tortured people would be forced to live in these ovens until the following Saturday, when they would be returned to their homes.

Some of the most interesting diving and driving can be found in Washington Slagbaai Park. This national Park is composed of 13,500 acres of wild, mostly undeveloped beauty.

Once only accessible to four wheel drive vehicles, the government has made sufficient improvements to the dirt roads to allow a regular automobile to pick along gently. This area is a true "must see" for all of those traveling to Bonaire.

Plan a full day in the park and make sure you start early. Bring a lunch, plenty of refreshments and also two tanks of air per diver.

Enter the park through Rincon and take the long route. One of the first stops is Playa Chiquito. This is a wild, windward side beach that has been plagued with a huge undertow problem. I would strongly recommend that you not swim. Generally, we forego Chiquito and make our first stop Boca Cocolishi. This is a cut into the windward side and a small beach that, if the conditions are right, is sheltered from the large waves and rough conditions by a small limestone reef. If the conditions are right, it can be one of the most spectacular swimming holes you have ever experienced.

Continue on and enjoy the scenery above water, but don't allow the beauty to let you forget that you came here for the diving. The first dive site that you will encounter is Boca Bartol. This is one of my personal favorites and it can entertain any skill level. There are two deep dives that can be made; one at the north end of the bay and another at the south. Once at the sand terrace on the south side of the bay, I spent nearly twenty minutes cavorting with two, five foot, spotted eagle rays. However, my favorite part of this dive is the shallow section which can be enjoyed by snorkel as well. In the official Bonaire dive guide *Guide to the Bonaire Marine Park*, by Tom van Hof (strongly recommended) it is referred to as "spurs and grooves". In essence, they are alternating coral ridges that, come within feet of the surface, and twenty and thirty foot sand channels. These features attract multi and varied sea life and while they are also present at the next site Benge, they are the best at Bartol.

Unfortunately, both Bartol and Benge can often be wiped out by bad surf. Please exercise caution.

Playa Benge is the second of the four dive locations in the park that you will encounter. Like Bartol, Benge also, has an array of spurs and grooves in the shallow areas; but the most spectacular parts of Benge are the wall and the cave. They are both deep, so if you plan on going down to see them, leave plenty of air to enjoy the shallows afterward. By world standards the next stop, Playa Funchi is a fantastic dive site. However, by my Bonaire standard it is only a regular dive and I will only dive here if Benge and Bartol are wiped out.

The last dive site in the park is Boca Slagbaai. In general, I like to make this my second dive in the park, because it offers so much. After having done a deep dive in the morning, we will stop to have lunch at Slagbaai. It offers a nice beach for sunning and swimming (with booties). There are some interesting old buildings that relate to the sites former plantation use. Most importantly, by this time one has been exposed to the effects of sun at eleven degrees of latitude for many hours and Slagbaai has some shade. Regarding the diving here, the dive book describes two dives, Slagbaai-Wayaka and Slagbaai-south. I have done both and strongly recommend the Slagbaai-south. The swim to the North is very long, about thirty minutes. As the guide book suggested save air for the last part of the dive; I swam the first thirty minutes on the surface. After arriving at the approximate position of what was described as "spectacular coral buttresses", I found that the visibility was totally obliterated because the Wayaka Salinas was disgorging fresh water and silt. I returned and dove Slagbaai-south, wracking up an hour and fifteen minute surface swim prior to putting a regulator in my mouth.

One of the first things I learned about Bonaire is that if you enjoy the night life, you better be ready to create it yourself, and I have some suggestions to that end.

Just outside and to the north of Kralendijk is a hill called Ceru Largu. Often times just before dusk my wife and I will drive there with a bottle of wine to enjoy the end of day and the start of darkness. The hilltop which is about four hundred feet above the surrounding land, is topped with a few benches that allow some of the more spectacular views of the island. Very rarely is anyone else up there, except the ever present goats, and as the sun sets, the viewer is afforded vistas of Klein, Kralendijk and the southern end of the island.

After darkness has fallen, I have often enjoyed taking a ride down south toward the salt pans to look at the stars. I believe that on a Bonairian, moonless night, one can see more stars than anywhere else on earth. Occasionally, during these night time safaris, I have bumped into a heard of white mules. I was once told that they were originally employed in the hauling of salt before mechanization and since that time have gone wild. I have never encountered them during daytime dive trips, but what a treat it is to bump into this herd of thirty or so white beauties in the midst of the Bonaire night.

If you haven't got your fill of bottom time during the day, a night dive is also a great way to spend the night. While most of the organized, boat dives will put you in the water just as the sun is going down, I have always found that one is better served by waiting for a couple of hours for night conditions to settle in. By giving it some time one allows the corals to more fully extend, the parrot fish more time to finish their cocoons and the squirrel fish a chance to do their wake-up calisthenics.

For those that are a bit apprehensive about night diving, I would suggest a small foray beneath the town pier. It is a shallow dive that provides columns every twenty or so feet and will provide the novice with a structural context within which to dive. In addition, a night time dive at the town pier also offers the diver some of the most spectacular configurations of orange cup coral. For those more experienced, I suggest swimming to the end of the Pier, settling in at the base of a column and turning off your dive light. The Tarpon that have been cruising the daytime ocean frequent this place at night. When that occasional five and six foot long creature silently glides by you will have witnessed one of Bonaire's great delights.

So Stop Di Hasi Pantomina (Don't act so crazy). Make plans to visit Bonaire soon. It is one of the worlds great dive destinations.

SCUBA AND SNORKELING FACILITIES QUESTIONNAIRE

NAME Sand Dollar Condominiums and Beach Club
ADDRESS Kaija Cobernador N. Deprot 79
Bonaire, Netherlands Antilles
CONTACT DEI
TITLE
TELEPHONE 617-723-7134   FAX 617-227-8145

CAPITAL: Kralendijk   GOVERNMENT: Dutch
POPULATION: 11,000   LANGUAGE: Dutch, Papiamentu, English
CURRENCY: Guilder, Dollar   ELECTRICITY: 120/50C
AIRLINES: Ayn Air Aruba   DEPARTURE TAX? $10
NEED VISA/PASSPORT?   YES   NO x   PROOF OF CITIZENSHIP? YES x NO

YOUR FACILITY IS CLASSIFIED AS: SCUBA CENTER x   RESORT x
BUSINESS HOURS: 8:30 a.m. to 5:30 p.m.
CERTIFYING AGENCIES: PADI 5-star IDC Training Facility
LOG BOOK REQUIRED?   YES   NO x Cert. Card
EQUIPMENT: SALES x   RENTALS x   AIR FILLS x
PRIMARY LINE OF EQUIPMENT: Sherwood, US Divers, Dacor, Sea Quest
PHOTOGRAPHIC EQUIPMENT: SALES x   RENTALS x   LAB x

CHARTER/DIVE BOAT AVAILABLE?   YES x   NO   DIVER CAPACITY 13-20 (84 boats)
COAST GUARD APPROVED?   YES   NO x   CAPTAIN LICENSED? YES   NO x
SHIP TO SHORE? YES x   NO   LORAN? YES NO   RADAR? YES   NO
DIVE MASTER/INSTRUCTOR ABOARD?   YES x   NO   BOTH at times

DIVING & SNORKELING: SALT x   FRESH
TYPE OF DIVING/SNORKELING IN AREA: WALL x   BEACH x   WRECK   REEF   CAVE   ICE
DIVING/SNORKELING IN YOUR AREA IS BEST SUITED FOR: BEGINNER x INTERMEDIATE x ADVANCED x BEST TIME OF YEAR FOR DIVING/SNORKELING: All year
TEMPERATURE: NOV-APRIL: 78 F   MAY-OCT: 78 F
VISIBILITY: DIVING: 100 FT   SNORKELING: 100 FT

PACKAGES AVAILABLE: DIVE x   DIVE STAY x   SNORKEL   SNORKEL-STAY
ACCOMMODATIONS NEARBY: HOTEL x   MOTEL   HOME RENTALS on site
ACCOMMODATION RATES: EXPENSIVE MODERATE x   INEXPENSIVE
RESTAURANTS NEARBY: EXPENSIVE MODERATE x   INEXPENSIVE
YOUR AREA IS: REMOTE   QUIET WITH ACTIVITIES x   LIVELY
LOCAL ACTIVITY/NIGHTLIFE: Discos, restaurants
CAR NEEDED TO EXPLORE AREA?   YES x   NO
DUTY FREE SHOPPING?   YES x   NO

LOCAL EMERGENCY SERVICES   NEAREST HYPERBARIC TREATMENT FACILITY
COASTGUARD: N/A   AUTHORITY: San Francisco Hospital
TELEPHONE: LOCATION: Kralendijk
CALLSIGNS: TELEPHONE:

LOCAL DIVING DOCTOR:
NAME: Dr. I.M. vanderVaart
LOCATION: Kralendijk
TELEPHONE: 011-599-7-8661

British Virgin Islands Diving

Jeff Williams started diving in 1973 in Pennsylvania quarries. He first experienced visibility better than 20 feet in Martinique in 1982 and immediately fell in love with Caribbean diving. Together with his wife Raine, he became a PADI Dive Instructor in 1989 to further pursue and enjoy the sport. That same year he left a ten year career in the computer industry to move to the British Virgin Islands where he and Raine began work as dive instructors. Together they logged over 800 dives throughout the BVI. During these dives, he compiled much of the information used in the writing of "The Guide to Diving and Snorkeling in the British Virgin Islands." Currently crewing a Moorings charter boat, Jeff and Raine live on board their sailboat "Fresco" when they are not on charter.

The British Virgin Islands offer world class diving from wrecks to reefs for divers of all experience levels. But what makes diving here unique is that most popular sites are accessible to divers on their own sail or power charter yachts.

The waters of the BVI are noted around the world as a sailor's paradise, and at any time of year crewed and bareboat charters can be seen throughout the islands.

Located near the U.S. Virgin Islands in the northeast Caribbean, the British Virgin islands (or simply the BVI) are centered around the Sir Francis Drake channel, a well protected waterway that is the primary attraction for boaters. With Tortola on one side and Virgin Gorda on the other, this channel is well protected from the vagaries of the Caribbean Sea to the south and the Atlantic Ocean to the north. While sea conditions outside the channel can reach intimidating heights, within the protection of the islands the waters are always calmer, making for great sailing and excellent diving.

The dive sites of the BVI are as varied as the personalities of the islands. Many shallow coral reefs surround the smaller islands.

Hundreds of species of fish, coral, sponges, anemones, and more make these sites especially colorful and entertaining. Some of the reefs have developed on walls which drop 60 to 80 feet to the sand floor, or on rock pinnacles which reach for the water's surface. These dives present the opportunity to observe the varied marine life at various depths on a single dive. Ship wrecks, including the famous Royal Mail Steamer Rhone, are also popular destinations for divers in the BVI. All popular BVI dive sites are less than 100 feet deep, allowing ample bottom time for exploring.

Charter boats are by far the most popular means of vacationing in the BVI. There are literally hundreds of boats on these waters year round. Within the BVI, there are about a dozen charter companies that offer sail and power yachts to experienced sailors. Boats ranging from 30 feet to 50 feet in length are common. In addition to bareboat cruising, in which you and your friends comprise the crew (and do the work!), most charter companies can arrange for a professional captain and/or chef to accompany you.

For people that have no sailing experience, or for those who have had enough, crewed yachts can provide the ultimate in convenience and comfort.

Staffed with a professional crew of two or more, these boats are maintained to the highest standards. While the vacation itinerary is still yours to control, you are relieved of the responsibility for the day to day operation of the boat. Couple this with the crew's extensive local knowledge and with gourmet food prepared daily, and the advantage of a crewed yacht vacation becomes apparent. Some crewed yachts cater specifically to divers, providing guided tours, instruction, equipment, onboard compressors, etc.

Another alternative for active divers is a diving liveaboard

These larger boats can carry up to 50 guests, combining the convenience of boat diving with the ambiance of a small guest hotel. On liveaboards, the dive plan for the week is generally more structured than on crewed yachts, but much more diving is typically available because of the size of the boats, their facilities, and the number of crew.

While most divers consider a boating vacation the ultimate for accessibility to diving, not everyone likes to spend their entire holiday afloat. For these people, the islands offer guest houses, small hotels, and rental apartments. Diving is accomplished with one of the dive companies providing the transportation and guidance. Most companies offer packages to hotel guests allowing the diver to tailor the amount of diving and the desired destinations to best fit in with the rest of the vacation plans.

To start planning a B.V.I. vacation, check with your travel agent for information on charter boats, charter companies, and hotels. Also, write to the B.V.I. Tourist Board for a current copy of the welcome Guide. This bimonthly publication has a listing of boats, hotels, restaurants, and ferry and flight information. Keep in mind that you can start your vacation either in the B.V.I. or in St. Thomas or St. John (both U.S. Virgin Islands).

If you are planning a sailing vacation, get a current copy of Sail or Cruising World magazine. Both of these carry articles and advertisements for charter boats and charter companies.

Finally (or firstly perhaps), get a copy of "The Guide to Diving and Snorkeling in the British Virgin Islands". This recently published guide book provides much of the information needed to plan safe and exciting dives in the B.V.I. Information in the book includes B.V.I. diving, the weather and water conditions, game laws, local marine life, and more. Seventeen prime dive sites are described in detail and include a detailed underwater map.

There are presently 5 dive operators in the B.V.I. that offer services like certification courses, rendezvous tours, and equipment rentals. Whether you are planning your first or fiftieth dive, you will find these companies ready to assist you. All are staffed by professional dive instructors - most PADI, some NAUI - and all operate daily dive tours to many of the sites described here as well as some of the more difficult to reach sites.

BASKIN IN THE SUNSAFARI
Prospect Reef Resort
P.O. Box 108
Road Town Tortola
(809) 494-2858

BLUE WATER DIVERS
Nanny Cay
P.O. Box 846
Road Town, Tortola
(809) 494-2847

ISLAND DIVER
Village Cay Marina
P.O. Box 3023
Road Town, Tortola
(809) 494-3878

KILBRIDE'S UNDERWATER ADV.
Saba Rock
P.O. Box 40
Virgin Gorda
(809) 496-0111

UNDERWATER
Moorings Marina
P.O. Box 139
Road Town, Tortola
809) 494-3235

(The following excerpts are from "The Guide to Diving and snorkeling in the British Virgin Islands". Provided by the author and DIVEntures Publishing.)

One of the pleasurably difficult parts of B.V.I. diving is deciding which of the many sites to visit. Shallow reefs, walls, and shipwrecks are all available.

Your selection will depend on the experience level of the divers in the group, the sea conditions, and the dive objectives being contemplated. Although every effort has been made to provide thorough and accurate information in this book, it remains the responsibility of every diver to determine the appropriateness of each dive and to conduct each dive in a safe manner. Sea conditions are constantly changing, and can change even during the dive itself. The dive sites themselves can undergo significant change as the result of severe storm and sea action. Always evaluate each dive site based on natural conditions such as weather, surge, and current, and on personal preparedness prior to entering the water.

By far the most abundant dive sites in the B.V.I. are coral reef areas. Some, such as The Indians, are shallow enough that they are popular snorkeling sites as well.

Others, like Alice's wonderland, are only accessible with scuba equipment. All of the dive sites listed here are excellent reef locations, whether deep or shallow. The life on each reef will vary from site to site but all sites have an abundance of fish, corals, sponges, and other invertebrate life.

In addition to the abundant reefs, there are several excellent wreck dives in the B.V.I. including the Royal Mail Steamer Rhone, the Marie L, and the Chikuzen.

For a diver to visit the B.V.I. without seeing The Rhone would be blasphemous. The wreck of the Royal Mail Steamer Rhone lies in 25 to 80 feet of water just off Black Rock Point on the southwest tip of Salt Island.

The ship's wreckage is strewn over the sea bottom in an area of about 100 feet by 400 feet, distributed in two major sections - the bow and the stern. The bow section is about 150 feet long and is still relatively intact. While not as well preserved as the bow, the stern section including the massive rudder and propeller still makes a great dive, providing visibility of the inner structure of the ship. All of the wreckage is covered with corals, sponges, and other life and is home to thousands of fish.

Certainly the most popular (and famous) site, the wreck of the R.M.S. Rhone is an underwater attraction that should be seen. Sunk in 1867 during a hurricane, the remains of this steamship lie scattered along the seabed in depths from 25 to 80 feet. Many parts of the ship are still recognizable today although all of the wreck has become encrusted with corals and sponges. The area around the shipwreck teems with fish thanks to the many divers who provide food. This site can be enjoyed by divers of all skill levels - from novice divers on the stern to advanced wreck divers who can penetrate the bow section.

The Marie L was a derelict tugboat that was sunk purposefully as a new dive site. Located near Cooper Island in 80 feet of water it is an easily accessible site for advanced divers and provides a very entertaining dive.

The Chikuzen was a refrigerated freighter that sunk in 1981 about eight miles north of Scrub island. Although the interior is not considered safe for penetration, the exterior of the ship is nearly intact making it an excellent dive. Because of the difficulty in locating the wreck, this dive is best made with a local dive operation.

You don't need to go to a hundred feet to find excellent diving in the B.V.I. For relatively inexperienced divers or for those who may not have been active for a year or more, there are a number of very good sites that offer interesting and plentiful life while still providing the safety of shallow, well-protected water.

The Indians, near Norman Island, is one of the best shallow reef dives in the area. Painted Walls on Dead Chest Island is a very good dive for novices as long as the seas are not running out of the east. Vanishing Rock, near Cooper Island, is a well protected site although occasionally subject to strong currents. At the Dogs, The Chimney is a very interesting dive that almost always has calm surface waters. Near Marina Cay, Diamond Reef has very good life, easy access, and protected waters.

If it's been a few years since your last dive, consider taking a tour with one of the dive operators before venturing out on your own. It is a great way to become reacquainted with your Scuba equipment and the diving environment.

The Indians are four rock pinnacles that project from a sandy bottom at 50 feet to a height of 50 feet above the surface. The dive site consists of the pinnacle walls, coral gardens, and some very interesting shallow pools. This site is probably the best shallow reef site that is consistently accessible and protected from bad seas. The site, by the way, is said to have been named by sailors long ago, for the similarity of the rocks to Indian teepees, obviously, the sailors had too much rum.

Painted Walls is an underwater series of canyons that reach from an average depth of 35 feet to just below the water's surface. At the terminus of the third canyon are two arches which are covered with encrusting sponges in an artist's palate of color (thus the name).

It is a difficult site to dive when the seas are running from the east or southeast as a result of the surge underwater and the wave motion on the boat; otherwise it is an excellent site for divers of all experience levels.

Blonde Rock is a pinnacle reaching from the 60 foot bottom to within 15 feet of the surface. Approximately 200 feet wide and 600 feet long, the site can be circumnavigated in a single dive by experienced divers. It's exposed location, between Dead Chest and Salt Islands, dictates that this site can only be dived on days when the seas in the area are relatively calm and flat However, when the opportunity permits, this is an exceptional dive; the reef life is abundant and larger fish are common.

Tortola
Wendy Canning Church

If you have heard that this destination is serene and unspoiled, a haven for yachtsmen as well as divers, offering crystal clear water and sheltered anchorage, then you have heard correctly.

The British Virgin Islands fondly known as the B.V.I.'s are comprised of 45 islands, islets and cays, many of which are uninhabited. Actually the entire area is part of the archipelago, along with the U.S. Virgin Islands, that stretches for some sixty miles east of Puerto Rico and lies between the Atlantic Ocean and the Caribbean Sea.

Their position within the belt of the tradewinds allows for a semi-tropical climate with 75-85F temperatures year round with winds of 10 to 20 knots. The exception is Christmas week when the winds are stronger. This makes for an ideal vacation destination.

You will not find Kentucky Fried Chicken, casinos, glitzy nightclubs or large resort complexes in the B.V.I.'s. What you will find are restaurants, some small and intimate, others with an island flavor, guest accommodations to fit any pocketbook, local entertainment and beautiful scenery, both above and beneath the sea.

It is rumored that when Christopher Columbus discovered the islands in 1493, he was told not to land because of the fierce cannibal tribe. In fact these islands were first settled by the Carib Indians who were driven away by the treacherous Arawaks who raped, pillaged and practiced cannibalism. They were hated and feared throughout the Caribbean.

Pirates holed up in the protected caves of Sopers Hole in the 1800's. The Dutch were the first settlers from Europe and were soon followed by the English who were the first to gain an economic stronghold.

Because of economic hardships, the 19th century was a time when most of the Europeans returned home, leaving their plantations to become overrun and by the 20th century, turned to ruin.

A small percentage of Europeans remained and to this day work hand in hand with the former slaves. One could never question that there is still a strong legacy of English culture still flourishing.

You can reach Tortola either by a small plane or by a ferry from St. Thomas (U.S.V.I.). We chose the ferry which runs on a frequent schedule from downtown Charlotte Amalie.

As the ferry slipped away and got farther out to sea an air of calm began to settle in. The first stop is St. John (U.S.V.I.). After a brief stop we headed for Tortola, 40 minutes away. The sheer beauty of the small green islands, sitting quietly in crystalline waters is simply magnificent.

Tortola is the largest island in the chain, being twelve miles long and three miles wide. The highest point on the island is 1710 feet above sea level and is in Sage National Park. We drove past this point as we made our way to the hotel past this beautiful spiral mountain range that runs through the island.

Our hotel was the **Prospect Bay Resort** which we chose for a variety of reasons. First it is located one mile from Roadtown, the capital, an easy 15 minute walk. Secondly, **Baskin' in the Sun**, the scuba center that we dove with has a satellite center at Prospect's marina. Thirdly, it is a most attractive hotel at the waters edge that offers a wide variety of services and accommodations to fit any pocketbook. It has 131 rooms, suites, and two, 2-bedroom villas on 40 tropical acres. Many rooms have kitchenettes, and the villas have full kitchens as well as a living room and dining room. They also have a nice beach and a natural pool enclosed by huge boulders.

General Manager, Graham Sedgwick, and his staff could not be more friendly nor helpful. Prospect Reef is for those divers who want to be close to town, the shops and restaurants, and a short walk to the dive shop.

Having a home away from home with your own kitchen can be a welcomed change from a hotel room. Each of the seaside rooms has a patio to take sun, read or dine.
For more information contact. **PROSPECT REEF RESORT LIMITED** - PO Box 104, Road Town, Tortola, British Virgin Islands. Tel. (809) 494-3311. Fax. (809) 494-5595. Reservations: (800) 356-8937.

We chose to dive with Baskin'in the Sun because they had been recommended numerous times for their safety standards, terrific dive sites, attitude of the staff and the warm and generous interest shown to each diver by the owners Eva and Alan Baskin. All of the above were found to be true.

They are undoubtedly one of the most organized dive operations we have ever seen.

We met at the Prospect Reef shop early in the morning. Baskin also has a scuba center at Sopers Hole. They will pick up and deliver divers at resorts anywhere on Tortola. All of their boats, both large and small, have ample room for divers, overhead canopy for sun protection, and heads.

The first morning we were off to Spyglass, a mini wall dive off Norman's Island. In earlier times pirates living on Norman's Island took advantage of the bight running past it. Ships making passage to St. Thomas would misconstrue the pirates' signals thinking that they would bring them through the bight and into St Thomas. As a result they ended up floundering on Norman's rocks and beaches.

Beach Bar in Tortola by Wendy Canning Church

(It is a beautiful island. For those interested, the sales price is $5 million dollars. The only drawback it that there is no anchorage.)

We rolled over into the water and followed our guide, Harold. We worked our way southeast, looking out for the pelagics who like these waters because of the bight. We saw a number of stingrays and a good size nurse shark. As we swam further along a beautiful spotted drum came into view. There were stovepipe and elephant ear sponges as well as shrimp living among the anemones.

Our bottom time was up and we ascended, stopping at 15 feet for 3 minutes even though the wall dive was not a decompression dive. This practice is one that is done on every dive with Baskin, which I believe is a good one and exhibits their high safety standards.

Our second dive was a shallow one exploring the north section of the wall. There were beautiful purple sponges, brown and black coral, lobster, trumpetfish, brain coral, schools of yellowhead, a spotted moray eel, parrotfish, squirrelfish, blue hamlet, butterfly fish, sergeant major, and black durgeon.

As you move along the wall look out occasionally to the left and you are likely to see rays and pelagics.

The following morning we dove Painted Walls situated on the southeast point of Dead Chest Island. This is a shallow dive 20 to 30 feet which gives one lots of bottom time to explore its three canyons which are so colorful that they are aptly named "Painted Walls". We descended to the shortest of the three and then swam back up the second and repeated this with the third. The hangings get longer and longer as you move to the ends. The sponges are a burst of color.

Swimming through the arches, we saw octopus, eels, brissel stars, feather dusters, arrowcrabs, turtles, rays and spade fish, large french angel fish, sea cucumber and a large porky. The walls are a myriad of colors and provide a fantastic backdrop for the abundant variety of sea life.

Our next dive was on the wreck of the R.M.S. Rhone, pride of the Royal Mail Steam Packet Company. She went down in a hurricane off Salt Island with 331 passengers aboard. She makes a good two-tank dive since after sinking she broke in two with both parts preserved.

Our first dive was on her bow section which lies in 80 feet of water on a sandy bottom. The forward mast and crows nest are intact. Descending further you can investigate the deck, cargo holds and inner chambers. Reef fish abound and coral has encrusted her belly. The bowspirit lies in the sand.

After a sufficient interval time, the second dive is on the stern section examining the engine, propshaft and very large propellers. Extensive footage for the movie "The Deep" was shot here.

Ginger Steps is another dive site close to Virgin Gorda. Dropping into the water one investigates the terrain at a 40 foot step, then the next step at 60 feet and another at 90 feet. We saw a great variety of fish life on this dive, eels, french angelfish, barracuda, feather dusters, schools of creole wrasse and snappers, queen trigger fish and sea turtles. Large conch shells appear as halos in the sand.

Caravel Rock is another interesting dive site. It's geological formation reminds one of diving off the coast of Hawaii. There were beautiful walls and ledges and all I could think of was mountain climbing.

The black coral was not only beautiful but abundant. A large turtle caught our eye along with a school of barracuda and angel fish.

A mooring system is in place throughout the British Virgin Islands and boaters strictly adhere to it. We commend this practice for it is one more step to saving the endangered underwater environment.

When not underwater, take time to explore Tortola. It is truly a beautiful island. We rented a Jeep and drove the entire island, stopping here and there to investigate other hotels, beaches and restaurants.

Cane Garden Bay is one of the most popular beaches and has wonderful snorkeling. Brewers Bay is secluded with tranquil estates and a campground. *Long Bay* is on the western side. It is home to the *Long Bay Hotel*. *Sugar Mill Hotel* which is a little further on has a long lovely beach and is a wonderful place for windsurfing and snorkeling. On the eastern side of Tortola you will find *Josiah's Bay* and *Lambert Bay*. These beaches are beautiful and wonderful for snorkeling or swimming.

Editor's Note: Nudity is an "offense" under the law.

West Side of Tortola by Wendy Canning Church

We dined out each night and found a number of wonderful restaurants, both funky and elegant.

Be sure to dine at the UPSTAIRS HARBOUR RESTAURANT at the Prospect Harbour Marina. Do dress appropriately, not fancy, but no jeans please. This is a lovely restaurant with good food and a wonderful atmosphere looking over the harbor. The owners take great pride in their cuisine and service.

You will find a PUSSERS RUM COMPANY STORE AND PUB in Road-town where you can get a variety of pub food which is quite good and they have a broad selection of beer and ale. Tel. 4-2467.

If you get a craving for Chinese food go to *Chopsticks*. Tel. 4-3616

The *Fort Burt Restaurant* is a short walk from Prospect Harbour. The food is excellent and served in a pleasant setting overlooking the Harbour. The fort was built in the 17th century by the Dutch and is an interesting piece of island history. Tel. 4-2587.

The Paradise Pub is situated right on the water and is also a short walk from the Prospect Reef. The food is simple but very good. Casual dress is acceptable. It has a happy hour and some form of entertainment nightly. It is a fun spot. Tel. 4-2608.

On the west end of the island you will find the *Sugar Mill Hotel* and its gourmet restaurant. Tel. 5-4355. Jeff and Jinx Morgan are hosts and owners. Do dress for a four course dinner in this enchanting location.

SCUBA AND SNORKELING FACILITIES QUESTIONNAIRE

NAME **Baskin In The Sun**
ADDRESS **P.O. Box 108**
Tortola, BVI
CONTACT **Alan Baskin**
TITLE **President**
TELEPHONE **800-233-7938, 809-494-5854**   FAX **809-494-5853**

CAPITAL: GOVERNMENT:
POPULATION: LANGUAGE:
CURRENCY: ELECTRICITY:
AIRLINES: DEPARTURE TAX?
NEED VISA/PASSPORT?   YES   NO **x**   PROOF OF CITIZENSHIP?   YES **x**   NO

YOUR FACILITY IS CLASSIFIED AS: SCUBA CENTER **x**   RESORT
BUSINESS HOURS: **7 days a week year round 8:00 a.m. - 18:00 p.m.**
CERTIFYING AGENCIES: **PADI, NAUI, CMAS**
LOG BOOK REQUIRED?   YES   NO
EQUIPMENT: SALES **x**   RENTALS **x**   AIR FILLS **x**
PRIMARY LINE OF EQUIPMENT: **Scuba Pro, Dacor, Sherwood**
PHOTOGRAPHIC EQUIPMENT: SALES **x**   RENTALS **x**   LAB **x**

CHARTER/DIVE BOAT AVAILABLE?   YES **x**   NO   DIVER CAPACITY **50**
COAST GUARD APPROVED?   YES **x**   NO   CAPTAIN LICENSED?   YES **x**   NO
SHIP TO SHORE?   YES **x**   NO   LORAN?   YES **x**   NO   RADAR?   YES **x**   NO
DIVE MASTER/INSTRUCTOR ABOARD?   YES **x**   NO   BOTH

DIVING & SNORKELING: SALT **x**   FRESH
TYPE OF DIVING/SNORKELING IN AREA: WALL **x**   BEACH **x**   WRECK **x**   REEF **x**   CAVE   ICE
DIVING/SNORKELING IN YOUR AREA IS BEST SUITED FOR: BEGINNER **x**   INTERMEDIATE **x**   ADVANCED **x**   BEST TIME OF YEAR FOR DIVING/SNORKELING: **Summer**
TEMPERATURE: NOV-APRIL: F   MAY-OCT: F
VISIBILITY: DIVING: FT   SNORKELING: FT

PACKAGES AVAILABLE: DIVE **x**   DIVE STAY **x**   SNORKEL   SNORKEL-STAY
ACCOMMODATIONS NEARBY: HOTEL **x**   MOTEL   HOME RENTALS
ACCOMMODATION RATES: EXPENSIVE   MODERATE   INEXPENSIVE
RESTAURANTS NEARBY: EXPENSIVE   MODERATE   INEXPENSIVE
YOUR AREA IS: REMOTE   QUIET WITH ACTIVITIES **x**   LIVELY
LOCAL ACTIVITY/NIGHTLIFE:
CAR NEEDED TO EXPLORE AREA?   YES   NO
DUTY FREE SHOPPING?   YES   NO

LOCAL EMERGENCY SERVICES   NEAREST HYPERBARIC TREATMENT FACILITY
COASTGUARD: **St. Thomas, USVI**   AUTHORITY: **Dr. David Boaz**
TELEPHONE: **809-774-1911**   LOCATION: **St. Thomas General Hospital**
St. Thomas, USVI
CALLSIGNS: TELEPHONE:

LOCAL DIVING DOCTOR:
NAME: **Jana Downing, MD**
LOCATION: **Road Town, Tortola, BVI**
TELEPHONE: **809-494-2763**

The Cayman Islands
By Wendy Canning Church

"He Hath Founded It Upon the Seas"
Cayman Motto

Lois Hatcher has been active in diving since 1982 when she learned how to dive off the frigid coast of western Canada. Since her first dive she was hooked and went on to become a PADI instructor. She has worked in Southern California, Canada, Thailand and Australia.

As the amount of dives she logged grew in number, so did her interest in Underwater Photography. She now resides in Grand Cayman where she owns a successful underwater photo/video shop and spends her days snapping pictures, teaching photo classes and shooting videos for visitors to the island.

Editor's Note

When I observed Lois on the Parrots Landing dive boat with her students, I was greatly impressed by both her professionalism and patience.

After the dive, I returned to the Center and looked at her photos which I thought were quite beautiful. Lois was kind enough to return to Stingray City twice so we could get a good shot for the article. She has also contributed other works to this book.

For photographers or "would be's", a visit with Lois on Grand Cayman is a MUST!

Purple Spotted Shrimp & Anemone by Lois Hatcher

The Cayman Islands lie 480 miles south of Miami, Florida in the Western Caribbean.

They consist of three islands, Grand Cayman, Cayman Brac and Little Cayman.

Cayman Brac and Little Cayman are referred to as "sister islands" since they are separated by a channel only seven miles long.

George Town, on Grand Cayman, is the capital.

The population of all three islands is 27,000 with the majority on Grand Cayman. The people are of English, Irish, Scottish, Welsh and African descent.

English is the official language.

Columbus landed there on May 10, 1503, naming them Las Tortugas or The Turtles after the large sea turtles that frequented the waters.

The Spanish never set up a permanent settlement.

Throughout the following years, pirates used the hidden caves and inlets for safe anchorage to repair their ships and hide their treasure.

Las Tortugas did not take hold as a name and some years later they were called Las Garotos.

This name, did not last either, the islands finally were called Caymans, derived from the Carib word for crocodile. History suggests there may indeed have been members of the crocodile family inhabiting the islands.

In the 1600's, the British arrived and in 1670 the "Treaty of Madrid" made the Caymans British property.

Today, a British Crown colony, the Governor is appointed by the Queen. The legislative assembly consists of 12 elected members with an executive council of three appointed and four elected members. Elections are held every four years.

Twenty-five years ago there was not a paved road on Grand Cayman. Today, it ranks as the fifth largest financial center in the world with approximately six hundred branches of global banks.

All three islands are situated on a coral reef that is eight miles long, descending to six thousand feet.

Couple this with a year round temperature of 77 to 86 degrees Fahrenheit, pristine waters, incredible visibility and a diverse and abundant marine life and you will see why 85% of the Caymans' income is derived from tourism.

Sun, sand, and sea are a perfect combination for a vacation. Finally, let us add one more, safety. Today, when one travels, this is a difficult mixture to find in a vacation playground.

The Cayman Island Marine Park rules are a model worldwide.

The marine environment, arguably the most important natural resource and tourist attraction of the Islands, has been the focus of most of the legislation over the last several years.

The Cayman Island Water Sports Association (30 members) meets frequently and sets rules for its members, prices, safety standards, maximum depth for diving (100 feet), ratio of dive masters to divers and what equipment must be carried aboard a boat for safety. Everyone adheres to these!

This is to be commended, for they realize, even though in competition for business, the safety of the diver, the well being of the sea life, the coral reef and fragile ecosystem depend upon a combined effort of everyone in the business and their clients' adherence to these set rules.

They have also established 200 permanent moorings.

The use of spearguns is forbidden. Divers cannot wear gloves.

Marine Park zones have been set up where no one can take any kind of sea creature, living or dead. "Take only pictures, leave only bubbles" is their slogan.

For visitors, especially divers and snorkelers, copies are made available of *Guidelines for the Prevention of Diver Damage*.

The Conference on EcoTourism was held in the Caymans in 1993 and resulted in the following laws:

No more than 3 cruise ships may be present in George Town Harbor at any one time or no more than 5,500 passengers.

Raised the fine for illegal dumping of sewerage in its waters to international standards.

Permanently established Marine Parks in certain areas and are looking to establish more (i.e., similar to Saba).

I think the above will give you some indication of how serious the Caymans are about protecting their most precious asset .... their waters! In 1978, the Cayman Marine Conservation department banned the taking of black coral from its waters. What you can buy comes from Belize and Honduras. Do discourage the taking of black coral. Do not buy any as a souvenir!

Grand Cayman, The Appetizer

When I was visiting Cayman Brac, I met two charming gentlemen from Canada who were filming a documentary for Canadian television: Jim Kozmik and John Robb of Aqua Images.

We became fast friends on the ride out to the dive site. They asked if I would be their underwater model. I was happy to oblige.

Aboard, we talked further about our occupations and I told them that I was compiling a book, a *Global Guide*, and that was my purpose for the visit.

They asked if they could shoot a short interview with me for their particular documentary. Again, I was only too happy to join their project.

The first question asked by John was how would I describe the Cayman Islands.

Without a moments hesitation I said that I felt Grand Cayman was the appetizer, Cayman Brac the entree, and Little Cayman the dessert. They thought it was a good analogy of the Islands and the more I thought about it, the more convinced I was that this would be a good way for a visitor to think about each island.

Grand Cayman is 28 miles long and 7 miles wide.

The high season is December through April and they get most of their rainfall from May through October.

From the minute you land at the airport, you will find every modern convenience you would expect on the mainland. This is both good and bad.

Good for the natives who need these services to run business and homes, but a shame for those visitors expecting an island unique in and of its own culture.

Grand Cayman *has* been discovered! You will find 4 and 5 star hotels, luxurious waterfront homes, American franchise takeout, very expensive restaurants, apartment condos, and all in all, what one might find in Miami.

On the other hand, with the Caymans ranking as one of the top ten dive destinations in the world, you will find that rare wonderment under its seas brings the same visitors back again and again each year.

If you have an inquisitive nature as I do, you will take a car and tour the entire island.

Once out of town and away from seven mile beach, town and the cruise ships, you get a feeling of what it *must* have been like twenty-five years ago.

I had planned an ambitious trip, covering all three islands in two weeks.

I began my visit on Grand Cayman, staying at *Coconut Harbor*. I chose this hotel because I wanted to dive with Parrots Landing who have a satellite scuba center at Coconut Harbor. 1/2 mile from their watersports park, three miles from the airport, and 1/2 mile from town, Coconut Harbor sits on the sea. All of the 35 rooms have mini kitchens, air conditioning and ceiling fans. There is a fresh water pool, jacuzzi and open-air, thatched roofed cabins, bar and restaurant.

"*Waldos Reef*" just offshore offers some excellent diving and snorkeling.

The staff couldn't be more hospitable and helpful. The rooms are clean and a good size. The food is simple, but quite good.

Coconut Harbor is a good bet for dedicated divers.

Coconut Harbor P.O. Box 2086 Grand Cayman, BWI
Tel: 1-809-949-7468 Fax: 1-809-949-7117

I chose to dive with Parrots Landing because it had been highly recommended to me. After the first day, I knew I had chosen correctly.

Seldom have I witnessed an operation that was so organized, its boat comfortable and ship shape, its staff professional and safety conscious, and genuinely helpful and friendly.

On an acre of land just a half mile south of downtown George Town, you will find Parrots Landing, a multi-faceted Watersports Park. Parrots Landing opened in February 1988 with something different in mind for divers and non-divers coming to Grand Cayman. They offer hassle-free diving and snorkeling, small to medium boat capacity, a little extra freedom and a different dive site each day. They operate 6 boats which go to remote and virgin dive sites along the North, South, East and West Walls. They have a full service dive equipment retail, rental and repair facility on site, a boutique and a photo lab headed by Lois Hatcher.

For the advanced computer diver, they offer the boat which departs at 8:30 a.m. This boat is limited to 6 divers and ventures to diver selected sites along the South Wall, West Wall and Northwest Point.

This non-guided buddy team type dive requires each diver to monitor his or her dive with a computer.

Multi-level diving and the use of a computer allows for better bottom time; however, the 100 foot maximum depth limits remain in effect.

There were 6 of us that departed on The Macaw bound for **Lemon Drop** at the North Wall. The Macaw is 23 feet long with 220 horsepower, roomy enough for gear and divers with a nice comfortable cabin and head. We buddied up and the dive plan was given. This would be a dive at 100 feet maximum. With giant stride entry we descended down the mooring line and made our way to the wall.

There was spectacular light from above so we had excellent visibility to explore even at that depth.

Here there was a good chance to see the pelagics, the occasional hammerhead or lemon shark for whom the reef was named.

Our first glimpse was of a ray lying partially buried in the sand. He darted away at the sight of divers.

The eagle rays go into the North Sound to feed. There is only a small channel so you can catch a glimpse of many eagle rays while checking out the wall. As you swim along, look behind you for that's how they cruise. We spotted three stingray.

These were followed by a huge lobster walking across the reef and a very large gray angelfish, a good size grouper, schools of spotlight parrotfish and all sorts of open water fish.

There are three large pinnacles separated by canyons and sand chutes. The black coral and gorgorians were especially beautiful.

As we ascended the wall, we came upon a large array of plate coral stacked one atop the other. At about 50 feet, we encountered all variety of reef fish. This is an impressive dive and not one to be missed.

Orange Canyon is made up of two ravines, nice and wide. We reached our maximum depth of 100 feet. There were schools of large tarpon, a great barracuda, lots of brain, barrel and plate coral. As we slowly ascended, there were gray green angelfish, trumpetfish, orange sponge and brilliant pink coral. A really pretty wall dive.

Tarpon Alley North Wall is a deep dive that is very close to stingray city. It is comprised of three canyons, one leads to a drop off, the others to open sand. Descending to a maximum depth of 70 feet, we reached sandy bottom. The tidal movements at that time of day brought us good luck. Schools of tarpon appeared before our eyes, their silver bodies shimmering in the dapple light from above. We encountered large barracuda cruising the wide, deep ravines.

Back aboard, we counted 5 spotted ray and another very large lobster that we'd seen.

Cheeseburger off George Town runs like a band, 50 feet wide by 300 to 400 feet long. The reef side has a sandy bottom with lots of caves you can swim through and then all along the reef. The coral side juts up abruptly and this is a sheer wall which is inhabited by schools of yellow jack. At shallower depths, gray angelfish, parrotfish, redband parrotfish, squirrelfish, black durgons and other reef fish were present. A nice dive to end the morning.

Rumor hath it that "Stingray City" is the most dived and snorkeled site in the world. Whether this is true or not, I never tire of diving or snorkeling it.

I have included this remarkable site in our chapter "Seven Underwater Wonders of the World".

The Stingray City dive and snorkel excursion, a most popular trip, is available everyday of the week at 2 p.m. There are many photographic opportunities as you feed squid to over 25 friendly southern stingrays. Divers and non-divers alike will certainly want to sail the "Cockatoo". This thrilling 60 foot ultra-modern Catamaran is a great way to relax and catch some sun. The "Cockatoo" sails from the North Sound and sets anchor at Stingray City. Squid is provided for snorkelers to hand feed the southern stingrays.

A 3-Tank boat trip is scheduled for Fridays and Sundays departing at 9:00 a.m. and returning around 4:30 p.m. This all-day trip is not for those inclined to be sea sick. The excursion includes 2 wall dives and one shallow dive. All divers are required to have a computer. Upon re-entering the boat, the Divemaster checks computers to ensure that the divers have not entered into a decompression dive or exceeded the profile. To qualify for the advanced dives, you must first be on one of Parrots Landing's daily 2-Tank boat dives and demonstrate your skills as a diver and knowledge of a dive computer.

The 2-Tank boat dive trips depart at 8:00 a.m. and 1:00 p.m. The dive sites are selected by the divers upon leaving the dock. The morning boats leave early to get the choicest dive sites before the other boat operators. The dive profile normally includes one deep wall dive (100 feet maximum) and one shallow (40 ft. to 50 ft.) reef or wreck dive. The extremely popular afternoon two-tank boat dive is a double shallow profile. Each reef and/or wreck dive is to a maximum of 50 feet. This is ideal for late sleepers, newly certified divers and photographers and videographers who want maximum bottom time to capture lots of fish and marine life.

The one tank boat night dives are scheduled on Tuesdays and Fridays. The night dive boat departs the dock around 6:00 p.m. or dusk. This is a great way not only to enjoy a Cayman Sunset, but also to observe sea creatures such as lobsters, crabs and octopus which come out at night to feed.

The North Wall boat departs Governors Harbour at 8:30 a.m. daily and you are certain to see Spotted Eagle Rays gliding by the wall. Twenty new moorings have been placed in the North Wall area making many exciting sites accessible.

All the boat dives included free tanks, weights, weight belts and unlimited shore diving for the entire day. Divers can take advantage of this unlimited shore diving by experiencing the waters at night. All they ask is that the tanks and rental gear be returned by 9:00 a.m. the next day. Transportation is also provided at no charge from your hotel or condo prior to and after all boat dives.

The diver training facility is ideal for anyone interested in Open Water Certifications, Check-Out Dives, Resort Courses, or advanced PADI or NAUI Certifications. The professional Instructors are available for all of your training needs. Interesting and educational courses can be combined with previously scheduled boat dives so that you can advance your skills without giving up dive sites.

"There's a place where the Caribbean is still gracious, the way it used to be" is the Carribean Club motto.

Built twenty-five years ago by Jerry Payne when beach front property prices on seven mile beach were not prohibitive and density was not a problem. Today it exists serene and picturesque at waters edge, retaining its age old aura of serenity and understated elegance. The 18 privately owned one and two bedroom villas are all individually decorated in a style of good taste and comfort. Each is centrally air conditioned, with color TV and kitchen. One can partake of all the sea and its toys at their doorstep. Tennis is also available on the premises. We dined at *Lantanas Restaurant* which is on the property but owned by outside managers. This restaurant serves gourmet cuisine, the service warm and unobtrusive in a toney atmosphere. *Lantanas* Tel: 809-947-5595 Fax: 809-947-5653

The Caribbean Club is something of an anomaly in the modern world of tourism. Indeed, the Caribbean Club of today is remarkably similar to that of a quarter century ago. The beach is still pristine, and the staff remains as amenable and welcoming as ever, which perhaps explains why many of the guests return year after year, some, in fact, for as many years as they have been open.

This is a little jewel of a resort.

Please, no children in winter season.
For more information, contact:

DEI
37 test Cedar Street
Boston, MA 02114
Fax: 617-723-7134

WHEN YOU COME UP FOR AIR

I had scheduled a voyage on the Atlantis Submarine and was looking forward to seeing the new form of entertainment they had added. Passengers are transported to the submarine by the Yukon II, the tender vessel which takes eight minutes to reach her. Built in Canada at a cost of $3.5 million, the Atlantis can accommodate 46 passengers. Once aboard and while slowly descending, safety procedures are explained and demonstrated.

> **One can view the impressive variety of fish through their own porthole or view point in an air conditioned comfortable seat.**

Kevin was our narrator for the voyage and not only pointed out and identified the sponges, corals and fish, but also gave us interesting tidbits about them and the sea they inhabited.

> **About three quarters of the way through the trip, the sub settles in a patch of sand and to everyone's amazement divers arrive on bright yellow scooters.**

They bring squid along and feed the fish which produces almost a feeding frenzy and a good subject for photos. (In order to take pictures, you must use 1000 or higher film speed and *do not* use a flash. Cover your automatic flash.)

> **The divers speak to the guests aboard the sub, "Nice visibility, barracuda, snappers, groupers, we are at 83 feet," etc.**

The addition of divers to the dive is whimsical and fun. This is truly a voyage for the *entire* family. It encompasses both delight to the eye and food for the brain. Don't pass this up!

The Atlantis Submarine
P.O. Box 1043
Grand Cayman, BWI
Tel: 809-949-7700

Enter Million Dollar Month, the International Fishing Tournament that takes place each June. Visit the Cayman Islands Turtle Farm. Play golf on a course designed by Jack Nicklaus and use the famous Cayman ball. Visit Pedro Castle. Built in 1780 it stands as Cayman's oldest structure. Pedro Castle lies on one of the most beautiful and peaceful spots on the south coast of Grand Cayman. Shop in downtown George Town for duty-free bargains. Jewelry, perfume, crystal, and many other gifts can all be found here. Visit the Cayman Islands National Museum. Visit the Treasure Museum where you'll learn about Cayman's seafaring and pirate lore. Go to Hell! Ironshore rock formations, more than one and a half million years old, look like the charred remains of a hellfire. You can send the folks back home a postcard from Hell! Enjoy a night out at the theatre. Check the Harquail Theatre for a schedule of current stage and musical productions from Cayman and other Caribbean countries. For the marine biologist in you, ride Research Submersibles Ltd., a two-passenger sub that reaches depths of 800 feet.

SCUBA AND SNORKELING FACILITIES QUESTIONNAIRE

NAME **Parrots Landing Watersports Park**
ADDRESS **P.O. Box 1995 George Town**
Grand Cayman, Cayman Islands, BWI
CONTACT **Larry Leonard**
TITLE **Reservations Manager**
TELEPHONE **809-949-7884** FAX **809-949-0294**

CAPITAL: **George Town** GOVERNMENT: **British Commonwealth**
POPULATION: LANGUAGE: **English**
CURRENCY: **Cayman Islands Currency** ELECTRICITY:
AIRLINES: **Cayman Airways, United** DEPARTURE TAX? **$7.50 U.S.**
NEED VISA/PASSPORT? YES NO **x** PROOF OF CITIZENSHIP? YES **x** NO

YOUR FACILITY IS CLASSIFIED AS: SCUBA CENTER **x** RESORT
BUSINESS HOURS: **8 a.m. - 6:00 p.m.**
CERTIFYING AGENCIES: **PADI, NAUI, SSI**
LOG BOOK REQUIRED? YES NO **x** C-card required
EQUIPMENT: SALES **x** RENTALS **x** AIR FILLS **x**
PRIMARY LINE OF EQUIPMENT: **Dive Gear**
PHOTOGRAPHIC EQUIPMENT: SALES RENTALS **x** LAB **x**

CHARTER/DIVE BOAT AVAILABLE? YES **x** NO DIVER CAPACITY **see attached**
COAST GUARD APPROVED? **Cayman Govt.** YES **x** NO CAPTAIN LICENSED? YES **x** NO
SHIP TO SHORE? YES **x** NO LORAN? YES NO RADAR? YES NO
DIVE MASTER/INSTRUCTOR ABOARD? YES **x** NO BOTH **x**

DIVING & SNORKELING: SALT **x** FRESH
TYPE OF DIVING/SNORKELING IN AREA: WALL **x** BEACH **x** WRECK **x** REEF **x** CAVERN **x** ICE
DIVING/SNORKELING IN YOUR AREA IS BEST SUITED FOR: BEGINNER **x** INTERMEDIATE **x** ADVANCED **x**
BEST TIME OF YEAR FOR DIVING/SNORKELING: **All year round**
TEMPERATURE: **NOV-APRIL:** 81-82 F **MAY-OCT:** 82-85 F
VISIBILITY: **DIVING:** 100 FT **SNORKELING:** 100 FT

PACKAGES AVAILABLE: DIVE **x** DIVE STAY **x** SNORKEL SNORKEL-STAY **x**
ACCOMMODATIONS NEARBY: HOTEL **x** MOTEL **x** HOME RENTALS **condos**
ACCOMMODATION RATES: EXPENSIVE **x** MODERATE **x** INEXPENSIVE **x**
RESTAURANTS NEARBY: EXPENSIVE **x** MODERATE **x** INEXPENSIVE **x**
YOUR AREA IS: REMOTE QUIET WITH ACTIVITIES **x** LIVELY **x**
LOCAL ACTIVITY/NIGHTLIFE: **Bars, restaurants, movie theater**
CAR NEEDED TO EXPLORE AREA? YES NO
DUTY FREE SHOPPING? YES NO

LOCAL EMERGENCY SERVICES NEAREST HYPERBARIC TREATMENT FACILITY
COASTGUARD: **Cayman Islands Port of Authority** AUTHORITY:
TELEPHONE: **949-2228** LOCATION: **George Town Hospital**
CALLSIGNS: **Channel 16 on VHF radio** TELEPHONE: **555 in an emergency**

LOCAL DIVING DOCTOR:
NAME: **Dr. Hetley**
LOCATION: **Crewe Road**
TELEPHONE: **949-7400**

Cayman Brac: The Entree:

Cayman Brac or the Brac (Gaelic for bluff) is situated some 89 miles Northeast of Grand Cayman and separated from its sister island, Little Cayman, by some five miles at its nearest point. Twelve miles long and one mile wide, it has become renowned for its scuba diving and snorkeling, bone fishing and, of course, its 140 foot high bluff of limestone. As you land at the small airport, you immediately get a sense of why its 1,400 permanent residents are content to live here.

Crime is almost nonexistent and they leave their windows open and doors unlocked.

As remote as you might feel, the hotels here are equipped with satellite T.V. and if you want to send a fax, they are prepared to do so.

We had received mixed reviews about the hotel on the Brac and quite frankly considered skipping the island altogether. That did not seem entirely judicious, so we went ahead and booked. Our choice of hotels was *The Brac Reef Resort*, run by the Tibbett family who have recently opened a new resort on Little Cayman. The resort is 5 miles from the small town and 2 miles from the airport. The newly renovated, two-story structure on the sea has 40 rooms. Rooms are good sized, with air conditioning, color T.V., beach, pool, dining on the premises (all meals – buffet style), patio bar, tennis courts, conference facilities and is handicapped accessible.

There are no phones in the rooms, but there is a phone center in the lobby. The scuba center is a short distance from the premises. The staff were friendly and helpful. My only suggestion is that they add a bellman to tote those heavy dive bags, etc. to the rooms which can be very far from the main lobby!

Winston McDermott owns the dive center and he has a good, comfortable 45 foot boat called the Reef Runner with a capable captain: Raymond Scott and crew. They carry a maximum of 25 divers and snorkelers. Everyone at the dive shop was most helpful.

DIVE SITES

Anchor Wall was 60 feet high and our maximum depth would be 100 feet.

This was an interesting dive with caves and crevices running perpendicular in the wall.

We came upon a 150 year old anchor belonging to a schooner of the late 1800's. It is eight feet tall so you can pass through it.

At 90 feet we went inside a cave filled with magnificent black coral. Their sign for black coral is money. We passed through the cave at 100 feet and began our ascent for home. After a safety stop, we went aboard.

The boat has an ascent and descent line along with a tag line. There is a bar over the side for safety stops along with a tank with hose for those low on air or in an out of air situation. She has VHS channel radio, carries oxygen, first aid and a backboard.

Interval time up, we prepared for our second dive at *Tarpon Reef* Southwest Side. The reef was exceptional with wonderful channels and crevices to explore.

Big Tarpon swam in schools. We spotted two nurse shark, a green moray eel, yellowfish, squirrelfish, blue hamlet, dusky squirrelfish, midnight parrotfish, gray angelfish, tiger grouper, banded butterfly fish, sergeant major, black durgeon, large spotlight parrotfish, and red-banded parrotfish.

A barracuda that we spotted on the descent line followed us the entire dive.

We had a mild to strong current and this would have made a perfect drift dive! The topography was really beautiful but unfortunately with *so* many divers having dived the site, a great deal of damage has been done to the coral. So many of the sea fans had been broken off and it truly brings home the need for more *diver damage control*!

The following morning we headed for the waters off Little Cayman to *Marilyn Cut* off Bloody Bay Wall.

The Reef Runner can hit speeds of 25 knots so a trip to Little Cayman takes a short time, weather permitting.

The wall starts at 25 feet when you take a right hand turn going in an easterly direction while slowly descending. Our maximum depth would be 100 feet and this should be closely monitored since the wall extends to some 800 feet. At the top of the wall we ran into a school of Nassau grouper. We played with a grouper and petted it and went on our way. We swam through the cut at 65 feet. The wall was so sheer and so spectacular that it was easy to lose sight of your depth.

Our second dive was **Mixing Bowl** off Little Cayman Northwest Side. The top of the wall is at 35 to 40 feet. Inside the wall is a sandy area where Southern Stingrays hang out. There were crevices and caves that enticed us but they were too deep for the second dive. There was lots of black coral on the edge of the wall and of course the friendly grouper who calls this place home.

Wendy Canning Church with Barrel Sponge by Jim Kozmik

These are two *great* dives. Don't miss them.

And when you come up for air, you might enjoy the other interesting activities offered on the Brac. Visit the bluff on Cayman Brac. Hikers may see hundreds of resident and migratory birds. For the truly energetic, ask for directions to the original bluff trail to the lighthouse and take the challenging 3.5 mile hike. You will be rewarded with some of the most dramatic scenery in the Cayman Islands, looking down at the islands from a 140 foot precipice.

Make an appointment to see the Parrot Reserve on Cayman Brac. This protected area, managed by the National Trust for the Cayman Islands, is dedicated to preserving the life of the endangered Cayman Brac Parrot.

Brac Reef Resort
P.O. Box 56
Cayman Brac, BWI
Tel: 1-809-948-7323
Res: 1-800-327-3835

SCUBA AND SNORKELING FACILITIES QUESTIONNAIRE

NAME **Brac Aquatics Ltd. (Brac Reef Beach Resort)**
ADDRESS **P.O. Box 89, West End, Cayman Brac**
Cayman Islands, BWI
CONTACT **Winston or Denise McDermot**
TITLE **Owners**
TELEPHONE **809-948-7429** FAX **809-948-7527**

CAPITAL: **Stake Bay** GOVERNMENT: **Elected, British**
POPULATION: **900** LANGUAGE: **English**
CURRENCY: **Cayman Is. Currency & U.S.** ELECTRICITY: **110v 60 cycle**
AIRLINES: **Cayman Airways** DEPARTURE TAX? **$7.00 U.S.**
NEED VISA/PASSPORT? YES NO **x** PROOF OF CITIZENSHIP? YES **x** NO

YOUR FACILITY IS CLASSIFIED AS: SCUBA CENTER **x** RESORT
BUSINESS HOURS: **8 a.m. - 5:00 p.m.**
CERTIFYING AGENCIES: **NAUI, PADI**
LOG BOOK REQUIRED? YES NO **x**
EQUIPMENT: SALES **x** RENTALS AIR FILLS **x**
PRIMARY LINE OF EQUIPMENT: **Dacor, Sherwood**
PHOTOGRAPHIC EQUIPMENT: SALES **x** RENTALS LAB **x**

CHARTER/DIVE BOAT AVAILABLE? YES **x** NO DIVER CAPACITY **20, 20, 18, 10**
COAST GUARD APPROVED? YES **x** NO CAPTAIN LICENSED? YES NO **x**
SHIP TO SHORE? YES **x** NO LORAN? YES **x** NO RADAR? YES NO **x**
DIVE MASTER/INSTRUCTOR ABOARD? YES **x** NO BOTH **x**

DIVING & SNORKELING: SALT **x** FRESH
TYPE OF DIVING/SNORKELING IN AREA: WALL **x** BEACH **x** WRECK **x** REEF **x** CAVE ICE
DIVING/SNORKELING IN YOUR AREA IS BEST SUITED FOR: BEGINNER **x** INTERMEDIATE **x** ADVANCED **x**
BEST TIME OF YEAR FOR DIVING/SNORKELING:
TEMPERATURE: **NOV-APRIL:** 80 F **MAY-OCT:** 84 F
VISIBILITY: **DIVING:** 120+ FT **SNORKELING:** 100+ FT

PACKAGES AVAILABLE: DIVE **x** DIVE STAY **x** SNORKEL SNORKEL-STAY
ACCOMMODATIONS NEARBY: HOTEL **x** MOTEL HOME RENTALS **x**
ACCOMMODATION RATES: EXPENSIVE MODERATE **x** INEXPENSIVE **x**
RESTAURANTS NEARBY: EXPENSIVE MODERATE **x** INEXPENSIVE **x**
YOUR AREA IS: REMOTE **x** QUIET WITH ACTIVITIES **x** LIVELY
LOCAL ACTIVITY/NIGHTLIFE: **Weekend only**
CAR NEEDED TO EXPLORE AREA? YES **x** NO **x**
DUTY FREE SHOPPING? YES **x** NO

LOCAL EMERGENCY SERVICES NEAREST HYPERBARIC TREATMENT FACILITY
COASTGUARD: **No** AUTHORITY: **Cayman Clinic**
TELEPHONE: LOCATION: **Grand Cayman**
CALLSIGNS: TELEPHONE: **555**

LOCAL DIVING DOCTOR: **Yes, at the local hospital.**
NAME:
LOCATION: **Stake Bay, Cayman Brac**
TELEPHONE: **809-948-2243**

Little Cayman: The Dessert

Please refer to Honeymoon and Anniversary section.

Please see chapter Seven Underwater Wonders of the World for the Deep Dive Submarine to 800 feet and Stingray City.

The Appetizer, Grand Cayman, gives a hint of what lies ahead for the worldwide diver seeking virgin diving.

Cayman Brac, The Entree, brings one closer to that quest.

Little Cayman, The Dessert, (often the best part of a dinner at many restaurants) doesn't disappoint the diver who has traveled far to find one of the last, almost untouched areas both above and under the sea. The quest for this dessert is well worth the time there and the price!

Editor's Note

In summer, Cayman Island rates are lower (April 16 - December 15).

Passports are not required for U.S. or Canadian citizens, but you must show your return ticket and proof of citizenship.

COSTA RICA
COCOS ISLAND
Gary Ratzke

NAUI Advanced Open Water Diver; Diving for six years; Public School Administrator

Diving is a natural for me, having degrees in the biological sciences, grown up in Southern California and living very near the Pacific ocean. As a little boy I always had a love for any body of water and anything that walked, flew, crawled or swam. I don't know why it took me so long to start diving, but I'm making up for lost time.

My current personal project is adventure diving of any type. My obsession is to place little diver flags in as many places as possible on the world map I have hanging on my wall at home. I'll sleep anywhere, eat anything and dive in the strangest places.

Dive experiences have included extensive beach and boat diving along the California coast and Baja. I have been diving at all of the California Channel Islands and open water in between. These waters are great and the kelp forests, seals, sea lions and open water blue shark diving should be experienced by everyone.

Venturing farther from home has found me diving the islands of Tahiti and Moorea, Cayman Islands, all of the Hawaiian Islands, Grenadine Islands, St. Thomas, Puerto Rico, Yasawa Islands in Fiji, Northern Bahamas, Jamaica, Cozumel Mexico, Papua New Guinea, Australian Northern Barrier Reef, Coral Sea, Borneo Malaysia and Sipadan Island, and Cocos Island in Costa Rica. Each of these hold special memories.

I once thought that my list of diving adventures was getting long. The more I dive, though, the more places and creatures remain to be experienced. Current interests await in the Red Sea, Yap, Palau, Truk, Belize, Honduras, Sea of Cortez, Bonaire, Thailand, the Florida Keys and the Galapagos. I am ready to go on short notice during the summer months and rarely like to make far ahead plans and reservations. If there is a vacant spot to fill or a special deal, I'm ready!

Diving interests center mainly on still underwater photography using both the Nikonos system and housed cameras. I'm not especially good but I make up for that in volume. I love interaction with the creatures and always have to touch them even if it sometimes gets me in trouble. I'm from the old school of diving that still feels a few beers in the evening in any old dive does not contribute to the bends.

Within the span of a few short years, Cocos Island has emerged as one of the premiere adventure dive destinations in the world.

Adrenaline levels soar as you step into the water with anticipation of schools of hammerhead, whitetip, and roaming whale sharks, dolphins, tuna and huge manta rays.

Cocos does not disappoint the fortunate diver soaring through its surrounding waters. Marine life is abundant and each dive is a different adventure.

Isla del Coco (Cocos Island) is an uninhabited Pacific island located approximately 260 miles off the coast of Costa Rica.

The main land mass measures approximately 4 miles long by 2 miles wide and is almost completely covered by rainforest. It is of volcanic origin and has many small rocky offshore islets. The island itself is rich in history with rock carvings dating back as far as the 1600s. Cocos displays a variety of indigenous tropical birds, plants; and an unbelievable number of waterfalls, making it a place not soon forgotten.

A trip to Cocos Island typically includes a flight into the main city of San Jose, Costa Rica with an overnight stay before making an overland trip by van to the port city of Puntarenas. There are numerous quality hotels in San Jose, and we stayed at the San Jose Palacio. The hotel is modern and first class with good restaurant facilities and even a small casino with complimentary coupons for free play.

Excellent rooms are available in the neighborhood of $60 and the staff is friendly and courteous.

The only way to get to Cocos Island is by boat. Since there are no facilities on the Island, the diving choice is one of the liveaboards visiting the island. Currently there are three boats regularly diving Cocos.

My choice was the Okeanos.

The two hour morning van trip to Puntarenas brought us to our liveaboard, the Okeanos Aggressor.

The Okeanos is a well maintained and designed boat and is well above the minimal standards for a dive vessel accommodating 19 divers.

Air conditioned staterooms are large and comfortable with ample storage space. There are four very large heads with hot water showers, a spacious comfortable lounge with TV and videos for entertainment and provisions for viewing videos taken on the day's dives. A separate dining room, individual on-deck storage space for dive gear, extensive camera storage areas, a mid-deck bar with additional table space and a third level sun deck with lounge chairs and a hammock all add to passenger comfort. Rental Nikonos cameras and accessories, E6 processing and a 110 volt strobe charging station are available. 80 cubic foot tanks, air, weights and weight belts are provided.

Upon arrival at the dock, the crew quickly unloads the van and places all gear aboard. Divers are treated to beer and soda to revive their spirits after the warm drive from the hotel. Guests are assigned cabins, dive lockers are selected and the Okeanos is soon under way. The trip to Cocos averages about 32 hours. The trip is smooth and comfortable and guests arrive rested and ready for first-class diving.

Good food was served buffet style three times a day, in variety and quantity, and ample snacks. Alternate choices were always available. Soda, beer and wine was available at nominal extra charge 24 hours a day.

The Okeanos crew was very friendly and helpful and quick to see what was needed without asking or reminding. On one dive, just prior to entering the water, my high pressure hose blew. I had barely shut off the air before a crew member appeared and attached his own regulator to my tank. I was in the water in probably less than two minutes and lost zero dive time! Help was always available for camera gear with loaner or rental gear readily available as needed.

Diving is done from two inflatables kept tethered to the Okeanos. The larger boat anchors in different locations each day but the actual diving is done from the inflatables to permit closer approach to the actual dive sites and for diver pick up when drifting in currents. Crew members do a good job of following bubbles and there is seldom a long wait or swim for pick up. Each dive location is often dived twice but on different days. This procedure is sometimes used because experience showed more frequent encounters with large fish by not remaining in one area too long. This seemed a good idea because the fish life was different and abundant on each dive.

The normal schedule is three dives per day at 8:00 a.m., 11:00 a.m. and 3:00 p.m. Generally, the Okeanos would move in the evening or early morning to anchor in a different bay for the next day of diving. Night dives were available to those interested and were done near the bay of anchorage. Night dives would leave every night at 8:00 p.m.

Wendy Canning Church TV Interview by John Robb. Photo by Jim Kozmik

The diving at two or three areas was so fantastic that we continued to return time after time by our request. Although the physical terrain remained the same, currents would change, animals encountered would vary visibility would differ from between 50 and 75 feet, sometimes less, thermoclines would be encountered in different locations and at different times. Water temperature varied between approximately 70 and 80 degrees Fahrenheit and a wetsuit was definitely in order because of some extreme thermoclines.

Most dives were very comfortable with a thin 1/8 inch or less wetsuit but some areas were quite cold. Some of our group added vests and switched to heavier wetsuits, and we were diving in the month of August! Diving depths ranged from about 40 to 130 feet with most dives between 60 and 95 feet. There were a few exceptional dives with large manta rays in about 20 feet of water over deep channels.

One of our favorite dives was Manuelita Islet. We had hoped to see at least a few hammerheads during the week but we saw them every dive. Groups of 10 to 15 were swimming but came no closer than 30 to 50 feet.

Moorish Idol by Gary Ratzke

Manuelita is a sharp cascading wall. There are shallow coral gardens with usual tropicals, eels and lobster, but the real action is the sharks. Sharks are everywhere. Whitetips were found stacked on top of one another, sometimes three high in groups of 8 to 10, resting on the bottom.

There must have been more than 30 of them swimming in a tight circle! We were able to position ourselves less than three feet from the mass as they brushed passed us. Apparently lunch was trapped in a large crevice in the rock and they were patiently waiting.

Dirty Rock was another outstanding dive area with similar physical characteristics. Again hammerheads were present in small schools and whitetips were abundant, with manta rays and a very large number of marble rays. Although the schooling hammerheads kept their distance, we did have a few close encounters with very curious large hammerheads. On at least two occasions I was approached much closer than I had preferred by large hammerheads. I had one come within two feet of my mask and turn away sharply! Although I think I personally reduced the visibility at that moment, I did get a good photograph of half his turning body, the side of his head and a big black eye!

Enough excitement? Enter a whale shark! Just as-on cue, he met us head on and slowly swam over the top of our group. The chase was on and we were able to swim at close distance. Some were fortunate to touch it and be barely missed by the huge tail. We estimated his size at about 45 feet.

Other areas explored included Viking Rock, Cathy's Lost Rock and Gates Rock; none compared to Manuelita and Dirty Rock. We kept going back for thrills of a lifetime. Recounting all dive areas, we were able to add to our sightings and/or photographs with oceanic white tip sharks, Galapagos sharks, turtles, dolphins, schools of jacks and yellowfin tuna, yellow and black puffers, trumpetfish, triggerfish, unusual starfish, whitetipped sea urchins, frogfish, and eels. Lacking is the abundance of colorful varieties of hard and soft corals shown in South Pacific photographs.

Cocos is the site of close encounters with the big guys. If you don't like sharks, don't come.

It should be noted that Cocos Island is not a trip for beginners. Cocos is for advanced divers used to diving in changing conditions and who are ready for the unexpected. The excellent diving around Cocos is mainly due to powerful ocean currents surrounding the island that guarantee an abundant food supply by bringing up enormous amounts of plankton. Vertical as well as horizontal currents sometimes accompanied by areas of reduced visibility, deep water and the remoteness of the location all call for diving experience. A calm dive today may be a frightening dive tomorrow, in the same location, for an inexperienced diver. Snorkeling at Cocos would be very disappointing and possibly dangerous considering the number of large sharks that could be excited by splashing on the surface.

Shore activities on Cocos are fun and interesting if you like rainforests, waterfalls, history and birds.

It is estimated that Cocos has over 200 waterfalls and there are many opportunities to go ashore and explore. There are many interesting old carvings on the rocks on the beach announcing the landing of ships from around the world. There are even tales of a treasure buried on the island. Hiking through the forest will present the opportunity to swim beneath a large waterfall and view beautiful frigate birds, gulls and boobies.

For more information on booking an Okeanos cruise contact: Divers Exchange International, 37 West Cedar Street, Boston, MA, 02114; or call (617) 723-7134.

CURACAO
A DIVE DESTINATION DISCOVERED
by Jerry Kassanchuk

Curacao as a dive destination is not exactly a well kept secret. It's just that while European divers have been enjoying the unspoiled reefs of this largest of the ABC islands for years, Americans have thought of it only as a plane change/stopover island near Bonaire. That's a pity, because in many ways Curacao has more to offer than Bonaire and other popular, Caribbean dive destinations like Grand Turk, Roatan and Grand Cayman.

To begin, Curacao is truly one of those places that has something for everyone. If you like quiet, off-the-beaten track seclusion with nothing but diving to take up your time, Curacao has it. If you like diving plus lots of non-diving activity in a European city atmosphere, Curacao also has that.

How about a huge coastline with more dive sites than one could possibly visit in a month including 42 well mapped dive sites providing great snorkeling for non-diving family members as well as a wonderful setting for between dive beach picnics.

Economy lodging, or major resort settings? Or exclusivity in a luxury two-bedroom condo in a quiet and remote setting with an incredible overlook of a large chunk of

Curacao coastline? Meals on a verandah with an ocean view and pounding surf or dress up fine dining in an elegant restaurant?

Wreck diving or virgin reefs? Curacao can, indeed, meet every diver's needs and desires.

The Aruba/Bonaire/Curacao group of desert islands lies about 35 miles north of Venezuela in the extreme southern part of the Caribbean. This location puts it out of the hurricane belt and provides the three weather constants that make missed diving days highly improbable. Those constants are: a year-round average temperature of 82 degrees; a very brief rainy season in late November/early December; and a predominantly northeast wind that gives divers 38 miles of protected, southwest-facing leeward shore.

Unlike other far-flung Caribbean dive destinations Curacao is easy to get to on any day of the week by flying KLM out of Miami. Layovers, island hopping, lost luggage and non-existent airline schedules need not be factored into the very precious vacation times of divers who choose Curacao. Aruba is sometimes a stopover but, since plane changing is not involved, it is very brief. Most travelers, after leaving their homes in the morning, should have plenty of time after arriving in Curacao to settle into their rooms, watch the sunset, eat dinner and still see some of the wonderful city of Willemstad. And if you don't want to waste any time getting into the water, you can even get in an easy shore dive from the beach in front of the Princess Beach Hotel.

Since Curacao has been serving travelers for a number of years it can fill any lodging need at almost any price. There are small and large apartments in Willemstad as well as hotels and dive resorts close to or on the beach. While the large places with their own dive operations can give package discounts you can sometimes do as well taking an apartment in town and having the owner line you up with an independent dive operation or dive guide. Choosing a Willemstad location keeps you close to the wonderfully Dutch-like atmosphere, shopping, dining and night life.

A moderately priced choice for the those who want more than diving on their vacations is the Curacao Plaza (a Canadian-Pacific Hotel). The Plaza is a high-rise at water's edge in the heart of downtown Willemstad. It was built on the site of and in fact, behind the walls of an historic fort at the entrance to Willemstad's harbor. The surroundings are very European and the hotel is complete with shops, music and dancing, lounges, shows, restaurants and a casino. Quaint, old-world Dutch waterfront shops are just a couple of blocks away. There is no on-site dive operation but diving can be arranged.

At the opposite end of the scale in price and ambiance is the Royal Gramma Apartments which promise very luxurious, fully equipped kitchen/dining room, living room, bedroom, and bathroom in 800 square feet of space. Royal Gramma, which is located in a quiet suburb, has cable television, phone, pool, and laundry facilities and is close to supermarkets, restaurants and various clubs. The owner/manager, Peter van den Broek, will provide two 3000 psi tanks and weight belt for about $13 per day including tips and directions on shore diving. He can also fix you up with free mileage, air conditioned cars and will meet you at the airport. Cost of a Royal Gramma apartment was $400 per week.

An alternative for families or those who want something homey with quiet surroundings and oceanside location is Sun-Reef Village, a collection of roomy, one to four person, freestanding units several minutes drive from Willemstad. Sun-Reef is in a residential area and the units on the water, in particular, offer a peaceful, private place to relax after a day of diving. They have their own dive operation but no on-site dive shop. A water's edge two bedroom unit goes for @ $625.

Las Palmas Hotel and Casino/Vacation Village bills itself as an ideal place for families. For couples and singles it has 100 rooms in the main hotel building, but it also has 100 two-bedroom villas for families or small groups who are willing to trade some personal privacy in order to share costs. Swimming pools and tennis courts are nearby and

Las Palmas offers every possible amenity except a dive operation. Diving can be arranged, however. They have beach access, but it is a couple of blocks away.

If diving is your primary concern and if you are used to, and satisfied with, a dive resort situation and atmosphere you have several from which to choose. At the highest end of the price/amenities scale is the Curacao Caribbean Hotel & Casino which is just ten minutes away from downtown. It has a fine restaurant, casino, pool, beach shops, entertainment and its own dive operation. The Holiday Beach Hotel has the same amenities but is five minutes closer and about 30 percent cheaper. Princess Beach Hotel also offers all amenities plus a Peter Hughes dive operation and a beach. It is very close to Seaquarium and to Curacao Underwater Park. In price it is halfway between Curacao Caribbean and Holiday Beach.

Even closer to the Underwater Park and very moderately priced are Lions Dive Hotel and Marina, a basic dive resort with just a few frills, and Bonbini Seaside Resort. Avila Beach Hotel, which is on the beach near the edge of downtown, is also very basic.

The absolute bargain-basement, though, is Trupial Inn. It is a comfortable family hotel located in a residential area close to shopping. It has a pool, cable television and a shuttle to the downtown area. Rates here are less than half that of the highest.

The far opposite end of the spectrum for divers is basing themselves in lodging at the northern end of the island away from the hustle and bustle of downtown and high-traffic diving. Actually, there is no high-traffic diving on Curacao. But, by way of comparison, consider this: All of the above mentioned resorts, plus a few not mentioned, have about 1500 rooms and are within easy diveboat distance of some prime diving in the southern half of the island; but there are fewer than 100 rooms available in the northern half of the island.

There are two places where divers usually house themselves in the north, and the difference between them is considerable. Coral Cliff Resort and Beach Club is a dive resort and has its own dive operator. The rooms are American motel quality, but large clean and with a bit of a kitchen. The rooms are dramatically perched on the edge of a cliff overlooking the ocean. The sights and sounds of the water sometimes gently lapping, sometimes beating on the shoreline are positively enthralling. The view and tranquillity inland are just as enthralling: a steep slope, covered with a large variety of beautiful, desert type vegetation rises a surprising distance. There is a single road into the resort and it carries only resort traffic. In short, this place is beautifully isolated and it's quiet.

The resort covers nearly twenty acres – a good part of which is beach. The dive shop, diveboat anchorage and guest equipment locker are located just down the hill from the resort office and the Santa Marta Terrace Restaurant. This very large, open-air restaurant, bar and social center is the only place to eat for several miles, so it's small wonder that guests congregate here. No problem; the menu has enough choices so one can try something new every day, and the food, while not overly plentiful, is very good.

Divers who want to economize can shop a local grocery store and then make use of the kitchens in some of the rooms. These kitchens are modest but adequate.

The other choice of lodging at this end of the island is literally at island's end. Kadushi Cliffs consists of a series of two-story, two-bedroom luxury condominiums that were begun in 1991. They aren't perched at cliffs edge but they are near the edge and that edge is very high above the water. Despite this seemingly great barrier to the water, Kadushi Cliffs residents do have access to all the usual water sports via a beach which must indeed lie at the very northern-most tip of the island. What this placement provides for guests is constant cooling breezes and a south facing view of the coast and the inland peaks which is positively breathtaking. Though it's just a bit pricey, it is the ultimate getaway location for small groups and families.

And that brings us to the primary focus of this piece: Curacao diving. The first thing one has to say is that there is a lot of it. The island's diving can be broken into roughly four parts: The Banda Abao Underwater Park begins at Wata Mula near Kadushi Cliffs and stretches almost halfway down the island to just north of Kaap St. Marie. It includes 21 boat dive sites. There are also 20 well mapped shore dive sites in this section –some of which have moorings for boats.

Central Curacao Underwater Park begins at the south edge of Bullen Baai near the middle of the island and extends to Princess Beach Hotel just north of Willemstad. The third part, Curacao Underwater Park, comprises the last fourth of the island from the Seaquarium to East Point. Last but certainly not least is Klein Curacao where virgin diving and frequent 150 foot visibility makes a boat ride of about 50 minutes well worthwhile.

That there are a large number of dive resorts in the southern half of Curacao compared to the north and, consequently, more divers. There are so many dive sites in Curacao Underwater Park that most divers couldn't possibly cover them in a week. The reefs in this Park include some of Curacao's finest. Also, since diving is so new here, the reefs are still pristine and, except for the busy season, dive boats on the Park's reefs are few and far between.

Incidentally, Curacao is very popular with Europeans, especially the Dutch. Many European businesses close during the summer months for employee vacations. This means that you might want to plan a Curacao trip for anytime except a four-week span from June into July.

Shore diving versus boat diving is a personal thing. If you've only done one and not the other Curacao is a good place to try the other kind of diving. But if you're a boat diver with a non-diving spouse and/or kids, Curacao's shore dives are a definite must. Shore diving automatically includes sightseeing, once you're away from the city, that can be very enjoyable.

Though Curacao is a desert island, it is very hilly and doesn't seem as arid as Bonaire. In fact, it has a lushness that is more reminiscent of an island like Roatan.

Hell's Hole produces a Black and White Crionid by Jerry Kassauchuk

A nice feature of Curacao is that many of the reefs start in shallow water so, while you're diving, your non-diving friends and families can be snorkeling.

Shore-dive beaches are great places to pass surface intervals and, depending on your timing, they are nice for picnics after you've done a couple of dives. Be advised, though, that Curacao's European flavor includes topless sunbathing and, on weekends especially, you are very likely to find this at most beaches.

Current for shore diving is usually not a problem. Obviously the first thing you need to do after you've started your dive is establish direction and strength of the current. If it's absent or very light you might be able to get two dives out of a given dive site, one in each direction. You'll be amazed at how different the reefs can be. If the current is strong or if you don't feel like fighting a current on your return leg, start your dive against the current and come back with it.

Some words of caution – particularly to shore divers: First, it is always important to dive with a dive buddy. Your snorkeling friends or family won't be any help if you're in trouble at 50 feet. Second, because many of the beaches are small, you should be well versed in natural and compass navigation so that you can return to your entry point.

Most writers, in reviewing dive destinations, take some time to highlight dive sites for their particular destination. It's somewhat difficult to do that about Curacao. First there is the sheer number of dive sites. Second is the size of the island and the difficulty in covering the great expanse of shoreline of Curacao not to mention Klein Curacao. Finally, there is the quality of diving. It'd be far easier to list the few dive sites that are so-so. This writer is, therefore, tempted to say simply that if you're not a well-traveled, globe-trotting diver, you'll like anything you try in Curacao and, believe me, you'll likely find something new, different and exciting at every dive site. If you've been diving for a long time and have seen everything except Curacao, you can't afford to pass it up.

I'll resist that temptation, but I won't even try to discuss every dive site. A brief overview will allow you to at least set some goals and priorities when you dive Curacao.

Dive sites in the Underwater Park are marked with numbered buoys beginning with buoy #1, *Oswaldo's Dropoff*. The dive starts as a shelf where you'll find a fish feeding station, heads of elkhorn coral as well as staghorn coral and gorgonians. Porgies and squid have also been seen here. After the drop-off at about 40 feet you'll find brain coral, leaf coral and sponges. If you go deeper you'll find a pile of cars but the only attraction of this attempt at an artificial reef is that some of the cars are very old.

From the Seaquarium divers and snorkelers can reach *Bapor Kibra* (*Papiemento* for "broken ship"), where the *SS Oranje Nassau*, a Dutch steamship was wrecked over 80 years ago. There are some lovely growths of elkhorn coral on the ribs of the ship. Beyond the shallow-water coral garden are a couple of pillar coral stands providing cover for an abundance of fish.

Continuing eastward is another dive/snorkel site, this one with a colorful and shallow undercut ledge. This dive site, which is called *Boda di Sorsaka*, has a two-tiered terrace. The upper level is solid rock covered with small coral as well as some elkhorn; the lower plateau, which is at a depth of about 30 feet, is covered with a delightful collection of different corals and gorgonians. Swimming to the left from the buoy for several minutes will bring you to a short vertical wall covered with different hued Cavernous star coral.

A little farther down the coast in the Park is another beach dive/snorkel site, *Jan Thiel*. Because of the sandy beach and a breakwater which provides protection, entry here is easy. The nicest part of the reef is at depths beyond 50 feet, so the reef itself will be more attractive to divers than snorkels. Snorkelers won't be cheated, however, because there is a lush shallow reef community here. Snorkelers should check out the edges of the bay and the area near the mooring.

Towboat (Buoy #8) is considered a perfect spot for snorkelers and underwater photographers. The tugboat wreck at this site lies in just 17 feet of water in an upright position and is overgrown with orange tube coral and different colored brain coral.

A very pretty wall begins just out from the wreck in about 30 feet of water. It is covered with orange elephant ear sponges and sheet coral.

Divers will find very wide and shallow terraces offshore at *Kabaya* (Buoy #9). Facing the ocean from the mooring take a heading toward the west for a short distance to the drop-off. A dramatic vertical wall, which starts at just 33 feet, offers cavernous star coral and gorgonians at its upper edge, then growths of black corals, encrusting sponges and wire coral. Brown chromis, creole wrasses and sergeant majors are abundant here. Just east of *Kabaya* is *Punt's Piku* (Buoy #10) which also features a shallow wall and terraces. Just east of the entrance to Fuikbaai is *New Port* (Buoy #11) a nice, shallow terrace dive with an abundance of fish, coral and gorgonians.

Other dive sites near the eastern end of the island are excellent and varied, but because of the relative distance from Willemstad and somewhat constant choppy seas, they are visited less often. This is unfortunate because one of the nicest, *Piedra Pretu* (Buoy #15), is located here. If you can get a boat to make the long and choppy trip to the tip of Curacao you'll be rewarded with a spectacular vertical wall. The dive starts very close to the wall near a field of staghorn coral. It begins at about 30 feet and drops straight down to a maximum depth of 110 feet. The wall is covered with a lush growth of black coral and, just past 80 feet, are small crevices filled with royal grammas (common name: Fairy Basslet. Note black dorsal spot) and an occasional green moray. Near the base are large flattened plates of sheet coral.

If your dive boat makes it this far you might also be able to dive *Basora*, the very last site on this end of Curacao. Diving here is somewhat similar to *Piedra Pretu* but you'll also find unusually shaped mountainous star coral as well as giant brain coral. Watch for a very tall pillar coral growth near the mooring just before the wall.

The first dive site northwest of Willemstad, *Superior Producer*, is a highly regarded wreck dive. The *Producer* is a completely intact freighter, which is said to have been overloaded, sank when some cargo shifted. Because it is a deep dive – the keel is at 110 feet, the bridge at 90 feet and the wheelhouse at 80 feet – and sometimes subject to strong current and surge, some advanced diving expertise and extra caution are a must. Some anemones and corals have made a home here and manta rays and porpoises are often sighted. Though access is rated difficult it can be reached from shore.

If beach night dives strike your fancy you should consider *Piscadera Baai*. Like other choice night dive spots this one is good because junk on the bottom makes for excellent hiding places for all those neat nighttime critters.

Be sure to get there before nightfall so you are oriented. Or, better still, make a day dive across the channel to the right of the entry area. It's a bit of a swim, but well worth the effort if you plan to return for a night dive.

Blaubaai is the third site in the Central Underwater Park area and is delightful. Though this is a boat dive site, it's one you might consider doing from shore during the week. The area to the right as you leave the beach is not worth diving but the area to the left is worth two tanks. For closer access to the actual dive site you should drive to the left well beyond the main beach to one of the small beaches. Entry is a bit more difficult but you'll save time, effort and air. Bring your camera; it's an exciting dive. A word of caution: near what would be a turnaround point for most divers is a sharp ridge and beyond the ridge is a strong flow of current out to the sea.

As always when you dive, keep an eye on the bend of soft corals so that you are not caught unaware. Watch for snake eels on the terrace before the slope and very large trumpetfish, French angelfish and high hats.

Port Marie Baai is another good shore dive site – as is *Daaibooi Baai* just a short distance to the east. Access from a sandy beach is easy and it's an attractive spot for a picnic.

Be sure to leave some time during your visit to Curacao to dive with Coral Cliff Divers. Owner/manager Mike Feytt and his wife are very helpful, low key people who are naturals at making diving fun and painless. Their divemaster, Cecil, is one of the best. He is well informed and is willing to share all he knows about local dive sites. If you dive with Coral Cliff Divers have them take you to *Mushroom Forest*. It is breathtaking. Once you get somewhat used to the enchantment, however, do take some time to look very carefully, of course for critters living in this forest and, especially, under the mushroom coral. Cecil can find you a scorpionfish, and spotted drums and rough limas are common.

There are many other good boat-dive sites in this area but one called *Hell's Hole* produced some of our more enjoyable sightings: black and white crinoids, slipper lobster, black coral and rough lima.

Other very picturesque shore dive spots are *Playa Lagun*, *Playa Jeremi* and *Knip Chikitu*. At *Playa Lagun* the water is protected by high bluffs and is always calm. Entry is easy and snorkeling, especially at the base of the cliffs, is very good. The fishing boats pulled up on the shore provide a colorful touch and some landside photo opportunities. *Play Jeremi* has an unusual beach composed of white sand and volcanic stones and *Knip Chikitu* has such a perfect white-sand beach that it is very popular with locals.

Playa Pikado di Westpunt is a wonderful place to watch the sunset. Like other dive sites in this far northwestern end of the island, high bluffs surround the bay and fishing boats pulled onto the shore makes one feel very removed from the hustle and bustle of civilization. Diving is good here, too, but getting to it is not nearly as easy as other sites because the reef is rather far out.

Playa Kalki, the only spot on the island that gave us pause, is also known locally as "thieves beach." We were advised that the way to avoid potential problems is to leave nothing in our rented car and to leave the car unlocked and the windows open. After a very short entry effort we found a reef similar to **Mushroom Forest**, though not as spectacular. We were more excited about a huge green moray that was out in the open and which seemed completely unbothered by our invasion. Our second dive here, this time to the east (left entry) produced a very large barracuda at reefs edge, scorpionfish, another large moray and a missed landmark when returning to our entry point.

> **With three of us using compasses that miscue served as a reminder that one cannot trust to luck – or a divemaster – when shore diving.**
>
> **Klein Curacao is the highlight of any dive day here because of the clarity of water, number and size of fish, and absolute virginity and variety of reefs.**

It is, however, a full day's effort and, if the seas are rough, it requires an uncomfortable crossing. Generally it has been once-a-week undertaking by most dive operators and then only when weather permits.

However, something new was recently added: One can now overnight on Klein Curacao at a home owned by Miss Ann Rentals, a boat service providing diving and fishing as well as trips to Klein.

In addition to the brief mention made of dive operators and guides above, we must recommend two additional dive operations: Wederfoort Diving School is a full service dive operation owned and operated by a delightful native of Curacao named Eric Wederfoort. His is a perfect example of what we call "down home" hospitality and graciousness. One day, after completing three dives, rinsing our gear and cleaning up for an evening exploring Willemstad, we dropped in on Eric. He and a couple of his sons had just come in from an instructional dive and hadn't even unloaded their truck. Yet he dropped everything and not only invited into his home for a visit but, before he would let us leave, took us on a brief tour of dive spots close to his home (Central Underwater Park), showed us the site of his new dive center and then stopped and bought us a large bag of mangos from a local vendor simply because we happened to mention how much we liked them.

The second, Atlantis Watersports, is a new and relatively small-scale operation. It is owned and operated by Roland de Knegt a divemaster and former instructor on the Antilles Aggressor. Roland is experienced and very knowledgeable. If you prefer smaller, more personalized diving, his operation should suit you perfectly.

How does one plan a trip to a Caribbean island that is off the beaten path and unknown by every travel agent in the U.S. that we talked to? For us it was with a great deal of difficulty. The Curacao Tourist Board was not very much help, so we had to make most of our arrangements blind. Then, just before we left for Curacao, Wendy Church of Divers Exchange International put us in touch with a travel agent, tour operator extraordinaire, and all around promoter of, and expert on, Curacao named Henry Veeris. He did an incredible job of fixing our mistakes and turning a potentially disappointing week into a smashing success. If there- is anything at all you need to know about Curacao, Henry can help you

Wendy Church, through Henry, can give you a tailor-made package.

Dominica

by Martha Watkins Gilkes

Martha Gilkes by Lucy Stickley

The underwater scenery of Dominica is as spectacular as the scenery on land, with rugged mountains continuing into the sea.

Shallow coral reefs lead out to dramatic drop-offs and sheer walls, most covered with tremendous black coral trees and huge barrel and tube sponges. The volcanic action has formed arches and caves, now heavily encrusted with marine life, Not found on many other islands, there is also a marine sub-aquatic hot freshwater spring just offshore in only 10-20 feet of water, know as "Champagne." Freshwater bubbles drift slowly through the black sand towards the surface, appearing like liquid crystal glistening in the sunlight. This was the perfect ending to a night dive as I ascended from the nearby reef to the hot bubbles to experience nature's sauna. On every night dive I have done at "Champagne" I have been greeted by schools of squid.

Some of the more popular dive sites are **Scotts Head Drop-Off**, a 20 foot ledge with a dramatic drop-off to over 120 feet, The walls are covered in large tube sponges and georgians and occasional black coral trees, The **Soufriere Pinnacle** rises out of Soufriere Bay from around 150 feet to within 5 feet of the surface. The pinnacle is covered with soft and hard corals and a variety of tropical reef fish. The **La Bim Wall** is an extensive 1.5 mile wall which drops off from a 20 foot ledge to over 800 feet in some places. Large schools of blue and brown chromis fish mass among the pillar and boulder coral on the 20 foot ledge. **Point Guignard** drops from 15 feet to 110 feet along the cliff face of blackbar soldier fish. I repeatedly dove one cave, which made a safe shallow dive. The cave is large enough for diver's to enter, penetrating the rock wall about 40 feet. A mass of blackbar soldier fish parted ranks as I entered and the roof is often inhabited by lobster.

More advanced dive sites on the Atlantic side of the island include **King David's Throne, Mountain Top, The Village** and **The Condo**. Boat entry and exit is usually difficult due to wave action and the site availability is limited. However, the visibility is generally excellent and the marine life is prolific. You often see massive sting rays, occasional nurse sharks, large school of margate, snappers and pelagic fish, Although I know there are numerous other exciting dives, I repeatedly return to this site! The large rock formation offers a network of three intertwining caves filled with soft corals, brightly coloured sponges, and large schools of blackbar soldier fish and assorted reef fish that gently part as divers swim through.

On all four sites, there are enormous coral overhangs providing shelter for a large variety of colourful reef fish and marine growth. Massive sting rays frolic on the nearby sand bottom and are easily approached if a diver is quiet. The northern end of Dominica does not provide the sheer, spectacular drop-offs, but offers some magnificent diving.

Grand Savanna, Trumpet Fish Reef, Point Roande, and **Berties Dream** are a few of the more popular sites, Some have permanent moorings installed to protect the coral reef against anchor damage.

Wreck diving does not feature prominently, although there are a number of known wreck sites. One dive shop frequents **The Barge**, a shallow site in 40 feet, used mainly as a night dive due to numerous basket star fish. **The Canefield Tug**, a 55 foot tug lying in 90 feet of water, is another site. She is home for schools of reef fish and features wire coral and hydroids, black margate, and large barracuda, jacks and mackerel also cruise around the site. However, the location is near the mouth of a river and the run-off can cause very low visibility so the site is not always diveable. The newest wreck on Dominica, intentionally sunk as a diving site in July 1990, is ***The Dowess*** located at Anse Bateau. She was cut into several parts so is not an intact wreck. Originally this 80 foot steel hull freighter plied the waters between the islands carrying produce. She now lies in 60 feet of water.

Are there any disadvantages to diving in Dominica? Well, Dominica sometimes experiences heavy rains and the run-offs from the numerous rivers can cause clouding of the sea near to the shore. The protected leeward side of the island suffers a lack of fish life as the traditional way of fishing with wire fish pots has taken a toll on the small reef fish. Attention is being focused on this issue in the hope of finding a solution. However, the spectacular drop-offs encrusted with the huge sponges and black coral trees still provide breathtaking underwater scenery.

The Dominica dive shops are well organized and equipped. The longest established scuba diving shop on the island, Dive Dominica, is a NAUI Dream resort and SSI Resort Member. It is run by well-known diver Derek Perryman, the first qualified diving instructor on the island, and his attractive wife, Ginette. Dive Dominica is operated in conjunction with Castle Comfort Diving Lodge and ten cozy rooms are run with a personal touch (complete with local home-cooking) by Derek's mother. Located by the dive shop, on the doorstep of the sea, the decor is marine-related.

There are two additional shops on the island, Dominica Dive resort which opened in 1988, and Castaways Water Sports and Dive Centre which opened in February 1990.

Dominica Dive Resort, run by Fitzroy Armour, has a dive shop at Anchorage Hotel, and a second at Portsmouth Beach Hotel.

Castaway Water Sports and Dive Centre, located at Castaways Hotel on the water front, is operated by Germans Gunther Glatz and Berthold Blaschek. Their operation is geared towards a European market, with equipment being metric and certifications offered being CMAS or VDTL, a German qualification. In addition to scuba diving, certificates and full training courses are given in windsurfing and sun fish sailing.

Not everyone wants to visit a Caribbean island that has few white sand beaches, no casinos, no duty-free shops and no glittering night life. Dominica appeals to people who want to immerse themselves in its lush mountain jungles- botanists, bird-watchers, nature-lovers, hikers and climbers. Adventuresome scuba divers come to seek unknown diving destinations. Dominica draws explorers who know there aren't too many places like this one left on Earth.

> **Dominica does not depend on super-highways, casinos and towering hotels. The lack of such "improvements" is why the reef life still abounds, especially when compared to nearby islands. The rush of rivers still drowns out traffic noise on the island roads, and the scent of fresh pungent lime is still stronger than exhaust fumes.**

And then there are the Dominicans, a warm friendly people, who are filled with pride for their beautiful island. They know they have something special that has slipped away from many of the other surrounding islands, and they are happy and proud to share it with their visitors. These things help keep this island the choice for the adventure diver who wants to escape the "realities" of tourism a while longer, and explore the unexplored.

HONDURAS
ROATAN
by Ron Streeter Photos by Louise Seddon and Ron Streeter

Roatan and the Bay Islands are magnificent tropical islands in the Caribbean Sea off the coast of Honduras. World renowned for their spectacular coral reefs, these islands contain a great diversity of plant life. Their individual rich cultural histories dates back to the ancient and highly advanced Mayan Civilization. Today the islands are blessed with a distinct mixture of cultures, customs, and traditions.

> **In the western Caribbean Sea about thirty miles north of Honduras, lies Roatan, about 49 square miles. Roatan rests on the Bonacca Ridge, an undersea extension of a mainland mountain range that rises above the Bartlett Trough.**

The tropical island temperature hovers between 77 and 84 degrees F. The annual rainfall exceeds 72" per year. The major population centers are Coxen Hole, French Harbor, and Oak Ridge. Roatan is the only island with an extensive road and communication system.

The history of the Bay Islands has created a cultural legacy as richly varied as the landscape. At least nine cultural groups have occupied Roatan. Columbus first arrived on his fourth voyage to the New World between 1502 and 1504. Over the next century, Bay Islanders were subjected to Spanish slave raids. They were put to work in gold mines, and later used for farm labor. Spanish olive jars are to this day frequently found in archaeological sites as well as by divers in the sea. Currency of the day was small knives, copper hatchets, obsidian-toothed swords, copper beads, crucibles for smelting, maize beer, and cacao beans. In 1683 the English attempted to establish an agricultural colony on Roatan, challenging Spanish rule. Pirate leaders, Morgan, Morris, Jackson, Sharp, and others occupied the islands at various times before British military occupation in 1742. Some believe that the treasure from Morgan's 1671 raid on Panama is buried somewhere on Roatan. Fort Key, offshore from Port Royal, shows evidence of the British military occupation. Fort George was built in the mid 1700's. The British signed a treaty with Spain and vacated Roatan in 1752. The first permanent settlers on the Bay Islands were the Black Caribs, a mixture of the island Carib Indians and transplanted Africans from Saint Vincent Island. They were forcibly moved to Roatan in 1797. Many left for Trujillo on the mainland but those remaining settled Punta Gorda. In 1989 when I was in Punta Gorda, the native people lived as they did in the late 1700's. Since then, electricity has become a normal part of life. White Cayman Islanders founded many of the settlements in Coxen Hole beginning in the 1830s. Emancipated slaves from the Cayman Islands followed shortly thereafter. Mid-century Great Britain annexed the Bay Islands as a colony. However, the United States helped force the British to cede the Islands to Honduras.

Seafaring has traditionally provided most of the income. The lack of subsistence agriculture and the presence of grocery shops in every village indicates the dependence on income remitted from the merchant marines, tourism and fishing to purchase food. Immigrants from the mainland have the advantage of jobs in the fishing industry. This influx of new immigrants adds greater diversity to an already rich cultural landscape.

Mangrove forests provide a vital service by protecting the coast from hurricane and storm damage. Several varieties of delicious fruit trees grow along the beach including coco plums and sea grapes. Hundreds of flowering plants have been recorded in the Bay Islands by botanist Cyril Nelson of the National University.

Invertebrates are the most abundant forms of life. Beetles and termites, locally called wood lice, feed on rotting wood and recycle vital nutrients to living plants. Bees play an important role in pollinating plants, including agricultural crops. However, after pollinating the flowers, the males harvest the sweet orchid scent to use like cologne to attract female bees. Most of the thirty-six species of reptiles and amphibians found here came from the mainland. Scientists have a variety of theories why this is so: Some animals may have been stowaways on ships, others may have been transported by birds, and many may have originally floated over on pieces of vegetation or small rafts of mangroves from the mainland. 120 species of birds are found in the Bay Islands, about one third are residents that live and nest here. The remainder are migratory species that pass through the islands or remain for a short period during winter. Only about a dozen mammal species inhabit the Bay Islands, a third of these are bats. The various bat species are adapted for dining on a specific menu. They carry out much of the important ecological work on island. The nectar-feeding bats pollinate flowers, and other economically important plants.

The Bay Islands are home to hundreds of different fish including most of those found anywhere in the Caribbean. Reef fish of Honduras are protected by law. No spearing or collecting, or disturbing their spawning activities.

When diving Roatan, the term "world class" is no exaggeration. The island is bordered by a healthy and extensive barrier reef with lagoons, and the entire range of deep and shallow reef types can be found here.

Hard coral, soft coral, sponge, fish, invertebrates, whatever your pleasure. Walls start between twenty to forty feet and there are 100-foot-plus wall dives off the beach.

I have done over 100 dives here in the past couple of years. On the Island of Roatan, you can find a dive resort tailored to your personal requirements.

Maya culture flourished in the city of Copan from approximately 200 AD to 900 AD 822 is the last carved record. By 1200 AD, the Maya Culture as known in Copan had vanished. The disappearance of the Mayan metropolis has been attributed to overpopulation, deforestation and war. The local people of the town Copan display their Maya culture when they smile at you.

Coco View offers diving to the hard core responsible diver that is unsurpassed by any other place I have been. They test your stamina and your computer. The gear room opens at 5 a.m. and closes at 12:00 midnight. A typical dive day at Coca View consists of 5 a.m. beach, wall, or wreck after breakfast, boat dive, drop off dive, lunch, boat dive, drop off dive, dinner, night beach wall or wreck dive. If you can keep this schedule for six days, you may be a candidate for dive buddy to my partner Louise. If you're not an experienced diver, or you are not sure of yourself, Cliff and/or any one on his staff will be happy to help you. You can get certified, or upgrade your certification, or do specials. If you would like to sleep in, read a book, our just be a beach bum, that's OK too. Island tours are available any time. Play ping pong, kayak, or teach one of the parrots a few new words.

A small fishing village on the southeast end of the island is the home of ***Reef House***. Water taxi is the means of transportation. Beach wall dives, boat dives drop off dives, night beach wall dives are available. A new boathouse dock, and dive shop have been constructed. There are several small restaurants within easy walking distance. Instruction is available along with kayaking, sunbathing, or just taking it easy. Good food and drink are served in the dining room and the bar.

Fantasy Island is a very upscale resort catering to heads of state, sales meetings, small conventions, honeymooners., and just plain vacationers. Here you will find diving, jet skiing, sun bathing, tennis, TV, air- conditioned rooms, and elegant dining. Native dancers accompanied by their own band using primitive instruments perform one night during the week. Fantasy Island has diving on both sides of the island. Fantasy Island is located on a key off the coast of Roatan connected by a modern bridge. All the amenities found at most resorts in the world are at Fantasy Island.

Roatan Beach Resort in its former life (a very short time ago) was an elegant estate. The mansion has been converted to a hotel. The dining room and the kitchen are in the center or main part of the house, with the rooms in wings on either side. The dining room is about three stories above the beach. At the east end of the dining room there is a two-story high fireplace made from native stone. The opposite end overlooks the balcony dining area. That is where breakfast is served, or you might enjoy a before-dinner cocktail and watch the sun set over the ocean. There are four rooms in a newly constructed guest house between the mansion and the beach. Sand beaches with palm trees and other tropical plants and trees are beautifully maintained. Some parrots freely roaming the grounds finish the tropical setting. Diving headquarters are located on the beach in a newly-built dive shop with a gear storage and rinse area. On the shore there is a dock where a 20-passenger dive boat is berthed. Above the dock is a sitting area for sunbathing, watching sun sets or relaxing. The dive boat goes out twice a day to excellent dive sites.

Sueno Del Mar is located in the town of West End. The resort is relativity new, very conveniently laid out, with excellent management. The rooms are large enough to house four photographers and all their equipment. Now that's big! Nicely appointed with tables and chairs in adequate supply, and ceiling fans. The rooms are fantastic, as is the diving. Crews are locals and very proud of their ability to show you nature's finest. The restaurant and bar are located in the center of the resort. The local business people gather for morning coffee and it seems to be the restaurant of local choice. Diving is fantastic here as is the staff. Volley ball, horseback riding, a walking tour of the town, beachcombing, and sunbathing, are a few of your options if you need a rest from diving.

Anthony's Key is for the diver who wants to be at a tropical dive location, but just can't be without pizza and ice cream. Anthony's Key is the largest dive resort on Roatan. The offices, dining room, bar, dive headquarters, dive boats, dolphin research center, hyperbolic treatment facility and more are nestled into the side of the hill at waters edge, festooned with tropical trees and plants, while the cabins are located on the key just off the mainland. Transportation to and from the key is by boat 24 hours a day. The grounds are manicured daily and the rooms are beautifully kept with a fantastic tropical decor. The view of the sunset from our room was second to none. Several different dolphin experiences are available, in fact, a dolphin specialty is offered along with all other types of certifications; PADI, NAUI, and PDIC. Happy Hour, and live music is a nightly occurrence, which is a nice way to end the day if you're not planing a night dive. The Museum at Anthony's Key Resort displays a spectacular assortment of artifacts, and for the "shop till you drop" diver, the gift shopping is the finest on island: many fine clothes and jewelry items in stock, plus sweats, tee shirts, shorts, jackets and swimsuits.

Wreck of The Prince Albert by Louise Seddon

Be it simple or elegant, whatever your tastes in accommodations and diving styles are, they can be found on Roatan. For a spectacular dive vacation, simply find the resort that suits your lifestyle best...then start packing!

In Memorium
Louise Seddon
1950-1994

In March of 1994 Louise Seddon became suddenly ill and passed away in a tiny hospital in her beloved Roatan. She was on a diving/photography excursion, of course.

Born in Murphysboro, Tennessee, Louise chose to become an educator; her sister, Rae, went on to become a doctor and an astronaut.

Teaching mathematics since the eighties at Cooper City High School in South Florida. Louise would spend weekends working as a divemaster on a charter dive boat. She has guided thousands of divers over the reefs and wrecks of all of South Florida. Still her love was Roatan.

In December of 1993, she logged dive number 2,000.

Perhaps the biggest tragedy of this event is the "why" of Louise Seddon's dying. Medivac aircraft were poised in Miami and Mexico to fly in and transport Louise to modern facilities but could not even leave the ground. Although the airport in Roatan is classified as "international", it has no runway lights. Louise died in the night waiting for the plane that couldn't come.

To the thousands of high school students and divers alike who had the chance to know this lady, the world is a sadder place. Gentle, yet feisty; unassuming, unpretentious, and never wanting anyone to mourn her passing, Louise was cremated, and her ashes scattered over a reef in the Atlantic.

Perhaps, now, we all have a chance to dive with her.

Editor's Note:
  Contact Bill Roe, Florida Scuba News, 305-943-8989 to give to the fund for Roatan runway lights.

Valentine Bouquet by Louise Seddon

MARTINIQUE

Nancy L. Marrapese is a Sports writer for the Boston Globe and has covered the Boston Bruins beat for the past six Seasons. She has been diving for the past six years and has done all of her diving off Grand Cayman island with the exception of one dive – a mid-July experiment off a beach in Nahant, Massachusetts a couple of years ago.

"I'll spend nine months a year in hockey rinks," she said, "And I've never before come close to being as cold as I was that day."

My first impression of Martinique was 'What took me so long to come here?' It's absolutely stunning, both above the sea and below. Whether it's the bustling capital of Fort de France or the tranquil St. Anne an the Southwest Coast or the quaint St. Pierre on the Northwest Coast, there is plenty to see in Martinique and probably not enough time to see all of it in one trip.

The island is a region of France, a level to which it was elevated in 1974 after being a Department of France for the previous 28 years. Originally discovered by Columbus in 1502, it was claimed by France 133 years later and in 1674, was annexed. France and Britain battled for the rights to the island until 1815 when it was restored to France.

141

The island is 50 miles long and 22 miles wide. The population is 359,572.

To vacation in Martinique it's not crucial that you speak French but it would be extremely helpful. I wouldn't hesitate to ask for help from the tourist board there, whom I found to be very friendly, very knowledgeable and interested in promoting tourism on the island.

I stayed at the Squash Hotel, located just outside the capital of Fort de France. It's a very nice place with a fitness center downstairs and a couple of squash courts. It also has a pool and a terrific restaurant called Le Bistro de la Marne. My impressions of it were that it's largely for business people. It's close to the airport and close to the Fort de France businesses. Unlike Anse Caritan and Novotel Diamant, it's not on the beach. For a beach bum on vacation, it's probably not what you want but it's a good place as a home base if you want to explore the island. The rooms are very nice, the staff is efficient and friendly and the food in the restaurant is marvelous.

It's a large island so it would be recommended that you rent a car.

Bannerfish by Ralph Mercier

I opted to take public transportation because I wanted to see what it was like. I enjoyed immersing myself into the everyday lives of the people of Martinique.

On my first day, I took a bus from Fort de France to St. Anne, which is about an hour and 20 minutes with all the stops etc. Anse Caritan is a lovely hotel on the beach. My host for the dive was Benoit Grondin.

We boarded a small motor boat and rode for about 15 minutes to a site known as "Green Garden." It was a good first dive because it had been about nine months since my last dive so I wanted an easy one and this was it. We saw lobster, a white spotted eel, a school of trumpetfish and Benoit yanked a large crab out of a barrel sponge that didn't seem to mind showing off for a minute or two.

The next day, I rode up to Diamond Rock or Rocher du Diamant and went diving with the crew from Novotel Diamant's Le Club de Plongee, hosted by Claude Carvezzal. The dive shop is nestled in a cove around the corner from the rock. Our party was made up of 10 divers, only one of whom spoke English (guess which one?) but we managed to communicate with a variety of hand signals and a lot of nodding.

Rocher du Diamant is truly a magnificent sight. Some in Martinique refer to it as the Caribbean's Gibraltar, which rises 600 feet from the sea.

There is vegetation on it and we watched as flocks of birds came and went from their nests. There were little caves along the side of the rock and it was like nothing I'd ever seen before.

I tried a new piece of equipment which I instantly loved. It was a wetsuit with a built-in BC. All you needed was a weight belt and off you went. It was so unrestricted and without the bulk of the regular jacket, it almost felt as if you'd forgotten a piece of your equipment.

The dive was interesting. There was plenty to see beneath the surface, interesting fish that are indigenous to the area but the rock itself was the most memorable part of the dive.

I've been diving for six years and without a doubt, the most amazing dive I've ever done was my last day in Martinique. I was finally able to rent a car (trust me, make your reservations early and pick up the car early in the morning because the companies, even though there are many, sold out very early).

I drove to Tropicasub Plongee located in St. Pierre. St. Pierre. It has been completely rebuilt because an May 8, 1902, Mt. Pelee erupted and the volcano wiped out the city and its 30,000 inhabitants in a matter of minutes.

Unlike the southern part of Martinique, with its white sandy beaches and gradual drop-offs, the sand on the Northwest Coast is black volcanic sand and the depths drop off more dramatically.

My hosts at Tropicasub were a terrific couple named Lionel and Francoise Lafont. Francoise spoke English and she gave me a tour of St. Pierre by boat and a fascinating history of the area. She also helped me select a dive site.

Naturally I chose the deepest dive on the biggest wreck and it was the most memorable dive of my life.

It was the wreck of the *Roraima*, a victim of the volcano. The site was only a five-minute boat ride from the shop. Francoise stayed up an board while Lionel and I descended.

We hit the stern at 140 feet, which is a very deep dive, but Lionel, as all the dive shops I'd dived with on the trip, was very safety conscious. The *Roraima* is unbelievable. It's 120 meters long by 20 meters wide and 25 meters high. It's upright and intact and had a very eerie feeling to it as we explored from stern to bow. We went into the machine room and looked around. It was remarkable how well preserved it was. The other wrecks I'd been diving on were either much smaller or they weren't intact. None of them had been in this deep water and that part was a little bit scary but very exciting too. I didn't experience any fear or discomfort. Lionel was diving with two tanks and we had another at our safety stop area so that all was accounted for. It was obvious Lionel had a lot of experience diving.

The most astounding part of the dive was when we descended over the top of the bow and down onto the sand in front, with the straight back at the ship and it was the most menacing and overpowering sight. the ship looked huge and as if it was on track to run us over. It was spectacular and took my breath away for a second.

Francoise told me that it was a Quebec ship, carrying half passengers and half cargo when it was sunk by the volcano.

We did three safety stops on the way up, which enabled me also to get a good look at the ship from above.

St. Pierre is beautiful to look at from the water. It's what you would imagine a quaint fishing village to be. I want to venture back here someday and would probably spend the bulk of my time here. It's the type of place that would be a perfect setting for writing a book or painting a picture or just sitting and taking it all in. It's a picture postcard kind of place. There are also several other wrecks offshore in St. Pierre and someday I plan to return to explore them all.

Saba

A Tiny Island with Lots of Excitement
Joan Curtis Bourque

Ten years ago I learned to scuba dive. As an artist living in New York City, I decided it was the perfect sport for me; it took me out of the concrete jungle and it gave me plenty of visual excitement. Within three years I found myself on Saba being a dive bum. Two more years, my dive bum buddy and I, my husband, Lou, opened Sea Saba Dive Center with the hopes of showing off the varried and numerous dive sites we'd found around this five-square mile island in the Eastern Carribean. Five years later, as an escape from the usual we started traveling to our neighboring islands to see something different, a busman's holiday. We found the best part of any diving vacation is returning to our home reefs and our friends with whom we've become so familiar.

Saba Sights by Joan Bourque

Everything on a small island is small scale, therefore very friendly. Sea Saba arranges dive packages with Julianas or Captain's Quarters, each ten rooms surrounded by colorful tropical gardens. Saba's quaint villages are nestled into the side of her lush green Mt. Scenery at 1200' above sea level which means, no mosquitos, breathtaking views, and cool-nights summer or winter. Restaurants and gift shops are a tropical 5 minute stroll away. Taxis and transportation are easily arranged. If you want something special, just ask. A unique way to enjoy Saba's hillside views are from the veranda of your own private cottage. Buy fresh lobster or fish and have a great barbeque.

The Saba Marine Park had 30 permanent moorings in place, which translates to no anchor, diving, or fishing damage. Our dive sites are as varied as they are rich in marine life. Our most praised sites are the underwater pinnacles; seamounts that rise up to 80' below the surface from over a thousand foot depth only a half mile offshore. Lot's of drama only a stone's throw away. These habitats are far enough out to be fed by healthy open ocean currents. Not only delicate brilliant corals but awesome pelagic life nearby. We always see big Nassau groupers, sparkling yellow tail snappers, metallic queen triggers, and quickly darting black jacks. Giant clusters of plump orange and yellow sponges help camouflage out often seen clever frogfish. All guides are instructors and very experienced in showing you around **Twilight Zone, Outer Limits,** and **Shark Shoals**.

For the best in a multi-level dive, **Diamond Rock** offers a 360° wall dive from the surface to 80'. Hundreds of rubbery looking Carribean anemones dance to the ocean's rhythm all around this pinnacle. Stingrays nap lazily in the sand bottom. Large schools of horse-eye jacks and big-eyes keep watch while blue tangs and rock beauties follow the divers everywhere.

Tent Wall Deep and **Tent Reef Shallow** are home to nearly every shape, size, or color of sponge. For the photographer it creates a tapestry of textures and patterns. Hawksbill turtles, garden eels, scorpionfish, and peacock flounders are just a few of the characters living there.

Sea Saba's surface interval is usually spent in a quiet cove called Torrens Point. Twenty feet below, coral and fish life delight snorkelers as they cool-off in between dives. Sea Saba's dive guides can identify every specie of fish or coral you can find. Apres dive contests usually include "name that fish."

Saba Poster by Joan Bourque

Your dive package will have a free day, use it wisely. There are trails from easy to a little strenuous. The most spectacular is to the top of Mt. Scenery, nearly 3,000 feet above sea level. Stone steps lead the way through tree ferns, wild orchids, heliconias, and misty clouds into a rain forest. Overlook the village from 1800 feet above. A walk past local houses usually comes with an invitation to sample Saba Spice, a homemade liquor and a chance to look at their delicate handicrafts of lacework and crochet souvenirs.

A visit to Saba immediately relaxes you. Two dives a day, lunch and a poolside nap leaves you rested for an evening of quiet conversation or lively dancing, whichever you prefer.

SCUBA AND SNORKELING FACILITIES QUESTIONNAIRE

NAME **Sea Saba Dive Center**
ADDRESS **P.O. Box 530 windwardside**
Saba, Netherlands Antilles
CONTACT **Joan Bourque**
TITLE **Owner**
TELEPHONE **011-599-46-2246**   FAX **011-599-46-2362**

CAPITAL: **The Bottom**   GOVERNMENT: **Dutch**
POPULATION: **1200**   LANGUAGE: **English**
CURRENCY: **N.A. Floins/U.S. Accepted**   ELECTRICITY: **110v**
AIRLINES: Winair via American SXM   DEPARTURE TAX? **$5.00 U.S.**
NEED VISA/PASSPORT?   YES   NO x   PROOF OF CITIZENSHIP?   YES x   NO

YOUR FACILITY IS CLASSIFIED AS: SCUBA CENTER x   RESORT
BUSINESS HOURS: 8 a.m. - 5:00 p.m.
CERTIFYING AGENCIES: **PADI**
LOG BOOK REQUIRED?   YES   NO x
EQUIPMENT: SALES x   RENTALS x   AIR FILLS x
PRIMARY LINE OF EQUIPMENT: **Sherwood**
PHOTOGRAPHIC EQUIPMENT: SALES   RENTALS   LAB x

CHARTER/DIVE BOAT AVAILABLE?   YES x   NO   DIVER CAPACITY **22**
COAST GUARD APPROVED?   YES x   NO   CAPTAIN LICENSED?   YES x   NO
SHIP TO SHORE?   YES x   NO   LORAN?   YES   NO x   RADAR?   YES x   NO
DIVE MASTER/INSTRUCTOR ABOARD?   YES   NO   BOTH x

DIVING & SNORKELING: SALT x   FRESH
TYPE OF DIVING/SNORKELING IN AREA: WALL x   BEACH   WRECK   REEF   CAVE   ICE
DIVING/SNORKELING IN YOUR AREA IS BEST SUITED FOR: BEGINNER   INTERMEDIATE x   ADVANCED x
BEST TIME OF YEAR FOR DIVING/SNORKELING: **Everyday**
TEMPERATURE: **NOV-APRIL:**   80 F   **MAY-OCT:**   80 F
VISIBILITY: **DIVING:**   120 FT   **SNORKELING: 100 FT**

PACKAGES AVAILABLE: DIVE x   DIVE STAY x   SNORKEL   SNORKEL-STAY
ACCOMMODATIONS NEARBY: HOTEL x   MOTEL x   HOME RENTALS x
ACCOMMODATION RATES: EXPENSIVE   MODERATE x   INEXPENSIVE
RESTAURANTS NEARBY: EXPENSIVE   MODERATE x   INEXPENSIVE
YOUR AREA IS: REMOTE x   QUIET WITH ACTIVITIES x   LIVELY
LOCAL ACTIVITY/NIGHTLIFE: **Hiking, relaxing**
CAR NEEDED TO EXPLORE AREA?   YES   NO x
DUTY FREE SHOPPING?   YES x   NO

LOCAL EMERGENCY SERVICES   NEAREST HYPERBARIC TREATMENT FACILITY
COASTGUARD: AUTHORITY: **Saba Marine Park**
TELEPHONE: LOCATION: **Saba**
CALLSIGNS: TELEPHONE:

LOCAL DIVING DOCTOR:
NAME: **Dr. Jack Buchanan**
LOCATION: **Hospital, Saba**
TELEPHONE:

St. Lucia

Nancy Marrapese

The island, which was fought over by the French and British, was granted sovereignty in 1979 and is now a member of the British Commonwealth.

I spent my first few days in St. Lucia, staying at a resort called Windjammer Landing Villa Beach Resort, located on the Northwest Coast with a breathtaking view of the sea.

Windjammer is a perfect place for families, honeymooners or people who just want to get away from everything to a place that has everything.

The villa I stayed in, No. 129, was a gorgeous and spacious one-bedroom with an airy feel to it. It was bright, sunny and tastefully decorated. It had a small kitchen with all the amenities and a large, comfortable bedroom with a small but nicely decorated bath.

It had a big balcony that looked out over the water and a view of the hillside. On a clear day, you can't see forever but you can see Martinique.

Resting at Shore by Wendy Canning Church

I went on a site inspection with marketing director Lisa Sampson, a friendly and well-informed member of the staff. We looked at one of the two-bedroom villas which seemed a perfect spot for a family or two couples.

In the main area down the hill on site is a minimart where you can buy groceries or other supplies and there are shuttle buses that run from the lobby up the hills to the villas.

It's great exercise to walk back and forth but it's a little much if you're laden with gear or kids or both. Also, they're great for bringing you down to dinner at night. The restaurants and bars are lovely and have extensive and creative menus.

I spent a day with Hilary Moise, who works with the tourist board. He was my guide and my time with him was an education. He gave me a history of the island and its people and took me to some fascinating sites.

Among the stops were Saline Point, which has a stunning view. We went to Pigeon Island National Park and Fort Rodney. From the top of Fort Rodney, you can see Martinique.

It's interesting talking to the local residents. When asked how I liked Martinique, I said I really did. They all said they found it to be stuckup and elitist, that it didn't cater to tourists. While I agreed that it wasn't as friendly as St. Lucia, I had a wonderful time.

The next day I toured the capital city of Castries and Marigot Bay (where they filmed Dr. Doolittle). The scenery is amazing. When you think of paradise, this has to be it. It's so unspoiled. Windjammer's staff does a good job of making sure its guests are taken care of. It's very isolated and caters more to couples and families than singles.

The only bad thing about St. Lucia is the roads. They are AWFUL. Very windy and full of potholes. It takes forever to get anywhere so most people travel by boat.

I went from Windjammer to Anse Chastanet, which is where the diving is and is known as one of the 100 best resorts in the Carribean. It's located on the Southwest Coast near the Pitons.

It's very easy to see why it's so highly regarded. It's owned by Nick P. Troobitscoff, whose wife Karolin Guler Kolcuoglu is the marketing director. The dive shop is run by Michael and Karyn Allard, a pair of native Californians. All are interesting, remarkable people and great hosts.

There are no phones or TVs in the open-air gazebo-like cottages. This to me is a blessing. There is no air conditioning. Large ceiling fans cool the rooms and the beds are huge and comfortable. Each cottage comes with a mosquito net over the bed but I found I didn't need it, for they are equipped with orange lights, which you leave on through the night and they keep the bugs away.

Anse Chastanet is built along a steep hillside on the north side of Soufriere.

At night, you could hear little else but the small waves lapping against the shore. It's a quiet, lovely place where it's early to bed early to rise. The sunsets are unique. The sky becomes slate blue in varying hues with the colors reflecting off the clouds along the horizon.

The dive shop, which is the only PADI five-star shop on the island, is located on the beach which is a short walk from the cottages.

To get to the cottages from the beach you have to venture up a very steep set of stairs and some more gradual stairs up the hillside after that but it's well worth the walk in both directions.

It's a nice location from which to shore dive and all the dive sites are close by, either by a short swim or boat ride. It's also worthwhile to do a night dive.

One interesting aspect of the diving there is the shortage of angel fish although there are parrotfish everywhere.

Here it's not necessary to dive deep.

Most of the sites are at the 50-60 foot range and the varied types of coral are worth photographing. The dive sites seem to have little wear and tear from divers and the divemasters are dilligent in reminding visitors that it's a marine park and to respect it as one.

If you stay at Anse Chastanet, you must venture to a restaurant called Dasheen, located near the Ladera Resort and is set high in between the Pitons. From the restaurant, you can see a Piton on each side of you, and Jalousie Plantation at the base of the valley leading to the sea. It's an overwhelming sight and the food is sensational.

Another two places worth visiting are the Sulpher Springs and the Botanical Gardens, which are a short ride from Anse Chastanet.

SCUBA AND SNORKELING FACILITIES QUESTIONNAIRE

NAME **Scuba St. Lucia**
ADDRESS **Anse Chastanet Hotel**
P.O. Box 216 Soufriere, St. Lucia
CONTACT **Nick P. Troobitscoff**
TITLE **Managing Director**
TELEPHONE **809-454-735415** FAX TELEX **0398/6370**

CAPITAL: GOVERNMENT:
POPULATION: LANGUAGE:
CURRENCY: ELECTRICITY:
AIRLINES: DEPARTURE TAX?
NEED VISA/PASSPORT? YES NO **x** **Driver's license or birth certificate is sufficient for American citizens.**

YOUR FACILITY IS CLASSIFIED AS: SCUBA CENTER RESORT **x**
BUSINESS HOURS: **Summer 8-6; Winter 8-5**
CERTIFYING AGENCIES: **PADI**
LOG BOOK REQUIRED? YES NO
EQUIPMENT: SALES RENTALS **x** AIR FILLS
PRIMARY LINE OF EQUIPMENT: **ScubaPro BC's, Mares regs for rental**
PHOTOGRAPHIC EQUIPMENT: SALES RENTALS **x** LAB **x**

CHARTER/DIVE BOAT AVAILABLE? YES **x** NO DIVER CAPACITY **Up to 100**
COAST GUARD APPROVED? YES NO **x** CAPTAIN LICENSED? **Not required**
SHIP TO SHORE? **Soon** NO LORAN? YES NO **x** RADAR? YES NO **x**
DIVE MASTER/INSTRUCTOR ABOARD? YES **x** NO BOTH

DIVING & SNORKELING: SALT **x** FRESH
TYPE OF DIVING/SNORKELING IN AREA: WALL **x** BEACH **x** WRECK **x** REEF CAVE **x** ICE
DIVING/SNORKELING IN YOUR AREA IS BEST SUITED FOR: BEGINNER **x** INTERMEDIATE **x** ADVANCED **x**
BEST TIME OF YEAR FOR DIVING/SNORKELING: **All year round**
TEMPERATURE: NOV-APRIL: F MAY-OCT: F
VISIBILITY: DIVING: FT SNORKELING: FT

PACKAGES AVAILABLE: DIVE **x** DIVE STAY **x** SNORKEL SNORKEL-STAY
ACCOMMODATIONS NEARBY: HOTEL **x** MOTEL GAZEBOS **x** HOME RENTALS **Beach units**
ACCOMMODATION RATES: EXPENSIVE MODERATE INEXPENSIVE
RESTAURANTS NEARBY: EXPENSIVE MODERATE INEXPENSIVE
YOUR AREA IS: REMOTE **x** QUIET WITH ACTIVITIES **x** LIVELY
LOCAL ACTIVITY/NIGHTLIFE:
CAR NEEDED TO EXPLORE AREA? YES NO
DUTY FREE SHOPPING? YES NO

LOCAL EMERGENCY SERVICES NEAREST HYPERBARIC TREATMENT FACILITY
COASTGUARD: **Ship "Defender"** AUTHORITY: **Barbados Defense Force**
TELEPHONE: **Vigie Tower 22426** LOCATION: **Barbados**
CALLSIGNS: TELEPHONE: **809-436-6185**
LOCAL DIVING DOCTOR:
NAME:
LOCATION: **St. Jude Hospital, Vieux Rort/Soufriere Casualty**
TELEPHONE: **46041** **809-436-6185**

U.S. Virgin Islands

St. Croix
By Bill Cleveland

I have done hundreds of dives on St. Croix, many serving as Dive Technician with the Aquarius Undersea Habitat program in Salt River.

I also have experience diving on St. Thomas, St. John, and the B.V.I., Saba, Australia's Great Barrier Reef, Lanai-Hawaii, and Cozumel.

Current Profession: Graduate student in concurrent M.B.A./Environmental Management degree program at Duke University.

Personal Introduction: I lived on St. Croix for over four years and really enjoyed the diving opportunities there. I liked diving so much that I got a job that included diving as part of my responsibilities. In addition, by organizing the Swim Around St. Croix, I got to know the entire coastline of the island intimately and have included what I feel are the most rewarding dive experiences. I hope my advice inspires you to experience some great diving.

St. Croix is the largest of the U.S. Virgin Islands. It is located about 100 miles east of Puerto Rico, 1,000 miles from Miami and 1,500 miles from New York. Airline service has increased over the last several years and there are daily flights from many U.S. airports.

The 84 square miles of St. Croix are contained in 23 miles running east-west and a maximum distance of 7 miles north-south. St. Croix is home to two main towns, Christiansted in the north center of the island and Frederiksted in the west. Christiansted is livelier at night and has more shops while Frederiksted is quieter and has more local flavor and better beaches.

St. Croix has a unique history, having been purchased twice, the latest time in 1917 when the U.S. purchased the U.S. Virgin Islands from Denmark.

Blackbar Soldierfish congregate on the East Wall at South River by William E. Cleveland

The Danes had purchased St. Croix from the French in 1733 and soon thereafter began sugar cultivation on the island. Plantation ruins can still be found throughout the island, and I've visited 119 windmill ruins and know at least 30 more were built between 1745 and 1845, the days when sugar was king. If you have an interest in history, don't miss the museum at Estate Whim along Centerline Road near Frederiksted where a plantation Great House and sugar factory have been authentically restored and furnished with period furniture.

If you are interested in shopping, the Virgin Islands has a generous duty free arrangement. The best buys are generally found on liquor and jewelry. If you would like to take home some local mahogany or other wooden pieces, the L.E.A.P. (better known as the 'Mahogany Shop') on Mahogany Road near Frederiksted is the place to look.

There are numerous types of hotels on St. Croix and certainly one for everyone's liking. The St. Croix Hotel Association can assist with particulars, tel. (809) 773-7117. There are a number of hotels in both Christiansted and Frederiksted which welcome divers as well as a number of full service resorts on St. Croix. If you want to stay close to the best beach diving, try the Cane Bay Reef Club (809) 778-2966 or the Waves at Cane Bay (809) 778-1805. If you are traveling with a group, renting a condominium or a private home may be most cost effective. Try Island Villas (809) 773-8821.

There are many dive operators who will both rent equipment and serve as dive guides. These operators are located in Christiansted, Frederiksted, along the north shore, and at the major marinas such as Salt River and Green Kay. I have never had a problem with any of the current operators in terms of safety and feel that all of them act professionally.

St. Croix has a lot of very accessible diving. Many dives are beach dives, especially in the northwest portion of the island. There are also plenty of great boat dives.

A panoramic view of St. Croix's north west shore looking past Davis Bay to Cane Bay by William E. Cleveland

A mooring system has recently been set up at the most popular dive sites to protect the local reefs. Great snorkeling is also found, especially in the north west portion of the island. Water temperatures generally stay around 80 degrees Fahrenheit.

With regard to personal safety in this American Paradise, act with the same precautions that you would when you visit any metropolitan area. In other words, don't leave your valuables on the beach for an afternoon's dive and expect them to be there when you return.

SALT RIVER CANYON:

Salt River is located on the north shore of St. Croix several miles east of Christiansted and is the home of the latest National Park, encompassing over 600 acres of land and sea.

Salt River is special not only for the natural beauty and ecological importance of both the underwater canyon and the land surrounding the bay but also for the fact that Salt River is the only location under the U.S. Flag where Christopher Columbus was known to land (on his second New World voyage on November 14, 1493).

The canyon has two walls both of which are great dives for any experience level. Visibility is over 50 feet, although unusually heavy rains can make for murky conditions, especially on the West Wall. The West Wall tops out in about 25 feet and descends to the sandy canyon floor at over 100 feet. The West Wall features spectacular geological formations as coral has formed towering pinnacles along the wall's edge which create numerous tunnels and mini-canyons to explore. All the nooks and crannies provide a home for plenty of lobsters and eels and plenty of sleeping space at night for the 40+ pound parrot fish living around the canyon. In addition, a pod of bottle nose dolphin are known to regularly frequent the Canyon, and there is one female that really enjoys playing tag, staying just beyond arm's reach.

The East Wall, like the West Wall, tops out at about 25 feet. I've always preferred to dive the East Wall in the afternoon as the sun beautifully illuminates the numerous gorgonians that cover the entire wall. There are often turtles and always barracuda on the East Wall as well as plenty of fish of all types, especially angel fish.

If you travel to St. Croix in the winter months, you may be fortunate enough to swim with some of the Humpback whales which nurse their newborn calves and have been seen near Salt River.

Salt River is best accessed by boat, as it is a long swim from shore. Depending on your schedule, you may like to take one of the several dive operators from Christiansted and stop at another site either to or from the canyon. If time is a concern, Anchor Dive (809) 778-1522 is located in Salt River Bay, a 10 minute boat ride from the spectacular canyon.

There is great beach diving to be found along St. Croix's north shore between Cane Bay and Davis Bay. Visibility is consistently over 60 feet. Cane Bay features a beautiful sand beach and is a great site for snorkelers as well as both beginner and advanced divers. A short distance from shore, a garden-like reef is found in about 20-25 feet. Just to the north of the extensive gardens, the wall drops off into vast blueness. The wall is covered by a mature and healthy spur and groove coral formation. In the many sandy grooves, over a dozen antique anchors can be found, relics of the days when sugar waved on the hillsides.

The dive at **Northstar**, just west of Cane Bay, is one of my favorite dives on St Croix. This dive is recommended for more experienced divers, as the beach entry can be tricky if the surf is up. The wall comes closest to shore at Northstar, just north of the lovely garden reef in about 20-25 feet. Invariably there are green turtles at the top of the wall. Over the edge of the wall, there is a vertical drop of over 40 feet. At the small ledge at 65 feet, an antique anchor lies outside a small cave which is the nursery for a school of adolescent squid, each one no larger than your pinkie finger.

To enjoy the dives along the north shore, you can take the boat ride from Christiansted or rent equipment from some of the nearby shops such as Cane Bay Dive Shop (809)773-9913 or Blue Dolphin Divers (809) 773-8034.

Frederiksted offers the greatest variety of dive experiences on St. Croix. In addition to the fantastic reef and gentle wall dives to be found along the coast, Frederiksted also is home to the famous **Frederiksted Pier** as well as the **Wrecks at Butlers Bay**. The reef diving in Frederiksted is spectacular for beginner divers as well as advanced divers. The conditions are almost always calm here and the visibility is consistently 60 feet or more.

> **The Frederiksted Pier is the best and most unique night dive site I have ever experienced. The quarter mile long pier has dozens of vertical piles which are covered with sponges and soft corals.**

As Frederiksted is a roadstead and not a harbor, the Pier provides the most dramatic relief along the coastline and attracts a tremendous amount of marine life. The Pier is famous for its microfauna such as seahorses, crabs, and mollusks and also for the creatures that regularly hang around at night such as octopus and eel. But it is the chance meeting that really make the Pier special. I have seen porcupine fish here over 3 feet long and even larger turtles. While diving the pier, be sure to orient yourself carefully as it is easy to get turned around while circling the pilings.

One last dive that deserves mention is the fish feed on **Long Reef** run by Dive Experience (809) 773-3307. This dive is off a wrecked barge in about 80 feet. Visibility is not much of a factor here as the fish feeding is done in a restricted area at one end of the barge. The great assembly of fish and eels make for a photographers dream as marine life swarms around and will even eat out of your hand. If you are prone to getting cold, you may think about a wet suit here as you generally stay in the same general area for the 35 minute dive.

St. John,
Wendy Canning Church

ABOUT THE PHOTOGRAPHER

In 1978, Steve Simonsen helped open the first dive shop in Boulder, Colorado. In 1979, he became a NAUI instructor. He first began using a Nikonos II in Cozumel, Mexico. Steve traveled to exotic destinations such as Moorea in French Polynesia, the Red Sea in Egypt, Martinique in the French West Indies, Cancun and Playa Blanca in Mexico.

Couple diving in coral by Steve Simonsen

Steve and his new family moved half way around the world to Micronesia in the Western Pacific where he started his current business entitled Marine Scenes. Lured back to the natural beauty of St. John's National Park, Steve now bases operations at Low Key Watersports. He can be found most days on the colorful reefs surrounding St. John photographing divers and marine life.

Take one island and add sun year round. Place it in close proximity to mainland U.S., but far enough away from the bustling crowds that one must land in St. Thomas, then take a ferry (runs on the hour every hour). Throw in topography that is comprised of beautiful flora and fauna (2/3 is a national park!). Then add a nice little downtown center, Cruz Bay, which is home to a variety of restaurants, small boutiques and a lot of nightlife. Sprinkle two five star hotels, a small group of comfortable condominium rentals and exquisite, understated villas. Place all ingredients in a 21 square mile area and garnish with some of the clearest and cleanest waters found anywhere and ... voila! vous avez St. John, la belle virgin.

We booked the forever elegant and tranquil Caneel Bay for our stay on St. John. It is situated on its own 170 acre peninsula with the lush green hills of the National Park as its backdrop. Please see our Honeymoon Section for more details.

On a previous visit, five months prior, my buddy and I stayed at Gallows Point. We were introduced to Gallows Point by an advertisement in the newspaper. We chose it because the ad mentioned a dive/stay package. On further inquiry we found out that the complex was only a short walk from town and only five minutes away on foot from the dive shop.

Gallows Point is a condominium complex that sits on the edge of the Cruz Bay and is made up of detached villas, two in each group, separated from the other groups by vegetation. The villa condos are lovely, furnished in native rattan and Caribbean fabrics. The kitchens are complete and the bathrooms are large. Each villa also has a balcony. There is a small pool, and you can swim and snorkel from the beach. There is also a restaurant on the premises called Ellington's.

We dove each day with Low Key Watersports. Low Key is probably one of the most organized and safety conscious centers we have come across. They offer a variety of dive sites. Owners Bob Shinners and Ann Marie Estes really take a hands on approach. Experienced divers are taken out in the morning. This was wonderful for us because it gave us time to explore the island and its secluded beaches in the afternoon for sunbathing and snorkeling. The snorkeling at these hideaways and at Gallows Point is terrific. Be careful, however, not to snorkel alone. You will be amazed at the variety and size of fish that you will encounter in shallow waters.

Each day Low Key took us to a new and interesting site. Jimbo, our guide on many dives, was a wealth of information. Here is just a sampling of what St. John has to offer:

Carval Rock: A reef dive good for the novice diver. Not recommended for snorkeling. On the top side there are two giant rocks and a bird nesting area.

> **Below you will find extensive marine life, sea fans, gorgonians, sponges, tarpon, angelfish, barracuda, turtles, and large schools of fry fish. The terrain drops off to 70ft where you will find an airplane wreck.**

The average water temperature at this site is 8OF and the average sea conditions vary from flat calm to north swell.

Tunnels at Thatch Key: Another reef dive that is good for novice divers on a calm day. Again, not recommended for snorkeling. The site is located in a bay surrounded by the rocky peninsula area of Thatch Key. Below you will see picturesque archways, large tunnels, and beautiful canyons to swim through. At this spot you will also see angelfish, tarpon, sea fans, hatchet fish, and enormous boulders of coral. The average water temperature at this site is 8OF and there is normally a surge. Not recommended to dive when there is a north swell!

Grass Cay: A reef dive that is good for both novice divers and for snorkeling. The entry is shallow and sandy at 20ft and then leads down to the reef at 30-50ft. Here you will see a lot of sea fans and corals. Heavily populated with coral -sheet, saucer, finger and club. The variety of coral, the small marine life, fire sponges and flamingo tongues make for great macro photography. The average water temperature is 78-82F at this site and the sea conditions are generally calm.

Wreck of the General Rodgers: A wreck dive not recommended for the novice diver and not good for snorkeling. This dive is best suited for the intermediate to advanced diver. The site ranges from 40-60ft, with visibility of 50-80ft. The boat ties onto the wreck's mooring and the divers follow the line down. Gloves are recommended due to possible heavy current. There is an abundance of marine life at this spot-snappers, yellowtail, groupers, jewfish, grunts.

> **The wreck is penetrable and makes a fun photo site! The surrounding topography is painted with sea fans, gorgonians, tube coral and sea rods.**

The average water temperature at this site is 78-82F and the air temperature is on average about 88F. The sea conditions are fairly calm, but occasionally there is a strong current.

Stevens: This is a shallow dive at 20-40ft that is good for both the novice and the snorkeler. The area is interspersed with a variety of beautiful corals: brain, rough star, butterprint brain coral, and fire (or stinging) coral. This site is home to many an angelfish, wrasse, butterfly fish, and grunt. On night dives you can also see lobster and turtles at this spot. There are also lots of sea urchins. The terrain starts off sandy, then gradually moves toward the spectacular coral formations. The sea conditions are calm with very little current.

Congo Cay: This is a reef dive that is good for the novice diver, but not for snorkeling. Good drift dive. The dive site is located north of St. John, west of Carval Rock. There is a bird nesting area at the site with boobies and pelicans. The dive drops off to 70ft and has sandy patches where you will find buried stingrays. There are a few caves in the rock walls for you to explore. Large sea fans, and brilliantly colored sponges and coral make this a beautiful day dive and an incredible night dive! You will also see turtles, barracuda and an occasional manta ray. The average water temperature at this site is 8OF and the air temperature is generally 85F. The sea conditions are flat, with a slight current.

Bob's Bump: A reef dive that is not recommended for either the novice diver or the snorkeler. It is more suited for the intermediate or advanced diver. The reef resembles a large "bump" that juts up to 60ft and is surrounded by sand flats at 75ft. The reef is made up of lots of hard and soft corals that create canyons and mysterious crevices. Large stingrays, lobsters, nurse sharks, jacks and snapper call this site home. The sea conditions are generally calm, but there are occasionally swells.

Do rent a car for at least one day in order to tour the island.

Delberts Hill's Jeep Rental is competitively priced. For more information, you can contact them at (809)776-6637 or 1-800-537-6238. If you are hikers, the trails at the National Park are superb and they have wonderful guides.

Be sure to have dinner at the **Paradiso** restaurant at Mongoose Junction. Its Northern Italian cuisine is exceptional. It is pricey, but worth it! For more information call (809) 776-8806. For steaks and fish try **Jumby's**. If you crave a pizza, **Paradise Pizza** is your best bet.

Pusser's, located in **Wharfside Village**, (the same complex where Low Key Watersports is located), is great fun for lunch or for a drink. The Village is open daily. It also has a Sports Bar. The Wharfside Village boutiques will tempt anyone with nautical interests.

Blue Carib Gems is a must see. They made me a beautiful pair of earrings. Stop in and see their variety of jewelry made of black coral as well as different minerals and stones.

The Cruzan Rum is wonderful. If you do not drink, it is worth it to bring some home for gifts (check duty free limit at time of purchase). You will need your passport if you are not a U.S. citizen or if you are a U.S. citizen and plan to visit the nearby British Virgin Islands. They can be reached by ferry and are equally as beautiful and interesting.

For more information or to book Gallows Point contact. Diver's Exchange International, 37 West Cedar Street, Boston, MA 02114-3303; or telephone (617) 723-7134; facsimile (617) 227-8145.

SCUBA AND SNORKELING FACILITIES QUESTIONNAIRE

NAME   **Low Key Watersports, Inc.**
ADDRESS   **P.O. Box 431**
             St. John, USVI 00831
CONTACT   **Ann Marie Estes**
TITLE   **Owner**
TELEPHONE   **809-776-7048**   FAX   **809-776-6042**

CAPITAL: GOVERNMENT: **U.S.A.**
POPULATION: **4,000**   LANGUAGE: **English**
CURRENCY: **U.S. $**   ELECTRICITY:
AIRLINES: **American/Delta**   DEPARTURE TAX?
NEED VISA/PASSPORT?   YES   NO **x**   PROOF OF CITIZENSHIP?   YES   NO **x**

YOUR FACILITY IS CLASSIFIED AS: SCUBA CENTER **x**   RESORT
BUSINESS HOURS: **0800 - 1800 Mon-Sun**
CERTIFYING AGENCIES: **PADI**
LOG BOOK REQUIRED?   YES **x**   NO
EQUIPMENT: SALES **x**   RENTALS **x**   AIR FILLS **x**
PRIMARY LINE OF EQUIPMENT: **Sherwood, US Divers, Dacor**
PHOTOGRAPHIC EQUIPMENT: SALES **x**   RENTALS **x**   LAB **x**

CHARTER/DIVE BOAT AVAILABLE?   YES **x**   NO   DIVER CAPACITY   **6**
COAST GUARD APPROVED?   YES   NO **x**   CAPTAIN LICENSED?   YES   NO
SHIP TO SHORE?   YES **x**   NO   LORAN?   YES   NO   RADAR?   YES   NO
DIVE MASTER/INSTRUCTOR ABOARD?   YES **x**   NO   BOTH

DIVING & SNORKELING: SALT **x**   FRESH
TYPE OF DIVING/SNORKELING IN AREA: WALL   BEACH   WRECK **x**   REEF   CAVE   ICE
DIVING/SNORKELING IN YOUR AREA IS BEST SUITED FOR: BEGINNER **x**   INTERMEDIATE **x**   ADVANCED
BEST TIME OF YEAR FOR DIVING/SNORKELING: **Summer - April - September**
TEMPERATURE: **NOV-APRIL:**   **78**   **F**   **MAY-OCT:**   **82**   **F**
VISIBILITY: **DIVING:**   **70**   **FT**   **SNORKELING:**   **30 FT**

PACKAGES AVAILABLE: DIVE **x**   DIVE STAY   SNORKEL   SNORKEL-STAY
ACCOMMODATIONS NEARBY: HOTEL **x**   MOTEL   HOME RENTALS **x**
ACCOMMODATION RATES: EXPENSIVE **x**   MODERATE **x**   INEXPENSIVE **x**
RESTAURANTS NEARBY: EXPENSIVE **x**   MODERATE **x**   INEXPENSIVE **x**
YOUR AREA IS: REMOTE   QUIET WITH ACTIVITIES **x**   LIVELY
LOCAL ACTIVITY/NIGHTLIFE:
CAR NEEDED TO EXPLORE AREA?   YES   NO **x**
DUTY FREE SHOPPING?   YES **x**   NO

LOCAL EMERGENCY SERVICES   NEAREST HYPERBARIC TREATMENT FACILITY
COASTGUARD: **St. Thomas/Waterfront**   AUTHORITY: **Dr. Boaz**
TELEPHONE: **809-776-3497**   LOCATION: **St. Thomas, USVI**
CALLSIGNS: TELEPHONE:

LOCAL DIVING DOCTOR:
NAME: **Dr. Boaz**
LOCATION: **St. Thomas, USVI**
TELEPHONE: **809-776-4605**

St. Thomas

Raymond Elman is an artist and writer living in Truro, Massachusetts on Cape Cod, and Lexington, MA near Boston. His has written travel pieces for various newspapers and magazines, and is the author of A Critical Guide to Cross Country Ski Areas, *published by Viking/Penguin, He has also published and edited several art magazines.*

Mr. Elman's paintings, prints, and drawings have been widely exhibited, beginning with his first exhibit in Provincetown in 1971. His work hangs in many U.S. embassies around the world, and in several museums.

He is also deeply involved with computer graphics and multimedia mediums, and currently serves as Director of Creative Services for Coopers & Lybrand.

When my wife Lee and I first announced that we were thinking about spending a week on St. Thomas (primarily because it was the only destination we could easily attain using our frequent flyer mileage), we were forced into second-guessing ourselves by the barrage of negative comments we heard from our friends. "Why St. Thomas?" they all asked. "It's crime ridden - it's like a U.S. suburb - it's like Miami Beach - it's overcrowded." Reluctant to admit that we had selected this particular slice of the Caribbean because we were short of disposable funds, we began to apologize for our choice even before we were asked the "why?" word. We whispered "St. Thomas" with an apologetic shrug of our shoulders, the way some people say the word "cancer".

My father used to admonish me whenever I said I hated something or someone, "If you look for the bad, you'll always find it, but if you look for the good, you'll find that too — and maybe you won't notice the bad." My travel agent will confirm how hard I looked for the good in St. Thomas - she said that my file of information requests was second only to a certain news producer at a local TV station. But my research and her patience were well rewarded.

We stayed at **Secret Harbour Beach Resort**, the only hostelry on St. Thomas that could match all of our requirements for a week in the tropics, which included: a one bedroom condominium smack on a beautiful secluded crescent of beach with gently lapping turquoise waters, abundant marine life for interesting snorkeling (we saw eagle rays, lobsters, squid, and the usual assortment of reef fish right in our little cove), tennis courts, an open air restaurant overlooking the water, a non-mega-resort ambiance, and a five star PADI dive center on the premises.

In 1917, the United States purchased St. Thomas, St, Croix, and St. John, the islands known today as the U.S. Virgin Islands, for the exorbitant sum of $25 million. What was the attraction? A slice of paradise? Commerce?

The islands were purchased to protect the Panama Canal from marauding German U-boats.

Since then, the islands have acquired U.S. territorial status, providing U.S. Virgin Islanders with all the rights of U.S. citizens, with the exceptions that they cannot vote for the president of the United States and they do not have representation in the U.S. Congress.

The first person form a northern hemisphere credited with visiting St. Thomas was the ubiquitous Christopher Columbus. He named the islands for St. Ursula and her 11,000 martyred virgins.

In 1666 the Danes began the colonization of St. Thomas, populating plantations with convicts and prostitutes. The Danes eventually prepared a purchase and sale agreement for the United States.

There are many remnants of Danish culture on St. Thomas, including names of towns and street, islanders who still speak Danish, and automobile traffic that travels on the left side of the road.

The U.S. Virgin Islands are approximately 1,100 miles southeast of Miami, and only 60 miles east of Puerto Rico.

American Airlines offers daily non stop flights from New York City to St. Thomas that take less than 4 hours.

Delta flies nonstop daily from Atlanta and/or Orlando.

There is no shortage of rooms on St. Thomas. Most of the better known accommodations are clustered around three areas: Charlotte Amalie, the capital and center of government, duty-free shopping, and cruise ships; Red Hook, the more secluded and fashionable East End of the island and embarkation point for the ferry to St. John and Tortola; and the southeast side of the island, where several mega-resorts are located.

Four Eyed Butterfly Fish by Peter Nesbit

By my standards, however, the only place worthy of our vacation dollars was **Secret Harbour Beach Resort**. Why? There are certainly more luxurious places - the recently opened **Grand Palazzo** aspires to be a resort of the Italian Riviera. There are newer resorts with more facilities - **The Sugar Bay Plantation** has 7 tennis courts including a stadium court, and 3 swimming pools.

> **But Secret Harbour had everything we needed (a dive center, tennis courts, a swimming pool that we never used, decent snorkeling, a fine open air restaurant, cuddled by a non-mega-resort low-key ambiance that made us feel very much at home.**

Another mark in the plus column for Secret Harbour is that it is the closest resort to the best dive site around St. Thomas, **French Cap Cay**. Secret Harbour is located in the East End, 4 minutes from the Red Hook ferries.

When we visit the Caribbean Islands, we prefer to eat native foods. On Providenciales in the Turks & Caicos, we ate conch fresh from the local conch farm in every conceivable con-conch-tion; in Jamaica we tried all sorts of over-salted and jerked dishes; on Tortola we savored rotis. But on St. Thomas it seemed like every restaurant recommended by the guide books and hotel staff featured dishes that I can find in Boston every day of the week. In other words, St. Thomas restaurants tend to cater to mainstream middle-American taste buds.

So our primary consideration for dining on St. Thomas became location - was the restaurant outdoors and on the water, something unattainable in Boston during the winter. By that standard we faced a plethora of choices. Our secondary criteria was distance (a subset of location). Enjoying the relative peace and quiet of the East End, we had no desire to travel 20-40 minutes into the downtown hubbub of Charlotte Amalie.

We enjoyed dining al fresco at the following restaurants:

Located right on the beach overlooking the sea at Secret Harbour Beach Resort, *Tamarind by the Sea* (775-6550) serves an eclectic melange of Caribbean and continental dishes. Our favorite was curried conch. Its decor is restrained Caribbean. It is arguably one of the prettiest restaurants on St. Thomas. *East Coast Grill* (775-1919) serves American style seafood, with an occasional conch fritter tossed in the mix. They are located right in the middle of Red Hook on Route 38, overlooking the harbor. They definitely have found their audience, because they're crowded most nights of the week.

When you pick a name like "For the Birds" (775-6431) your food should be great to compensate for the obvious possibility that the name of your restaurant will be used to describe the quality of your food. I can't say that the combination of Tex/Mex and seafood dishes they serve is great, but their location on Scott Beach near Compass Point is pretty sweet.

The best dive operators on St. Thomas are:

Aqua Action Secret
Harbour Beach Resort
6501 Red Hook Plaza
St, Thomas,, USVI 00802
Phone: (809) 775-6550 ext. 274
(809) 775-6285

Dive In Sapphire
Beach Resort
Route 38, Smith Bay Road
St. Thomas, USVE 00801
Phone: (809) 775-6100

We only went diving with Aqua Action, our choice dictated by location - they were 100 yards from our beach-front patio. Nevertheless, we dove with people staying at other resorts who preferred Aqua Action. One of Aqua Action's principle advantages is that they are the closest dive center to St. Thomas' best dive sites.

The staff of Aqua Action is friendly and dependable. They allowed their patrons to help choose dive sites, and were not married to a tight time schedule. Some of their gear was a little worn, but all was serviceable.

St. Thomas' best dive site is French Cap Cay, located 30-40 minutes south of Secret Harbour Beach.

It's important to dive **French Cap** on a relatively calm day, seas can build quickly at this spot, disturbing visibility and stomachs. **French Cap** is a small hunk of rock and coral, the dive sites closely ringing the cay. Two popular spots are called "**Pinnacles**" and "**North Side**". There is a large variety of coral life at French Cap and the usual variety of reef fish and critters (lobsters and eels). One of the most fun parts of diving **North Side** is an excursion through a short tunnel into the cay's bedrock. The tunnel doglegs to the left into a space with a hole in the roof that allows a light to flood a small cavern.

My second favorite dive sites surrounded neighboring **Capella Island** and **Buck Island**. 15 minutes closer to Secret Harbour., these two small islands lie in calmer waters – on days when **French Cap** is an adventure for the stomach, relatively calm anchorage can be found around **Capella** and **Buck Islands**.

My favorite dive at this site is called **Coral Bowl**. Beginning at about 35 feet, marked by a large old coral encrusted anchor, **Coral Bowl** fans out like an amphitheater, dropping to about 80 feet.

The bowl is loaded with a huge variety of coral. There is also an abundance of fish, though the most exciting life we saw were schools of barracuda.

Another favorite dive in the area is the wreck of the Cartanser Senior. This 190 foot wreck sits in just 35 feet of water off Buck Island and is also a popular snorkeling spot.

A word about **snorkeling** in the immediate vicinity of both St. Thomas and St. John. The coral community in those areas looks sickly, though there is still an exciting variety of marine life to be viewed. Most of the coral appears to be either dying or covered with a fine silt. We heard people blame everything from Hurricane Hugo to destruction of the natural filtration system for fresh water run-off to urinating swimmers.

Nevertheless, while snorkeling we saw more interesting sea creatures than while SCUBA diving. Snorkeling, we saw several sea turtles, large eaglerays, squid and exposed lobster.

OTHER ACTIVITIES

Duty-free shopping is the major league sport on St. Thomas. There are tennis courts at several of the hotels. Golf. Bill Fishing. And, of course, anything that can be done with a sail on warm water can be done here: windsurfing, para-sailing, and sailing.

SCUBA AND SNORKELING FACILITIES QUESTIONNAIRE

NAME **Aqua Action Dive Center**
ADDRESS **6501 Red Hook Plaza, Suite 15**
St. Thomas, USVI 00802
CONTACT **Robert Kreisel**
TITLE **Manager**
TELEPHONE **809-775-6285**   FAX **809-775-1501**

CAPITAL: **Charlotte Amalie**   GOVERNMENT: **U.S. Territory**
POPULATION: **100,000**   LANGUAGE: **English**
CURRENCY: **U.S. $**   ELECTRICITY: **110**
AIRLINES: American/Delta   DEPARTURE TAX? **No**
NEED VISA/PASSPORT?   YES   NO **x**   PROOF OF CITIZENSHIP?   YES **x**   NO

YOUR FACILITY IS CLASSIFIED AS: SCUBA CENTER **x**   RESORT **x**
BUSINESS HOURS: **8:00 - 4:30 daily**
CERTIFYING AGENCIES: **PADI, NAUI**
LOG BOOK REQUIRED?   YES **x**   NO
EQUIPMENT: SALES **x**   RENTALS **x**   AIR FILLS **x**
PRIMARY LINE OF EQUIPMENT: **Sherwood, Scubapro**
PHOTOGRAPHIC EQUIPMENT: SALES   RENTALS **x**   LAB
CHARTER/DIVE BOAT AVAILABLE?   YES **x**   NO   DIVER CAPACITY   **12**
COAST GUARD APPROVED?   YES **x**   NO   CAPTAIN LICENSED?   YES **x**   NO
SHIP TO SHORE?   YES **x**   NO   LORAN?   YES   NO **x**   RADAR?   YES   NO **x**
DIVE MASTER/INSTRUCTOR ABOARD?   YES **x**   NO   BOTH

DIVING & SNORKELING: SALT **x**   FRESH
TYPE OF DIVING/SNORKELING IN AREA: WALL   BEACH **x**   WRECK **x**   REEF **x**   CAVE   ICE
DIVING/SNORKELING IN YOUR AREA IS BEST SUITED FOR: BEGINNER   INTERMEDIATE **x**   ADVANCED
BEST TIME OF YEAR FOR DIVING/SNORKELING: **Summer - April - September**
TEMPERATURE: **NOV-APRIL: 78   F**   **MAY-OCT: 83   F**
VISIBILITY: **DIVING: 75-125 FT**   **SNORKELING: 50 FT**

PACKAGES AVAILABLE: DIVE **x**   DIVE STAY **x**   SNORKEL   SNORKEL-STAY
ACCOMMODATIONS NEARBY: HOTEL **x**   MOTEL   HOME RENTALS
ACCOMMODATION RATES: EXPENSIVE   MODERATE **x**   INEXPENSIVE
RESTAURANTS NEARBY: EXPENSIVE   MODERATE **x**   INEXPENSIVE
YOUR AREA IS: REMOTE   QUIET WITH ACTIVITIES **x**   LIVELY
LOCAL ACTIVITY/NIGHTLIFE: **Quiet, Steel Band**
CAR NEEDED TO EXPLORE AREA?   YES **x**   NO
DUTY FREE SHOPPING?   YES **x**   NO

LOCAL EMERGENCY SERVICES   NEAREST HYPERBARIC TREATMENT FACILITY
COASTGUARD: **St. Thomas/Waterfront**   AUTHORITY: **St. Thomas Hospital**
TELEPHONE: **809-776-3497**   LOCATION: **St. Thomas Hospital**
CALLSIGNS: **Ch. 16**   TELEPHONE: **809-776-8311**

LOCAL DIVING DOCTOR:
NAME: **Dr. Boaz**
LOCATION: **St. Thomas, USVI**
TELEPHONE: **809-774-8998**

CARRIBEAN LIVEABOARDS

Carribean Explorer
The Liveaboard Experience
Fin Loose and Fancy Free in Paradise

By Bill Roe with photographs by Ron Streeter

There are many wonderful dive destinations in the Caribbean.

One of the newest and most pristine hot spots in this part of the world is certainly the island of Saba.

Almost from it's discovery as a dive destination, Saba was declared a marine sanctuary. The Saba Marine Park was created to ensure that it's unspoiled wonder would remain for all time. That divers would have the experience of swimming among marine life unafraid of man, giving photographers and videographers countless opportunities to bring that perfect memory, or award-winning shot back home, but the best way to see Saba and other spots such as the island reefs off St. Kitts, is by taking a liveaboard trip to journey through this part of the Caribbean.

As of this writing, the only liveaboard offering this eclectic lifestyle year round is the 100 ft. MV Caribbean Explorer. If you have experienced liveaboard diving before, you'll be surprised. If you've never been on a liveaboard before, you are in for a treat. This boat is one tough act to follow. Save your pennies, take out a second mortgage if you must., but DO take a trip with this first-class operation.

When you book with the Caribbean Explorer, you will receive a packet of information, the most comprehensive this writer has ever seen, that gives you literally all the information you would need to prepare for this week-long sojourn into diving delights not found anywhere else in the world.

If you have a passport check it's expiration date, if you don't have one, order one today, you will need it when you want to go. But the information packet tells all that and so much more.

Based out of Sint. Maarten, a three-hour flight from Miami, the Caribbean Explorer is docked at Bobby's Marina in Phillipsburg which is the capital of the Dutch half of this multi-cultured island. The other half being French makes for a unique blend of language and local cuisine in this sun drenched eastern Caribbean paradise. If you let the Caribbean Explorer know when you are arriving, they will arrange to have a cab meet you. The fare from the airport to Bobby's Marina was pretty standard at $10 at the time of this writing. The twenty minute ride from the airport winds through mountains and affords some breath-taking views of quiet coves dotted with sailboats from all over the world, who trek to this mecca for sun and sea worshippers.

You check into the boat anytime after 3:30 p.m. on a Saturday and then have the option to explore Phillipsburg until 6:30 p.m. or so when a complete dinner is served aboard, or if you wish, check out the town and report to the boat around 10:00 p.m. to receive your introductory presentations to the ship and its crew.

The heart of the crew are the co-managers. There are two sets of co-managers who alternate on six-month rotational shifts. Our co-managers for this voyage were the team of Luc Callebaut and Jackie Lee. This couple has worked dive operations literally all over the world. Together with a highly skilled international crew consisting of a dive master, an engineer, a cook, and a stewardess. Their single purpose is to make your dive vacation as near perfect as possible. Friendly, flexible, and accommodating would be the best words to describe this group.

In the introductory briefing, you learn that the Caribbean Explorer supplies towels for diving, washcloths and towels for bathing and, with a washer and dryer on board, the laundry is done daily. At the end of the night dive, you are handed a fresh *warm* towel and hot chocolate. What a treat!

The boat also subscribes to an ecological approach to operations, Everything is recycled that is possible to recycle.

There are no paper cups. There are plastic tumblers that get washed and reused daily. You also learn that all beverages, soda, beer, wine and liquor are supplied as well. The alcohol is reserved for after the dive day is concluded obviously, but they also provide the tastiest non-alcoholic beer anyone on our trip had ever encountered, a brew called Buckler, imported from Holland by Heineken.

This is one class act. As 11:30 approaches, the Caribbean Explorer fires up its two massive diesel engines and prepares to head for Saba. Pulling away from the marina, the lights of St. Maarten give a panoramic view of the island. Lights appear and vanish between the valleys and hills beneath a blanket of stars. The humming of the engines and the light roll of the sea lull you to sleep.

Saba

You awake to the smells of fresh coffee and breakfast being cooked. On deck you are amazed at the first sight of the tiny island of Saba. Volcanic in origin, it juts straight out of the sea, sheer walls dotted by wild goats that wander the precarious slopes feeding on the sparse vegetation that clings to the rock.

The boat is moored in Ladder Bay. Halfway up the mountain is a tiny building at the end of a series of steps carved out of the rock. This was the customs house until the eighties when it was moved to "The Bottom" around the time when the waters surrounding Saba became a national Marine Sanctuary.

The towns (more like villages) all have interesting names. For the most part, they derive their names from a viewpoint of Dutch practically, "The Bottom" has the lowest elevation of any town on the island. St. Johns boasts the oldest Anglican church on Saba. "Windwardside" is on the windward side of the island, and "Hells Gate" is atop one of the most rugged parts of Saba. All are connected by a single road that threads it's way up from The Bottom through Wind-wardside to Hells Gate. From the lookout at Hells Gate, you have a commanding view of the Saban Airport. Is has the distinction of being the world's smallest international airport. The runway compares to an aircraft carrier for length, and only small "commuter" type air-

Octopus off Saba by Ron Streeter

craft can make the landing. If you wish to visit Saba but don't wish to do so on a live-aboard, you can fly in from Sint.Maarten and stay at one of the small resorts.

Local lore explains that before the road was built, everything was moved around the island by hand up either by steps carved in the rocks, or on trails through the lush, but foreboding interior.

The legend goes on to tell of several attempts by the Dutch government to build a road that would connect these towns that all ended in failure. Eventually the Dutch gave up saying it was impossible. Shortly thereafter, a local sea captain sent away to the United States for a correspondence course in civil engineering, and once completed with the course, he built the "impossible" road. The road was built entirely by hand, pick and shovel. It took twenty five years to complete.

Although the population is now about 60% 'outsiders' (primarily Americans), the true Saabs descend from only four founding families. The Sabans have a tradition of painting their buildings white with red roofs. Custom dictates a new paint job every two years, and a wreath of gaily colored flower gardens encircle each building. It makes for a very clean and beautiful island.

There are quaint shops and restaurants on the island. They are clean and inhabited by charming shopkeepers and servers. There are many places that sell local crafts and a liqueur that is locally made. The local currency alternates between Netherlands Antilles Guilders (or florins which shows up as NAF on price tags) or, the U.S. dollar which is more widely used.

There are several establishments that only offer one or two guest rooms or cottages. Several resorts on the island have more rooms and amenities. One place that stands out is "Captains Quarters". Ten spotlessly clean apartments overlooking a small swimming pool. Captains Quarters also has a restaurant/bar/activity center that is perched on a cliff with a breathtaking view of the mountainside overlooking the deep blue Caribbean. You could sit there and take in the scenery for hours on end.

The sound of the dive master blowing on a conch shell horn, signals the divers to gather around for the pre-dive briefing. We learned we were to make several dives that morning in Ladder Bay. On one bulkhead on the dive deck is a list of the days, dive sites, and depths. On an adjacent wall another board gives a graphic description of the dive site you are about to visit and a list of the various sea life and topographical features you should encounter. Normally, right before the dive, the spacious camera bench is a flurry of activity.

As this is the first dive of the week, you are also instructed on the various safety procedures, the points of entry and exit on the boat and the emergency diver recall procedure, as well as site description. A weighted down line is hung over the side at the stern of the boat. It will be used as a reference point for a safety stop at the end of the dive, The diver recall system is simple, functional and, foolproof (a mighty whack on one of the massive stern cleats with a 16 lb.sledgehammer). You can enter the water from a gate amidships on either side or from the wide dive platform at the stern. The side gates make for a quick entry but it is about a six-foot drop. The best entry is made feet first, both fins hitting the water flat rather than a classic giant stride. Once in, a quick OK to the dive master and you are on your way to the wonders below.

As the island is literally a giant volcanic rock that over time has had many massive pieces break off and fall into the sea to become a home for reef building corals. The coral grows on these ancient rocks, there is little if any true "reef", but it makes for an interesting series of dives, winding around these encrusted boulders between the sandy bottom which is made up largely of a pumice like material and has a volcanic gray color to it.

The profiles afford some interesting photo/video opportunities that is characteristic of diving all around Saba. Another pleasant surprise, you will find upon return to your boat, your cabin is cleaned, straightened and the bunk made and turned down (complete with a mint on the pillow). I told you this is a class act.

Sleepy Pufferfish by Ron Streeter

Another series of dives off Saba is made on Tent Reef. The origin of the name here could not be determined, but it did provide more fantastic photo opportunities.

A long ledge, fifteen to twenty feet high, is bordered by more boulders allowing you to swim in the trench and photograph or videotape creatures hiding in the nooks and crannies. Large anemones, fearless fish will let you almost swim up and shake hands.

They seem to love to have their picture taken, so don't disappoint them.

Lunch is served on the top deck under the canopy. Typically sandwiches with salads and side dishes are served. The Caribbean Explorer has a habit of delivering more than is promised.

The average number of dives per day is five with the last one being a night dive. A chemical light stick for each diver is required, as is a dive light. It is recommended that a third, back-up dive light per buddy team be part of the program. Be it your first, fiftieth or more night dive, night diving on Saba is a treat.

Dinner is hearty and plentiful, served in the air-conditioned salon followed by a sumptuous dessert and a video or two. Usually after the meal, you are reminded of any "optional" activity, such as a land tour, that will be available the following day. It seemed that each day we were being 'sold' something after dinner, but it was always a soft sell and more informative than bothersome.

The two large dining tables in the main salon conceal large light tables you can view the days slides after the E6 processing is done in the ship's photo lab.

Smokers are welcome aboard the Caribbean Explorer, but the top (sun) deck is the only area aboard where it is allowed.

The cabins have several configurations of sleeping accommodations. The bunks will comfortably hold a six-foot diver, but if you choose a cabin with a double bunk below a single, the headroom between the two is a little tight. It is not advisable to bolt upright in the night. If you do, you usually only do it once.

The following day, another set of spectacular dives complemented with more great food and fun. That evening the Caribbean Explorer will make way for St. Kitts and the diving thrills it holds. Not to worry though, we will be back in Saba in two days for more diving as well as an island tour. As the tiny Dutch island fades in the distance, all the passengers are smiling and filled with anticipation.

St. Kitts

Celebrating it's tenth anniversary of independence from the British crown in 1993, the island country of St. Kitts (and sister island Nevis) is a lush and lovely contrast to Saba's nearly vertical terrain. First discovered by Columbus on his second voyage in 1493, parts of the island have changed flags of ownership many times, and is rich in history and the lore of New World discoveries.

The Caribbean Explorer moors offshore the capitol city of Bassetere. The morning of the first day visiting this island, a bus tour is organized. Passengers are ferried via inflatable to the docks at Bassetere. Bus is a relative term here. The roads outside the city are too narrow to accommodate anything stateside dwellers would deem a bus. The bus is actually a van, much smaller and narrower than anything found in the U.S. But the driver is charming and knowledgeable in the history of the country. Probably the first inhabitants of the island were Carib Indians. Our guide stops at a place along Old

Road where samples of their glyphs, long ago carved in stone, with little known meaning, lie in a silent testament to a bygone time.

Along our way, the driver stopped for a rest and a photo opportunity. Across the road from the islands oldest Christian church and cemetery sat a ramshackle (spell that island quaint) building, barely wide enough for three grown men to stand abreast, that somehow served as a store of sorts. This was our rest stop. We chose between some fascinating local beverages, "Ting" a soft drink (I have found for sale in Key Largo Florida) and "Caribe" a very light and tasty beer, or the more standard fare available stateside. As we sipped our drinks, the architecture of these hopelessly old buildings held out a certain charm. On the "house" next door to the store, you could see where some island carpenter had tried, eons ago, to replace some ancient gingerbread trim and obviously failing to have any decorative pattern available to him, he traced his hand and forearm several times on a board, and cut them out for the decoration.

> **The island is more than pretty beaches. It is a rich, old culture that today is in the throws of painful political adjustment while keeping a smile on it's face and its head held high.**

You could see it on the weather worn tombstones in the church yard, testaments to the courageous who founded this island paradise at great cost. You could see it on the smiles of the workers in the various shops, stores and the batik factory. You could feel it in the air at Brimstone Hill.

Our driver waived us back to our van and en route to Romney Manor with our final destination, the Fort at Brimstone Hill beyond that, he filled us in on more of St. Kitts' history.

The island was visited by a succession of 15th century vessels under many flags, but it was not actually settled until a brave band of British led by Sir Thomas Warner wandered ashore with the intention of staying around 1623. But while the English settled happily nestled by the bay near Sandy Point, in the central part of the island, the French were busily moving in on both ends. The series of battles and general hassles that evolved from this co-habitation situation, re-sulted in construction of the fort at Brimstone Hill to protect the British settlement.

This was all the driver had time to say as we threaded our way up and down the foothills, now well off Old Road heading for Romney Manor. He stopped near an old sugar plantation and allowed those who wished, to get out and walk past the sugar mill and along the last part of the small road that led to the Manor through the jungle like foliage. There were wonderful scenes of rare flowers and birds along the path. So many, you could burn out a camera lens if you weren't careful. But that was only a preview to the sumptuous gardens around the Batik factory at Romney Manor. Handmade, in a multiple step process of waxing, dying, and boiling over and over, this fabric is unique in the world. Somewhat pricey, mind you, but it is the only place in the world you can get it. We again boarded the van (some of us now toting shopping bags) and got back on the road leading to Brimstone Hill.

Island of Saba from Brimstone Hill Turret by Ron Streeter

165

The construction of the fortress at Brimstone Hill was started in 1680; growing from one entrenched battery, it evolved over the years to encompass several acres or at least seven levels along the hillside. After changing hands a few times between the British and French, it was abandoned altogether over one hundred and thirty years ago.But from one specific gun turret on the hillside, you could look out over the Caribbean and see Saba in the distance, twenty eight miles away. You could feel what it would have been like to be peering out into the royal blue waters searching for enemy vessels or pirates. The light whistle of the Trade Winds through the stonework of the turret added the perfect sound effect to the fantasy. Tomorrow we would dive in the shadow of those long silent cannon where many spent rounds still lie encrusted on the ocean floor.

There is a small tourist shop, at the fort where you can buy local crafts, post cards, drinks and snacks as well as locally produced island music on cassettes. The currency is either American dollars or E.C. Dollars (which stands for Eastern Caribbean, an economic consortium of island countries in the region) and of course American Express, Master Card and Visa are widely accepted throughout the Caribbean. A few minutes in the shade, enough time to enjoy a cold drink in this tropical warmth, and our driver gathers us back into the van for the ride back to Basseterre.

The Old Road hugs the sheer coast, only evenly spaced concrete stumps separate a vehicle from the straight drop to the sea below. An occasional missing post marks the spot where some poor motorist had their day ruined. We arrive back at the capitol of this twin-island country with about an hour left before the tender comes back from the Caribbean Explorer. Enough time for a short walking tour of downtown Basseterre. An hour was just about enough for the casual window shopper, an honest to goodness, hard core, shopper could probably spend days. A mall at the dock is primarily for the convenience of the cruise ship passengers. There are many duty free shops there, but the more folksy stores hover along the main streets that lead to the town square. If we had needed a cab there it would have been no problem. Without a cruise ship in port you almost trip over them, their drivers all crying "Taxi? Taxi?". I almost thought these people were looking for someone *named* Taxi.

Back on the Caribbean Explorer, we contentedly made our way to the first of two natural shipwrecks (not artificial reefs) we would dive that day. The "**Talata**" lay twisted, resting on the bottom at 50 feet. The growth along the hull, huge tube worms 8-10" long or more festooned the wreck as a solemn great barracuda inspected the thousands of tropical fish, all kinds and sizes, that darted among the growth. The hull, broken as she was, provided infinite nooks and crannies to support any kind of reef creature. It was fantastic. Being the first dive of the day, we had lots of bottom time, and the film went buzzing through the cameras all too quickly. But as we hung out on our safety stop, all we could think of was the next wreck, and the night dive.

As we motored to the next dive site, we learned that there are no true "dive shops" (at least by American definition) on the island of St. Kitts. There are some operators on the island who have gear, fill tanks, a boat, and the knowledge to find the dive sites, but don't expect a refresher course as of this writing. Now some of the resorts have water sports concessions that do include scuba, but only for their guests. Truly the best way to dive St. Kitts, is from a liveaboard.

The "**River Taw**" was the second freighter we dove. Again in 50 feet, she was different from the "**Talata**". While one was sunk from storm damage, the other simply rusted to death and sank at anchor one night. You can find some unusual photo opportunities along those old chains across the sometimes sandy bottom up to the mammoth anchors. The abundant fish population coupled with the combination of hard and soft corals that had worked their way into the fiber of this wreck were amazing. Back on the dive deck, we agreed this would be an excellent choice for the night dive. It was.

After dinner, up on the top deck you had a spectacular view of Mt. Misery overlooking the town of Basseterre. The street lights and city lights that hung over the town looked like a jeweled necklace of diamonds, amber, sapphires and rubies. We watched the lights grow brighter as the sun set behind the mountain, someone had put a Jimmy Buffett tape on, and the upper deck was bathed in island music.

"Ya' know? It doesn't get any better than this" was a line from an old beer commercial that rolled through my mind as darkness set in. It is hardly ever really dark down there, on any clear night the starlight beams down. That night, a full moon crept up around ten. (It doesn't get any better than this.)

The following morning, we sampled the wonders of **Paradise Reef** for a few dives. The corals and sea life were as prolific, but now in a more natural surrounding, with more light, the imaging opportunities were endless. Old cannon balls and encrusted armament almost littered the bottom in some places. At dives end, the deck was filled with excited hoots and "Wow" and "Did you see the...". **Paradise Reef** was aptly named. But the crew of the Caribbean Explorer had more in store for us. In the afternoon we moved to a site called **Anchors Aweigh**.

On that site we found large anchors, chain, spent shot, and old artifacts all frozen into the reef structure. This was the spot viewed the day before from the turret on Brimstone Hill. How much of this coral encrusted debris was placed there by nature, and how much by man, was impossible to tell.

> **But swimming among the bones of ships and probably men, you could sense the history that was passing by your faceplate, almost hear the groans of the sailors as they struggled at the windlass lifting those masses of metal. Now, they are visited by the occasional reef fish and diver. Truly a memorable dive.**

By nightfall the photo lab aboard the Caribbean Explorer was rolling in high gear. The following night would be the ship's weekly photo contest, and the photographers were hot to win. The light tables in the galley burned into the evening. Then a video show or optional night dive back to **Anchors Aweigh**. It never ceases to amaze me that, no matter how marvelous a dive site is by day, and then you come back at night, to the very same spot, how it seems totally different.

In the night, the Caribbean Explorer had quietly made the crossing back to Saba where we were once again greeted in the morning by the goats skimming over the cliffs at Ladder Bay.

The day was to be filled with dives at **Tedron Wall, Diamond Dock, and Man O' War Shoals. Diamond Rock** is a twin sea mount with one peak broken off. The sea passes between a narrow channel between the two tops. You can start the dive at eighty feet or so, and work your way up into tidal pool conditions (if the waves co-operate) along the sloping side.

Today the black durgeons showed up in force. Not found in great abundance in most areas of the Caribbean at **Tedron Wall** they had to be 'shooed' away to get shots of the giant anemone and huge tube sponges that covered the rocky bottom. **Man O' War Shoals** offered more marine life and some nifty swim throughs, more chances for that "perfect" shot.

> **The water around Saba has an almost magenta hue to it, the blues show up very rich and contrast perfectly with the brighter colors of the reef and its inhabitants.**

Mid-afternoon the diving was over. Tonight we were to tour the island and have dinner at a local restaurant. Given the height of Saba, we would need a bit of a surface interval before getting near the top.

The driver was charming, a true native descended from one of the two Dutch founding families. He answered the questions we had and punctuated the answers with the lore and history of this tiny vertical paradise. Stopping first at the Saba decompression chamber, then at shops and points of interest along the way, we were eventually led to a spot near the top of Mount Scenery where we would take the ancient island path down to the town below.

As sunlight crept behind the foliage and the rocks, sounds of the forest night filled the air. Old jungle movies came to mind. It seemed funny to be in such a harsh and primeval environment on an island filled with such gracious and friendly people.

We ate at the Brigadoon, a quaint place converted from a house, owned by a transplanted Californian. The local food was the star. After the opportunity for home-made dessert, coffee or a cordial, our group stepped out into the night to find our driver waiting to shuttle us back to the boat. On the way back down, we learned that the government scours the single road daily for rocks that have fallen into the roadway the day before, and they are always busy. We also learned that any gear beside first, second, and reverse on any vehicle on the island, was a waste of metal. So steep and winding is the road, it is simply suicide to use a higher gear.

The morning found the divers doing a "fun" dive the crew had cooked up for them. I am promised to secrecy on the details, but it's fun, trust me. After that we dove a shallow reef and even had a chance to get in a final snorkel near the island's rock face on the lee of the wind and waves. A final sumptuous lunch and it was time to head back to Sint. Maarten.

The town of Phillipsburg is the Capital of the Dutch side of the island. Two main roads, aptly named Front Road and Back Road are tied together by streets (or Steegs or Steegjes). If you look closely you will find that the street signs are resourcefully made from old drum lids. A quaint touch, no doubt with it's roots in Dutch frugality. The island street vendors and the locals who come into town make a colorful mix of people. There are blocks of shops of international fame mingled with T shirt emporiums, duty free camera, and jewelry shops. There are a number of wonderful waterfront watering holes and restaurants, and hotels from the lavish to the adequate. There are a few casinos, they lack the litter and glitz of Las Vegas, barely seeming to exude even the faint glimmer of hope of winning in their dark and sullen rooms. If you go off onto the back streets, you can even find some fast food places. Almost all seemed hopelessly overpriced, and in some cases lacking in quality as well. Not to say there are not fine meals and fair prices to be found, but it does pay to shop around first, whatever the commodity. When the cruise ships are in, the streets writhe with shoppers crowding in and out of stores, wildly dodging vehicles that dart through the narrow streets. It is a town with a unique flavor and local color, it should probably be experienced at least once. The Dutch florin is coin of the realm, but it shares the limelight with the dollar, the franc, and all major credit cards.

After dark, the divers meet with Luc and Jackie for drinks and a farewell meal together. The conversations were made up of re-hashing a certain dive, assorted promises of writing each other, of coming back real soon, and simple warm feelings shared between people who a week ago were strangers. The restaurant was filled with locals, cruise ship passengers and both land and water borne tourists. The air was shaking to the band, playing loud enough to be heard back on Saba. The dancers were shaking to it with the same fever. Content, but with our ears still ringing, our party slowly returned to the ship where the starlight and the island night waited up on the top deck for us. Tomorrow we headed home, the week long dream had ended.

The entire crew of the Caribbean Explorer was professional, friendly, and always willing to lend a hand. Given the quality of food, service, accommodations, and the overall experience made possible by the entire staff of owner Clay McArdle, this is one of the finest dive vacations you could ever ask for.

**Explorer Ventures LTD. 10 Fencerow Drive Fairfield CT. 06430
800-322-3577 or in Connecticut (203) 259-9321 FAX (203) 259-9896.**

The Star Flyer

Bill Waschko

My first love, professionally speaking, is the news media and communication. I have been employed with WAZL-AM and WWSH-FM for twenty years, beginning my career as D.J., then developing into the technical, promotional, programming, television and production aspects of the media. I am presently Operations Director.

A communications/media profession keeps you actively involved in community growth and development and so I host charitable telethons and prepare and present high school career oriented programs.

Activities and interests include: active membership of the Board of Directors of the Hazleton/Carbon County Easter Seal Society.

I fell in love with diving and snorkeling back in 1979 when I was vacationing in Bonaire.

I am President of the Mountain City Scuba Club, member of the Luzerne County Sheriff's Dept., Scuba Division and amateur photographer, both above and below the water, a member of Divers Alert Network, The Cousteau Society, International Association of Dive Rescue Specialists, International Oceanographic Foundation, and, of course, Divers Exchange International.

The Star Flyer by Bill Naschko

My diving experience in PA includes ice dives, dives in lakes, and abandoned strip mining cavities. Eastern Coastal dives include wrecks off the coasts of Delaware, Maryland, New Jersey and New York. Also many Caribbean islands.

This diving experience was not at all routine to me. For me, a diving vacation consists of rising early, loading up the dive boat and performing two dives, then getting back to our rooms at approximately 2 pm, grabbing something to eat, snorkeling, then later in the evening, a night dive. This is repeated the next day and the day after.

These trips are great. However, not so for the spouse who is not a diving enthusiast. Such was the case when my wife and I were planning a sailing cruise. After careful research, and considering my love for scuba diving, we chose the "Star Flyer".

The "Star Flyer" sails the Virgin and Leeward Islands, alternating weeks. We sailed the Leeward Islands and our itinerary included stops at St. Kitts, St. Eustatius, Antigua, Iles Des Saintes, Nevis and St. Barts.

The cruise sails Sunday to Sunday. We decided to arrive on Saturday and the "Star Flyer" arranged for us to stay at the Great Bay Beach Hotel in Phillipsburg. Great Bay is just within walking distance to the exclusive shopping district and fine restaurants in Phillipsburg, which is the Dutch territory of St. Maarten. Our rooms were recently renovated, very spacious and clean and in just minutes you can cool off at poolside or the ocean.

After boarding the ship, we were greeted by the officers and crew, Caribbean Steel Band music, hors d'oeuvres and infamous rum punch.

The sailing ship was magnificent with its 226 foot mast height and sail area of 36,000 square feet.

The cabins were spacious and accommodating, equipped with air conditioning, a marble bath with shower, a hair dryer, reading lamps, telephone and closed circuit television. This was not roughing it!

The captain held "Story Time" each morning at approximately 10 a.m. At this time he would inform his passengers on what adventure we would be debarking upon that day; what tours and activities would be available to us, as well as a history lesson on that island. The captain's green parrot, Loretto, sat on his shoulder while he spoke. Routinely, all interested divers were informed to meet in the ship's library.

Our first island adventure was St. Eustatius. I sacrificed this dive to show my wife I didn't have to dive on our very first Caribbean venture. Instead we both chose to climb a volcano, the Quill. This tour was a 5 minute ride to the base of the volcano. Our guide provided us with self confidence and when we reached the summit, a glass of orange juice. Only, a handful of our co-cruisers chose to climb the Quill. It was truly an adventure for those physically fit, not those who think they are!

The Quill has been inactive for a few hundred years and as we climbed the path to the top, were engulfed in rich, green vegetation, blooming flowers, singing birds and many species of butterflies. We were able to see a magnificent view of our ship in the silvery horizon as we climbed higher to the summit. We didn't have enough strength to climb down into the volcano, but later a co-cruiser, (also an archeologist and journalist) informed us that the inside of the Quill was even more spectacular ... thick jungle, radiant flowers and fruit trees and a rain forest.

The first night's entertainment and activities included a "crab race". Needless to say, my crab finished last! Also, just chatting with the crew members and new friends and strolling under the moonlight was entertainment by itself.

St. Kitts was our next stop. It was breathtaking that morning as the ship anchored at Friar's Bay, which is secluded somewhat from the populated area of Basseterre.

In addition to offering diving, the ship's crew planned a beach trip and also provided snorkeling, wind surfing, and beach games.

Of course, just lying on the sandy, tropical beaches and soaking up the rays was quiet entertainment worth welcoming. I signed up for the St. Kitts dive. It seemed that a few of the other divers aboard ship took a diving refresher course that day with the ship's diving instructor, Pontius Svanberg. Today's dive was a drift dive at **Nag's Head**, located south of where the ship had anchored. We loaded our Zodiak dive boat and in no time we were skirting the sheer cliffs near **Nag's Head**. The cliffs appeared as great masses of stone which had fallen into the sea and we were advised to keep our distance from where the sea and masses of stone met. A kaleidoscope of undersea species were seen and the dazzling blue, gold and white corals proved to be a photographer's dream come true. All divers "bundled up" as our crew member and diver, Jeremy, stayed in the Zodiak boat above us keeping watch. Diving conditions were perfect and effortless and on this particular dive, we saw marvelous banded worms swimming around us. I only wish I had brought my macro camera attachment instead of my wide angle lens, although the wide angle lens was perfect for photographing the crinoids as they danced in the soft current. It was a relaxing dive as we smoothly floated with the current. Our deepest dive was 55 feet and lasted 45 minutes. Jeremy helped us with our gear and helped us into the Zodiak. (It may take a few tries and a few extra hands to get back into this inflatable Zodiak boat).

Our dive master thought we could do some snorkeling as we were returning back to our ship. This would be a test snorkeling site, then perhaps he could bring other passengers back to this site in the afternoon. This location, near **Nag's Head**, had a pleasant mystique about it; star coral and purple sponges.

Back aboard ship, I changed and took a tender (50 passenger motor boat) to Friar's Bay and then a taxi to the shopping area of Basseterre.

St. Kitts is a very green, mountainous, friendly island. New shops and real estate are developing in the southern region, and as my taxi cab driver drove me from the beach to the shopping area, I could see fields of vegetables and livestock. It's a place I'd like to spend the entire week!

Our next adventure was Antigua.

Antigua's diving is excellent and I photographed many exotic species of marine life and stony corals. Night diving is an excellent choice at Antigua.

The next morning our ship anchored in Falmouth harbor and a short distance away is the very picturesque English Harbor and Nelson's Dockyard. Nelson's Dockyard is named after Admiral Horatio Nelson. This harbor was originally established as a British naval base in 1720. The fort, museum and historical buildings and culture were truly interesting to me, as I am a history buff and amateur photographer. We journeyed on to St. John's shopping district by taxi and took the last tender back to the ship. Tonight's entertainment will feature Steel Band Music and a Costume Party.

It's Thursday and as I look through our porthole, I can see a small group of velvety green islands, "Iles Des Saintes". The dive master, Pontius, informs divers that he will explore a dive spot for later that afternoon. Meanwhile, we anchored off Terre D'En Haute, the largest of the islands and strolled about Bourg Des Saintes, which is the only town and shopping area. I also climbed to the top of Fort Napoleon. This climb was almost as vigorous as the Quill, very steep and a twisting and turning road path, but the View of Terra-De-Hauts, the quaint villages and terra cotta rooftops and surrounding harbor, made it well worth the climb! Back down the twisting and turning road and back to the ship for my afternoon dive.

Back aboard ship, our diving gear is loaded on the Zodiak and this trip we have 8 divers as we make our way to our virgin dive spot. The excitement intensified as we got closer to our sight.

The visibility was excellent upon descending; and there were no discarded fishing nets or rusty beverage cans

The fish life was colorful and plentiful, the coral growth abundant as we explored this hidden pleasure. Many eels swam the sea floor. We named the dive sight, "Pte A'Vachell", or "Cow Point".

The week was passing by too quickly and it was Friday. Our ship slowly approached an island with a snowy white cloud hanging overhead. This island whose name meant snow, was Nevis.

Our sailing adventure is almost over; it's Saturday and this stop takes us to St. Barthelemy. There will be two dives offered on this island and I will be diving both of them. Our dive master, Pontius, is careful to check our Sunday flight schedule in order to allow at least 24 hours between our last dive and flight departure. The ship anchored in Gustavia Harbor and the first dive was at **Pain Du Sucre**, which was a massive rock. There were some undersea fish and plant species on the dive, but nothing magnificent.

The second dive was grand. It was a wreck dive, a large private yacht equipped with helicopter pad and jacuzzi. This wreck was sunk in only 45 feet of water and unbelievably, its contents were intact. Dishes, appliances, a toilet and even a full size mirror lies in place, unbroken.

The current is very strong at this wreck dive site and I must check my air quite often since I am using more air due to my vigorous fin action.

It's time to hurry back on the ship and I'm just in time to make the snorkeling excursion and beach activities. After doing two very strenuous dives in strong current waters, I was planning to snorkel just a few minutes and spend the rest of the afternoon lying on the beach soaking up the rays.

I found that this snorkeling experience was the best one yet! The sea life was so diverse, so magnificently colorful, and the multi-hued corals were so

breathtaking, I found myself spending only a few short minutes on my beach blanket and the entire afternoon snorkeling.

I rate my best snorkeling experience at Columbier Beach, St. Barts.

This must be an excellent sight for a night dive! My final day, Saturday, was spent wholly exploring and savoring the Caribbean Sea, a place where divers, snorkelers and sun worshippers can ultimately find paradise. Our ship sailed on to St. Maarten.

Our "Star Flyer" sailing dream cruise was over and it was back to the Pocono Mountains in Pennsylvania.

I rate their diving operation, headed by Pontius Svansberg, an A+. If you are a beginner or intermediate diver, a closer watch will be kept on you, and if you are a more experienced diver, the dive master will match you with a comparable diver. Safety is top priority when diving the "Star Flyer".

Again, this sailing cruise is perfect for the diver traveling with a non-diver and for the diver who has a desire to see many islands and make a few dives in between sightseeing.

For more information on the "Star Flyer" contact: Divers Exchange International, 37 West Cedar Street, Boston, MA 02114; or call (617) 723-7134.

Cyprus

Cherry Dobbins

Cydive, Ltd. is a well established British Sub-Aqua Club and PADI school, run by two British divers, Mark and Cherry, who are qualified instructors and have many years experience diving around Cyprus.

Dive trips for qualified divers (one star or above) are organized twice daily at 9.00 and 14:00 hrs. They return to the center between dives to allow for those who prefer to make only a single dive each day.

Safari trips are available which take you through some beautiful remote parts of the island, normally inaccessible, and include two dives with barbecue or buffet. Safaris are only available April to October.

Besides the "safari" they organize day trips by Landrover or boat when numbers and conditions are suitable. Divers' family and friends are welcome when space is available. Night dives with beach barbecue and full day boat trips are also possible.

Cydive is a recognized BSAC and PADI five star school, and as such, runs courses to all levels and in specialist subjects, such as Photography. For those without underwater cameras, Cydive has both movie and still equipment for hire.

Cydive has a large stock of good quality equipment for the use of visiting divers. For shore dives they use a long-wheel base Landrover and for boat dives a 10 meter wooden dive boat with radio, echo sounder, boarding platform and shade from the sun for those who prefer it. Non-diving relatives and friends are always welcome on dives when there is space in the Landrover and, for a small fee, on the boat.

Courtesy of Cherry Dobbins

Other watersports are available in Paphos including wind-surfing and water skiing.

In the true tradition of Cyprus, a warm and friendly atmosphere prevails and Cydive is fortunate to have Dougie and Gill next door serving breakfast, snacks and drinks in their bar, the Divers Den. Evening entertainment may include a slide show, barbecue or visit to a local tavern for a meze.

DIVE SITES

The Wreck of the Achilleas

A Greek vessel which mysteriously sank in 11m. of water in 1975. It is in three main sections and good condition. There are still some portholes. The bronze propeller is still attached and the bow section may be entered. The winch and large grab are also of interest.

Big Steps
20 minutes by boat from the harbor is this site which drops down to 25 meters in a series of small drop-offs. Lots of small holes to examine and plenty of marine life.

The Shoals
This site is an isolated rocky area about 3 kilometers from the shore.

> **The rocks come just to the surface and in ancient times a large number of ships were wrecked there. The rocks are littered with amphorae, mostly broken, and in some places concreted together in the shape of the hold of the ship from which they came.**

There are many other remains such as stone anchors but none of the artifacts can be removed. The site takes 20 minutes to reach by boat. Depths are between 2 to 10 meters.

The Valley
Takes less than 15 minutes to reach by boat. The site is an underwater "valley" of about 100m. length and about 60m deep. The deepest end of the valley is 26m. There is much encrusting marine life under the overhanging walls of the valley and there are a few small caves.

Wreck of the Vera K
This wreck is near some small islands called moulia rocks. It takes 25 minutes to reach the site by boat. The Vera K went aground in 1972. It was blown up as a hazard to shipping in 1974. The vessel is a large Lebanese freighter of about 200m length. The wreck is in four main sections and is completely submerged. It lies in a "crater" in the sea-bed which is 8m deep. Just beside the wreck is a large rock archway where a family of groupers live, the largest of which (1.5m) is known to local divers as Uncle George. Close to the archways there is a system of fairly narrow tunnels suitable for experienced divers.

Valley of Caves
A large valley with many small caves and 100m away a large crater contains large boulders and more caves. Maximum depth 15m.

N.E. Reef
A popular site not far from the valley. Rocky bottom, lots of small holes and interesting marine life. Maximum depth 18m.

100 Foot Dive
An interesting dive to depths of between 26 and 34m. The clear water means the boat is visible from the bottom. Lots of small caves and low drop-offs.

Bream Bay
A favorite dive site. Sand and rock bottom with many crevices, valleys and tunnels in 26m of clear water and lot of marine life. The beautiful red and purple algae and coral encrust many of the holes so taking a torch is a good idea. Maximum depth 30m.

The Slope
A rocky bottom area with small holes and interesting marine life. The remains of a Roman anchor (lead cross bar) may also be seen here. The area slopes down from 16 to 26m fairly quickly.

The Column
The pieces of amphorae to be seen at this site suggest a Rhodian wreck (similar to the Kyrenia wreck). It was carrying building materials, the column with fitting holes is clearly discernible.

The Roman Rubbish Tip
An area with a great many shards of amphorae and pieces of artifacts. Archaeologists believe this to be "Anchorage Gash"- Broken items junked by sailors.

30 Walrus Flats
No Walrus have ever been spotted here but a very attractive site. Sandy bottom with rocky outcrops, valleys and small caves.

Grouper Holes
A popular site only 15 minutes by boat from harbor. Depth 16 to 23m. An area with gullies and small holes inhabited by grouper. Also a good area to see pina clams and fan worms.

Deep Slope
Only 10 minutes by boat to this site, then down the shot line to 40m and a calcified coral bed on a fairly steep slope.

Anchor Reef
An interesting dive in depths between 9 and 20m. Rocky bottom with small gullies. The site is so called because of a large Danforth anchor and a very large admiralty pattern anchor only 200m apart.

THE FOLLOWING SITES ARE ACCESSIBLE BY SHORE

Corallia Point
A variety of caverns, craters, archways and tunnels make this a good dive for scenery and interesting marine life, especially fan and peacock worms in the shallower caverns. Also to be seen is the lovely red and purple coral and algae that encrusts most of the caves around Paphos.

Moray Cove
Half a mile past Corallia Point, a small white cliffed bay is a popular site. Attractive underwater scenery of small drop-offs down to 20m. On the far side of the bay a stepped crater was once thought to be a submerged amphitheater.

Wolf Bay
Past Moray Cove, the next small bay gives yet another marvelous dive for scenery and marine life.

The Old Harbor Wall
Opposite the center is a submerged line of rocks where one can find the remains of the original Roman harbor wall and numerous small fish, sponges and octopus.

Also to be seen are amphorae remains and the spare propeller from the Achilleas. Maximum depth 7m. Excellent for a first or night dive.

Octopus Point
A popular and well protected dive site with very easy access. An interesting rocky bottom with small holes and crevices, leading to 14m. Some broken amphorae.

Saint George
From the beautiful small fishing harbor of Ayios Yeorgos is this shore dive in depths down to 14m, with a large crater, cavern, archway, and plenty of amphorae.

Lighthouse Wreck
Only 5 minutes from Cydive, this is an ideal snorkel or first dive in 6m. The Ektimon was a 5,000 ton Greek freighter which ran aground in 1971. It is very broken up but the two propellers are still here.

Pistol Bay
This is normally a shore dive, and is about a 20 minutes drive from Paphos. It is near the island of Ayios Yeorgios. Maximum depth is about 12m. The main feature of this dive is a system of tunnels over 100m long. To fully explore the caves a torch is required. The caves are not suitable for novice divers.

Manijin Island

This dive can be made from the shore, in which case it is a 10 minute snorkel to reach the island.

To reach the site by land takes 30 minutes and by boat 90 minutes. For this reason, we usually go by boat if we go for a day trip and will make a second dive elsewhere the same day. This is considered to be one of the best dives by most divers. The island is small enough to swim around during a dive. There are drop-offs, caves, a large archway, and a lot of marine life. Maximum depth is 22m close to the island.

The Maze

As the name suggests, the site is a maze of channels, tunnels and archways in 12m of water. An "out of the way" site, but well worth a visit.

A short drive from Kato Paphos gives access to many beautiful quiet beaches and coves. On the more popular beaches windsurfing and water skiing are for hire and lessons are available. Alternatively one may use the water sports facilities at Kato Paphos harbor.

Paphos has recently been placed on the "World Heritage" list by UNESCO. There are many sites of antiquity, including the famous Mosaics, Tombs of the Kings and a lovely amphitheater.

The old harbor of Paphos, sentried by a small fort from Crusader times, is a popular attraction. Here are a number of taverns and bars where you may sit and watch the local fishing boats.

Nor should one miss a day in the Troodos Mountains with the cool, pine clad slopes, streams, waterfalls, monasteries and Byzantine Churches.

Cyprus has many local handicrafts including lefkara lace, pottery, filigree, silverware and basket work. These may all be purchased from the shops in Kato Paphos or one can visit the villages and see the crafting in progress. Mesoiya, only a few miles from Paphos is famous for its basket work and the village of Yeroskipos makes Turkish Delight.

Paphos has a very low crime rate and is safe for everyone to walk at all hours of the day and night.

Cydive organizes slide shows at the center with a barbecue afterwards and Meze nights at local restaurants. A meze is a Cypriot meal of about twenty different dishes.

There are numerous bars and restaurants in Kato Paphos and many restaurants have displays of local dancing on certain nights each week.

There are three discotheques and a number of "Bouzouki" night clubs. At the latter you will find live music and singers.

A visit to some of the village taverns is a must for very good food and local color.

SCUBA AND SNORKELING FACILITIES QUESTIONNAIRE

NAME **Cydive**
ADDRESS **One Poseidon Avenue**
K. Paphos
CONTACT **Cherry Dobbins**
TITLE **MS**
TELEPHONE **(06) 234271**   FAX **(06) 235307**

CAPITAL: **Nicosia**   GOVERNMENT: **Republic of Cyprus**
POPULATION: **Cyprus @ 200,000**   LANGUAGE: **Greek**
CURRENCY: **Cyprus Pounds**   ELECTRICITY:
AIRLINES: DEPARTURE TAX:
NEED VISA/PASSPORT?   YES **x**   NO   PROOF OF CITIZENSHIP?   YES **x**   NO

YOUR FACILITY IS CLASSIFIED AS: SCUBA CENTER **x**   RESORT
BUSINESS HOURS: **8:00 - 17:30**
CERTIFYING AGENCIES: **PADI, BSAC**
LOG BOOK REQUIRED?   YES **x**   NO
EQUIPMENT: SALES **x**   RENTALS **x**   AIR FILLS **x**
PRIMARY LINE OF EQUIPMENT: **Seaquest. Spiro, Oceanedge**
PHOTOGRAPHIC EQUIPMENT: SALES   RENTALS   LAB

CHARTER/DIVE BOAT AVAILABLE?   YES **x**   NO   DIVER CAPACITY **25**
COAST GUARD APPROVED?   YES **x**   NO   CAPTAIN LICENSED?   YES **x**   NO
SHIP TO SHORE?   YES **x**   NO   LORAN?   YES   NO **x**   RADAR?   YES   NO **x**
DIVE MASTER/INSTRUCTOR ABOARD?   YES   NO   BOTH **x**

DIVING & SNORKELING: SALT **x**   FRESH
TYPE OF DIVING/SNORKELING IN AREA: WALL **x**   BEACH **x**   WRECK **x**   REEF   CAVE **x**   ICE
DIVING/SNORKELING IN YOUR AREA IS BEST SUITED FOR: BEGINNER   INTERMEDIATE **x**   ADVANCED **x**
BEST TIME OF YEAR FOR DIVING/SNORKELING: **September and October**
TEMPERATURE: **NOV-APRIL: 16 C**   **MAY-OCT: 26 C**
VISIBILITY: **DIVING:**   80-100 FT   **SNORKELING:**   80-100 FT

PACKAGES AVAILABLE: DIVE **x**   DIVE STAY   SNORKEL   SNORKEL-STAY
ACCOMMODATIONS NEARBY: HOTEL **x**   MOTEL **x**   HOME RENTALS **x**
ACCOMMODATION RATES: EXPENSIVE **x**   MODERATE **x**   INEXPENSIVE **x**
RESTAURANTS NEARBY: EXPENSIVE **x**   MODERATE **x**   INEXPENSIVE **x**
YOUR AREA IS: REMOTE   QUIET WITH ACTIVITIES **x**   LIVELY
LOCAL ACTIVITY/NIGHTLIFE: **Bars, restaurants and restaurants with dancing**
CAR NEEDED TO EXPLORE AREA?   YES **x**   NO
DUTY FREE SHOPPING?   YES   NO **x**

LOCAL EMERGENCY SERVICES   NEAREST HYPERBARIC TREATMENT FACILITY
COASTGUARD: **Paphos Harbour-Marine Police**   AUTHORITY: **Akrotiri R.A.F.**
TELEPHONE: **242911 Channel 16 Cyprus Radio**   LOCATION: **Akrotiri R.A.F. Base**
CALLSIGNS: TELEPHONE:

LOCAL DIVING DOCTOR:
NAME: **Dr. Chris Theophanides**
LOCATION: **Rochester Medical Center**
TELEPHONE: **233966**

GREECE

Corfu

Wendy Canning Church

The wooded isle Corfu (Keri Keri), named Corcyra in ancient times, sits peacefully and stately alone in the north Ionian Sea. The island stretches out in front of the coast of Epirus and Albania. It was separated from the mainland by only a narrow strait some millennia ago.

Founded in 734 BC by the Corinthians, Corfu fell under Roman control in 229 BC, but regained independence in the 6th century.

Homer sang Corfu's praises. Shakespeare selected it as a background for his Tempest and it is the place which Ulysses chose to make a last stop before his long journey home to Ithaca after a 20 year absence.

Corfu, by its very location and place in history provides an island of contrasts. Gracefully and successfully it has managed to offer beauty and history to the traveler whilst at the same time offering comfort.

The climate is Mediterranean, thus moderate, attracting the year-round guest. This ancient land of the Phoenicians has risen nobly to the occasion providing modern accommodations and amenities for any pocketbook.

Corfu Town

The first day's destination was to the west side of the island to the village of Agios Gordis. Armed with a map and directions we set off. We made our way along the shore and into the capitol, also named Corfu. It is the only urban center on the island. Of Corfu's 92,000 inhabitants, 29,000 live in Corfu town.

We approached the Spinanada or Esplanade. This is the town green, the largest square in all of Greece and some say its most beautiful. On one side of the square are shops and restaurants, to the left are the stately Venetian homes, a reminder of their long centuries of occupation. In 1402 the Venetians paid the King of Naples 30,000 gold ducats for the right to rule and inhabit Corfu.

The civic center which unfolds around the Spinanada is another example of Venetian architecture. Built in 1663 as a club for Venetian nobility, it was later a theater and in 1902 became a town hall. The Corfu branch of the Greek National Tourist Association is housed here. During our visit we made many calls on them and they were most helpful.

A little further along the shore route one comes upon the Heraion Acropolis, the Venetian fortress cut off from town by a moat. To this day, of all its occupiers, the Venetians, are beloved and respected throughout Corfu.

Coast of Corfu by Wendy Canning Church

As we wandered about, the different architectural influences were apparent. The Neapolitan Cantounia houses, which are French in style, are side by side with the English Georgian style houses. Farther along are the Byzantine churches. What an architect's delight. This melange somehow works, making Corfu town an eclectic delight to the eye.

We visited some of the shops. Many of the smaller ones are located down narrow back alley ways that are paved with blocks of stone, (Kantounia). No cars are allowed to drive here, making touring even easier. The quality of merchandise ranges from expensive furs and leathers to souvenir shops. Here the visitor finds gold jewelry, much of it fashioned after museum pieces. They are exquisite!

If you are a shopper Corfu is your town. If you are not a shopper browse anyway. Look at the local wares for they tell a great deal about the people and their culture.

Gastouri

Nine kilometers from the city we came upon Gastouri, a town of old world charm. It is here that many of the aristocratic families of Greece built their summer homes. The Empress Elizabeth of Austria was so taken by its beauty that she built her summer palace here. She named it the Achillion Palace in honor of the mythical figure Achilles. At the palace she sought refuge from the indifference of her husband and the intrigues of the Hapsburg Court.

We returned to the Achillion some days later and toured the neoclassical Palace and gardens which have a commanding view of the sea and the entire northern coast. The interior of the Palace has wonderful decorative ceilings and inlay, the furnishings are tasteful and simple.

A stroll in the garden will introduce you to Gods and Goddesses of pure white marble. Plantings of all varieties abound. In the rear courtyard the hero of this home, Achilles, depicted by two statues is found. The first shows the seated, wounded Achilles with an arrow in his foot, yet looking brave and noble. The second statue at the far end of the courtyard is in distinct contrast. Achilles stands 11'6" high in full military dress ready for battle. The statue overlooks the sea and entire valley beyond. A fitting place, a majestic view for this warrior.

In recent years past the palace has served as a museum during the day and a casino at night. The casino has since moved to the Hilton.

We traveled through what seemed to be miles of olive groves. We noticed something curious and inexplicable. Tucked in one branch of every olive tree was a roll of black mesh. Whatever for?

On inquiry we were told that many olive trees are too tall for the farmer to pick the olives. Therefore, when the olives ripen, the mesh is unrolled, placed under the trees, the trees are then shaken and the olives gathered in the mesh.

The cultivation of olives has been a great source of income for Corfu. This is yet another positive contribution left by the Venetians centuries ago.

Buena Vista Restaurant

Right next to the Archillon Palace is the Buena Vista restaurant. Two nights later we dined by candlelight there on fresh fish, fresh vegetables, fruit and one of the best bottles of wine we had ever savored.

The food was perfect, the view from the terrace sensational. Our table overlooked the sea. The full moon, the candlelight, and the lights of Corfu town twinkleling in the distance illuminated the rugged coastline.

DIVING AGIOS GORDIS

Each morning or early afternoon we would wind our way to Agios Gordis, a distance of 16 kilometers or one half hour from Corfu town. We always took a different route, allowing extra time to discover and photograph the sun-splashed seaside villages or the historic old towns tucked away in the large luxuriant valleys between the mountains.

The true photographic rewards were the townsfolk. Many would look, hesitate, then smile at us, but most scrutinized us carefully and then continued on about their daily chores in the same fashion as their ancestors did centuries before them. The women are very shy however and it is difficult to get close for a photograph. One woman, perhaps for vanity or prosperity, stopped for us, removed her shawl and said: "Please.

Our first glimpse of Agios Gordis was from high in the hills. Tall, noble, cypress trees and flowering cactus parted before us, as if on schedule. Our eyes were bedazzled by the glistening sea, seemingly stretching to infinity.

What seemed only a tiny dot bobbing up and down near the shore, was our boat and the sea beckoning to us.

The topography and architecture of the town unfolded before us. The small houses snugly fit into the hills that ran down to the sea and the beach.

The beach, long, sandy, beautiful and one of the most swimmable on Corfu, is where the action takes place both day and night.

Here you will find not only restaurants and discos but hotels and pensions as well.

A myriad of activities are offered beach side, some of which are water-skiing, parachuting, pedal boats and canoes. For those content with sun and a book, sun beds and parasols are for hire.

The Calypso Diving Center and its adjacent restaurant with pension behind are located here.

Calypso Diving Center

Flying Fish by Andreus Dukakis

A family operation, Mr. and Mrs. Dukakis run the 27 year old restaurant and pension. Their son, Andreas, runs the scuba center. The restaurant specializes in Italian cuisine, but Greek favorites are also offered. The food is simple, fresh and delicious. Most of these waters have been over fished but Andreas knows where these critters hide, so fresh fish is always available.

For those on a budget the Diving Center offers an inexpensive dive/stay package. Andreas also offers two bedroom apartments with kitchenettes for families or a small group. The apartments are simple but charming. We feel those who want quieter surroundings should opt for a hotel further from town or better still the Corfu Hilton.

Please see Honeymoon and Anniversary section for the Corfu Hilton.

The Center carries a full line of Mares equipment. It's up to date, well serviced and available for hire or purchase.

For years scuba diving has been at best very limited and restricted in Greece. It is only allowed with a special permit. Treasure hunters abound worldwide and the Greek government is adamant that none of their artifacts yet uncovered beneath its water leave the country!

You can imagine our enthusiasm when we learned that the Calypso Diving Center had obtained a permit to dive the entire western coast of Corfu and that we would be able to explore, learn about and film its beauty.

So, our gear was loaded in the boat and the small group boarded. We were a mix of divers, snorkelers and non-divers. The divers aboard talked about favorite worldwide destinations offering what each of us considered to be the best of virgin diving. Twenty minutes later we arrived at the dive site.

FOUR METER REEF AT PALEOKA STRAITS

The dive plan was given, we buddied up and dropped into some of the clearest and bluest water I have ever seen. We descended down the anchor line to 40 feet and swam toward the reef. To my amazement the reef's topography resembled a Roman amphitheater. The coral had been formed in a semi-circular shape with ledges running from 40 feet almost to the surface.

Andreas and I had buddied up. He introduced me to the undersea photographic opportunities.

The Dive Center schedules special scenic photography outings. They will point out different species of fish and vegetation and later educate you as to their unique habits.

A moray eel caught our eye as it peered out from inside a crevice in the ledge. It made its way toward us, mouth open, looking as if we might be lunch. The first time I saw a moray I was quite apprehensive. Then I learned that the moray eel breathes through its mouth, thus it is always open, not just when he is hungry!

Swimming further along the reef we caught sight of two 30-40 pound grouper at about 60 feet. We dropped down and swam along with them. They soon became bored with us however, and took off. We gave chase but they were too fast for the likes of mere mortals.

Our bottom time up, we ascended. The wind had come up and the currents had become strong, so we opted for a slow scenic tour back.

We pulled into a little sandy cove embraced on either side by two large caves. We went shell collecting on the beach and in the caves. There were few shells for the collectors, in fact there are very few shells in these waters.

While we are on the subject of collecting: **Do not even think about bringing home an artifact if you are lucky enough to cross its path underwater! It is a definite no-no and also illegal!** The Greeks are passionate about their national treasures, both discovered and undiscovered. This is the main reason why scuba diving is not encouraged throughout Greece and why so few permits are given to individuals or scuba centers.

We returned to the boat and continued along the coast. Andreas pulled the boat close to shore and maneuvered it into the mouth of a large cave. Here, beneath the water lies the remains of a British ship dive bombed by a Messerschmidt during World War II. The ship is still intact and you will see many objects aboard. What you will not see is fish life. There is very little fish life in the cave, but it is found on the reefs.

OFF ERMONES BEACH

The winds and the sea were up, so a decision was made to use the inflatable. After the gear and the divers were abroad we headed off into the choppy seas.

We anchored off two huge rocks. The dive plan was to drop off, descend the anchor line, drop 50 feet and then swim towards the rock. We were then to pass through a huge arch and return to the boat. We were warned not to go on the north side for the currents would carry us to out to sea. There would be were many crevices to investigate so we took our dive lights.

With our lights we were able to see both families of shrimp and an upside-down crayfish in the crevices.

We had two shark fanciers along with us that day. They had inquired on the way out to the site about the possibility of seeing sharks in these waters. It seems that back in July 1990 the first sharks were seen in Corfu waters. They ranged in size from 7-20 feet. The "yellow pollution" however prevailed in the Italian waters last summer and the sharks swam down the channel. So sorry folks, no sharks seen on this dive, but to my delight we found the antheas, the world's smallest grouper.

Homeward bound, our guide, Stephen Dye, (who has since returned to Scotland), a charming, capable young Scotsman had a delightful surprise. We pulled up to a small islet out of the wind. The waters were calm and were the most beautiful shades of crystal clear emerald green one will ever see.

We noticed well worn stone steps reaching up the side of the cliff. We all disembarked and climbed to the top where we found a small church, simply but lovingly fashioned, and bleached white by years of salt air, sun and rain..

Upon entering we were awestruck to find beautiful icons, intricate hand-painted frescos and a silver chalice. Each year on August 15th worshippers make the short journey over the water and climb these steps to this tiny chapel to celebrate the Feast Day of the Virgin Mary.

Outside we toured the grounds. It was mid-October but the plantings of yellow cactus and prickly pear were in full bloom. We looked out to the sea at the two huge boulders where we had just dove.

In less than three hours we had discovered and learned about two unique and wondrous places, one above and one beneath the sea. These experiences are the true gifts of travel.

Does the diving compare to the world's virgin spots such as the Red Sea, Roatan, Palau or Australia? The answer is yes and no.

There is certainly not the abundance of fish life, but there is the beauty of the drop-offs and caves, the wrecks, the clarity of the water, the reef formations and the interesting family of fish that is endemic to these waters compensate for the abundance of fish live one finds in other parts of the world. And you shark fanciers, remember last July!

The Center caters to divers of all levels of experience and separates them accordingly. Divers dive in small groups. At intervals strong winds can blow in making for rough seas. Divers of every level should use caution and commonsense before booking a dive!

The guides are experienced and knowledgeable. An anchor line is dropped along with a safety line at the bow. The buddy system is adhered to. Andreas informs me that divers diving with the Center are covered by insurance which allows evacuation to the decompression facility in Italy. P.S. at this writing they have never had to use it!

The Center plans a variety of excursions which include trips to quaint villages like Sinarades which produces some of the island's best wine, a boat trip to Paxi, museums and nights out at local discos, and restaurants such as the Tripa.

The Tripa

Run for generations by the same family, the Tripa is famous throughout Greece. The food and wine you are served comes from their farms and vineyards.

On first approach the Tripa seems a simple Tavern. Once inside, you find a small dining room at the front. The walls are filled from floor to ceiling with every wine and liquor imaginable. Many of these are hundreds of years old. Further back there is a large garden for dining in good weather.

Across the street the upstairs of a small house caters to very large groups. Here they have live music and I expect this is where the plates are broken a la Zorba.

There is a set menu. One begins with mezes followed by grilled, herbed lamb, small potatoes braised in cheese and a very long pasta dressed with a light red sauce. Table wines both white and red from the Tripa vineyards are served throughout dinner.

Dessert is several different fresh fruits, rum and raisin cake, a white cake and the most heavenly yogurt topped with honey from their own hives.

The Tripa is a must for travelers to Corfu!

AN ISLAND OF CONTRASTS

Corfu is an island of contrasts, the modem and the ancient, they do not blend but rather dwell in concert, side by side, offering those rare opportunities to feed the mind whilst at the same time soothing one's soul. Corfu is a kaleidoscope of color, bright, clear and dazzling to the eye.

As your journey unfolds, the patterns and colors will not change but rather interchange as when one moves their kaleidoscope. They will never lose their clarity nor you your awe.

We urge travelers to Corfu to rent a car or scooter and set out to explore all of Corfu. Begin your journey along the shores where sun-filled skies meet gin clear waters in hues of emerald and blue. Pause and delight or join in the activities of bathers, boatmen or fishermen before you are on your way again.

Climb into the hills and with every turn notice how resplendent the valleys are dressed in lush green vegetation. The oak pine, cypress and olive trees share lovingly their space with fruit trees and flowering cactus.

Noble, stately villas will amaze you when you notice they are perched precariously in the hillside in order to be perfectly situated to catch the gentle winds and view of the sparkling sea beyond.

At the many points in your journey there will be clearings. Stop and take in the mesmerizing view. At times the entire coast will stretch before you. You will soon become aware of shrines along the roadside usually built at a curve in the road. The shrines have either colored or white facades. Most are simple but some are expensive and ornate.

When we asked about these we were told that the shrines were memorials. The white shrines were memorials to those who had died in traffic accidents, the others were for those who had survived. These shrines are attended by the victims' families. Some attend them daily, refilling the water and wine bottles or replacing flowers. These are considered sacrifices to God and to give thanks and ask for His continued blessings for the car's occupants.

As you approach the densely built villages you learn to use caution driving through the narrow cobblestone streets fit for only one car or, heaven forbid, a town bus to pass at a time. Beware of the natives on donkeys loaded with wares going to or coming from market. They are around every corner. Learn to exercise caution and always think there is something very big coming around the next comer. Many times you will be correct. It's the Mercedes buses that really get your attention.

The order and cleanliness of each small sun-washed house adds an air of quiet and order, and a feeling that all is well with those people.

Every town has a church, their interiors are beautifully appointed with frescos and icons. Enter and reflect in one of these.

On your return home perhaps the sun will be setting. Stop at a tavern and take a glass of local wine. As you slowly sip it perhaps you will feel as we did, that we began to understand the pace and continuity of these people and the serenity evidenced in their lives lived day by day, century after century in sweet, honest rhythm.

SCUBA AND SNORKELING FACILITIES QUESTIONNAIRE

NAME **Calypso Diving Centre**
ADDRESS **Marsan 124**
Corfu, Greece
CONTACT **Andreas Doukakis**
TITLE **Director**
TELEPHONE **661-53101** FAX

CAPITAL: GOVERNMENT:
POPULATION: LANGUAGE:
CURRENCY: ELECTRICITY:
AIRLINES: DEPARTURE TAX?
NEED VISA/PASSPORT? YES **x** NO PROOF OF CITIZENSHIP? YES NO

YOUR FACILITY IS CLASSIFIED AS: SCUBA CENTER **x** RESORT
BUSINESS HOURS:
CERTIFYING AGENCIES: **PADI**
LOG BOOK REQUIRED? YES NO
EQUIPMENT: SALES RENTALS AIR FILLS
PRIMARY LINE OF EQUIPMENT: **Holiday Diving**
PHOTOGRAPHIC EQUIPMENT: SALES RENTALS LAB

CHARTER/DIVE BOAT AVAILABLE? YES **x** NO DIVER CAPACITY **varies**
COAST GUARD APPROVED? YES **x** NO CAPTAIN LICENSED? YES **x** NO
SHIP TO SHORE? YES NO **x** LORAN? YES NO **x** RADAR? YES NO **x**
DIVE MASTER/INSTRUCTOR ABOARD? YES **x** NO BOTH **x**

DIVING & SNORKELING: SALT **x** FRESH
TYPE OF DIVING/SNORKELING IN AREA: WALL **x** BEACH **x** WRECK **x** REEF CAVE ICE
DIVING/SNORKELING IN YOUR AREA IS BEST SUITED FOR: BEGINNER **x** INTERMEDIATE **x** ADVANCED
BEST TIME OF YEAR FOR DIVING/SNORKELING: **July - September**
TEMPERATURE: NOV-APRIL: F MAY-OCT: F
VISIBILITY: DIVING: FT SNORKELING: FT

PACKAGES AVAILABLE: DIVE DIVE STAY **x** SNORKEL SNORKEL-STAY
ACCOMMODATIONS NEARBY: HOTEL MOTEL HOME RENTALS
ACCOMMODATION RATES: EXPENSIVE MODERATE INEXPENSIVE **x**
RESTAURANTS NEARBY: EXPENSIVE MODERATE INEXPENSIVE
YOUR AREA IS: REMOTE **x** QUIET WITH ACTIVITIES **x** LIVELY
LOCAL ACTIVITY/NIGHTLIFE:
CAR NEEDED TO EXPLORE AREA? YES NO
DUTY FREE SHOPPING? YES NO

LOCAL EMERGENCY SERVICES NEAREST HYPERBARIC TREATMENT FACILITY
COASTGUARD: AUTHORITY:
TELEPHONE: LOCATION: **Athens or Italy**
CALLSIGNS: TELEPHONE:

LOCAL DIVING DOCTOR:
NAME:
LOCATION:
TELEPHONE:

Crete

Orville S. Carman

I am a 35 year old male who has been in the Navy since 1975 (out of high school). I have spent most of my time overseas. By profession I am a U.S. Navy Mineman and part of the Military Police/Customs operation. My primary job is to test, build and deliver U.S. Naval underwater mines to the Planting Agent

I received my Open Water certification in 1987. I have not been able to do much diving lately due to work and the distance to the only legal site for foreigners to dive.

I have had the chance to go snorkeling with the Greek EOD that is a bomb disposal unit. We found a 200 pound W.W.II naval gun shell.

I do a lot of snorkeling, but I have no favorite place. Anywhere on the coast is nice. The water is cool, but not too bad. I do not use a wet suit There is not much to see however. These waters have been picked over for years. I have seen some small fish and some cuttlefish, octopus, and shells.

Jellyfish by Wendy Canning Church

PUBLIC SNORKELING SITES

Kalathas Beach has a restaurant that is open in the summer only and three bar/water stands. This is the main beach that the U.S. Navy personnel go to. It is also where I found the W.W.II gun shell.

Tavros Beach has one restaurant and one bar/water stand. It also has a marina and is the second beach that the American Navy uses.

The coast line between these two beaches is filled with caves, most of which do not have great depth, but some do. You can snorkel in these, but without a light you cannot go in very far.

ACTIVITIES

Both beaches are topless. They also have a volleyball area. Kalathas has water-skiing and jet-skiing, windsurfing, and a better restaurant. It is also closer to Hania, which is the main city. There you can find bars, restaurants, cafes and museums. Hotels also abound in Hania. The average price of a room is $30.00/night.

There is one dive center on the island but I have not dived with them. I have enclosed information. It is best that any diver check them out with other divers familiar with this center.

Aegean Dive Shop 31 Pandoras St. Glyfada 166 74 ATHENS Tel: 8945409-8952698

Now is your chance to discover the underwater world of Southern Crete. We offer services for all levels of experience, gentle Underwater slopes or steep walls, caves with beautiful colours and much more.

Our experienced and multilingual team is eager to welcome you and introduce you to this newly- opened diving area. We offer: * Diving for experienced divers (incl. boat dives) * PADI and VIT courses * Specialty courses * Beginner courses * Introduction Dives Diving for everyone. Call us today!

Mykonos

Chris Politopoylos

I, Chris Politopoylos, am the diving instructor (PADI & NAUI) and owner of the diving center -"Lucky Scuba Divers." My diving experience includes being in the Underwater Destruction Team as an officer of the Greek Navy for ten years 1970-1980.

Mykonos and "Lucky Scuba Divers"

Discover why both of them are able to make you never forget your holidays. We take your fun very seriously. Visit the famous island of Mykonos, queen of Cyclades and explore the fantastic underwater world with "Lucky Scuba Divers" and let us surprise you with our hospitality. "Lucky Scuba Divers" welcomes you in Mykonos. You can find us in Ornos Beach and a few meters from the beach you can see our traditional 17 meter boat named Agios Andreas.

The dive sites where we go for diving or snorkeling are:
1. Dragon Island
2. Paradise Reef
3. Lazaros Island
4. Green Islands
5. Paraga Reef etc.

All of these sites are about 5-30 minutes away from our diving center.

The places we go for diving or snorkeling have a combination of walls, reefs, wrecks, caves and offer a variety of fish life.

The most interesting site of all and one different from all the other places all over the world is the archaeological site of Mykonos which is under the surface of the sea at the places we diving.

Lady in Repose by Wendy Canning Church

There you can enjoy what has been left by our ancestors and their great civilization like amphorae, house walls of old cities, etc. They have all been there for thousands of years. The visibility of the water is 80 feet for diving and 65 feet for snorkeling. The temperature is about 70F.

All levels from beginner to advanced are suited for the site. The location's scuba and snorkeling facilities are so good that nobody has ever left the place disappointed. For us safety is more than just a slogan.

For accommodations there are rooms for rent, houses, villas and apartments,, etc.

There is great entertainment in our restaurants with a variety of Greek and any other kind of food. Excellent seafood, traditional Greek hospitality and exciting night life.

On diving and snorkeling information and scuba diving laws:
1. All the international dive certifications can be used in our country.
2. Everybody can use a spear gun for fish, lobster, octopus, etc. But without using a scuba tank.
3. There are no licenses or fees in our country.
4. The scuba gear Lucky Scuba Divers offers is Scubapro, US Divers, Dacor, Sherwood, etc. and our compressor is a Bauer.

For more information contact. Chris Politopoylos, Lucky Scuba Divers, (Summer) Ornos Beach, Mykonos 84600, Greece. Tel: 0030-289-22813; Fax: 0030-289-23764. (Winter) Artemidos 3, Aegion 25100, Greece. Tel: 0030-691-21849; Fax: 0030-691-2133.

SCUBA AND SNORKELING FACILITIES QUESTIONNAIRE

NAME **"Lucky Scuba Divers"**
ADDRESS **Summer - Ornos Beach, Mykonos, Greece**
Winter - Artemidos 3, Aegion 25100, Greece
CONTACT **Chris Politopoulos**
TITLE **Diving Instructor**
TELEPHONE **691-21849** FAX **691-21331**

CAPITAL: **Athens** GOVERNMENT: **Presidential Democracy**
POPULATION: **9,500,000** LANGUAGE: **Greek, English**
CURRENCY: **Greek Trahma** ELECTRICITY: **220 volts**
AIRLINES: **Olympic Airways** DEPARTURE TAX? **18%**
NEED VISA/PASSPORT? YES **x** NO   PROOF OF CITIZENSHIP? YES   NO **x**

YOUR FACILITY IS CLASSIFIED AS: SCUBA CENTER **x** RESORT
BUSINESS HOURS: **10.00 - 18.00**
CERTIFYING AGENCIES: **Esco-Reisen - Tuireisen, ITAS**
LOG BOOK REQUIRED? YES **x** NO
EQUIPMENT: SALES   RENTALS **x**   AIR FILLS **x**
PRIMARY LINE OF EQUIPMENT:
PHOTOGRAPHIC EQUIPMENT: SALES   RENTALS **x**   LAB **x**

CHARTER/DIVE BOAT AVAILABLE? YES **x** NO   DIVER CAPACITY **40**
COAST GUARD APPROVED? YES **x** NO   CAPTAIN LICENSED? YES **x**   NO
SHIP TO SHORE? 60 ft.   NO   LORAN? YES **x**   NO   RADAR? YES **x**   NO
DIVE MASTER/INSTRUCTOR ABOARD?   YES **x**   NO   BOTH **x**

DIVING & SNORKELING: SALT **x**   FRESH
TYPE OF DIVING/SNORKELING IN AREA: WALL **x**   BEACH **x**   WRECK **x**   REEF   CAVE **x**   ICE
DIVING/SNORKELING IN YOUR AREA IS BEST SUITED FOR: BEGINNER **x**   INTERMEDIATE **x**   ADVANCED **x**
BEST TIME OF YEAR FOR DIVING/SNORKELING: **Middle May to Middle October**
TEMPERATURE: NOV-APRIL: F   **MAY-OCT: 70   F**
VISIBILITY: **DIVING: 80 FT**   **SNORKELING: 65 FT**

PACKAGES AVAILABLE: DIVE **x**   DIVE STAY **x**   SNORKEL **x**   SNORKEL-STAY **x**
ACCOMMODATIONS NEARBY: HOTEL **x**   MOTEL **x**   HOME RENTALS **x**
ACCOMMODATION RATES: EXPENSIVE   MODERATE **x**   INEXPENSIVE **x**
RESTAURANTS NEARBY: EXPENSIVE   MODERATE **x**   INEXPENSIVE **x**
YOUR AREA IS: REMOTE   QUIET WITH ACTIVITIES **x**   LIVELY **x**
LOCAL ACTIVITY/NIGHTLIFE: **Nightlife in Mykonos**
CAR NEEDED TO EXPLORE AREA? YES **x**   NO
DUTY FREE SHOPPING?   YES   NO **x**

LOCAL EMERGENCY SERVICES   NEAREST HYPERBARIC TREATMENT FACILITY
COASTGUARD: **Mykonos Island (Greece)**   AUTHORITY: **Marine Hospital**
TELEPHONE: **0030-289-22218**   LOCATION: **Piraeus**
CALLSIGNS: **VHF Channel 12 5 16 "Marine"**   TELEPHONE: **0030-1-4654611**

LOCAL DIVING DOCTOR:
NAME: **Stambolis Filippos**
LOCATION: **Mykonos Island, Greece**
TELEPHONE: **0030-289-22930 or 23530**

HONG KONG

By Don Lanman

From the Great Wall of China the mighty Kun Lun Shan mountain range, of central Asia snakes south to the coast like a giant serpent. Where the great mountains submerge into the South China Sea there's a magical place that Chinese spiritual teachers, "Fung Shui Masters", say the Dragon lives. This place is Hong Kong.

The area surrounding Hong Kong is known as Kowloon or "Nine Dragons" after the eight hills that surround it to the north. Local legend holds that a Chinese Emperor arrived in search of the Nine Dragons, throwing himself into the sea when he counted only eight, never understanding that he represented the ninth.

With a strong desire to dive the Dragon, I arrived in Hong Kong at the peak of the Typhoon season (June to August). Before leaving, I uncovered information on diving facilities, requirements, conditions, and the environment.

This research turned out to be a great journey in itself. Local dive shop owners simply laughed, asking why would I dive in that cesspool. So much for the "no sea to rough" mentality.

> **Of equal help, Skin Diver Magazine, PADI and NAUI could provide no information to assist me in preparing for diving in the South China Sea. Finally I contacted Divers Exchange International and learned that information was sparse for this dive location. In fact the only dive operation on file was Bunn's Divers Institute Ltd.**

As it turns out Bunn's is the only official dive operation in Hong Kong. Formed in 1958 to produce diving equipment, Bunn's is a full service dive operation with divers certification training, equipment sales/service, dive trips and a wide variety of water sports activities including: water skiing, wind surfing and snorkeling.

The dive operation is licensed for several organizations including: PADI, NAUI, British Sub-Aqua Club (BSAC) and the Confederation Mondiale Activities Sub Aquatiques (CMAS). Bunn's offer a full range of classes from beginner to dive master, with a sincere focus on safety through "Equipment, Knowledge and Technique".

> **There are two drawbacks to Bunn's; they schedule dive trips on the weekends only and preference is given to local club members. This severely limits the diving opportunities and requires at least two weeks advance reservations.**

In addition, they have only two dive boats, the newest being an 80 ft. custom boat named "DiversPro". While it's comfortable, air conditioned and fully equipped, there is only room for 20 divers, again limiting access to divers.

The dive masters and instructors seemed competent and attentive to safety. However, there is a language issue to consider, so I found it important to speak and listen very carefully to each dive briefing. While many divers do not associate Hong Kong with scuba diving, given the high level of pollution in the harbors, the destination is growing in popularity.

> Outside the harbor areas, the eastern waters have remained relatively clear and support a wide range of marine life.

The typical visibility is only about 30 feet and sea temperatures range between thirteen and twenty-eight degrees Celsius. This wide variety of temperature creates an environment for many temperate and tropical marine species to exist.

> There are no true coral reefs however there are over 50 species of coral growth on wrecks and other solid objects.

The sea is void of any large fish due to unrestricted fishing in the area.

> However there are a nice variety of other sea creatures including; crabs, sea slugs, miniature octopus, small damselfish, and pink and white fan worms. If you are lucky you may see a small reef sharks and sea bass.

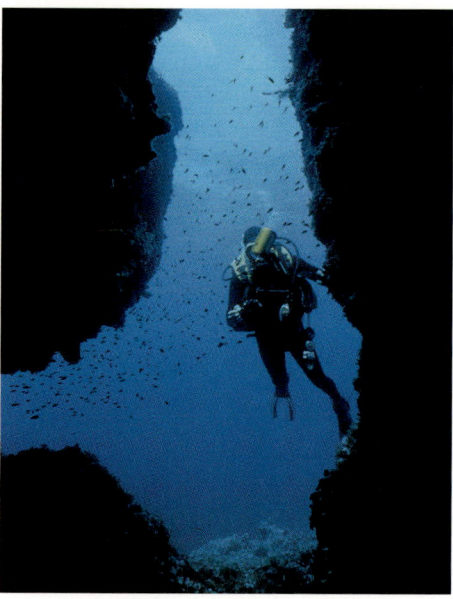

Hong Kong diver by Kwan Ito

In an attempt to protect the environment the World Wide Fund for Nature Hong Kong, and other government departments, have set aside the first marine protected area in the Hoi Ha Wan Bay located at the mouth of the Tolo Harbor. The plan is to build a marine studies center at the bay for students, visitors and divers.

From Ping Chau in the North to Po Toi in the South, there are over 235 islands in the region, most of them uninhabited. This provides the adventurous diver with an unlimited source of dive locations including great spots like Tap Mun, Breaker Reef, Fung Head, Long Ke and Pak Kwo.

> For the snorkeler there are some great spots at Repulse Bay, Clear Water Bay and Stanley Bay.

Stanley, once an old pirate city, still resembles a sleepy fishing village like you might find in Mexico. It has interesting sights, shopping, old English Pubs and plenty of history.

As a tourist destination, Hong Kong has much to offer. Sensational shopping, fabulous food, great night life, diverse sightseeing and a remarkable cultural heritage.

In addition to being a dive destination, Hong Kong is a fascinating fabric of local culture, state-of-the-art shopping complexes, bobbing sampans, English tradition, modern world influence and the history of an Eastern civilization that dates back thousands of years. So, if you're looking for a unique dive location, then Dive the Dragon.

SCUBA AND SNORKELING FACILITIES QUESTIONNAIRE

NAME   Bunns's Divers Institute, Ltd.
ADDRESS   Kwong Sang Hong Building, Shops E & G,
              188 Wanchi Road, Wanchi, Hong Kong
CONTACT   Anthony C.F. Ho, Simon K.K. Yu
TITLE   Manager and Centre Manager
TELEPHONE   852-893-7899   FAX 852-834-0039   TELEX 81003 BUNNS HK

CAPITAL: Hong Kong   GOVERNMENT: English Crown Colony
POPULATION: 6 million   LANGUAGE: English & Chinese-Canton
CURRENCY: Hong Kong Dollar   ELECTRICITY: 220 volt, 3 pin British type
AIRLINES: UA, Cathay, Singapore   DEPARTURE TAX? $20 U.S.
NEED VISA/PASSPORT?   YES   NO   PROOF OF CITIZENSHIP?   YES   NO

YOUR FACILITY IS CLASSIFIED AS: SCUBA CENTER x   RESORT
BUSINESS HOURS: 10:00 a.m. - 6:00 p.m. Weekend diving only - advance booking
CERTIFYING AGENCIES: PADI, NAUI, BSAC, CMAS
LOG BOOK REQUIRED?   YES   NO x
EQUIPMENT: SALES x   RENTALS x   AIR FILLS x
PRIMARY LINE OF EQUIPMENT: Complete Pro Shop, custom wet suit
PHOTOGRAPHIC EQUIPMENT: SALES x   RENTALS x   LAB

CHARTER/DIVE BOAT AVAILABLE?   YES x   NO   DIVER CAPACITY   20
COAST GUARD APPROVED?   YES x   NO   CAPTAIN LICENSED? YES x   NO
SHIP TO SHORE?   YES x   NO   LORAN?   YES x   NO   RADAR?   YES x   NO
DIVE MASTER/INSTRUCTOR ABOARD?   YES x   NO   BOTH x

DIVING & SNORKELING: SALT x   FRESH
TYPE OF DIVING/SNORKELING IN AREA: WALL x   BEACH   WRECK   REEF   CAVE   ICE
DIVING/SNORKELING IN YOUR AREA IS BEST SUITED FOR: BEGINNER   INTERMEDIATE x   ADVANCED
BEST TIME OF YEAR FOR DIVING/SNORKELING: September to November
TEMPERATURE: **NOV-APRIL:**   60-75 F   MAY-OCT: 75-90 F
VISIBILITY: **DIVING:**   35 FT   **SNORKELING: 20 FT**

PACKAGES AVAILABLE: DIVE x   DIVE STAY   SNORKEL x   SNORKEL-STAY
ACCOMMODATIONS NEARBY: HOTEL x   MOTEL   HOME RENTALS
ACCOMMODATION RATES: EXPENSIVE x   MODERATE x   INEXPENSIVE x
RESTAURANTS NEARBY: EXPENSIVE x   MODERATE x   INEXPENSIVE x
YOUR AREA IS: REMOTE   QUIET WITH ACTIVITIES   LIVELY x
LOCAL ACTIVITY/NIGHTLIFE: Unlimited
CAR NEEDED TO EXPLORE AREA?   YES   NO x
DUTY FREE SHOPPING?   YES x   NO

LOCAL EMERGENCY SERVICES   NEAREST HYPERBARIC TREATMENT FACILITY
COASTGUARD: On file with Dive Shop   AUTHORITY: Hong Kong, Royal Navy
TELEPHONE: LOCATION:
CALLSIGNS: TELEPHONE:

LOCAL DIVING DOCTOR:
NAME: Any local hospital. On file with dive shop.
LOCATION:
TELEPHONE:

INDONESIA

BALI

Jochen Kem, DEI Member

Dear Wendy, Let me give you my impression on Bali and its scuba diving. "It's fantastic!"

Sanur, Kuta and Nusa Dua are the famous lodging areas and each area has its own scuba centre. Most visitors to Bali stay in these areas, using them as a base, diving and snorkeling them, and then taking day trips to more remote areas, getting to know Bali both above and under the water.

Pulau Menjangan is located on the north-west coast of Bali. Here you will find the most marvelous wall reef with a drop to 140 feet.

The reef is protected and you must obtain a license at the small security station for $2 U.S. A boat brings you to the island, taking about 20 minutes and costing around $20 U.S. The boat is great carrying 10 people including diving equipment. You must bring your equipment from your hotel, 2 tanks for a 2 tank dive, spare O rings and your lunch.

Make sure you have underwater photography equipment because the 80ft visibility will reveal a fantastic assortment of marine life including clams, pearl mussels, sea anemones, umbrella anemones, lobster, sea shells, flyer snails, all kinds of coral fish, large jacks and if you are lucky, the monstrous 40 foot shark wall - outstanding!

Make sure you stop on the road on your return and drink a coffee Bali - one of the real strong ones!

Pulau Menjangan is a four hour drive from the hotel area. You will leave in the morning at 8 am and arrive at the island at 12 noon.

P. S. Make sure when diving this beautiful Menjangan wall reef that you don't break anything or carry anything away. The reef is protected and anyway I want to go back and enjoy the reef just like my last dive.

SINGARADJA

40 minutes after Padangbay in the direction of Singaradja on the east coast road to Bali (opposite Lombog) offshore, only 20 minutes from the stoney beach, can be found the wreck of the **S.S. Liberty**.

The **S.S. Liberty** was a U.S. Navy transport, torpedoed by the Japanese in World War II. She lies on her right side in depths of 8 to 40 feet making this of interest to both the snorkeler and scuba diver.

The engine room and other parts are filled with sand and volcanic ash from the 1962 mountain eruption. This beautiful site unveils a myriad of marine life. Your offering of bananas or bread brings you to a centre of thousands of colorful fish.

The wreck is 2 hours by car from the major hotel resorts. Remember, you drive on the left side and must have an international drivers license.

Make sure to check your vehicle for damages before hand and show any small scratches to the renter to guarantee a disturb free return!

Benzene (gasoline) is very inexpensive, the roads are very nice and the countryside beautiful, with wonderful scenery of rice fields and palm trees.

THE KILLERSHELL PLACE

20 minutes after Padangbay is another dive called "The Killershell Place." The dive at 40 feet must be entered through a barricade of heavy waves.

PADANGBAY HARBOR

One more destination is behind the Padangbay Harbor. You can visit a cave with depths of 40 feet and see up to 20 sharks sleeping on the ground without movement.

BENOA

In Benoa there is a passage to the open sea to the right of Turtle Bay and to the left of Nusa Dua passing into the harbor of Benoa. This passage is fantastic for drift diving and has depths of 80 feet. There are large lobster colonies, a few big sharks, pilot fish and many small coral fish.

NUSA PENIDA ISLAND

South of Sanur is the large island of Nusa Penida comprised of channels with depths of 150 feet. You must travel by boat for 3 hours. Most of the boats are deepsea fishing boats so you will have a chance to catch marlin, dolphin, jack and tuna. These may be cooked and served free in the fisherman's restaurant at the Hyatt Hotel. A full days' charter includes lunch and equipment. Nusa Penida has heavy current and therefore you should dive with not only your buddy but a guide that knows these waters.

Divers by Dick Snow

SANUR

South of Bali is Sanur one of the richest hotel areas and also my former workplace.

Sanur is fronted by a wall reef. On the island site of the reef it is 6 feet deep. Perfect for snorkeling or diving and over the wall on the sea side the depth is 30 feet. There is a break in the center which makes a passage for the wooden outriggers, the local boats called Sakung.

The reef is fully alive with marine life. All kinds of coral fish, watersnakes, lobster, young barracuda, schools of octopus, large ball fish, small sharks, seasnails, prawns, fire fish, stone fish and moranes can be found.

The current can be strong! Make sure you wear a wet suit or heavy t-shirt and gloves as the water is not deep and a collision with coral is possible.

A second site is perfect for the snorkeler or diver as at its deepest it is 10 feet. You can leisurely visit the home of beautiful sunfish or stingrays, yellow and black angelfish, the gracious looking trumpet fish and more, more, more.

Snorkelers and divers beware and don't forget the reef passage on the right side from land to sea is very dangerous! Please stay at the left side only!

Baruna is the biggest dive shop operator in Sanur having 5 shops and offering complete dive tours.

NUSA DUA

Nusa Dua is the newly established tourist area. Like Sanur it is fronted by a wall reef which is mostly dead but still has some marine life.

The depths outside the reef are 60 feet. The Scuba Centre next to the Nusa Dua Beach Hotel is run by my friend Ketut, an instructor, who gave me your address two and a half years ago and was my teacher.

> **Ketut organizes dive trips and you can be sure that with him you will dive safely!**

Wendy, when you go to Bali give my regards to this island of the Gods.

> **Make sure your equipment is in good shape because there is no decompression chamber on Bali.**

You can count on good equipment from Ketut or Baruna.

I'm off to China to work. Diving in China is still new and there may be diving on Hainan Island. If I hear of something, I'll let you know.

SCUBA AND SNORKELING FACILITIES QUESTIONNAIRE

NAME	**Bali Marine Sports**
ADDRESS	**J.L. By Pass Ngurah Rai, Blanjong - Sanur,**
	Denpasar 80228, Bali, Indonesia
CONTACT	**I Ketut Ena Partha**
TITLE	**Director**
TELEPHONE	**0062-0361-89308, 88829**	FAX **0062-87872**

CAPITAL: **Denpasar**	GOVERNMENT: **Indonesia**
POPULATION: **2,000,000**	LANGUAGE: **Indonesian, English**
CURRENCY: **Any currency**	ELECTRICITY: **220 volt**
AIRLINES: **Garuda Indonesia etc**	DEPARTURE TAX? **Rp 11.000**
NEED VISA/PASSPORT? YES **x** NO	PROOF OF CITIZENSHIP? YES **x** NO

YOUR FACILITY IS CLASSIFIED AS:	SCUBA CENTER **x**	RESORT
BUSINESS HOURS:	**6:30 a.m. - 11:00 p.m.**
CERTIFYING AGENCIES:	**PADI**
LOG BOOK REQUIRED?	YES **x**	NO
EQUIPMENT:	SALES **x**	RENTALS **x**	AIR FILLS **x**
PRIMARY LINE OF EQUIPMENT:	**US Diver and ScubaPro**
PHOTOGRAPHIC EQUIPMENT:	SALES	RENTALS **x**	LAB **x**

CHARTER/DIVE BOAT AVAILABLE? YES **x** NO	DIVER CAPACITY **14**
COAST GUARD APPROVED? YES NO **x**	CAPTAIN LICENSED? YES **x** NO
SHIP TO SHORE? Radio **x** NO LORAN? YES NO	RADAR? YES NO
DIVE MASTER/INSTRUCTOR ABOARD? YES **x** NO	BOTH **x**

DIVING & SNORKELING:	SALT **x**	FRESH
TYPE OF DIVING/SNORKELING IN AREA: WALL **x** BEACH **x** WRECK **x** REEF CAVE **x** ICE
DIVING/SNORKELING IN YOUR AREA IS BEST SUITED FOR: BEGINNER **x** INTERMEDIATE **x** ADVANCED **x**
BEST TIME OF YEAR FOR DIVING/SNORKELING: **All the year round**
TEMPERATURE: **NOV-APRIL:** **80 F**	**MAY-OCT:** **80 F**
VISIBILITY:	**DIVING:**	**70 FT**	**SNORKELING:** **80 FT**

PACKAGES AVAILABLE:	DIVE **x**	DIVE STAY **x**	SNORKEL **x**	SNORKEL-STAY **x**
ACCOMMODATIONS NEARBY: HOTEL **x**	MOTEL	HOME RENTALS
ACCOMMODATION RATES: EXPENSIVE **x**	MODERATE **x**	INEXPENSIVE **x**
RESTAURANTS NEARBY: EXPENSIVE **x**	MODERATE **x**	INEXPENSIVE **x**
YOUR AREA IS:	REMOTE	QUIET WITH ACTIVITIES	LIVELY **x**
LOCAL ACTIVITY/NIGHTLIFE: **Bar, disco, etc.**
CAR NEEDED TO EXPLORE AREA? YES **x** NO
DUTY FREE SHOPPING?	YES **x** **3 duty free shops in our area**

LOCAL EMERGENCY SERVICES	NEAREST HYPERBARIC TREATMENT FACILITY
COASTGUARD: **Kuta Beach, Bali, Indonesia**	AUTHORITY: **Indonesian Navy Hospital**
TELEPHONE: **0062-0361-51999**	LOCATION: **JL. Gadung No. 1, Surabaya**
CALLSIGNS: **YC 9 ZRV**	TELEPHONE:

LOCAL DIVING DOCTOR:
NAME:	**Not available in Bali, only in Surabaya (East Jawa)**
LOCATION:	**Indonesian Navy Hospital in Surabaya (East Jawa)**
TELEPHONE: **0062-031-816053**

Manado

LUCKY HERLAMBANG

Calling all nature lovers, especially divers and other sea lovers. If you have been yearning for an exciting and unusual destination for your next holiday, your first choice should be Manado, a beautiful city on the north tip of Sulawesi, the orchid shaped island with the ancient name Celebes. It is the south of The Philippines and split in two by the equator.

In this tropical paradise, friendly expert local divers will help you explore the world's most unspoiled marine wilderness area. These marine parks are fully protected from spearfishing, coral, or fish collecting:

Bunaken - Manado Tua Marine Preserve of 75.265 hectares, off the north coast of Minahasa peninsula, in Celebes Sea, including the 5 islands of Bunaken, Manado Tua Old Manado, Siladen, Montehege and Nain.

Lembeh Island and Pulau Dua Island (sister island), off the south coast of Minahasa peninsula, in Molucca Sea.

Each island is surrounded by a white sand beach with breathtaking beauty of colorful shallow coral reefs and magnificent deeper coral gardens. The water is usually calm and visibility often exceeds 30 meters (100 feet). The water temperature remains about 30 degrees centigrade (84 degrees Fahrenheit) all year round. The excellent diving can be found anytime of the year, only disturbed by the occasional monsoon west wind. Then the diving will be on the opposite coast.

Coral reef formation begins with a flat reef to about five meters (15 feet) deep, then slopes down forming underwater valleys, or drop-offs vertically down to hundreds of meters. This forms fantastic "underwater great walls", cut with many narrow vertical clefts, large caves and hanging masses of corals.

> **On these unique coral reefs a tremendous collection of marine life thrives, red and orange encrusting sponges, christmas tree worms, basket and tube sponges, soft and hard corals of all colors, sea anemone stocked with clown fish, red-blue-pink and brown starfish, bright colored crinoids, giant tunicates, sea-whips, nudibranch. Spanish dancer, transparent and red stripped coral shrimps, lobsters, mollusks, thousands of ornamental coral fish and large pelagics, often seen giant Napoleon wrasse, angelfish, cattlefish, turtles, blue ribbon eels, moray eels, stingray and eagle ray, harmless sea snakes, sharks, barracuda, tuna, snapper and dolphin.**

Night life begins after the sun sets. Take your underwater torch to observe sleeping fish, mating shells and invertebrates, the swinging lantern fish and colorful feeding corals.

> **Completing the diving experience are the exciting W.W.II wrecks in 25 meters (80 feet) of water. These are encrusted with marine life such as color sponges, soft and hard corals, deepwater gorgonians and serve as a home for large schools of fish including lionfish, stonefish, the upside-down shrimpfish, batfish, trumpetfish, jacks and mother of pearls. Shallow water snorkeling and observation through a glass bottom boat provides an excellent experience as well as diving.**

Awaiting you on the surface is the fascinating land of the Minahasa region. Here you will meet the delightful light skinned Minahasan people with their quick smiles and keen interest in visitors. In this region you have many optional activities: Climbing volcanoes to see the smoking cauldron and colorful crater lake.

Exploring the rain forest to observe species unique to Sulawesi such as: the tarsius, at 15cm it is the smallest carnivorous monkey in the world; the maleo, a small pigeon with 10cm eggs; the tailess black monkey; the marsupial kukus; babirusa (pig-deer); anoa the dwarf buffalo; hornbill birds and hundreds of other bird and butterfly species.

Touring by car to enjoy the mountain scenery, beautiful lakes, sulfuric hot springs, clove, nutmeg and coconut plantations, vanilla and tropical vegetable farms, cinnamon trees on the road side and all sorts of tropical flowers and fruits. Especially interesting are the "Waruga", stone burial containers dating from the pre-Christian anemist days of megalithic age.

The city of Manado is fully stocked with your needs for medicines, film and film processing, book stores and markets of every kind. You can buy souvenirs, clothes and spices. There are inexpensive quick service tailors who will make suits, shirts or dresses from Indonesian batik, silk sarongs or kerawang (pulled thread embroidery). You can also play golf, tennis or enjoy an expert oriental massage or accupressure.

Divers Statue at Manado by Lucky Herlanbang

Manado, an accessible travel destination, offers many unique and unmatched sea and land attractions, especially the fascinating dive sites and endless variety of dive programs, shallow or deep dives on the colorful flat reefs or dramatic drop-offs, drifting or current dives, the wreck dives and night dives. All of these should keep even the most experienced diver busy for at least ten days.

Besides the many hotels in the city of Manado, just 15 minutes from the central city, 25 minutes from the airport and 30 minutes from the marine park, is the **Nusantara Diving Center** or **N.D.C.**, your inexpensive joyful home base for exploration, in the seaside village of Molas.

Nusantara Diving Center is owned, operated and dedicated to divers. It was the founder of diving activities in Manado. Established in 1975, this organization received the Kalpataru Award in 1985. This is the highest honor for pioneering works in environmental conservation. Kalpataru means "tree of life".

N.D.C. only organizes small group tours in their typical outrigger dive boats. This assures you a completely hassle free, cheerful vacation with uncrowded exploration to remote dive sites. Daily two-dive programs depart at 9 a.m. and return at 4 p.m.

Pink Coral by Lucky Herlanbang

This dive center offers you a homey atmosphere with 20 rooms in local type seaside cottages that are fan-cooled with western-style private baths and hot water. Superb home cooked meals of Indonesian, Chinese, European and regional specialties. Don't plan to loose weight. Also for your pleasure: mini-bar, disco, bamboo music band, billiards, aquarium, volleyball court, motor bike rental and game fishing

Manado is not tourist oriented yet. It is a delight to know and dive with young competent Indonesian divers as an individual instead of part of a large group. They are qualified and look after your every need. At night they entertain you with a singsong, guitars, Manadonese Bamboo music, marimba or dancing.

The airport meeting, send off, transportation into town, welcoming and farewell or birthday party is included in your accommodation package.

SCUBA AND SNORKELING FACILITIES QUESTIONNAIRE

NAME **Nusantara Diving Centre (NDC)**
ADDRESS **Molas Dusan 3.**
P.O. Box 15, Manado, Indonesia
CONTACT **Loky Herlambang**
TITLE **AOWI-SSI**
TELEPHONE **0431-3988** FAX TELEX **74100 BCA MO & 74228 BCA MO**

CAPITAL: GOVERNMENT:
POPULATION: LANGUAGE:
CURRENCY: ELECTRICITY:
AIRLINES: DEPARTURE TAX?
NEED VISA/PASSPORT? YES **x** NO PROOF OF CITIZENSHIP? YES NO

YOUR FACILITY IS CLASSIFIED AS: SCUBA CENTER **x** RESORT **x**
BUSINESS HOURS: **Summer & Winter**
CERTIFYING AGENCIES:
LOG BOOK REQUIRED? YES NO
EQUIPMENT: SALES RENTALS **x** AIR FILLS **x**
PRIMARY LINE OF EQUIPMENT: **Best Scuba Dive Tours**
PHOTOGRAPHIC EQUIPMENT: SALES RENTALS **x** LAB **x**

CHARTER/DIVE BOAT AVAILABLE? YES **x** NO DIVER CAPACITY **20**
COAST GUARD APPROVED? YES NO **x** CAPTAIN LICENSED? YES **x** NO
SHIP TO SHORE? YES NO LORAN? YES NO RADAR? YES NO
DIVE MASTER/INSTRUCTOR ABOARD? YES **x** NO BOTH **x**

DIVING & SNORKELING: SALT **x** FRESH
TYPE OF DIVING/SNORKELING IN AREA: WALL **x** BEACH **x** WRECK **x** REEF **x** CAVE **x** ICE
DIVING/SNORKELING IN YOUR AREA IS BEST SUITED FOR: BEGINNER **x** INTERMEDIATE **x** ADVANCED **x**
BEST TIME OF YEAR FOR DIVING/SNORKELING: **April till December**
TEMPERATURE: NOV-APRIL: F MAY-OCT: F
VISIBILITY: DIVING: FT SNORKELING: FT

PACKAGES AVAILABLE: DIVE **x** DIVE STAY **x** SNORKEL SNORKEL-STAY
ACCOMMODATIONS NEARBY: HOTEL **x** MOTEL HOME RENTALS
ACCOMMODATION RATES: EXPENSIVE MODERATE INEXPENSIVE
RESTAURANTS NEARBY: EXPENSIVE MODERATE INEXPENSIVE
YOUR AREA IS: REMOTE QUIET WITH ACTIVITIES **x** LIVELY **x**
LOCAL ACTIVITY/NIGHTLIFE:
CAR NEEDED TO EXPLORE AREA? YES NO
DUTY FREE SHOPPING? YES NO

LOCAL EMERGENCY SERVICES NEAREST HYPERBARIC TREATMENT FACILITY
COASTGUARD: **Harbour of Manado City** AUTHORITY: **Indonesian Navy**
TELEPHONE: **51875** LOCATION: **Surabaya & Jakarta**
CALLSIGNS: TELEPHONE:

LOCAL DIVING DOCTOR:
NAME: **Dr. W. Warouw**
LOCATION: **Manado City**
TELEPHONE: **0431-3090**

Tropical Princess Live-Aboard

Glenn Mullin San Francisco, CA USA Certification date: 1986 experience in Monterey California diving, Pacific Northwest, Caribbean, GBR, Australia, Indonesia, Hawaii.

Shark by Lucky Herlanbang

I have been diving twice on the Tropical Princess and have been equally impressed. American, Japanese and Taiwanese divers book expeditions and have been interesting and fun to dive with. The diving expeditions are never the same as the Dive Master and Captain can adjust the sites to conditions and guest consensus.

There are more dive sites within range of the Tropical Princess than can be visited in ten expeditions.

There are three notable dive sites: Mapia, Asia, and Ayu. The diversity of fish and coral species is amazing and the submarine terrain is made up of a seaward reef front with sand terraces, vertical walls and drop-offs. The reefs are decorated with Gorgonians and black corals. Nearly all dive sites will interest deep or shallow divers. Night dives were spectacular with giant Spanish dancers and many lobsters.

There are over 250 different common species in some areas including pelagics, gobies wrasse, damselfish, groupers, blennies, cardinalfish, moray eels, butterflyfish, surgeonfish, pipefish, parrotfish, scorpionfish, jacks, snapper, snake eels, emperors, wormfish, dartfish, triggerfish.

Read up on the fishes to be seen in *Micronesian Reef Fishes* (Myers).

The safety of the boat and crew is excellent and the Zodiac crew is excellent at spotting surfacing divers. Post dive return to boat is very quick.

The meals are excellent with fresh vegetables and a wide assortment of meats and fish. Snacks were always available. The cabins and public areas of the ship are well thought out and very spacious. Bring a couple of favorite compact discs or choose a video from the ship's large movie library.

An expedition on the Tropical Princess may visit a small (100 person) fishing village on one of the remote islands or visit W.W.II Japanese caves.

Do not be dismayed by the long flight to Indonesia. Biak is rare in that one can fly to such a remote area of the world without first transiting through a city or another country first.

SCUBA AND SNORKELING FACILITIES QUESTIONNAIRE

NAME	**M.V. Tropical Princess**
PORT	**Biak, Irian Jaya**
CONTACT	**Wendy Church**
TITLE	**Booking Contact**
ADDRESS	**DEI, 37 West Cedar Street, Boston, MA 02114-3303**
TELEPHONE	**617-723-7134** FAX **617-227-8145**

CAPITAL: **Jakarta, Java**   GOVERNMENT:
POPULATION: LANGUAGE: **Bahasa Indonesian**
CURRENCY: **Rupia**   ELECTRICITY: **220 vac**
AIRLINES: **Garuda Indonesia**   DEPARTURE TAX? **11,000 Rupia or $6 U.S.**
NEED VISA/PASSPORT?   YES **x**   **Issued upon entry - good for 3 months**

YOUR FACILITY IS CLASSIFIED AS: LIVEABOARD **x**   RESORT
BUSINESS HOURS:
CERTIFYING AGENCIES:
LOG BOOK REQUIRED?   YES   NO **x**
EQUIPMENT: SALES   RENTALS **x**   AIR FILLS **x**
PRIMARY LINE OF EQUIPMENT: **Scuba Pro**
PHOTOGRAPHIC EQUIPMENT: SALES   RENTALS   LAB   **E-6 slide processing on board x**

CHARTER/DIVE BOAT AVAILABLE?   YES **x**   NO   DIVER CAPACITY
COAST GUARD APPROVED?   YES   NO   CAPTAIN LICENSED?   YES **x**   NO
SHIP TO SHORE?   ICOM, SSB **x**   LORAN?   YES   NO   RADAR?   FURUNO **x**
DIVE MASTER/INSTRUCTOR ABOARD?   YES **x**   NO   BOTH

DIVING & SNORKELING: SALT **x**   FRESH
TYPE OF DIVING/SNORKELING IN AREA: WALL **x**   DRIFT **x**   SLOPING REEF **x**   CAVE   ICE
DIVING/SNORKELING IN YOUR AREA IS BEST SUITED FOR: BEGINNER   INTERMEDIATE **x**   ADVANCED **x**
BEST TIME OF YEAR FOR DIVING/SNORKELING: **February to November**
TEMPERATURE: **NOV-APRIL:**   **84 F**   **MAY-OCT: 84 F**
VISIBILITY: **DIVING:**   **150 FT**   **SNORKELING: 150 FT**

PACKAGES AVAILABLE: DIVE **x**   DIVE STAY **x**   SNORKEL   SNORKEL-STAY
ACCOMMODATIONS NEARBY: HOTEL **x**   MOTEL   HOME RENTALS
ACCOMMODATION RATES: EXPENSIVE   MODERATE   INEXPENSIVE **x**
RESTAURANTS NEARBY: EXPENSIVE   MODERATE   INEXPENSIVE **x**
YOUR AREA IS: REMOTE **x**   QUIET WITH ACTIVITIES   LIVELY
LOCAL ACTIVITY/NIGHTLIFE: **On-board video library, CD & Cassette System**
CAR NEEDED TO EXPLORE AREA?   YES   NO   **x**   **Can take taxi**
DUTY FREE SHOPPING?   YES   NO **x**

LOCAL EMERGENCY SERVICES   NEAREST HYPERBARIC TREATMENT FACILITY
COASTGUARD: AUTHORITY:
TELEPHONE: LOCATION:
CALLSIGNS: TELEPHONE:

LOCAL DIVING DOCTOR:
NAME:
LOCATION:
TELEPHONE:

IRELAND

Simon Nelson has 17 years of diving experience and has dived in Ireland, the United Kingdom, the Meditterean, Kenya, the Red Sea and the Caribbean. With his wife, also a keen diver, they run a small dive shop and marine chandlery. After 7 years working around the world as an engineer they settled in West Cork six years ago to indulge their passion for scuba diving and to provide facilities for others wishing to enjoy the wonders of this beautiful corner of a beautiful county.

The rugged coastline of County Cork at the southwestern corner of the Republic of Ireland offers some of the best cold water diving that is available anywhere in the world.

Off its most southwesterly point lies the famous Fastnet Rock -the last piece of Ireland seen by those emigrants that left for America in the last century. The adjoining coastline is deeply indented with bays and towering headlands and a scattering of quiet towns and villages.

Being at the very edge of Europe and in the path of the Gulf Stream, the area has clear unpolluted water and an abundance of marine life.

The area is remote and under-developed and facilities for the diver are few and far between. However, for the intrepid diving group that is looking for more than an easy trip to a popular reef which has been dived by thousands, here there is spectacular diving in an area that has yet to be explored.

The village of Schull, just nine miles from Fastnet Rock, has become popular in recent years with those on holiday and has a good range of accommodations. Schull also has the only dive shop in the area. It is possible to rent tanks and weights, but you must bring all the rest of your gear with you, or rent it in Dublin. You must also bring your own diving buddy, as you are unlikely to find any lone divers to match up with. Similarly, any boat diving is by way of boat charter. There are no scheduled boat trips to join up with. So much for the difficulties! Here is a sampling of the myriad of possible dive sites:

Fastnet Rock lies 3 miles southwest of Cape Clear Island and is 9 miles from Schull. It is topped by a magnificent lighthouse that seems to grow from the very rock itself. It is at the tip of an underwater reef that is about 1 mile long and 200 yards wide. The reef rapidly plunges down to 50 meters on all sides. It is an area of tricky currents and an experienced local skipper is a must for safe diving. The visibility underwater is always good and in settled weather you can easily see the boat from 30 meters down. The reef is split into a maze of gullies whose rock faces are carpeted with jewel anemones of every possible color. Huge shoals of pollack and mackerel abound and can all but block out the light as they swim overhead. This is an advanced dive and you need to keep your wits about you, but on a good day it is a world beater.

Lying close under the cliffs of Cape Clear Island lie the remains of the 400 ft ship, the Nestorian. She ran aground early in 1917 and sank in 20 meters of water.

Being exposed to the full force of the Atlantic storms for 75 years means there is little structure left intact. However, its cargo of large steel ingots and empty shell casing lie scattered amongst the plates of this once proud vessel. Being close up under a westerly facing cliff means this site is inaccessible if there is any swell rolling in from the open Atlantic. When conditions are calm however, it makes a splendid scenic setting to an interesting wreck dive with good visibility and extensive marine growth on the pinnacles and rock faces.

The coastline is dotted with small isolated landing points, built in the last century to promote fishing in the bays. These now offer the diver some excellent sites for shore diving. They are easy to find given a good map and a bit of local advice. The best of them all is **Toor Pier** which is a lonely spot near the end of Dunmanus Bay about 12 miles from Schull. As with shore diving in the area, it is vital to check that you can cope with the somewhat limited facilities for entering and leaving the water. Slippery and broken concrete steps can be difficult with the water surging around you with the swell.

This site offers excellent diving starting at 10 meters and running down into deep gullies at 25 meters with their tops in 15 meters. Visibility is usually excellent and the marine life extensive. Swimming the other way brings you to a large arch that runs right through the rock and is the home to several inquisitive seals. With a maximum depth of 10 meters and rocks reaching almost to the surface, this is an excellent area for advanced snorkelers as well.

Lough Hyne Marine Reserve is one of the first marine reserves to be set up in Europe, this one mile square lough is connected to the open sea by a narrow set of rapids and reaches depths of 50 meters in places. However, the area of main interest is in 15 meters close to the entrance of the rapids. An exciting experience is to snorkel through the short stretch of rapids where the tide runs at about 10 knots, is then easy to climb out and return by foot.

> **This world renowned wild "Dingle Dolphin" has lived close to the town of Dingle for the last 7 years and has sought out human company. It is easy to snorkel out to his "playground" at slack water and the experience of meeting a 10 foot dolphin who just wants to come and play is very exciting.**

Dingle is about a three hour drive north of Schull through stunning scenery and the trip can easily be made in a day.

During the summertime the water temperature is 15 C and a 6 mm wetsuit is the minimum needed for diving in comfort.

It is illegal to pick up any shell fish or to use a spear gun while using SCUBA.

A permit is required to dive in the Marine Nature Reserve at Lough Hyne. It can be obtained for free by writing to: Conservation Section, Wildlife Service, OPW, Leeson Lane, Dublin 2. All wrecks over 100 years old are protected and a permit is required to dive them. There is no legal requirement to hold a diving certificate to dive or rent gear. However, you should be competent in dealing with diving in a thick wetsuit, sudden low visibility and rough surface conditions.

The national federation coordinating diving in Ireland is the Irish Underwater Council, Haigh Terrace, Dun Laoghaire, Co. Dublin.

The local dive shop is Schull Watersports Centre, the Pier, Schull. Telephone 028-28554 or 28351. They can also help arrange accommodations.

In case of emergencies the local doctor is trained in diving medicine and the nearest recompression chamber is only one and a half hours away.

Non diving activities include: golf, sailing, pony trekking, spectacular walks and enjoying the relaxed Irish way of life!

SCUBA AND SNORKELING FACILITIES QUESTIONNAIRE

NAME			**Schull Watersport Centre Ltd**
ADDRESS		**The Pier, Schull**
			Co. Cork, Ireland
CONTACT		**Simon Nelson**
TITLE			**Owner**
TELEPHONE	**028-28554 or 28351**			FAX

CAPITAL:		**Dublin**				GOVERNMENT:
POPULATION:	**4 million**				LANGUAGE:		**English**
CURRENCY:	**Irish Pounds**			ELECTRICITY:		**240v**
AIRLINES:		**Air Lingus**				DEPARTURE TAX?
NEED VISA/PASSPORT?		YES **x**	NO		PROOF OF CITIZENSHIP?		YES	NO

YOUR FACILITY IS CLASSIFIED AS:	SCUBA CENTER **x**	RESORT
BUSINESS HOURS:				**9:30 a.m. to 18:30 in the Summer**
CERTIFYING AGENCIES:
LOG BOOK REQUIRED?			YES **x**	NO
EQUIPMENT:					SALES **x**	RENTALS **x**	AIR FILLS **x**
PRIMARY LINE OF EQUIPMENT:
PHOTOGRAPHIC EQUIPMENT:		SALES		RENTALS	LAB

CHARTER/DIVE BOAT AVAILABLE?	YES **x**	NO		DIVER CAPACITY	**10**
COAST GUARD APPROVED?		YES		NO		CAPTAIN LICENSED?	YES	NO
SHIP TO SHORE?	YES **x**	NO		LORAN?	YES	NO	RADAR?	YES	NO
DIVE MASTER/INSTRUCTOR ABOARD?		YES	NO **x**	BOTH

DIVING & SNORKELING:			SALT **x**	FRESH
TYPE OF DIVING/SNORKELING IN AREA: WALL **x**	BEACH **x**	WRECK **x**	REEF **x**	CAVE	ICE
DIVING/SNORKELING IN YOUR AREA IS BEST SUITED FOR:	BEGINNER	INTERMEDIATE	ADVANCED **x**
BEST TIME OF YEAR FOR DIVING/SNORKELING:		**May through September**
TEMPERATURE:	**NOV-APRIL:**		20	C	**MAY-OCT:	15	C**
VISIBILITY:		**DIVING:**		20	M	**SNORKELING: 15 M**

PACKAGES AVAILABLE:		DIVE		DIVE STAY		SNORKEL		SNORKEL-STAY
ACCOMMODATIONS NEARBY:	HOTEL **x**		MOTEL		HOME RENTALS **x**
ACCOMMODATION RATES:		EXPENSIVE		MODERATE			INEXPENSIVE **x**
RESTAURANTS NEARBY:		EXPENSIVE		MODERATE **x**		INEXPENSIVE
YOUR AREA IS:				REMOTE		QUIET WITH ACTIVITIES **x**		LIVELY
LOCAL ACTIVITY/NIGHTLIFE:	**Traditional Irish music in bars**
CAR NEEDED TO EXPLORE AREA?	YES **x**	NO
DUTY FREE SHOPPING?			YES **x**	NO

LOCAL EMERGENCY SERVICES				NEAREST HYPERBARIC TREATMENT FACILITY
COASTGUARD: **Baltimore Lifeboat Station**		AUTHORITY:	**Irish Naval Services**
TELEPHONE:	**028-20119**					LOCATION:	**Haulbowline Naval Base, Cork**
CALLSIGNS:							TELEPHONE:	**021-871246**

LOCAL DIVING DOCTOR:
NAME:		**Dr. Larry O'Connor**
LOCATION:	**Meevane, Schull, Co. Cork**
TELEPHONE:	**028-28311**

JORDAN

Aqaba

Cass Lawson is a retired managing director of an office equipment company, now spending time traveling the world. 41 years young, going through a second childhood by traveling the diving world earning a living wherever possible. The only possible lifestyle desciption is "World Diving Gypsy".

The Hashemite Kingdom of Jordan is located in the "Middle East" an area which unfortunately is renowned for its political instability. However this should not deter the enthusiastic diver who wishes to visit the Red Sea and dive in the beautiful waters. Jordan has boundaries with Israel to the west, Saudi Arabia to the south, Iraq to the east and Syria to the north. The only coastline in Jordan is in the south and is at the most northern point of The Gulf of Aqaba which is an integral part of the Red Sea.

Glass Fish in soft coral by Victor Organ

The coastline stretches for approximately 18 miles. It may seem only a short distance, but in that length of coastline are crammed some of the most beautiful soft and hard corals as well as an abundance of fish of many species.

Accommodation in Aqaba are plentiful and range from the Alcazar and Holiday Inn to smaller hotels with less amenities for locals who also accommodate divers on a budget. It is difficult to rent apartments if you are outside Jordan, but with local contacts it is sometimes possible to arrange this type of accommodation. One of the better Diving Travel Agencies in Britain is Aquatours (telephone number 448-1399-6953 who operate a large number of diving packages to Jordan.

The Al Cazar hotel is a Three Star rated hotel situated near the centre of Aqaba, a few minutes walk from the town centre where there is a large selection of local shops and market stalls. The hotel has two bars, an International restaurant as well as a small gymnasium, sauna, jacuzzi, outdoor pool and full Scuba Diving centre.

There are a number of other hotels locally including Aqaba Gulf Hotel and numerous small hotels who cater for the locals more than tourists.

About six miles along the coast is a government run camp site which is designed for the hardy traveler. Although it has all the usual facilities, it has not yet become popular enough to attract major budgetary attention from the local Aqaba regional Authority.

The dive operation of Sea Star Watersports is situated in the complex of the Alcazar Hotel. Sea Star is a PADI centre and school as well as being a British Sub Aqua (BSAC) centre and school and is also affiliated to C.M.A.S. Currently the instructors are British with ample experience in teaching all nationalities and there is a local divemaster who has been diving the Red Sea for the last 12 years. Full equipment hire is available and there is a small retail outlet encompassed in the operation.

DIVE SITES

BLACK ROCK: A pleasant and easy dive for the snorkeler as the coral starts in six feet of water.

Also a good site for the first dive of a vacation as there is a gentle slope allowing the diver to acquaint themselves with the sea and it's myriads of inhabitants. Black Rock has been known to have it's own semi-resident hawksbill turtle.

Eel Canyon: An aptly named site with several types of moray eels including green and snowflake morays. These eels thrive in the cracks and crevices of the many coral heads.

Saudi Border (The Drop Off): A good dive for beginners as the reef starts at about four metres, but then it descends abruptly to a wall to over 50 metres turning it into a spectacular dive for the more advanced diver. Small caverns are to be found at the 30 metre depth level with large coral pinnacles providing a home for the large variety of fish.

Bull Nudibranch by Victor Organ

Gorgons 1 and 2: Similar dive sites as they are only a short distance apart, however Gorgon 2 has a more varied terrain and descends to around 18 metres whereas Gorgon 1 allows a dive to only 14 metres. These are great as second dive sites in a morning or as a days shooting for any budding photographers!

THE "CEDAR PRIDE" WRECK: This is the spectacular remains of an 80 metre long Lebanese freighter sunk by command of Prince Abdullah as an extra attraction for divers.

The wreck lies about 120 metres offshore and spans two coral reefs allowing the experienced diver to swim completely underneath it. There is an plethora of soft corals and the wreck makes a natural home for nearly all types of Red Sea fish. Quite simply, stunning.

Jordan is steeped in Biblical and Roman occupational history and offers a wealth of interesting places to visit.

Wadi Rum is a massive canyon which provides a natural backdrop for superb sunsets. See the places where Lawrence Of Arabia was filmed, meet the Bedouin Police mounted on camels who patrol the area rescuing unfortunate tourists who need their expert guidance to explore the barren wastes of red rocks, and you can even arrange tours to include an open fire cooked meal whilst enjoying the sunset

Petra, the Rose Red City lives up to it's name. Carved out of solid rock for and by the Romans it stands in splendour in the Arabian sunshine as close runner up to the eight wonders of the world. Words are hard to describe it, a visit is a must.

Restaurants are plentiful in Aqaba. Try Captains Table directly across the road from The Alcazar Hotel for inexpensive and spicy local food, or on a visit to the market place arrange a detour by Ali Baba's Restaurant, they are known in Aqaba for their Lebanese mezze. More often than not it is difficult to finish a main meal after several mezze dishes. Aqaba has a Chinese restaurant which provides a far eastern flavour to the already delicious food. If you want to be more adventurous, try the street vendors who sell felafel and beans with rice, or hot kebabs fresh off the spit. For those with more of a sweet tooth try the amazing selection of nuts wrapped in pastry and then drenched in honey. And to cool the palate try some great ice cream at Ata Ali's in nearly as many flavours as Haagen Dazs. There is something for everyone.

SCUBA AND SNORKELING FACILITIES QUESTIONNAIRE

NAME **SGA Star Water Sports**
ADDRESS **Al Cazar Hotel, P.O. Box 392**
Acuba, Jordan
CONTACT **Cass Lawson**
TITLE **Operations Manager**
TELEPHONE **962-3.314131** FAX **962-3.314133** TELEX **62242**

CAPITAL: **Amman** GOVERNMENT:
POPULATION: LANGUAGE: **Arabic and English**
CURRENCY: **Dinars** ELECTRICITY: **220v**
AIRLINES: **Royal Jordanian** DEPARTURE TAX?
NEED VISA/PASSPORT? YES **x** NO PROOF OF CITIZENSHIP? YES **x** NO

YOUR FACILITY IS CLASSIFIED AS: SCUBA CENTER **x** RESORT
BUSINESS HOURS: **8:30 a.m. to 6:00 p.m.**
CERTIFYING AGENCIES: **PADI, BSAC, CMAS**
LOG BOOK REQUIRED? YES NO **x** **(C-cards only)**
EQUIPMENT: SALES **x** RENTALS **x** AIR FILLS **x**
PRIMARY LINE OF EQUIPMENT: **Spiro (US Divers)**
PHOTOGRAPHIC EQUIPMENT: SALES RENTALS LAB **Rental lab across the street**

CHARTER/DIVE BOAT AVAILABLE? YES NO **x** DIVER CAPACITY
COAST GUARD APPROVED? YES NO CAPTAIN LICENSED? YES NO
SHIP TO SHORE? YES NO LORAN? YES NO RADAR? YES NO
DIVE MASTER/INSTRUCTOR ABOARD? YES NO BOTH

DIVING & SNORKELING: SALT **x** FRESH
TYPE OF DIVING/SNORKELING IN AREA: WALL **x** BEACH **x** WRECK REEF CAVE ICE
DIVING/SNORKELING IN YOUR AREA IS BEST SUITED FOR: BEGINNER **x** INTERMEDIATE **x** ADVANCED **x** BEST TIME OF YEAR FOR DIVING/SNORKELING: **All year**
TEMPERATURE: **NOV-APRIL:** **18** **C** **MAY-OCT: 30 C**
VISIBILITY: **DIVING:** **80** FT **SNORKELING: 60 FT**

PACKAGES AVAILABLE: DIVE **x** DIVE STAY **x** SNORKEL **x** SNORKEL-STAY **x**
ACCOMMODATIONS NEARBY: HOTEL **x** MOTEL HOME RENTALS
ACCOMMODATION RATES: EXPENSIVE MODERATE **x** INEXPENSIVE **x**
RESTAURANTS NEARBY: EXPENSIVE MODERATE **x** INEXPENSIVE **x**
YOUR AREA IS: REMOTE QUIET WITH ACTIVITIES **x** LIVELY
LOCAL ACTIVITY/NIGHTLIFE:
CAR NEEDED TO EXPLORE AREA? YES **x** NO
DUTY FREE SHOPPING? YES NO **x**

LOCAL EMERGENCY SERVICES NEAREST HYPERBARIC TREATMENT FACILITY
COASTGUARD: AUTHORITY:
TELEPHONE: LOCATION:
CALLSIGNS: TELEPHONE:

LOCAL DIVING DOCTOR:
NAME:
LOCATION:
TELEPHONE:

Mexico

AKUMAL

Bill Hull is a former teacher and researcher of children's thinking. He continues to explore these interests by studying his own learning of physical skills, especially ice dancing and table tennis. He lives in Cambridge, Mass.

Tulum Ruins by Wendy Canning Church

From the international airport at Cancun the drive to Akumal is about 65 miles.

> Divers Exchange International arranged for a rental house, a pleasant "Casa" about a mile to the north of the dive shop. Several more Topes and a tended gate soon accustom everyone to a more leisurely pace, and ensure an atmosphere of peace and quiet for watching the water, sky, birds, lizards and insects.
>
> Our Casa was right on the Yal-Ku, a relatively shallow lagoon with a protecting reef at its mouth. We could swim right from our front steps or walk a short distance to the head of the bay to begin explorations of its upper regions.
>
> The Yal-Ku has been described as a natural aquarium and coral garden.

Why are there so many fish? Are they attracted by the flow of fresh water from the head of the bay? Has someone been feeding them? On our first swim from the front steps we encountered French grunts, three-spotted damselfish, small Spanish hogfish, a spotted ray with a stubby tail and a golden spotted eel. On a later excursion we startled a small sea turtle. In the lagoon itself, the layering of fresh and salt water sometimes produces a "halocline" that blurs the scenery.

The more we discovered the more interesting it became. We found a group of large, midnight blue parrotfish. What were they eating? I thought their diet was largely coral and there isn't a great abundance in the Yal-Ku. I watched carefully- but all I saw was some nibbling on vegetation growing on rocks. In addition to schools of sergeant majors there were quite a few larger fish such as gray snappers and Bermuda chub. On one dive we saw many Atlantic needlefish, some solitary others in schools. There were trumpet fish, brittle stars, very large sea urchins: such a variety of creatures to see that it is hard to remember, or identify all that was encountered. One is apt to see more fish when swimming very slowly or drifting.

On our first swim in the upper Yal-Ku I was preparing to slip into the water from a convenient rocky shelf — mask, snorkel, fins, wet suit and weight belt all adjusted — when there was a sudden impact on my dangling calf — no blood drawn, but it was startling. When I checked it out from below I discovered a line of small and fiercely territorial damsel fish. Their impact is all out of proportion to their size. Exclamations from others, preparing to swim by cooling their legs off as I had done suggested that generations of damsel fish from this short stretch of shore had been practicing full speed head-on collisions on relaxed calf muscles.

We chose Akumal for a family vacation because we wanted easy access to the water and favorable conditions for introducing two grown daughters to SCUBA diving.

My wife and I had received our certification two years previously in Culebra, but had not had an opportunity to practice our skills. Most of all we wanted an opportunity for extended observation of underwater life. I have had a long term fascination with diving and was particularly interested that other members of our family have an opportunity to experience the richness and complexity of SCUBA diving in a safe and supportive setting.

Diving has always had a compelling fascination for me, perhaps because it is a strong challenge to one's senses to operate in such a different environment. I was very excited to find that it was possible to float at any depth by adjusting the amount of air in my lungs or buoyancy compensator. The ability to go up and down so easily in three dimensions is fascinating in itself. Gliding down the side of reefs, controlling buoyancy by the amount of air in one's lungs gives a sense of effortless flying in worlds of incredible diversity and beauty.

The resort refresher course at the Akumal Dive Shop was very well handled.

The shore, session packed a great deal of information into a short time and then we waded into the water with small tanks to check out the equipment, practice clearing the regulator and masks, breathing from our buddy's octopus, etc. We hadn't understood that this was to be followed by a boat dive the same morning, but we were soon wading out to a dive boat. This time carrying full-sized tanks.

The trip through the reef entrance seemed very rough, but it was a short trip to the "Escuela" or school site where there was a mooring. The pitching was less in deeper water, but still a bit intimidating for beginners who found themselves being asked to roll over backwards under these conditions. La Escuela is a fine location for a beginning dive. I wish we had been able to return there. The sand bottom with coral canyons to swim through at a depth of 25 feet and the abundance of marine life was marvelously exciting.

Two members of our family had difficulty compensating; one developed a nosebleed, and both had ear troubles which lasted for several weeks. I was able to help but it could have become complicated if others had also needed assistance. Johanna, our guide, had her hands full with a party of seven. I explained our problem to Dick Blanchard who suggested that we sign on with David who was especially experienced in working with beginners.

Two dives with David on nearby reefs went well.

The best dive was off Akumal Point a mile or more to the south and well offshore. The water was much clearer and the bottom visible at 70'. One member of our party, missing his mask and snorkel recalled that he might have rested it on the rail alongside of him. Tough luck. David descended in a shallow glide, suddenly I saw the lost mask in the sand alongside a coral ridge. I hadn't realized that David had been looking for it. I was impressed that he was able to locate it at that depth from a boat that had been drifting for several minutes while we were getting ready.

Rental villa at Akumal by Wendy Canning Church

With such good visibility we could get a good overhead view of the reef configuration on our slow descent. The bottom was sandy with coral forming vertical walls and canyons. It was similar to the Escuela site, but on a much larger scale. I had the sense that I was viewing something quite ancient. How many years had this reef been here in a similar form, I wondered?

Tulum and Coba make wonderful cultural excursions for non-dive days, and a nearby biosphere reserve, which we did not visit, may offer possibilities as well.

For more information on diving centers and villa rentals contact; Divers Exchange International, 37 West Cedar Street, Boston, MA 02114 Telephone; (617) 723-7134; Fax: (617) 227-8145

SCUBA AND SNORKELING FACILITIES QUESTIONNAIRE

NAME	**Excursiones Akumal**
ADDRESS	**Postal 1345**
	Cancun, Q.ROO, Mexico
CONTACT	**Richard Blanchard**
TITLE	**Instructor**
TELEPHONE	FAX

CAPITAL: GOVERNMENT:
POPULATION: LANGUAGE:
CURRENCY: ELECTRICITY:
AIRLINES: DEPARTURE TAX?
NEED VISA/PASSPORT?   YES   NO **x**   PROOF OF CITIZENSHIP?   YES   NO

YOUR FACILITY IS CLASSIFIED AS: SCUBA CENTER **x**   RESORT **x**
BUSINESS HOURS: **8:30 to 5:30**
CERTIFYING AGENCIES: **PADI, NAUI, SSI, NSS/COS, NACO**
LOG BOOK REQUIRED?   YES   NO
EQUIPMENT: SALES **x**   RENTALS **x**   AIR FILLS **x**
PRIMARY LINE OF EQUIPMENT: **Sherwood**
PHOTOGRAPHIC EQUIPMENT: SALES   RENTALS **x**   LAB **x**

CHARTER/DIVE BOAT AVAILABLE?   YES **x**   NO   DIVER CAPACITY **6**
COAST GUARD APPROVED?   YES   NO   CAPTAIN LICENSED?   YES   NO
SHIP TO SHORE? YES   NO   LORAN?   YES   NO   RADAR? YES   NO
DIVE MASTER/INSTRUCTOR ABOARD?   YES **x**   NO   BOTH

DIVING & SNORKELING: SALT **x**   FRESH **x**
TYPE OF DIVING/SNORKELING IN AREA: WALL **x**   BEACH **x**   WRECK   REEF   CAVE **x**   CENOTE **x**
DIVING/SNORKELING IN YOUR AREA IS BEST SUITED FOR: BEGINNER **x**   INTERMEDIATE **x**   ADVANCED **x**
BEST TIME OF YEAR FOR DIVING/SNORKELING: **All year**
TEMPERATURE: NOV-APRIL: F   MAY-OCT: F
VISIBILITY: DIVING: FT   SNORKELING: FT

PACKAGES AVAILABLE: DIVE **x**   DIVE STAY   SNORKEL   SNORKEL-STAY
ACCOMMODATIONS NEARBY: HOTEL **x**   BUNGALOW **x**   CONDOS **x**   HOME RENTALS **x**
CASITAS **x**   ACCOMMODATION RATES: EXPENSIVE   MODERATE   INEXPENSIVE
RESTAURANTS NEARBY: EXPENSIVE   MODERATE   INEXPENSIVE
YOUR AREA IS: REMOTE **x**   QUIET WITH ACTIVITIES **x**   LIVELY
LOCAL ACTIVITY/NIGHTLIFE:
CAR NEEDED TO EXPLORE AREA?   YES   NO
DUTY FREE SHOPPING?   YES   NO

LOCAL EMERGENCY SERVICES   NEAREST HYPERBARIC TREATMENT FACILITY
COASTGUARD: AUTHORITY:
TELEPHONE: LOCATION: **Cozumel and Isla Mujures**
CALLSIGNS: TELEPHONE:

LOCAL DIVING DOCTOR:
NAME:
LOCATION:
TELEPHONE:

Cancun

Jeffrey Ray Noordhoek

Originally from Nebraska, Jeffrey now lives in Boston. He is a Senior Financial Analyst for the Investment Banking Department at State Street Bank. He is 27 years old and enjoys hunting, fishing, and the performing arts. The following story describes Jeff's first scuba diving experience.

Being a lover of the outdoors I have always been curious about the mystical underwater world of scuba diving and anxious to learn how to dive. Many of my friends belong to Diver's Exchange International in Boston and have found Wendy Church, its founder and President, to be a wealth of information. Therefore, when I was planning my trip to Cancun, Mexico I solicited advice from Wendy as to where to get certified while I was on vacation.

I was staying at Club Med which only offers a "Club Certification," and I had heard rumors of overloaded dive boats

Diver amongst coral by Wendy Canning Church

diving reefs with other overloaded dive boats. These horror stories obviously made me a bit leery of "Club" diving and I wanted to receive a full certification that I would be able to use all over the world not just at Club Meds. Wendy highly recommended Scuba Cancun, so I decided to dive with them.

I wrote to the owners Edith and Louis Hurtado to inquire about their certification course and to set up a meeting with them upon my arrival in Cancun. The day I arrived at Club Med I took a taxi into town to meet them and to schedule my classes and open water dives. I was to meet with my instructor everyday for the next 5 days. It was a rigorous schedule for one week, but well worth it.

Edith assigned me to a personal instructor, Juan Carlos Marin. He is everything anyone would want in an instructor and in a friend. He is a professional diver with over 15 years of diving experience, 7 of which were spent in the Gulf of Mexico working on off-shore oil wells. He has only one motive for being an instructor - to introduce those in search of adventure to the incredible beauty and magic of the underwater realm.

He manages to accomplish this while also adhering to the highest level of safety possible. Juan Carlos is a PADI instructor and does everything by the book. He had me read each of the five modules in the book before I viewed the video that accompanies each module. This would be followed by classroom instruction and a quiz.

One of Juan Carlos' greatest attributes is his uncanny ability to simulate underwater sounds, sights and human reaction. The demonstrations were humorous, yet they completely prepared me for what I was about to experience. He made me feel comfortable with my equipment and my skills, making any traces of apprehension disappear. We practiced my underwater skills again and again until we both felt that I was completely prepared for the open water dives.

The actual open water dives were beyond imagination. It is almost impossible to describe the sensations and sights that I experienced during my first "adventures" underwater.

On my very first dive I saw sea turtles, six foot barracuda, lobsters, and so many fish that I am still attempting to learn all their names. On another I had the opportunity to play with an eel and swim amongst enormous schools of jacks.

The waters of Cancun are an ice blue, yet warm and abound with plant and fish life.

The current is strong however, and so most of the dives are drift dives where the boat follows your bubbles and picks you up when you surface after your dive.

I was also impressed with the other staff members at Scuba Cancun. For my last two dives we went out with 6 other divers and we had 2 dive masters aboard. We were given a full description of the site and the dive plan. We were told how we would proceed, what order we would get into the water, how deep we would be going, what we could expect to see, the current conditions and changes along the way, and how long we would stay down. The dive itself was equally as organized and professional.

On a scale of 1 to 10, I would give my overall certification experience a 12. Edith and her husband Luis and their entire staff are a delight. The shop also has the only hyperbaric chamber in Cancun, another plus!

Scuba Cancun is located downtown and is on the Hotel route so you can reach it by bus from any of the hotels for a mere 5,000 pesos, which at the time was about 85¢, a much better deal than the taxis. You can leave your equipment at the shop if you are diving for an extended period, so you only need to cart yourself back and forth.

I will undoubtedly return to Scuba Cancun for more pleasure diving - and maybe even an Advanced Certification! I highly recommended it to all!

SCUBA AND SNORKELING FACILITIES QUESTIONNAIRE

NAME **Scuba Cancun (PADI 5 Star Training Facility)**
ADDRESS **P.O. Box 517**
Cancun, Quintana Roo, Mexico 77500
CONTACT **Edith and Luis Hurtado**
TITLE **Owners**
TELEPHONE **988-4-23-36 and 3-10-11** FAX

CAPITAL: **Mexico City** GOVERNMENT: **Democratic**
POPULATION: LANGUAGE: **Spanish**
CURRENCY: **Peso** ELECTRICITY: **110v**
AIRLINES: Various DEPARTURE TAX?
NEED VISA/PASSPORT? YES **x** NO   PROOF OF CITIZENSHIP? YES **x** NO

YOUR FACILITY IS CLASSIFIED AS: SCUBA CENTER **x** RESORT
BUSINESS HOURS: 9:00 a.m. to 5:00 p.m.
CERTIFYING AGENCIES: **PADI**
LOG BOOK REQUIRED? YES **x** NO
EQUIPMENT: SALES RENTALS **x** AIR FILLS **x**
PRIMARY LINE OF EQUIPMENT: **Seaquest**
PHOTOGRAPHIC EQUIPMENT: SALES RENTALS **x** LAB

CHARTER/DIVE BOAT AVAILABLE? YES **x** NO   DIVER CAPACITY **14**
COAST GUARD APPROVED? YES **x** NO   CAPTAIN LICENSED? YES **x** NO
SHIP TO SHORE? YES **x** NO LORAN? YES **x** NO   RADAR? YES   NO **x**
DIVE MASTER/INSTRUCTOR ABOARD? YES **x** NO   BOTH

DIVING & SNORKELING: SALT **x** FRESH
TYPE OF DIVING/SNORKELING IN AREA: WALL   BEACH   WRECK **x**   REEF   CAVE   ICE
DIVING/SNORKELING IN YOUR AREA IS BEST SUITED FOR: BEGINNER **x**   INTERMEDIATE **x**   ADVANCED **x**
BEST TIME OF YEAR FOR DIVING/SNORKELING: **April to October**
TEMPERATURE: **NOV-APRIL:** 80 F   **MAY-OCT: 80+ F**
VISIBILITY: **DIVING:** 80 FT   **SNORKELING: 80 FT**

PACKAGES AVAILABLE: DIVE **x** DIVE STAY   SNORKEL   SNORKEL-STAY
ACCOMMODATIONS NEARBY: HOTEL **x** MOTEL   HOME RENTALS
ACCOMMODATION RATES: EXPENSIVE **x** MODERATE **x** INEXPENSIVE
RESTAURANTS NEARBY: EXPENSIVE **x** MODERATE **x** INEXPENSIVE **x**
YOUR AREA IS: REMOTE   QUIET WITH ACTIVITIES   LIVELY **x**
LOCAL ACTIVITY/NIGHTLIFE: **Lots**
CAR NEEDED TO EXPLORE AREA? YES   NO **x Plenty of taxis, tours and buses**
DUTY FREE SHOPPING? YES **x** NO

LOCAL EMERGENCY SERVICES   NEAREST HYPERBARIC TREATMENT FACILITY
COASTGUARD: **Isla Mujeres**   AUTHORITY:
(8 miles from Cancun)   LOCATION: **Scuba Cancun Dive Shop**
TELEPHONE: **2-00-34**   (only one in Cancun)
CALLSIGNS: **VHF Ch 16 and Ch 18**   TELEPHONE: **4-23-36 and 3-10-11**

LOCAL DIVING DOCTOR:
NAME: **Dr. Jorge Garcia**
LOCATION:
TELEPHONE: **4-65-23 and 4-55-30**

COZUMEL

Jane Goulston

Dive Master, Water Safety Instructor, Lifeguard, Adapted Aquatioc Dive Master.
I am very happy to say that I have the largest in water Easter Seal Program in MA. With many of the population being physically challenged, it is important to realize that scuba and swimming offers some unique opportunities to these people. These fall into three major areas: physiological, psychological and socialogical. The opportunity to do something well and to enjoy the feeling of success is special importance to an individual with a physical challenge. Many impairments are far less evident when the individual is in the water, the buoyancy of water makes movement, which would be impossible or highly difficult to perform on land, much easier. Working in the field of adapted aquatics has given me the understanding that it is a demanding, but rewarding one.

Diver ascending by Margory Clair

The adventure starts as you are flying into Cozumel and peering out of the airplane's window, looking down at the island. You'll notice the current hugging the entire coastline. Great diving is in store for you! Cozumel is my secret getaway...lazy white sand beaches, surrounded by unexplored jungle and breathtaking dramatic aquamarine waters. Welcome to the beautiful waters of Cozumel! There are bountiful beaches to swim and snorkel from. Every beach on the island is capable of fullfilling your dream of relaxing in the 80 degree water. You'll also find a large number of quality restaurants that not only tempt your palate with some down to earth Mexican cooking but also keep you within your travel budget. Most of the restaurants accept major credit cards, but I'm sure they'll accept your cash. It is most important to hold on to those receipts in case of currency exchange or billing errors. No need to bring the high heels and suit jackets, just throw on your Berkenstocks and enjoy! The array of eclectic shops range from those specializing in great cotton throw rugs to those that sell primitive art made by the local Mayan people. The people of Cozumel expect you to barter for the items that you are interested in purchasing and believe me, it can be fun! Accomodations on the island are varied. I stayed in a small motel on the water which was more than adequate. You can stay in a fancy hotel or a small bungalow on the beach. The choice is yours. I chose the small motel because I knew that I wouldn't spend a lot of time in my room between diving, eating and touring. The scuba shops are friendly, knowledgeable and will guarantee you a good dive vacation. I used the "Dive Paradise" shop. The manager's name is Apple and she is most helpful with any and all of your diving needs and questions. She is dedicated to safety, which I find most improtant. The price of trips are around $40.00 for a two tank dive with a dive master. Make sure that the operator is fully sanctioned by PADI etc. You will see C.A.D.O. (Cozumel Association for Dive Operators) and S.S.S. (Decompression Center). We had to pay $1.00 a day for the Decompression Center (I hope you will never need it but its very nice to know it is on the island!). Cozumel is drift diving! The new diver or one not familiar with drift diving, should have the dive master take them down for a test run. They should also verify the dive master's certification.

I did see a lot of small boats with many people on them and many more in the water so check for the type of diving you want. The people of Cozumel show evidence that they are working on the management of their resources, primarily their reefs. All reefs are in extremely good condition and are fascinating to dive through. One of the dives that I went on was the **Chancanab Reef Dive** with a maximum dive depth of 55 feet. Night diving is done here as well. Another excellent dive was the **San Francisco Reef Dive**, broken into three sections. This is Cozumel's most shallow wall dive, the list is endless. One of my favorites is the **Santa Rosa Wall**. It's impressive caves and tunnels are breathtaking as well as exciting for the more advanced diver. In addition the **Maracaibo Dive** will offer the experienced a challenge. For the most challenging dive go to deep **Palancar** which a 120 foot descent. It is not suggested for the novice diver. I can carry on all day about the colors, coral, marine life...etc...! But your dive master will guide you through Cozumel's underwater paradise. Culturally speaking, the Mayan people are always sweet and have a sensitive quality inherited from their ancestors who worshipped the sun. I did take a day off to go and see the ruins of Tulum and Xel-Ha. This tour involved being transported first by Hydrofoil boat and then by air conditioned bus from Cozumel via Playa Del Carmen. If you have a tour guide by the name of Mr. Pinky, a man with candor you will definitely have an interesting experience. If my best friend were to ask me where to go get a bit of interesting culture, an amazing underwater experience, lovely white sand beaches, friendly people and not spend the next 100 paychecks on a vacation, I would definitely suggest Cozumel, Mexico.

SCUBA AND SNORKELING FACILITIES QUESTIONNAIRE

NAME **Dive Paradise**
ADDRESS **P.O. Box 222, 601 Rafael Melgar Ave.**
Cozumel, Quintana Roo, Mexico 77600
CONTACT **Tom and Dusty Hartdegen**
TITLE **Owners**
TELEPHONE **011-52-987-21007 direct from U.S., after hours, 011-52-987-21061**

CAPITAL:	GOVERNMENT:
POPULATION:	LANGUAGE:
CURRENCY:	ELECTRICITY:
AIRLINES:	DEPARTURE TAX?
NEED VISA/PASSPORT? YES **x** NO	PROOF OF CITIZENSHIP? YES NO

YOUR FACILITY IS CLASSIFIED AS: SCUBA CENTER **x**   RESORT
BUSINESS HOURS: **Winter: 8:00 a.m. - 9:00 p.m. 7 days/week**
CERTIFYING AGENCIES: **PADI, SSI, IDEA**
LOG BOOK REQUIRED? YES   NO
EQUIPMENT: SALES   RENTALS **x**   AIR FILLS **x**
PRIMARY LINE OF EQUIPMENT: Sherwood, Mares
PHOTOGRAPHIC EQUIPMENT: SALES   RENTALS **x**   LAB available

CHARTER/DIVE BOAT AVAILABLE? YES **x**   NO   DIVER CAPACITY **12**
COAST GUARD APPROVED? YES **x**   NO   CAPTAIN LICENSED? YES   NO
SHIP TO SHORE? YES   NO   LORAN? YES   NO   RADAR? YES   NO
DIVE MASTER/INSTRUCTOR ABOARD?   YES **x**   NO   BOTH

DIVING & SNORKELING: SALT **x**   FRESH **x**
TYPE OF DIVING/SNORKELING IN AREA: WALL **x**   BEACH **x**   WRECK   REEF   CAVE   ICE
DIVING/SNORKELING IN YOUR AREA IS BEST SUITED FOR: BEGINNER **x**   INTERMEDIATE **x**   ADVANCED **x**
BEST TIME OF YEAR FOR DIVING/SNORKELING: **April 15 - November 15**
TEMPERATURE: NOV-APRIL: F   MAY-OCT: F
VISIBILITY: DIVING: FT   SNORKELING: FT

PACKAGES AVAILABLE: DIVE **x**   DIVE STAY **x**   SNORKEL   SNORKEL-STAY
ACCOMMODATIONS NEARBY: HOTEL **x**   MOTEL   HOME RENTALS
ACCOMMODATION RATES: EXPENSIVE   MODERATE   INEXPENSIVE
RESTAURANTS NEARBY: EXPENSIVE   MODERATE   INEXPENSIVE
YOUR AREA IS: REMOTE   QUIET WITH ACTIVITIES   LIVELY **x**
LOCAL ACTIVITY/NIGHTLIFE: **Lots**
CAR NEEDED TO EXPLORE AREA?   YES   NO
DUTY FREE SHOPPING?   YES   NO

LOCAL EMERGENCY SERVICES   NEAREST HYPERBARIC TREATMENT FACILITY
COASTGUARD: **Useless unless you speak Spanish**   AUTHORITY:
TELEPHONE: LOCATION: **Cozumel**
CALLSIGNS: TELEPHONE:

LOCAL DIVING DOCTOR:
NAME:
LOCATION:
TELEPHONE:

MICRONESIA

Palau

Betsy A. Blacher received her PADI certification in 1980 and has had extensive diving experience. She currently resides in Boston, Massachusetts where she manages tax free funds for Keystone, a major mutual fund firm. Her search for remote diving spots remains a priority in her life.

The crime and stress of city life incited dreams of diving. We chose Palau as our March destination because it rang true of escape; distant and tropical. Palau is a tiny island in Micronesia, located between Guam and the Philippines. Remoteness does have its price however; flight time totaled nearly twenty hours. Seven rubbery chicken meals and lack of sleep led to irrevocable jet lag for the first few days of our fantasy vacation.

Since information regarding Palau was not abundant at the time, we feared that "modest accommodations" might mean no plumbing or potable water. As a result, we chose to stay at the Palau Pacific Resort, a Japanese-owned luxury hotel, located in the capital of Koror. It was costly but worth it to those who desire quality service and beautiful landscaping. Several dive operations serviced our hotel, all at one dock less than a hundred yards from our rooms.

We dove with Fish In Fins, an experienced operation run by the island's most eminent entrepreneur, Francis Toribiong. Francis' son, Melvin, was our dive master. Its dive boat was rather crude with no platform and no cover from sun or rain. Occasionally, it rained heavily while returning from a late afternoon dive and several of us sought refuge in the cabin's cramped crawl space.

Travel time to dive sites ranged from 30 minutes to over an hour, and the boat ride was loud and bumpy. Despite the bouts with weather and sore derrieres, however, the scenery was spectacular. We wove through the maze of Rock Islands daily; clusters of small, tree-covered islands formed from ancient coral reefs and limestone.

> **Hundreds of these islands exist with no two alike; it was a topiary of imaginary figures, small and round, oblong, or mushroom shaped.**

Some of the Rock Islands contained sandy beaches or hidden lagoons. Many were replete with wildlife such as crocodiles, sea turtles and fruit bats.

We came to Palau primarily to see large sea life and we were not disappointed. Powerful crosscurrents, at a dive site called **Blue Corner**, provided an intersection of sea life traffic.

> **Backtip sharks and schools of sea turtles appeared like magic both times that we dove Blue Corner.**

The strong currents made this site a difficult dive, however; on certain days, it was necessary to manually hold onto our masks. In addition, cloudy water limited visibility to 50-75 feet, though occasional clarity allowed for 100+ feet of viewing. We found the water to be sparkling clear only sporadically.

Another dive site called **Ngemelis** offered an entirely different experience. This was a wall dive with a 900' drop-off. Here the water was frenetic with activity as dense schools of smaller fish swam along the steep wall, hundreds of yellowtail, wrasse, and snappers would repeatedly merge together, then disperse into their separate schools, creating a kaleidoscope of color.

A third site, **Blue Hole,** proved to be more adventurous than spectacular. The dive began with a 110' drop into a hole, or vertical tunnel, about twelve feet in diameter. At the bottom we exited the tunnel by swimming past a sign with Japanese lettering, (We later discovered that the sign was a monument to two Japanese women who panicked in the Blue Hole and lost their lives.) The remainder of the dive was fairly standard for Palau; huge coral heads, and black sponges were abundant, as were large grouper, and gray reef sharks. Unfortunately, the current proved problematic once again. During our return to the boat, we swam against the current (which had shifted without warning) and I found myself working extraordinarily hard just to stay still. I looked toward Melvin, our dive master, and was shocked to find him grasping onto rocks and pieces of jutting coral in order to pull himself slowly along the wall. In the process, he broke off coral and disturbed sea creatures, upsetting nature's beautiful living reef.

Clearly, there is a need for underwater regulation in Micronesia.

The incident left me wondering if Melvin's concern for his divers was as cavalier as his attitude toward the environment. While I had confidence in Melvin's diving skills and knowledge of his native waters, I would hesitate to recommend the Fish In Fins operation to a novice diver.

The folks at Fish In Fins were, however, accommodative and flexible with regard to our desires. They truly worked at varying our daily routines. One day we stopped for lunch at an isolated Rock Island. It was only about an acre in size, but boasted a pure white, sandy beach, tropical flora, and giant tridacna clams just a few yards from shore in shallow water. While some members of the group feasted on freshly caught sushi and dozed lazily in the sun, others donned fins and explored the giant clams.

These enormous shells, roughly the size of Volkswagon beetles, made storybook fantasies come alive. Their mouths opened and shut with every languid breath, while a blanket of purple and turquoise velvety flesh rolled in and out like a giant tongue.

The following afternoon, we made an excursion to Jellyfish Lake which was situated in the center of a Rock Island. After hiking through several hundred yards of jungle landscape, we found the marshy stream which served as the entry to the lake. A fifty yard snorkel through rocky water was required in order to reach our destination, the center of the lake.

Coral garden courtesy of Palau Pan Pacific Hotel

Thousands upon thousands of jellyfish swarmed about us, pulsating, translucent and pink.

While I knew intellectually that they were stingless (no enemies co-exist in their environment, which is sheltered from the open sea), it took several minutes before I had the courage to touch one. Soon I was in heaven, patting their amorphous, slimy heads and naming each one of them.

After awhile of frolicking in the water, we extracted our pet crocodile, Elvis, from a BC pocket. Elvis is plastic and harmless, but our dive master did not know this when his peripheral vision caught Elvis briefly. Since the Rock Islands are a known habitat for unfriendly crocs, it was a cruel joke to play on an unsuspecting dive master.

Locally caught fish and sushi were the best meals in Palau- understandably, given the huge Japanese influence on the island. We ate several meals at Furusato, a modest one-room restaurant which served fresh, bountiful sushi at fabulous prices. On one occasion, the president of Palau and his entourage dined at the table next to us.

On another night, we decided to try more upscale dining at the Osel Plaza. My dive buddy and I indulged in an eight-course meal (approximately $30 each) which included lots of oriental style noodles with generous helpings of vegetables and of course, fresh fish. The meal did NOT include the island specialty; bat soup. We watched in awe as others ordered a tureen filled with pinkish, gray broth garnished with the furry rodent sitting upright in the center.

Our final trip to the Palau airport was a sad one as we silently reflected upon the week's adventures. The van bumped along the winding road past a grove of lush trees, and around the bend overlooking a bay of turquoise water. Off on the distant horizon, we caught our last glimpse of the majestic Rock Islands.

At the steamy, overcrowded airport, we passed the time over tepid coffee. The airport walls were decorated with large posters depicting major world cities: London, Paris, Tokyo, directly across from us, Manhattan's World Trade Center loomed large. An elderly Palaun gentlemen stared dreamily at it as he expressed his desire to visit New York City. "In New York, everyone is rich, everyone is happy," he proclaimed, I leaned forward to correct him, to share my knowledge of the real world; the hardships, the crime, the poverty to which we would return from our Palauan paradise. I felt a tug at my elbow, as my friend stopped me, "Don't," he urged, "don't burst his bubble, If he believes THAT is better than this, let him dream."

SCUBA AND SNORKELING FACILITIES QUESTIONNAIRE

NAME   **Palau Pacific Resort**
ADDRESS   **P.O. Box 308**
                Koror, Republic of Palau 96940, Western Caroline Islands
CONTACT   **David S. Feinberg**
TITLE   **General Manager**
TELEPHONE   **680-488-2600**   FAX **680-488-1606**   TELEX **8920 Resort PW**

CAPITAL: **Korror**		GOVERNMENT:	**UN territory; Under guardianship of US, English & Palauan**
POPULATION: **15,000**			
CURRENCY: **US $**			
AIRLINES: **Continental**		LANGUAGE:	**English, Palauan**
NEED VISA/PASSPORT? YES **x** NO		ELECTRICITY:	**115v/60 cycle**
PROOF OF CITIZENSHIP? YES **x** NO		DEPARTURE TAX? **$10.00**	

YOUR FACILITY IS CLASSIFIED AS: SCUBA CENTER **x**   RESORT **x 5-Star**
BUSINESS HOURS: **Splash Dive Operation 8:00 a.m. - 7:30 p.m.**
CERTIFYING AGENCIES: **PADI**
LOG BOOK REQUIRED?   YES   NO **x**
EQUIPMENT: SALES **x**   RENTALS **x**   AIR FILLS **x**
PRIMARY LINE OF EQUIPMENT: **Scubapro**
PHOTOGRAPHIC EQUIPMENT: SALES   RENTALS   LAB **x**

CHARTER/DIVE BOAT AVAILABLE?   YES **x**   NO   DIVER CAPACITY   **Up to 18**
COAST GUARD APPROVED?   YES **x**   NO   CAPTAIN LICENSED? YES **x**   NO
SHIP TO SHORE? YES **x**   NO   LORAN?   YES NO   RADAR? YES **x**   NO
DIVE MASTER/INSTRUCTOR ABOARD?   YES **x**   NO   BOTH

DIVING & SNORKELING: SALT **x**   FRESH
TYPE OF DIVING/SNORKELING IN AREA: WALL **x**   BEACH **x**   WRECK **x**   REEF   CAVE   ICE
DIVING/SNORKELING IN YOUR AREA IS BEST SUITED FOR: BEGINNER **x**   INTERMEDIATE **x**   ADVANCED **x**
BEST TIME OF YEAR FOR DIVING/SNORKELING: **Year round**
TEMPERATURE: **NOV-APRIL:**   80-84 **F**   **MAY-OCT: 80-84 F**
VISIBILITY: **DIVING:**   Unlimited   **FT**   **SNORKELING: 100 FT**

PACKAGES AVAILABLE: DIVE **x**   DIVE STAY **x**   SNORKEL **x**   SNORKEL-STAY **x**
ACCOMMODATIONS NEARBY: HOTEL **x**   MOTEL   HOME RENTALS
ACCOMMODATION RATES: EXPENSIVE **x**   MODERATE   INEXPENSIVE
RESTAURANTS NEARBY: EXPENSIVE   MODERATE **x**   INEXPENSIVE
YOUR AREA IS: REMOTE   QUIET WITH ACTIVITIES **x**   LIVELY
LOCAL ACTIVITY/NIGHTLIFE: **Guest activities program; nightly entertainment in restaurants; slide shows; movies**
CAR NEEDED TO EXPLORE AREA?   YES **x**   NO
DUTY FREE SHOPPING?   YES **x On property**

LOCAL EMERGENCY SERVICES   NEAREST HYPERBARIC TREATMENT FACILITY
COASTGUARD: AUTHORITY: **Mac Donald Memorial Hospital**
TELEPHONE: LOCATION: **Koror, Palau**
CALLSIGNS: TELEPHONE: **680-488-2554, 2553, 2813**
LOCAL DIVING DOCTOR:
NAME:
LOCATION: **Mac Donald Memorial Hospital**
TELEPHONE: **680-488-2554, 2553, 2813**

NEW GUINEA

Papua

Carol Boone, a native of Austin, Texas, began her fascination with photography at age twelve. She has traveled extensively since then, capturing images throughout the world.

Carol graduated in 1982 from the University of Texas with a B.S. in Communications, and studied photography at Brooks Photographic Art Institute in Santa Barbara. She has been published in numerous publications on photography, diving, science, nature and travel. She has also had exhibits in Austin, Santa Barbara, Aspen and Houston.

Today, Carol has her own portrait business in Austin, and travels to photograph the sea. She has photographed in the Caribbean, Hawaii, California, New Guinea, Australia, Micronesia, the Red Sea and Suborn Islands.

"After 13 years of diving, the beauty and serenity of the underwater world continues to enchant me. I cannot see enough; every dive seems too short when I realize that I must surface. I never run out of air, just film. I cannot carry enough cameras to capture the endless array of underwater images. I feel that in focusing in God's underwater creation, I can share this wonder with others for generations to come. The sea is another world to be shared through my lens."

Far away in the South Pacific lies the charming and primitive islands of Papua, New Guinea. These islands have a magic, charm and special aura of primitive life that does not exist in our fast paced day-to-day world. It is a land where people have different values for money, time and space.

I left on August 13th to go on my journey across the Pacific with eight other divers and photographers. After flying form Austin to Los Angeles to Honolulu to Sydney, I arrived in Port Moresby, the capital of Papua.

This was my first glimpse of the New Guinea people. The natives are friendly with grinning faces, red-stained mouths from chewing beetle nut, callused soles from wearing no shoes and dry, dark skin from the daily, hot sun.

Seven hundred languages are spoken, gold is abundant and coffee is rich on this second largest island in the world. There are more runaways here than any other place in the world. It is a land of volcanoes, palm trees, azure blue water, hot springs and endless reefs.

How does one even begin to unfold the treasures of such a place? It is like a time lock to which one has a key to step back in time-an ancient land!

We entered Rabaul, a small village, and photographed the natives. My camera had the entire village enthralled.

The purpose of my trip was to explore-to dive where no one has been before, to discover unknown reefs and territories. The boat was now my home. For the next twelve days there would be no television, phones or newspapers; just water, reefs, air and my camera.

We steamed all night to arrive at the first dive site. As I descended on this first dive, I swam toward the untouched reef which was endlessly soft and seemed to continue forever. No one else had ever entered this little domain of space underwater.

I saw corals, fish life and richness like nowhere else in the world. During the almost 50 dives I did in 12 days, I experienced wonders most people will never see. There were no other boats, planes or people in sight.

We saw a few villagers, who were surprised at the sight of white men and women. Their only encounter with white people has been with the few missionaries, who have tried to penetrate their lifestyle.

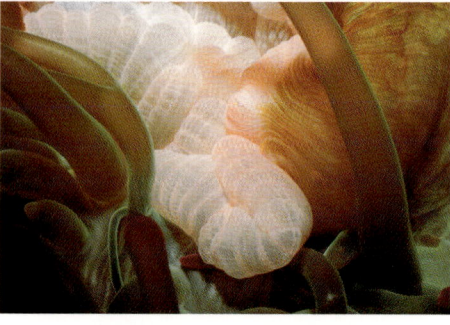

Anemone Mouth by Carol Boone

A circus of life thrived on the reef, including gray reef sharks, dog-toothed tuna, oceanic silver tip sharks, hammerhead sharks and the infamous clown fish with their anemone homes, safe from other predators of the sea.

On one descent, I was approached by a 10-foot silvertip and swam under a 12-foot hammerhead whose eyes were closely focused and my body was briefly paralyzed with fear of the large Pelagics. The reef is a place where the shark is king: a majestic, stunning, swift and bold creature.

This territorial beast rules his king-dom. Fast, quick and smooth, with an ability to maneuver unlike any other fish or animal like a torpedo of the sea. When the 10 foot silvertip approached, it left me feeling small, helpless and low on the new scale of life I was discovering. He swam in swiftly and aggressively, leaving no room for others. This was his home and no one was to question this!

The currents flowed, keeping the water rich with other forms of sea life. Hundreds of silver schooling jacks, schools of oho and many large, curious barracuda swain by me. Pelagics were cruising as if they were on their own highway. Sea turtles were occasionally spotted as well as the gorgeous, but poisonous lion fish. Cone shells also thrive in New Guinea waters.

Shrimp in soft coral by Carol Boone

Night diving in New Guinea was an enchanting experience, similar to a colorful, underwater jungle.

I spotted many red velvet crabs, cuttle fish, fluorescent octopus and a huge puffer fish.

As my dive light burned my path, the richness of color abounded into the darkness of the Bismarck Sea. Tiny shells, colorful nudibranchs and a basket starfish glowed in the small, macroworld of the reef.

Our New Guinea dive guide, Michael, took us to visit his village. We met the Witch Doctor, traded biscuits for shells, and gave Life Savers to the children.

The village people value pigs and dug-out canoes more than the Kena (the New Guinea dollar), because money is of no value to them. Food, bread, water and earth are what their lives consist of. Each day evolves around getting fresh water, nursing the pigs, fishing the reefs and just staying alive. Their average life span is 50 years.

I have so much to share that sometimes I feel like a volcano near eruption, wanting to flow into other people's lives, sharing my world and my discover -ies. The world is in my soul, waiting to be shared. Through my lens, I hope to accomplish this.

Native by Carol Boone

NEW ZEALAND

Paul Snowman has been scuba diving since 1979 and has completed over 1,000 dives. He is a First-Class Diver Rating from the N.Z. Underwater Association. He is also a C.M.A.S. 4 Star Diver and N.A.U.I. Openwater II.

He is 34 and married with 2 children. He works for a local government organization administering Harbour Laws. This involves 80% of his time on boats in the Sounds.

He is a keen scuba diver with interests in underwater photography, marine biology, marine conservation and continually looking for exciting dive sites.

If you take a globe of the world and rotate it so that the New Zealand is in the center you will see more than land. "Our" half of the world is 91% ocean, with nearly half the remaining 9% made up of the continent of Antartica.

New Zealand is at the center of the water hemisphere. This makes us the most maritime nation on earth.

New Zealand has a long Coastline (approx. 15,000km or 9500 miles). Our coast is varied and includes fiords, sounds, vast bays, harbors, beaches and cliffs. We have everything except coral reefs and icebergs. Almost all of New Zealand is accessible by car or boat with the sea never more than 120km (75 miles) away. New Zealand's human population of a little over 3,000,000 is small when distributed over a land area approximately equivalent to Japan or the British Isles.

The waters of New Zealand lie between the 33rd and 47th parallels which includes the subantartic to the subtropical, the shallow continental shelf to the abyssal depths. Because our country lies in the "Roaring Forties" (westerly winds circumnavigating the earth at 40 degrees to the South) the west coast is rugged and almost incessantly pounded by ocean waves and high winds. Our proximity to Antartica affects our water temperatures which range from winter lows of 10 degrees centigrade (50 degrees Fahrenheit) to summer highs of 22 degrees centigrade (72 degrees Fahrenheit), depending on your location. Obviously, the further south you go, generally, the colder it gets. January and February are our warmest months (25C-30C) with July the coldest (-5C-12C).

Picton

Because diving in New Zealand is so varied I'll concentrate on the area where I live–Picton.

Picton lies at the base of the Marlborough Sounds, at the very top of the South Island. Picton is a quiet town of 4,000 people and because of its role as a "Getaway to the South" it prides itself on its tourist oriented outlook. The numerous restaurants, motels, hotels and retail outlets are geared to accommodate the tourist, with all budgets catered for.

Eating houses range from cafes and dairies ($10/person) to top of the line restaurants ($25-$40/person).

View from the top of Okuri Bay looking west across south end of D'Urville Island. D'Urville is the western border of the Marlborough Sounds. Nearby is "French Pass", a narrow passage near D'Urville Island and mainland New Zealand. By Paul Sowman.

Accommodations range from backpacker hotels ($12-$16/person/night) to top class hotels/motels ($63-$76/room/night). There are no diving resorts in Picton, but a number of resorts in the Sounds cater to dive groups.

Picton is the South Island terminal for an inter-island ferry service and this as well as the scheduled bus, train, and plane transport is regular and convenient. Picton also sports a large fleet of rental vehicles with all the major companies represented.

Pre-bookings for accommodation and all modes of travel can be made through the Picton Information Center, The Station, P.O. box 332, Picton, New Zealand. Phone (03) 5738838 within New Zealand. **Diver's World – Picton** is the sole dive retail center in Picton and boasts a full range of both hire and retail equipment. The store has full testing and filling facilities and undertakes recognized Scuba training (PADI & SSI) by qualified instructors. Dive charters are also arranged with groups of 4-16 divers. Trips do not normally include a dive master, but can if required.

Diving from Picton centers on the Marlborough Sounds, 1,400km (900 miles) of coastline containing a unique drowned valley system. The vast collection of bays, islands and subtidal reefs create numerous habitats supporting a great variety of New Zealand's endemic marine species.

Water temperatures range from 14 degrees centigrade (57F) to 20 degrees centigrade (68F) with the warmest water and more settled weather usually being experinced from January to April. Year round diving is possible although 7mm wetsuits are the norm regardless of the seasons. Water clarity is not comparable to the tropics, ranging from 2m (6ft) in bad weather to 20m (65ft) in good.

Novice divers will find excellent safe scenic diving within the Sounds at sites such as **Cooper's Point, Motuara Island** or the wreck of the **Koi**. These sites are also suitable for snorkelers, diving shallow rocky reefs covered in kelp and supporting large varieties of marine life.

The more ambitious experienced diver is catered for at sites such as **Cape Koamaru, Cape Jackson, Brother's Island** and the more distant **D'Urville Island**. These sites are generally kelp covered, rocky reefs with some tidal currents experienced resulting in exhilarating diving. Fish life is prolific with both conservationist and hunter being satisfied.

The Sounds sports numerous wrecks from small launches to 100 year old sailing ships and coastal steamers to our most recent, the 20,000 ton Russian liner *Mikhail Lermontov* which struck rocks and sank in the outer Sounds in February 1986. This wreck is imense and needs many dives to gain a perspective of its size. The ship lies on its side in 36m (120ft) with 13m (45ft) at its shallowest point. However, due to the regular poor visability and the numerous "enticing" windows and doors accessing the wreck, this is not a dive for the beginner and like all wreck dives, requires proper planning with local knowledge preferable.

No scheduled dive operation runs to the *Lermontov* but trips for groups of 4 or more can be arranged but can cost up to $120/day per person.

Several other, much older, shipwrecks lie in the outer Sounds many with opportunities for photography, relic hunting or just observing the resident fish population.

Excellent snorkling opportunities exist in Troy Channel for spearfishing. Paua (Abalone), pronounced "Par-wah", hunters; photographers; or just content to observe.

Because the Marlborough Sounds are largely sheltered from the effects of ocean waves and winds, there is always a dive site available for all levels of diving ability. Dive charters are available at the Picton town wharf. Self-drive charter vessels ranging from 5.0m runabouts ($50/person) to 12.0m launches and sailboats ($150/person/day) are available for independent divers while skippered charters costing $30-40 per person per day are available for groups of four to sixteen divers. Because the best dive sites are 35km (21 miles) from Picton, it is advisable to set a full day (or more) aside to do justice to the area.

The best diving value would have to be as a guest of the Picton Underwater Club which runs monthly dive trips into the Sounds.

Most trips are held on the 2nd or 3rd Sunday of the month, so timing your arrival in Picton for this event would ensure your participation.

The club (30 members) has good local knowledge and by using members private boats, cost for 3-4 dive day are kept below $40 per person. The boats used by the club are fast runabouts, so dive sites are accessed within 30 minutes of Picton compared tp 2-3 hours taken for charter launches.

Contact with club members can be made through the dive store in Picton.

Diving in Marlborough Sounds or indeed any part of New Zealand will be an experience you will fondly remember. If you decide to come here, I wish you safe happy diving.

All prices in this article are indicative only. New Zealand currency is approximately 55 U.S. cents to our dollar. No special adapters are required for dive equipment. American retail equipment is standard here.

One of the many different species of anemones found.
by Paul Sowman

SCUBA AND SNORKELING FACILITIES QUESTIONNAIRE

NAME **Diver's World - Picton**
ADDRESS **London Quay, Picton**
New Zealand
CONTACT **Bill Lines**
TITLE **Manager**
TELEPHONE **03-5737323** FAX **03-5737323**

CAPITAL:	**Picton**	GOVERNMENT:	**New Zealand**
POPULATION:	**4,000**	LANGUAGE:	**English**
CURRENCY:	**NZ Dollar**	ELECTRICITY:	**230v ac**
AIRLINES:	**Air NZ/United/Continental**	DEPARTURE TAX?	**$20 NZ Dollars**
NEED VISA/PASSPORT? YES **x** NO		PROOF OF CITIZENSHIP? YES **x** NO	

YOUR FACILITY IS CLASSIFIED AS: SCUBA CENTER **x** RESORT
BUSINESS HOURS: **0830 - 1730**
CERTIFYING AGENCIES: **PADI, SSI**
LOG BOOK REQUIRED? YES NO **x**
EQUIPMENT: SALES **x** RENTALS **x** AIR FILLS **x**
PRIMARY LINE OF EQUIPMENT: **Sherwood**
PHOTOGRAPHIC EQUIPMENT: SALES RENTALS LAB **x**

CHARTER/DIVE BOAT AVAILABLE? YES **x** NO DIVER CAPACITY **4-15**
COAST GUARD APPROVED? YES **x** NO CAPTAIN LICENSED? YES **x** NO
SHIP TO SHORE? YES **x** NO LORAN? YES NO **x** RADAR? YES **x** NO
DIVE MASTER/INSTRUCTOR ABOARD? YES **x** NO BOTH **x**

DIVING & SNORKELING: SALT **x** FRESH
TYPE OF DIVING/SNORKELING IN AREA: WALL **x** BEACH **x** WRECK **x** REEF CAVE ICE
DIVING/SNORKELING IN YOUR AREA IS BEST SUITED FOR: BEGINNER **x** INTERMEDIATE **x** ADVANCED **x**
BEST TIME OF YEAR FOR DIVING/SNORKELING: **Summer/Autumn**
TEMPERATURE: **NOV-APRIL: 70 F** **MAY-OCT: 60 F**
VISIBILITY: **DIVING: 15-65 FT** **SNORKELING: 15-65 FT**

PACKAGES AVAILABLE: DIVE **x** DIVE STAY SNORKEL **x** SNORKEL-STAY
ACCOMMODATIONS NEARBY: HOTEL **x** MOTEL HOSTELS **x**
ACCOMMODATION RATES: EXPENSIVE **x** MODERATE **x** INEXPENSIVE **x**
RESTAURANTS NEARBY: EXPENSIVE **x** MODERATE **x** INEXPENSIVE **x**
YOUR AREA IS: REMOTE QUIET WITH ACTIVITIES **x** LIVELY
LOCAL ACTIVITY/NIGHTLIFE: **4-wheel drive tours, wine trails, harbour cruises, hotels, restaurants, nightclubs**
CAR NEEDED TO EXPLORE AREA? YES **x** NO
DUTY FREE SHOPPING? YES NO **x**

LOCAL EMERGENCY SERVICES NEAREST HYPERBARIC TREATMENT FACILITY
COASTGUARD: **Picton Police** AUTHORITY: **Canterbury Area Health Board**
TELEPHONE: **03-5736439** LOCATION: **Princess Margaret Hospital, Christchurch**
CALLSIGNS: TELEPHONE:
LOCAL DIVING DOCTOR:
NAME: **Dr. John C. Welch**
LOCATION: **Picton**
TELEPHONE: **03-5737901**

THE PHILIPPINES

Lynn Funkhouser is a world recognized leader in dive travel adventure as well as in underwater photography. Diving since 1967, she has circled the globe in her pursuit of discovering and capturing the underwater world. She created Lynn Funkhouser Photography, which specializes in environmental, nature-oriented, travel, architectural, and underwater images.

Her spectacular photos have been published in major magazines, catalogues, and ads, notably in "Ocean Realm", "Audubon", "Skin Diver", "International Wildlife", and "Sierra." Her works have also appeared in calendars and books, including the Audubon Nature Yearbook-State of the Reef, and in Aquatic Life, published by the John G. Shedd Aquarium.

Nikon has featured her images in "The Philippines", a projector slide show. Lynn is a popular and frequent speaker at major conferences, as well as scuba shows around the world. Her professional multi-projector slide presentations have attracted a steady and dedicated following. She has served as photo judge in international competitions.

She actively pursues her dedication to an environmental commitment and serves as the Vice-President of the International Marine life Alliance, Inc. which works to preserve coral reefs and the harmony of humans with the sea.

Lynn was honored to have received the Lifetime Achievement Award from The Philippine Aquatic and Marine Life Conservationists' Association, Inc. (PAMARCON) and her "outstanding contributions on behalf of the conservation and preservation of the marine environment of the Philippines." She is also listed in the 1990-1 edition of Who's Who in Photography.

Lynn is currently working on a book which will offer readers intimate insight into the inner inhabitants of the watery reef world.

A Philippines Foursome
Lynn Funkhouser

The Philippine Islands stretch for over 1,000 miles along the western edge of the Pacific Ocean.

The archipelago is made up of 7,107 islands, and the surrounding waters support what's said to be the largest variety of marine life in the world.

To date, over 2,000 species of fish have been identified, and no doubt there are more yet to be discovered.

Of the more than 7,000 islands, less than 800 of them are inhabited, and these by a cultural mix as diverse as the islands themselves. Malayo-Polynesian, Chinese, Indian, Spanish and American influences can all be seen in varying degrees on the different islands. Seventy languages and dialects are spoken, although English is spoken almost everywhere.

Filipinos are among the warmest, most friendly people in the world, and this makes traveling in their country all the more delightful.

Dorio Nudibranch by Lynn Funkhouser

Because I have traveled extensively throughout the Philippine Islands, I'm often asked about the country's political instability and if I ever fear for my safety. My answer to that is simple: for the past 15 years I've spent an average of two months each year in the islands, and I have yet to have any problems, whether out in the countryside or on the crowded streets of Manila.

Another misconception about the Philippines is that all of its reefs have been damaged or destroyed. According to some reports, 70 percent of the reefs are in poor to fair condition. While I think that this figure is grossly exaggerated, let's say for the sake of argument that it is accurate. That means, then, that the remaining 30 percent of the country, or 2,132 islands, are relatively unspoiled. (Compare that to the Caribbean which has a total of only 800 islands.) I can only say that the reefs and marine life you will experience in the Philippines are some of the finest in the world.

Since to cover the entire archipelago could fill volumes, let's take a look instead at four diving areas that I feel rank among the best in the Philippines.

WORLD FAMOUS TUBBATAHA REEF

When talking about diving in the Philippines the name that most frequently comes to people's minds is Tubbataha Reef in the Sulu Sea. This place has everything: awesome walls starting as shallow as 10 feet and plunging to depths unknown, mantas, large schools of fish, lots of white tip sharks and often 200 foot visibility.

After diving the sheer walls which seem to pulsate in shades of purple, pink, red and yellow, you ascend to the shallow areas where every patch of coral seems to have been perfectly placed, like in an underwater garden. It becomes a matter of "Which way do you look?" as you are torn between admiring all the nudibranchs, corals, sea fans, shells and clownfish and watching the blue water behind you for the pelagics. (Whale sharks are often seen here.)

> Dusk is an especially exciting at Tubbataha. Huge schools of fish - thousands of them - come sweeping into the reefs to find places to spend the night. And then the night critters come out, and the underwater night life begins, complete with predatory maneuvers and mating rituals.

Then at dawn, this underwater world transforms, and entirely new daytime vistas unfold before you.

Tubbataha is accessible only by live-aboards. They depart from Puerto Princesa, Palawan, which is about a one and a half hour flight from Manila on Philippine Airlines.

Tubbataha Reef is divided up into North Islet and South Islet. The southern islet has a lighthouse. If you get a chance, make sure to go ashore to photograph the sea birds. Tubbataha is diveable March through June only. Water temperatures average around 85 degrees.

ESCAPE TO EL NIDO

Located on northern Palawan in a scenic section of the island, El Nido derives its name from the swallows' nests built high in the cliffs which are harvested for bird's nest soup.

Accessible via private aircraft from Manila, you know something special is about to happen when you fly over this beautiful area and touch down on a dirt airstrip surrounded by bougainvillea. As the plane rolls to a stop you are met by a cart pulled by a caribou (water buffalo) which transfers your baggage to a large banca (outrigger-style boat) which will take you on a scenic half hour ride out to the El Nido Resort.

El Nido resort is nestled between several black marble mountains and features a crescent shaped white sand beach.

Feather Star by Lynn Funkhouser

There are seven cottages built on stilts over the water and fourteen garden cottages surrounded by beautiful tropical flower gardens. Three of the cottages are located up some very steep stairs which afford a spectacular view, but can be difficult to get to if you have lots of camera equipment.

Diving is excellent year-round, although the best times to go are from March to June. Right in front of the resort is a fish feeding station where you can find those fish that are so hard to photograph elsewhere as they pose for your camera while waiting for their daily handouts.

One dive to 100 feet has about 15 volitan lionfish hanging out over forests of black coral. Another diver offers lots of blue spotted stingrays in about 50 feet of water. There is also a spot where you can find large crevices and caves in 10 to 20 feet of water swarming with silver sides.

In between dives there are wonderful beach lunches or buffets back at the resort featuring fresh seafood, chicken, pork, fresh vegetables and fresh fruits. Or, you can opt to be put on a private beach of your choice with food, beverages, blankets, your favorite dive buddy and your fantasies, with instructions to be "rescued" only when you're ready.

El Nido Resort offers only two dives per day and no night diving, so it is not a place for "gorilla" divers. But if you want an incredibly beautiful place to relax, where you can enjoy spectacular daytime diving, explore secluded lagoons with caves and gorgeous beaches, and then return to the resort to be pampered with beach lunches and extravagant sunset dinners, then El Nido is the place for you.

The only drawback to El Nido may be the communal bathrooms, but they are immaculately maintained and so well situated that you don't mind the inconvenience. "Trips" allow you to take a walk through gardens and enjoy the flowers and wildlife - eagles, a monkey, guinea fowl, ducks, cranes, show pigeons and occasionally wild parrots fly in to take advantage of the feeding stations.

BOHOL FOR AVID DIVERS

Juvenile Semicircular Angelfish by Lynn Funkhouser

A smaller island located between the eastern islands of Cebu and Leyte, Bohol Island and its surrounding waters have a lot to offer divers of all levels.

The Bohol Beach Club is a resort located along a beautiful white sand beach rimmed with palm trees. There is an open air, thatched roof dining room, lounging areas, a swimming pool, tennis courts, pool tables and a bar, as well as wind-surfing and diving facilities.

Two 65-foot bancas transport divers to the various dive sites. In a country where dive masters are extremely helpful, Joey Vaenzuela and his staff still deserve a mention. Even though we experienced an unseasonable Force 11 typhoon, we only lost one day of diving and were able to make up those dives later. The most appreciated service provided was to rap on their tanks while I was shooting macro subjects to let me know that enormous schools of pelagics were passing behind me.

The dive sites of Bohol are many and varied.

To the southwest Pamilacan Island is named for the manta rays which breed there between February and May. Balicasag Island brings to mind Tubbataha with its dense corals and vertical drop-offs. Here the clownfish are plentiful, and pelagics cruise by like they were on a timetable. Both species of flashlight fish can also be seen here on night dives as well as lots of shells, octopi and spanish dancers.

Balicasag is a wonderful place for beach lunches. Local children and friendly vendors provide lots of bargaining and photo opportunities.

One of the few places where you can see lots of black and white banded sea snakes is **Cervera Shoal**, just west of Pamilacan Island. When the currents cooperate, dive masters organize expeditions to the shoal, where you'll also find huge expanses of coral, volitan lionfish and maroon clownfish.

But you don't have to wander far from the Bohol Beach Resort to find some excellent diving. A whale shark passes right in front of the resort daily and a wall teeming with sea life is just a short distance away.

In addition to the wonderful sights underwater, there is so much to do topside that you may want to take a day or two off from diving to take a river safari, explore some of the local caves or hike through the mahogany forests. This is an excellent destination to take along a non-diving spouse or the whole family.

To reach Bohol, you have to take Philippine Airlines to Cebu City on the island of Cebu, the second largest city in the Philippines, and transfer to a small plane to Tagbilaran City on Bohol. If you happen to find yourself with several hours on your hands in Cebu City, hire a jeepney (agree to the price beforehand) and take a tour of the Island (connected to Cebu by road) to see the Lapu Lapu Monument, where the Filipino Lapu Lapu killed the explorer Ferdinand Magellan and many of his troops.

The best time to visit Bohol is November through May, but diving is possible all year.

Underwater Beauty of Batangas

Batangas is a province on the southern end of the island of Luzon located approximately 50 miles south of Manila. If you travel from Manila by car and you are an avid photographer, allow plenty of time to get to Batangas. Early morning or late afternoon you might find the wonderful rattan-laden gypsy carts drawn by beautiful white or brown caribou traveling in caravan. For a few pesos (20 pesos = $1) you can have the whole caravan pull off the highway for a photo session. Traveling along the road you may also see farmers and their caribou plowing rice fields, families planting or harvesting crops, women washing clothes in the streams, and beautiful fruit and produce stands along the road lined with exotic flowers and tropical plants.

If you go through Tagaytay, there are spectacular views of Lake Taal and the volcano. Batangas City is worth stopping in if you want to see a thriving provincial market.

During the best diving season between October and June, Batangas water temperatures average 75 degrees and a rich plankton environment supports an incredible number of fish and invertebrates. Crinoids in all colors are everywhere, as are many species of nudibranchs. Sea cucumbers range in size from the beautiful yellow inch-long variety to the four-foot-long species. There are at least a dozen species of clownfish, and some of them live in anemones the size of wagon wheels. And all of this can be found in 10 to 20 feet of water.

Bonito Island Resort is on its own island, located just off the east end of Maricaban Island at the mouth of Batangas Bay. Bonito Island is accessible by boat from the Batangas City dock (either one dollar per person on the ferry or hire your own banca for $15 to $25, but it is probably best to make arrangements through Bonito Island Resort owner Jun Marcelo or a tour operator.)

There is a fish feeding station near the resort that attracts swarms of butterflyfish. One unique dive in shallow water has actual sea goblins - strange looking fish that look like a cross between scorpionfish and sea robins. At that same point you'll find beautiful white nudibranchs with large orange spots, a species that I haven't seen anywhere else.

Just off Bonito is **Malajibomanoc** (or chicken feather) **Island** which has an underwater hot springs about 30 feet deep. Its fun to swim through the champagne-like bubbles, and it is said that you can cook an egg if you bury it in the sand there. There are lots of large sea fans, huge sponges and many macro critters along its perimeter.

Each one of these Philippine dive locales could keep you busy for weeks, and they are just four spots in an island chain with countless similar diving op-portunities. You could vacation in the Philippines every year for the rest of your life and never even begin to cover the exceptional dive locales the islands offer, but these are good places to start.

For Additional Information on the Philippines: Philippine Dive Versions - A book by Gretchen Hutchinson & Edgar Ventura with Lynn Funkhouser.

Elegre In Northern Cebu

Captain Victor Organ

Diving Experience: I started diving 1965 at the age of 14 in Palm Beach, Florida. I hold certifications from NAUI, SSI, PADI and I am currently an Instructor Trainer for PDIC and IDEA. Over the last 26 years I have logged over 1,800 dives of which 1,600 were made in the Red Sea.

Other diving locations and experience include the Atlantic off the Florida Coast and Keys, St Croix USVI, Mediterranean Sea from Cyprus and Italy, Seychelles in the Indian Ocean, Sea of Siam off Thailand, China Sea and Zulu Sea in the Philippines, Hawaii in the South Pacific and altitude and ice diving in the Flaming George, Wyoming.

Red Tube Worms by Victor Organ.

I have written several articles for local dive club news letters and have had pictures featured in Ahlam Wahsalam, Saudia's flight magazine, the Wild Life Book of Saudi Arabia and numerous advertising layout for local hotels and companies.

For the more discriminating diver Elegre Beach Resort in Northern Cebu is a destination not to be missed. Even the name 'Alegre', which is Spanish for "the good life" promises refreshing dives, swimming in warm tropical waters and relaxing in the sun by the sea. Elegre has 21 bungalows with 2 rooms each, beautifully laid out on seven hectares overlooking the Camotes Sea. Each room has either a king sized bed or two queen sized beds, central air-conditioning and a well stocked mini bar. Satellite T.V. is available and each room has a private verandah facing the beach. When our group visited Elegre, we had our dinner served each evening on this verandah and watched the moon rising on the distant Leyte Islands. The most striking feature of these apartments was the size of the rooms, especially the bathroom. It featured a tub set in marble, separate showers roomy enough to hang, wet suits and other gear to dry and an elegant double vanity set in locally mined marble. The buildings are constructed in block, plastered in a Spanish stucco style and the roofs are grass thatched. This harmonious combination blends the old Hacienda style with the well manicured grounds.

The grounds are beautifully landscaped in local and imported plants with coral walk ways leading to the resort's many other features. These include the split level swimming pool next to the restaurant and lounge with its circular bar which overlooks the pool and sea.

Elegre has the first sand filled grass tennis court in the Philippines built to international standards and an archery range for those who wish to try something different. But it is the variety of water sports that will interest the diver most.

Florescent Jellyfish by Victor Organ.

The resort is built upon a small bluff or cliff which forms three distinct beaches from which the Leyte Islands can be seen miles across the Camotes Sea. The Southern cove is called Natures Cove because it was left exactly as found other than the stone walk down to it. The Center Cove is by far the largest which features two stone walks down to the Coconut Trees and a large Talisay tree after which the beach is named. Here one can swim, sunbathe or relax in the shade while enjoying the cool drinks served from the beach bar. 'Habibi' meaning shell cove is where Aqua Sports Facilities which are certified by the Philippine government is located. Wind surfing, hobby cat sailing and jet skiing are available.

It is from Habibi Beach that your diving adventure will begin whether it will be a beach dive or by boat.

Beach diving can be done by walking in or by boat. The reef is 42 feet deep and stretches out to sea about two hundred feet before the coral wall drops off to a one hundred foot bottom.

There is easily a quarter mile of wall diving just in front of Elegre and because the resort is new a diver can explore and find new dive locations within two or three miles up the coast in either direction.

One outstanding location I visited was the cavern directly in front of Talisay Cove. The wall stops back towards the reef instead of the sea and as result seafans, sponge and other marine life are abundant, and extremely colorful, as there is no build up of sands or silt. While night diving this wall Jamie Holman, (the Project Manager building Elegre) and I found a cavern at about 80 feet. The opening is forty-feet wide and goes back under the wall thirty-five feet or so. The entrance is fifteen feet high and ceiling tapers back to four or five feet. The top of the cavern is covered with black corals, tube worms,, sponges and yellow sea anemones. We found six blue spotted rays buried in the silty sand bottom and plenty of holes dug up by feeding rays that suggest these creatures reside here.

The whole area is a macro-photographers dream come true. The shrimp nudibranchs and the famous Philippine feather star fish are abundant in many colors and type. Don't forget the wide angle lens or video because there are jacks, tuna, coral grouper and other schools of reef fish to photo along the wall.

Just a half mile North of Elegre is the "Hole in the Wall" site. This is a cave that starts on the outside wall at about fifty feet that does a half twist up towards the surface at fifteen feet. Sea fans and black coal line the walls and there is plenty of room for a diver to pass without disturbing either. If caught just right, the mid-morning sun dances through to put on a light show for the diver or photographer.

One of the best sites that I have dived in the Philippines is Capitancillo. This reef is a half mile long, runs North to South and is surrounded by fifteen hundred feet of water. The reef can be reached by driving thirty minutes North of Elegre and taking an hour "banka" ride towards Leyte to the century old light house that can be seen from shore. Bancas are Philippine boats with two bamboo outriggers, varying in size from ten-foot and hand paddled, to the twenty to thirty-foot 'in-board' powered variety used for fishing, trade, transport and scuba divers. Usually, the Capitancillo dive excursion is done as a day trip with divers drift diving the wall along the west side on the first dive. Lunch is then served on Capitancillo Beach on the Southern end of the light house and divers have a break to explore the small island or snorkel for the many shells that are washed up on the beach daily. A shallow reef dive on the east side in forty to fifty-feet of water can be made safely without worrying too much about 'bottom time' on a second dive.

On my next visit to Elegre I plan to travel to Kalangaman Island and the Quattro Islands. Twenty minutes from Capitancillo is Kalangaman island. A semi inhabited island. Kalangaman is surrounded by an extensive coral reef offering outstanding snorkeling as well as diving.

The depths at Kalangaman are not as deep as those at Capitancillo, reaching maximums of 30 meter (100'). Broad, white, powder sand beaches make Kalangaman an excellent lunch stop on a day's excursion.

Further afield, just off the Leyte coast, lies the Quattro Islands. As the name implies these are four small islands close together. A two and a half hour trip.

Quattro offers the most beautiful coral gardens to be found in the Camotes Sea. Beach dives are the rule here as the reefs run less than 10 meters (30') from the shore. Very large brain and table coral are scattered across the cavern riddled reefs. Large fish populations abound.

Elegre is situated in the municipality of Sogod 65 kilometers north of Cebu City.

Air conditioned transportation for guests from the international airport at Mactan is provided free of charge and takes approximately an hour and a half. Air transport to Cebu is provided by 8 daily flights from Manila on Philippine Airlines. Direct international flights to Cebu originate from Tokyo, Singapore and Sydney. Charter flights are available from Hong Kong on both Cathay Pacific and PAL.

The Red Sea

Paul & Liz James

Paul: B.S.A.C Dive leader and Fire Brigade Officcer
Breathing apparatus instructor for Lancashire County Fire Service
Diving for ten years all around British Isles and Mediterranean, Red Sea, Forida, and the Caribbean
Liz: B.S.A.C sports diver. Diving for five years
Profession: College Administrator

In June having heard so much talk about the Red Sea diving from our fellow club members, diving books and monthly publications, we decided to take a look for ourselves.

As we flew over the vast sprawl of Cairo, the largest city in Africa, the pilot advised us to look out of the starboard windows, there was our first sight of ancient Egypt, the pyramids. We landed and straight away felt the fierce heat which was to accompany us for the next fortnight.

After an age going through immigration, we took a taxi to Hurghada, a well known dive location approximately 230 miles south of Cairo. Sharing our journey was a fellow diver from Texas called Rick Palmer.

We advise anyone to fly from Cairo to Hurghada, it only costs about $75. The taxi ride will scare the hell out of you and cost you $35.

In the USA you drive on the right, in England we drive on the left, in Egypt, they drive on the right and on the left. They also have a quirky habit of switching their headlights off as they pass each other on the road at night.

We stayed at a hotel complex called the Princess Club. As we booked in, we were met by our dive guide, Diana, who then took us for a welcoming drink. She asked about our previous diving experience. It was then that I became envious of Rick's dive log, as our dive guide read out "Truk Lagoon". My experience of wrecks was the German fleet in the cold waters of Scapa Flow, while Rick had been diving the Japanese fleet in lovely warm waters.

Our charter boat was roomy and had only six divers on the first day. A big toothy grin from the skipper, Saed, said we were in for a fun day. We were to dive an outer reef of the Giftun Islands called **Carless**. The journey took about one and a half hours. We talked as all divers do of previous dives and equipment .

When we arrived at Carless and dropped anchor, three other dive boats were in attendance. We looked over the side and both agreed that it would be a shallow dive of about five to ten meters. As we jumped overboard and hit the surface of the water, we were surprised at just how warm it was. 87 f registered on Rick's thermometer! We started to descend, 10m, 15m, 17.5m.

At the bottom, we could still see the markings on the hull of the boat almost 60 feet above us - fantastic visibility. I can only say of that dive, that I didn't

ever want to surface. I have never seen such a profusion of color both in fish and coral.

Parrot fish of every shade of the rainbow, scorpion fish, lion fish, turkey fish, pipe fish, morays, stingrays, angels, clown fish, grouper, shark, you name it and it swam past you.

We spent the day there snorkeling around the reef until it was time to dive again.

In the afternoon we dived the opposite side of the reef, it was just as wonderful as the morning's dive, with possibly even more fish.

Our first week of diving was over very quickly. We had dived most of the outer reefs around the Giftun Islands, with names such as Giftun Picola, El Aruk Giftun, Abu Ramada Nord, Gota Abu Ramada West and my favorite, Shabbrur Umm Gamar.

This dive had everything! Depth, if you wanted it, hundreds of fish, from sharks to morays, from angels to pipe fish, and a wreck of a torpedo boat, which had been sunk by the Israelis.

Red Sea Spanish Dancer by Lynn Funkhouser

The wreck was broken up and housed tame groupers and large Napoleon wrasse. The whole dive was unforgettable, luckily we had another week's diving to come.

All the dive sights visited were a photographers' heaven, with clear warm water, very co-operative fish and something unusual around every coral head. Don't forget your Nikonos or you'll kick yourself.

The Red Sea isn't all a delight however, as it has its nasties which you will have to stay away from. It boasts over a thousand species of fish, more species than any other comparable body of water and out of these, approximately 100 are dangerous in some way.

Some are dangerous to touch, others dangerous to eat and some are dangerous to come face to face with. There are fire corals and stinging hydroids which can be extremely painful if accidentally touched.

There are numerous species of shark, including the tiger and hammerhead.

Other fish to be cautious of are stonefish, turkey fish, some species of surgeon fish, rabbit fish, barracuda and some of the large moray eels. All are beautiful to look at but if in doubt, don't touch. A recommended read prior to your visit is 'Red Sea Safety' by Peter Vine-Immel Publishing. It tells you all you need to know to ensure that your dives are safe ones.

All diver grades can safely dive the area. Most dives are shallow at around 15-20 meters, however, there are wall dives and drift dives for the more adventurous and when you can still see the bottom of your dive boat at 40 meters, you must agree, the visibility is fantastic.

While we were there a number of people gained qualifications. All associations are catered for, but PADI and BSAC seemed to be most popular. The nearest hyperbaric chamber is to be found 3 to 4 miles south of Hurghada in the Magawish Resort Village and is run by two brothers who also run a diving operation. They are specialists in decompression and diving related medicines.

The port of Hurghada, offers a wide range of accommodation to suit all travelers, from those who wish to conserve their funds to those who can afford and expect the height of luxury. Remember, when booking into any of the 30 or 40 hotels and villas in and around Hurghada, air conditioning is an absolute must. Temperatures can reach upwards of 140 f on a windless summer's day.

There are several diving centres in Hurghada and most of the hotels offer diving for their guests, some even boast their own diving centre twinned with the hotel. Diving cost approximately 30 to 50 dollars for two dives, cylinder and weights included. All diving is from hard boats, 40 to 50 ft in length and lunch is usually provided aboard for an additional fee. Most boats leave dock at 8:30-9:00 am to ensure that both dives are comfortably taken to enable the skippers to comply with the port authorities, that insist that all boats are back in port by 4:00 pm. Special permission can be obtained for night dives.

Non-divers are catered for handsomely in the hotel complexes or villages with bars, swimming pools and sports of all descriptions, including water skiing, jet skiing, and one of the Egyptians' favorite sports, soccer, for the more energetic. There are a host of trips to take.

You can take the coach journey 200 miles inland to Luxor to see the valley of the kings and queens and experience the classical tour of Karnak Temple, the Colossi of Memnon, Luxor Temple and many more breathtaking sights. A journey to Luxor is like stepping back in time.

Remember that inland from Hurghada is the Eastern desert. It is extremely hot. You must go equipped with a hat and clothing that will protect you from the burning sun. Large bottles of cool water are essential.

Don't forget your camera! Trips down the Nile can also be arranged both on luxurious boats equipped for about 100 guests (floating hotels) or after some serious bartering, experience a journey on a felluca. Do remember that buying anything in Egypt is usually done by barter and they are better at it than you are, so be careful.

Returning to the coast, snorkeling is probably the activity enjoyed the most by non-divers.

Boats are available every day to take snorkelers out to the shallow reefs. With a stop off for lunch on one of the many uninhabited islands.

The reefs are so scenic, some being likened to underwater gardens. Fish abound, but be careful what you touch.

Crocodile Fish by Lynn Funkhouser

RUSSIA

Val Darkin

Val Darkin has visited the United States for about 200 days all together. He participated in two symposiums of the AAUS in 1990-1991. His main goal is to bring to the Russian recreational and scientific diving community modern systems of divers training, education, and safety. It is a self-supported and self-developed international diving programme and his company is the base for realizing it.

After years of successful operations with a 52 foot live-aboard dive boat, First Russian recreational SCUBA Diving Company ACFES-VECTOR is going to launch a 96 foot live-aboard dive boat, converted from a former all-weather marine rescue boat.

Thanks to sponsorships and encouragement from PADI, NAUI, American Academy of Underwater Sciences, DAN, International Association of NITROX Divers, Ocean Divers - Key Largo, Professional SCUBA Inspectors, Inc., Truth Aquatics - Santa Barbara, Russian pioneers in recreational SCUBA diving are growing up as true international SCUBA diving facility with high standards of diving training and safety.

Both boats are based in Vladivostok and operated in the Bay of Peter the Great within 10-50 miles range from Vladivostok. So, the best dive sites in Russia become available for western divers. New dive sights every day from 8-10 include about 20 offshore islands, at least 3 wrecks; great wall diving down to 130 feet and much more.

Summer water temperature reaches 75F/23C with average temperature 60-70F/15-21 C. Visibility ranges 40-100 feet/12-30 metres.

The main underwater creatures are giant octopus dolphin (up to 80 pounds); king or Alaskan crab, giant and colourful starfishes.

SCUBA AND SNORKELING FACILITIES QUESTIONNAIRE

NAME **Acfes-Vector**
ADDRESS **P.O. Box 2661**
Vladivostok 690090, Russia
CONTACT **Mr. Valeri (Val) Darkin**
TITLE **Dive Manager of Acfes-Vector**
TELEPHONE   FAX **4232-254920**   TELEX **21 3115 ABC SU**

CAPITAL: **Valdivostok**   GOVERNMENT:
POPULATION: **2,000**   LANGUAGE: **Russian**
CURRENCY: **Ruble**   ELECTRICITY: **220v**
AIRLINES: **Aeroflot, Alaska Air**   DEPARTURE TAX? **No**
NEED VISA/PASSPORT?   YES **x**   NO   PROOF OF CITIZENSHIP?   YES **x**   NO

YOUR FACILITY IS CLASSIFIED AS: SCUBA CENTER **x**   RESORT
BUSINESS HOURS: **Splash Dive Operation 8:00 a.m. - 7:30 p.m.**
CERTIFYING AGENCIES: **PADI**
LOG BOOK REQUIRED?   YES   NO **x**
EQUIPMENT: SALES **x**   RENTALS **x**   AIR FILLS **x**
PRIMARY LINE OF EQUIPMENT: **Scubapro**
PHOTOGRAPHIC EQUIPMENT: SALES   RENTALS   LAB **x**

CHARTER/DIVE BOAT AVAILABLE?   YES **x**   NO   DIVER CAPACITY   **Up to 18**
COAST GUARD APPROVED?   YES **x**   NO   CAPTAIN LICENSED? YES **x**   NO
SHIP TO SHORE? YES **x** NO   LORAN?   YES NO   RADAR? YES **x** NO
DIVE MASTER/INSTRUCTOR ABOARD?   YES **x**   NO   BOTH

DIVING & SNORKELING: SALT **x**   FRESH
TYPE OF DIVING/SNORKELING IN AREA: WALL **x**   BEACH **x**   WRECK **x**   REEF   CAVE   ICE
DIVING/SNORKELING IN YOUR AREA IS BEST SUITED FOR: BEGINNER **x**   INTERMEDIATE **x**   ADVANCED **x**
BEST TIME OF YEAR FOR DIVING/SNORKELING: **Year round**
TEMPERATURE: **NOV-APRIL:**   80-84 F   **MAY-OCT: 80-84 F**
VISIBILITY: **DIVING:**   Unlimited FT   **SNORKELING: 100 FT**

PACKAGES AVAILABLE: DIVE **x**   DIVE STAY **x**   SNORKEL **x**   SNORKEL-STAY **x**
ACCOMMODATIONS NEARBY: HOTEL **x**   MOTEL   HOME RENTALS
ACCOMMODATION RATES: EXPENSIVE **x**   MODERATE   INEXPENSIVE
RESTAURANTS NEARBY: EXPENSIVE   MODERATE **x** INEXPENSIVE
YOUR AREA IS: REMOTE   QUIET WITH ACTIVITIES **x**   LIVELY
LOCAL ACTIVITY/NIGHTLIFE: **Guest activities program; nightly entertainment in restaurants; slide shows; movies**
CAR NEEDED TO EXPLORE AREA?   YES **x**   NO
DUTY FREE SHOPPING?   YES **x On property**

LOCAL EMERGENCY SERVICES   NEAREST HYPERBARIC TREATMENT FACILITY
COASTGUARD: AUTHORITY: **Mac Donald Memorial Hospital**
TELEPHONE: LOCATION: **Koror, Palau**
CALLSIGNS: TELEPHONE: **680-488-2554, 2553, 2813**

LOCAL DIVING DOCTOR:
NAME:
LOCATION: **Mac Donald Memorial Hospital**
TELEPHONE: **680-488-2554, 2553, 2813**

SAUDI ARABIA

Jeddah

Captain Victor Organ arrived in Saudi Arabia in August of 1982 as a Project Manager for ROLACO Engineering, holding a SSI Advanced Open Water Certificate. After a few weeks of settling in, he made his first dive during a local holiday related to the Hajj, which is an obligatory religious pilgrimage for Muslims around the world. Victor lives and works in the Jeddah area which is on the Red Sea Coast just 40 miles west of Meccah, the Islamic Holy City. The coast line for forty miles north and south of Jeddah offers a coral wall varying in depth from six to ten feet, down to one hundred feet or more. You can imagine his excitement when he found hundred foot visibility just a couple of hundred feet off shore. Victor was born and raised in West Palm Beach, Florida and other than diving the Palm Beach inlet you had to charter a boat to reach the reef below the Gulf Stream, so unlimited beach diving in the Red Sea was a dream come true. After snorkeling over the reef and seeing the bottom one hundred feet below, even the most casual of divers would be hooked. He enrolled in one diving class after another and in 1985 became an instructor. He has certified over eight hundred divers since then as an Instructor Trainer for PDIC and IDEA and has logged over 1600 dives in the Red Sea.

Jeddah has changed as much in the last ten years as South Florida has over the last fifty.

Many of the coastal dive sites are no longer available, so in 1986 Victor bought a twenty-eight foot Willson boat, and started chartering to the many reefs of the Jeddah coast on the weekends. Today, the Al Saif Charter Service has the only custom built Dive Boat in Saudi Arabia. The Al Saif, meaning "The Sword" in Arabic is forty-five feet long, has 50 tank racks and can accommodate up to thirty Divers. Charters are available daily to over ninety dive sites that are stored in her Loran-C, seven of which are wrecks. Night diving, overnight trips, deep walls, spear fishing, photography, drift dives and caves are available. In fact, Al Saif Charters offers everything but ice diving, though there is no shortage of ice in the drinks.

Gogle Eyed Conch by Victor Organ

The divers don't have to worry about bad weather, the sun shines almost 365 days a year and because the reef comes all the way to the surface, good snorkeling and smooth water is practically guaranteed.

Water temperature in the winter is 72 to 75 degrees Fahrenheit and the rest of the year it is a warm 80, so lycra skins and light wet suits are all that is needed to stay comfortable.

Saudi Air Lines is the official carrier into the Kingdom of Saudi Arabia and offer the only direct flight from New York to Jeddah. The Al Bilad Hotel, situated on the Red Sea, caters to divers, and have their own beach complex. They also offer exclusive packages for divers that include bus service to the airport, beach and to the Al Saif. A word of caution to anyone who is eligible to come to Jeddah. "Don't bring alcohol or drugs", and familiarize yourself with other customs and laws of the Kingdom. This is an Islamic culture and the Saudi Authorities strictly enforce the law. Diving permits are required by the residents, visitors can secure a temporary permit from the Department of Fisheries.

Weekends in Saudi Arabia are on Thursdays and Fridays. Many of the expatriates from America and Europe head for the beach or the Al Saif for a relaxing day. People fly in from such exotic places as Riyadh, Dammam, Tabuk and Taif to take advantage of clear waters and blue sky.

Many of the servicemen from Desert Storm took a break on the Al Saif, some of which learned to dive while waiting for action.

On a typical day, divers will arrive about 7:30 to process their papers to exit Abhor Creek Coast Guard Station where the Al Saif is moored. The number of passengers, the destination and expected time of return is recorded with the Coast Guard along with a passenger manifest. This completed the Al Saif exits Abhor Creek to cross a five mile wide channel along the coast to enter into what is known as the Eliza Shoals, which is about ten miles wide and twenty miles long. There are about four hundred reefs that come up to the surface in the shoals with an unlimited amount of sea mounds, coral pinnacles and vertical walls.

When divers make the switch from shore to boat diving, the first thing they ask for are wrecks. They are seldom disappointed for there are several wrecks in the area.

Known locally by exotic names like **Chicken Wreck, Woody's Wreck, The Staphonos, Toilet Wreck, Ann Ann** and the newest wreck found by the Al Saif - **Willi's Wreck**. The names came from their bow marking (Ann-Ann and Staphonos) their cargo (frozen chicken and toilet/sanitary wears) or who found them or dived them first (Elwood Pridgen and Captain William Victor Organ). All are in eighty feet of water or less so they afford the diver plenty of bottom time. Most of the wrecks went down in the late seventies while the now airport was being built. At that time, the rule of thumb for navigating the Red Sea was stay in the middle and at the first set of bright lights on the horizon come hard to port. It's been reported by old timers like Woody that with construction going on around the clock, twelve miles north of Jeddah, some unsuspecting captain ran aground almost monthly. Most of the ships were unloaded and towed off the reefs. **Willi's Wreck** is by far the oldest. It is believed to be a steam ship. Judging from the large brain corals and the deterioration of the hull, it is estimated that she's been down over seventy years.

One of our most popular afternoon sites is **Marilyn's Gardens.** This cut 100 meters long by 50 meters wide lying between Marilyn's Reef and Al's Reef just North of Woody's Wreck is a photographers dream. The bottom is 35 to 40 foot deep and scattered across it are small coral heads. Table top coral and fire coral with soft corals growing in between them are in abundance. These give the photographer or diver a very pleasing array of figurations to explore and photograph. There are two small pinnacles that raise twenty feet from the bottom which are fully covered in soft corals. On the North end of the cut there is a very large bed of sheet coral, usually inhabited by sweet lips. jacks and red snapper that swim though the cut feeding on the many small bait fish and almost all the sixteen local varieties of grouper have been seen there on one dive or another. In order for the visibility to be good and the soft corals to be in bloom or feeding, the current should be running at a moderate speed, preferably from the North West. This brings in clear water with lots of micro-organisms for the coral to feed on. The only drawback is that divers must negotiate the current and anchoring can be tricky in order to keep the boat off the rocks. This is a nice site for a second dive after **Woody's Wreck**, unless photography is the main objective. In that case, it is suggested to check the site out before mid morning for clarity, then dive when the light is best. Spear Fishing is not allowed at this particular site.

Sunset on Kings Island by Victor Organ

One of the favorite sites for deep divers is the **Black Coral Canyon**. This lies on the Eastern drop-off of the Eliza Shoals about seven miles Northeast of Abhor Creek. The bottom has a variety of soft and hard corals at a depth of about ninety feet. There is a series of canyons formed by coral ridges that slope Eastward into the deep channel. On the ridges above the canyons there are four very large black coral "Trees". The largest of these stands over twelve feet in height, has an eight-inch base and is over ten feet in diameter. Schools of jacks and tuna run these ridges in search of food and eagle rays and deep water sharks are common.

Speaking of sharks, there never has been a recorded attack in the area, in fact, many divers with over 100 dives in the Red Sea have never seen one. When people request a shark experience, the site to head for is **Allah I**, a reef which is the only known sea mound in the area. Allah's Reef rises from 1500 feet to a depth of 35 feet and is 100 yards long and 50 yards wide at the top. On the East side there is a shelf at a hundred feet so this is an excellent location for a deep dive. Experienced divers and plenty of guides are required considering the depth and the resident shark population.

> **This has to be one of the best locations for large fish in the area, couple that with one hundred fifty foot visibility and sharks in blue water, even the most experienced diver will experience a "divers rush". Practically every dive, white tip sharks are seen.**

They vary in size from the three to four foot reef variety, to the larger and more aggressive oceanic white tips, six to ten feet in length. Hammer heads, threshers and gray sharks occasionally visit the reef and a twelve foot tiger shark was spotted once. There are several coral heads that feature gregorian soft corals and sea fans in which coral grouper, moray eels and soldier fish reside. Large jacks, snapper, barracuda and tuna schools constantly ply the waters in search of food.

If spear fishing is your thing the outer reefs of the Eliza shoals like **Ritas Reef** is the place to head. Named after IDEA Instructor Rita Gieges, one of the first female instructors in the Kingdom, this reef produces big fish in good numbers year after year. To insure that the population remains high the Al Saif only visits it every other month.

> **The reef is interesting to snorkel and pleasure dive as well because the depth is ten feet or more so the Al Saif can anchor right on top. Reef fish and soft corals are abundant so it makes an interesting trip for all.**

> **In addition to the diving, Jeddah offers the traveler the opportunity to step back in time with a visit to the "old souk" or Jeddah Museum and the sunsets from the Corniche (highway along a sea side or water front) will not be soon forgotten.**

SCUBA AND SNORKELING FACILITIES QUESTIONNAIRE

NAME   **Al Saif Charter Service**
ADDRESS   **P.O. Box 171**
                 Jeddah, Saudi Arabia
CONTACT   **Marilyn Organ**
TITLE   **Sales Manager**
TELEPHONE   **02-6603094 ext. 144**   FAX **02-6605383**

CAPITAL: **Jeddah**   GOVERNMENT: **Kingdom**
POPULATION: **2 million**   LANGUAGE: **Arabic/English**
CURRENCY: **Riyal**   ELECTRICITY: **50/60 MH**
AIRLINES: **Saudia**   DEPARTURE TAX?   **No**
NEED VISA/PASSPORT?   YES **x**   NO   PROOF OF CITIZENSHIP?   YES **x**   NO

YOUR FACILITY IS CLASSIFIED AS: SCUBA CENTER   RESORT **x**
BUSINESS HOURS: **0700 - 2300 daily**
CERTIFYING AGENCIES: **PDLI, IDEA, BSAC**
LOG BOOK REQUIRED?   YES **x**   NO
EQUIPMENT: SALES **x**   RENTALS **x**   AIR FILLS **x**
PRIMARY LINE OF EQUIPMENT: **US Divers, Tabata**
PHOTOGRAPHIC EQUIPMENT: SALES **x**   RENTALS **x**   LAB **x**

CHARTER/DIVE BOAT AVAILABLE?   YES **x**   NO   DIVER CAPACITY **30**
COAST GUARD APPROVED?   YES **x**   NO   CAPTAIN LICENSED? YES **x**   NO
SHIP TO SHORE? YES **25mh**   NO   SITEX YES **x** NO RADAR? YES   NO **x**
DIVE MASTER/INSTRUCTOR ABOARD?   YES **x**   NO   BOTH **x**

DIVING & SNORKELING: SALT **x**   FRESH
TYPE OF DIVING/SNORKELING IN AREA: WALL **x**   BEACH **x**   WRECK **x**   REEF   CAVE **x**   ICE
DIVING/SNORKELING IN YOUR AREA IS BEST SUITED FOR: BEGINNER **x**   INTERMEDIATE **x**   ADVANCED **x**
BEST TIME OF YEAR FOR DIVING/SNORKELING: **Year round**
TEMPERATURE: **NOV-APRIL:**   **75 F**   **MAY-OCT:**   **80 F**
VISIBILITY: **DIVING:**   **100+ FT**   **SNORKELING: 100+ FT**

PACKAGES AVAILABLE: DIVE **x**   DIVE STAY   SNORKEL   SNORKEL-STAY
ACCOMMODATIONS NEARBY: HOTEL **x**   MOTEL   HOME RENTALS
ACCOMMODATION RATES: EXPENSIVE   MODERATE **x**   INEXPENSIVE
RESTAURANTS NEARBY: EXPENSIVE **x**   MODERATE **x**   INEXPENSIVE **x**
YOUR AREA IS: REMOTE   QUIET WITH ACTIVITIES   LIVELY
LOCAL ACTIVITY/NIGHTLIFE: **Nightlife/Shopping**
CAR NEEDED TO EXPLORE AREA?   YES   NO **x**
DUTY FREE SHOPPING?   YES   NO **x**

LOCAL EMERGENCY SERVICES   NEAREST HYPERBARIC TREATMENT FACILITY
COASTGUARD: **Al Kawais, Jeddah, KSA**   AUTHORITY: **GMP Clinic**
TELEPHONE: **Commander Ahmed Assad 6435422**   LOCATION: **Jeddah, KSA**
CALLSIGNS: **Jeddah Radio, Jeddah Radio, Jedda Radio**   TELEPHONE: **6823300**

LOCAL DIVING DOCTOR:
NAME: **Dr. Prescott**
LOCATION: **GMP Clinic**
TELEPHONE: **6823300**

SCOTLAND

Stephen John Dye

Fife, Scotland
Diving Qualifications: Royal Navy ships diver, H.S.E. Part III commercial diver, British Sub Aqua Club dive leader. Experienced in Naval diving, civil engineering diving, and sports diving.
Current Occupation: Robert Gordon's Institute of Technology Survival School. Involved with training offshore workers in the oil industry. Training includes free-fall lifeboat abandonment, fire fighting, underwater helicopter escape, in water survival techniques.

Diving in Scotland can be cold and hazardous and the ill-prepared diver could quickly find his/herself in trouble. Water temperature changes from winter to summer are in the range of 5C to 15C, give or take a few degrees. Subsequently air temperatures can range from below freezing in winter to 60C - 70C in summer.

Winter diving presents the stiffest challenge and I would strongly recommend the following equipment: Dry suit with direct feed, thick neoprene gloves, a good hood, stabilizer/ABLJ with emergency air supply, S.M.B. (surface marker buoy to mark position of divers), compass, depth gauge, watch, and torch.

In summer many divers prefer a wet suit or semi-dry suit, although I much prefer to wear my dry suit with less undergarments. I would also recommend wearing a hood all year round although gloves may not be necessary.

The sea state can change quickly from calm to rough so seeking a weather forecast before setting out is essential.

Launching a boat can be tricky, waves and swells are factors which can make diving from a R.I.B. uncomfortable. By Stephen Dye

Divers should always indicate their position by attaching S.M.B. lines to themselves, which let the dive boat know the divers position but also warn other approaching boats. The dive boat should have on board a radio set (VHF is sufficient) and the Coast

Guard should be informed of any diving which will take place and the location. H.M.S. Coast Guard should be contacted by VHF radio on channel 16 or by dialing 999 in an emergency.

The visibility depends on the time of year and the sea state. The best visibility is found on the west and can be anything up to 30m, the visibility on the east coast tends to be about half that.

On the east the diver finds himself in the North Sea which can be cold and treacherous and lies on the continental shelf. The west faces onto the Atlantic Ocean and is affected by the warmer water of the North Atlantic Drift.

Oban, which is situated on the west coast of Scotland, is a dive site I have been visiting for the past five years. I would describe it as the diving 'mecca' of Scotland, everything is here -dive sites to suit all levels of diver, equipment hire, boat hire, plus plenty of accommodation and public houses to provide comforts.

On several of our expeditions there we have stayed at the Oban Divers camp-site. The accommodations we chose can be best described as a bunkhouse, bunk-beds three high with a cooker, heater and sink. Showers are next door in the washroom (be prepared to queue). It sounds basic, but for only a few pounds per night it is good value and is an ideal 'divers residence'. No need to worry about getting carpets dirty, or messing up a nice kitchen while preparing the 'catch' for dinner.

A popular dive in Oban is on the wreck of the S.S. Breda. This is a wreck of a British convoy vessel which was bombed in World War II and is very well preserved.

Bass Rock is home to many seabirds and seals. Very interesting diving all around rock, steep drops, caves, plenty of marine life, and broken wrecks. Watch out for strong tides. This dive would be suitable for experinced divers. By Stephen Dye

It lies upright and pretty much intact on the sea-bed which is at the 30m mark, although a diver on the deck would be nearer the 20m mark, which would suit the more experienced diver.

On one particular visit to the S.S. Breda we decided to launch our RIB from a beach close by (the wreck is not far offshore), in search of the wreck which we found using transits. Upon fixing our position we dropped a short line on which we would descend and ascend for safety. On reaching the sea-bed we saw we were close to the stern. Swimming along the deck level the fish life was excellent, shoals of cod and pollock taking of the food the wreck provides. Sitting perfectly intact on the deck about midship is a 4 ton lorry, although the tyres are a bit flat now. On returning across the sandy seabed to the shoreline I came across a cuttlefish, which when startled by my approach changed color instantly and shot off at an angle, brilliant to see. Unfortunately, as we had touched 30m our no-stop time was twenty minutes and our dive was over all too soon, but still very rewarding.

Another excellent dive close by Oban is a drift dive round Maiden Island, which is a relatively small rock island inhabited only by seabirds and seals.

This particular dive provides me with my favorite underwater pursuit, diving for scallops. It provides a challenge, a purpose for the dive, and the reward of the highly prized shellfish which is delicious. Again this would suit the more experienced diver and is reached by boat, although is only a very short distance offshore.

Jimmy (my buddy) and myself rolled over the side of the inflatable and descended down the sloping rocky face. On making bottom, we swam a short distance away from the rock face and onto the sandy bottom which is the home of the scallop. Each armed with a net bag, we set off in pursuit, which we soon found to be successful by indented half-moon crescents in the sand which gave their position away.

While drifting along we also encountered a large edible crab which unfortunately only had one claw and so we let it be. Further on we drifted past an angler fish, the first one I had seen underwater and was great to see. As the deepest we reached was 18m we had plenty no stop time and we surfaced after forty five minutes with a haul of about twenty largish scallops between us.

Oban also provides plenty of good dives for the novice with good visibility and interesting marine life.

One particular site is at **Gavannack Beach** where divers can enter the water from the beach and swim through the kelp forests full of fife and rocky coastline in depths around the 9m mark.

The coastline on the west is very different to the east, it is generally very broken and rugged with many islands dotted along its coast (many of these islands cater to the diver and offer excellent diving sites).

There are also many beautiful beaches with fantastic scenery along its shore. Hill walking, scenic coach tours, sailing and windsurfing are all pursuits available to the holiday visitor.

Accommodations range from expensive hotels to bed and breakfasts to campsites for pitching tents. Hotel prices tend to range from fifty pounds up, bed and breakfasts from fifteen to twenty pounds and campsites from a few pounds per night. Prices and availability obviously depend on the season, summer being busiest (May-August) although Easter (April) and Christmas and New Year are very popular times for people to get away.

The east coast of Scotland provides many good dive sites, many which are rarely, if ever, dived. Unfortunately the east has not been developed for the scuba diver. There are however many boat skippers who will charter their boats to divers, and regularly do so. Equipment hire as far as I know is not available, (although further south this may not be the case), but air is available from certain sources (dive shops and commercial outlets). For this reason the east would suit divers who have the necessary equipment.

The water along the east coast is the North Sea which is known for its cold and hostile waters.

Lying on the Continental Shelf the depth increases very gradually out from the shore (9m is about as deep as the diver would expect to find going from the shore). Tides can be quite strong and shore dives should ideally be planned to coincide with incoming tides around hightide/slack water for safety. Further offshore, however, greater depths are available to the diver (the North Sea is several hundred meters deep).

Before diving it is always a good idea to contact the local Coast Guard station for a weather report and to inform them of your intentions.

Dive sites that I have first hand knowledge and experience of are: Crail (a shore dive which suit novices, but still a very interesting dive), Bass Rock and May Isle, both of which lie offshore and would suit the experienced diver.

May Isle lies about 6 miles out from the Firth of Forth and **Bass Rock** lies to the south of the island. Both are uninhabited and offer wonderful sanctuaries to both seabirds and seals. Visitors landing must keep to pathways and respect birds nesting and not get too close. The islands are very impressive sites from a small boat and stand very high with rocky faces. Many boats offer charter trips for either people wishing to visit the islands and study the wildlife or for divers. My investigation has shown that although many boats are available I have not come across any skippers who hire equipment, but many are experienced in taking divers and have a good knowledge of the sites.

Scattered around the rocky islands are the remains of many wrecks but as is the case on most of the east the are very broken and scattered.

Close into the island are many caves, drop-offs and rocky reefs leading to sandy bottoms. Depths range from roughly 70m (210 ft). Seals and other forms of marine life can be studied at close quarters and are great attractions.

Summer would be the ideal time to visit these sites as the seas are warmer, air temperatures higher, and sea conditions calmer.

The winter can be very cold and rough seas make venturing out very dangerous.

The date was February 2nd, the air temperature was slightly above freezing and we had recorded the sea temperature at 3.6 degrees centigrade. We had just arrived at Crail on the Fife coast for our first dive of the year. We planned to take advantage of the calm seas resulted of two weeks of windless westerly weather. The visibility was good, light green and dark patches indicating the varying bottom conditions.

Suited up we made our may to the waters edge and fitted our fins. We fitted our masks, regulators in place and submerged our heads into the icy water. The first couple of minutes are the worst, then numbness takes over and comfort is felt, the hard part of the dive over.

We swam out on an easterly compass bearing for approximately twenty minutes (a compass is a very useful tool here for navigation, no need to surface for direction, also poor surface conditions may exist) On our way out we encountered little fish life as they move further offshore in winter, which is in total contrast to summer when wrasse, lobsters, edible crabs, codling, flatfish, starfish and sea urchins are just a few of the species which may be encountered. Although we did see plenty of starfish and sea urchins and a sea lemon as we swam over areas of kelp forests, sandy bottom and rock outcrops. After deciding we had swam for enough out (the cold helped us decide!) we turned around 180 degrees and swam westwards back in.

This location provides very good diving. Shallow bays provide good dives for novices. Further offshore dropoff's, drift dives, scallop beds, lobster all very interesting and exciting for the more experienced. By Stephen Dye

On surfacing, we inflated our jackets, spat out the regulators and remarked to each other how good the visibility was with numb mouths. At this point Stuart realized his fingers were too numb to remove his fins for the walk ashore, even though he was wearing neoprene gloves (another essential). Luckily my gloves had proved more effective and I was able to help him (for a small fee!).

254

Once out of our drysuits we bought ourselves back to life with a hot cup of coffee which Stuart brought along (yet another essential piece of equipment). Looking back the challenge of winter diving in Scotland was well worth the effort of all the preparation, planning and the cold water.

Apart from diving there are plenty of other attractions for the visitor along this part of the coast. There are rages of magnificent beaches to walk along, one beach I particularly like is Tentsmuir. This beach is home to a large gray seal colony which are not too shy and it is possible to view them at close quarters. Further north to Tentsmuir is Dundee and to the south is St. Andrews, the world famous home to golf, historic ruins, beautiful beaches and golf courses. There is also very good accommodation and restaurants in and around St. Andrews.

Charter a boat to May Island/Bass Rock. No equipment is for sale or hire. Be sure a knowledgeable skipper/ex-diver who knows the dive sites and is experienced with divers accompanies you. Both these sites are only for experienced divers.

Note: I would suggest that if any of you intend to visit Scotland with the intention of diving you should order a copy of the magazine "Diver." This is a monthly edition which is the official British Sub Aqua Club magazine. Included in the magazine are many addresses of locations, dive schools, shops, etc. which is very comprehensive.

SCUBA AND SNORKELING FACILITIES QUESTIONNAIRE

NAME
ADDRESS **30 Dreelside**
Anstruther, Fife, Scotland, UK
CONTACT **Jim Raeper**
TITLE **Mr.**
TELEPHONE **0333-310103**   FAX

CAPITAL: **Edinburgh**   GOVERNMENT:
POPULATION: **1 million**   LANGUAGE:
CURRENCY: **Sterling**   ELECTRICITY: **Yes**
AIRLINES: DEPARTURE TAX?
NEED VISA/PASSPORT?   YES **x**   NO   PROOF OF CITIZENSHIP?   YES **x**   NO

YOUR FACILITY IS CLASSIFIED AS: SCUBA CENTER   RESORT
BUSINESS HOURS:
CERTIFYING AGENCIES:
LOG BOOK REQUIRED?   YES   NO **x**
EQUIPMENT: SALES   RENTALS   AIR FILLS
PRIMARY LINE OF EQUIPMENT:
PHOTOGRAPHIC EQUIPMENT: SALES   RENTALS   LAB

CHARTER/DIVE BOAT AVAILABLE?   YES **x**   NO   DIVER CAPACITY
COAST GUARD APPROVED?   YES **x**   NO   CAPTAIN LICENSED?   YES **x**   NO
SHIP TO SHORE?   YES   NO **x**   LORAN   YES   NO **x**   RADAR?   YES   NO **x**
DIVE MASTER/INSTRUCTOR ABOARD?   YES **x**   NO   BOTH

DIVING & SNORKELING: SALT **x**   FRESH
TYPE OF DIVING/SNORKELING IN AREA: WALL **x**   BEACH   WRECK **x**   REEF   CAVE **x**   ICE
DIVING/SNORKELING IN YOUR AREA IS BEST SUITED FOR: BEGINNER   INTERMEDIATE **x**   ADVANCED **x**
BEST TIME OF YEAR FOR DIVING/SNORKELING: **May-October (Summer)**
TEMPERATURE: **NOV-APRIL: 40-50   F**   **MAY-OCT: 60 F**
VISIBILITY: **DIVING: 50 FT**   **SNORKELING: FT**

PACKAGES AVAILABLE: DIVE   DIVE STAY   SNORKEL   SNORKEL-STAY ACCOMMODA-
TIONS NEARBY: HOTEL **x**   MOTEL **x**   HOME RENTALS
ACCOMMODATION RATES: EXPENSIVE   MODERATE **x**   INEXPENSIVE
RESTAURANTS NEARBY: EXPENSIVE   MODERATE **x**   INEXPENSIVE
YOUR AREA IS: REMOTE   QUIET WITH ACTIVITIES **x**   LIVELY
LOCAL ACTIVITY/NIGHTLIFE: **St. Andrews/Edinburgh is fairly close**
CAR NEEDED TO EXPLORE AREA?   YES **x**   NO
DUTY FREE SHOPPING?   YES   NO

LOCAL EMERGENCY SERVICES   NEAREST HYPERBARIC TREATMENT FACILITY
COASTGUARD: **Forth Coastguard, Fifeness & Crail**   AUTHORITY: **Rosyth Naval Base**
TELEPHONE: **0333-5066/Emergency Dial 999**   LOCATION: **Rosyth (Firth of Forth)**
CALLSIGNS: **Channels 16 on VHF radio**   TELEPHONE:

LOCAL DIVING DOCTOR:
NAME:
LOCATION:
TELEPHONE:

SCUBA AND SNORKELING FACILITIES QUESTIONNAIRE

NAME   Oban Divers, Ltd.
ADDRESS   Cologin Homes, Lerags by Oban
            Argyll, Scotland, U.K.
CONTACT   Henry Woodman
TITLE   Mr.
TELEPHONE   0631-64501   FAX

CAPITAL: GOVERNMENT:
POPULATION: LANGUAGE:
CURRENCY: ELECTRICITY:
AIRLINES: DEPARTURE TAX?
NEED VISA/PASSPORT?   YES   NO PROOF OF CITIZENSHIP?   YES   NO

YOUR FACILITY IS CLASSIFIED AS: SCUBA CENTER x   RESORT
BUSINESS HOURS: Varies
CERTIFYING AGENCIES: BSAC
LOG BOOK REQUIRED?   YES x   NO
EQUIPMENT: SALES x   RENTALS x   AIR FILLS x
PRIMARY LINE OF EQUIPMENT: Scuba
PHOTOGRAPHIC EQUIPMENT: SALES   RENTALS   LAB

CHARTER/DIVE BOAT AVAILABLE?   YES x   NO   DIVER CAPACITY
COAST GUARD APPROVED?   YES x   NO   CAPTAIN LICENSED?   YES x   NO
SHIP TO SHORE? YES   NO x   LORAN   YES   NO x   RADAR?   YES   NO x
DIVE MASTER/INSTRUCTOR ABOARD?   YES x   NO   BOTH

DIVING & SNORKELING: SALT x   FRESH
TYPE OF DIVING/SNORKELING IN AREA: WALL x   BEACH x   WRECK x   REEF   CAVE   ICE
DIVING/SNORKELING IN YOUR AREA IS BEST SUITED FOR: BEGINNER x   INTERMEDIATE x   ADVANCED x
BEST TIME OF YEAR FOR DIVING/SNORKELING: Summer
TEMPERATURE: NOV-APRIL: 30-50   F   MAY-OCT: 50-60 F
VISIBILITY: DIVING: 100 FT   SNORKELING: FT

PACKAGES AVAILABLE: DIVE x   DIVE STAY x   SNORKEL   SNORKEL-STAY
ACCOMMODATIONS NEARBY: HOTEL x   MOTEL x   B&B's   HOME RENTALS x
ACCOMMODATION RATES: EXPENSIVE x   MODERATE x   INEXPENSIVE x
RESTAURANTS NEARBY: EXPENSIVE x   MODERATE x   INEXPENSIVE
YOUR AREA IS: REMOTE x   QUIET WITH ACTIVITIES   LIVELY
LOCAL ACTIVITY/NIGHTLIFE: Oban - Bars, restaurants, nice walks, scenic and hillwalking
CAR NEEDED TO EXPLORE AREA?   YES x   NO
DUTY FREE SHOPPING?   YES   NO

LOCAL EMERGENCY SERVICES   NEAREST HYPERBARIC TREATMENT FACILITY
COASTGUARD: AUTHORITY: Fasclane Naval Base
TELEPHONE: Emergency Dial 999   LOCATION:
CALLSIGNS: Channel 16 on VHF radio   TELEPHONE:

LOCAL DIVING DOCTOR:
NAME:
LOCATION:
TELEPHONE:

SOUTH AMERICA

Brazil
Beyond Carnival
Wendy Canning Church

"Carnival", celebrated each February, an occasion similar to Mardi Gras in New Orleans, has always been the most played up attraction in Brazil. As much local color, excitement, and fun this celebration brings to both native and visitor, we feel that there lies a Brazil that world travelers should know about.

Brazil was discovered in 1500 by the Portuguese Navigator Pedro Alvares Cabral. Brazil remained a colony for 300 years until the Portuguese King arrived in 1808 and set up court in Rio de Janeiro. John Pedro I ruled as Emperor but was forced to resign. His son, Pedro II, ruled until 1821 and in 1822 declared independence from Portugal and declared Brazil an empire.

After his death in 1831, his son Peter, only 5 years old, became ruler. He declared himself Emperor in 1841 when only 14 years old. He could speak 8 languages and proved to be a very progressive leader, bringing positive changes to the country. In 1872 he invited Alexander Graham Bell to install the beginnings of a telephone system. He reigned as Emperor from 1841-1889 and died at age 63.

Peter II became Emperor, and proclaimed Brazil a Federal Republic in 1889. The landed gentry were not happy with this because it came hand and hand with abolishment of slavery. The New Republic came to an end in 1930. The country and its people were soon to be as they are now, living in a democratic state.

Brazil, meaning wood, is the world's fifth largest country. It is boarded by every country in South America except Ecuador and Chile. Most of its population of 127 million residents are under twenty-four and descend from European, African, Asian, and native American backgrounds. The Portuguese language tends to set Brazil apart from its neighbors in South America.

Brazil has some 8,000 kilometers or 5,000 miles of beaches making it one of the best locations in the world for water sports. Couple this with warm temperature throughout the year because of its location in the southern hemisphere and you have an unbeatable combination for fun and sun!

Before playboy President Fernando Collor de Mello resigned, he made some extreme changes (some good, some bad) in the modernization of Brazil.

There is severe poverty and conversely, great wealth in Brazil. The middle class is struggling. Can this not be said of many countries?

Yes, there is crime. One should not travel with expensive jewelry or flaunt a camera in crowded areas. Isn't this true of any big city?

On the plus side, Brazil is one of the most beautiful countries you will ever visit. With its size, almost that of the United States, you have a range of topography from lush high mountain ranges, plains covered in colorful fragrant orange groves, cattle ranches, the verdant jungles, the sea and its islands which hold not only untold treasure from sunken wrecks but which offer the scuba diver and snorkeler a world that is almost virgin.

You will be astounded by the variety of fruits and vegetables, the high caliber of cuisine and the immense portions which you are served.

And the people ... well, all I can say as a world traveler, you'd have to go a long way to find a friendlier, more helpful group. Everywhere I went, I was presented with a gift, whether it was a small flower or a piece of native art.

Would I return? You bet your life ... in a heartbeat!

Historic colonial house by Wendy Canning Church

Rio de Janeiro: The River of January

We left Boston on a very cold November evening connecting out of J.F.K. International Airport in New York via Varig Airlines and landed in Rio de Janeiro early the next morning in spring.

We planned to spend three days in Rio for a little R & R and some sightseeing. The **Hotel Inter-Continental** was our choice of hotels. We wanted to be far away from the hustle and bustle of Copacabana and Ipanema, yet near enough to take advantage of the hotels free shuttle to visit and yes, be part of the action ... and action there surely is! Under the watchful eye of Director of Marketing and Sales, Paulo Senise, this hotel-resort is run with the utmost of professionalism. The entire staff have been expertly trained and are truly warm and helpful.

You really never need to leave the compound for everything is provided for the traveler whether their mission is pleasure or business. The rooms and suites are large and tastefully decorated, many with views of the beach which stretches for miles.

> **At sunset, the lights of Rio come an and it's Christmas all over again as they twinkle and light up the night and the beat goes on to the Latin rhythms until the wee hours of morning.**

The hotel has three swimming pools set in exuberant tropical gardens, a small pool on the upper deck for more privacy, or swim in the pool with waterfalls, or savor a cool drink at the swim-up bar. There are three tennis courts with a multi-lingual pro shop and cabana bar adjacent to a spectacular eighteen-hole golf course. Surf fans can catch waves on the beach, while hang- gliding, squash and ice skating are all available just a few minutes from the hotel.

The 9 million Rio natives or "cariocas" love life and like to play night and day.

All beaches are public and this is taken advantage of both during the week and on weekends. My advice would be to sightsee on the weekends, especially Sunday, or book a dive or a boat cruise because it is really body to body at the beach.

To watch the parade go by is better than any movie. No matter what age the girls from Ipanema and for that matter Copacabana, love the thong bikini, jokingly referred to as "dental floss". They say the bikinis are so small they can be wrapped up in the price tag.

We loved the fruit bars or "suco" where for very little money you can purchase freshly squeezed mango, papaya, passion fruit or watermelon juice. Vendors also pass with coconuts. They cut off the top and you drink the fresh milk. Afterwards you use the top to scrape out the meat. This is not only delicious, but apparently good for you and any stomach ailment. The local beer, Brahma, is not bad either!

Little shops are filled with local handmade crafts. The more fashionable sell precious stones in beautiful settings, leather goods and gold. These are good buys and if budget allows, take advantage of them.

On January 1, 1502, Captain Gaspar de Limos and his Portuguese fleet landed in Guanabara Bay and called it Rio de Janeiro or River of January. Salvador, in northern Brazil, was the first capital until gold was discovered inland. Rio was the nearest seaport to transport the gold to Portugal so it became the capital and remained so until 1960 when it was moved to Brasilia. Rio is divided into two areas, Zona Sue and Zona Norte. These lie to the North and South of the business district in the center.

One will marvel at the beautiful neoclassic style mixed with the modern architecture dispersed throughout these districts. The neighborhoods or "barrios" where you will find the population especially concentrated are Ipanema and Copacabana. They are where most tourists stay in the many hotels lining the beach. A quieter barrio is Leblon. It is quite beautiful and the one I prefer.

The Opera House is a copy of the one in Paris, only smaller, in jewel-like colonial style. The original customs house, its architecture of Moorish style, is now used by the Brazilian Navy.

The **Maracana** or soccer stadium is the largest in the world, holding 200,000 fans. It was constructed in 1950 for the world cup match between Brazil and Uruguay. In the final game, Uruguay won. It is common knowledge that the Brazilians are passionate about soccer so you can imagine the riot that followed this game.

There is a saying in Brazil that when you see a man playing dominoes, you know he is a senior citizen because he has given up soccer.

Don't miss the museums: Museu Nacional de Belas Artes; Museu de Arte Moderna; Museu da Republica; Museu Historico Nacional; Museu do Indio and Jardim Botanico.

Most of us are familiar with two other sites in Rio. The first in the Southern end is Sugar Loaf Mountain (1,300 feet high) which is reached by cable car. Here you can get a spectacular view of the city. The second is situated inland on Hunch-back Mountain, a 2,400 foot peak where an enormous statue of Christ stands with arms outstretched. This statue can be viewed from almost any point in Rio. When you see it you wonder if the Brazilians are correct when they state, "God is a Brazilian."

We set out early in the morning for Angra Dos Reis, an area on the Green Coast, which is located to the Southwest of Rio.

Family snorkeling by Wendy Canning Church

One-half hour out of the city, the hustle and bustle gives way to the serenity of sights of vast mountains and colorful lush hillside running to meet the sea.

A two hour ride brought us to Angra Dos Reis, an archipelago of 360 jungle covered islands and pristine tropical beaches.

Settled in the 18th century, almost the entire area was owned by the Frade family who were bankers. They developed it into a rich ranching and farming community under the then popular feudal system.

In the 1970's they built four splendid hotels.

The **Hotel Portobello** is a five star hotel in every sense of the word and we had a tour and luncheon with the very knowledgeable and charming General Manager, George Court. The buffet was not only tasteful to the eye, but to the palate as well. The entire complex is situated on a calm bay with mountains behind. Each room has direct access to the beach. They are air conditioned, with T.V. and mini bar. The public rooms are light and airy, furnished in Brazilian style with wonderful woods and colorful fabrics. The Hotel's landscaping is lush, the hibiscus and bougainvillea were especially breathtaking.

When or if you tire of the scenery, you can take advantage of the myriad of activities offered. There are tennis courts, jet skis, windsurfers, volleyball and Laser sailboats. If ping-pong is for you, then grab a partner. Deep sea fishing is offered, or you can charter a yacht for the day at their private marina to investigate the many islands. Children will be delighted with the area designed especially for them filled with all sorts of games.

There is a gift shop on the premises, sauna and massage are also offered.

Across the street from the hotel is their farm which can be reached by foot, buggy ride, or bicycle. Many guests like to jog back and forth.

A new addition here is the **Safari**. On Safari guests learn about all the flora and fauna and the animals that inhabit the rich surroundings of the Atlantic forest, a nature preserve.

The hotel runs a school for the children of those that work on the farm. We found this truly admirable.

As you can see, the **Portobello** is no ordinary hotel, but one where a guest can not only be refreshed but where they can learn and be part of the Brazilian environment.

In early afternoon we departed for another but completely different Frade Hotel, **The Portogalo**, forty-five minutes away by car from Portobello, 2 1/2 hour by bus or car from Rio. It is here that we would stay for five days and do our scuba diving.

The Portogalo Hotel is situated on a hill overlooking the Bay of Angra, linked to the island and port through a chair lift from 8 a.m. until midnight. This is really fun. There are beaches and a small restaurant at the bottom of the lift.

The 80 rooms and 20 suites all face the bay are air conditioned and have a small patio. All the public rooms overlook the bay and are open except the main dining room. The large pool satisfies those who do not wish to take the lift to the beach but rather laze about in the sun with a cool drink from the pool bar. All meals in the dining room are buffet style. There is also an a la carte menu for lunch and dinner. The food is fresh, and simple, with fantastic desserts.

If you have $12 U.S. dollars to spare, treat yourself to one of the most incredible massages you will ever have. Yes, I said $12 U.S. There are tennis courts on the premises. Paddle tennis is also available which is a favorite of the Brazilians. Car rental, baby-sitting, foreign exchange, safe deposit box, game room, sauna, and room service are on premises.

The staff is helpful and friendly. Even though there is a language difference, they somehow find out your wishes.

We dove with *Aqua Life* run by Joselio Da Silva, a former Brazilian Navy Seal.

The boat we used was quite small, but he assured us if there is a larger group he can secure a larger boat.

He runs a good, safe operation, following all safety regulations.

There is a boat person on board at *all* times. My only critique would be that this small boat had no canopy. The last day was spent entirely in the sun and the Brazilian sun sure can be brutal! So when you book him, ask for a boat with a canopy. All our dives were off **Ilha Grande**, about a 1/2 hour boat ride from the hotel.

Our first dive was a wall of about 60 feet. As we descended to a sandy bottom, we made our way to the wall. The entire bottom was covered with black and purple sea urchins. There was a tremendous variety of fish, star fish, moorish idol, sergeant majors, yellow goatfish, four-eye butterfly fish, porkfish and a large Nassua grouper.

This was a good first dive and you could tell that Joselio had picked a mellow one so he could size up our experience. I always respect that with a guide.

The wind really was kicking up so we decided to call it a day and head for the little island of Ilha Granda. Since it was Thursday, the island was very quiet and we had a good chance for a complete tour. Victor, our guide for the entire trip, took us into a little Pousada and introduced us to the owner. We decided to come back over the weekend and spend a night there.

The next day we dove off **Abraao Island**, a very small island off Ilha Grande. Rolling over, we descended to 30 feet and swam to the reef. It was covered with red and orange sponges, sea stars, and sea urchins covered the boulders.

There must have been a thousand sand dollars on the sandy bottom between the reef and the boulders.

Grooved brain coral, elliptical star coral, and smooth star coral were also abundant. There were crabs and spiny lobster and tiny jellyfish. Although this was a shallow dive, it was really interesting for there was current and we just went with it, gliding in and out of the boulders and through openings in the reef.

On Friday we headed out for Ilha Grande late in the day. We had dinner at one of those small little seaside restaurants and just watched the world go by.

On Saturday morning we dove **Enseads Das Pamas**. This was a rock wall dive with sandy bottom. As we descended, a small ray darted past us. As we went deeper, we came upon a moray eel hidden amongst the rocks in the wall. It was quite long and came out to investigate us, winding in and out of his rock. Ocean triggerfish, smallmouth grunt and porkfish swam along with us.

I can highly recommend the Aqua Viva Pousada in Ilha Grande. It is not just clean and neat, it is a little gem. Carlos and his wife are charming proprietors of this resting place. You really shouldn't pass up seeing the island even if just for the day.

There is ferry service from Portogalo.

Before we left Portogalo, we made a day trip to the 18th century colonial town of Paraty, an hours trip southwest by car or three hours from Rio. In the 18th and 19th century this beautiful, historic town was one of Brazil's most important ports. It was from here that gold and sugar cane were shipped back to Portugal.

Rich landowners, merchants and shipping magnates, along with those who controlled the mines (they received 1/4 of the price of gold, Portugal retained the other 3/4) built beautiful houses both in and around Paraty. It has a charming town which reached its height in 1750. As gold ran out, so did Paraty's power. When the Empire came into being in 1822, Paraty became all but forgotten.

It was left to decay until UNESCO stepped in and declared it a national monument and began refurbishment. No renovation can be made unless permission is granted by UNESCO. No cars are allowed in most parts of the city; therefore, one can walk about and marvel at its architecture.

As you travel throughout the historic cities of Brazil, you will notice that the shutters of the buildings are painted in various colors. The royal family or palaces of the Emperor were white with pink shutters. Blue was attributed to the second degree of royalty, the Barons. One could become a Baron by virtue of wealth as well as birth. The

"Coffee Barons" appeared from 1830-1850. These titles were bestowed by the Emperor.

The old families of Rio would utilize white with green shutters. Throughout Paraty we could distinguish the owners position in society by the colors of the shutters.

Today, the town has almost been completely restored and Paraty has become an antique and arts center. If you are lucky enough to find a piece of furniture made from Jacarava, grab it, for this wood is 600 years old and quite novel in its appearance.

There are boutiques to roam through, open air markets selling native crafts and wonderful little restaurants. We wandered down to the port and had fish, salad and dessert which was simple yet delicious and made with fresh ingredients. Served with a smile, it cost very little.

Paraty is not to be missed if you are in the area and even worth a trip from Rio. There are many Pousadas where one can overnight.

We made our way out of Paraty and arrived at Fazenda Murycana about 20 minutes out of town. Today it is home to a zoo, restaurant and a distillery, where the Caipirinha Sugar Cane Rum is made.

Angelita Murycana, second wife of the owner, now runs all three. She is both delightful and interesting and gave us a private tour and a tasting of the many varieties of liquor.

It seems her husband purchased the land for a cattle farm, but soon it became the first farm in the region to produce sugar cane.

Twenty years ago, they began to travel worldwide and collected exotic animals, beginning the zoo.

There is a restaurant on the premises which serves food produced on the farm. All meat is cooked on a wooden stove and is fantastic!

Her husband, rumored to be a violent man, never drove an automobile although they owned several. Each day he would ride into town on his horse, dressed like a cowboy complete with pistols at his side. One year ago whilst just inside the farm, three shots were fired, he was killed. To this day, no one knows why!

Drink the Murycana over ice with lime. This is the typical Brazilian drink.

As you ride through the countryside, take note of the beautiful old colonial farm houses, two stories in height. On the first floor the stock was kept and the second floor was the residence. The right side of the house, was the commercial side where the farmers conducted business. The middle of the house served as the social center, and on the left side, parents hid their daughters until marriage so they would go to their marriage bed pure not only of heart but body. Behind the house there was a winter garden. Slaves were kept in small buildings away from the main house.

The aristocracy planted four Imperial Palms in front of their homes. In front of houses were large rock walls where coffee would placed and dried. From the 17th to the 19th century, rich landowners thrived and were very much part of the power structure.

We set out for Cabo Frio in early afternoon. A four hour drive from Portogalo or two hours from Rio. We passed through Rio and within 15 minutes were in the countryside where all one could see for miles were orange groves.

Brazil is the second largest exporter of oranges in the world.

Just outside of Cabo Frio, the sea salt mines came into view. This is also the place that each year, September to December, you can stop along the roadside and buy shrimp and crab. They come in such quantities that they cost very little.

Cabo Frio is still the most important fishing port in Brazil and has the best octopus fishing on the coast, catching 50-150 octopus a day. It has the richest fish life in Brazil because the current of the Falklands passes through and the plankton comes up, making a food chain.

We stayed in Arraial do Cabo, a moderately large sea side village. Quiet in off season, it really swings from December 15th until March.

We stayed in the delightful Thalassa Pousada run by Giselle and Bernard Rebiere, an elegant and lovely ex-patriot Frenchwoman and her husband.

Patrick, their son, handles the scuba and snorkeling end of the operation.

Beds are dressed in ironed linens. Baths are furnished with French soaps. Flowers grow profusely from the center atrium that runs through the Pousada.

Breakfast is included. It will be the typical Brazilian fare of juice, fresh fruit, rolls, bread, ham, cheese and, of course, wonderful Brazilian coffee.

Madame will surprise you each morn-ing with one of her homemade goodies, i.e., tomato preserves.

There is a central room where groups can gather, games to occupy children, and a T.V. set.

The rich marine life of Arriaial do Cabo is due to the phenomenon of the flora of the cold, deep waters (around 350 meters/1140 ft.) which, despite their richness in nutrients, are not productive as they are out of sunlight's reach. With the resurgence of the deep waters, the phytoplankton, the most basic level of marine life, receive solar energy, and then are consumed by plankton, which in turn feed the other species on up the food chain. The result of this process are rich and varied waters that make it possible to see both whales and sunfish in the same dive. The diving conditions on the leeward side of Cape Island are excellent with the bay reaching a maximum depth of 65 feet, visibility from 10 to 65 feet, and a sandy bottom which meets the coast with burrows and small coral banks. Diving among the ruins of the English vessel "**Wizard**", shipwrecked in 1821, is an added treat. Among the marine life to be found here are lobster, sea turtles, starfish, rays and moray eel.

Cabo Frio Octopus by Helio

On the windward side of the island, the conditions are quite different; huge walls between 100-150 ft., and cold waters of 13 degrees Celsius, producing the resurgence phenomenon, and visibility of between 10-100 ft. The bottom is sandy with pebbles near the deep walls. There is a big cave with a submarine entrance and an exit to a chimney about 260 ft. inland.

We loaded our gear on the little "putt putt" and were off on a sunny morning. A small cove about an hour from shore was chosen as our first dive. Since it was out of season, there were only two divers an the boat, Jezzeco, my buddy (who by the way, holds the world record for free diving 320 ft.) and myself. Not a bad buddy!

We rolled over and descended to 45 feet to inspect a beautiful long wall. I couldn't believe the diversity of fish. Each time one of us would find another variety we thought that would be our last great find of the dive, but then another fish appeared. All in all, we came upon a conger (sea snake), spotted flounders, two sea horses, pufferfish, French angelfish bluewing sea robin, black-ear wrasse, spotted scorpionfish, porkfish, squirrelfish, Atlantic spadefish, rock beauty crevalle jack, snowy grouper, scarlet lady and moan jellyfish. The entire sea floor was covered with vegetation that resembled a field of lettuce.

As we surfaced, alas, there was no boat. It seems that the sea had come up and as this was a drift dive, the boat had lost sight of us. Shore was near so we swam to it and waited. Finally, we heard the "putt putt" sound.

Happily, we were not at open sea.

The **Thetis** was a British frigate serving Spain. She sank in 1830 while returning to port. It was quite foggy and she mistook a cave for the opening to the Harbor.

She lies off a cove in open sea 25 feet to 69 feet. The visibility was not more than five feet. I had no hood and my wet suit was not thick enough so that bottom time for me was only 20 minutes.

> **If you dive this area any time of year, you will need a thick wet suit, hood and gloves. The weather and water temperature can change by the hour! Calm seas can become treacherous ones in a matter of minutes. This is not an area for the faint of heart!**

FUENTAS DAS MULHERES - The Cove of Women

> **This British boat sunk in 1906 in 66 feet of water. She was transporting French prostitutes from Rio.**

Half the women drowned.

THE WIZARD - Saco Do Leste

The Wizard was a British Steamer sunk in 1831. She lies in 90 feet of water in open sea.

IMBETIBA - Praia Grande

Here these waters are *always* cold.

The Imbetiba, caught in the fog in 1888, got stuck in the sand and the waves broke her to pieces. She's only 50 to 100 feet from the beach so she can also make for a good snorkel. There is a rich population of fish on her.

You *must* come prepared to dive these waters. Cabo Frio means cold coast so as I have said, travel with correct gear. One day it can be warm with wonderful visibility, but on a moment's notice, it can change.

If you are willing to brave the cold waters, it is a location you MUST dive! Remember, even the most experienced diver might have to sit out a day or two, but there are other activities in the vicinity. For those who wish to come in a group and want to rent a villa, there is a beautiful 5 bedroom, 5 bath villa that sits high in the hills, overlooking the ocean. It has its own pool and there are steps to the beach. Maid service is provided. This villa assures the ultimate privacy.

For villa information in the U.S. fax: 617-227-8145.

Recife: The Venice of Brazil

Recife is the fifth largest city in Brazil (incorporating nine towns). Its population of 2.8 million comprises Portuguese, Indians, French, Dutch and Africans. The first settlers were the native Indians. The Portuguese brought slaves from Africa in 1526 to fight the Indians and to tend the sugar cane crops. Recife became a commercial port during colonial times, exporting sugar cane, tobacco, and cotton.

Thirty years ago, the city was discovered by developers and since then it has become one of the favorite resorts for both Brazilians and world travelers.

> **It is known as the *"Venice of Brazil"* because of its many bridges and rivers which criss cross the area and eventually run into the sea.**
> **We stayed at the Petribu Sheraton Hotel whose five stars are well deserved.**

It is fifteen minutes from the airport and offers the traveler a quiet oasis from the busy downtown area. Opening in November 1991; its owners were determined to create an ambiance of local color. Therefore, its architecture, furnishings paintings, ceramics and carpet are fashioned by Brazilian artisans. The flowers throughout lend a touch of grace. The Hotel faces the Atlantic Ocean. The public rooms are large and airy with intimate areas for meetings whether social or business. Rooms are large and comfortable, with marble baths, cable T.V., direct dial phones, mini bar, safety deposit box and 24 hour room service. There is a *hotline* so that if a guest has a problem or questions, they will be attended to immediately. Fax and telex are available. There are two pools, one for children, one for adults, and a pool bar and restaurant. The "Quebra" is the tastefully decorated dining room, serving local food always arranged beautifully in buffet style or a la carte.

On Fridays and Saturdays, the Ocean Reef Club and lounge which sits on the top floor of the hotel is open. This is a special place to dine and take in the commanding views of Recife. Be there for the sunset!

Sauna, massage, hairdresser, and boutiques are on premises. Babysitting can be arranged. Golf, tennis, and scuba diving are nearby. A doctor is on call. The beach that stretches for miles down the coast is a wonderful one to walk and catch all the local color. There is a hotel guard at the gate to the beach. Please do not take any valuables or cameras with you. Just don your swimsuit, that's all you need!

There are apartment buildings and private homes along the beach, and since all beaches are public, local vendors set up their booths or carry their wares up and down the beach, selling hats, suntan lotion, ice cream, etc.

The *Jangadas*, replicas of the age old fishing raft, sit on the beach, awaiting to take you for a ride. Originally for fishing, they are made of wood, very-flat and truly seaworthy.

Sunday is family day, so everyone goes to the beach. This is where you will observe the real Brazilian family at play. This is a good day to take in the local attractions!

There are many tourist attractions and one that surely should not be missed is the *Museu Do Homan Do Nordeste*, the Museum of Northeastern Man. Gilberto Freyre, a sociologist, is responsible for its creation. The museum, although not large, depicts the history of Recife from its first inhabitant to modern times.

The Governor's Palace is also quite beautiful and there is a very good modern art museum.

Outside of Recife, the little town of Olinda is where the artists live. Here you will find beautiful museums, monasteries and convents. The architecture spans many centuries and styles. Olinda was the liveliest of all the towns surrounding Recife.

If you want to skip carnival in Rio, remember there is one held in Recife which starts a week earlier. This is so they can practice for Rio, but rumor hath it that it is because the natives of Recife want a week's more of "anything goes".

Recife means reef, and reefs abound but are not charted. Most of the diving is wreck diving far out at sea.

We dove with **Brasmar**, a company which was highly recommended to us. From my first encounter with Joel, the owner, and a tour of his facility, I could understand why.

Brasmar is a full service scuba center with diving trips and certification.

Joel does not believe in taking the students from the pool to the open ocean to do open water check outs. He has built a cylindrical tank (the only other one we know of is in San Paolo), of concrete and 120 ft. high. Students are trained in the pool, then checked out in the tank and then taken to the open ocean for final check outs.

It is such a terrific idea! How many times have you seen divers panic on their open water check outs? This is a wonderful alternative. A security blanket, if you will, to ease them into the comfort of the kind of depth they will eventually encounter.

Joel has a good boat, well maintained, with a permanent canopy to shade you from the sun, a deck topside for sun worshippers and more than ample room for tanks, gear and divers.

Our dive was on The Pirapama, a steamboat carrying cargo which collided with another ship, the Vapor de Bahia, in 1889.

Her frame is still intact, including a giant paddle wheel. Our trip from the dock was about 1 1/2 hours. No one on board spoke English, but somehow we had a running conversation and a great many laughs.

Our first dive was to 72 feet which gave us enough time to inspect the entire wreck and the abundance of sea life which has grown an her and plays in and around her frame.

On descending, we spotted a large turtle swimming around the wreck. Further on, yellow jack, blue tang, Portuguese man of war, squirrelfish, fairy basslet, rock beauty and plume worm were sighted.

A long, whip-like tail hidden in the sand gave evidence to a large ray that, once spotted, darted off. The corals, both hard and soft, growing on the wreck were in various colors, especially purple, pink and orange.

Bottom time up, we ascended, took time for a safety stop, reboarded and had soft drinks and sweets while waiting out our interval. For those of you who get hungrier, I suggest having the hotel pack you a box lunch. This is a long day.

Because the seas were high and the visibility became less clear, we choose to do the second dive in the same spot.

Our real dive reward was the spotting of five rays, one right after the other. They stayed quite close this time which is unusual for rays in open water. This gave us a chance to study them.

Training Tank in "Brasmar Center" recife by Joel Calado

Recife is the perfect place for the diver who loves to explore the graveyards of the sea.

It is about 1 1/2 hour flight from Recife to Natal on the Northeastern shore of Brazil.

My plan was to overnight at the Genipabu Hotel in Natal and the next day catch the small plane that flies to Fernando Di Noronha. The Hotel's complimentary bus transfers you to and from the airport.

Founded in 1500, Natal is in the most Eastern part of Brazil. The entire archipelago is 26 square km. During the Ice Age it was part of Africa.

Wreck of the Pirapania by Joel Calado

Its topography is really quite interesting. Miles and miles of beach not good for scuba but a favorite of surfers with its awesome waves. Its hillside resembles a desert.

During World War II, Natal was the site of the largest U.S. Air Force Base outside the United States.

It was built from scratch in 1941 with the help of the Brazilians, 440 buildings included lodgings, supply, hospitals, and aircraft maintenance.

The base employed 6,000 Brazilians and housed anywhere up to 15,000 troops. No one knows the exact number. By 1943, it was handling outgoing aircraft every three minutes. It could accommodate 1,000 people in transit overnight. In addition, it was a base of operations for submarine surveillance, ferrying aircraft and crews to Europe, and the support system for the North African invasion. From Dakar to Casablanca one could travel to anywhere in Europe.

Hitler, in two major speeches, singled out Natal for destruction. Because of this, there were untold blackouts.

On August 26, 1942, Brazil declared war on Germany and from that time on they were U.S. allies. Brazilians served with our 5th Army in Italy as General Mark Clark's "Brazilian Expeditionary Force".

You could fly from Washington to Natal in 21 hours. Therefore, many VIPs were transported through here. USO shows used this route and President Roosevelt came through twice. The United States gave the base free of charge to the Brazilian government in 1945. They use it as their international airport and a training school for air force pilots.

Perched high in the hills was *Genipabu*. Its setting and architecture gives you an immediate sense of a less hurried world. The 24 double rooms are quite large with balconies overlooking the valley aglow with all color of vegetation, and the desert-like hillside that runs to the sea. They are furnished in a way which reminds one of the Orient, simple yet beautiful. T.V., mini bar, no phone or air conditioners, just a ceiling fan.

After lunch, Victor suggested a buggy ride on the dunes. I thought this a splendid idea which should teach me never to say yes until I have inquired just what a new adventure entails.

It takes a *very* experienced driver for this sport because of the strong wind from the sea and the desert sands shift constantly from area to area. It is definitely similar to a roller coaster ride, only I'm not sure which makes my heart beat faster.

Along the way we encountered a father and his sons, who give donkey tours of the dunes. I shall never forget the father's face, so weathered, so gentle, and the boy, so young but a little man. It can be a hard life in Brazil.

The next afternoon our small plane took off for the hour trip to Fernando De Noronha.

Here we were to dive with Patrick Muller, husband of Ana, who own the Genipabu Hotel in Natal.

Patrick had come to Fernando De Noronha to secure a license for a scuba diving operation, (not an easy feat since the government in 1988 declared most of this island a National Park) and they are very dubious about any new development or enterprise, especially by non-Brazilians.

Father and son offering Donkey rides in the dunes by Wendy Canning Church

Juan de la Luca, sailing from Portugal, discovered this vast archipelago two hundred miles off the coast of Natal, comprising six main islands and fourteen rocky outcroppings.

As our plane flew over, we viewed the steep pinnacle rocks, in varying shapes and sizes rising from the sea, beautiful deserted beaches and century old buildings in a state of disrepair. It was as if time had stood still in this naturalist's paradise.

The government allows only a certain number of visitors per day, and this is strictly enforced.

When you land you must fill out a form with length of stay, Pousada, passport number and pay a fee or tax which goes towards preserving these islands.

There are few places to stay at this writing. Most are very rustic and do not have hot water. If you can do without fancy amenities, you will partake of some of the finest diving anywhere.

Patrick's boat, the *Atlantis*, is 32 feet long with two 155 horsepower engines, head, permanent canopy, flybridge, bow for sunning, and enough room to comfortably hold 8 divers and their gear.

We motored out of the small cove, heading towards our destination about forty-five minutes away. This gave me a good opportunity to see the island close up. What a beauty it must have been in her hey day when the wood exporting business gave it riches and prominence.

As we passed the "Bay of Dolphins", a group of them came out and followed the boat. They are such gentle and friendly creatures, I marvel at how they move through the water at great speed and wonderful grace.

The seas were very high. Finally reaching our dive site, *Iuias*, in front of Cape Cabacas, we entered the water by-giant stride for a drift dive.

We descended and were quickly in calm water with a slight current. We swam amongst many huge rocks and through caves and tunnels. The variety and size of fish was unbelievable. Catching sight of a 12 foot nurse shark, we watched it as it slept, then awakened by the Nikonos, dart away.

There were turtles, barracuda, French angelfish, schools of squirrelfish, parrotfish, African pompano, blackjack, quelly jack, Atlantic spadefish, a large horse eye jack, a green triggerfish with the brightest yellow tail I have ever seen, spiny lobster, dog snapper, banded butterfly fish, yellow pea chub, silver porgy, tiny shrimp and black margate. The barracuda who met us on our descent followed us the entire dive. I can honestly say this was one of the best dives I've ever made.

Patrick apologized for the rough seas and the visibility. He told me in good weather the visibility is 200 feet.

My retort was, "Forget the swells and visibility. I saw more just now than I have seen in most places I have dived."

When our interval time was up, the swells had gotten higher so we decided to dive one of the many grottos close to shore.

Descending, we swam into the grotto at **Sapata Cave** and investigated any hiding places for fish. We spotted another large nurse shark, a school of barracuda, spotlight parrotfish, blue tang, butterfly fish, coney and black margate. We caught the sight of a jewfish that weighed at least 150 pounds and followed it for the rest of our dive.

On my next trip to Brazil I will head here first and just dive dive, dive. I can put up with simple accommodations for the world class virgin diving it offers.

Patrick is both an able and safety conscious fellow who is determined to create a full service scuba center for worldwide divers. He is also probably one of the most charming and accommodating fellows you will ever meet!

We flew back to Rio the next day and I confess, I vegged out after this whirlwind trip. Because I enjoyed the Sheraton in Recife so much, I decided to book the 5 star Sheraton Rio Hotel and Towers. The hotel offers enough luxury and privacy to please any celebrity.

The Sheraton Rio Hotel & Towers is the only hotel located directly on the beach in Rio with sea view, and recreational facilities. The tennis courts, are ranked among the 10 most beautiful in the world by Tennis Magazine.

Rentamar Turismo planned our entire itinerary for us. They called upon Victor Lima who plans and leads adventure tours throughout Brazil to be our guide and interpreter.

Victor is not your cookie cutter guide; on the contrary, he will show you not only the should sees but will introduce you to the real Brazil! You will leave with a sense of its culture and people both of yesterday and today.

Editor's Note
When flying to another country, I always like to use the nation's carrier.

My advice is do a background check on any airline you have not flown, also ask others who have traveled to that country which airline they used.

After inquiry of our Brazilian friends, we knew Varig was for us.

Founded in 1927 in Brazil, it is one of the world's oldest airlines. In continuous operation for 65 years by its employee owned staff, it flys to many other countries.

So highly regarded is Varig's maintenance operation that the Brazilian government uses Varig to service its military air craft. Now that's saying something!

Well, my last word on Varig is that the food is delicious and served with a wonderful sense of international warmth.

SCUBA AND SNORKELING FACILITIES QUESTIONNAIRE

NAME Joselio Sebastiao Da Silva
ADDRESS Aqualife Conceieao De Jacarei - Mangarafibs

CONTACT Fjevitour/Rio - 7 Setembro 92/1706
TITLE 2 stars instructor - Navy
TELEPHONE 507-2211   FAX 224-6319

CAPITAL: **Rio/Brasilia/Brazil**		GOVERNMENT: **Democratic**
POPULATION: **145 million**		LANGUAGE: **Portuguese**
CURRENCY: **Crueeiros Peais**		ELECTRICITY: **110v**
AIRLINES: Varig		DEPARTURE TAX? **$16 U.S.**
NEED VISA/PASSPORT? YES x NO		PROOF OF CITIZENSHIP? YES NO

YOUR FACILITY IS CLASSIFIED AS: SCUBA CENTER x   RESORT
BUSINESS HOURS: **9 a.m. - 6 p.m.**
CERTIFYING AGENCIES: **International**
LOG BOOK REQUIRED?   YES x   NO
EQUIPMENT: SALES   RENTALS   AIR FILLS
PRIMARY LINE OF EQUIPMENT: **Luxfer Aluminum/3000 PSI USI Divers**
PHOTOGRAPHIC EQUIPMENT: SALES   RENTALS   LAB

CHARTER/DIVE BOAT AVAILABLE?   YES x   NO   DIVER CAPACITY **3**
COAST GUARD APPROVED?   YES x   NO   CAPTAIN LICENSED?   YES x   NO
SHIP TO SHORE? YES   NO x   LORAN   YES   NO x   RADAR?   YES   NO
DIVE MASTER/INSTRUCTOR ABOARD?   YES x   NO   BOTH x

DIVING & SNORKELING: SALT x   FRESH
TYPE OF DIVING/SNORKELING IN AREA: WALL x   BEACH x   WRECK x   REEF x   CAVE x   ICE
DIVING/SNORKELING IN YOUR AREA IS BEST SUITED FOR: BEGINNER x   INTERMEDIATE x   ADVANCED x
BEST TIME OF YEAR FOR DIVING/SNORKELING: **Summer**
TEMPERATURE: **NOV-APRIL: 21 C**   **MAY-OCT: 17 C**
VISIBILITY: **DIVING: 30 FT**   **SNORKELING: 36 FT**

PACKAGES AVAILABLE: DIVE x   DIVE STAY x   SNORKEL x   SNORKEL-STAY x
ACCOMMODATIONS NEARBY: HOTEL x   MOTEL   HOME RENTALS x
ACCOMMODATION RATES: EXPENSIVE x   MODERATE x   INEXPENSIVE x
RESTAURANTS NEARBY: EXPENSIVE x   MODERATE x   INEXPENSIVE x
YOUR AREA IS: REMOTE x   QUIET WITH ACTIVITIES x   LIVELY
LOCAL ACTIVITY/NIGHTLIFE: **Weekends**
CAR NEEDED TO EXPLORE AREA?   YES x   NO
DUTY FREE SHOPPING?   YES   NO x

LOCAL EMERGENCY SERVICES   NEAREST HYPERBARIC TREATMENT FACILITY
COASTGUARD: **Yes**   AUTHORITY: **Marine/Navy Capitania**
TELEPHONE: **Yes**   LOCATION: **Angra Dos Reis**
CALLSIGNS: TELEPHONE:

LOCAL DIVING DOCTOR:
NAME:
LOCATION: **Angra Dos Reis**
TELEPHONE:

272

SCUBA AND SNORKELING FACILITIES QUESTIONNAIRE

NAME **Brasmar**
ADDRESS **Boa Viagem, Recife, Brazil**

CONTACT **Joel Calado**
TITLE **Owner**
TELEPHONE **081-326-0162** FAX **same**

CAPITAL: **Brasilia** GOVERNMENT:
POPULATION: LANGUAGE:
CURRENCY: **Crueeiros Peais** ELECTRICITY:
AIRLINES: **Varig** DEPARTURE TAX?
NEED VISA/PASSPORT? YES **x** NO PROOF OF CITIZENSHIP? YES NO

YOUR FACILITY IS CLASSIFIED AS: SCUBA CENTER **x** RESORT
BUSINESS HOURS: **9 a.m. - 10 p.m. all year round**
CERTIFYING AGENCIES: **CMAS**
LOG BOOK REQUIRED? YES **x** NO
EQUIPMENT: SALES **x** RENTALS **x** AIR FILLS **x**
PRIMARY LINE OF EQUIPMENT: **Sherwood**
PHOTOGRAPHIC EQUIPMENT: SALES **x** RENTALS **x** LAB **service only**

CHARTER/DIVE BOAT AVAILABLE? YES **x** NO DIVER CAPACITY **18 + 12**
COAST GUARD APPROVED? YES **x** NO CAPTAIN LICENSED? YES **x** NO
SHIP TO SHORE? YES **x** NO LORAN YES NO **x** RADAR? YES NO **x**
DIVE MASTER/INSTRUCTOR ABOARD? YES **x** NO BOTH **x**

DIVING & SNORKELING: SALT **x** FRESH
TYPE OF DIVING/SNORKELING IN AREA: WALL BEACH WRECK **x** REEF **x** CAVE **x** ICE
DIVING/SNORKELING IN YOUR AREA IS BEST SUITED FOR: BEGINNER **x** INTERMEDIATE **x** ADVANCED **x**
BEST TIME OF YEAR FOR DIVING/SNORKELING: **October until May**
TEMPERATURE: **NOV-APRIL: 81 F** **MAY-OCT: F**
VISIBILITY: **DIVING: FT** **SNORKELING: FT**

PACKAGES AVAILABLE: DIVE DIVE STAY SNORKEL SNORKEL-STAY
ACCOMMODATIONS NEARBY: HOTEL MOTEL HOME RENTALS
ACCOMMODATION RATES: EXPENSIVE MODERATE INEXPENSIVE
RESTAURANTS NEARBY: EXPENSIVE MODERATE INEXPENSIVE
YOUR AREA IS: REMOTE QUIET WITH ACTIVITIES LIVELY
LOCAL ACTIVITY/NIGHTLIFE:
CAR NEEDED TO EXPLORE AREA? YES NO
DUTY FREE SHOPPING? YES NO

LOCAL EMERGENCY SERVICES NEAREST HYPERBARIC TREATMENT FACILITY
COASTGUARD: AUTHORITY: **State Police Hospital**
TELEPHONE: LOCATION: **Derby Square**
CALLSIGNS: TELEPHONE: **Dr. Pantoja's Office**

LOCAL DIVING DOCTOR:
NAME: **Dr. Paulo Pantoja**
LOCATION: **State Police Hospital**
TELEPHONE: **081-326-3165/325-4424**

SCUBA AND SNORKELING FACILITIES QUESTIONNAIRE

NAME **Patrick Rubiere**
ADDRESS **Rua Bernardo Lenz, 114 Pousada Thalassa**

CONTACT **Figuiton — Pousada Thalassa**
TITLE **Tour Angene Pousada (Hotel)**
TELEPHONE **502-2211 0246-222285**   FAX **2246319**   TELEX **021-21408 EEFP - BR**

CAPITAL: **Rio**	GOVERNMENT: **Democracy**	
POPULATION: **14 million**	LANGUAGE: **Portuguese**	
CURRENCY: **Crueeiros Peais**	ELECTRICITY: **110v**	
AIRLINES: Varig	DEPARTURE TAX? **$17 U.S.**	
NEED VISA/PASSPORT? YES x NO	PROOF OF CITIZENSHIP? YES x NO	

YOUR FACILITY IS CLASSIFIED AS: SCUBA CENTER x   RESORT x
BUSINESS HOURS: **9 a.m. - 6 p.m.**
CERTIFYING AGENCIES: **Figuitoun**
LOG BOOK REQUIRED?   YES x   NO
EQUIPMENT: SALES x   RENTALS x   AIR FILLS x
PRIMARY LINE OF EQUIPMENT: Boat 26 ft. - 12 bottles Beauchrat - Regulators/B.C.
PHOTOGRAPHIC EQUIPMENT: SALES   RENTALS   LAB

CHARTER/DIVE BOAT AVAILABLE?   YES x   NO   DIVER CAPACITY **8-30**
COAST GUARD APPROVED?   YES x   NO   CAPTAIN LICENSED?   YES x   NO
SHIP TO SHORE? YES   NO x   LORAN   YES   NO x   RADAR?   YES   NO
DIVE MASTER/INSTRUCTOR ABOARD?   YES x   NO   BOTH x

DIVING & SNORKELING: SALT x   FRESH
TYPE OF DIVING/SNORKELING IN AREA: WALL x   BEACH x   WRECK x   REEF x   CAVE x   ICE
DIVING/SNORKELING IN YOUR AREA IS BEST SUITED FOR: BEGINNER   INTERMEDIATE   ADVANCED
BEST TIME OF YEAR FOR DIVING/SNORKELING: **Summer**
TEMPERATURE: **NOV-APRIL: 14-25 F**   **MAY-OCT: 14-25 F**
VISIBILITY: **DIVING: 60 FT**   **SNORKELING: 60 FT**

PACKAGES AVAILABLE: DIVE x   DIVE STAY x   SNORKEL x   SNORKEL-STAY x
ACCOMMODATIONS NEARBY: HOTEL x   MOTEL   POUSADA x   HOME RENTALS x
ACCOMMODATION RATES: EXPENSIVE x   MODERATE x   INEXPENSIVE x
RESTAURANTS NEARBY: EXPENSIVE x   MODERATE x   INEXPENSIVE x
YOUR AREA IS: REMOTE   QUIET WITH ACTIVITIES x   LIVELY
LOCAL ACTIVITY/NIGHTLIFE: **Bars with live music**
CAR NEEDED TO EXPLORE AREA?   YES x   NO
DUTY FREE SHOPPING?   YES   NO x

LOCAL EMERGENCY SERVICES   NEAREST HYPERBARIC TREATMENT FACILITY
COASTGUARD: AUTHORITY: **Capitania - Navy**
TELEPHONE: LOCATION: **Arraial Do Cabo/Cabo Frio**
CALLSIGNS: TELEPHONE: **0246-432840**

LOCAL DIVING DOCTOR:
NAME: **Angelo Lima**
LOCATION: **Arraial Do Cabo**
TELEPHONE: **0246-222218**

SCUBA AND SNORKELING FACILITIES QUESTIONNAIRE

NAME **Atlantic Divers**
ADDRESS **P.B. 59067-010 Natal in Brazil - Genipabu Hotel**

CONTACT **Patrick and Ana Muller**
TITLE **Owner**
TELEPHONE **084-2252063 - 2318206** FAX **084-2314602**

CAPITAL: **Natal** GOVERNMENT: **Democracy**
POPULATION: **700,000** LANGUAGE: **Portuguese**
CURRENCY: **Cruzeiros Reais** ELECTRICITY: **220v**
AIRLINES: DEPARTURE TAX? **Natal Park US$ 3/day**
NEED VISA/PASSPORT? YES **x** NO PROOF OF CITIZENSHIP? YES **x** NO

YOUR FACILITY IS CLASSIFIED AS: SCUBA CENTER **x** RESORT
BUSINESS HOURS: **9 a.m. - 5 p.m.**
CERTIFYING AGENCIES: **PADI**
LOG BOOK REQUIRED? YES **x** NO
EQUIPMENT: SALES RENTALS **x** AIR FILLS **x**
PRIMARY LINE OF EQUIPMENT: **Luxfer - Sherwood**
PHOTOGRAPHIC EQUIPMENT: SALES RENTALS LAB

CHARTER/DIVE BOAT AVAILABLE? YES **x** NO DIVER CAPACITY **8**
COAST GUARD APPROVED? YES **x** NO CAPTAIN LICENSED? YES **x** NO
SHIP TO SHORE? YES **x** NO LORAN YES NO **x** RADAR? YES NO **x** GPS **x**
DIVE MASTER/INSTRUCTOR ABOARD? YES **x** NO BOTH

DIVING & SNORKELING: SALT **x** FRESH
TYPE OF DIVING/SNORKELING IN AREA: WALL **x** BEACH **x** WRECK **x** REEF **x** CAVE **x** ICE
DIVING/SNORKELING IN YOUR AREA IS BEST SUITED FOR: BEGINNER **x** INTERMEDIATE **x** ADVANCED **x**
BEST TIME OF YEAR FOR DIVING/SNORKELING:
TEMPERATURE: **NOV-APRIL:** 28 **C** **MAY-OCT:** 28 **C**
VISIBILITY: **DIVING:** 5 Mtrs **SNORKELING:** 100 Mtrs

PACKAGES AVAILABLE: DIVE **x** DIVE STAY SNORKEL **x**
SNORKEL-STAY ACCOMMODATIONS NEARBY: HOTEL **x** MOTEL POUSADA **x**
HOME RENTALS
ACCOMMODATION RATES: EXPENSIVE MODERATE **x** INEXPENSIVE
RESTAURANTS NEARBY: EXPENSIVE MODERATE **x** INEXPENSIVE
YOUR AREA IS: REMOTE **x** QUIET WITH ACTIVITIES LIVELY
LOCAL ACTIVITY/NIGHTLIFE: **Presentation about environment - Brazil music**
CAR NEEDED TO EXPLORE AREA? YES **x** NO **Can be done on trekking**
DUTY FREE SHOPPING? YES NO **x**

LOCAL EMERGENCY SERVICES NEAREST HYPERBARIC TREATMENT FACILITY
COASTGUARD: AUTHORITY: **IBSMA**
TELEPHONE: LOCATION:
CALLSIGNS: TELEPHONE:

LOCAL DIVING DOCTOR:
NAME:
LOCATION:
TELEPHONE:

Columbia

Renee Burt

Is it extremely difficult to answer the question as to what my favorite dive spot is in Colombia, it would be impossible to name just one. But, here are a few of my favorite places.

You cannot come to Colombia without visiting the islands of San Andres and Providencia. The Hawaii of Colombia, it is a favorite place for honeymooners and vacationers from the surrounding countries

Flower garden by Humberto Nahim

The natives speak Spanish, English and Papiamento. Located 480 km north of Colombia on the Caribbean sea, it is a diver's paradise.

Another good diving location is Santa Marta, a big Colombian tourist spot and home of the legendary "Lost City" of the Sierra Nevada mountains.

Santa Marta is the capital of the Magdalena department of Colombia (pop. 300,000), the third Caribbean port, and is 96 km east of Barranquilla, at the mouth of the Manzanares River. Santa Marta lies on a deep bay with high shelving cliffs. The climate ranges seasonally from hot, to hot and pleasant in February and March.

A friend and I went last year and found a nice diving school called Pro-Buzos de Colombia. The instructor, Alvaro Riascos, took us on two excursions either out of the goodness of his heart or because he liked American women. We ended up paying a nominal fee for air and transportation and had an unforgettable diving experience. Be sure to visit the little fishing village of Taganga. The natives build their boats and fish the same way they did over 100 years ago.

Bahia Solano is also a nice, place to dive. It also happens to be the area I took my first open water diving lessons.

When I was there the waters ranged from 20-25 Centigrade with a visibility of 10-15 kms. It is also much smaller and more primitive than the other sites I previously mentioned.

Capurgana is located in the Gulf of Uraba, and is very close to Panama. The Calypso Hotel is a first-class luxury hotel with air conditioning, satellite television, a swimming pool, playground, and tennis and basketball courts. They also have excursions to the beaches of Panama and the San Blas islands. I have never been diving there, but I hear if you have your own equipment, there is a place that will fill your tanks and take you via speed boat to the nice diving areas.

Bahia Solano and Capurgana are not your typical tourist locations so some degree of Spanish is necessary as no-one speaks English there.

Cartagena is a very popular vacation spot, especially for Canadians, and most natives speak English. It is also one of the most interesting cities in South America. It is old and steeped in history.

In the 1600's Cartagena was one of the storage points for merchandise sent from Spain and for treasure collected from the Americas to be sent back to Spain.

A series of forts protecting the approaches from the sea and the walls that were built around the city made it impregnable.

Of more interest to the diver however, are the Rosario islands. About 45 minutes away from the city by speed boat.

Any of the major hotels have daily excursions to the islands. We made reservations to stay at La Isla Pirata (The Pirate Island) for two nights which included a nice cabana and food. Be sure to get tanks filled in the city beforehand as there are no diving facilities on the islands. It's a hassle but well worth the effort.

Cali

Karen Rodriguez
Apartado Aereo 6963 Cali, Colombia
Telephone 515008 Fax 688452

I received your folder just the other day and want to help your readers out with some information on diving off the Pacific Coast of Colombia. Mr. James Baker put Cali and our road to Buenaventura on the map. I can't say that makes me very happy but I suppose it forces me to put our dive expeditions on the high adventure list.

Let me give you a little background information on myself and the area I know and love. Born in Pampa, Texas, an Air force brat, and having traveled all over the world I eventually got to Cali, Colombia with my Colombian husband. I learned to dive in Cali and became a Fedecas instructor five years ago. I have also become a PADI and NAUI instructor. For the past seven years I have organized live aboard trips to the Pacific Coast using anything I could get my hands on as long as it would float. A year and a half ago my partner Harold Botero, also a NAUI instructor, and myself took out a loan and bought a typical Colombian banana boat. It floated, but just barely! In the meantime we have redone the hull and put in navigational equipment for safety. We still have a long way to go. We provide clean sheets and fresh water to bathe in from a faucet, good food and wonderful diving.

You can fly from Miami to Cali direct on Avianca or American Airlines in three and a half hours. I pick you up at the airport and babysit you for your entire stay. Cali is three hours from the Pacific Coast where we keep the Asturias, (our banana boat). Now I know Mr. James Baker is an important person and should know what he was talking about but... I have not had any trouble in fifteen years either in Cali or driving the road to Buenaventura at any hour of the day or night.

Diver entering cave by Humberto Nahim

There are two places that we divers go to. One is Gorgona National Park. It is a 10 hour crossing to this park which is the mating ground for the humpback whale from July through November. A beautiful lush jungle island with white beaches and coconut trees. It was once a prison island but now only receives 60 park visitors at a time.

Spearfishing is not allowed. You may fish with a line, and you are only allowed to take photographs and memories home with you. You will see the big stuff here but not much in the way of corals. At different times of the year we have devil mantas, hammerheads, whale sharks, huge snappers, amberjacks, tuna and barracuda. I have always seen white tips. We can see everything in less than 100 feet but the visibility can be anything from thirty to eighty feet. Most of the time the temperature is around 78f but I recommend a light wetsuit for protection. I take open water students to Gorgona for certification. Advanced divers enjoy some of the advanced dive spots.

I'm a mother hen... And since our chamber is a good nine hours away, I keep an eye on all divers. We dive in small groups with an instructor or dive master guiding the way.

My high-high adventure trip on our "Regressor Banana Boat" is to Malpelo Island which is a 35 hour trip. It is well worth the wait. A stark rock, 400 meters high, with lots of smaller rocks scattered around. There are tunnels, sheer walls, and more fish life than most people see in a lifetime. Unfortunately the Colombian government can't protect this outpost from fishing trawlers. I fear the schooling hammerheads are in danger. We do spearfish there but only by free lung and we are only going to take what we can eat. Other divers are discovering this treasure and if we are going to continue to go there we must protect it! This is an eight day trip for experienced divers only. I would expect any divers to use all standard required equipment and come with an internationally recognized certificate and log book. There are no special fees for sport diving here in Colombia. At the Gorgona National Park there is no spearfishing or taking by hand of aquatic life. In other areas there is no enforcement of any kind.

Wendy, I know this is lacking in information but it will give the flavor of what I want to say. I have understated the conditions somewhat because I would rather have people pleased with what they find than upset because too much was promised.
Best regards,
Karen Rodriguez

SCUBA AND SNORKELING FACILITIES QUESTIONNAIRE

NAME **Aquarium Dive Shop**
ADDRESS **P.O. Box 1692**
San Andres, Isla-Colombia-Sur America
CONTACT **Pablo E. Montoya A.**
TITLE **PADI Open Water Scuba Instructor - CMAS 3-Star Instructor**
TELEPHONE **6649- Home: 6378** FAX TELEX **40126 Hansa CO**

CAPITAL:	GOVERNMENT:
POPULATION:	LANGUAGE:
CURRENCY:	ELECTRICITY:
AIRLINES:	DEPARTURE TAX?
NEED VISA/PASSPORT? YES x NO	PROOF OF CITIZENSHIP? YES NO

YOUR FACILITY IS CLASSIFIED AS: SCUBA CENTER **x** RESORT **x**
BUSINESS HOURS: **All the time, Summer & Winter**
CERTIFYING AGENCIES: **PADI, CMAS, FEDECAS**
LOG BOOK REQUIRED? YES   NO
EQUIPMENT: SALES **x** RENTALS **x** AIR FILLS **x**
PRIMARY LINE OF EQUIPMENT: **Sales and Rental**
PHOTOGRAPHIC EQUIPMENT: SALES   RENTALS   LAB

CHARTER/DIVE BOAT AVAILABLE? YES **x** NO   DIVER CAPACITY **20**
COAST GUARD APPROVED? YES **x** NO   CAPTAIN LICENSED? YES **x** NO
SHIP TO SHORE? YES **x** NO   LORAN YES **x** NO   RADAR? YES **x** NO
DIVE MASTER/INSTRUCTOR ABOARD?   YES **x**   NO   BOTH

DIVING & SNORKELING: SALT **x** FRESH
TYPE OF DIVING/SNORKELING IN AREA: WALL **x** BEACH   WRECK **x** REEF   CAVE **x** ICE
DIVING/SNORKELING IN YOUR AREA IS BEST SUITED FOR: BEGINNER **x** INTERMEDIATE **x** ADVANCED **x**
BEST TIME OF YEAR FOR DIVING/SNORKELING: **All year**
TEMPERATURE: NOV-APRIL: F   MAY-OCT: F
VISIBILITY: DIVING: FT   SNORKELING: FT

PACKAGES AVAILABLE: DIVE **x**   DIVE STAY   SNORKEL **x**   SNORKEL-STAY ACCOMMODA-
TIONS NEARBY: HOTEL **x**   APARTMENT **x**   HOME RENTALS
ACCOMMODATION RATES: EXPENSIVE   MODERATE   INEXPENSIVE
RESTAURANTS NEARBY: EXPENSIVE   MODERATE   INEXPENSIVE
YOUR AREA IS: REMOTE   QUIET WITH ACTIVITIES **x**   LIVELY
LOCAL ACTIVITY/NIGHTLIFE:
CAR NEEDED TO EXPLORE AREA?   YES   NO
DUTY FREE SHOPPING?   YES   NO

LOCAL EMERGENCY SERVICES   NEAREST HYPERBARIC TREATMENT FACILITY
COASTGUARD: AUTHORITY: **Juan Martin Velasquez - Fabio Acevedo**
TELEPHONE: LOCATION: **Hospital Santander - San Andres Isla**
CALLSIGNS: TELEPHONE:

LOCAL DIVING DOCTOR:
NAME: **Juan Martin Velasquez**
LOCATION: **Hospital Santander, San Andres, Isla**
TELEPHONE: **3596**

SCUBA AND SNORKELING FACILITIES QUESTIONNAIRE

NAME **Karen Rodriquez**
ADDRESS **Apartado Aereo 6963, Cali, Colombia**

CONTACT
TITLE
TELEPHONE **515008** FAX **688452**

CAPITAL: **Bogota** GOVERNMENT: **Democratic**
POPULATION: **30 million (approx)** LANGUAGE: **Spanish**
CURRENCY: **Peso** ELECTRICITY: **110v**
AIRLINES: American/Avianca DEPARTURE TAX?
NEED VISA/PASSPORT? YES **x** NO PROOF OF CITIZENSHIP? YES **x** NO

YOUR FACILITY IS CLASSIFIED AS: SCUBA CENTER RESORT
BUSINESS HOURS:
CERTIFYING AGENCIES: **PADI, NAUI, FEDECAS**
LOG BOOK REQUIRED? YES **x** NO
EQUIPMENT: SALES **x** RENTALS **x** AIR FILLS **x**
PRIMARY LINE OF EQUIPMENT: **Variety**
PHOTOGRAPHIC EQUIPMENT: SALES RENTALS **x** LAB

CHARTER/DIVE BOAT AVAILABLE? YES **x** NO DIVER CAPACITY **18**
COAST GUARD APPROVED? YES **x** NO CAPTAIN LICENSED? YES **x** NO
SHIP TO SHORE? YES **x** NO LORAN GPS **x** NO RADAR? YES **x** NO
DIVE MASTER/INSTRUCTOR ABOARD? YES **x** NO BOTH

DIVING & SNORKELING: SALT **x** FRESH
TYPE OF DIVING/SNORKELING IN AREA: WALL **x** BEACH WRECK REEF CAVE ICE
DIVING/SNORKELING IN YOUR AREA IS BEST SUITED FOR: BEGINNER **x** INTERMEDIATE **x** ADVANCED **x**
BEST TIME OF YEAR FOR DIVING/SNORKELING: **All year**
TEMPERATURE: **NOV-APRIL: 78-80 F** **MAY-OCT: 78-80 F**
VISIBILITY: **DIVING: 40 FT** **SNORKELING: 40 FT**

PACKAGES AVAILABLE: DIVE **x** DIVE STAY **x** SNORKEL **x** SNORKEL-STAY **x**
  ACCOMMODATIONS NEARBY: HOTEL **x** MOTEL HOME RENTALS
ACCOMMODATION RATES: EXPENSIVE MODERATE **x** INEXPENSIVE **x**
RESTAURANTS NEARBY: EXPENSIVE MODERATE **x** INEXPENSIVE **x**
YOUR AREA IS: REMOTE **x** QUIET WITH ACTIVITIES LIVELY
LOCAL ACTIVITY/NIGHTLIFE:
CAR NEEDED TO EXPLORE AREA? YES NO **x**
DUTY FREE SHOPPING? YES NO **x**

LOCAL EMERGENCY SERVICES NEAREST HYPERBARIC TREATMENT FACILITY
COASTGUARD: **Naval Base, Bahai Malaga** AUTHORITY: **Naval Base**
TELEPHONE: **34114-34120** LOCATION: **Bahia Malaga, Pacific Coast, Colombia**
CALLSIGNS: TELEPHONE:

LOCAL DIVING DOCTOR:
NAME: **Carlos Botero**
LOCATION: **Buenavetura, Colombia**
TELEPHONE: **34865**

Venezuela

"The Best Kept Secret in the Caribbean"

Wendy Canning Church

February was the coldest winter in the Northeast in 15 years and frankly, I'd had enough of ice and snow!

We had covered Brazil in November and had such a rewarding trip that when a friend mentioned Venezuela I thought, "Why not?" Near the equator, the seasons are the reverse of North America. Actually its climate is warm year round Caracas can get cool at night since it is in the plateaus. Warm, that was for me. I went to see if it was "The Best Kept Secret in the Caribbean".

In 1498, on his third voyage, Columbus discovered Venezuela. But like so many of his findings, he never laid down a permanent settlement. Amerigo Vespucci followed in 1499 and mapped much of the area.

One of his favorite spots was Lake Maricaibo which Indian tribes had settled. They lived in houses built on stilts, traded along the waters in dugout canoes. This reminded him of Venice, thus he named the country Venezuela, meaning "Little Venice".

Wendy Church against black coral by Humberto Nahim

Spain, with its lust for gold, had a strong foothold for the next 300 years. Simon Bolivar, then and now a hero, an aristocrat born only 57 miles from Caracas, overthrew the tyrants and Little Venice became a democracy.

Today, Venezuela remains a democracy of over 20 million people, the preponderance of which are under 40 years of age.

Situated in the Caribbean with 1,800 miles of coastline and seventy-five islands, it is bordered by Guyana, Columbia and Brazil. Its 352,150 square miles are comprised of some of the most diverse and beautiful topography one will find anywhere. Stretches of jade green mountain ranges run throughout. The wild, verdant Amazon, bubbling rivers, deserted islands, huge waterfalls, solitary beaches in colors of perfect gemstones are yours to discover. Its waters are crystalline clear, virgin and most are protected by the government as Reserves.

It is a country of dichotomies like so many, in South America. There are the old, great fortunes made from gold and new from oil, and then there are the favelas of the city which one always wants to turn an eye from.

Caracas, the Capital, is the most populous city. There, four million people live in a city of cosmopolitan charm with many historic sites.

I was amazed to learn that a large percentage of the population are Italian and that one can find 5 star Italian cuisine at little cafes throughout Caracas and, for that matter, the country. This country holds many surprises for the guest.

Once again, we inquired of our friends about flights to Venezuela. Viasa Airlines, formerly owned by the government but now privately managed, was their choice.

Although they do not fly everyday from North America, we found their schedule suited us since they left Kennedy in early afternoon and were less expensive than the other carriers.

We chose correctly. Why cannot most carriers serve palatable food? Our luncheon was served to each guest individually from a beautifully appointed cart.

The movie was in English with Spanish subtitles and there was a good selection of magazines, papers and duty-free shopping aboard.

Just because an airline is not familiar to you, don't pass it by. Check it out with other travelers. *Do be at the airport* at least two hours ahead of time and re-confirm 24 hours before departure, especially when leaving Caracas. There is a great deal of paperwork. You pay taxes at a counter other than the check in. There are at least two securities checks before boarding the aircraft. This is for your protection so greet it with a smile and patience!

Viasa flys worldwide. The North America gateways to Caracas are Kennedy, Miami, and Houston.

No matter what anyone tells you, you do need a Visa! Don't lose it or you'll spend two days going through a lot of red tape at your Embassy.

Los Roques: (The Rocks) Venezuela

ABOUT THE PHOTOGRAPHER
Humberto Ramirez Nahim

Born: Caracas, Venezuela. Began diving at the age of 13, and began taking underwater pictures at the age of 19.

His photographs have been published in magazines like Mecanica Nacional, Caza y Pesca, GeoMundo, Corpo Vaz, Carta Ecologica y News Sport, also has been publishing 61 photos in a book made by the Provincial Bank in Venezuela, call Mochima. Also he makes documentaries for television in Hi8 Video Format.

92 miles north or one hours flight from the sophistication and activity of Caracas lies Venezuela's largest group of islands, the archipelago of Los Roques.

They wait to be discovered by those who wish to escape to the sounds of silence for a day or a week.

Unhurried, uncrowded, no phone, faxes or newspapers.

You will find a sleeply little village whose local livelihood depends on the lobster and conch found beneath its waters. It is a spot on the map on its way to becoming a picture perfect destination.

Declared a National Reserve, the entire village is being brought back to life under the watchful eye of the government.

Surrounded by the Caribbean Sea, the archipelago comprises some 350 islands curving around a central lagoon. Most are uninhabited and unnamed.

As the plane approaches the main island of Gran Roque, which is home to most inhabitants, and the Posadas and watersports center, you will notice the diverse topography. Ten thousand years ago, volcanic eruptions opened the sea floor and this chain of lava islands was created. Over the centuries, exfoliation and the winds wore away the sharp volcanic peaks into chunks of rock that give way to the highlands of sand-covered limestone. Tropical flatlands sweep from the plateaus to the beaches below.

Off-shore, this same volcanic activity laid down the hard bottom necessary for coral lava to establish colonies. Today we have a pristine, virgin underwater environment for watersports especially for the scuba diver, snorkeler and bone fisherman. This is practiced on a fish and release system which is commendable.

In earlier days, the island salt flats provided a lucrative economy for the town. One sees the parts of wonderful structures with high ceilings, terra cotta floors and beautiful old wooden doors and shutters in the ongoing renovations.

We stayed at a charming, newly renovated Posada, **El Pelicano Club**, situated in the center of town.

Each guest room overlooks an open air, central courtyard with beautiful plantings and native pottery runs the length of the Posada.

There is no air conditioning, but the high ceilings, fans and fresh sea breezes prove more than adequate. One takes showers with water heated by the sun since there is no hot water but this proves no hardship.

Meals are taken several yards away in the Posada's attractive dining roam. Food is simple but plentiful with an emphasis on fresh fruits, vegetables, pasta, rice and fish. El Pelicano Club makes a perfect resting spot. It is run with an iron fist in a velvet glove by Frank Ibarra and his staff. Everything is immaculate and a nice touch is their perfumed soaps and shampoo in the bath. As in all of Venezuela, the staff will grant your request with genuine warmth and friendliness in an atmosphere of relaxed hospitality.

Frank personally escorts all groups to the islands. His passion is fishing but he is also an avid diver.

Los Roques is the new paradise in the world for bonefishing. You can catch more than twenty fish per day and they will be in the 6 to 10 pound range. You can use fly fishing, like most of the fishermen, or you can try with light spinning gear.

Sesto Continente is the dive center an the island. Their center in Caracas was the first to open there 11 years ago. This center gets top rating for upholding high safety standards and their professionalism. Their true love of diving and interest in each diver really impressed me.

All equipment is provided and all dives are drift dives.

Our first dive, a 35 minute boat ride from Gran Roque was **Boca de Cota-Este**.

Depending on the current, this is a site suited for all levels. The site comprises spectacular underwater cliffs going down to a maximum depth of 180 feet.

On our descent we encountered four very large barracuda who kept a watchful eye on us. The reef was resplendent with hard and soft corals and sponges.

Tube coral, elephant ear, flower color, common plate coral, leafy stinging coral, brain and fire coral along with tub and barrel corals were in every color and hue.

Schools of blue and brown cromis swam above, through and beneath us. A large trunkfish, spiny lobster, giant yellowjack, scrawled filefish, black durgeons, harlequin bass, and every member of the parrotfish family were all spotted. The sponges were breathtakingly beautiful, like bright colored flowers. The plum worms were especially *lovely*.

We all agreed even though there was a good abundance of fish life, the topography was undoubtedly the best feature of the dive, a brilliantly colorful spectacle of flora and fauna, similar to a field ablaze with flowers in summer.

We motored to a nearby island owned by local fishermen. Dropping anchor, we went ashore and were greeted as guests.

Many of these islands have small houses on them where the fishermen stay for three months at a time, collecting lobster and conch for the bigger boats that pass by to purchase them for Caracas and export. To my amazement the small house, open to the air, was made out of varied materials and had a sand floor, it was immaculate. The floor had been newly raked.

Lobsters and conch which are caught are kept in man made lagoons until they are purchased.

There are immense mounds of conch shells which had been opened to remove the meat.

We were astounded by the size and variety of sea creatures spotted on or near the reef at **Boca de Cote Nord**.

Squirrelfish fish, French angelfish, spotlight parrotfish, spotfin butterfly fish, high hat, spotted drum, large pufferfish, yellowtail damselfish, juvenile tang, hundreds of blue hamlets, large Nassau grouper, schools of bluestriped grunt, yellow goatfish, schools of bar jack, French grunt, black grouper, and schools of horse-eye jack were seen by all.

> **As we ascended, I was convinced that what people had told me about the diving in these islands was true. Here was a rich underwater kingdom comprising major reefs with a large repository of sea life.**

Our second day took us to **Piedra de La Guasa** (Rock of Grouper) situated about fifteen minutes off Gran Roque and aptly named. It is a very large rock sitting in 120 feet of water where you sight grouper in varying sizes. These creatures, along with other fish life, red snapper, barracuda, horse-eye jack, queen angelfish, French angelfish and spiny lobster, swim in and around the multi-colored sponges and hard and soft corals. A really pleasant day dive; it is also a favorite spot for night diving.

> **Throughout these waters sailors must be very careful to monitor their charts and approach each channel with utmost caution for the waters suddenly become deceivingly shallow.**

Madriequi is a particularly beautiful island with a stretch of white sandy beach. We took time to walk it leisurely.

The top dive of my stay was at **Cayo Sal**, an hour and one-half away, almost at the end of the archipelago is made up of vertical cliffs adorned with some of the healthiest underwater vegetation one will find in any waters. As we made our way down to one of the seven caves in this area, there was a plethora of black coral.

> **It was as if one were swimming through a virgin forest, the backdrop of which was black coral in every shape and size. Interspersed were sponges in a rainbow of colors.**

We entered the first cave and spent the rest of the dive studying and filming the beautiful hard and soft coral and sponges which grow in profusion.

Seles Qui by Huberto Nahim

Interval time was spent at a deserted nearby island. Here we picnicked under the shelter of an umbrella in an abandoned fisherman's house. He had taken the roof with him until his next round of duty here.

The second cave at Cayo Sal was incredibly beautiful, its base is adorned with bright sun colored orange sponges. Descending and ascending, the majestic black coral surrounded us. Never have I seen this quantity of black coral. It was worth the entire trip to Los Roques!

It was late in the afternoon, but we had planned to visit the *Fundacan Cientifica Los Roques*, the biological research station where turtles are raised and then released. Turtles are an endangered species here and it is strictly forbidden to take them. On all our dives, I never saw one which says a great deal. The station is quite interesting and well worth a visit. Buy a T-shirt to help support their work.

Our fourth and last day we to returned to **Boca de Cote Este and Nord**. The light was good, the fish and sea vegetation abundant and we got some good photos to show the wonders of these waters.

The usual school of barracuda greeted and followed us on both dives.

> The beauty of this virgin topography must be seen. It is similar to an underwater English garden.

As we began our ascent, the biggest, greenest moray eel I have ever seen greeted us from an outcropping. First its head only visible, then it slowly sashayed out as if to say "Goodbye."

OTHER DIVES - OFFERED:

Boca del Medio	Entry east of the archipelago, clear and shallow waters (10 to 15 m./30 - 45 ft.) with a great variety of coral.
Noronqui:	Formation of "antler corals" (Acropora Palmata). Inside this labyrinth lives a great variety of species.
Nordisqui:	North of the archipelago, formations of flat coral stones and canals, many lobsters as well as a few shipwrecks.
Boca de Sebastopol:	The southeast entrance of the archipelago, varied fauna. You can easily observe sharks and rays.

> Quite near Caracas, in the area off the La Guaira Bank, you will find the world's second best place for fishing (after Cuba). It is most famous for its billfishing and is the home of the World and IGFA tournaments. You will find white and blue marlin, sailfish, dorados, and yellow fin tuna in this area. It is very uncommon to end a day of fishing without seeing at least one marlin.

After Los Roques, we stayed at the *Sheraton Macuto* in Caracas. The Sheraton is a complete resort with a lovely beach on one side and the backdrop of verdant mountains running to an inlet on the other. There is a state-of-the-art marina. R&R by the pool, dip in the ocean, play tennis or golf, dine by candlelight in its 5 star Italian Restaurant or veg out with room service and watch a movie. You'll be tempted by its boutique carrying a unique selection of bathing suits, wraps and casual wear. Far enough away yet near enough to the historic sights, I found it a perfect choice.

I especially must thank Stephen Sharpe in the head office. I ran into a couple of difficult travel snags that could have been disastrous without his help and Loren Iriarte in Guest Relations. I probably should have sent them to Los Roques for a rest after dealing with my traumas!

> In this day and age when many big chains can seem impersonal, the Sheraton Macuto's staff either knows inherently the manner in which guests should be treated or have been superbly trained. I suspect a little of both. All certainly lived up to their motto, "Our World Revolves Around You"

An all inclusive package to Los Roques is available for scuba divers, snorkelers and fishermen which includes an overnight upon arrival and departure at the Sheraton Macuto and private air charter to Los Roques.

Puerto La Cruz

One half hour flight on Viasa Airlines to Barcelona or a four hour drive from Caracas, gets you to Puerto La Cruz also known as "The Gateway to the East".

Just ten short years ago, this area resembled Los Roques, a remote fishing village, on the map overlooked by tourists. Today, the traveler will find a humming city replete with five star hotels, beautiful waterfront villas, condos, and marinas in whose berths lie fabulous yachts. There is also the American infusion of McDonalds and Burger Kings. Whether their introduction was due to the Americans working the oil fields or demand from the locals is anyones guess.

You will be a bit dazzled by the area's facelift and its obvious building boom geared to the rich and famous. If you spend a little time you will find the old city, built in colonial times, with small cafes serving delicious cuisine and little shops selling charming handicrafts.

Once out on its waters, the true beauty of the area becomes apparent. Many small islands lie off shore that are surrounded by waters protected by the government. They were designated a Marine Park five years ago. The government judiciously patrols the Park.

Scuba divers can take nothing dead or alive from the waters. There is no spearfishing. Fish can only be taken on a line. Limits are set for the fishermen and there are times of the year when allocated species may be caught.

New housing cannot be built upon the islands in the Park. Call it poetic justice if you will, but a group of wealthy people built expensive houses without permission. The government tore them down, allowing only the small, modest houses of the fisherman whose livelihood has been culled from these waters for centuries to remain.

> **You can sail for miles and never see another boat. Every island has a reef. Some islands have more than two! Most of the islands are deserted. The reefs are virgin, the waters pristine. Couple this with a year round temperature of 80 degrees and you have a perfect destination for lovers of watersports.**

We dove with Lolos, a first class operation situated about one-half hour from our Hotel, *The Golden Rainbow*, Maremares Resort and Spa. Some days we would be picked up by Eddy Revelant, our dive master, at the Hotel and we would leave from the scuba center. Other days, he and the captain would bring the boat around and we would leave from the marina at the Hotel.

Lolos has three boats, all in good condition, comfortable, with enough room for divers and equipment and canopy for shade from the intense sun.

> **The scuba center is up to date. The equipment provided is in good shape and well serviced.**

They carry wet suits which you will need. Don't laugh, but a hood and gloves are also necessary. Even though it was April the waters were quite cold!

Day 1 - Dive I - The Bubble off East Las Caracas Island

This is a wall dive suited for all levels. We rolled over and descended to a maximum depth of 100 feet.

> **As we descended we saw bubbles rising to the top. Eddy stopped along the way and showed me different areas where hot water was coming out of the rocks.**

The bubbles are caused by natural gas coming out from under the bottom of the wall at 100 feet.

As we ascended, there was a field of beautiful corals and reef fish, parrotfish, angelfish, grunt, squirrelfish, deep water grouper, small snapper, sergent major, and a pair of spotted drum. The abundance of healthy corals was astounding, star corals, brain, knobby brain, large flower corals with brilliant red and green coloring. It was a really pretty and interesting dive.

Dive-2 Las Penas off Santa Fe Gulf

A reef dive suited for all levels depending on the time of year and current. This applies to almost every dive in Venezuela, if there is heavy current drift dives are done.

The pinnacle reaches almost to the surface. The dive plan is to begin at the last pinnacle in shallow water and make your way to the west side which is comprised of a sandy slope. The hard and soft corals were beautiful. The entire dive site was covered with anemones which resembled bouquets of flowers. Small shrimp were hidden amongst the rocks along with arrow crabs and a large variety of reef fish. We spotted two moray eels, stone fish, and sea cucumbers littered the sand.

> **This dive used to be called, *Anemone Garden*, and one can understand why. We swam through fields of them our entire dive. I was impressed with this first days dive!**

2nd Day The Cathedral off Barracuda Island

This is a reef dive suited for every level and a good site for a night dive.

We dropped down to forty-five feet and swam along the reef toward the northwest side where there is a cave in the wall. The cave is full of passages filled with sea life and beautiful colored sponges. It has two openings at the top.

Ascending, I heard a voice. Eddy said "Hi." Obviously, we had hit an air pocket. These happenings underwater are what get us divers hooked!

We came out of the cave and descended to 60 feet. There were parrotfish, angelfish, a snake eel, a green moray eel, and something strange which I first thought might be an octopus, but rather it was fire worms eating eggs of other fish.

The second dive was *La Ballena* off Borracho Island. We approached the reef by going under a large ledge of rocks. It resembled an amphitheater. Its slope, made up of hard corals, went downward. There were schools of red snapper, two huge blue parrotfish, schools of butterfly fish (which I have never seen) swam along with us.

We headed back against a very strong current and as we reached the top of the slope we noticed the different hard corals. There was a crater-like hole in the middle. As we moved on, there were tube corals growing in profusion in bright sun orange. Hundreds of silversides or sardines swam underneath and out of the ledge at us.

Tiquitique is a reef dive, that is shaped like a mountain so you can dive both sides, the deepest point being 120 feet.

Here we spotted the big fish, manta rays, nurse shark, grouper and big red snapper.

Because the area is too open this would not make a good night dive.

On our third day, Michael Bryant, an American expatriot, joined us. They just don't make them any better than Michael. One would never imagine seeing him on the boat or underwater that he is physically challenged. He is a most competent diver, holding an advanced C card. He would make anyone a well-trained buddy! On our last day he brought his boat and captain along with a wonderful picnic. Many-thanks to him for his friendship and generosity.

Lolo has innumerable dive sites but on our last day the first dive's visibility was poor. We decided to go further inland and find better visibility. This was a new site. It was a wonderful dive. I liked this very much about the operation. They never stuck to a strict dive site plan. Their flexibility were always keyed not only to the safety of the diver, but their enjoyment of the site. Lolo's is first rate and I thank them all for a wonderful underwater stay-in Puerto La Cruz.

The *Golden Rainbow*, Maremares Resort and Spa, is situated only 20 minutes from the airport and minutes from town. It is definitely *the place* to stay in Puerta La Cruz. A five star hotel by Venezuela's standards, it is the most complete resort you will find in the area.

Guests are lodged in attractive rooms with private baths and balconies in three-story pink pastel buildings. I don't think anyone could possibly get bored with the myriad of activities offered. The food is delicious.

The world class spa is a joy. Lifestyles of the Rich and Famous filmed it for one of its T.V. episodes. Interestingly enough, by the world's standards and prices, the Golden Rainbow is very affordable.

Diving in Venezuela is an all day affair. You start off early in the morning, motor to your first site, complete the dive, then set out for an island to picnic. In early afternoon, a second dive is done and you are back on shore between three and four. This makes a nice relaxing day. Those not wanting to go each day can opt for every other and just relax or sightsee on off days.

Old Town is worth a visit. It is very picturesque. Walk to Boulevard El Paseo Colon. When oil was discovered, the big American companies ran the refinery until they were bought out by the Venezualan government. Here you will see the American influence. It is an interesting contrast, restaurants, hotels and craft shops situated on the sea. You will not find any big shopping malls yet; little souvenir shops abound.

If avid shoppers need their "fix", Margarita Island makes a good day trip.

When we inquired of knowledgeable dive operations in Venezuela about good diving areas. Margarita Island was sold to us more as a duty-free port than a dive destination. A ferry service runs each day from the end of Boulevard El Paseo Colon, it is a four hour trip.

Or you can take a plane and visit *Angel Falls*, named for American aviator, Jimmy Angel. In 1937 on a quest for gold, his plane crashed on top of "Auyan-Zepuy" or table top mountain. The party survived and when they emerged from the forest they came upon this waterfall, the highest in the world.

Spotted Moray Eel by Eddie Revelent

SCUBA AND SNORKELING FACILITIES QUESTIONNAIRE

NAME **El Pelicano Club**
ADDRESS **Los Roques**

CONTACT **DEI**
TITLE
TELEPHONE **617-723-7134**   FAX 671-227-8145

CAPITAL: **Gran Roque**		GOVERNMENT: **Democratic**	
POPULATION: **1,000**		LANGUAGE: **Spanish, Little English**	
CURRENCY: **Bolivar**		ELECTRICITY: **110v, 60 cy**	
AIRLINES: **Charter Flight Aeroejecutivo/Aereotuv**		DEPARTURE TAX? **National Park Fee**	
NEED VISA/PASSPORT? YES **x** NO		PROOF OF CITIZENSHIP? YES **x** NO	

YOUR FACILITY IS CLASSIFIED AS: SCUBA CENTER   RESORT **x**
BUSINESS HOURS: 7:30 a.m. - 7:00 p.m.
CERTIFYING AGENCIES: PADI
LOG BOOK REQUIRED?   YES   NO **x** **Certification is required**
EQUIPMENT: SALES **x**   RENTALS **x**   AIR FILLS **x**
PRIMARY LINE OF EQUIPMENT: **Seaquest - Technisub**
PHOTOGRAPHIC EQUIPMENT: SALES   RENTALS **x**   LAB **None**

CHARTER/DIVE BOAT AVAILABLE?   YES **x**   NO   DIVER CAPACITY **10 people w/each D.M.**
COAST GUARD APPROVED?   YES **x**   NO   CAPTAIN LICENSED?   YES **x**   NO
SHIP TO SHORE? YES   NO   LORAN   YES **x**   NO   RADAR?   YES **x**   NO
DIVE MASTER/INSTRUCTOR ABOARD?   YES **x**   NO   BOTH **x**

DIVING & SNORKELING: SALT **x**   FRESH
TYPE OF DIVING/SNORKELING IN AREA: WALL **x**   BEACH   WRECK **x**   REEF **x**   CAVE **x**   ICE
DIVING/SNORKELING IN YOUR AREA IS BEST SUITED FOR: BEGINNER **x**   INTERMEDIATE **x**   ADVANCED **x**
BEST TIME OF YEAR FOR DIVING/SNORKELING: **May - October**
TEMPERATURE: **NOV-APRIL: 80 F**   **MAY-OCT: 80 F**
VISIBILITY: **DIVING: 40- 80 FT**   **SNORKELING: 80 FT**

PACKAGES AVAILABLE: DIVE **x**   DIVE STAY **x**   SNORKEL   SNORKEL-STAY
ACCOMMODATIONS NEARBY: HOTEL   MOTEL   HOME RENTALS **x**
ACCOMMODATION RATES: EXPENSIVE **x**   MODERATE **x**   INEXPENSIVE **x**
RESTAURANTS NEARBY: NONE **x**   EXPENSIVE   MODERATE   INEXPENSIVE w/package
YOUR AREA IS: REMOTE **x**   QUIET WITH ACTIVITIES   LIVELY
LOCAL ACTIVITY/NIGHTLIFE: **During high season there are parties in the plaza**
CAR NEEDED TO EXPLORE AREA?   YES   NO **x**
DUTY FREE SHOPPING?   YES   NO **x**

LOCAL EMERGENCY SERVICES   NEAREST HYPERBARIC TREATMENT FACILITY
COASTGUARD: (Has emergency helicopter)   AUTHORITY: **Centro Clinico Hiperbarico**
TELEPHONE: **VHF Channel 16**   LOCATION: **La Guaira**
CALLSIGNS: **Guardacosta Los Roques**   TELEPHONE: **35.29.33/242.84.77/242.93.25**

LOCAL DIVING DOCTOR:
NAME: **Dr. Adolfo Gonzalez Poarrio**
LOCATION: **Centro Clinico Hiperbarico, La Guaira**
TELEPHONE: **35.29.33/242.84.77/242.93.25**

SCUBA AND SNORKELING FACILITIES QUESTIONNAIRE

NAME **Lolo's Diving Center**
ADDRESS **Sector Punta De Meta Guantamarina Guanta Edo, Anzoategui**

CONTACT **Pedro Rodriguez/Eddy Revelant**
TITLE **President/Marketing Director**
TELEPHONE **081-683052 014-801543 014-205073**   FAX **081-682885**

CAPITAL: **Barcelona**   GOVERNMENT:
POPULATION: **1,00**   LANGUAGE: **Spanish, Little English**
CURRENCY: **Bolivar**   ELECTRICITY: **110v, 60 cy**
AIRLINES: **Charter Flight Aeroejecutivo/Aereotuv**   DEPARTURE TAX? **National Park Fee**
NEED VISA/PASSPORT?   YES **x**   NO   PROOF OF CITIZENSHIP?   YES **x**   NO

YOUR FACILITY IS CLASSIFIED AS: SCUBA CENTER   RESORT **x**
BUSINESS HOURS: **7:30 a.m. - 7:00 p.m.**
CERTIFYING AGENCIES: **PADI**
LOG BOOK REQUIRED?   YES   NO **x**   **Certification is required**
EQUIPMENT: SALES **x**   RENTALS **x**   AIR FILLS **x**
PRIMARY LINE OF EQUIPMENT: **Seaquest - Technisub**
PHOTOGRAPHIC EQUIPMENT: SALES   RENTALS **x**   LAB **None**

CHARTER/DIVE BOAT AVAILABLE? YES **x** NO   DIVER CAPACITY **10 people w/each D.M.**
COAST GUARD APPROVED?   YES **x** NO   CAPTAIN LICENSED? YES **x**   NO
SHIP TO SHORE? YES   NO   LORAN YES **x** NO RADAR? YES **x**   NO
DIVE MASTER/INSTRUCTOR ABOARD?   YES **x**   NO   BOTH **x**

DIVING & SNORKELING: SALT **x**   FRESH
TYPE OF DIVING/SNORKELING IN AREA: WALL **x**   BEACH   WRECK **x**   REEF **x**   CAVE **x**   ICE
DIVING/SNORKELING IN YOUR AREA IS BEST SUITED FOR: BEGINNER **x**   INTERMEDIATE **x**   ADVANCED **x**
BEST TIME OF YEAR FOR DIVING/SNORKELING: **May - October**
TEMPERATURE: **NOV-APRIL:**   **80 F**   **MAY-OCT:**   **80 F**
VISIBILITY: **DIVING:**   **40- 80 FT**   **SNORKELING: 80 FT**

PACKAGES AVAILABLE: DIVE **x**   DIVE STAY **x**   SNORKEL   SNORKEL-STAY
ACCOMMODATIONS NEARBY: HOTEL   MOTEL   HOME RENTALS **x**
ACCOMMODATION RATES: EXPENSIVE **x**   MODERATE **x**   INEXPENSIVE **x**
RESTAURANTS NEARBY: NONE **x**   EXPENSIVE   MODERATE   INEXPENSIVE **w/package**
YOUR AREA IS: REMOTE **x**   QUIET WITH ACTIVITIES   LIVELY
LOCAL ACTIVITY/NIGHTLIFE: **During high season there are parties in the plaza**
CAR NEEDED TO EXPLORE AREA?   YES   NO **x**
DUTY FREE SHOPPING?   YES   NO **x**

LOCAL EMERGENCY SERVICES   NEAREST HYPERBARIC TREATMENT FACILITY
COASTGUARD: **(Has emergency helicopter)**   AUTHORITY: **Centro Clinico Hiperbarico**
TELEPHONE: **VHF Channel 16**   LOCATION: **La Guaira**
CALLSIGNS: **Guardacosta Los Roques**   TELEPHONE: **35.29.33/242.84.77/242.93.25**

LOCAL DIVING DOCTOR:
NAME: **Dr. Adolfo Gonzalez Poarrio**
LOCATION: **Centro Clinico Hiperbarico, La Guaira**
TELEPHONE: **35.29.33/242.84.77/242.93.25**

THAILAND

Since I am reasonably sure that no one reading this will be interested in my professional curriculum vitae, I will encapsulate it into one sentence.

My professional career as a clinical chemist ended a few years ago with retirement.

Born on the West Coast of Scotland in the halcyon days midway between the two world wars, my lot was a happy one. At a very early age I was exposed to books and travel. Both of which have been life-long addictions. It would be difficult to say which has had the greater impact. However, since most people reading this will be more interested in travel than in bibliography I will confine myself to a condensed version of that aspect of my life.

I associate travel with a kaleidoscope. Often, and for no particular reason, video-like images flash through my mind.

The images may be of a place, an incident, a chance encounter, a meal, a conversation or even a very unnerving experience. When associated with either a very pleasurable or a very traumatic event, it is understandable that such an incident would be indelibly stamped on one's mind. It is, however, less comprehensible why one retains equally vivid mental images of events, people and places which are in no way associated with either of those emotional extremes.

Hence a kaleidoscope - a thing of random images - colorful, stimulating and forever changing. Even the disasters are amusing when viewed in retrospect. If travel teaches no other lesson, very early in the game you do learn to cope.

It has been my good fortune to see a great deal of the world. Since I had been trailed around from a very early age, my two sons have been subjected to similar treatment. I have not heard any complaints. Also I have found that traveling with children is an unique experience. For the rest of your life you associate certain places with the strangest things. The list is innumerable.

Without question my "one spot above them all" is Kenya. Not as good as it used to be but I'll still did not turn down the highlands any time! Our favorite spot is LEWA DOWNS, a large (45,000 acres) private farm close to Isiolo. Absolutely a unique experience. On the other hand, the coast of Kenya leaves me cold. From my experience if you want good diving and or snorkeling, there are many better places to go.

In 1974 the family went on a diving trip to CEDAM headquarters in the small village of Akumal, on the Yucatan coast of Mexico. Four years later we went back, purchased a lot on the Yalku Lagoon and started to build a family vacation "hide-away". That was an experience not easily forgotten! Let us not laugh too loudly over the promises of electricity, water, etc. made by the landowner-seller. However, we finally managed to complete the building and though it is not the hide-away it was even ten years ago it still is a great place with wonderful snorkeling in the coral garden right off the property. Unfortunately, Cancun is now totally ruined by mass tourism. Hate the place.

Travel is such an individual thing. Having rather catholic tastes many places hold very fond memories for me. The Far East, India, Egypt, the Caribbean, Mexico and

South America all have their own very special attractions. Europe with its marvelous museums, architectural wonders, exciting cities and marvelous food (another of my addictions) will always tempt me. Even while complaining that "I've seen Europe in better times", it does still retain the culture and characteristics unique to each specific country. Scotland is, of course, for me "home" and my bias might show if I said anymore on that subject.

Happy roaming.
Agnes C. Haff

Bangkok

Since Bangkok will almost certainly be your take-off point en route to Phuket, please don't miss seeing something of this city. In my opinion, one of the world's most colorful and exciting. I have had the good fortune to visit it many times but never tire of its charms. First priority is to find yourself a good hotel. While Bangkok has a number of very good ones I, personally, will eat rice and beans for a month to really indulge myself by staying at The Oriental in a river-view room in the Garden Wing (used to be known as the Authors' House. It is generally considered to be the finest hotel in Asia, indeed, many people claim it is the best in the world, myself included.

Now it's time to become oriented and no better way than to take a long- tailed motorized boat (hang yao) at the hotel's dock and see the sights along the Chao Phraya River - the main artery of the city - and the klongs (or canals) branching off it. Even if you can't make The Oriental you should try and stay in one of the other hotels on the river. Both The Royal Orchid Sheraton & Shangri-La Hotel are so situated. Many of the more famous temples (wats) can be seen from the river and the boat will stop and give you time to wander and sight-see.

The water taxis are convenient and cheap and there are also water buses.

A visit to the Royal Palace is very much recommended. Taking a water bus or taxi up the river to Chinatown is a fun thing to do some morning. While snakes are not really my thing, if you would like a snake skin handbag, belt or shoes you can get very nice snake skin merchandise very cheaply at the shop adjoining the Snake Farm. Thai silk is, of course, justifiable world famous and the city abounds with excellent silk stores and tailors. Always one of lifes great temptations.

Should you have some extra time, there are many interesting day trips out of the city. Three of the most popular are those to Ayuthaya (the former ancient capital), Damnoen Floating market and the National Museum.

There are many others and the choice is very dependent on personal tastes and interests. There are many good restaurants in the city. One that is quite special, however, is the Sala Rim Naam across the river from The Oriental. Since it is owned by the hotel the boat ride over is free. A favorite place for lunch is Lord Jim's in the hotel proper, and the Riverside Terrace is very pleasant for dinner. Beside The Oriental is a very nice Chinese restaurant in an old house, unfortunately the name escapes me at the moment but it is easy to find.

Phuket

Probably at this point you're wishing I would get on with it. What about scuba-diving, skin-diving, snorkeling underwater photography and related water oriented activities? Just catch a flight out of Bangkok to Phuket - ThaiAir is a good airline and in approximately an hour your are in Phuket and it's all there waiting for you.

Having globe trotted quite a bit in my time I consider the Andaman Sea to be a real treasure. Crystal clear waters which are home to an astounding variety of species of fish while coral of all shapes and colors bewilder the eye.

Snorkeler by Melindi Ran

All this in today's world and, so far, still not spoiled by mass tourism. There are, unfortunately, few places left that fall into this very special category. Already the warning signals can be seen that this will be a very different place a few years hence. Bitter experience has made me all too well aware of what can happen to a mini-paradise when the developers and mass tourism move in.

There are a number of diving centers on the island. Personally, I have not done any diving while in Phuket. The snorkeling is so impressive that I take the easy route and confine myself to that and a few boat trips to one of the many small off-shore islands for more snorkeling. The boat trips in themselves are fun with the beautiful waters and the flying fish cavorting around the boat. At this point let me interject two warnings. While it is possible to rent the various pieces of necessary equipment, I would recommend that you take your own mask if you have a particular favorite - as I happen to have. The other thing that could spoil an other-wise perfect trip would be allowing yourself to be burned to a crisp. The sun is very strong and unless you have developed a perpetual tan from long time exposure to the tropical sun, it can be lethal. It is a good idea to wear a long-sleeved cotton shirt when in the water or on a boat trip and it is also some protection against coral scrapes, etc. There are a number of hotels of various types on the island. I have only first hand experience of one - the Phuket Yacht Club Hotel. It is a very pleasant place with good food, a really lovely pool area and a nice beach. Built in a series of units set into a hill side and surrounded by lush tropical landscaping makes for an interesting and pleasant setting. Each unit has its own private balcony from which you have a spectacular view over the gardens of Promthep Cape and the Andaman Sea. You can rent equipment, arrange for boat trips, etc. at their beach shop. A short walk up the beach are long-tail motorized boats which you can hire quite cheaply. The Yacht Club is located at the far end of the island from the airport. You can either rent an Avis car at the airport or arrange with the hotel to pick you up on your arrival. Should your plans not call for much driving around the island the latter is probably the better choice. With so many incomparable water oriented activities available, it is difficult to get too excited about doing much else.

The best months are November to March but December and January are considered to be the ideal time to go.

During this period the visibility of the waters around the Similan Islands (85 km.) N.W. by boat from Phuket often extends to 30 meters and are considered to be a paradise for both scuba and skin divers.

Underwater photographers claim they have found their Nirvana.

Since this area is a marine national park no overnight accommodations are available. Closer to Phuket, there are many more small islands most of which are highly recommended by the diving fraternity. Read up on them and take your pick. Accommodation on the smaller islands are usually rather primitive if, indeed, there are any at all. Some have little shacks where you can get a fish lunch, and they may have beach chairs and umbrellas which you can rent for a few baht. Most of the hotel boats will pack a lunch and soft drinks to take along with you.

The following are some of the various organizations operating in Phuket.
1) Reef Explorers, P.O. Box 230 Amphur Muang Phuket, Thailand.
    Fax: (076) 381-325
2) Marine Divers, Kata-Karon Beach, Phuket, Thailand
    Fax: (66-76) 213604
3) Andaman Sea Diving, 47/12 Viset Rd. Chalong Bay, Phuket.
    Fax: (076) 381-834

Note: Would like to try this one sometime. It is a house boat type of arrangement where you eat and sleep aboard and arrange your own diving schedule.

4) For the deep-sea fishing enthusiast try:
    Phuket Big Game Fishing Charter Co., LTD
    82/85 Soi Bangla, Patong Beach, Phuket, Thailand
    Fax:(076) 321357

TONGA

Anne Harvey is Vice President of DALBAR Financial Services, a Boston based publishing and research firm which conducts syndicated and proprietary surveys for the mutual funds, insurance, banking and brokerage industries.

Anne is a graduate of the University of Nebraska and holds degrees in journalism and marketing. She is the publisher of the mutual fund trade publications FACS, The Journal of Mutual Fund Services and FACS of the Week specializing in industry news and information.

She and her husband Louis currently reside in Cohasset Massachusetts. They are avid divers and have made a hobby of traveling the globe to discover new and interesting dive sights.

We first became aware of The Kingdom of Tonga during an annual Caribbean charter. After several years of sailing the Caribbean, nearly exhausting our supply of adventures there, we decided to turn our sights to a place that would stand up to our hopes for remote and distinct.

TONGA. It sounded so exotic. A poll of the group revealed of our collective geographic incompetence...no one had a clue as to its location. That was enough to proclaim Tonga a new destination. Next year's trip would be a pilgrimage to discover this lost paradise "somewhere" in the South Pacific.

We began our research by inquiring at The Moorings, our boat charterer. To our good fortune, David the coordinator in Grenada had personally established the Tongan operation. After an hour with David we were sold on the description of this remote and foreign island group located approximately 800 miles to the southeast of Tahiti and 1000 miles northeast of New Zealand.

The Kingdom of Tonga consists of five island groups. It is composed of 170 volcanic and coral islands with a total land area of 600 square miles.

The islands are both short plush mounds, and high rugged coast peaks rising directly from the ocean. The population is just over 100,000 people primarily of Polynesian origin.

Travelers to Tonga will arrive in Tongatapu and find commuter fights on Air Tonga to the other island groups where most of the cruising and diving occurs. Flying into Tonga is perhaps one of its greatest visual delights. Multi-shaded blue rings resulting from the abundant coral reefs present an endless rainbow of colors from above. A brief stay in Nuka'alofa, Tongatapu may be of interest to visit the palace and get a glance at Tongan royalty. Yes, Tonga is the only functional monarchy in the world. King Taufa'ahua Tupou IV is head of state and is responsible for all functions of government including allocation of land to the people of Tonga. The Tongans we spoke with found this system equitable although the expanding population has put limitations on the land size per family. Consequently, many young Tongans are leaving the kingdom for greater opportunities. The Kingdom has also made headlines for recently entering into an agreement with a satellite concern to utilize Tonga as a cable satellite launching location for the South Pacific.

Local customs are well defined and visitors are asked to observe the proper rules of Tonga. Women are asked not to expose shoulders and to wear skirts or pants, rather than shorts. Men are asked not to be seen barechested. And, all are asked to observe the Sunday day of rest which includes no swimming in public areas. Boaters and divers will find these rules to be less a problem as they are usually in less public locations.

Depending upon the type of traveler you are, this is a word of caution, or a word of encouragement.

> **To the rustic adventurer, Tonga will be an untouched tropical paradise filled with friendly people, the decedents of an ancient and tumultuous history. To the traveler who is accustom to four star accommodations, lavish dining and entertainment, Tonga would best be given over to its neighbors such as Tahiti or Fiji.**

To illustrate this point, Tonga has a grand total of 400 telephones in the entire country.

Tonga is for the adventurer who loves aquatic life both above and below the surface.

> **Below the surface we encountered vibrantly colored reefs and walls still unfettered by over diving. Both the snorkeler and the diver will find a multitude of choice locations in Tonga**

We began our underwater sojourn at Hunga in the Vava'u Island group and snorkeled a wall in clear shallow water with abundant sea life. Hunga, as in many of the dive and snorkeling sights, is easily accessible by boat. One could see the wide array of reef fish in addition to rare, black and white striped water snakes, usually found in dark caves. (Pretty to look at, but poisonous to touch).

Perhaps the most interesting underwater experience in Tonga is **Mariner's Cave**. Steeped in mystery, this cave can only be reached by an underwater entrance. There is a tale of a Tongan chief who hid his lover who was scheduled for execution, in Mariner's Cave for two weeks before he could safely transport her to Fiji. To enter the cave one must descend eight feet to the entry of the cave and proceed fourteen feet through the passage and then up into the cave. Once inside and above the surface we encountered the surge of waves and the consequent change of air pressure which surrounded us in a blue haze. To many in our group, this was unpleasant, disorienting and difficult to breathe. To us, it was a magical, eerie place which drew blue light reflected from the floor of the sea. The cave walls were rugged and moist. One could hear the sound of the surge lapping the rock and feel the constant air pressure changes that make Mariner's Cave a complete sensory experience.

The secret to Mariner's Cave is this. Tackle it at low tide, unless you are an experienced free diver or have scuba gear. (We learned this the hard way entering at full high tide!). Next, send your strongest diver in first. Once "in" this diver can dangle their fins from the entrance as a guide to the others. This allows the others a way to pace their dive and avoid surfacing too soon. The surge is unforgiving to the individual who surfaces too soon as one of our group learned.

Scuba diving in Tonga is spectacular for one thing, it is still relatively virgin. We dove with Dolphin Pacific Divers located at The Tongan Beach Resort (FAX 001676- 70380) in the Vava'u group. We highly recommend Dolphin Pacific for its safety and knowledgeable staff. The story of Dolphin Pacific begin with Patty Field. Patty has been a diver her entire life, her father having introduced her as a child in their home in California. Patty became a successful hospital administrator, but yearned for something more. It was on a Tonga Moorings yacht charter she decided that her hospital days were over. Shortly after she waved good-by to California and began her endeavor to establish a dive operation in Tonga.

I asked Patty what it was like to come to a country with such a foreign culture and set up a business.

"It isn't like doing business in the U.S. There are a different set of rules here. First you must find a native sponsor who will own a share of the business. I found my sponsor here at the resort. Although European, my partner was married to a Tongan and the first hurdle was crossed".

Patty laughs and describes her first encounter with purchasing business supplies and equipment.

"I made my order and was ready to buy the materials when the merchant insisted I must have a island man's permission to take the purchase".

Those obstacles are far behind Patty who now runs a very successful dive facility. Those wishing to book dives with Patty can stay at The Tongan Beach Resort or she will be happy to pick divers up at their boats. Safety comes first with Dolphin Pacific. Patty and her staff are certified dive masters and the equipment is state of the art.

Dolphin Pacific met us at our yacht for C-Card inspection and equipment fitting. We had two dives, a wall and a cave dive. Tonga is filled with finger caves wide enough for one person. Our dive master claims to find a new one each time. We funneled through several beginning at the bottom, moving upward toward the surface observing silvery spoon fish and colorful coral formations.

We shared the cave dive with Sandy the nurse shark who permitted our company at a respectful distance.

Tonga has an abundance of unexplored reefs and caves. Patty informed us that she and her staff delight in virgin diving to discover new areas with experienced divers. We'll be back for that.

It is recommended you try a Tongan feast. The islanders give proper meaning to the word feast. Guests sit on mats and are often invited by a native to try kava. Kava is a ground root drink served in social settings from a large wooden bowl where a carved cup is passed. Kava has the appearance of muddy water and tastes rather like one would expect a ground root to taste. It creates a mild numbness to the back of the throat and in abundance will have an intoxicating effect.

After kava, a spread of food is presented on enormous palm leaves. Fingers only, we opened green leaf pouches containing steamed pork, octopus, chicken, vegetables and fresh fruit. During the feast guests are entertained by dancers and musicians where it is common practice to place money on the dancers coated in coconut oil. All quite folksy, but a good opportunity to exchange tales with other sailors in the area.

If you are anywhere near the Vava'u islands, and if you are a connoisseur of the somewhat bizarre, do not miss La Peala. The owners, a couple from Spain came to Tonga circuitously. With absolutely no knowledge of sailing. the couple set out with their baby from Spain, crossed the Pacific and eventually ended up in Tonga where they established this restaurant, a hut really. You will be ready to eat after ascending the steep and rocky path; a flashlight is a must if you value your life. The couple also provides entertainment and note that the more sangria you consume, the better Edwardo sounds and the more he looks like the real Charles Manson. The food is delicious and the atmosphere boarders on raucous.

The best time of year to travel to Tonga is between April and June to avoid the rainy season and the find the best wind for sailing.

The Moorings can provide more information regarding arrangements, but most travelers to Tonga fly via Hawaii or do as we did and tour New Zealand first.

When the trip was all said and done there were mixed reviews. Some of our group longed to be back in the familiar waters of the Caribbean complete with its amenities. As for us, we found the diving, and snorkeling to be some of the best we had seen largely due to the fact that Tonga is remote enough not be have been exploited.

TURKEY

A Tapestry

Wendy Canning Church

Turkey is a beautiful country with a land mass of 780,000 square kilometers that is populated by some 60 million inhabitants.

One might compare its six centuries of continuous but diverse culture to an antique tapestry. A bit threadbare, yet finely woven by the influence of the Hitites, Frigians, Urartuans, Lydians, Ionians, Persians, Macedonians, Romans, Byzantines, Selijuks, and Ottomans into a work of art that touches every sense.

If you are fortunate enough to visit this remarkable country, your mind will be stretched by Turkey's history and your eye delighted by its natural beauty and architectural heritage.

Quite subtly a sense of a higher power will be awakened or heightened by the essence of spirituality that embraces the panoramic views of pine forests sloping to the seas, olive groves stretching as far as the eye can see, indented coastlines and hidden inlets in a panoply of color where one hears families laugh while playing, swimming, or fishing, the grandeur of century old monuments, mosques, synagogues, and churches who call for pause. Her ancient cities, some in ruins, set the mind to roaming with their history and mythology.

The official language is Turkish, but it seems most of the population speaks fluent or passable English. I delighted in their love of things American. I have yet to find friendlier people.

Religion plays a great part in their lives with 99% being practicing Moslems.

Tourism is one of the main sources of revenue.

I felt as safe in Turkey as in any country I have traveled. From Istanbul down the coast to Kas there is a very low crime rate.

Agriculture is another lucrative industry. I was amazed at the freshness and variety of fruits and vegetables.

A perfect meal begins with raki (a drink similar to anisette) mixed with water which is referred to as "lions milk." This is taken with meze (an assortment of hot and cold hors d'oeuvres prepared with different meats, fish, foul, vegetables and rice). The cuisine is similar to French or Chinese.

I must admit breakfast was a bit difficult to become accustomed to. The typical fare is olives, tomatoes, cucumbers, feta cheese, bread, hard-boiled eggs and Turkish coffee.

The famous Turkish baths (public bath houses or hamman) date back to medieval times. I had two while in Turkey. There are separate facilities for men and women. My first experience was a bit unsettling, more because of a brusque attendant than the ritual. (Kadinlar Hamami on Capanoglu Sokagi - Turkish Bath for Ladies). My second one was at the Cirogen Palace Hotel and was wonderful! You disrobe, wrapping a towel around yourself, then enter a room and lay on a large heated stone. When you have perspired the required amount of time, the attendant takes something similar to a loofa and rubs your body down. Intermittently, the attendant throws cool water from a metal bowl over you. This is followed by a shampoo. If you really want the complete treatment, ask for the Sultans Delight. You will not be sorry.

Tourists will find good buys on carpets, copper, silver and onyx jewelry, embroidery, suede and leather, as well as native handicrafts.

How will you ever be the same after you have visited the shrine of the Virgin Mary which was her last home. Christ, before he died, asked St. Paul to take her here and tend to her. Or after you have climbed to the top of the summit where the enormous Temple of Artemis, (the Golden Goddess), built in 3 B.C. once stood (numbered amongst one of the seven wonders of the ancient world) or walked the marble streets in Etes, or taken a moonlight swim in the Dardanelles as the phosphorescent waters danced about you, or tied a piece of cloth to the wishing tree at the Temple of Athena, Goddess of Love, or dived the world's oldest known intact Bronze Age shipwreck.

I suggest you begin your visit in Istanbul once called Constantinople. At one time, Constantinople and Rome were the two greatest capitals of the Western World.

Today, Istanbul is the commercial center of the Turkish Republic.

Ciragen Palace by Wendy Canning Church

Since 1910, there has been a constant migration from rural to urban. It has one foot in the past and one in the present. Towering office buildings, new 5 star hotels and couture boutiques live in harmony with small wooden structures, houses in the 18th century, they are now small guest hotels.

The Grand Bazaar covers 5 acres. Under its roof are 4,000 small shops. Here it is a sin not to bargain. It is approached from a street filled with shops catering to lovers of haute couture.

There are small, intimate native restaurants nested near those of 4 and 5 star caliber.

Istanbul is similar to Sydney, Australia as much of daily life revolves around the water. Commuters take ferries to and from work. Many of these go from the Asian to the European side across the Bosphorus Strait. In Istanbul Europe meets Asia either by ferry or the Galata bridge.

The itinerary was planned for me by Orion Travel. The Turkish Department of Tourism (821 U.N. Plaza, New York, New York, 10017, Telephone 212-687-2194, Fax 212-599-7568) was of great assistance with hotels in Kas and Bodrum. They sent me reams of information.

Awakening early, we set out for the old-city, visiting the Hippodrome. In Byzantine times, this was the center of cultural events and the very popular chariot races. The entire edifice was surrounded by columns and statues. Today, only three of these remain. Look for them: the obelisk of Theodosius, the bronze serpentine column and the column of Constantine.

Next we visited the Museum of Turkish and Islamic Art originally built as a private residence by Ibrahim Pasa. It is said to have been the most opulent private house in the Ottoman Empire. The museum houses some of the oldest carpets in Turkey, a collection of textiles, ceramics, metalwork, miniatures and calligraphy. Take special notice of the architecture. The beautiful high ceilings for ventilation, enormous fireplaces for heating and cooking and the exquisite woodwork throughout.

We walked across the boulevard to the Blue Mosque. The Blue Mosque is famous for its delicate blue ceramic tiles. We visited Saint Sophia across the street. This church-

Trojan Horse in Troy by Wendy Canning Church

turned mosque-turned museum takes one's breath away with the sheer size of its interior and its magnificent dome. We visited the spectacular Topkapi Palace, built on one of the seven hills of Istanbul. This huge complex commands views of the Sea of Marmata, the Bosphorus and the Golden Horn. It was the seat of government for the Ottoman Empire for many centuries (1453-1852).

The following morning started with a visit to the aromatic Spice Bazaar, where the smells of cinnamon, cloves and thyme rise from colorful muslin bags at every store-front. We then boarded our ferry boat for a relaxing cruise along the shores of the legendary Bosphorus, the natural gateway that divides Asia and Europe. As you sit back and enjoy Turkish coffee or well-brewed tea from traditional small cups, summer palaces and palatial homes pass by on either side. Disembarking at the northern end of the Strait, we proceeded to a restaurant for a tasty meal of local fish. We traveled by car to the Suleymaniye Mosque, built by master architect Sinan during the reign of Sultan Suleyman the Magnificent, the Lawgiver. The last stop was the Grand Bazaar which is a most attractive shopping center and the biggest "souk" in the world with nearly 4,000 shops.

On our third day we began our trip to Canakkale. It's best to have a car with air conditioning in the summer. There is only a two lane highway with a speed limit of 140 kilometers per hour (around 85 m.p.h.). Take your time. About one half hour out of Istanbul the pace begins to slow and another Turkey shows its face.

We passed well-tended farms with many varieties of fruits and vegetables, miles of sunflowers grown for the seeds, and small ranches with cattle, goats and donkeys. The houses are small and built with mud and sticks.

> **The countryside opened up to us and we climbed into the mountains with breathtaking views of the sea and descended through acres and acres of olive groves.**

We stopped along the way for water and gas or a sandwich and coffee. You see very few women and the cafes are filled with men.

> **There in the countryside they still lead a life of century old customs.**

> **We began our scenic drive down to Gallipoli, historically famous for being the site of many battles during WWI.**

Following a lunch break, we crossed the second strategic waterway, the Dardanelles, and landed in Asia and proceeded to Troy or Canakkale. Referred to in Homer's "Iliad" and "Odyssey," Troy is in fact nine cities superimposed one upon another.

> **Troy VI pertains to the famous Trojan War of Homer where the legendary heroes included Agamemnon, Achilles, Ulysses and Nestor on the Greek side, and Priam, Hector and Paris on the Trojan side.**

We checked into the Hotel Tusanin Canakkale for the evening which I thought was a good choice. Simple, comfortable, on the sea, with excellent cuisine.

On our journey to Izmir we stopped by the hauntingly beautiful Pergamon. Among the impressive structures of this city, dating from 399 BC., we saw the Altar of Zeus, Temple of Dionysus and the 200,000 volume library which was surpassed only by the one found in Alexandria. The Asclepieum of Pergamon was a famous health center where methods of treatment included blood transfusions, music therapy, and meditation. Leaving Pergamon behind, we settled at the Hilton in Izmir. It has all the modern amenities. Lovers of gambling will delight in the casino where all attendants are dressed as cowboys and cowgirls. Free drinks and cigarettes are offered, and American music is played.

Dancing Bear by Wendy Canning Church

The old section of Izmir called Kadife Kale was a bastion built by Alexander the Great when he moved the city to this commanding location over the Bay of Izmir. Heading further south, we arrived at the ancient city of Ephesus and visited the Basilica of St. John, who came here with the Virgin Mary and wrote his Gospel. To the southwest of the Basilica stands the Isa Bey Mosque and further in the same direction is the Temple of Artemis, another of the seven wonders of the ancient world. Ephesus was one of the most important cultural centers of the ancient world. Impressive structures included the Library of Celsius, Temple of Hadrian, and the Theatre and Odeon. We also visited the Museum of Seljuk.

Close by is the House of the Virgin Mary where she is believed to have spent her last years. On August 18, 1961, Pope John XXII proclaimed the House of the Virgin Mary at Ephesus sacred.

You can take a phial of Holy Water from the Sacred Spring.

We left early and journeyed to Priene which is a fine example of an ancient city, that dates back to the 10th century BC. Highlights include the Temple of Athena Polias, the Ecclesiasterium and the Agora. We next visited Miletus where the Philosopher Thales was born. He coined the phrase "Know Thyself." We inspected the Delphinion, Baths of Faustina and the Council Chamber. Our last visit was to Didyma which served as a religious sanctuary to the god Apollo. The oracular inscriptions date as far back as 600 BC. Among the highlights are the Temple of Apollo and the Stadium.

Bodrum

We proceeded down the Southwest Coast to the Bodrum Peninsula where the Mediterranean meets the Agean. In Bodrum I began my exploration of Turkey's underwater life.

We drove through the steep mountain ranges and at intervals caught glimpses of the sea which seems to stretch to infinity.

On the outskirts of Halinarnassu (Bodrum) as it was called in the 4th century BC. (the birthplace of Heredotus, where the tomb of King Mausolus was built in the 4th century and considered another of the seven wonders of the ancient world), we began to get a feeling for the town.

White washed, sun bleached houses dot the lush green hillside where orange and tangerine orchids grow. Boats in the harbor appear as miniature models bobbing up and down, fanned by the gentle warm breezes.

On the other slope we caught a glimpse of new high rise apartment houses and villas of modern design. These were a sign to us that our little secret was no secret. Bodrum has been found and has started to develop into a major tourist center. Yet as we became more familiar with it, our fears were slightly calmed, for it is a community of artists that dwell here.

Motif Dive Center was the facility I chose to dive with. They offer a dive stay package in a comfortable, hotel right on Gumbet Bay. The Antique Theatre Hotel was highly recommended to me, and as the car pulled into the driveway, I knew I had chosen correctly.

The Hotel is perched high on a hill with a panoramic view of all of Bodrum. Rooms are approached by sun washed, stucco steps with bougainvillea in all their glorious color running along the sides, giving off a wonderful scent. My room was comfortable and large, with adequate bath, and air conditioning. The windows were shuttered against the mid-day sun. I opened mine and discovered my own terrace awash in plantings.

The view from my window was postcard perfect. I could take in all from my private little terrace, the guest rooms on separate levels, the turquoise pool, beautiful small villas fitting snugly in the lush and colorful ledges and the calm bay with all matter of vessels from fishing boats to luxury yachts.

The 15th century medieval castle of St. Peter, built by the Knights of Rhodes and now the Museum of Underwater Archeology lay in the distance.

After unpacking I met Catherine Woods, a delightful Canadian lady from *Motif Divers*, who became a good friend. She checked my certification card, log book and medical form and told me about the center and our schedule.

Every diver in Turkey is covered by insurance which is rolled into the price of their dive. No one is allowed to dive or get their tank filled without presenting a recognized certification card and log book. They cannot dive without a guide.

All divers and snorkelers are picked up and delivered to their respective hotels free of charge.

The next morning, bright and early, Catherine was at the hotel in the minivan. We made our way to the Bay of Gumbet where our ship the Viking was docked. She is a 55 foot replica of the ancient ships. A woody, built in 1986 and to my eye, more of a yacht than a dive boat. Simply, she is beautiful, comfortable and roomy; adequate for a day's outing or long charter.

These Bodrum built Gullets are exact replicas of the ancient ships except for the modern amenities of galley and head. They are built locally at one of three yards which have been in existence for centuries. The ships have pointed bow, broad beam and rounded stern, making them especially comfortable. During the Gulf War when tourism was off they sold for $8,500.

The Viking leaves her berth at 10 A.M. and returns at 4:30. The site dived or snorkeled depends on sea conditions. There are numerous sites on the Viking's roster.

After reaching the site, the vessel is moored, the dive plan given and divers and snorkelers from all corners of the globe suit up. The ratio of diver to guide is 1 to 4. There is a lead guide and a follow up guide.

One of the great features of the yacht is the ladder Zeki (part owner) de-signed. It is stationary so a diver can enter the boat fully equipped (sans fins of course).

We moored that day off (Karaada) *Black Island* which is about 1/2 hour from Gumbet Bay. There were small swells and the visibility was 75 feet.

Antique Theater Hotel, Bodrum by Nusin Brown

Even though it was August and the temperature was 100 degrees Fahrenheit and the water was 85 degrees, there were cold rushes of current at spots throughout the dive. This occurred on every dive. At first I laughed when I saw the crew put on heavy wet suits, gloves and hoods. Believe me, after a day or two I didn't think it hilarious.

We entered the water and slowly descended to the reef. Leveling off at 60 feet where we began to investigate the territory. There was a giant grouper who was king of the reef. Different species of wrasse swam by. There were many caves and tunnels to investigate. Seals used to live in them but the great number of divers drove them away.

Ascending slowly we made our way along the wall. I marveled at the beautiful sea pans. I had never seen these before. They are tube like and had the most beautiful bright pink flowers. When you touched the flower, it receded back inside.

On the bottom we spotted pieces of amphora. At closer range we could see the inscription on the inside. It looked as if these were all parts of larger vessels. What a wonder to see and feel an object of art and beauty thousands of years old.

There were sea urchins, octopus, moray eels and starfish. The wall was ablaze of orange coral in all different hues. Bottom time up, we ascended, made a safety stop and reboarded.

Guney Ucu, our second site, was on the opposite side of Black Island. We dropped down to a grassy area and swimming further on came to a sandy bottom and the reef, resplendent in all colors were sponges and hard and soft coral. We made our way to the wall which was covered in peacock weed. Small tunnels and caves turned out to be hiding places for huge sea urchins. Small multicolored reef fish, wrasse and bleeny swam by. A bright green moray eel pushed out, seemed bored, and tucked its head back in. On this dive we came across beautiful bright orange sea pans. Average visibility was 80 feet.

The second day we sailed to *Little Reef* right off the Bay of Gumbet. A deep dive at 90 feet maximum. The interesting feature of the dive was the topography. The reef had a wall all around it like a ledge. The Aussies call it a Bombie. Water was quite cold at this depth. We did see large groupers, crayfish, played with an octopus at the end of the dive and then slowly ascended. The current and swells picked up so we pulled anchor and headed for Gorecik Island.

These waters were calm and crystal clear, good for both divers and snorkelers.

This is the site of many wrecks. Greek galleons and Turkish merchant ships would come around the corner from the other side of the island not knowing about the treacherous reef – their ships would be broken like match sticks.

There were huge black sponges, hollow in the middle with broken shells and pebbles inside. We spotted many pieces of amphora, surely the last remnants of those unfortunate ships that met their end on the reefs.

Amphora – Motif Dive Center

This is a good site for beginners and snorkelers and a good place for a night dive. The seas are calm which makes for stable anchorage.

On our third day our routine changed. It was Monday and it seems every Monday in summer a group of Scandanavians book a group for resort courses. We took two boats for we had 25 people for the resort course and three scuba divers. We would return to Black Island and dive at Kagakgi Kouv. Because we had so many resort course divers and because Zeki by now had assessed my level of diving, he suggested all three certified divers go off on their own.

There were slight swells but no current and we were moored in a very shallow protected cove. We decided to swim out to a further depth and descend to 80 feet to check out the wall. Despite the slight swells, once under water we had good visibility. There were few fish but the topography once again was quite interesting.

We descended to a sandy bottom laden with orange starfish and swam along coming to a nice wall with hundreds of little ledges. To our surprise, the more we looked, the more little critters and sea life we found hiding in them, i.e., lots of shrimp. Sea pans covered the walls and they were now in varying shades of pink and orange. A baby octopus came out to play.

Motif's motto is "Our Promise Safety Enjoyment Service".

All of this is true of them. If I may, I would like to add one, "New Friendships".

For those of you who want to take time off from diving, Bodrum offers many alternatives. For the shopper there are boutiques, small shops with handmade crafts and little booths down the alleys by the marina. There are many little cafes, bars, and discos as well as elegant water-side dining.

Do not leave without a visit to the Museum of Underwater Archaeology.

For information on diving or chartering at Bodrum with Motif Dive Centre contact DEI; 37 West Cedar Street, Boston, MA 02114.

We left Bodrum and continued down the Southwest coast towards the small town of Kas (pronounced Kash).

It seemed the deeper we drove into the countryside, the more modern architecture and customs faded away. Houses constructed in the same centuries old fashion were visible throughout our journey. Donkeys were used by many to transport themselves and goods from village to village. The fields were tilled and plowed using cattle. The preponderance of women were dressed in black from head to toe.

The countryside is exceedingly lovely with forested hillsides harboring remote villages awash in the colors of nature's fruits, flowers and vegetation. All this interspersed by ancient ruins.

Some time later, we arrived in the small town of Kas known in ancient times as Antiphillos, it's meaning "across from Phellos."

The remains of the Lycian culture can

Stone anchor from wreck of Uluburum, Kas
by Don Frey

Aqua Park Hotel, courtesy of Aqua Park Hotel

today be seen in the form of ruins in sarcophagi, rock tombs, cisterns, ancient inscriptions and an open air theatre.

Out of town, high in the hills, the Aqua Park Hotel is a wonderful complex of accommodations. Here you can in-dulge in the sun and serenity only 5 km away from all the activities of town. The hotel runs a complimentary shuttle bus all day and into the evening to Kas. The positioning of the hotel is such that it lies on a sloping area and you have breathtaking views of the Mediterranean, and Turkish and Greek islands just off the shore.

I had one of the 31 apartment rooms which are large and spacious, fully air conditioned, with well equipped kitchen, terrace with sea view, satellite T.V. and direct dial telephone.

If one were not a scuba diver they would probably spend most of their vacation at the hotel (with side trips into town) for the Aqua Park Hotel is a complete resort.

It has a 400 sq. mt. swimming pool, children's pool, waterfall, pool bar, B.B.Q., beach bar, disco, mini market, fitness room, billiards, games room, table tennis, and a 103m water slide. I found the food to be excellent. Every morning there was a bountiful buffet with a delicious variety of foods. The service was excellent and executed with warmth and charm. Apartments have daily maid service. There are also 39 standard rooms bringing the hotel units to 70. The new manager, Abdullah Bayrak, is seen throughout the hotel, making sure that all is in tip top shape for his guests.

My three days diving and snorkeling on the site of the *Uluburun* prohibited me from doing much diving off Kas but I really wanted to check out *Barakuda Club*. I called owner Ugur Eroghu, a CHAS, 2 star instructor, to book a dive. Their dive boats go out at 9:30, 12, 3 and 4:30. Each trip offers a one tank dive.

We met at 9:30 at the dock in Kas the next morning where one of the two boats (The Barracuda) Ugur and his wife, Gabrielle, operate. The craft is well suited for diving. She is 16 meters long, 5 wide with a 210 horsepower engine.

She can carry a maximum of 25 divers at a good clip to the more than 15 dive and snorkeling sites offered along the coast or near one of the islands lying offshore.

The vessel is coast guard approved, has a radio, loran, carries a backboard, first aid kits, oxygen supply and a blood pressure monitor. Our dive and snorkel site that morning was the **Flying Fish II**, about 1/2 hour from the marina.

We headed toward the reef, descending to a maximum of 30 meters (90 ft.), then make our way over to the wall and were back at the boat with no less than 500 PSI (50 Bar). The seas were calm with average visibility of 90 feet. The slight current carried Ugar and I over the reef where we investigated blue snails (without shells), lobsters and two moray eels. We drifted along the wall which was really beautiful, bedecked in all colors of anemones.

A special highlight of the dive was a broken amphora which we both lovingly picked up. To our elation, its parts fit together perfectly. We placed them back very gingerly.

It was time to return to the boat and as we did, a school of larger grouper swam by leading our way.

Aboard, delicious hot apple tea (a favorite drink in Turkey) was ready for us. This was welcomed, for as I have told you, the waters are cold in Turkey even in August.

As we cruised home, a watermelon was cut and offered along with cold drinks.

I would book an apartment at the Aqua Park, take advantage of their shuttle to Kas, and dive with Barakuda. The town is bustling both day and night and it's great to have the serenity of Aqua Park to return to.

Do take some time and investigate the little town.

They sell local handicrafts and practical goods ... it's similar to a flea market. There are also little grocery shops, small bakeries and little "delis", and innumerable restaurants. I marveled at the beautiful jewelry more valued for its workmanship than gems. The cost was embarrassingly little and if you leave Turkey without buying a carpet, you will regret it.

Perhaps now you have some idea why I left Turkey with the feeling it had been one of my best trips. I was sad to leave this wonderful town of Kas.

Many thanks to the Director of Tourism, Ferhat Moilcan for his help and that of his staff. The office in the middle of Kas is small, but they offer a wealth of information both written and oral.

I arrived at The Ciragan Palace in Istanbul very late in the evening. But despite the hour, all at the front desk greeted me in a very warm and friendly manner with just the right air of professionalism, living up to the five star Kempinski Hotel chain standards.

My room overlooked the Bosphorus and to my right I had a wonderful view of the Palace.

The hotel is linked to the historical Ciragan Palace. A Palace worthy of the world of Scheherazade, brilliant white marble facade, classic Ottoman architecture, international flair, Ciragan pronounced Shi-ra-gan is Turkish for "torches." For torches once illuminated the Palace so extravagantly that they named it Ciragan Palace, "Palace of The Torches."

The Palace dates back to the 16th century and was destroyed many times. Completely refurbished in the 1990's, it gives guests all the luxurious modern amenities while at the same time keeping its historical integrity. Downstairs you will find a grand ballroom and conference rooms. Upstairs, a handful of luxurious suites.

General Manager, Willi Dietz, runs a tight ship. The lovely and charming Oya Batuk, Public Relations Manager, sees that both royalty and guest alike have their stay perfectly orchestrated, whether for banquet, conference, or vacation.

Every service is available, 24 hour room service, valet, hairdresser, Turkish bath, shopping gallery, a casino, business service, wonderful small and large restaurants serving fine cuisine and vintage wines. The only word I can think of is Indulgence. Do indulge yourself for one night or many nights, whatever your pocketbook allows. This is a perfect way to begin or end your trip to Turkey.

Sarcophagus, Kas courtesy of Aqua Park Hotel

In the morning awaken early, as the sun is rising over the Bosphorus. Take in both the view of the Asian and European sides, don your swim suit

and go to the large beautiful pool which looks as if it's waters run right into the sea. Have a leisurely breakfast beside the pool among the exquisite plantings, know that at that moment your being is both in the past and in the present. Then promise yourself, "One day I will return."

Editor's Note Please see chapter on Seven Underwater Wonders of the World for Bill Charlton's story on the Ulubrun. My invitation to visit the site for three days and dive her was probably the greatest honor any sport diver could receive since those schooled in underwater archaeology are hand-picked to work this dig. Texas A&M is grateful for contributions or membership to sponsor projects worldwide.

SCUBA AND SNORKELING FACILITIES QUESTIONNAIRE

NAME **Zeki Arslan - Motif Diving Center**
ADDRESS **Neyzen Tevfik Cad. no: 80**
Bodrum, Turkey
CONTACT **Zeki Arslan**
TITLE **Owner**
TELEPHONE **614-62997** Home; Work: **614-66252** FAX **614-63522**

CAPITAL: **Ankara** GOVERNMENT: **Democratic**
POPULATION: **70 million** LANGUAGE: **Turkish**
CURRENCY: **Turkish Lira** ELECTRICITY: **220v**
AIRLINES: **Delta** DEPARTURE TAX?
NEED VISA/PASSPORT? YES **x** NO PROOF OF CITIZENSHIP? YES **x** NO

YOUR FACILITY IS CLASSIFIED AS: SCUBA CENTER **x** RESORT
BUSINESS HOURS: **10:00 a.m. - 5:00 p.m.**
CERTIFYING AGENCIES: **PADI, CMAS**
LOG BOOK REQUIRED? YES **x** NO
EQUIPMENT: SALES RENTALS **x** AIR FILLS **x**
PRIMARY LINE OF EQUIPMENT: **Scubapro, Cressi-sub, Spiral**
PHOTOGRAPHIC EQUIPMENT: SALES RENTALS LAB

CHARTER/DIVE BOAT AVAILABLE? YES **x** NO DIVER CAPACITY **25**
COAST GUARD APPROVED? YES **x** NO CAPTAIN LICENSED? YES **x** NO
SHIP TO SHORE? YES **x** NO LORAN YES NO RADAR? YES NO
DIVE MASTER/INSTRUCTOR ABOARD? YES **x** NO BOTH **x**

DIVING & SNORKELING: SALT **x** FRESH
TYPE OF DIVING/SNORKELING IN AREA: WALL **x** BEACH WRECK REEF **x** CAVE **x** ICE
DIVING/SNORKELING IN YOUR AREA IS BEST SUITED FOR: BEGINNER INTERMEDIATE ADVANCED
BEST TIME OF YEAR FOR DIVING/SNORKELING: **May - October**
TEMPERATURE: **NOV-APRIL: 80 F** **MAY-OCT: 100 F**
VISIBILITY: **DIVING: 100 FT** **SNORKELING: 50 FT**

PACKAGES AVAILABLE: DIVE DIVE STAY **x** SNORKEL SNORKEL-STAY
ACCOMMODATIONS NEARBY: HOTEL **x** MOTEL HOME RENTALS
ACCOMMODATION RATES: EXPENSIVE **x** MODERATE **x** INEXPENSIVE
RESTAURANTS NEARBY: EXPENSIVE **x** MODERATE **x** INEXPENSIVE **x**
YOUR AREA IS: REMOTE QUIET WITH ACTIVITIES LIVELY **x**
LOCAL ACTIVITY/NIGHTLIFE: **Wide variety**
CAR NEEDED TO EXPLORE AREA? YES **x** NO
DUTY FREE SHOPPING? YES **x** NO

LOCAL EMERGENCY SERVICES NEAREST HYPERBARIC TREATMENT FACILITY
COASTGUARD: AUTHORITY: **Ali Erkal**
TELEPHONE: **VHF** LOCATION: **Bodrum**
CALLSIGNS: **Channel 16** TELEPHONE: **614-61143/62491 F: 614-62492**

LOCAL DIVING DOCTOR:
NAME: **Sezgin Gokmen**
LOCATION: **Bodrum**
TELEPHONE: **614-62385**

SCUBA AND SNORKELING FACILITIES QUESTIONNAIRE

NAME   Barakuda Diving Center (Gabi 2 Ugur Eroglu)
ADDRESS   PK 55
        Kas/Antalya/Turkey
CONTACT
TITLE
TELEPHONE   242/8362987   FAX   242-8362997

CAPITAL:	Ankara	GOVERNMENT:	Turkish Republic (T.C.)
POPULATION:	Turkish	LANGUAGE:	Turkish
CURRENCY:	Turkish Lira	ELECTRICITY:	220v
AIRLINES:	Thy, Istanbul Airlines	DEPARTURE TAX?	
NEED VISA/PASSPORT?	YES x NO	PROOF OF CITIZENSHIP?	YES NO

YOUR FACILITY IS CLASSIFIED AS: SCUBA CENTER x   RESORT
BUSINESS HOURS: Everyday
CERTIFYING AGENCIES: CMAS
LOG BOOK REQUIRED?   YES x   NO
EQUIPMENT: SALES   RENTALS x   AIR FILLS x
PRIMARY LINE OF EQUIPMENT: Scubapro
PHOTOGRAPHIC EQUIPMENT: SALES   RENTALS   LAB

CHARTER/DIVE BOAT AVAILABLE?   YES x   NO   DIVER CAPACITY   25
COAST GUARD APPROVED?   YES x   NO   CAPTAIN LICENSED?   YES x   NO
SHIP TO SHORE? YES x   NO   LORAN   YES x   NO   RADAR?   YES   NO
DIVE MASTER/INSTRUCTOR ABOARD?   YES x   NO   BOTH x

DIVING & SNORKELING: SALT x   FRESH
TYPE OF DIVING/SNORKELING IN AREA: WALL x   BEACH x   WRECK x   REEF x   CAVE x   ICE
DIVING/SNORKELING IN YOUR AREA IS BEST SUITED FOR: BEGINNER x   INTERMEDIATE x   ADVANCED x
BEST TIME OF YEAR FOR DIVING/SNORKELING:
TEMPERATURE: **NOV-APRIL:**   Closed F   **MAY-OCT:**   20-28 C
VISIBILITY: **DIVING:**   40 Mtr   **SNORKELING:** 50 FT

PACKAGES AVAILABLE: DIVE x   DIVE STAY   SNORKEL   SNORKEL-STAY
  ACCOMMODATIONS NEARBY: HOTEL x   MOTEL   HOME RENTALS
ACCOMMODATION RATES: EXPENSIVE   MODERATE x   INEXPENSIVE x
RESTAURANTS NEARBY: EXPENSIVE   MODERATE x   INEXPENSIVE x
YOUR AREA IS: REMOTE   QUIET WITH ACTIVITIES x   LIVELY
LOCAL ACTIVITY/NIGHTLIFE: Live music, bars, few discos
CAR NEEDED TO EXPLORE AREA?   YES x   NO   But minibuses are inexpensive and go everywhere
DUTY FREE SHOPPING?   YES x   NO

LOCAL EMERGENCY SERVICES   NEAREST HYPERBARIC TREATMENT FACILITY
COASTGUARD: 3226-^^ 85   AUTHORITY: Deco-Chamber Ulu-Burun
TELEPHONE: LOCATION: Deco-Chamber Bodrum
CALLSIGNS: On ship, radar   TELEPHONE: Deco-Chamber Istanbul

LOCAL DIVING DOCTOR:
NAME: Dr. Aydin
LOCATION: Kas, Turkey
TELEPHONE: 3226-^20^

UNITED STATES

Alaska

Hal Livingston

Born in Colorado Springs, Colorado in 1932, Hal did not find himself in Alaska until he arrived as a freshman at the University of Alaska. He graduated in 1956 with a B.S. Geology, He then served as a U.S. Army Engineer at Fort Belvoir, VA from 1956-1958. Hal has also completed graduate Geology courses at the University of Ann Arbor, MI.

Hal then returned to Alaska where he was self employed from 1959- 1962. Since 1962 he has worked as an Engineering Geologist.

Hal Livingston was certified in 1984, and since has done over 100 dives in Alaska and Hawaii. He has been married (to the same woman) for over forty years and has four grown sons, three are certified divers.

His other hobbies include hunting big game to feed his family, fishing, gardening, mushroom hunting, and flaking arrowheads. His avocation is Commercial Beekeeping and he has 40+ colonies in Alaska and Hawaii.

Snorkeling in Alaskan waters is restricted to a fairly narrow zone near the shore, because of the many deep glacially carved fjords. The zone that is shallow enough to snorkel is only 10 to 200 feet wide.

Whittier

Diver's Cove, also called **Smitty's Cove**, is a popular training spot where many new divers are certified each year. These divers come primarily from Anchorage and Fairbanks and enjoy the varied diving in the cove along the south coast of the glacial fjord. Depths range from 15 feet to more than 100 feet, although most diving takes place in the 15 to 50 foot range. Winter diving provides the best visibility. Temperatures range in the low 50's during the summer and can drop down to 38 degrees Fahrenheit during the winter.

Some divers use quarter inch wetsuits, but drysuits are more popular. Diver-placed underwater destinations include several fishing boats and an airplane. Diving air is not available locally.

Juneau

Two popular dive destinations are the **Sophia** and the **Princess Kathleen**; both early shipwrecks in water ranging from 30 to 190 feet. The local wharf is popular with divers looking for old bottles.

Many dive sites are accessible out of Juneau including **Sitka, Tenake Springs, Funter Bay** and others. Air for diving is available in Juneau and Sitka.

Valdez

Local diving ranges from the mud bottom at RV Point, also called **Salmon Point**, where lost lures are sometimes an objective, to **the Ferry Dock**, where china is sometimes found. Depths at the Ferry Dock range from 30 feet near shore to more than 100 feet a short distance out. The rocky bottom descends steeply to depths most divers avoid, so take precaution when diving this spot.

The small boat harbor should be avoided because of the number of boats people live on year round. Traffic is busy here and the plain mud bottom with its effluent is not a fun place to dive.

Diver with fish by Jim Jones

Many of the best dive spots are accessible by boat just few miles away in Prince William Sound. **Galena Bay, Rocky Point,** and other locations are remote, and visited infrequently - except by a few fishermen, bears and eagles.

Beaver Sports in Valdez has dive air and gear.

INTERIOR LAKES AND RIVERS

Limited diving does take place in the clear water streams of the Fairbanks area. The Chatanika and Chena Rivers are less than 8 feet deep, and are snorkeled. Some of the deeper stretches are dived by recreational divers looking for lost fishing lures. A few places in these rivers have been scoured carefully by divers hoping to find gold nuggets - none have been reported. **Birch, Harding and Quartz Lakes** are all dived to some extent, as is the largest artificial water body near Fairbanks, the **Chena Lakes Recreation Area**

The lakes range from 40 to 140 feet deep, most have mud bottoms and have the best visibility during Spring and Fall before the thermocline develops. Visibility goes to 6 inches or less below the well-developed thermocline layer, which usually forms at about 8 feet.

Artic Fire Supply and the local dive club members can supply diving air. **Beaver Sports** carries dive gear as do some of the other sporting goods stores, but the latter have less of a selection.

Denali Sports in Wasilla, 40 miles north of Anchorage, carries dive gear and air. There are several sporting goods stores in Anchorage that carry dive gear and a few supply air as well.

> **Because of the limited road access in the state, many of the diveable marine waters are inaccessible except to the lucky few who have boats or can afford to rent them. It pays to befriend fishermen by offering to retrieve lost tools, anchors and other small jobs in return for a ride to dive sites.**

Chartering boats to dive destinations like **Kodiak Island** for king crabs is challenging because of the need to carry numerous air tanks and coolers in addition to routine dive gear.

The range of marine life in Alaskan waters is wide and wondrous; the 3 foot white anemones at Galena Bay, the octopus of many colors at Whittier, the abalone and bay scallops near Sitka, the ribbon kelp of Diomeda Island, the king crabs of Kodiak, the many bright-colored nudibranchs widely distributed in most Alaskan waters, and the seals, sea lions, killer whales, gray whales, sea otters to say nothing of the halibut, salmon, cod, and wolf eels.

California

Diving in Los Angeles
Kurt Turner

I grew up in Northern New York State, where I survived several early near drowning accidents. Initial underwater experiences include snorkeling and an attempt at building an underwater breathing apparatus to retrieve soda pop bottles from beneath piers and docks.

I Joined the Navy in 1960 and was introduced to their style of diving in 1964. After 8 years of service I settled in Los Angeles for over 20 years, I am a graduate of Pepperdine University.

Presently, I live in Florida where I am active in the diving community. I hold numerous diving certifications including Instructor Cards from NAUI, and YMCA.

The visitor to Los Angeles will find a wide variety of diving adventures awaiting their pleasure. From the kelp beds of Leo Carrillo State Park to the urchin encrusted reefs of Laguna Beach, the conditions qualify as world class. As is so often the case however, you must know how to get around and where to go. If not, you will come away with the attitude that a lot of good water is going to waste.

Upon arrival at Los Angeles International Airport (LAX), the first problem you face is contending with Southern California geography. If you expect public transportation to fill your needs, you will be setting yourself up for frustration and disappointment.

There is only one way to cope. Get a car.

The Yellow Pages list a wide variety of rental agencies. A phone call to one of them from the airport lobby will have you on the Freeway in 30 minutes.

Where do you stay? Since Pacific Coast Highway follows the coast line, I would recommend you stay on this route. This will keep you located near the water, and this route is home to many good restaurants. Since you are contemplating dive activity, I recommend renting a motel room. The large hotels do not deal well with wet dive gear in their lobbies. Stay with a national chain such as Holiday Inn, Motel 6, or Best Western. Be sure to ask for a ground floor room. Carrying equipment up several flights of stairs will not improve your disposition.

Cleaners by Rich Cassens

For SCUBA diving purposes, divide the beaches of Los Angeles and Orange counties into two groups. West facing beaches offer good conditions when seas are from the south. South facing beaches are better when the seas are from the west. This places the surf action at an angle to the beach offering easier entry and exit. Don't worry about seas from the north. Due to the shape of the coast, waves never come from the north. Occasionally, there is a hot wind called the Santa Anna that blows from the deserts lying to the east. During these Santa Anna conditions, diving is near perfect. The ocean blows flat and an upwelling begins.

The shape of the coastline gives each beach its unique character.

At the north end the coast follows an east-west direction. This gradually curves to the south as it passes Malibu and Santa Monica resulting in a north-south coastline to Palos Verdes. There it wraps around the cliffs again going east-west through Long Beach. The Long Beach area does not offer diving because the beautiful beach lies within the Federal breakwater. It is illegal to dive on the harbor side of the breakwater. Some locals do dive the ocean side, however, this would be quite foolhardy for the visitor. The caves formed by the large boulders could be very dangerous. After Long Beach, the coast again curves to the south through Laguna Beach. This is a popular west facing diving area. Here the reefs come to within a few feet of the shoreline and offer spectacular underwater conditions.

Initially, consider the south facing beaches. The first of these is in the Malibu area. Go north on the Pacific Coast Highway. After you pass through Malibu and before you get to the Ventura County line, you will see signs for Leo Carrillo State Beach. Parking is plentiful. Next to the parking lot is a broad, sandy, beach. This is a large area offering many entry and exit points. Check in with the lifeguards and seek their advice about the local area.

After entering the water, you notice several large kelp beds on the reefs that run parallel to the shore and out 25 to 50 yards. The depths here are shallow (20 to 35 feet) inside the kelp beds. You should be able to spend all day making 3 or 4 dives without falling off the tables.

Don't go on the outside of the kelp beds as there is a sharp drop off and the rip currents can be unpredictable.

The second South facing beach is White Point near the Eastern end of the Palos Verde Peninsula. The trip begins on Pacific Coast Highway. From there turn south on Western Avenue. Stay on Western Avenue to the coast in San Pedro. Turn right on Paseo Del Mar then again to the right at the entrance to Royal Palms Beach. At the bottom of the hill bend to the left and go as far as you can. You'll see the ruins of a hotel foundation in the water. These ruins are seaward of the rocky beach entry area.

The diving here is shallow. I have been out 1/2 mile and still only found 45 feet of water. If you swim out 1/8 to 1/4 mile, you will have no more than 35 feet.

This is an unique area. Several underwater hot springs spew forth mineral water you will visually notice them first as a patch of black sand.

Position yourself over the patch and you will feel the hot water. Very noticeable in the area are strings of fungus that look like egg whites. They are harmless but quite interesting, as they live on the sulfur from the hot springs. Purple sea urchins cover most of the rocks. There are also some large octopuses. Plan on spending the whole day here and making 3 or 4 dives.

In Los Angeles County there are only two west facing beaches worth mentioning. They can both be done in a single day. The first is Veterans Park in Redondo Beach. Start again from Pacific Coast Highway and turn westbound on Torrance Blvd. This street will dead end at Veterans Park. The parking lot is on the south side and access to the beach is by concrete steps. The bottom drops off quickly. You'll be in 40 feet of water within 75 yards of the beach. It then drops very quickly into the Redondo Canyon. You'll probably see many sheep crabs and a few rays. There are many fish here and some get to be quite large. Pay special attention to the sandy bottom and you'll spot some good size halibut. Plan on making only one dive here. It will be a deep dive, but stay above 90 feet so you'll have time left on the tables at the next site.

Our second west facing location is Malaga Cove, a few miles to the south. Go back to Torrance Blvd. and then turn south on Pacific Coast Highway. Turn south bound on Palos Verdes Drive Vest. As you pass Malaga Cove Plaza, turn right on Via Corta which becomes Via Almar. Turn right on Via Arroyo and as you pass the Malaga Cove school you will be on Paseo Del Mar. You'll see a large parking area with a gazebo on one end. From that vantage point you can see the area quite clearly. To the north is a sandy beach that stretches all the way to Ventura. To the south are the rocks and cliffs of the Palos Verde Peninsula. Suit up in the parking lot and follow the steep path down to the shoreline. This transition point from a flat sandy beach to rocky cliffs is an interesting dive site. Here is a combination of rocks, reefs, and sand. The added kelp bed to provides cover for a variety of aquatic life. On the sandy side you'll probably see some angel sharks near the rocks. In the rocks you'll find lobsters, abalone, and rockfish.

The kelp bed will be home to schooling fish.

These dives will be shallow, 20 to 30 feet. Plan on doing as many as the tables will safely allow.

The remaining West facing beaches are at Laguna Beach located in Orange County. Go south on Pacific Coast Highway and as you enter Laguna Beach look for Fairview Street or Wave Street. A right turn on either one will put you on Cliff Drive, which runs parallel to the ocean. Many well marked sites are available along this street. They are all easily accessible. Although quite similar, each spot has an individual flavor. Sometimes it is difficult to find parking in this area. On weekends it is not uncommon to see a dozen classes. It is for good reason that instructors select these sites. Usually the surf is only 2 or 3 feet, so wave action is negligible. Visibility is between 15 and 30 feet, and there is plenty of beautiful reefscape to enjoy. The bottom terrain includes both rocks and sand with all the attendant creatures. There are numerous gorgonias, nudibranchs, and anemones adorning the rocks. Also in abundance are the ever present Garibaldi, constantly begging the diver to break open a sea urchin which they readily devour.

I would like to offer a word of caution on the taking of game to eat. You will see many legal fish, scallops, lobster, and abalone, but my advice is not to take any. Enjoy them visually. Those that come behind you will be grateful. Furthermore, eating these critters is not a safe practice. The Santa Monica Bay is a dumping area for sewage effluent and over flow. The waters off Palos Verde were a chemical dumping ground for decades. Most notably, DDT and heavy metals lie in the silt leeching their way into the food chain.

A portion of Orange County is a game refuge, but even if legal I wouldn't want to eat anything caught there.

The storm runoff carries all manner of pollution into the ocean. The filter feeders absorb this chemical stew and the food chain becomes polluted. If you wish to eat fresh seafood, go to one of the fine restaurants in the area. They offer a menu of government inspected items that are safe to eat.

The most important step to insure a successful dive boat trip in Southern California is planning the schedule.

This is because you need reservations for anything to do with a boat. They fill up fast. Your primary tool for making a reservation is the publication entitled "Dive Boat Calendar and Travel Guide." It lists the charters by destination, and provides a telephone number to call for your reservation.

Most of the charters in the Los Angeles area operate out of 22nd Street Landing in San Pedro.

This is an excellent facility, recently remodeled and offering plenty of convenient parking. It is easy to find and offers special access to off load passengers and gear. Most of the boats allow you to board the night before. They provide a bunk complete with blanket and pillow. I strongly recommend that you take advantage of this service. Doing so removes all the anxiety of trying to find your way to the dock during the morning commuter rush. You'll wake up to hot coffee after a pleasant sleep, and be able to enjoy the harbor dawn without a care. When you call to make your reservations, get good directions to the dock, and tell then you wish to sleep on board.

Boat diving destinations usually are the Channel Islands with the most common being the "near side" of Catalina Island. This is an excellent choice.

There is a wide variety of dive sites for the captain to choose from. Depths can range from 20 feet to over 100 feet, so use caution in forming your dive plan. If you are lucky enough to catch a boat going to the "back side" of Catalina Island you are in for a real treat. Farnsworth Banks is an advanced site that never fails to deliver some exciting activity. The banks consist of two peaks rising from the ocean floor. One comes to within 60 feet of the surface and the other to 90 feet. The actual depth depends upon the daily sea conditions. These peaks fall off very sharply, straight down in some places. As a result there is the need to monitor depth and bottom time carefully. The peaks exhibit a wide variety of sea life. One worth noting is the purple coral. Also it is not uncommon to see several species of sharks and rays.

Local dive shops are a valuable resource for gaining insight into the current diving scene. They can offer invaluable advice about the conditions at the beach.

It is not unusual for dive conditions to change on a weekly basis. A good shop operator can tell you what is hot on any particular day.

The shops book boat charters, and offer specialty courses that may interest your party. In addition most of them sell copies of the "Dive Boat Calendar and Travel Guide."

While at the shop, inquire about any additional equipment that you may need to buy or rent. In addition to the basics, you will definitely need a wet suit. The minimum is 1/4 inch if cold doesn't bother you. For myself, I use a 3/8 inch complete with hood and gloves. Remember to adjust your weight. Many of the shops have a training pool on their premises. Ask if you can try out the wet suit and get yourself neutrally buoyant. If you are neutrally buoyant in fresh water, add 2.5% of your fully suited weight to your belt. That should be just right for the ocean.

As you contemplate diving in the varied beach areas, you must realize that it is of utmost importance that you have the necessary training. This will add to your enjoyment of the area, and it will enhance your safety. In this regard, you must be comfortable in traversing the surf line.

A very frightening scene is that of inexperienced and untrained divers, caught in a moderate surf. The wave action will toss then about, out of control, and in a state of panic. They will lose equipment and possibly suffer serious injury. Such a disaster is avoidable with a course of instruction in surf diving. To receive the finest instruction, contact the Underwater Instructors Association. The Los Angeles County Department of Parks and Recreation, Underwater Unit, Carson, Ca., will provide a roster. Telephone a couple of the members and be specific in your request. Tell then that you wish to learn how to deal with sandy beach and rocky beach surf. A day of instruction will enable you to enjoy some excellent beach diving in safety and comfort. Most of these instructors are also available for guide service.

Don't overlook the fun of linking up with a local dive club. There are at least two dozen in the area that are very active with monthly boat trips and many beach activities. The mid-week meetings are open to the public.

Potential buddies will swamp you with offers of diving trips, once the members learn you are a visitor. A partial listing of clubs is available in the "Dive Boat Calendar." Take the time to contact one or more of them. You are sure to add some lasting friendships to your diving adventures.

There are many other sites available. For the visitor, however, these few offer the best access and reasonable assurance of good beach diving conditions. Now that I have whetted your appetite for blowing bubbles, make plans to visit some of the finest sites for world class diving. Even if you spend a full two weeks exploring the area, you will only see a small portion of what is available. I guarantee that you will want to return. As you become more familiar with the area, you will discover that it offers an endless variety of conditions. Enjoy them and bring your friends!

San Diego

Richard H. Cassens was born and reared in Glen Cove, Long Island, New York. Growing up within six blocks of the sound, my water experience started as soon as I could walk.

At the age of ten, with mask, snorkel and fins, I discovered that with a spear I could get eels hiding in the grass.

In 1959, at age 14, I made my first Scuba dive. I loved it. The visibility was 10 feet, and the bottom was sand. I still love that dive.

After completing my degree in 1974, I signed on with the U.S. Peace Corps, Finding myself in Jamaica, W.I., where the waters are warm and clear, I resumed free diving.

Returning to the U.S. of A., it was time to get my certification in SCUBA. In 1983 I completed the NAUI Instructors certification course, directed by Mark Flahan, at San Diego State University, San Diego.

Since my instructors course, I have introduced and certified over 350 new divers and over 50 advanced divers. I have also received a U.S. Coast Guard Captains License (100 ton).

After leaving my position as Senior Industrial Engineer, General Dynamics, Convair Division, I started America II, SCUBA Diving Charters in Mission Bay, San Diego.

My current profession is SCUBA Diving Charter Boat Captain, America II, Islandia Sports Fishing Landing, Mission Bay, San Diego, California.

SNORKELING: LA JOLLA, CALIFORNIA.
The following locations are recommended for the Beginners:

Scripps Pier, No. La Jolla   La Jolla Cove
La Jolla Shores   Casa Cove
Marine Room, So. La Jolla

SNORKELING AND SCUBA DIVING:
The following locations are recommended for the experienced Skin and Scuba Divers:

Devils Slides   Casa Cove
La Jolla Cove   Hospital Point (Whale View Point)
Goldfish Point   Horseshoe Reef
Shell Beach   Big Rock Reef

BEACH DIVING THE LA JOLLA AREA
Hospital Point

Note: Beach/Surf experience is a must for this area. Check with the lifeguards for information and conditions. Hospital Point is located off the 300 block of Coast Blvd., La Jolla, San Diego. It is also known locally as Whale View Point. Hospital Point is located between Wipeout Beach to the North and Horseshoe Reef to the South.

317

La Jolla by Rich Cassens

The Hospital Point Reef is made up of sand channels, giant kelp forest and parallel reef structure that extends to a depth of approximately 55 feet. The extensive reef and kelp forest offers the diver a large lobster population, abalone and all forms of kelp life. The reef structure offers the photographer excellent photo opportunities. Whale View Point is a very beautiful dive site. It's well worth the time devoted to learning the area by talking to local divers and the San Diego lifeguard personnel. The more the divers know about the area, the more enjoyable the dive will be. At Hospital Point Reef, care must be taken in getting into and out of the water. Because of the constant surf and slippery moss covered rocks, the divers must be ever alert to conditions of the area.

Casa Cove or also known as "The Children's Pool"

The Children's Pool, depending on conditions of the day, is grand diving for the beginning diver all the way to the most advanced. Always check with the lifeguard on duty for conditions and tips on diving the area. The entry into the ocean is easy because of the rip current, but knowledge of the area is a must for returning to the beach. The lifeguards or local divers will be happy to give you a detailed description of proper technique to exit. It's not hard, but the proper method must be utilized.

> **The Children's Pool offers a variety of vertical reef walls, the giant kelp forest of South California and great varieties of kelp life. The Children's Pool also offers beautiful photo opportunities both in and out of the water.**

Casa Cove is perhaps one of the most popular dive sites in the La Jolla area for both new and "old divers" alike.

> **Because of the variety of reef structure, kelp forest and marine life, it offers the chance to cavort with local sea lions, poke at the resident lobster or be thrilled by the sight of a moray eel.**

The Casa is a varied and diverse diving area.

Sunken Observation Tower off San Diego Wreck Alley provides Oil Rig Style Dive.

Selecting a dive site along the California coast can be difficult – there's just so much to choose from. One favorite site off the coast of Southern California is the N.O.S. sea tower. The tower rests off Mission Beach in San Diego in an area known as Wreck Alley.

Local divers say the sea tower, formerly used as an observation tower, can be compared to an oil rig dive. The tower went down in January, 1988 and rests in 60 to 65 feet of water on the sandy bottom about one half mile offshore.

The rig, approximately 150 feet long, attracts an abundance of marine life to the area, including calico bass, sand bass, and blacksmith. Soft corals, starfish and a multitude of sponges have taken up residence, and an occasional white anemone can be seen.

Giant stars and nudibranchs also abound. Spearfishing is allowed, but divers need to be aware of local regulations and seasons.

Divers say the tower, lying on its side, looks like a big jungle gym covered with corals and growth. The top can be reached at 30 feet, the bottom at 65 feet.

This boat dive is for intermediate to advanced divers. Several local charter boats run out of Mission Bay. It is only a 10 minute boat ride from the dock.

It is possible to dive this area year-round, but the best time is during the fall months of October, November and December when visibility is best. During this time visibility ranges to 40 feet; the rest of the year it averages 20 feet.

For the non-diver and/or for after diving, the San Diego area offers plenty of activities, including visiting SeaWorld, and the Zoo, shopping, sightseeing at local historical sites and sporting events.

Peak Season:	Diving can be done year-round, but the best visibility will be found October through December.
Depth:	Depth ranges from 30 to 65 feet.
Visibility:	During peak season, visibility ranges to 40 feet. The rest of the year, it averages around 20 feet.
Temperature:	Temperature ranges from high 40s to 60 degrees with an average of 55 degrees during peak season.
Bottom Composition:	Sandy, silty bottom.
Restrictions:	Spearfishing is allowed, but a state license is required. Check dive store for local regulations.
Dive Support:	There are several dive stores in the Mission Bay area.
Hazards:	Possible hazards include fishing line and boat traffic. Also divers should be aware of the possibility of surges.

Ten exciting shark dive dates have been booked aboard the dive boat America II in Mission Bay, San Diego.

Divers will be assisted by the professional crew of the America II. The experience and knowledge of the Captain, Rich Cassens, will add to your thrill of a lifetime. 6 divers maximum.

SCUBA AND SNORKELING FACILITIES QUESTIONNAIRE

NAME American II, Scuba Diving Charters
ADDRESS 4010 South Hempstead Circle
San Diego, CA 92116
CONTACT Richard H. Cassens
TITLE Owner/Captain
TELEPHONE 619-584-0742   FAX

CAPITAL: GOVERNMENT: **Democratic**
POPULATION: LANGUAGE: **English**
CURRENCY: **US $**   ELECTRICITY:
AIRLINES: DEPARTURE TAX?
NEED VISA/PASSPORT?   YES   NO **x**   PROOF OF CITIZENSHIP?   YES   NO

YOUR FACILITY IS CLASSIFIED AS: SCUBA CENTER   RESORT **x**
BUSINESS HOURS: **Summer and Winter**
CERTIFYING AGENCIES: **NAUI, Instructor #6973**
LOG BOOK REQUIRED?   YES   NO
EQUIPMENT: SALES   RENTALS **x**   AIR FILLS
PRIMARY LINE OF EQUIPMENT: **Charter, Scuba Diving**
PHOTOGRAPHIC EQUIPMENT: SALES   RENTALS   LAB

CHARTER/DIVE BOAT AVAILABLE?   YES **x**   NO   DIVER CAPACITY **6**
COAST GUARD APPROVED?   YES **x**   NO   CAPTAIN LICENSED?   YES **x**   NO
SHIP TO SHORE? YES **x**   NO   LORAN   YES **x**   NO   RADAR?   YES **x**   NO
DIVE MASTER/INSTRUCTOR ABOARD?   YES **x**   NO   BOTH

DIVING & SNORKELING: SALT **x**   FRESH
TYPE OF DIVING/SNORKELING IN AREA: WALL **x**   BEACH **x**   WRECK **x**   REEF   CAVE   ICE
DIVING/SNORKELING IN YOUR AREA IS BEST SUITED FOR: BEGINNER **x**   INTERMEDIATE **x**   ADVANCED **x**
BEST TIME OF YEAR FOR DIVING/SNORKELING: **October - April**
TEMPERATURE: NOV-APRIL: F   MAY-OCT: F
VISIBILITY: DIVING: FT   SNORKELING: FT

PACKAGES AVAILABLE: DIVE **x**   DIVE STAY   SNORKEL   SNORKEL-STAY
ACCOMMODATIONS NEARBY: HOTEL   MOTEL   HOME RENTALS
ACCOMMODATION RATES: EXPENSIVE   MODERATE   INEXPENSIVE
RESTAURANTS NEARBY: EXPENSIVE   MODERATE   INEXPENSIVE
YOUR AREA IS: REMOTE   QUIET WITH ACTIVITIES **x**   LIVELY **x**
LOCAL ACTIVITY/NIGHTLIFE:
CAR NEEDED TO EXPLORE AREA?   YES   NO
DUTY FREE SHOPPING?   YES   NO

LOCAL EMERGENCY SERVICES   NEAREST HYPERBARIC TREATMENT FACILITY
COASTGUARD: **Coastguard Marine Society Office**   AUTHORITY: **San Diego University Hospital**
TELEPHONE: **619-557-5860**   LOCATION: **San Diego**
CALLSIGNS: **Radio/Marine #16-22, & 23**   TELEPHONE:

LOCAL DIVING DOCTOR:
NAME: **San Diego University Hospital**
LOCATION: **San Diego**
TELEPHONE: **Emergency Medical System 911**

Florida
Crystal Springs

Tom Boyd
Rockfish Productions
10736 Magnolia Boulevard #9
North Hollywood, CA 91601
Phone: 818-985-1736

    Tom Boyd is President of Rockfish Productions, Inc., a video/film production company that produces environmentally themed documentaries. Rockfish recently completed a mini-documentary on the Florida Manatee.
    Before forming Rockfish, Tom managed two dive shops in the Northeast. Tom is a NAUI Open Water Instructor and has been diving for 16 years. His dive experience ranges from New England, New Jersey and New York, throughout the Caribbean and California.

Joseph R. Tatosky
    The enclosed slide is a shot that I took about six years ago at Crystal River. Florida had been hit with three successive hurricanes in a row thus Crystal River was anything but crystal clear. Nonetheless, Tom and I still had a great time due to this one particular manatee that I affectionately named "Murry" after the large nosed character in the Odd Couple sitcom. Murry approached Tom and I and played with us for a solid forty-five minutes. It truly was one of my most memorable experiences.
    The shot was taken in about ten feet of water. A Nikons 5 with a 15mm lens along with two SB103 strobes was used. Settings were full power manual mode F16. Subject distance was about three feet. We were snorkeling due to scuba restrictions in Crystal River and I had to free dive, turn and shoot as the Manatee approached me. What I liked most about this shot was the eye contact that "Murry" made with me and the hazed surroundings (actual visibility) that could be perceived as a fleeting view of a truly endangered species.

    In my 16 years of diving, I'm often asked, why do I dive? Aren't you afraid of sharks? How deep have you gone? I've given a lot of different reasons for being a diver but, I think what draws me to dive most is the sense of adventure it gives. The idea of exploring an alien world and seeing creatures possibly unseen by anyone else. I dive because I want to share the ocean experience with all the different creatures the oceans have living in them; including sharks.
    Recently, I produced a documentary on the Florida Manatee and the need for protecting their precious environment. The documentary was filmed at Crystal River, a dive site that I've been visiting on and off for about 12 years. Crystal River is situated on the west coast of Florida about an hour north of Tampa. I've been a witness to its development and it isn't the sleepy little town it used to be. There is a power plant, plenty of homes and too many boats. Each dive at Crystal River becomes ever more meaningful to me as I'll never be sure if it is to be my last encounter with the manatees.
    The Florida Manatee is probably one of the gentlest creatures in the marine environment. I feel privileged to have been able to dive with them, especially since their survival is doubtful.

I've taken numerous newcomers to encounter a manatee and after snorkeling and diving with them, everyone seems to be wearing a grin and walking on water.

"Murry," Manatee by Joseph R. Tatusky

That's why I dive. I don't believe I'll ever become bored with the feelings of awe when I see something new or am able to make a connection with a marine animal.

Every year between November and March the manatees head into the warm springs of Florida.

Crystal River is one of the main areas that the manatees come to and the only place I know of that you can snorkel/dive with them.

Snorkeling is the preferred way to encounter a manatee as they don't seem to like the noise and bubbles created by scuba gear.

King's Spring is the main spring and is about 30 feet deep, The river itself isn't very deep and around the spring it can be only 8 to 10 feet (plenty of room to enjoy a meeting with a manatee). Be aware there are strict laws governing harassing a manatee, classified as an endangered species. They also have restricted sanctuary areas where no one is allowed so the manatee has a place to get away when it wants to be left alone. If you are lucky enough to have a manatee approach you and initiate contact, enjoy the opportunity to touch its almost leather-like hide (although the authorities prefer you don't). Don't think about grabbing onto or chasing the manatee as there are stiff fines and any decent diver would understand this action could force the manatee into colder waters of the river which is harmful to their health. A word to the wise for divers and snorkelers, due to the large number of boats in the manatee sanctuary areas stay within the area of your dive flag.

Although visibility in the river isn't always crystal you'll know when you are about to have a manatee encounter, they are about 10 feet long and can weigh up to 3,000 pounds.

A month ago, I was shooting some footage of a manatee calf and was having a great time. He seemed to love having his picture taken and I thoroughly enjoyed his company, Wherever I went he kept right along side.

I felt honored to have such a unique friend as a dive buddy.

As we came near the main spring my new friend drifted quite close until a group of inconsiderate divers began to chase him. I knew I had connected with this manatee because as I was shooting this sequence of events, he turned looked at me and decided to beeline to my side keeping distance between him and his undesired pursuers (I will always cherish that footage). Needless to say, the divers weren't happy with the calf's adopted bodyguard but my friend obviously felt safe and the feelings I have are virtually indescribable.

The following quote I discovered while working on the manatee documentary and which I feel could possibly summarize why I dive; my love of shark encounters; sightings of beautifully colored tropical fish; the whales and manatees; and the hope that my manatee buddy will be around for a very long time.

> *"For in the end we will conserve only what we love.*
> *We will love only what we understand.*
> *We will understand only what we are taught."*
> -Baba Dioum: Senegalese Naturalist

The Florida Keys

Beginning writing at age seven, owning his first printing press at nine, Bill Roe was inspired by his grandfather, both a writer and a deckhand aboard the classic windjammers in the pre-turn of the century Merchant Marine.

Being raised around the fishing pier in Deerfield Beach, FL in the late fifties, Bill strengthened his bond with the sea., and learned to SCUBA dive in 1962.

In the early eighties, Bill began writing features and reviews for Florida Scuba News, a Florida Dive Magazine. His travels for the Magazine have taken him throughout the Keys a dozen times each year. Bill expressed happiness when offered the chance to share "his Keys" with D.E.I members and readers.

Still writing and selling advertising for Florida Scuba News Bill and his wife Shirlee have branched out into a typesetting, marketing, and advertising service, Coastal Associates Publishing Services specializing in marketing support for the Dental field (Shirlee's special area of expertise), utilizing Bill's creative writing and advertising background in a field sorely overlooked by the mainstream.

Both divers, Bill and Shirlee travel the state of Florida and the Caribbean.

If you would like to discuss Keys diving, or inquire about Coastal Associates services, call (305) 942-1424.

Photographer, Ron Streeter

With over 30 years experience as a hunter in Northern woods, first with a firearm, then with a camera, he learned that being close to nature, and understanding it, was the only way to photograph it.

Ron made an easy transition to U/W photography back in 1985. Since then, he averages 300 dives a year in search of the perfect shot.

Shooting literally thousands of slides annually as he travels the Keys and the Caribbean, Ron processes each one himself to achieve control of the quality of his work.

Ron uses housed cameras, with a combination of strobes he mixes and matches to get proper light for his photos. Drawing from his long time "real job" as an Electronic Engineer, he often finds himself on the phone to various manufacturers, discussing improvements to these devices.

With thousands of slides on file already, Ron has become his own "stock house", and is in the process of forming one, in conjunction with several other South Florida photographers.

If you have need for some quality underwater shots, or wish to discuss an assignment either topside or below, call him in Ft. Lauderdale at 305-561 8879.

America's Caribbean Island Chain
by Bill Roe

Home to Indians, then Spaniards, wreckers, cutthroats, and thieves from all Nations, the Florida Keys have endured a rich history that predates the landing at Plymouth Rock. Even today it doesn't hurt to have a little pirate in your soul if you live there.

The waters surrounding these islands hold the last great natural coral reef system in the country, the bones of ships and their cargo, some dating back nearly 400 years and an abundance of maritime history. That is where SCUBA diving comes in, and there is plenty of it, as diverse as the island chain itself. In almost 120 miles, the Keys offer different lifestyles in different places, and great diving wherever you go. There are five different areas of the Keys. Each has it's own flavor and uniqueness, both above and below, the water. Those areas are, Key Largo, Tavernier/Islamorada Marathon, the Lower Keys, and of course Key West. These magical isles are linked by the Overseas Highway, also know as U.S. 1. It starts in Fort Kent, Maine and wanders down the country, terminating in Key West. It is "main street" in the Keys.

A pioneering developer and railroad owner, Henry Flagler built a railway down the east coast of Florida. As he went, he would build magnificent hotels for the tourists who rode his trains. His dream was to terminate in the southern most city in Florida, the seaport town of Key West. The majority of the Overseas Highway is laid on the old railroad bed of Flagler's railway after it was washed away in a 1929 hurricane. The original "Seven Mile Bridge" below Marathon was built to carry rail cars before it carried autos.

Most travelers fly into Ft Lauderdale or Miami and drive down from there, although both Marathon and Key West have airports with commercial links. Driving south along Florida's Turnpike until it ends in Florida City, you pick up the Overseas Highway and progress down the "Eighteen Mile Stretch." Eighteen miles of two lane road that has claimed the life and limb of many an impatient driver. This is the ideal time to get into

"Keys Time", a relaxed, unhurried state of mind that slows the pace of life to an island beat.

Although this was the only part of the area actually affected by Hurricane Andrew, you can still see dozens of Osprey nests, perched atop power poles and road signs. In the late winter and early spring, you can see the young sea hawks testing their wings at nests edge. The damage from the storm was largely contained to property in Florida City and to the Australian Pines that line either side of the "stretch". They have been topped and in some places, the little tufts of greenery left after the storm have thrived and add an eerie look to the landscape, almost post apocalyptic.

Lobster by Ron Streeter.

As you near the end of the "stretch" water appears on either side as you ride the ribbon of asphalt between the waters, Key Largo is dead ahead, just past Lake Surprise. Lake Surprise is actually a narrow strip of land that is the first piece of the roadway to flood in a hurricane, (surprise!).

Key Largo is the largest of all the islands in the chain. It boasts John Pennekamp Underwater State Park, and the Key Largo National Marine Sanctuary, as it's neighbors.

Some of the most legendary diving in the country is done around Key Largo. It seems to be the unwritten law in diving, that you HAVE to dive "The Statue" in Pennekanmp park.

French Reef is punctuated with small caves and swim throughs that are often home to clouds of glassy sweepers and other small fish.

Molasses, The Elbow, Carysfort, all beautiful, all served by any and all of the operators.

Besides, there are some other extraordinary experiences to be found beyond the Park boundaries that get much less exposure.

Lodging in Key Largo is varied from rustic campgrounds, to the ubiquitous Mom & Pop roadside motel, to the absolute lap of luxury. For sheer comfort, at a modest price, the Best Western Suites of Key Largo is my favorite. Upstairs master bedroom with a phone, T.V. and private bath, downstairs, a sofa that opens to a queen size bed, separate bath, a full size kitchen, another T.V. and phone. All with a commanding view of the dive boat fleet that twice daily runs out to Pennekamp.

You can also get a glimpse of the original "African Queen" of the classic Bogart/Hepburn movie, ferrying passengers about from her base at the Holiday Inn.

Across the canal is Marina Del Mar, another fine hotel, loaded with night time fun. The view from their rooftop sundeck shows Key Largo in all her splendor unlike any other vantage point on the island. Housed in Marina Del Mar is Ocean Divers, dive shop and Hyperbarics International, where veteran dive instructor and diving pioneer Dick Rutkowski teaches "nitrox" diving.

Nitrox is rapidly coming to the forefront in sport diving discussions today, and is a useful skill to have if you want to take full advantage of diving the Bibb or the Duane, twin Coast Guard cutters, sunk as artificial reefs several years ago. In over 100' of water, just outside Park boundaries, these ships are huge, and nitrox diving can maximize safe bottom time for viewing these awesome wrecks.

You can scuba or swim with the Dolphins Plus, advance reservations are required though. This little known attraction does have a waiting list at times.

Restaurants are not in short supply, the bill of fare is wide, but through out the Keys, seafood is clearly the mainstay. Senior Frioles', offers great Mexican food and a great sunset view.

For a neat yet out of the way waterfront dining experience, try Snappers, a little south of Key Largo proper. As you leave the main business district, heading toward Tavernier, notice the beautiful three-story mural on your left that welcomes you to the Keys and then lets keep heading down.

> **Tavernier and Islamorada have more of a small town feel than the comparative hustle and bustle of Key Largo. Even the dive operators have a more laid back style.**

Without the hype of Pennekanmp, they are less pressured, and you will find most of the boats carry either 6 or 12 passengers max. For dive operators, the gang at Floridaze Dive Center, Rainbow Reef, The Dive Shop, or Conch Republic Divers will charm you and treat you to personalized service you won't soon forget.

Ken and Pat Koch (pn: Cook) have one of the arguably more charming operations in the area. Rainbow Reef Dive Center is tucked away in the rustic Pirates Cove Hotel and Marina on Windley Key. They can put you up there, or at any number of places a short drive away, while overseeing your stay with true Southern Hospitality. When you dive with these people, you know they want you to have a good time.

Or stay with Brad Neat, at his Island Bay Resort. Clean tastefully decorated apartments, on the gulfside, with Brad's dive boat, the Do Wa Diddy, docked right there. Brad has a compressor on site and runs complete dive charters. One of the most experienced and respected of the operators in Islamorada, he has been known to occasionally gift his guests with a complimentary bottle of wine. They can enjoy it at sunset with their feet propped on a circa 1733 cannon at waters edge. Brad recovered the cannon in the 70's, let him tell you about it.

If you want a unique experience, try a submarine ride with the Conch Republic Divers. The little yellow sub can whisk you along walls and reefs, and the ultimate in stability for shooting u/w video. They even offer a shark cage dive, (or at least they will when they can find some sharks) they do have the cage.

Recently, NOAA has deployed an underwater habitat in the area, for the purpose of conducting numerous and varied manned experiments. The media blackout on this is just starting to lift. Many operators are running occasional dives to "the habitat" but not publicizing it too much. Recreational divers are "tolerated" for now, attempting to enter or touching any equipment outside the submersible is strictly forbidden. If the divers lucky enough to experience this site continue to abide these and other rules, there is hope it will be available to others.

Now, if you like to blend some hard partying in with your dive vacation, you should probably check in at the Holiday Isle, and not need your car again, until it is time to go home. Accommodations range from near royal to economy. The Holiday Isle now is compromised of several hotel properties all linked by shuttle service when not within walking distance.

The main Hotel is a complete, self contained resort. A dive shop and boat, a huge fishing fleet, boat rentals, jet ski rentals, several of the areas best eateries, all the shopping you could do plus...the legendary TIKI BAR, where the classic Keys RUMRUNNER was born and still reigns as king. One of the hottest night spots in the Keys, many don't make it any further south on their vacation than the Holiday Isle. Those that do will find wonderful dining at the Whale Harbor, the seafood buffet at the Cart Grill (the locals call it the "Oral Thrill", is another "must" for seafood lovers, as is the Green Turtle Inn, except on Monday when...."the turtle rests."

For diversion, you can spend an afternoon at Theater of the Sea. A long time attraction, it puts you close to the many ocean inhabitants and is an ideal way to introduce non divers of all ages to the wonders we experience. You will probably learn a few things yourself, I always do.

Diving is different here than in Key Largo. It is a place where you can see if your depth gage works below 35 feet. Where your dive can be as rewarding if you carry a camera bag, a bug bag, (in season, with a license) or a pole spear (license required also).

If you can, rent a boat and go snorkeling around Alligator Light, and visit the historical Indian Key Park, accessible only by boat. You will learn about the early days of Florida, when people lived by "wrecking", when this tiny island was the first Dade County county seat, why the Indians wanted the white men out, what they did to achieve this, and what little the Government could do to stop it. It all makes for a fascinating story.

There is allegedly a state run boat to ferry tourists out to the island, I have yet to see one running. Before we go down to Marathon, a few last fond memories, sitting on the deck of the Lady Cyana III in the sunlight, coming back from two great dives, and just smiling... bringing my own boat down on a trailer and staying at the Drop Anchor Motel.

You can get on Keys time very quickly in Islamorada.

MARATHON ..... THE HEART OF THE KEYS

Almost exactly halfway between Miami and Key West, the community of Marathon was born in 1904. Now, ninety years later, the area is losing it's status as one of the Keys best kept secrets for divers. The word has gotten out.

Home to Indians as far back as 2000 BC., the reefs off Marathon saw many a Spanish Galleon and British Merchant vessel alike break their backs and die on the coral in storms and in darkness. There are wrecks still being discovered here today, laden with booty and history. The rich fisheries on both the Atlantic and Gulf sides of the islands attracted only a handful of hardy settlers by the early 1900's.

Marathon gained it's name during pioneer Henry Flagler's headlong rush to build a railroad through to Key West. Flagler built a major construction camp on the island of Key Vaca as midway depot to house men and materials to complete the project. Because of the frenzied push for completion, a worker was heard to say, "Building this railroad has become a regular Marathon!" That was enough to give the camp a name. The name stuck.

Today the railroad is gone, and as I said, U.S. 1, the Overseas Highway, has replaced the rails and beams with a ribbon of asphalt that runs down the spine of the keys and leads divers to a host of Middle Keys diving delights. The Marathon area begins with Duck Key, Mile Marker (M.M.) 61 and wanders down to the Seven Mile Bridge at M.M. 45. Along this expanse the coastline offers divers dozens of reef sites and The Thunderbolt, a deep wreck that is quickly becoming as much of a "must" for traveling divers as the "Statue" in Pennekanmp Park

More of a "must" is Sombrero Reef, a labyrinth of coral caves and arches, home of Marathon's first mooring buoy project. Tying off to one of these buoys saves the reef from anchor damage, while putting divers on some of the prettiest "bottom" in all the Keys.

There are a number of operators in the area, most do not run any farther south than Sombrero Reef for they don't need to. Marathon is even blessed with a Gulf Side body of water that is deep enough and diverse enough in plant and fish life to make for an exciting dive.

Marathon is still a fishing community. The marinas and dockside moorings are littered with long liners and shrimpers. Aged and with their nets drying in the sun, they stand as a testimony to the generations of fishermen who have sought a living from the sea, and who remain here today. Many times throughout the year sponge divers are seen plying their trade on the Gulf side. The sight is a tribute to the ability of nature to rejuvenate herself, and a reminder of our oceans struggle to supply mankind with it's needs, at the same time.

Enough of that, the important thing to remember is, in Marathon, the Gulf side can still provide diving thrills when the Atlantic can't. In the shallows of the "inside", you are more or less in the nursery of the ocean. It is here that you can witness another strata of the food chain, much less visible in the open sea. Even if the weather is perfect for open water diving, you might elect to check with an operator and take one of these more ecologically oriented underwater tours. Days when it is a total "blowout" are almost non existent.

From the 25'-30' tall coral formations at the Pillars off of Duck Key, to the fantasy of arches and "swim throughs" that Sombrero Reef touts, Marathon diving has it's own unique and diverse menu.

Rule of thumb says the depths average 40'-60' on the reefs, but at places like Coffins Patch, the depth can be 10' or less. Ideal for snorkelers, bottom time like you can't believe for scuba divers.

For deeper wreck thrills, the Thunderbolt offers the challenge. Sunk a few years ago as an artificial reef, she lies in 110' with appropriate growth to make photographers giggle in their regulators with glee.

Other sites include the Fish Market, East Washerwoman, Delta Shoals, the Delta Shoal Wreck, the wreck of the Ignacio, and the Ivory Wreck.

For some reason divers either stop much further up in the Keys, or drive past in search of other things. Marathon is a well kept secret by many divers. The lack of fear in the marine life when approached proves this.

Aside from Marathon being a fishing community, many commercial tropical fish collectors are based here alongside the shrimpers and long liners. Some offer special "collecting" charters, and while it may be fun to learn the habits of these animals and the thrill of actually catching them, shipping them home can be a costly, logistical headache, equal to having a "trophy" fish mounted and shipped home.

Accommodations in the Marathon area can satisfy any budget and taste. Most operations are the "Mom & Pop" variety; clean rooms and friendly attention highlight them, many have boat ramps and dockage available to guests. There are nationally advertised chain hotels, (Days Inn, Howard Johnsons) and some truly first class "Resorts" that will pamper you silly. Some give package rates for divers.

Hawk's Cay located on Duck Key, is one of the most elegant resorts in the Caribbean let alone the Keys. Designed in a 50's island style, if you like chocolates on your pillow at night, and never lift a finger service, stay here. Of the few, Triple-A listed, five star restaurants in the lower Keys, two are on the premises of Hawk's Cay, as is Marathon Underseas Adventures, the dive shop. They have been honored for their work with the Handicapped Scuba Association (HSA) and have certified more student instructors than nearly any operation in Florida.

The Diving Site offers both reef and Gulfside ecology-oriented tours as well as great, friendly diving.

Good things to say for Tilden's Pro Dive, Bill and Heidi at Abyss Pro Dive Center, and CJ's Dive Center as well.

For breakfast or lunch, try The Wobbly Crab, or Brian's in Paradise. If you are not eating dinner at the Sombrero, or Hawk's Cay, Perry's is a sure favorite, and Brian's is also open late night, with a great menu, reasonably priced.

As for nightlife, the larger hotels have clubs, there are a number of restaurants and night spots that offer live entertainment and dancing. Margaritas and moonlight dancing on the water to an island backbeat. If you don't feel like diving, try a seaplane ride or a flying lesson. Marathon has a large airport serviced by commercial air carrier connecting links. You can fly to your dive destination!

If you have the chance, stop in at the Dolphin Research Center on Grassy Key. There are some very dedicated people doing amazing things to learn from, save, and protect those wonderful mammals.

Your donation for admission will give you access to some rare and insightful information on these cetaceans. You will walk away feeling a little 'different', and you will have helped support this ongoing program. The Marathon area is rich in diving delights, and steeped in maritime history.

Crab on Purple Fan Coral by Ron Streeter

The Lower Keys-Looe Key

At the end of the Seven Mile Bridge is Bahia Honda. One of the Nations 10 most beautiful beaches can be found here.

A Mecca for campers who either fish or dive and bring their own boat, you can literally just walk around the premises and feel refreshed and relaxed. The skeleton of Flagler's old bridge/trestle stands to one side of the 'new' Overseas Highway, a historic reminder of days past. If you can, stop for a picnic at Bahia Honda, from here down to Big Coppitt Key, the lodging is "mom & pop" style with the exception of the Sugar Loaf Lodge and Looe Key Reef Resort.

The main attraction for diving in this area is the Looe Key Marine Sanctuary, and rightly so.

Director Billy Causey's high-profile style of management has put this place on the map. Each July, the Sanctuary holds it's Underwater Music Festival, another unique Keys event. The local radio station provides programming that Park Rangers relay to divers in the Park via hydrophones. Gliding among the coral heads to a slow island beat as the fearless groupers and myriad tropical fish swim past is a treat. (Sorry I can't say the same about the insurance commercial I heard, the fish didn't seem to be too impressed either.)

Looe Key was named after the wreck of H.M.S. Looe, a frigate lost around the turn of the century.

Big Pine Key is one of the largest, and most interesting islands in the Keys, although you would not guess so by your passage along the Overseas Highway. The island is much wider than what you experience on U.S. 1, and most of it is a refuge for the rare (and endangered) Key Deer. These deer are so tiny, a full grown male would not necessarily come up to the height of your car fender. They wander across the road at all times of the day and because of their size are in constant danger of being hit by unobservant drivers. (The 45 mph day/35 mph night speed limits are strictly enforced).

The Key Deer National Refuge is on Big Pine Key, and a few miles of country road driving can put you in another place on earth and time. A primeval landscape of scrub pine and palmetto, the Refuge has a visitor station and supplies maps to spots where you might see one of these tiny creatures

sneaking a drink of fresh water, or crossing a path. If you have the time and like to see nature before it's all gone, stop in.

In Big Pine, Underseas, Inc. is your connection. Marianne Rockett, the owner and her staff operate one of the Keys oldest and best stocked dive shops. They can also run you out to the reef any day and many nights. Onward to Key West, if you stop at Looe Key Reef Resort on Ramrod Key you can have it all.

Spacious clean rooms, the dive boat out your back door, a restaurant and pool side Tiki bar at your front door, where do you need to go?

If you don't need the Tiki Bar and all it's attendant fun, look up Parmers' Place on Little Torch Key, it's a little hard to find, but absolutely Key's quaint and a spotlessly clean establishment,

If you stay there, dive with Les and Diane at Reef Runner Dive Center. Les is a Keys native and retired educator who will tell you the history of the area in an eloquent style; punctuated with the local draw. A fascinating dive trip every time.

Compared to other areas of the Keys, the Lower Keys area is probably the slowest paced, "closest to nature" part of the island chain. You can come to the Lower Keys to truly get away from it all. It's time to move on toward Boca Chica, the Key West lifestyle beckons.

Heading down, ever deeper into the Keys, the throaty, roaring whine of military jets overhead from Boca Chica Naval Air Station, heralds your approach into Key West.

A diving treat, and the ultimate party town.

Reefs, wrecks and even a wall highlight the diving around the Key West area.

And no where else in the world can you be so totally immersed in a divergent atmosphere, steeped in the lore of the sea, rum runners, smugglers of all kinds, as well as heroes both of military and artistic legend. Rouges of all descriptions have haunted the narrow streets of Key West.

Where after dive entertainment can begin with a walk at sunset on Mallory Square, as a man balances a bicycle on his chin while bagpipe music fills the air. Or watching the sunset from a sailboat, champagne in hand. Maybe a walk through a museum stuffed with the treasure of long dead kings or the quaint gingerbread homes passing by as you view them from a motor tour. "People that say, there's not much good diving in this area," says Tim Taylor of Looker Diving, "Haven't had a good look around these parts."

There are plenty of great spots around the Key West area. Sand Key is probably one of the more familiar reefs and Western Dry Rocks is also recorded in a lot of logbooks Their spur and groove formation give many a diver a thrilling view of spotted eagle rays (the most I have seen at one time).

There is a wall on another portion of Western Dry Rocks that trails from 35-40 feet down to 110. It is a small area but one worth seeing if you are a wall diver.

"One nice thing about our island is that it doesn't have a "Gulfside". said Mimi Dye of Lost Reef Adventures. We've got diving all around us. When the wind is strong on one side, we just dive the calmer, better visibility of the other side.

Dive sites for all tastes are available. From shallow brightly colored snorkeling reefs that are perfect for resort course and checkout divers to deep wrecks and even treasure hunting on the bones of sunken galleons.

The named sites in Key West include: Rocky Key, Nine Foot Stake, Western Sambo, Little Sambo and Pelican Shoals. Boats sailing out of Key West are as varied as the sites they dive. From the muted thunder of powered charter boats, to the silent whisper of sails pushing you out to the Marquesas and Dry Tortugas in search of underwater excitement and pleasure. You can even put on a trench coat and pretend you're an underwater spy riding the "James Bond Boat" (the Sea Eagle).

Or you can sail away on intimate liveaboards and trace the path of treasure hunters and roques in the Marquesas or the Dry Tortugas.

If your diving tastes lean toward the deeper, technical side of the sport, stop in at Key West Diver, on Stock Island just before coming into Key West. Capt. Billy Deans is one of the most experienced in this highly specialized area, he has visited the Andria Doria, and even dove the Monitor.

When it comes to lodging, food and nightlife, Key West has it, hands down. At the Ocean Key House, at the end of Mallory Square, you can luxuriate in a two bedroom suite with a Jacuzzi in your master bath, with balconies that overlook both the square and the sea.

The sunset view from the rooftop bar at La Conchia will take your breath away.

Key West is also rife with quaint little B&B's, nestled in refurbished, but authentic "Conch" houses, many over 150 years old. A real taste of the Old Town, but inconvenient at best lugging wet dive gear up and down the stairs and halls. If you want to stay at a B&B, best rent the major share of your gear.

If you prefer staying a little farther from the maddening crowd, the other side of the island, away from Mallory Square, offers ocean view hotels and motels with the beach across the street.

There is also some liveaboard boats that run weekend trips out to Fort Jefferson in the Dry Tortugas. You can dive this unspoiled wonderland with The Yankee Freedom or the M.V. Spree. They both offer a great trip, excellent diving, and a tour of historic Ft. Jefferson. If you want to see the Fort, "home" to Dr. Samuel Mudd after Lincoln's assassination without taking the time for the diving and the cruise you can fly out to the Fort via a number of seaplane charter operators.

If you really like to walk on the wild side, try to be here in October when Fantasy Fest is going on. It's Key West's answer to the Mardi Gras, a wilder time, you won't soon find.

Don't forget, this is also "Margaritaville", and if you don't like Jimmy Buffett songs, wafting from bars everywhere, you'll have trouble adjusting.

Home to Hemingway, and a host of famous writers, both living and dead, Key West is also an artists colony, many recognizable names and faces float around the town

You might even catch a glimpse of Mel Fisher, the world famous treasure hunter, using a small gold bar for a swizzle stick. Hit Sloppy Joe's, The Hog's Breath Saloon, The Turtle Kraaln and the Half Shell Raw Bar.

See at least one sunset at Mallory Square.

Check out the Art, both in the Galleries, and with the street vendors.

Take one sunset, champagne sailboat cruise.

Try not to buy a T-shirt in every shop that sells them.

Thanks for letting me share my Keys with you.

Palm Beach

Don Lanman

A PADI Rescue level diver with over 27 years of diving experience. Hundreds of dives around the world including: Hong Kong, Truk Lagoon, Honolulu, Maui, Kona, Bahamas, Netherlands Antilles, Bimini, Cabo San Lucas, Puerto Vallarta, Cozumel, Grand Caymen, Australia, Florida, Nevada, Ohio, Arizona, New Mexico, Texas and California. Don owns a Direct Response Advertising Agency in Sausalito, California with a focus on the travel industry.

It was about 10 am when I entered the crowded shop. I was seeking the treasure map I knew had to be hidden among the scores of books, trinkets and dive equipment that littered the little shop.

The bright sunlight reflected off the water and streamed through the windows casting an eerie glow on the everything in the shop including a group of browsing patrons who resembled a school of barracuda.

But I was looking for a specific map, a guide that would lead me to the location of scores of sunken galleons and their cache of silver coins, gold and pieces of Eight. I had to move quickly for fear the "Cudas" would get there first.

From the corner of my eye I could see the hint of a rainbow reflecting off a shelf of books and I knew it marked the spot. Not wanting to alert the others, I moved slowly toward the location to secure the book containing the map, as quietly as possible, and slip away unnoticed.

Just then the tall slightly built young man with a deep tan, long tangled yellow hair and a pirates earring moved swiftly toward me and in a soft voice said..."May I help you Sir?"

In an instant my daydream adventure had evaporated.

The shop was filled with interesting friendly people, the type you usually find at a dive location but this scene was unusual since this was a Pro Shop, a pro shop for divers.

In fact this pro shop was part of a dive company called the Scuba Club, a country club setting designed specifically for divers and located in one of the most beautiful Caribbean like settings in the world...West Palm Beach!

Florida is renowned for its diving, however the focus is usually on the Keys. Interestingly, however some of the best diving these emerald green waters have to offer is north from Miami to Vero Beach.

Easy to reach, low cost, no foreign exchange or difficult third world travel, the Palm Beaches offer everything a diver could want and more. From warm Gulf Stream waters that average 78 to 84 degrees Fahrenheit to diving with visibility that frequently reaches 100 feet or more.

The Gulf waters of the Palm Beaches are teaming with all the types of sea life that you generally expect to find only in more exotic locations like Truk or Nevis.

Almost every dive produces encounters with a variety of creatures, some of them in the water, including; turtles, lobster, barracuda, sharks, moray eels, stripers, groupers, amberjacks, rays and an amazing variety of sea fans, soft and hard coral.

To make this U.S. location even more exciting it has one of the largest artificial reef systems in world, not to mention the scores of Spanish Galleons lost over the years.

So if your passion is wreck diving you have hundreds to chose from by diving this part of the Gold Coast.

The Scuba Club itself is a 20 year old diving country club that was formerly known as the Norene Rouse Scuba Club. They have a pro shop, dive boats, swimming pool, deep tank, hot showers, steam room, photo lab and picnic area. Best of all the diving is only 30 minutes from the dock.

The key to this country club is fun and safety. They offer NAUI, PADI and YMCA courses. All visitors are welcome, the rates very reasonable and memberships are available but not required. However, if you are a first time guest be prepared to show your C-Card, log book and demonstrate your basic proficiency, if you've not been down for a while. There is a hyperbaric chamber in Miami, but who needs that type of trouble.

The dive sites are numerous and exciting including exotic sites like; the **Breakers**, **Ron's Reef**, **North Hook**, **Jupiter High Ledge**, wrecks of the **Esso Bonaire**, **Mizpah**, **Amarylis** and a **Rolls Royce** car (honestly).

Of all the sites, however, my favorites are the **Mizpah** and **Amarylis**. The Mizpah is a Greek luxury liner. She is intact and very easy to penetrate. Since she has been down for over 20 years there is a wonderful collection of sea life from great barracudas to turtles and groupers.

The Amarylis is a beautiful wreck of a 400 foot freighter. There's not much left except for the ribs but drifting over her grave gives one the feeling of being in a surrealistic painting.

Beyond the wrecks, reefs, walls; the warm clear water and sea life you always have the chance of drifting over a 300 year old Galleon. So as you see if diving adventure has a name, it must be...

West Palm Beach, the Golden Palm of the Caribbean.

SCUBA AND SNORKELING FACILITIES QUESTIONNAIRE

NAME **The Scuba Club Inc.**
ADDRESS **4708 North Dixie Highway**
West Palm Beach, FL 33407
CONTACT **Mr. J.D. Duff**
TITLE **Manager**
TELEPHONE **407-844-2466** FAX **407-844-8256**

CAPITAL:	**Tallahassee**	GOVERNMENT:	**Democratic**
POPULATION:		LANGUAGE:	**English**
CURRENCY:	**US dollar**	ELECTRICITY	**120v**
AIRLINES:	**All major U.S. carriers**	DEPARTURE TAX?	
NEED VISA/PASSPORT?	YES NO **x**	PROOF OF CITIZENSHIP?	YES NO **x**

YOUR FACILITY IS CLASSIFIED AS: SCUBA CENTER **x** RESORT **x**
BUSINESS HOURS: **Tuesday-Sunday 8:00 am to 5:00 pm**
CERTIFYING AGENCIES: **PADI, NAUI, SSI**
LOG BOOK REQUIRED? YES **x** NO
EQUIPMENT: SALES **x** RENTALS **x** AIR FILLS **x**
PRIMARY LINE OF EQUIPMENT: **US Divers**
PHOTOGRAPHIC EQUIPMENT: SALES **x** RENTALS **x** LAB **x**

CHARTER/DIVE BOAT AVAILABLE? YES **x** NO DIVER CAPACITY **25**
COAST GUARD APPROVED? YES **x** NO CAPTAIN LICENSED? YES **x** NO
SHIP TO SHORE? YES **x** NO LORAN YES **x** NO RADAR? YES **x** NO
DIVE MASTER/INSTRUCTOR ABOARD? YES NO BOTH **x**

DIVING & SNORKELING: SALT **x** FRESH
TYPE OF DIVING/SNORKELING IN AREA: WALL **x** BEACH WRECK **x** REEF CAVE **x** ICE
DIVING/SNORKELING IN YOUR AREA IS BEST SUITED FOR: BEGINNER **x** INTERMEDIATE **x** ADVANCED **x**
BEST TIME OF YEAR FOR DIVING/SNORKELING: **Year round**
TEMPERATURE: NOV-APRIL: **70-80F** MAY-OCT: **75-85F**
VISIBILITY: DIVING: **100+FT** SNORKELING: **50FT**

PACKAGES AVAILABLE: DIVE **x** DIVE STAY **x** SNORKEL SNORKEL-STAY
ACCOMMODATIONS NEARBY: HOTEL **x** MOTEL **x** HOME RENTALS **x**
ACCOMMODATION RATES: EXPENSIVE **x** MODERATE **x** INEXPENSIVE **x**
RESTAURANTS NEARBY: EXPENSIVE **x** MODERATE **x** INEXPENSIVE **x**
YOUR AREA IS: REMOTE QUIET WITH ACTIVITIES **x** LIVELY **x**
LOCAL ACTIVITY/NIGHTLIFE: **All available**
CAR NEEDED TO EXPLORE AREA? YES **x** NO
DUTY FREE SHOPPING? YES **x** NO

LOCAL EMERGENCY SERVICES   NEAREST HYPERBARIC TREATMENT FACILITY
COASTGUARD: AUTHORITY:
TELEPHONE: LOCATION:
CALLSIGNS: TELEPHONE:

LOCAL DIVING DOCTOR:
NAME:
LOCATION:
TELEPHONE:

The Hawaiian Islands

The Kona Aggressor
A Sampling of Hawaii's Best Dives

Please Refer to Honeymoon Chapter For
The Kahala Hilton
Kona Village Resort
The S.S. Constitution

Wendy Canning Church

The Hawaiian Islands are situated some 2,000 miles from the American Continent and some 2,000 miles away from any other major island making them the most isolated archipelago in the world.

The island chain is less than 6,500 square miles. The chain's topography is made up of vast mountain ranges, sloping green valleys leading to coastal flatlands, and beyond coral reefs.

Only in the last few decades has the science of archaeology been utilized to ascertain its peoples origins which are thought to be Asian.

It is believed, through the use of carbon dating, that the first settlers came from the Marquesas Islands in the 8th century.

The Polynesians dated events by generations and reigns of Chiefs, thus an exact chronology is difficult to confirm.

It is thought that settlements were in small groups. Their governments were tribal with the Chief as ruler.

They worshipped many Gods and the priests brought the Gods' messages to the people.

Their diet consisted of fish and poi (a paste made from cooked and processed taro root), and a variety of fruits and meat. The main occupations were agriculture and fishing.

By the time white settlers arrived in the late 18th century, 300,000 people populated the largest islands in the chain which were Hawaii, the big island, Maui, Molokai, Lanai, Kahoolawi, Oahu, Kauai and Niihan.

British Captain James Cook on his third mission to find a sea passage from the Pacific to the Atlantic across the north of the American continent came upon Oahu on January 18, 1778.

Oahu meaning "The Gathering Place" is 40 miles long and 26 miles at its widest point, an area of 595 square miles.

In its earliest days Oahu was known to sailors worldwide as the crossroads to the Pacific because it had the only safe protected harbor on its southeastern shore.

Today Oahu is noted for its tourism. It also houses major military bases, four sugar plantations, three pineapple companies and a large service industry to accommodate the tourists and year round population.

On his fourth mission Captain Cook landed with his two ships H.M.S. Discovery and H.M.S. Resolution in Keolakekua Bay on January 17,1770 and Hawaii or the "Big Island" was discovered.

The Kona Aggressor

Wendy Canning Church

We boarded our Hawaiian Airlines flight to Keohole Airport at the Kailua-Kona with just two minutes to spare. When they ask you to be at the airport at least one hour before departure they are serious! The lines were very long and there were no porters in sight. It was a nightmare!

After a short thirty minute flight, we arrived. One of the crew from the Kona Aggressor, greeted us with a wonderful smile, hug and a lei. The lei is a customary welcome in these islands, yet each time I am greeted this way it is touching. These handiworks of beauty, so delicate, emitting a sweet, subtle fragrance embody the essence of the Hawaiian islands.

Luggage loaded in the van, we were off on a ten minute trip to Honokolau Harbour where the yacht lay before us, 110 feet long, 22 feet wide, painted in red, white and blue. She was beautiful.

Rumor has it that the Kona Aggressor ran hundreds of thousands of dollars over budget having to adhere to the stringent safety standards for chartered yachts in the Hawaiian waters.

She is a comfortable yacht and perfectly outfitted for the scuba diver and the best of its kind in these waters. The yacht sleeps fourteen guests in seven double cabins and is served by a crew of five. Each cabin has a queen size bed with a single bed on top. There is a sink in the cabin with a separate shower and toilet. Each cabin is air conditioned with its own controls.

The following morning we awoke to the sound of engines. No need for an alarm clock on this boat. At seven o'clock the captain starts the engines and heads off to a new destination. Meals are an-nounced by the crew by blowing a conch shell.

Our cruise was to take us along the western shore of Hawaii and the Kona coast. There we found waters filled with multi-colored fish of all varieties and sizes and bays and villages steeped in Hawaiian history. We cruised not more than a mile from shore so that at all times were able to video and photograph the mountain ranges, jagged hills and green valleys interspersed with lava flow and waterfalls stretching to the sea.

Eighty-five miles long, the Kona coast offers a moderate climate, warm during the day and cooled by evening tradewinds. It is these same tradewinds shifting suddenly that can drive a sailor in search of a safe harbor. This was to be our luck for the next two days.

> **The captain told us that one of the reasons that there are so few private charters in these waters is due to a dearth of moorings. He and the crew have put down thirty such moorings along the coast. They chart their location and let others use them.**

Our destination for the next two days was Keolakekua Bay.

> **On our way we watched in awe as whales breached off our bow. We even saw a pair breach which is quite unusual.**

The whales frequent these waters this time of year where they come to mate and calve.

As we cruised toward the bay, we were given a dive briefing. No alcohol was to be consumed until after a diver's last dive of the day. This meant that if you were night diving forget your cocktail hour. This is a safety measure that I wish I saw enforced more often. The Kona Aggressor upholds these standards. One can do repetitive dives as long as they adhere to the Navy tables. Diving must be in buddy teams. If a guest does not have a buddy, a staff member will happily accompany you.

The stern is where the action takes place most of the day and after dinner. Each diver has a locker and behind each locker are two tanks refilled after each dive. There is an area for drying wet suits. A very large camera station with rental equipment, battery charges and space for personal equipment. An E-6 processing lab is also aboard.

There is a large dive platform and two ladders. Entry is a step off. A rinse tank is provided for cameras. There is a hot shower and towels after the dive. A blackboard is provided and a map of the area is sketched out along with the names of fish, plant life and coral you might see. A bar is thrown over the side for ascents and a regulator for out of air situations.

The salon is where meals are taken buffet style. There is a large screen television and VCR. Guests are invited to bring their favorite tapes and videos. Meals are simple but the food is fresh and well-prepared. Snacks are available twice a day. Soft drinks, wine, beer and liquor are included in the charter.

We pulled into Keolakekua Bay, our home for the next two days. This proved no hardship. The bay was calm and beautiful and steeped in history. Captain James Cook, landed here on January 17, 1779 during festival time. His welcome was a warm one. He set out again on February 4, 1779 but returned because of a storm and damage to his ship. During the night a boat from his flagship H.M.S. Resolution was stolen. Captain Cook went ashore to take Chief Kala-nipuu as hostage. A fight broke out and Cook fired on the natives. Captain Cook was struck down, bludgeoned to death and his flesh eaten. A lovely stark white obelisk stands at water's edge, a memorial to this courageous man, Captain, chart maker, a leader of men, and explorer.

Coral Garden by Wendy Canning Church.

There are one hundred and seventy-six species of fish endemic to these waters.

The Aquarium is aptly named for it is here that the scuba diver or snorkeler will find a myriad of reef fish. Depths range from relatively shallow to 110 feet.

Swimming toward the reef we noticed that the area was abundant with finger coral. We dropped down to fifty feet making our way along the wall. We were armed with peas, a favorite of the nenui, gray in color so you must watch closely for them. Dozens of pink tail durgeons sashayed by followed by pennant fish, yellow tang, barred fire fish, snowflake, yellow margin zebra, Hawaiian squirrelfish and saddle wrasse.

About thirty minutes into the dive I came across my first white mouth moray eel. It came out of its cave and wound itself in and out of the coral. I watched it with caution as should be the way with many sea creatures which can behave unpredictably at times. I spent the remainder of the dive photographing my new acquaintances.

Basket Starfish at night by Carol Boone

Our second dive of the day was in an area below the jagged cliffs. The cliffs form a sheer wall stretching from the sea. There are large crevices in these cliffs where Hawaiian royalty were buried. Their bodies would be lowered on ropes with slaves accompanying them to bury them in the caves. The ropes were then cut and the slaves joined their masters in the deep sleep. Their bodies have since been removed to a state burial ground.

The sun was high and shone brightly through the water making a flash for cameras unnecessary. Schools of butterhead parrotfish, forcept fish, butterfish and yellow tang came out for the shoot and what actors they were! At one point I just remained still and watched the parade go by!

That evening, the divemaster gave us a lecture and slide presentation on what we might expect to see on the night dive:

The **Raccoon Butterfish** has a bar in front of its eye. They travel in pairs, are monogamous and mate for life. If you see one alone chances are they have lost their mate.

The **Long Nose Butterfly** is found in two species. One's nose is longer than the other allowing it to feed deeper in the crevices of the rock. The longer nose butterfly is another example of evolution and its advantages.

The **Hammerhead Butterfly** are the cleaning fish. Cleaning not only keeps the fish population healthy, but at the same time creates more food by opening up a new whole food source.

The **Parrotfish** forms a mucous cocoon around themselves at night which protects them from the abrasion of the reefs and from the moray eel that likes to feed on them. This fish feeds off the reef excreting the particles, and further evolving the food chain.

The **Puffer Fish** continuously swallows water to become half again its size discouraging the larger fish which cannot get their jaws around them.

Just outside of the bay is Hammerhead Point. It is here that one can make a date with Barney the turtle at exactly 8:45 each morning. Make sure you bring Barney breakfast, he expects it!

Barney and Wendy Canning Church.
"Barney comes to breakfast punctually each morning at 8:45"
By Carol Boone

The yacht pulled in close to the site where the visibility was 100 feet. We descended down to 40 feet. Our guide was armed with a goodie bag. Barney didn't keep us waiting. Much to the consternation of his buddies, Barney had center stage. Definitely the lead in this shoot! He frolicked and ate, swam around us, left us, turned around and came back.

Barney had so captured our hearts that five days later on our return to home port we stopped to make a final visit. The seas were very rough with 6 foot swells crashing on shore. Barney never showed which proves he's a lot smarter than a bunch of crazy divers, but we were appeased by finding a baby octopus.

As we cruised up the coast the snow capped mountains of Mauna Kea came in view. Snow skiing in the tropics? You bet, it is true. Most years from December through March, only one hour away by car from the warm Pacific ocean, you will find skiers whisking down the slopes. They have cross-country skiing and slalom races in February on President's Day. A four-wheel drive vehicle is necessary to reach the runs since there are no lifts.

That day our destination was to be the bays off of Milolil. This tiny village is the oldest continuous settlement on Hawaii where natives earn their living entirely from the sea.

Although fishermen now use outboard motors for their canoes they still haul their boats up the rocky shores by hand. The fish are salted and dried in the sun.

We went ashore to photograph its stone walls covered in night blooming Cereus, a charming yellow church, small straw huts and canoes. There is nothing to buy, only a tiny grocery store but it was good to be on land for a while and to walk an interesting stretch of black lava shoreline.

Our first dive off Milolii was **Tabastrea Tunnel**. On this dive you are likely to find turtles, mantas, octopus, and eagle rays.

Be sure to bring your light and perhaps you will see the white tip shark which inhabits one of the three caves. They were not present that dive. We were especially delighted however, by the beautiful cup coral and the nudibranchs.

After lunch we dove the **Lighthouse**. We found that the site was of interest not so much for the fish life, but rather for the topography. The archways were magnificent. There were peaks and valleys and one felt as if they were discovering a mountain range beneath the water with the sun glistening down and waters gushing against its slopes.

It was time to begin our journey home. We stopped along the way and dove **Kauluoa Point**. Here we found a three room cave. As if one of the Gods knew our cruise was coming to an end they sent out ghost shrimp, pin cushions, sea stars, lionfish, conger eels, leaf fish, cowles and Hawaiian slipper. Unfortunately Cozy, the conger eel, was somewhere else that day.

Our second dive of the day was at **Rob's Reef**. In Skull Cave there were nudibranchs, blennies, gobys, and other divers came upon yellow margin, moray eels, conger eels, fatworms, but no sale sharks or manta rays which are usually present.

Dome Cave was our next site. For photographers this is known as "Nudibranch Haven." Sailfish, tangs, eels, cowries also were spotted along with all types of reef fish. There is a complex of caves filled with fascinating topography.

The charter runs from Saturday to Saturday. I have never seen a crew work harder or longer hours.

Mohalo to the crew of the Kona Aggressor.

Note: Due to seasonal and unexpected seas, we suggest inexperienced divers check weather conditions when booking.

Editor's Note: A new Kona Aggressor has been built, quite different from the original one and she plys the same route as we took along the coast of Hawaii.

A Sampling of Hawaii's Best Dives
Ed Robinson

In 1975 Ed Robinson began his own underwater photography business, "Hawaiian Watercolors". In 1981, he began his dive charter business under that same name. Two years later, Ed joined forces with his wife Susan who came to Maui as a tourist. According to the Robinsons, it was "love at first dive." Today, she is a Captain, a Dive Master and an accomplished underwater videographer. Sue handles most of the day-to-day business operations, and organizes and leads special arranged trips several times a year to extraordinary international dive destinations.

In January of 1989, the Hawaiian Watercolors dive operation changed is name to Ed Robinsons Diving Adventures; the name Hawaiian Watercolors was retained for Ed's photography business.

The crew has been personally trained by Ed Robinson and has years of experience. For example, Roger Pannier, Captain and Dive Master, has been on Maui for over 10 years, diving 6 days most weeks. In fact, he made his 2500th dive on Ed's 60th birthday. He's the oldest diving Captain on Maui, chronologically speaking, Ed's often described as "65 going on 30."

Ed's photography has been published by the National Geographic Society, Audubon, Oceans, and Sunset Books, as well as hundreds of national, international, and local magazines and books. Sport Diver Magazine has said that Ed has the "eye of a scientist and the soul of an artist." His most recently published books are Underwater Guide to Hawaii, and a new children's book, From Sand to Sea.

1001 Species

Roger thinks this dive is the closest he has seen in Hawaii to the reefs of Plau - and that's saying a lot!

Healthy coral reefs roll quickly to depths beyond and are adorned by multiple schools of butterfly and other tropical fish. We usually do this as a drift dive at 20 to 80 feet since current is often present. It is appropriate for all levels of divers.

Shoal Reef (or Boulder Reef)

On the far side of Kahoolawe lies a large shoal. Around large boulders and lava ridges divers find a mixed bag of animals and invertebrates at about 40 feet, some rarely seen around Maui. It is a long trip, but worth the time it takes to get to this distant and untamed area.

Scarecrow Point

A mile around Kahoolawe, back toward Maui from Shoal Reef, lies one of the least dived and most interesting areas. On this 10 to 70 foot dive you can expect to see pufferfish by the dozens, lobster by the bushel, and schools of squirrel fish that block the way through caves. It is one of the best exploratory areas we have, but access depends on the weather.

Sgt. Major Reef

Nine miles across the channel from Maui lies Lanai, and one of the first dive sites along the coast is Sgt. Major Reef named for the large schools of Sgt. Major damsel fish. The reef consists of three lava fingers, which create picturesque underwater gorges with thousands of hiding places for fish and invertebrates. Forty feet shallow, it is appropriate for those long second dives we are known for. Sgt. Major Reef is also good for wide angle and macro-photography.

First Cathedral

This is probably the second most popular dive from Maui (after Molokini). As divers enter his large cavern they are met with the feeling of entering a large (you guessed it!) cathedral. The central room has a porous ceiling; light streams around and illuminates the large alter (boulder) below.

It's large enough to hold a dozen divers easily, with elbow room to spare. There are lots of openings, so no one needs to worry about getting lost. In the same area we also find a pinnacle covered in orange tube coral and red sponges. In the other direction from the Cathedral lies a great wall and arch lofting 60 ft off the bottom. This is a very picturesque wide-angle or macro-photography area.

Fish Rock

As the name implies, there are lots of fish. The schools surround an exposed rock just off Manele Bay. We do this as a shallow, long dive with lots of photographic opportunities. The eastern side is a 40 ft. wall that breaks the surface, and the western side resembles rolling foot-hills in miniature. The shallows are covered with pastel colored moon (soft) coral, dancing sunlight, and clouds of inshore tropical fish.

Knob Hill

The 40 or 60 ft depth gives us lots of time to explore this area. Acres of lava ridges, arches, and small caves make this an exciting exploratory dive. We often see rays and an occasional turtle.

> **The "Knob" is shallow, and the hollow underside is a macro-photographers dream. Brightly colored sponges, tube coral, cowry shells, and a multitude of other invertebrates inhabit the underside**

Second Cathedral

It's probably a toss-up between divers whether First Cathedral or Second Cathedral is most exciting. The interior of Second Cathedral is large and sectioned into numerous smaller chambers branching from a vaulted central arch - great for dramatic wide-angle diver shots and for exploring. From black coral to lobster and prawns, there is lots to find inside. This is also one of the Lanai dive sites where we have pet (tame) eels.

Grand Canyon

Take a 150 ft lava fracture, place it from the surface to 60 ft, and add a lot of area to explore. That's the Grand Canyon. The to-pography is picturesque, and the animals found while exploring are many. Grand Canyon is not widely known, so it is dived infrequently.

Shark-Fin Rock

Around the corner, on the "back side" of Lanai, there is a rock protruding from the sea. Yes, it does resemble a shark fin! Through the years the butterfly fish have

Lemon Milletseed Butterfly Fish by Ed Robinson.

become accustomed to divers and are tame. The wall along the north side of the rock is one of those dramatic areas a photographer can spend an entire dive working. Between 10 and 60 feet you will see tube corals, red sponges, jagged lava, butterfly fish, and lots of animals hiding in the cracks that keep the dive interesting from beginning to end.

Mokuhooniki-Rock

> **You won't find a dive in Hawaii that's more exciting than "Elephant Rock" on a good day. Like "the land time forgot," we have seen the biggest fish, shells, octopus, and sharks here - a real adventure dive with current and large specimens.**

The rock is situated at the mouth of the Pailolo Channel and is exposed to all the seas and gusts the tradewinds can generate. In other words look for a calm, "Kona" day before asking to go here. It's best done as a private charter. We do not go here often, but we do go when we can.

Hidden Pinnacle

The Kahakuloa side of Maui has many hard-to-get-to adventure dive sites. This is one of them. A pinnacle rises from a 120 ft bottom to the surface and is covered with soft corals and sponge seldom seen on the leeward side of Maui. Swarms of plankton-feeding fish rise in the water column as the current, which is sometimes strong, brings a new supply of food. We suggest a private charter if you want to get this area - weather permitting.

Turtle Cove

The second dive of a north trip usually takes place here. Half a dozen lava pinnacles rise from 70 ft to about 10 ft below the surface. Some pinnacles are hollow, some have caves, and some form canyons. They are covered with healthy hard and soft corals and house more sea cultures (including turtles) than we find in almost any other region. About the only time we can get here is when winter Kona conditions prevail.

Reprinted with permission, from his book "The Ultimate Dive".

SCUBA AND SNORKELING FACILITIES QUESTIONNAIRE

NAME **Kona Aggressor**
ADDRESS

CONTACT **Wendy Church, DEI, 37 West Cedar Street, Boston, MA 02114**
TITLE **Booking Contact**
TELEPHONE **617-723-7134**   FAX **617-227-8145**

CAPITAL: **Honolulu**   GOVERNMENT: **USA**
POPULATION: **1,500,000**   LANGUAGE: **English**
CURRENCY: **US $**   ELECTRICITY: **110/220**
AIRLINES: **United, Aloha**   DEPARTURE TAX?
NEED VISA/PASSPORT?   YES   NO **x**   PROOF OF CITIZENSHIP?   YES   NO **x**

YOUR FACILITY IS CLASSIFIED AS: LIVEABOARD **x**   RESORT
BUSINESS HOURS: **7:00 to 17:00 Mon-Sun**
CERTIFYING AGENCIES:
LOG BOOK REQUIRED?   YES **x**   NO
EQUIPMENT: SALES **x**   RENTALS **x**   AIR FILLS **x**
PRIMARY LINE OF EQUIPMENT:
PHOTOGRAPHIC EQUIPMENT: SALES **x**   RENTALS **x**   LAB **x**

CHARTER/DIVE BOAT AVAILABLE?   YES **x**   NO   DIVER CAPACITY **21**
COAST GUARD APPROVED?   YES **x**   NO   CAPTAIN LICENSED? YES **x**   NO
SHIP TO SHORE? YES **x**   NO   LORAN   YES **x** NO   RADAR? YES **x**   NO
DIVE MASTER/INSTRUCTOR ABOARD?   YES **x**   NO   BOTH **x**

DIVING & SNORKELING: SALT **x**   FRESH
TYPE OF DIVING/SNORKELING IN AREA: WALL **x**   BEACH **x**   WRECK   REEF   CAVE **x**   ICE
DIVING/SNORKELING IN YOUR AREA IS BEST SUITED FOR: BEGINNER **x**   INTERMEDIATE **x**   ADVANCED **x**
BEST TIME OF YEAR FOR DIVING/SNORKELING: **All year**
TEMPERATURE: **NOV-APRIL:**   **77-78 F**   **MAY-OCT:**   **80-81 F**
VISIBILITY: **DIVING:**   **110 FT**   **SNORKELING:**   **70 FT**

PACKAGES AVAILABLE: DIVE **x**   DIVE STAY **x**   SNORKEL   SNORKEL-STAY
ACCOMMODATIONS NEARBY: HOTEL **x**   MOTEL   HOME RENTALS
ACCOMMODATION RATES: EXPENSIVE   MODERATE **x**   INEXPENSIVE
RESTAURANTS NEARBY: EXPENSIVE   MODERATE **x**   INEXPENSIVE
YOUR AREA IS: REMOTE   QUIET WITH ACTIVITIES **x**   LIVELY
LOCAL ACTIVITY/NIGHTLIFE: **Good**
CAR NEEDED TO EXPLORE AREA?   YES **x**   NO
DUTY FREE SHOPPING?   YES   NO **x**

LOCAL EMERGENCY SERVICES   NEAREST HYPERBARIC TREATMENT FACILITY
COASTGUARD: AUTHORITY:
TELEPHONE: LOCATION:
CALLSIGNS: TELEPHONE:

LOCAL DIVING DOCTOR:
NAME:
LOCATION:
TELEPHONE:

SCUBA AND SNORKELING FACILITIES QUESTIONNAIRE

NAME   **Ed Robinson's Diving Adventures**
ADDRESS   **P.O. Box 615**
                Kihei, Maui, HI 96753
CONTACT
TITLE
TELEPHONE   **1-800-635-1273 or 808-879-3584**   FAX

CAPITAL: GOVERNMENT:
POPULATION: LANGUAGE:
CURRENCY: ELECTRICITY:
AIRLINES: DEPARTURE TAX?
NEED VISA/PASSPORT?   YES   NO   x   PROOF OF CITIZENSHIP?   YES   NO

YOUR FACILITY IS CLASSIFIED AS: SCUBA CENTER   RESORT
BUSINESS HOURS: **Summer: 8 - 9; Winter: 8 a.m. - 9 p.m.**
CERTIFYING AGENCIES: **PADI, NAUI**
LOG BOOK REQUIRED?   YES   NO
EQUIPMENT: SALES x   RENTALS   AIR FILLS
PRIMARY LINE OF EQUIPMENT: **Scubapro**
PHOTOGRAPHIC EQUIPMENT: SALES   RENTALS x   LAB

CHARTER/DIVE BOAT AVAILABLE?   YES x   NO   DIVER CAPACITY   **6 or 12**
COAST GUARD APPROVED?   YES x   NO   CAPTAIN LICENSED?   YES x   NO
SHIP TO SHORE? YES   NO   LORAN   YES   NO   RADAR? YES   NO
DIVE MASTER/INSTRUCTOR ABOARD?   YES x   NO   BOTH

DIVING & SNORKELING: SALT x   FRESH
TYPE OF DIVING/SNORKELING IN AREA: WALL x   BEACH x   WRECK x   REEF   CAVE   ICE
DIVING/SNORKELING IN YOUR AREA IS BEST SUITED FOR: BEGINNER x   INTERMEDIATE x   ADVANCED x
BEST TIME OF YEAR FOR DIVING/SNORKELING: **All year**
TEMPERATURE: NOV-APRIL: F   MAY-OCT: F
VISIBILITY: DIVING: FT   SNORKELING: FT

PACKAGES AVAILABLE: DIVE x   DIVE STAY   SNORKEL   SNORKEL-STAY
ACCOMMODATIONS NEARBY: HOTEL   MOTEL   HOME RENTALS
ACCOMMODATION RATES: EXPENSIVE   MODERATE   INEXPENSIVE
RESTAURANTS NEARBY: EXPENSIVE   MODERATE   INEXPENSIVE
YOUR AREA IS: REMOTE   QUIET WITH ACTIVITIES x   LIVELY
LOCAL ACTIVITY/NIGHTLIFE: **Golf, snorkeling, tennis, biking, shopping, sightseeing**
CAR NEEDED TO EXPLORE AREA?   YES   NO
DUTY FREE SHOPPING?   YES   NO

LOCAL EMERGENCY SERVICES   NEAREST HYPERBARIC TREATMENT FACILITY
COASTGUARD: **Maalaea Harbor, Maui Hawaii**   AUTHORITY:
TELEPHONE: **808-244-5256**   LOCATION: **Honolulu, Hawaii**
CALLSIGNS: TELEPHONE:

LOCAL DIVING DOCTOR:
NAME: **Dr. Hoskinson**
LOCATION: **41 E. Lipoa, Kihei, Maui, HI 96753**
TELEPHONE: **808-874-8100**

Seven Underwater Wonders of the World

The Blue Hole – Belize, Central America

Wendy Canning Church

I can honestly say that I have never had a bad dive. Now this may seem a bit far fetched to those of you who must see a shark in order to be satisfied. To me, the sea is a place of wonderment and I treasure every moment I spend under it. If you speak with other seasoned divers, they will tell you that you if you remain quietly in one spot for 20 minutes, you will see the real parade of marvels go by.

There are a handful of dives, that will satisfy and intrigue everyone, those that I can recall as if I just surfaced, even if I have dived them years before. One of these is "The Blue Hole" in Belize. Lying in Light House Reef, "The Blue Hole" is actually a sunken cavern, 800 feet in depth. This is a dive for the experienced diver only and one that requires both preparation and a guide, no matter what depth you are planning to dive. The best time of year to dive this site is between March and July.

The day before our group was scheduled to dive the Blue Hole, each of us was taken down to a depth of 120 feet and tested for nitrogen narcosis. Only those who pass the test are allowed to embark on the adventure.

The next day our group of three descended into a world unknown to any of us except our guide. We made our way along the reef towards the inner edges of the cavern.

As we entered the mouth of the hole, I was struck by both the clarity and the color of the water. It was an unbelievably beautiful robin's egg blue, then as I looked down into the depths, there was nothing but complete darkness. As we continued our descent, I found myself looking up towards the surface. At one point I spotted two hammerhead sharks lurking above me like two bouncers, guarding the opening of the hole.

At 60 feet, we began to swim past a series of truly magnificent stalactites. They were shaped liked icicles and hung as if stretching to reach the bottom. They covered the outer walls and lined the hole for at least 120 feet. We found ourselves fascinated by the patterns they made along the wall.

At 160 feet, this magical band of stalactites stop and ledges, jutting out from the walls of the cavern, form. These ledges are at 170 feet. This is a absolute "No, No" for the sport diving limits, so do not even be tempted to head for them.

Unfortunately, one of the members of our group was tempted and swam down to stand on one of the ledges. I motioned to him to ascend, but he merely smiled back at me, clearly "narced". Our guide had to descend down to retrieve him. The diver had not only put the guide in danger, but the rest of us as well. We were forced to begin our ascent, our dive plan now broken, in order to compensate for the other diver's carelessness and selfishness.

Blue Hole by Hermando Ramones

Looking up, the pair of hammerheads still stood in our path, but appeared to be oblivious to our presence. We took the opportunity to swim near enough to touch the stalactites. Coming upon them, they sparkled against the black background of the cavern walls. They looked like diamonds scattered across sapphire velvet. I wanted to remain here forever, caught up in the beauty and understated elegance of these formations, but our time was quickly running out. The drama was ending and somehow I knew I would never return, and if I did, the wonderment I felt at that moment would never be the same.

I looked downward into the darkness beyond one last time and then continued my ascent. As we made our way safely past the pair of hammerheads, we found ourselves once again surrounded by clear crystalline water. We returned to the boat to make our safety stop.

It is important to remember when doing deep dives to remain within the limits. One does not need to push the limits to have a good time. I dived the "Blue Hole" safely within these limits and it was exciting and adventurous. Be sure to stick with your dive plan to ensure your safety and that of those diving with you. Never push your luck as the member of our group did. This will allow you to safely enjoy your dive and to take the memories away with you that the sea so generously gives up.

The added bonus to diving is that it is a sport that you can enjoy for the rest of your life. So adhere to the tables and the limits and protect that life. There is a big sea out there and you sure want to be around to explore it!

Dive The Ghost Fleet–Truk

DON LANMAN

The damp heat of the midnight air surprised me as I stepped out of the airplanes air conditioned cabin and climbed down the narrow ladder. As I made my way toward immigration I observed all manner of humanity filling the humid terminal from travelers to the locals who meet every plane as a form of entertainment. You see there's simply not much to do on this remote Banana Republic Island...unless you dive!

The tall sandy haired man, with a rugged complexion, signaled and I knew he must be our contact. My brother and I hurried through a crowd of brown, white and black faces to a waiting pick-up and without a word drove off into the night.

Diver on aircraft courtesy of Captain Lance Higgs

Wheels complained as the old Toyota rounded the corner of a dark alley, I was beginning to wonder if we had made the right choice in selecting this destination. The truck came to a halt as our equipment was yanked from the truck bed and heaved onto the deck of the waiting Zodiac.

I could barely make out the shape of the mighty THORNFIN in the distance, as the Zodiac bounced across the waves. It was like a scene from a cheap mystery thriller as we approached the large vessel and boarded her in the dead of night.

Welcome aboard! Lance finally said, as he helped us stow our dive gear. We were led on a brief tour, provided some snacks and shown to our accommodations amid ships.

"Breakfast is between 6 am and 9 am", Lance remarked, "with the first dive at 7 am. I'll need to know your dive history, however, and if it's been over 6 months since your last dive then you'll need a shallow test dive first. You see, in the middle of the South Pacific safety is a key issue on this liveaboard."

The S.S. THORNFIN was originally designed as an open ocean whaling ship in 1952. Converted and upgraded in the late '80's, she became the first liveaboard in Truk Lagoon. Measuring 170' from bow to stern she can accommodate 26 divers comfortably and cruise at 13 knots. She's anchored in the middle of the lagoon affording easy access to any wreck within minutes. Her crew is made up of Lance Higgs, the skipper, and local dive masters who have been diving these waters longer than any other group in Truk.

Too excited for sleep, I began re-reading the history of this "Pearl Harbor" for the Japanese that the Americans called Operation "HAILSTORM"!

Wine bottles courtesy of Captain Lance Higgs

There was no warning as hundreds of Navy F-6 Hellcats, CABOT's and VF-10's, from the massive Carrier Fleet, supported by land based B-24 bombers swept down on the sleepy lagoon that early morning in September 1944.

It was payback time! The Japanese were completely surprised and by the end of the operation over 60 major ships, from warships to tankers lay on the bottom of Truk Lagoon. It was the beginning of the end for the Imperial Japanese Fleet in that part of the South Pacific.

Now over 45 years later this Ghost Fleet rests quietly in its silent grave on the ocean floor a museum, a monument, a tribute to the gallant warriors who fell that fateful day.

The names of lost vessels reads like a Samurai Warriors honor roll. Destroyers; including the mighty Fumitsuki, Maikaze, Oite, Tachikaze. Cruisers; Katori and Naka plus 26 cargo laden merchantmen including the famous Fujikawa Maru, Hoki, Nagamo, Nippo and San Francisco Maru.

The new aluminum skiffs were waiting as we double checked our dive equipment. 6 am had come early but by 7 am we were prepared for the first dive. Safety was the watch word on the THORNFIN including a complete dive briefing for each wreck site, log checks and proficient local dive masters who knew each wreck like the palm of their hands.

The warm 79 degree water greeted us as we plunged into the lagoon. The dive objective was the famous **Hino Maru** or "**Gun High**" wreck. The 200 foot 900 ton vessel lies in only 40 feet of water with the frequently photographed deck gun rising to within 3 feet of the surface, visibility was over 75 feet. It was a great acclimation dive, shallow, interesting and easy.

By the third day, my brother and I had earned the distinction of "Gorilla Divers" because we were averaging 5 to 7 dives a day. Naturally the only safe method for this level of diving activity is computers. In addition, we paid careful attention to surface interval and scheduling of succeedingly shallower dive locations as each day progressed.

At the time of our dive trip there was a hyperbaric chamber on the island, however Lance did not give me a good feeling that it was managed by experienced professionals. So extreme caution should be exercised since the next best opportunity for medical assistance is Guam, two hours away by plane.

The deep, the mighty **Aikoku Maru**, a 500 foot 10,000 ton Armed Merchant Cruiser, was the most exciting wreck. This decompression dive required extensive planning since the wreck begins at 125 feet and reaches to over 200 feet.

Clearly an advanced dive, we planned a quick decent to the highest deck and penetrate the wreck for a maximum of 10 minutes.

This wreck is famous since it was recorded by Jacques Cousteau in his 1969 film and was found to contain the remains of over 400 sailors. Most of the remains were later recovered and given a Shinto burial ceremony.

As we entered the wreck I followed the dive master as if we were attached at the hip. We descended from deck to deck in the dark passageways to the massive boiler room. The walls of the wreck seemed to have been painted only yesterday, a tribute to the depth and unique pH factor in the water which does not support the sea worms and other parasites. In fact wooden boxes, chairs, tables and even some paper items are still remarkably intact.

No sooner had we arrived in the boiler room, then it was time to leave. As we made our way toward a breach in the hull I was filled with the spirit of Truk and the wonder of diving in a history capsule surrounded by memories from another time.

By the end of the week we had logged over 19 dives to 22 different wrecks from Betty Bombers and Zero fighters to destroyers. The artifacts were truly remarkable including fragile Sake bottles, cups and 18 inch artillery shells originally destined for the mighty battleship, Yamato.

As dawn arrived on the final day the same Zodiac which had delivered us to the THORNFIN was waiting to take us back to the island in time to make our flights. The crew of the THORNFIN had been wonderful, the food great and the diving unbelievable.

A quick luggage inspection at the airport, to assure we had not liberated any artifacts from the wrecks, and we were on our way with the haunting memory of the Ghost Fleet and a singular feeling that of all the dive locations I have visited this was the most inspired. I'll return to Truk.

Stingray City
North Sound, Grand Cayman

Wendy Canning Church

It is said that Stingray City is the most dived and snorkeled site in the world. I can surely believe it for its sea conditions are perfect year round. Despite the number of divers however, Stingray City still remains intact and undisturbed and contrary to most dive sites, the more divers the rays come in contact with, the friendlier they seem to get.

Years ago, fisherman discovered that this site, located just inside the North Sound Reef, had become a home and breeding ground to the rays. The fisherman dumped whatever they were not taking back to shore with them in this spot. The reef also acts as a barrier between the ray and the shark, its major predator. And so, generation after generation of rays are able to feed and romp freely in this shallow haven.

Word of the discovery spread throughout the island, and boats carrying scuba divers and snorkelers began making this a daily excursion. There has also been a tremendous amount of positive press coverage of the breeding ground, and so it has quickly become the world's favorite dive site. This dive is a must for anyone traveling to Grand Cayman and it makes a great dive for the entire family. Often, it is the first time a young person is introduced to the world of the sea as it is a perfect first dive for those just learning to dive.

Both my daughter and I have dived there many times and never tire of it. In fact, during our first trip to the Caymans, we dived there 3 times!

As most divers and snorkelers know, it is difficult to get close to a stingray in open water. Why is it so different here? Why do the rays allow you to rub their tummy like the family pet? It is because they feel protected. Here they are not only safe, but also the dive boats bring food with them. Due to the fact that the deepest water is at 30-35 feet, the divers and snorkelers are also comfortable. They are not worrying about air consumption or keeping up with the pack. They are free to swim along with the rays or to stay put and watch as the rays swim by and rub up against them. As a result, the rays have come to associate divers with food and with safety.

As you enter the water, squid in hand, the rays are no where in sight. But before you can blink, one family, then two, then three, then four appear from behind, above, left and right. Great big ones, little tiny brand new ones – they come in all shapes and sizes. When you squeeze the squid the rays immediately pick up the scent. You can feed them, touch them, rub them or just let them rub against you. Because of the depth you can use one of the new disposable underwater cameras. Even the amateur underwater photographer can capture the moment.

You will be amazed at how soft and docile these creatures are. On other dives you are lucky if you catch a sighting as they dart out from underneath you from their hiding place in the sand. No more squinting to see these magical figures as they disappear into the dark waters beyond. At Stingray City you are able to study their entire configuration for as long as your bottom time lasts. It really is the most remarkable and enjoyable experience that truly makes you feel like a child again – a petting zoo for adults.

For more information contact: Cayman Island Department of Tourism, 6100 Blue Lagoon Drive, Suite 250, Miami, Florida, 33126, (305) 266-2300.

Wendy Church and stingrays by Lois Hatcher

The Ultimate Wall Dive

Wendy Canning Church

How would you and a buddy like to dive to the depth of 800 feet and still manage to stay dry? Well, now it is possible, but only on Grand Cayman and only in the Atlantic Research Submersible.

Billed as "The Ultimate Wall Dive", the brochure promises a trip that you will not forget. "You are aboard the Atlantis Deep Sub, poised to begin your exciting decent to the spectacular Cayman Wall. The sub glides gently and quietly as you begin your exploration of the seas deeper mysteries. As the ambient light begins to dim, your pilot activates the sub's powerful quartz lights to expose the brilliant colors of the sponges, corals and other forms of deep marine life. Weather permitting, you will explore the *Kirk Pride*, a sunken ship balanced on a ledge of the great wall."

This brief description was enough to tempt me to sign up for the trip. But I warn you, if you are going to Grand Cayman, be sure to book this excursion weeks before hand, because it has become one of the islands favorite attractions.

My buddy and I were taken out to the submarine and introduced to the pilot. We climbed aboard and sat down in front of a large round window/porthole. The pilot sits above and behind the passengers. The submarine is 22 feet long, weighs 8 tons and carries only 2 passengers and the pilot. It is capable of going down to depths of 1200 feet.

Before we began our descent, all of the features of the submarine were explained to us and we were given a presentation regarding safety procedures. A launch remains on the surface that checks in with the pilot every fifteen minutes.

For this kind of dive you need a good deep wall that is close to shore and water with good visibility. Grand Cayman is fortunate enough to have extremely good visibility in most of its waters allowing the light to penetrate the depths.

Where the wall begins at 100-150 feet the topography resembles a deep terrace and is filled with the most abundant variety of sea life. Both the pink barrel and bird's beak sponges are exceptionally beautiful. Blackcap baislet, blackjacks and hovering gobi are all found in mind boggling numbers.

At 300 feet, the outer ledges are draped with both rope and melon sponges. You will notice black dots on the sponges, which indicates new growth is coming. The colors at this depth are simply magical. Most of the varieties of sponges depth are of the Sclero group, which is Latin for hard sponges.

As you continue even deeper, you pass through the thermal line. There is an abrupt change in temperature with a difference in density. At 500 feet, the sponges begin to become scarce and corals begin to dominate the scene.

The *Kirk Pride* lies at 600 feet and was discovered by the sub in 1985. The freighter is 170 feet long and went down in a storm in 1976. The submarine gets close enough for you to see into the galley and a Volkswagen Thing still on board.

At 700 feet, blocks and out crops of limestone come into view that resemble haystacks. There is also an abundance of black coral, fan coral, sea lilies, and feather stars. We also saw several specimens of deep water anemones, a 14 inch arrow crab, and a few spiny lobsters.

Descending down to 720 feet, we found some beautiful gargonias, which were 6 or 7 feet high and thought to be almost 700 years old.

Throughout the dive, you will notice that things appear smaller than they actually are due to the glass that is used in the window/porthole. I was fortunate enough to change seats with the pilot at one point and got a wonderful perspective of the world at 800 feet at its true size.

It was truly amazing to see all that life at such incredible depths! A pair of seahorses, snapper, and gobbies. We even saw rusticities, which are similar to stalactites, which were first identified on the Titanic. Soft corals, hard corals, wire corals, white fragile coral (madricis), branching stony coral, orange sea fans, cup corals, water inflated corals (soft corals that inflate themselves in water), plankton feeding fish, and black coral whips all in one dive! Who ever thought such a small craft could deliver such a great deal of adventure and entertainment!

For more information contact: Research Submersibles Ltd., Box 1719, Grand Cayman, BWI,(809) 949-8296. Children over the age of 8 are welcome. Each passenger receives a certificate and a free T-shirt and bring along your camera loaded with 400 ASA film.

Submarine by Dennis Denton

Portofino, Italy

Wendy Canning Church

No matter how many of the rich and famous visit the Italian Riviera each season, there are inhabitants, many of whom are fisherman, who have lived there for centuries quietly and simply. This is how we found Portofino when we arrived, a breathtaking town with a delightful mix of the sophisticated and the simplistic.

On one of our last scheduled dives, we disembarked from the Star Clipper and set out on their Zodiac. As we headed toward the lush shoreline which promised to hold a number of subaqueous caves and marble quarries, the sun tracked us and lifted the chill from the early morning. There was a gentle breeze that carried the fragrance of the vegetation and flowers that covered the surrounding cliffs. We journeyed at a slow pace as not to miss any of the beauty of the town just waking from slumber, surrounded by a blanket of turquoise water.

Once we arrived at our destination, we were briefed on the dive plan. We rolled over the side of the Zodiac and plunged into the warm waters of Italy. We descended slowly to a depth of 40 feet, expecting to explore a nearby reef and the belly of a grotto. We made our way through tall grasses, watching as many small fish darted in and out between the waving blades.

Ten minutes into our dive, we came upon a statue of Jesus Christ. He stood there with his arms stretched out towards the heavens. He appeared to be welcoming us and the fish that swam about him. We were awestruck as we had merely anticipated a mellow shallow dive that would serve as a way to ease ourselves away from these treasure filled waters. My husband (and buddy) turned to look at me and together we made the sign of the cross.

Swimming closer, we all moved slowly, almost as if we were sleepwalking. Separately, each ascended to clasp the hands that seemed to beckon us. I felt as if I had been blessed in my own way and to this day remember every detail of that moment.

The statue was commissioned by the local fisherman so they would be protected while at sea, ensuring a bountiful catch, and that no harm would come to them, their boats or their lines.

I can only speak for myself, and it is certainly not my intention to offend anyone practicing another form of religion, but this dive reconfirmed my belief in a higher power that I feel is infinitely good and watches over mankind.

I want to thank the fishermen for sharing their gift with all of us who were on that dive. I shall never forget the experience. A photograph has been purposefully omitted, so that you may bring your own image and interpretation to this dive.

Aliwal Shoal, Natal, South Africa

Wendy Canning Church

Shark by Andy Cobb

When Divers Exchange Member Al Venter invited me to South Africa to write about its beauty, above and below its waters, I was both elated and apprehensive. Faxes flew back and forth, the last of which was an article on Aliwal Shoal and the sharks that frequent this reef from June to December. A "P. S." was scribbled across the bottom informing me that this would be our last dive destination and that Al was certain we would encounter many sharks as we would be there in November. This got my attention. Aliwal Shoal is not home to your ubiquitous and mostly harmless nurse shark. Here you will find the raggie tooth (raggies), black tip, hammerheads, and sometimes the great white!

As it turned out, Aliwal Shoal was our first dive destination. On the hour plus drive from Durban I kept reminding myself that, as Franklin Roosevelt once said, "the only thing we have to fear is fear itself"– right?

On arrival we met with Andy Cobb, the Skipper of our boat and our dive guide. Aliwal Shoal sits six kilometers offshore. In good weather and at high tide boats are launched from the mouth of the Umkomas River. At other times, like the morning we dove the site, boats have to launch from the beach.

We were each handed a life jacket and told to position ourselves at various points on the inflatable. We were then instructed to "heave ho" after each swell of the ocean abated. We complied and our craft was set afloat. Have you ever ridden on a roller coaster and had that unexplainable feeling in the pit of your stomach? You told yourself that if you actually survived the nightmare you would never, ever, let anyone talk you into it again…I harbored these feelings as our inflatable made its way to the dive site over the rolling and angry sea.

With these sea conditions one must have a skipper who knows the waters intimately. The skipper must find a break in the swells and surges for passage to the open sea. This is done by steering straight into the swells. Just before they break the craft is quickly turned about and heads toward the shoreline in order to ride the crest. One mistake means flooding or capsizing. This maneuver continues little by little until you find an opening and make your way out through the breakers and into the calmer seas beyond.

Arriving at Aliwal Shoal we were given a dive profile, and buddy teams were assigned. Johnny, an instructor and dive guide, was assigned as my dive buddy. I got the feeling he had been carefully briefed, not so much regarding my diving ability, but rather as to what my reaction might be on this first encounter with the sharks of Aliwal

Shoal. We rolled over into the sea and descended slowly swimming along the reef towards the mouth of a cave. Andy told me later that he usually keeps his divers outside the cave and they observe the sharks at a distance. Today was to be an exception...

Johnny and I were at the entrance of the cave observing some 20 to 30 raggies from a safe distance when I felt a sudden push from behind. I found myself inside the belly of the cave–thanks Al! Al motioned to my buddy and then came and took my hand as we swam closer to the sharks now numbering close to 100.

At first it appeared that they did not notice us, but as the numbers grew they became aware of the divers. I had the feeling that they were curious as to what these floating objects were that were intruding on their territory.

In turn, I observed them in awe and wonderment. I was a visitor in their world, yet could not help but feel a sense of oneness with these majestic creatures. My fear and apprehension vanished and was replaced by delight and excitement at this incredible and truly magical experience.

We made our way towards the far side of the cave observing the raggies from afar. Johnny began to sift through the sand and found both a raggie's and a black tip's tooth which he gave to me. I keep these on my desk and when I see them I remember the beauty of the Aliwal Shoal and the sharks that call it home.

Sharks do not like human flesh. They generally only attack when provoked or if there is blood in the water. The number of registered shark attacks in comparison to the number of dives made is minimal. In fact, when the conditions are right, Aliwal Shoal is one of the world's seven best dive sites.

When Al asked me to write about my impressions of the dive I sat and wondered how I could possibly describe something that should really only be experienced first hand. The ride, the reef, the cave, the sharks–its all part of a magnificent adventure that you feel yourself giving into despite all the concern and apprehension. I left wanting to stay, and cannot wait to return. In fact, I could have spent the entire week diving the shoal. Of course, it helps that Andy Cobb runs one of the finest dive operations in South Africa and has only the best skippers and crew. He and his crew operate an incredibly safe and professional dive operation.

Thank you Al, Andy, Johnny and the rest of the crew for an experience I shall remember for the rest of my life...

William H. (Bill) Charlton Jr. is a retired U.S. MarineCorps Officer, former karate instructor, current practitioner of Tai Chi Chuan, and a SCUBA Diving Instructor with the International Diving Educators Association (IDEA), He served twenty-nine years in the Marine Corps, retiring in 1989, and is now pursuing his Master's Degree in Nautical Archaeology at Texas A&M University,

The Institute of Nautical Archaeology (INA) is a non-profit organization operating mainly on grants and donations. Anyone interested in learning more about nautical archaeology and aiding INA in its world-wide efforts is invited to join. Members receive the quarterly INA Newsletter, scientific reports, and book discounts (Regular member - $25; Contributor - $50; Supporter - $100; Life - $500; Benefactor - $1000; Student/Retired - $15). Write: Institute of Nautical Archaeology, P.O. Drawer HG, College Station, Texas 77841-5137,

Uluburun, Turkey
Diving on the World's Oldest known Shipwreck

I started diving in 1967 along the coast of Southern California, and got wet every so often over the next fifteen years, all uncertified. In the early 1980's I decided to get some professional training and went on to win my SCUBA Instructor rating. I've done most of my diving in the Far East, mainly around the island of Okinawa, where I taught recreational diving while in the U.S. Marine Corps.

When Wendy asked me to write an article for this book, I told her the sport diving area I was most familiar with was Okinawa, but since I hadn't been there in over four years I wouldn't be providing the most up-to-date information. But, given my preference, I'd rather not write about diving that just anybody could do, but about one particular diving experience that only a very few people from around the world would ever have the opportunity to take part in. I told her about my participation in the underwater archaeological excavation of a Late Bronze Age shipwreck at Uluburun, Turkey, and she consented.

THE PROJECT

Under the direction of Dr. George F. Bass, considered by many to be the father of underwater archaeology, and his field director, Cemal Pulak, the Texas A&M University-based Institute of Nautical Archaeology (INA), in cooperation with the government of Turkey, is excavating the remains of a ship that sank at Uluburun (Grand Promontory) on the southwestern coast of Turkey sometime around 1300 B.C. This is generally acknowledged as the oldest known shipwreck in the world. There are older sites where ships' cargoes have been found, but hull timbers have not been found with them. These are probably incidents where ships capsized and dumped their cargoes, and floated off to sink elsewhere. The Uluburun wreck is, without a doubt, an intact shipwreck.

The excavation began in 1984 and will continue through at least 1994. Each season begins around mid-May and ends in early to mid-September; bad weather and rough seas the remainder of the year make diving unsafe. With only rare exceptions all members of the excavation team are either current or former students in the Texas A&M Nautical Archaeology Program, or INA staff members from the U.S.A. or Turkey. One noted exception is the Turkish government representative on the excavation, the "Commissioner," who comes from the Bodrum Museum of Underwater Archaeology and is usually a diving member of the team.

This excavation is so important, archaeologically and historically, that many students choose to participate for more than just the two or so years during which they attend Master's Degree classes at Texas A&M; some have stayed with the project for its full run. All in all, fewer than one hundred people have had the privilege of working on this project during the ten years it's been active.

PREPARING FOR THE EXCAVATION SEASON

The camp at Uluburun is built from the ground up at the beginning of each season, and completely dismantled at season's end – if not, rough winter seas would destroy it and carry the building materials away. Around the 20th of May an advance party of five or six Nautical Archaeology students from Texas A&M meet Robin Piercy, the camp supervisor from the INA staff in Turkey, at the little sea-side town of Kas (rhymes with wash). For about a week before this a local work crew has been transporting the required building materials from a storage warehouse in Kas out to the campsite at Uluburun, to await the camp-building crew. The crew rides out to Uluburun on a little 25-foot boat owned by a local retired school teacher, about an hour-long trip. This is also the boat that brings food, drinking water, and supplies from Kas to the camp each day of the season, except on the rare day when the seas are too rough to make the trip. This same man and his boat have provided these services for the INA team at Uluburun since the excavation began.

Preparing stone anchors for lifting to the surface at the end of the 1991 season. By Donald Frey

Camp-building goes from sun-up to sun-down; there's a lot to do and not much time to do it in. The first to go up is the kitchen and dining hall, and our Turkish cook and his helper, the only non-diving members of the crew, arrive as soon as they are completed. In all, we put up the kitchen/dining hall, three team sleeping huts, the cook's sleeping hut, a conservation laboratory, a combination headquarters office and work room for keeping the excavation site plan, and the head.

The remaining team members arrive one-by-one during campbuilding week, all hands must be on site and all of the construction must be completed by the end of May. Excavation is scheduled to begin on the first day of June.

THE SHIPWRECK

Our ship was a merchantman that sailed the Mediterranean at about the time Tutankhamen was Pharaoh in Egypt, or shortly thereafter. In fact, she was carrying such a rich assortment of cargo that she may have been a royal envoy, according to Professor Bass. This included ingots of pure copper and tin which, when combined, yielded bronze for weapons and tools; ingots of beautiful cobalt-blue glass, raw materials for makers of glass objects all around the eastern Mediterranean; raw ivory in the form of an elephant tusk and hippopotamus teeth; amphoras (two-handled clay jars) containing terebinthine resin, possibly used as incense in Egyptian religious ceremonies, or in the making of perfumed oils in the Aegean; unworked logs of African blackwood, called hbny, or ebony, by the Egyptians; jewelry of gold, silver, agate, faience, and baltic amber; new Cypriot pottery carried inhuge pithoi (clay storage jars [sing. pithos]) that served as ancient china barrels; and a variety of bronze tools and weapons.

We suspect the ship wrecked in stormy seas by hitting the barren, rocky, Uluburun cliff. It slid beneath the water at the base of the cliff and on down the sloping seabed, coming to rest between a rock ledge and a huge boulder-like rock outcropping; the stern would have rested at a depth of about 140 feet, and the bow just below 160 feet. As the wooden hull came apart over the years, due mainly to the effects of wood-eating marine

Toredo worms, the cargo spilled out. Some of the large clay storage jars rolled down slope to almost 200 feet; might there be more still deeper that we haven't found yet?

The shipwreck at Uluburun is the oldest yet found anywhere in the world, and, without doubt, the most important from the standpoint of what it will teach us about the ancient world. It is also the oldest and deepest shipwreck ever to be completely excavated with the same meticulous care as any land excavation.

My purpose here, though, is not to talk about the importance of this excavation to scholars, but to relate to the general diving community the thrills and hazards of diving on the world's oldest known shipwreck. I worked as a member of the excavation team during the 1990 excavation season and as the excavation's Divemaster and Diving Safety Officer for the 1991, '92, and '93 seasons. Interested readers will find detailed information on the excavation in the publications I'll list at the end of this article.

The diving at Uluburun is arduous, to say the least. The remains of the ship and its cargo lie at depths from 140 feet to nearly 200 feet. As all divers know, bottom times at these depths, diving on compressed air, cannot be very long. We dive with four-person teams using the following profiles: a morning dive of 20 minutes bottom time, followed by 20 minutes of decompression on pure oxygen at a depth of 20 feet; a minimum five-hour surface interval; and an afternoon dive of 20 minutes, followed by 25 minutes of decompression at 20 feet on pure oxygen.

These diving profiles were developed during the first years of the excavation under the supervision of Dr. Yancey Mebane, the Divers Alert Network's (DAN's) Training Director, and other hyperbaric physicians. They began with very conservative use of the U.S. Navy Dive Tables (in other words, using the next-deeper-depths and next-longer-times), and later added in-water decompression on pure oxygen. The profiles I've described, tailored specifically for this excavation, were finalized in 1988 by Dr. Richard Vann of Duke University, and are now referred to as the Vann Tables. As a result of the very strict control exercised over the diving on this project, we've experienced only two major cases of decompression sickness in over 15,400 individual dives, totaling some 4,948 hours of bottom time, logged since the excavation began. A very impressive record, but more about that later.

Diver uses a lifting baloon to raise an oxide-shaped copper ingot by Donald Frey

We dive with standard scuba equipment, but we're often considered by modern sport divers as being a little old fashioned. We carry double 10-liter tank rigs with built-in shoulder straps and waist belts, and horse-collar BC's, Most of our equipment is made by Cressi-Sub of Italy. Cressi has been an active supporter of the Uluburun excavation since its beginning.

The visibility is generally good, from 80 to 100 feet on most days. Rarely do we experience turbidity during the summer months, especially below 140 feet. For the first two to three weeks of June, the water is quite cool, as low as 65° Fahrenheit. You don't really feel the cold while working on the bottom, but hanging on the decompression stop for 20 or 25 minutes after a 20 minute dive is almost painful for some. This is heavy-wetsuit-and-hood diving. From the end of June through the middle of August, the water is quite comfortable; some of our divers strip down to thin shorty wetsuits.

Then it starts to cool off again toward the end of August, back on with the heavy wetsuits and hoods.

There are those who feel the 45 minutes per day spent on the decompression stop is wasted time. Some innovative individual years ago discovered that a paperback book, properly prepared by soaking for a day in a bucket of sea water, handled carefully, and kept in a zip-lock bag in the decompression stop bucket when not in use, will last an entire season underwater. It's amusing to see four divers, either floating freely or hanging on to the stop-bucket handles, all reading. One team member studies Turkish for 45 minutes every day while decompressing. I've actually heard two divers at Uluburun, who are otherwise good friends who work well together, practically beg the Director not to put them on the same dive, not because they don't want to work together, but because they're both reading the same book during decompression.

There's a lot of marine life around the wreck, great in quantity, but not in variety, as I'm used to in the tropical waters of the western Pacific. During my first few dives on the wreck in 1990 I counted seven large groupers in and around the wreck area. Then a long-time member of the team told me there was an old seaman's superstition that these represented the original crew of our ship. Were there seven people on board when she crashed against the cliff? Eerie, isn't it?

We never wear footgear while working on the wreck. This makes us much more aware of where we're putting our feet, and reduces the potential for damage to the wreck. But we have to be especially watchful on the bottom; there are stone fish everywhere. And there are several moray eels that live in the rocks around the wreck area and under some of the large stone anchors. One day we jumped into the water to find ourselves surrounded by large jacks, some as long as five feet. It was quite exciting, descending through a school of dozens of these predators, knowing they were eyeing you as food as they circled around. But they only stayed around for a couple of days and we haven't seen them since. We often see two or three large dolphins in the area, usually in the early mornings or late afternoons. They sometimes look like they're putting on a show just for us. They truly are magnificent animals to watch, especially up close. We see manta rays and large sea turtles and monk seals, as well.

The diving we do at Uluburun is deep and dangerous, even with all the safety precautions built into our procedures, As the Divemaster, each time a team goes into the water I glance to the heavens with a quick prayer. Our divers are well-trained, though; I know! During my four years on the excavation I taught deep diving to all first-time team members, but the closest hospital is in Kas, almost half an hour away in our fast Zodiac, and there are no hyperbaric physicians and no decompression chamber at that facility. If we had to depend only on local medical support, excavation of this shipwreck would be out of the question.

But we do not, for two reasons. First, we always have a hyperbaric physician on the excavation team; and second, is our research vessel, the trusty VIRAZON, a 65-foot-long much-modified1950's-vintage U.S. Army inland-waterways cargo ship. She is crewed by two Turkish members of the INA staff in Turkey: TufanTuranli is the Captain and Murat Tilev the Chief Engineer. VIRAZON was donated to George Bass many years ago for use in his field work. When not involved in the Uluburun excavation or surveying the Turkish coast for other ancient shipwrecks, VIRAZON is berthed in the harbor at Bodrum, the ancient city of Halicarnassus, and the location of a Crusader castle which houses the Bodrum Museum of Underwater Archaeology, the only museum in Turkey specifically dedicated to artifacts from beneath the sea. INA's Turkish headquarters is also located in Bodrum, not far from the castle.

Within what was VIRAZON's cargo hold now sits a double-lock decompression chamber and bunk space for nine. This space also houses the oxygen and air cylinders required for operation of the decompression chamber. Just forward of this space is a small galley. The cargo hatch was welded shut once the chamber was installed, and the dive team's gear is now stowed on the main deck in racks fabricated atop the old hatch cover. Adjacent to these gear racks are racks holding the eight oxygen cylinders that supply the decompression stop regulators and four large air cylinders which make up the cascade system for the scuba tank filling station. Both the oxygen and air sources can be shunted as backups for operation of the decompression chamber.

Just aft of the pilot house are head and shower and a small "day cabin" used for team meetings and as a shady indoor relaxation space. Above the day cabin is a sun deck covered by an awning - the sun does get intense on the Mediterranean coast of Turkey in the middle of the summer. Aft of the day cabin is a small stern deck, below which is an equipment storage compartment.

Down in the engine room, alongside the main engine and primary and backup electrical power generators, the additional machinery required to support an underwater archaeological excavation has been installed. These include an air compressor for filling scuba tanks and two air pumps which power the underwater airlifts. The Chief Engineer's workbench and tool storage area are also down here.

Our days start at about 6:30 am, when the supply boat arrives. We off-load food, supplies, and visitors, and pump fresh water from a tank in the boat to two tanks in the camp. There is no fresh water in the area of the camp; it comes to us from the public water system in Kas.

We often get visitors at Uluburun, but they must have prior approval from the excavation's Field Director, Cemal Pulak. If not, they are not allowed to board the supply boat in Kas, or if they come in private boats, they may not come ashore. Providing guides for visitors disrupts the diving schedule, unless planned for in advance. The general public is not allowed to visit the site either for the same reason. Local dignitaries and police officials, government officials, and groups from other archaeological projects in the area, sometimes visit. Crews from Turkish Television do documentaries on our project for broadcast across Turkey, and INA conducts archaeological cruises along the Turkish coast for those wanting to visit ancient sites while cruising the beautiful Turkish waters; a visit to Uluburun is the highlight of these cruises.

Breakfast goes at 7:00 A.M. and usually consists of water, diced tomatoes with oregano sprinkled on top, black olives, white cheese (feta) and yellow cheese, Turkish bread and jams, and sometimes eggs, followed by strong Turkish tea. Take my word, it's a wonderful way to start the day.

The team goes out to the VIRAZON at 8:00 A.M. in our twelve-foot aluminum runabout powered by a fifteen horsepower outboard motor. The first dive team suits-up and is in the water by about 8:20 A.M. The divers go in like clockwork after that. With a normal complement of about 24 divers on the team, minus one or two out with medical complaints on any given day, we usually run between four and six dives per morning and afternoon session,

The noon-time break begins with lunch, the usual water and bread, and heavy on the vegetables, followed by tea. On this, as on all archaeological projects, there are many duties to perform in addition to excavation: photography, conservation, artifact recording, site plan updates, and routine equipment maintenance. Much of this work is done during the noon-time break.

The afternoon dives begin at 3:00 P.M. and continue until almost 7:00 P.M. when dinner is served. Again, water, bread, and vegies, and often a meat dish - chicken, mutton, fish, or beef - followed by that wonderful strong Turkish tea. Depending on your workload, you'll either go back to work on your additional duties or relax for a while after dinner. A small electrical generator provides camp lighting from sun-down until 10:00 pm.

We maintain a schedule of six days of diving and one day off for three and a half months. Unlike many archaeological projects which run multiple sessions with different crews during a summer excavation season, Uluburun runs straight through the summer with only one crew. Considering the length of time it takes to train and acclimatize new divers, and the short amount of time we put in on the wreck because of restricted bottom times, we must have the same crew for the entire summer to be effective. The average team member at Uluburun will make nearly 150 dives in one season. Counting bottom time and decompression time, that's over 100 hours in the water per season.

Everyone looks forward to Friday, our day off. You can stay in camp and either relax, catch up on your additional duty workload, or get away from camp and go to Kas when the supply boat returns to town. Whichever you choose, you are expressly forbidden from diving on this day. This is one of the key elements of Professor Bass' dive schedules, which he has included since beginning his career in underwater archaeology in the early 1960's - one day off per week to facilitate off-gassing of nitrogen.

While I completely agree with and support this ban on day-off diving, I sometimes wish it were different. I've gotten to know instructors from two of the sport diving services in Kas, one is a former Turkish Navy diver (who trained for a time with the U.S. Navy SEALS), and the other is a Turkish/German man/wife team; both have invited me to dive with them on Fridays, but understand why I cannot.

For sport divers interested in diving in Turkey, I suggest arrangements be made through a travel service familiar with these matters. Sport diving is strictly controlled in Turkey, one of the main reasons being that there are antiquities everywhere. The sea floor is littered with anchors and clay jars and other remnants of the past, and the government is interested in keeping them in Turkey. Diving services are licensed by the government, and then closely monitored. Instructors and Dive masters are charged with protecting the environment, as well as the antiquities. Shell collecting is forbidden and there are severe penalties for attempting to take antiquities out of the country.

Now, after all those admonitions, if you're still interested in diving in Turkey, go for it! Though I haven't been able to sport dive there myself, I've talked to many tourists in Kas and I'm told there are many beautiful places to dive in the area. I do know that in the summer the dive services rarely lack business and their dive boats are almost always full; all internationally-recognized certification cards are accepted.

Kas is a little town that's now about twice the size it was five years ago. Tourism has taken over. Lodging facilities, restaurants, and souvenir shops are everywhere. And, of course, it's a real treat for us to get out of camp and see new faces on Fridays. There are good places to eat, bargains to be had by souvenir hunters, and the people are very friendly, especially when they find out we're "from VIRAZON." They may not know all of our faces, but they do know what VIRAZON is doing out at Uluburun. Unfortunately, though, this short one-day-a-week break doesn't give us enough time to visit many of the numerous land archaeological sites in the area.

I had quite a pleasant surprise in Kas early in the summer of 1991 when I met three of the local people who were trying to learn Tai Chi Chuan. Since I've been a practitioner of this Chinese martial art for twelve years, they asked if I would workout with them. I spent two to three hours with them every Friday for the rest of the summer, quite an enjoyable and unexpected experience.

I mentioned earlier two serious cases of decompression sickness that had been suffered on this project. Neither of these were attributed to problems with the dive tables or improper or unsafe practices by the divers, while diving. One case was caused by not waiting long enough to recover from a stomach illness, and the other from dehydration during the day off. The classic, and most serious case was of a team member who went to Kas one Friday, hiked around the hills outside of town all day without drinking any water, had a few beers with dinner that night, and dived the next morning. He was hit on his first dive. Fortunately, because of the chamber on the VIRAZON, he received immediate treatment and recovered fully, as did the other case.

Scuba diving is an inherently dangerous activity which we try to make as safe as possible by practicing safe diving measures. Deep diving, especially as deep as we dive at Uluburun, is much more dangerous. To insure the safety of our divers, each first-time member of the team is taken through a deep diving course before being allowed to dive on the wreck. They are then assigned as buddies to the experienced excavators, and spend two to three weeks acclimatizing at wreck level before being allowed to begin excavating on their own.

At the beginning of each season all divers are taken through a stepped sequence of acclimatization dives - 60, 100, 130, and 160 feet - before any work is done on the wreck. This sequence is repeated any time a diver is out of the water for longer than three days.

Possibly the most important duty at Uluburun, one that is shared by all members of the team on a rotating basis, is that of Timekeeper. The Timekeeper ensures that buddy-checks have been completed, and gives all signals for dives to begin and end. Time is kept on two sets of clocks and specific times of each dive are recorded in the master dive log. Underwater signals are sent by an underwater sound transmitter controlled by the Timekeeper in the pilot house: a warning signal at eighteen minutes and the come-up signal at twenty minutes. Divers may either free-ascend to the decompression stop twenty feet below the VIRAZON, or follow a safety line tied between the decompression stop and the bottom, but buddy-teams must ascend together.

Safety features on the bottom include the just-mentioned safety line, which is tied between the decompression stop and one of the truly innovative safety features of underwater archaeology, the underwater telephone booth, developed by Michael Katzev, a student of Professor Bass, many years ago. The telephone booth is so named because it originally held a telephone for communication between the bottom and the surface, but this became more trouble than it was worth and was discontinued; the underwater phone booth remains as a valuable safety feature, though. It consists of a large hemispherical plastic dome chained to a heavy steel base plate. The dome is filled with air and provides an emergency haven for a diver in need, or a place where two or three divers can remove their masks and regulators and talk, although your voice at these depths is pretty high-pitched and squeaky. We have two phone booths on the bottom, one at 135 feet, the upper end of the wreck site, and one at 170 feet, the lower end. Air in the phone booths is refreshed weekly (or more often, if used) by releasing air into them from freshly-filled tanks. Spread around the wreck site we also have five safety tanks, full scuba tanks with regulators attached. No matter where on the wreck a diver is working, he is never more than a few feet from a safety tank or a phone booth, should an emergency occur.

I've been diving for many years and I've seen many things beneath the sea, but nothing can match the thrill I feel each time I descend to the wreck area at Uluburun. It's like taking a time machine back 3,300 years. Sometimes, while floating down toward the wreck, I fantasize, trying to imagine what our ship looked like, whole, intact, and sailing proudly across the ancient Mediterranean. Each time I touch an artifact, whether a glass or copper ingot, or a clay jar, or a bronze weapon, or a piece of wood, I thrill with the realization that another human being fashioned this piece some 33 centuries ago, and that I am able to aid in the effort to recover it from the depths so that people of my own time can marvel at it. I don't know where, when, or if it will ever happen, but it's going to take an awful lot to top my experiences at Uluburun, because, for me, this is the ultimate diving experience.

Can any diver be a nautical archaeologist? Well, probably not just any diver. First, you must have an appreciation for the past and a desire to bring the material remains of the past into the light of the present day, not for their intrinsic value, but for what they can tell us about their time. Quite often the more valuable items, such as gold and silver, are of much less interest to the archaeologist than those of lesser value. Take, for instance, tin. Tin is much less valuable than gold, but finding ingots of pure tin on the Uluburun wreck, the first ever from the Bronze Age, has shown us for the first time how the ancients transported one of the key ingredients of bronze.

Secondly, you must truly care about the physical properties of the artifacts you're handling. Many items that have spent 3,300 years in sea water are severely deteriorated and require great care to insure they aren't destroyed in the process of excavation. Sometimes just touching a clay or glass vessel in the wrong way can break it into a thousand pieces. Wood that has spent that many years in the ocean often has a consistency somewhere between wet cardboard and cottage cheese. It's a terrible feeling to pick up a piece of wood and watch it crumble and float away with the current like dust in the wind. Training in the delicate art of underwater excavation can only take place-underwater; it cannot be learned in the classroom, and I'm fortunate to have been able to learn from two of the masters, Professor George Bass and Cemal Pulak, at Uluburun.

Professor Bass reminds his students, especially those of us who are long-time divers, that we were not accepted into his Nautical Archaeology Program because of our diving skills. The all-around nautical archaeologist must first be a competent scholar, and then a competent diver. Bass often says it's easier to train an archaeologist to dive than to train a diver to be an archaeologist.

I'm often asked what we do with the artifacts we recover at Uluburun - do we get to bring them home? Do we get to keep them? NO and NO! Unlike years ago when archaeologists took everything they possibly could, all those things from ancient times that now populate the great and not-so-great museums of the world, everything we raise from the Uluburun shipwreck goes into the Bodrum Museum of Underwater Archaeology. On the rare occasion that we need to take samples back to America for material identification or dating, we obtain special permission from the Turkish government to do so.

For us, one of the unfortunate misconceptions is that underwater archaeologists and treasure hunters are one and the same. They are not! In the opinions of many underwater archaeologists treasure hunters are interested only in plundering shipwrecks for personal gain. On the other hand, underwater archaeologists, like their terrestrial brothers, are concerned with raising artifacts from earlier times for the purpose of adding to our knowledge of the past. The two are assuredly not the same.

Gold jewelry (clockwise from left): pendant with nude Canaanite goddess who clasps a gazelle in each hand, the Nefertiti scarab, a pendant with a Canaanite star motif, and a crescent-shaped pendant.
Photo by Donald Frey

People in general, and divers in particular, should know and appreciate that a shipwreck is a storehouse of information about an earlier time, and an irreplaceable one, at that. Unlike a land archaeological site, which may span hundreds, or even thousands, of years, a shipwreck is a complete slice of life from a particular time in history, often providing more information about that specific time than any land site. Much can be learned from an intact shipwreck; this is greatly diminished, though, when the wreck has been looted.

It's heartbreaking for an underwater archaeologist to investigate a shipwreck, only to find that it's been plundered in a search for "treasure." Such a wreck might look as if a Tasmanian Devil has gone through it, "worthless" items strewn about, cast aside in the frenzied search for "loot." If you come across a shipwreck, report it to the proper authorities. And please, keep your distance! It's deceptively easy to destroy important information on a wreck. Many ancient wrecks are so fragile that even the movement of fins near the wooden hull can destroy the wood. And diving on some wrecks can be extremely dangerous, as well. Let the archaeologist excavate and publish the shipwreck, properly conserve the artifacts, and display them for all to see. And don't buy artifacts from the treasure hunters, it only encourages them and keeps them at their nefarious trade.

One of the most important lessons I've learned in my many years of diving, both from teaching sport diving and now from my work as an underwater archaeologist, is the importance of getting the proper training for the type of diving you want to do. Deep diving and wreck diving are known to be dangerous. Wendy tells me of untrained divers dying on the wreck of the Andrea Doria. These losses are tragic, and avoidable. There are many exciting things to do under the water, deep diving, cave diving, wreck-diving, and ice diving, to name a few, but they all require specialized training. When you want to try a new experience in diving of any type you didn't learn about in your Open Water diving course, take a specialty course. Then go out and enjoy your new experience with the confidence that you really do know what you are doing.

As I said earlier, my main purpose in writing this article was to tell about the experience of diving on the world's oldest known shipwreck, but maybe I've sparked the interest of some who would now like to know more about this particular excavation from the archaeological standpoint, as well. Popular articles on the subject, readily available in most libraries, include: *"The Search for a Bronze Age Shipwreck"* by Cemal Pulak and Don Frey in the July/August 1985 edition of Archaeology magazine; *"Oldest Known Shipwreck Reveals Splendors of the Bronze Age"* by George F. Bass in the December 1987 edition of National Geographic magazine (my favorite); and *"Civilization under the Sea"* by George F. Bass in the April-May 1989 edition of Modern Maturity magazine.

Those interested in greater detail should read the following scholarly reports:
In the International Journal of Nautical Archaeology and Underwater Exploration -

>1984 edition - "A late Bronze Age shipwreck at Kas, Turkey,"
>Bass, Frey, and Pulak.
>In the American Journal of Archaeology -
>1986 edition - "A Bronze Age Shipwreck at Uluburun(Kas).
>1988 edition - "The Bronze Age Shipwreck at Ulu burun, Turkey.
>1989 edition - "The Bronze Age Shipwreck at Ulu burun: 1986 Campaign,"
>Bass, et al.

My sincere thanks to Dr. George F. Bass and Cemal Pulak for their comments on this article.

HONEYMOON & ANNIVERSARY SECTION

Wendy Canning Church

The Ocean Club Golf and Tennis Resort
Nassau, Bahamas

The Ocean Club (mentioned in the Bahamas chapter), lies discreetly tucked away between Merv Griffin's private home and the three other hotel properties which comprise his compound on Paradise Island.

Paradise Island has an interesting history. It has developed from a hog farm into one of the best managed and marketed properties in the Bahamas. The Ocean Club has always been a hideaway for the "Rich and Famous." Situated just minutes away from the hustle of downtown Nassau, it truly is a "Shangri-La," as it was aptly named by its second owner, who purchased the property in 1939 for a winter hideaway. Dr. Axel Werner-Gren, a Swedish industrialist considered it his private utopia. Unfortunately, in the 30's the good doctor's finances were running low and he sold his utopia to Huntington Hartford for $9.5 million. Mr. Hartford had very definite plans for Shangri-La. He wanted to turn it, and the adjacent land, into a world class resort.

The name "Hog Island" was not synonymous with his plans, so in 1962 he petitioned the government to let him change the name to Paradise Island.

The Ocean Club was built adjacent to Shangri-La and had 52 rooms and four cottages. Unfortunately, in 1966, after Resorts International Inc. brought the complex, the eastern section of the hotel and Shangri-La were burned to the ground.

The hotel was restored and now contains 71 rooms, suites and villas. Guests arrive at the entrance of a small colonial style building with a Bahamian presence. At once, you are reminded more of a southern mansion than of a hotel. The hotel's size gives it a sense of elegance and intimacy.

The public rooms resemble libraries, and there are many intimate corners in which to have a drink, play backgammon, sit and read, or just reflect. The balconies overlook the turquoise Bahamian waters. The villas are decorated similar to the guest rooms, and have private patios and jacuzzis.

You may dine each evening in the beautiful Courtyard Terrace Restaurant. As twilight falls, international cuisine is served among gentle cascading fountains and exotic foliage.

The fun of staying here is that its sister resort, the Paradise Island Resort and Casino, is a stroll down the beach or a short taxi ride away. Here you will find 12 restaurants that are part of the "dine around" program and a 30,000 square foot casino, complete with all the entertainment of a Las Vegas style show.

"Angels in Love" statue at Gardens Ocean Club, Nassau
by Wendy Canning Church

While a guest, do not forget to take a stroll through the unforgettable Versailles Gardens. The gardens extend for a quarter of a mile in a north-south direction from the Ocean Club. Werner-Gren designed the original gardens and Huntington Hartford continued to beautify them. Mr. Hartford purchased a twentieth century Augustinian Cloister from William Randolph Hearst and had it shipped from France to the island, where it was reassembled. This structure and the nearby terraced gardens filled with marble statuary and fountains are breathtaking. There is a swimming pool at the Cloister's entrance where guests can have luncheon. They have Harter tennis courts and golf is nearby. From its private beach you can choose from an array of watersports and have lunch at the beach club restaurant as well.

As times pass, so do great gems of hotels. They are either torn down or go the way of modern glitz. The Ocean Club retains that sense of good taste that is timeless, while never losing sight of its commitment to the ultimate comfort of its guests in an atmosphere of understated luxury.

Versailles Gardens, Ocean Club, Nassau courtesy of Ocean Club

All these amenities make the Ocean Club perfect for a honeymoon or anniversary.

The Ocean Club Golf and Tennis Resort, Paradise Island, Bahamas. In U.S. toll-free (800) 321-3000 or (809) 363-3000.

NOTE: *There is scuba diving nearby at Bahamian Divers.*

Barbados

Wendy Canning Church

Sand Lane Hotel and Golf Club

As you enter the gates of the Sandy Lane Hotel and Golf Club and make your way down the winding driveway you feel separated from the outside world and enclosed in your own paradise. The landscaping is beautifully understated and decorated with terra-cotta fountains. I stepped out of the limousine and through the entrance into an open room. This room houses

Sandy Lane Hotel, Barbados courtesy of Lou Hammond & Associates, N.Y.

367

the reception desk and serves as a passage way to the other areas of the hotel. The room is surrounded by glass with a balcony that looks out over the beach and the sea beyond. The view is spectacular.

From April 1991 until its reopening in November 1992, 86 of the guest rooms received extensive renovation, enlarging them and extending their balconies even further towards the sea. New terrazzo was also placed throughout the public areas. During the renovation period the staff was sent overseas to receive further training! The upper terrace and the Starlight Terrace remain unchanged, for who needs to improve upon perfection.

My room was one of the newly renovated in the north wing, decorated with quiet pastels and marble floors. A fruit basket and a complimentary bottle of Bollinger Champagne awaits each guest, in addition to the small refrigerator that is packed with delights. A complimentary newspaper also arrives every morning. I stepped onto the balcony and looked out upon a delicate fountain surrounded by manicured gardens and the sea beyond. The 91 rooms and 30 suites have a view of either the garden or the sea; I was fortunate to have both.

Under the able management of Richard Williams, born and raised in Barbados, each guest is ensured the ultimate in comfort and luxury. Sandy Lane has a staff of 370, a ratio of 2 for every guest. They also offer 24-hour room service, a maid who will even unpack for you, staff who will bring you a drink as you bask in the sun at the mere raise of your flag, or will even fetch the chilled champagne and pate from your room.

With two oceanfront restaurants you can either dine in a formal or a more relaxed atmosphere. Breakfast is served on the terrace. Sandy Lane does offer a dine around program with the Elegant Resorts of Barbados. Cobblers Cove, Coral Reef, Glitter Bay, Royal Pavilion, Sand Piper, Settlers Beach and Treasure Beach all participate in this program.

Jeans, T-shirts and shorts are not accepted in the public areas of the hotel after 19:00 hours. In the winter months, Wednesday and Saturday evenings, gentlemen wear jacket and tie in the Sandy Bar restaurant, and dress is casually elegantly in the Seashell restaurant. On Christmas and New Year's Eve, gentlemen are required to wear jacket and tie in all public areas of the hotel.

One can keep busy on the 5 championship tennis courts, 2 with floodlights; or you can tan and engage in various watersports on the 250 meters of beach. Complimentary watersports are available for as many sessions per day as required but there is a fee for scuba diving. They offer water-skiing, snorkeling, Hobie Cats, Sunfish sailing and windsurfing. There is also a fresh water swimming pool, where one can dine as well. Sandy Lane also hosts the only 18 hole golf course on Barbados, par 72, 6600 yards. Green Fees are complimentary for all hotel guests (minimum handicap men 28, women 36 preferred). Along the upper balcony and terrace one will find a golf and tennis shop, as well as an in-house boutique and duty-free shop.

Sandy Lane is the perfect setting for a honeymoon or anniversary. They can arrange weddings for those who wish to celebrate the ceremony as well as the honeymoon in Barbados.

For more information see our chapter on Barbados or contact. Sandy Lane Hotel and Golf Club, St. James Barbados, West Indies. Telephone: (809) 432-1311. Facsimile: (809) 432-2954.

Lantana Colony Club, Bermuda

In 1948, the Youngs bought ten acres at Somerset Bridge and built a small, charming hotel which they named Ledgelets.

In 1958, an adjacent ten acre onion farm became available. The land was for sale for two reasons, first the Bermuda onion was now being harvested in Texas at a lower cost, and second, land values had soared in Bermuda which made the continued cultivation of the crop economically unsound. The Youngs purchased the property and created a Bermudian cottage colony with the sole objective of offering international guests the highest of vacation values. In 1960 John Leseur, M.B.E., married Penny Young and they run the Club with the senior Youngs.

Topiary, Lantana, Bermuda by Wendy Canning Church.

Tom Young's handiwork is witnessed throughout the property's landscaping. One catches glimpses of him throughout the day tending to his "children." The former onion farm left terraced acres running down to the sea. Mr. Young has taken full advantage and utilized them as back drops for plantings of many shades and varieties.

As you walk to the beach, pool, dining areas, or other activity, elegant bronze statuary and gently bubbling fountains beckon you to pause and reflect rather than rushing from one spot to another. Small formal gardens, a mixture of English and French landscaping, are situated throughout the property. An enormous topiary elephant and chicken startle and amuse the walker.

Sixty-four air-conditioned suites and cottages dot the landscape. Each cottage is named. The setting overlooking the manicured grounds and out to the Great Sound resembles the Cote d'Azur. Accommodations are comprised of large bedrooms, baths, sitting areas and patios. Some are entered through wooden or iron grated gates which give the guest a feeling of being in a private villa rather than in a hotel suite.

Although ultimate privacy is ensured, this does not mean that guests are not offered a host of activities that one might expect at a much larger hotel. The Club has a private beach on Great Sound as well as a freshwater pool with an adjacent sun deck. Two all-weather tennis courts, a putting green, croquet and a variety of watersports are offered. Water-skiing, windsurfing, O'Day sailboats, glass bottom peddlers, Boston Whalers, and snorkeling equipment are available for guests at the private dock. Scuba diving is available fifteen minutes away at the Royal Navy Dockyard. The operation is Dive Bermuda: before 9:00 a.m., 234-0225 and after 9:00 a.m., 234-3547.

The Club has two dining areas: La Plage by the Sea, which serves luncheon daily and dinner once a week, and in the main clubhouse there is a large dining room, bar and solarium. The solarium is a delightful and unique spot for dinner. As one dines, the sun sets, night envelopes the area and the moon glistens into the room which is filled with semi-tropical floral and fauna. The cuisine is delicious; the menu is continental; the wine list is first rate; and the service is impeccable. Coffee and liqueurs are served on the terrace.

Lantana is also a member of the Carousel Dining Program.

On Monday evening, guests are invited to a Blister Party hosted by the Youngs and Paul and Penny LeSeur. We had the pleasure of meeting them at this party. Mrs. Young is an international tournament croquet player. The croquet field at Lantana is meticulously cared for and hosts many tournaments. Paul Le-Seur oversees the management of the hotel with his most able Resident Manager, Alan Paris.

Paul has been a major force behind the Maritime Museum at the Royal Navy Dockyard as well as an active participant in the Hotel and Travel Group of Bermuda. If you look closely you will see that it is his signature on the Bermudian $50.00 bill.

Lantana Colony Club, P.O. Box SB90, Somerset Bridge, SBBX Bermuda. Tel. 1 809-234-0141 or 1-800-468-3733 direct from the U.S.. Fax. 1 809-234-2562.

Editor's Note: For the romantic getaway, book the "Pool House" at Lantana. It is far away from everyone is reached by a private bridge, and has its own pool. Lantana closes for the month of January.

Little Cayman, Cayman Islands British West Indies

Pirates Point

THE DESSERT

The smallest of the three islands, this coral atoll lies seventy miles northeast of Grand Cayman.

The island is cigar shaped and is surrounded by a diamond bright sea.

We landed at Edward Bodden International Airport which consisted of a grassy air strip and a small shack to handle cargo and passengers.

Disembarking, I heard a loud voice say "Wendy, I'm over here. Come say Hi' while they sort the luggage."

I greeted Gladys Howard, owner and my hostess for the next three days at Pirates Point Resort.

Gladys' personality, professionalism and warmth are as big as the State of Texas from which she hails—Tyler, Texas to be exact.

We loaded my gear into her jeep and soon arrived at the resort which was built in 1989.

Guests are accommodated in octagonal shaped cottages. The interiors have high ceilings, are good sized, furnished in rattan with tasteful chinz. There is air conditioning but no telephone or TV.

The bathrooms have showers with wonderful soap, fluffy towels and all the hot water you would want. Believe me, this is a real luxury on such a remote island. They have a reverse-osmosis plant.

The main building houses the kitchen, dining room, bar, boutique and Gladys' office.

Don't even think about roughing it at Pirates Point. Before she became a hotelier, Gladys was a celebrated caterer in Texas and studied under the likes of Julia Child and James Beard.

Luncheon is casual but served with linen and silver, al fresco, under the shades of a perfusion of sea grape trees.

Dinner is served with all the amenities of a five star restaurant, linen, fine crystal and candlelight dress the tables.

Gladys presides over the buffet dinner, greeting and serving each guest.

After unpacking and a cold drink, Gladys asked if I would like a tour of the island.

We both climbed back into the jeep and for the next hour this crackerjack of a lady filled me in on the history, topography, scuba diving and gossip of this island which is 9 miles long and 1 mile wide with only 30 permanent residents.

As we drove along the road (which was one way), other vehicles would appear and each driver pulled over to greet the other. "We're having a good old fashioned barbecue tonight, ribs and chicken. Do you and the family want to join?" "Sounds great Gladys, expect us there at 7ish."

Little Cayman has its pirate legends. On Spot Bay Road which cuts clear across the island the pirates could walk through on foot and have an exit and entrance to the sea on either side.

We passed papaya trees growing along the road and Gladys remarked how they make great meat tenderizers. We stopped to smell the Star of Bethlehem flowers. The fragrance is similar to lime. We picked and tasted the seeds from the Nase berries. They are round and look like big seeds and taste like a cross between an apple and a pear. Further along, we picked cockspur seeds from the cockspur vine. These are used to play the game of Waurie that dates back to the time of the pirates and now is played on a special board.

Gladys is Chairman of the National Trust for the island and knows the scientific name of the birds and plants both indigenous and those brought to the island. She is adamant about preserving the wildlife and I wouldn't want to be one to tread on her philosophy.

The island has the largest sanctuary for red footed boobies in the Eastern Hemisphere, and the frigate and sula sula.

We rode past a 15 acre tarpon pond, a small shopping center (the only one on the island), The Iguana, a souvenir shop, and the state-of-the-art dump. The only problem with the dump is they can't find anyone who wants to be the trash man – any takers?

The island really is a beautiful one, a small model of perfection. The bright red flamboyant trees touching the Northfolk pine intermingled with all varieties of fauna, the wild iguana, the egrets and boobies, the tarpon pond, all these surrounded by a sea with some of the best bone fishing, scuba diving, and snorkeling to be found anywhere.

As I bade goodnight to Gladys, I asked about dive time. She said very casually, "Oh, about ten o'clock. Our guests are here on vacation to rest. No sense in rushing anyone."

Pirates Point, Little Cayman, Lazy Living for Lovers by Wendy Canning Church

> "My style of management makes Pirates Point more of a second home for my guests than a resort. My guests set their own schedules for diving and fishing, and the kitchen never closes. I have travelled and dived all over the world and I have incorporated into this small resort all the things that I have liked the best. Here I have the opportunity to get to know my guests and to cook for them creatively, which I enjoy. I feel Pirates Point provides a unique experience that our guests will never forget." I could not have said it better.

The next morning we all loaded our gear in the truck and were off to board, what else but, The Yellow Rose. She's a 34 foot boat with a permanent canopy for shade, room for sunning and a head. There is cold juice, fresh fruit, and fluffy towels on board. There is always an instructor on board. The Yellow Rose has a VHS radio, oxygen mask and carries a backboard for injuries. A giant stride is made from a roomy platform and a ladder is used for re-entry. You are asked not to feed the fish. Gloves are not allowed.

MIXING BOWL

Twenty minutes from shore, this site is situated between Jackson Reef and Bloody Wall.

It's an interesting dive since the sand holes change as you make your way over to Bloody Bay at 90-95 feet and gradually up the wall, being back on the line at 700 PSI at 15 feet for a 5 minute safety stop.

As you descend, you are at the top of the wall at 18 to 20 feet and then drop down where there are many holes and crevices. You go through the wall at 100 feet gradually ascending.

Turtles, schools of yellow jack, tiger grouper, queen angelfish, schools of snapper, banded butterfly fish, spotted drum, grouper, jewfish, black durgeon, ocean trigger, file fish and trumpet fish were spotted.

The topography was incredible. The most impressive sight was a sponge, the color of celedon china.

Our next dive, **Bloody Bay** off the Great West Wall, is an incredible dive for the wall is sheer. You descend to 18 feet and then it's like going over the side of a building. Keeping to the right at 50 feet, we swam along spotting a pea green moray eel. Making our way further along, we saw lobster, a yellow and an orange sea horse, hog fish, grouper, black durgeon with wrasse cleaning them, a huge rainbow parrotfish and sea slugs. Leafy lettuce covered almost the entire area. We had a tremendous amount of light even at that depth which made for outstanding visibility.

Unfortunately, I only had time to make these two dives at Little Cayman because of my flight schedule.

But I agree with the gentleman and his wife that I met in the Bahamas. He asked, "Have you dived Little Cayman?" I said "No." He retorted with, "Get there before it's found!"

WHEN YOU COME UP FOR AIR:

Take a walk around Little Cayman. You may be lucky and encounter an iguana taking his daily sunbath along the side of the road.

Bird watchers! You'll see the most beautiful bird life in the woodlands and wetlands. Some of the birds you'll see are mangrove cuckoos, bananaquits, woodpeckers, and the colorful and rare purple gallinule.

Take a row boat from Little Cayman to Owen Island, just 200 yards away. The untouched island is only 11 acres with a white sandy beach and a blue lagoon — the most beautiful place to picnic and spend a peaceful day.

Enjoy a game of waurie, a strategy game reputedly enjoyed by Hemingway and Blackbeard. The game was brought to the West Indies by slaves from Africa.

When I think of Little Cayman, I remember a beautiful, remote spot where God's handiwork is mostly untouched. An island where one is reminded, when diving, of a paperweight. You turn it upside down, then upright and the entire underwater scene is of a perfect undersea garden where nature's beauty has been left intact, surrounded and filtered by the radiant soft light of the sun. I remember a lady that I would not hesitate to call aunt or Mom who was at all times gracious, and warm to all the guests; someone you really would like to see again.

Little Cayman and Pirates Point are the perfect compliment and to be shared with that special someone. When you depart, somehow, someway, you will be filled up again with a peacefulness that is difficult to find today, that feeling which only comes from being part of unfettered nature.

SCUBA AND SNORKELING FACILITIES QUESTIONNAIRE

NAME Pirates Point Resort
ADDRESS Little Cayman
Cayman Islands, British West Indies
CONTACT Gladys Howard
TITLE Owner, Manager
TELEPHONE 809-948-4610   FAX 809-948-4611

CAPITAL: George Town   GOVERNMENT: British
POPULATION: 25,000   LANGUAGE: English
CURRENCY: C.I.   ELECTRICITY: 120v
AIRLINES: DEPARTURE TAX? $7.50 U.S.
NEED VISA/PASSPORT? YES x NO   PROOF OF CITIZENSHIP? YES x NO

YOUR FACILITY IS CLASSIFIED AS: SCUBA CENTER   RESORT x
BUSINESS HOURS: 7 a.m. - 11 p.m.
CERTIFYING AGENCIES: **PADI, NAUI**
LOG BOOK REQUIRED?   YES x   NO
EQUIPMENT: SALES x   RENTALS x   AIR FILLS
PRIMARY LINE OF EQUIPMENT: **Tabata**
PHOTOGRAPHIC EQUIPMENT: SALES   RENTALS   LAB

CHARTER/DIVE BOAT AVAILABLE? YES x   NO   DIVER CAPACITY 16
COAST GUARD APPROVED?   YES x   NO   CAPTAIN LICENSED? YES x   NO
SHIP TO SHORE? YES x NO   LORAN x YES NO   RADAR? YES x NO
DIVE MASTER/INSTRUCTOR ABOARD?   YES x   NO   BOTH

DIVING & SNORKELING: SALT x   FRESH
TYPE OF DIVING/SNORKELING IN AREA: WALL x BEACH x WRECK x REEF CAVE ICE
DIVING/SNORKELING IN YOUR AREA IS BEST SUITED FOR: BEGINNER x INTERMEDIATE x ADVANCED x
BEST TIME OF YEAR FOR DIVING/SNORKELING:
TEMPERATURE: **NOV-APRIL:**   78 F   **MAY-OCT:**   82   F
VISIBILITY: **DIVING:**   200 FT   **SNORKELING:** 100 FT

PACKAGES AVAILABLE: DIVE x   DIVE STAY   SNORKEL   SNORKEL-STAY x
ACCOMMODATIONS NEARBY: HOTEL x   MOTEL   HOME RENTALS
ACCOMMODATION RATES: EXPENSIVE   MODERATE x   INEXPENSIVE
RESTAURANTS NEARBY: EXPENSIVE   MODERATE   INEXPENSIVE
YOUR AREA IS: REMOTE x   QUIET WITH ACTIVITIES   LIVELY
LOCAL ACTIVITY/NIGHTLIFE:
CAR NEEDED TO EXPLORE AREA?   YES x   NO
DUTY FREE SHOPPING?   YES x   NO

LOCAL EMERGENCY SERVICES (Grand Cayman)   NEAREST HYPERBARIC TREATMENT FACILITY
COASTGUARD: AUTHORITY:
TELEPHONE: LOCATION:
CALLSIGNS: TELEPHONE:

LOCAL DIVING DOCTOR:
NAME: **Dr. Hetley**
LOCATION: **Grand Cayman**
TELEPHONE: **949-7400**

Cote d'Azur, France
Vista Palace Hotel

To celebrate our 25th wedding anniversary, my husband and I booked five days at the spectacular Vista Palace Hotel, before setting sail on the Star Clipper, which is docked in Nice.

In 1978, the hotel "Vistaero," built in 1963, became the "Vista Palace Hotel" of the Max Grunding Foundation. The setting is very romantic. Set on a cliff 1,000 feet above the Mediterranean Sea, the hotel offers grand views of Monte-Carlo and the French Riviera. A warm reception and unique setting await guests. The hotel was completely renovated and enlarged in 1987. The Vista Palace is a four star property with 68 rooms of which 21 are junior suites, and 5 are apartments. All rooms have a balcony overlooking the sea and are fully equipped with state of the art amenities: remote-controlled curtains, blinds and lamps, direct-line telephones, mini-bar, personal safe and a stereo. Video is available in the suites. Four suites offer a private pool and junior suites are equipped with jacuzzis.

The hotel is part of a 45,000 square feet property which includes:
- a gourmet restaurant, "Le Vistaero."
- a bar-lounge, "Icare," which offers panoramic views and is open all day.
- a piano-bar, "Le Cap," which opens when the coastal lights start to sparkle and remains open well into the night.
- a pool dug into the rocks and heated at 84 degrees F.
- a fitness center, "Le Corniche Club," surrounded by a garden, which includes a Finnish sauna and hammam, massages, tanning, gymnastic and body-building equipment, and squash, all of which are free of charge for hotel guests.

"Le Panorama" restaurant and its terrace is perfect for business functions, weddings and dancing. It overlooks Monaco and the views are magical, especially at night!

The service and ambiance are impeccable, due to the hotel's direction of the very capable and charming Patrice Glogg, who literally conducts a daily "white glove" inspection of the entire premises. Both Patrice and his lovely wife live on the premises, which I consider to be a great bonus!

If you feel you must leave this paradise, a free shuttle bus connects the hotel to Monte Carlo, only two and a half miles away. It also connects to the Monaco heliport and the golf and tennis clubs. Monaco is where you can "shop till you drop" at the numerous boutiques, gamble at the casinos, or just stroll about and embrace its beauty and character.

Editor's Note: When making a reservation, be sure to request one of the two suites that have a private pool and garden. The views of Monte-Carlo from these rooms are breathtaking!

GREECE

CORFU HILTON

We must have looked very frazzled for the staff at reception quickly checked us in.

We entered our room. The sun was setting on the Ionian Sea. Stepping out onto the balcony the sweet fragrances, the beauty and the serenity of the island welcomed us. This was our home on Corfu and we had chosen wisely.

Travel and world weary we decided to dine in-house that evening. The Esplanada Dining Room was already a buzz with diners conversing in several languages. We glanced at the menu and something called meze or mezedes caught our eye. We found meze to be a selection of Greek hors d'oeuvres. These we ordered with a bottle of Greek wine.

Eight different selections arrived: a Greek caviar spread; meat rolled in grape leaves; fried squid; cheese wrapped in streudel; pickled octopus; deep fried zucchini; cucumber yogurt; garlic spread and feta cheese.

It was lobster night so we ordered grilled lobster, fresh vegetables and fruit for dessert.

After dinner we went upstairs to the terrace and ordered brandy. Metaxa is the Greek brandy and we think it wonderful. The local Corfu brandy is made from kumquats and is very sweet. We would opt to put it on fresh fruit or crepes. It is sold in variously shaped, fun bottles, is inexpensive and makes a nice gift to take home.

Corfu Coast, Corfu Hilton Greece by Coleman F. Church III

We floated to our room. The long hours of travel were offset by a perfectly orchestrated dinner.

Awakening to a sunshine filled morning we had breakfast on the terrace and watched the activity below. Swimmers were already in the olympic-sized salt water pool while small groups of families were making their way down the long winding path to the beach.

A curious sight at the dock was unfolding. What looked like two Viking ships were loading groups of people who were happily singing in German. This no doubt was one of the many day trips scheduled to the small islands, perhaps Paxi, 3 hours away.

Many guests were content to spend their entire vacation on the premises, and who could argue with them for the Corfu Hilton is a complete resort. Perfect in every sense, 5-star facilities and service.

HAWAII
KONA VILLAGE RESORT

We had booked a stay at the Kona Village Resort before returning to Boston in order to get our land legs after a week at sea on Bottom Time II and to become reacquainted with the "Big Island."

We pulled off the Queen Kaakumanu Highway and after a short distance, we approached a gatehouse, giving our name the guard waved us on. This procedure is a preamble of the attention to detail the Kona Village Resort gives to each guest's privacy and comfort.

Proceeding down the long road, the resort's beauty unfolded before us. Lush greenery was interspersed with century old jet black lava flow. In the distance the sea sparkled in various shades of sapphire and emerald.

The Kona Village Obana (family) numbers two hundred and thirty. Fred Duerr, General Manager for thirty years, is referred to by some of the guests as "Father." You will meet Fred at the managers' cocktail party on Tuesday night.

The first member of the Obana at the reception area greets one with a beautiful lei and the warmest of smiles.

While you sip fresh pineapple juice or a rum punch, you are registered and presented with a complete information packet on the resort.

Waiting for our baggage we overheard three guests re-booking for a year in advance. We consider ourselves very organized with firm travel schedules but to book so far ahead caught our attention.

Our baggage collected, we were whisked off to our hale (thatched cottage). Our hale was one of the twenty-five built in 1987 when the resort underwent a four million dollar renovation.

Aerial View of Kona Village Resort, Kona, Hawaii.
courtesy of Kona Village Resort

There are 125 individual hales, the largest group in all Hawaii. The hales rest on eighty-two private acres and are situated either on the lagoon, in the gardens or on the sea. They are surrounded by thousands of acres of undeveloped land, at the foot of Mount Hualalai and running to the water's edge.

According to ancient legend, the fire goddess Pele unleashed her anger in 1801 on Mount Hualalai. The mountain erupted and its fiery entrails were strung over the small fishing village. Miraculously, one small area around the Kahuwai Bay and fifteen acres of petroglyphs were spared. In 1965, one hundred and fifty years later Johonno Jackson built his paradise on this very spot steeped in history.

In those days there were only forty hales. Guests and supplies arrived by boat or plane since there was no road. Each arrival was an event. Guests and staff would turn out not only to greet new arrivals but to check out the shipments of supplies.

Our hales' architecture is representative of one of the lighter styles of ancient Polynesian culture. It sat on stilts and was the embodiment of the South Pacific.

We found our now home to be sun splashed and spacious. The decor was in pastel shades. There was a king-size bed and an alcove which doubled as a dressing room and another sleeping area. A small refrigerator was stocked with mineral water and juices. There was a coffee maker with built-in coffee grinder and local Kona coffee beans – a nice touch for early risers.

After unpacking I stepped out on the balcony, listening to the sounds of silence. When man works in harmony with nature, he creates a beautiful canvas.

What you will not find in your room are TV, radios, phones, or air conditioning.

We set off for luncheon which is served in the oceanside Hale Moana. Luncheon is buffet style. It is not only pleasing to the eye but replete with a wide variety of selections to satisfy any palate. Breakfast is also served at the Hale Moana.

At dinner time guests have the option of dining at the Hale Moana or the Hale Samoa where gourmet dining is available every night except Wednesdays and Fridays.

On Wednesday evenings a Pariolo (cowboy) steak fry is served at the Ho'okipa Hospitality House set on the beautiful lagoon and gardens. Here, on Fridays, guests enjoy a luau and Polynesian show.

If adults are not content to swim in one of the two pools or the bay and sunning or reading is not their choice, then there are myriad of other activities offered which are included in the daily rates; such as unlimited use of sunfish, sailboats, snorkeling gear, outrigger canoes, and tennis courts.

Throughout the week, lessons in lei making and snorkeling are scheduled for the guests.

There is also a tennis clinic.

Scuba diving, catamaran sailing and tennis lessons are optional.

Golf can be arranged at a nearby 18 hole course.

Willie Ward is in charge of the scuba diving. One can become certified, take advanced courses, have a video made or book a dive. Willie says he separates divers on dive tours according to their level of experience. From what we've seen in these waters, a dive/stay at the Kona Village Resort would delight any diver!

The Kona is a superb choice for the scuba diver traveling with a non-diver or snorkeler because it provides many optional interesting activities.

Although its atmosphere is a sophisticated one, this resort is very family oriented.

There is a daily children's program supervised by junior hosts and hostesses.

A children's pool was built in 1987. We think a very nice option is the early children's dinner hour at 5:30 pm. This gives parents the opportunity to dine leisurely at a later hour.

Children's movies are shown after dinner.

It is no wonder that families return year after year.

The business traveler is warmly received. What a perfect spot not only for a pre or post conference visit but also a setting for the international business person to have meetings.

After touring the grounds, we just relaxed sitting on the beautiful beach.

Later I discovered some outstanding shelling in two tiny inlets below the jagged cliffs. We returned to our room to rest before dinner. You place a pineapple outside your door which means "Do Not Disturb."

The following day we arranged for a car and toured the island. There was a great deal to see. A complimentary van transports guests to the airport five and a half miles away to pick up your car. A van will return you to the hotel in the afternoon. Remember to request a picnic the night before.

Only a short drive away is the petroglyph field, Pu'abonua 0 Honacnau, or "The Place of Refuge." It was here that ancient Hawaiians would come to be given a second lease on life.

You will find ancient carvings of frogs, turtles, fish and stick figures on the rocks telling stories of earlier times.

On your return modified room service can await you. There is no meal room service but one can order hors d'oeuvres.

The Kona Village Resort is elegant yet informal; offering a choice of activities in a leisurely atmosphere. Its setting reflects ancient times yet offers twentieth century amenities. Its aura is serenity, simplicity and good taste reminding you of a time when life was sweeter and gentility was more a rule than an exception.

SCUBA AND SNORKELING FACILITIES QUESTIONNAIRE

NAME   **William Ward - Kona Reef Divers**
ADDRESS   **Kona Village Resort**
              Queen Kaahumanu Highway, Kailua-Kona, Hawaii 96740
CONTACT   **William Ward**
TITLE   **Owner - Dive Instructor**
TELEPHONE **808-325-5555**   FAX **808-325-5124**

CAPITAL: **Honolulu**		GOVERNMENT: **USA**	
POPULATION: **2 million**		LANGUAGE: **English**	
CURRENCY: **US $**		ELECTRICITY: **110v**	
AIRLINES: **United Airlines**		DEPARTURE TAX? **N/A**	
NEED VISA/PASSPORT? YES NO **x**		PROOF OF CITIZENSHIP? YES NO **x**	

YOUR FACILITY IS CLASSIFIED AS: SCUBA CENTER **x**   RESORT **x**
BUSINESS HOURS: **8:00 a.m. to 5:00 p.m. Monday through Saturday**
CERTIFYING AGENCIES:
PADI, NAUI
LOG BOOK REQUIRED?   YES   NO **x**
EQUIPMENT: SALES **x**   RENTALS **x**   AIR FILLS **x**
PRIMARY LINE OF EQUIPMENT: **Scubapro**
PHOTOGRAPHIC EQUIPMENT: SALES   RENTALS **x**   LAB

CHARTER/DIVE BOAT AVAILABLE? YES **x** NO   DIVER CAPACITY **12**
COAST GUARD APPROVED? YES **x** NO   CAPTAIN LICENSED? YES **x**   NO
SHIP TO SHORE? CB/VHF **x** NO LORAN YES NO **x**   RADAR? YES NO **x**
DIVE MASTER/INSTRUCTOR ABOARD?   YES **x**   NO   BOTH

DIVING & SNORKELING: SALT **x**   FRESH
TYPE OF DIVING/SNORKELING IN AREA: WALL **x**   BEACH **x** ARCHWAYS **x**   REEF   CAVE **x**   ICE
DIVING/SNORKELING IN YOUR AREA IS BEST SUITED FOR: BEGINNER **x** INTERMEDIATE **x** ADVANCED **x**
BEST TIME OF YEAR FOR DIVING/SNORKELING: **July through October**
TEMPERATURE: **NOV-APRIL:**   **74 F**   **MAY-OCT:**   **80 F**
VISIBILITY: **DIVING:**   **80 FT**   **SNORKELING:**   **FT**

PACKAGES AVAILABLE: DIVE **x**   DIVE STAY **x**   SNORKEL   SNORKEL-STAY
ACCOMMODATIONS NEARBY: HOTEL **x**   MOTEL   HOME RENTALS
ACCOMMODATION RATES: EXPENSIVE **x**   MODERATE   INEXPENSIVE
RESTAURANTS NEARBY: EXPENSIVE **x**   MODERATE   INEXPENSIVE
YOUR AREA IS: REMOTE   QUIET WITH ACTIVITIES **x**   LIVELY
LOCAL ACTIVITY/NIGHTLiFE:
CAR NEEDED TO EXPLORE AREA?   YES **x**   NO
DUTY FREE SHOPPING?   YES   NO **x**

LOCAL EMERGENCY SERVICES   NEAREST HYPERBARIC TREATMENT FACILITY
COASTGUARD: **Hilo, Hawaii**   AUTHORITY:
TELEPHONE: **808-935-6370 or 808-961-6181**   LOCATION: **Honolulu, Hawaii**
CALLSIGNS: TELEPHONE:

LOCAL DIVING DOCTOR:
NAME: **Dr. Stephen H. Denzer**
LOCATION: **Kealakekua, Hawaii**
TELEPHONE: **808-324-1133**

Oahu

The Kahala Hilton

Arriving at the Kahala Hilton, I was reminded of the charm and international ambiance that I had experienced on my last visit.

In an era of new, glitzy-mega resorts, the *Kahals Hilton* retains the grace and elegance of another era while at the same time sacrificing nothing to maintain a high standard of service.

Its location lends to the aura of serenity for it is situated in Oahu's exclusive Waialai, Kahalai residential neighborhood. One has the Koolau Kahalai mountain range as a backdrop with the frontage on the waters of Manualua Bay.

We booked the *Lagoon Terrace Wing* again which had undergone a complete renovation. I didn't think one could improve upon this wing, but they did!

Our room was spacious overlooking the lagoon with the pool and sea beyond. It was furnished in light pastels with comfortable sitting area, mini-bar and a wonderful terrace to take breakfast, read or sun.

For those who were not content to laze in the sun between dining in one of the three uniquely different restaurants that serve the finest of foods. There are a myriad of activities offered.

Kahala Hilton, Oahu, Hawaii
courtesy of Kahala Hilton

If you are a shopper, the many boutiques will entice you with their tasteful wares. Do you play chess or backgammon? Perhaps shuffleboard is your game. Do you wish to snorkel, windsurf or scuba dive? All this is available on premises.

The Maunalua Bay Club is minutes away by complimentary shuttle. This oceanside tennis and fitness club is for the use of members and guests of the hotel.

Don't leave the children behind. Despite its sophistication, the Kahala Hilton has hosted the same families year after year. Kamp Kahala is run for ages 6-12. It is supervised by junior hosts and hostesses each day from a.m. to 3 p.m. Except for transportation and admission fees for tours, the children's program is free. Babysitting services are available.

The discriminating executive will find the Kahala a perfect, quiet retreat while at the same time conducting business in an international atmosphere.

When booking, request the rooms overlooking the lagoon. They are more expensive, but worth every penny.

Kahala Hilton
Telephone: 808-734-2211
5000 Kahala Avenue, Honolulu, Hawaii 96816-5498
Telex: 379148 KHI UD - Cable: KAHILTON–HONOLULU
Fax: 808-737-2478
For reservations: Call toll-free 800-367-2525,
your travel agent, or Hilton Reservation Service

Watersport Center

"*Bubbling Enterprises*" is owned and operated by Jack S. and Adele Pappas. They provide a full range of water activities. They offer NAUI and PADI openwater through instructor level courses; night and twilight dives, spear fishing and lobster hunting.

Try the excitement of a jet-ski trip, the beauty of viewing Oahu from a parasail soaring along the coast, or the heart-stopping thrill of an open jet boat ride. Whatever your favorite water activity – they can help to make it safe and fun. Twenty years of showing the beauty of Hawaii's ocean to visiting friends make this the place to call in planning your Hawaiian Ocean Adventure. (See completed questionaire.)

Jack Pappas is an instructor, guide and raconteur. After knowing Jack, it is no wonder that when guests fill out the hotel questionaire upon departure they mention Jack as one of the most helpful persons at the Kahala Hilton.

Jack has wonderful sense of humor and always amazes us with his wealth of information. For example, the state fish is the Humuhumu-nukunukua Pua's. There is a legend that if you look closely at this fish you will eventually see the blue stripe which represents the ocean and the red along-side which represents a volcanic lava floor.

BEST SNORKELING AREAS

Alii Beach – in Haleiwa, a profusion of coral varieties with a depth of 3 to 20 feet.

Sharks Cove – a marine sanctuary with a depth of 5 to 25 feet; clear, calm waters with a tremendous variety of fish.

Hanauma Bay –world renowned for the shallow fringing reef, this nature reserve offers everything from beginner to ad-vanced snorkeling.

Keehi Lagoon – shallow, calm and protected; feed the fish by hand and perfect for underwater photos.

DIVE SITES

Haleiwa Trench – this is a wall dive with visibility of up to 100 feet. It has an abundance of varied coral formations –finger coral, mushroom coral, crip coral, razor coral and a thriving colony of the green sea turtles, an endandered species, some of which weigh up to 400 pounds. Most divers see 7 to 14 of these rare and graceful creatures with an occasional manta ray. The shallow coral area (up to 40 feet) is perfect for beginners while the deeper wall dive is tops foe experienced divers.

Pupukea (or Sharks Cove) – on the beautiful north shore is a protected marine reserve with mazes of lava tubes and caverns. The protected bay with tremendous schools of fish and curious and friendly octopi is for the beginner diver while the lava tube system is a once-in-a-lifetime experience for the experienced diver.

Lanai Lookout – this spectacular dive site on the rugged east coast is definitely for experienced divers. A current dive with arches, caves, 80 foot depth and average visibility of over 100 feet. It is a don't miss area for every experienced diver.

Magic Island – this area is also known as Rainbow Reef due to the unparalleled number of colorful reef fish which congregate there. Turtles, spotted eagle rays. Magic Island is also world renowned for the rare varieties of nudibranch. Suitable for both beginners and experienced divers with a maximum depth of 40 feet and an average visibility of 70. Perfect for underwater photos.

Kahe Point – on the quiet west shore of Oahu, Kahe Point offers 100 foot visibility and large schools of fish attracted by the warm water exhaust of the Electric Plant. Suitable for both beginner and certified divers with an average depth of 30 feet.

Jack had planned a special trip to the Village of Turtle Cove, a nice little rustic, country town, that reminded me of how Oahu used to be.

It's a beautiful ride from the Hilton to the north shore. On the way we had a chance to catch up. Jack's a new father!

We reached the dive site "*Sharks Cove*" and Jack wouldn't let me do a thing.

He sets up all your gear and practically carries you to the dive site.

This is really a interesting dive because of its many tunnels, caverns and lava tubes. It's a good spot for a beginner or experienced diver and for snorkelers.

This dive is best done from April to October.

We walked out to the edge of the lava formation and slipped gently into the warm, azure blue waters.

The next 40 minutes were spent investigating the topography which was very unusual, reminding one of a honeycomb.

When you are halfway through the dive, Jack surprises you with what he refers to as "water elevator". You can enter a cavern and then ascend through the opening and out onto the sea's surface. It was lots of fun...very different and interesting.

We stopped and had lunch at a great little spot, Kua Aina, in the heart of old Haleiwa Town. Don't pass it up!

It seemed that everyone knows Jack and he introduced me to his many friends.

Jack insisted we stop for brownies. There I put my foot down! We split one. We spent time browsing in the little shops carrying local handicrafts. They are charming.

We laughed and joked all the way home. I never tire of being with him or diving with him. He's as good a guide and instructor as he is a human being. That's saying alot these days!

And so our trip to these enchanted Islands had to come to an end.

We had chosen wisely and would take home warm memories to savour and to share with friends and readers.

SCUBA AND SNORKELING FACILITIES QUESTIONNAIRE

NAME   **Bubbling Enterprises**
ADDRESS   **c/o Kahala Hilton**
                 5000 Kahala Avenue, Honolulu, Hawaii 96816
CONTACT   **Mr. Jack Pappas**
TITLE   **Owner**
TELEPHONE   **808-735-8979**   FAX **808-737-2478 c/o Kahala Hilton**

CAPITAL: **Honolulu**   GOVERNMENT: **USA**
POPULATION: **100,000**   LANGUAGE: **English**
CURRENCY: **US $**   ELECTRICITY: **Yes**
AIRLINES: **All major carriers**   DEPARTURE TAX: **$3.00**
NEED VISA/PASSPORT?   YES   NO **x**   PROOF OF CITIZENSHIP?   YES   NO **x Not for US citizens**

YOUR FACILITY IS CLASSIFIED AS: SCUBA CENTER   RESORT **x**
BUSINESS HOURS: **0800 - 1700**
CERTIFYING AGENCIES: **PADI, NAUI**
LOG BOOK REQUIRED?   YES   NO **x**
EQUIPMENT: SALES **x**   RENTALS **x**   AIR FILLS **x**
PRIMARY LINE OF EQUIPMENT: **Scuba PRC**
PHOTOGRAPHIC EQUIPMENT: SALES   RENTALS **x**   LAB

CHARTER/DIVE BOAT AVAILABLE?   YES **x**   NO   DIVER CAPACITY   **14**
COAST GUARD APPROVED?   YES **x**   NO   CAPTAIN LICENSED? YES **x**   NO
SHIP TO SHORE? YES **x**   NO   LORAN YES **x**   NO   RADAR? YES **x**   NO
DIVE MASTER/INSTRUCTOR ABOARD?   YES **x**   NO   BOTH **x**

DIVING & SNORKELING: SALT **x**   FRESH
TYPE OF DIVING/SNORKELING IN AREA: WALL **x**   BEACH **x**   WRECK **x**   REEF   CAVE **x**   ICE
DIVING/SNORKELING IN YOUR AREA IS BEST SUITED FOR: BEGINNER **x**   INTERMEDIATE **x**   ADVANCED **x**
BEST TIME OF YEAR FOR DIVING/SNORKELING: **April - November**
TEMPERATURE: **NOV-APRIL:**   **75-85 F**   **MAY-OCT:**   **80-90 F**
VISIBILITY: **DIVING:**   **50 FT**   **SNORKELING:**   **50 FT**

PACKAGES AVAILABLE: DIVE **x**   DIVE STAY   SNORKEL **x**   SNORKEL-STAY
ACCOMMODATIONS NEARBY: HOTEL **x**   MOTEL   HOME RENTALS
ACCOMMODATION RATES: EXPENSIVE **x**   MODERATE **x**   INEXPENSIVE **x**

RESTAURANTS NEARBY: EXPENSIVE **x**   MODERATE **x**   INEXPENSIVE **x**
YOUR AREA IS: REMOTE   QUIET WITH ACTIVITIES   LIVELY **x**
LOCAL ACTIVITY/NIGHTLIFE: **Everything and anything**
CAR NEEDED TO EXPLORE AREA?   YES **x**   NO
DUTY FREE SHOPPING?   YES **x**   NO

LOCAL EMERGENCY SERVICES   NEAREST HYPERBARIC TREATMENT FACILITY
COASTGUARD: **Pier 4 Honolulu**   AUTHORITY: **USCG - Art Arnold, MD, Dive Medicine**
TELEPHONE: **808-541-2064**   LOCATION: **Honolulu, Hawaii 42 Ahui Street**
CALLSIGNS: **KQ21 531**   TELEPHONE: **808-523-9155**
LOCAL DIVING DOCTOR:
NAME: **J. Wood Ferren**
LOCATION: **K-K Medical Centre**
TELEPHONE:

The S.S. Constitution
"Hawaii's Floating Island"

Last year on our anniversary, we took a cruise through the Italian Islands scuba diving and visiting historic sites at each port. It was such a delight and relaxing respite from our busy lives that we thought a perfect way to celebrate our anniversary this year was to book another cruise, this one through the Hawaiian Islands.

We could choose between the sister ships the S.S. Independence or the S.S. Constitution.

These two classic ships are the only American built, flagged, staffed and owned ocean going cruise ships in operation.

Since the S.S. Constitution had planned a special theme week, "Aloha Festival," (a local festival celebrated for one month each year throughout the Islands) we chose her.

From the minute we arrived at the airport in Honolulu and saw the sign carried by one of the crew reading the S.S. Constitution, we were taken back into mother's arms and pampered and entertained for an entire week.

S.S. Constitution courtesy of Michelle Corbin, Public Relations Director, American Hawaii Cruise Line

S.S. Constitution: Saturday embarkation in Honolulu, Oahu;
Sunday at sea;
Monday in Nawiliwili, Kauai;
Tuesday & Wednesday in Kahului, Maui;
Thursday in Hilo on the Big Island;
Friday in Kona on the Big Island;
Saturday debarkation in Honolulu, Oahu.

She is 682 feet long, 89 feet wide and her speed is 17 knots cruising 22.5 knots maximum. There are 9 passenger decks and 23,000 squarefeet of open deck.

The Constitution was designed by Henry Dreyfuss, a respected industrial designer who also designed the Coke bottle and the classic Studebaker.

The Constitution has a wonderful history of hosting numerous celebrities.

She was built for transatlantic crossing and Grace Kelly chose the constitution to carry her wedding party to the principality of Monaco. One can go for a quiet game of checkers, letter writing, or to read a book in the *Grace Kelly Library*. Part of the movie classic, "An Affair to Remember" with Cary Grant and Debra Kerr was filmed on her.

There are 395 cabins (176 outside cabins and 219 inside cabins).

She has three bars: Tradewinds Terrace, Beachcomber Bar, and Lahaina Landing, two dining rooms Bird of Paradise and Hibiscus, a nightclub/conference room Tropicana Showplace, convention center, disco Lahaina Landing, theater, fitness center two fresh water swimming pools, barber shop/ beauty salon with sauna and massage facilities, boutique, shopping arcade, photo gallery, children's playroom and youth recreation area, deck sports area, and hospital.

Our cabin was quite large with a walk in closet, built in drawers, dressing table and bathroom complete with tub. This was a real luxury.

I truly expected a different kind of ship, more like the newer glitzy ones. Our floating hotel was the antithesis of this. She was a grand dame in every sense of the word.

Dinner was open seating and we took advantage of this by getting to know some of our fellow travelers.

After dinner we went up on deck. The lights of Oahu glimmered in the dark. It was time for "sail away." We stood at the railing and watched as Honolulu became a faint glimmer.

The moon led our way to the cabin.

Each evening when we would return from dinner, our bed was turned down, a chocolate on our pillow. The next day's activities printed in the ship's newsletter "Tradewinds" would be waiting for us.

There was such a variety of activities to choose from.

One could easily remain on board throughout the journey. We decided to partake of both on and off shore activities with emphasis on water sports.

The first day is spent at sea, and this is wonderful, for many had traveled long distances and this gave all a chance to relax.

Low and behold, we discovered there were games on deck.

Beer drinking contest aboard the S.S. Constitution by Wendy Canning Church

My husband, never one to turn down a good beer, entered the beer drinking contest. I just watched and shook my head in sheer amazement. They split the group in two teams – the prize, a beer mug with the Constitution logo.

People of all ages joined in and really let all their inhibitions go as we sailed along the beautiful shores of Molokai. Hurray! My husband's team won. We all laughed, cheered and took lots of pictures.

Molokai is famous for its leper colony and Father Damien who tended them for years. There are only a few lepers still alive.

Molokai's huge mountains, dressed in lush greens, rose from the sea and seemed to almost touch the clouds in the egg blue sky. Intermittently, waterfalls tumbled down their sides into the sea.

The ship moved in pace with the cumulus clouds above, leisurely.

Larry, the ship's very capable tour director, tried to find us a scuba center to dive with on Kauai: The Garden Island.

I knew of Fathom Five *before* they were sold a few years ago two divers and the *old* owners had been highly recommended to me. We called them but it seemed that they had no one to take out, so they didn't want to accommodate just me on their boat. I asked if I could do a shore dive with one of their crew. No, they were not interested.

I opted to take the half day Na Pali Coast tour with my husband. We hired a car and drove about 45 minutes to Hanalei where we met the boat, crew and other guests.

The boat, *Meliakai*, is 30 feet, having 3 seats on one side, two on the other, one-half has a canopy to protect from the sun. It was captained by Craig Wall, a NAUI instructor, and his very capable second mate, Emilio. She is moored in the Hanalei River, where there are two miles of sandy beach and is one of five navigable rivers in the Islands–all on Kauai.

From October to April the sea is too high to make the trip, but as you can imagine one of the best places to surf at that time. We were lucky to be there in September for it really was an unforgettable trip.

Craig is steeped in the history of Hawaii especially Kauai and this made the trip not only magical to the eye, but interesting as well on our 14 mile ride.

High cliffs rise from the sea, caves both large and small dot the topography, and waterfalls cascade to the coast below.

We reached a beach about half way that is only accessible by boat. It stretched endlessly.

We saw hikers in the hills above as we cruised along the entire coast. One can obtain a permit for five days and camp on the beach at different spots along the way. I am not a camper at heart, but given the opportunity, would surely return to the Na Pali coast and make the trip inland to this spectacular haven.

We moored the boat at a safe cove for the swells were beginning to form at sea. We snorkeled for about half an hour and saw all matter of reef fish off this gently curved beach.

Along the entire trip we saw turtles. They live to be 100 years old and grow to some 300 pounds. They are part of the reptile family and can hold their breath under the water for hours.

We went into caves and underneath waterfalls and past turquoise lagoons while Craig filled us in on little tidbits of Kauai history.

This tour practices good safety precautions, there is no smoking and those who cannot swim, must wear a life jacket at all times.

We were served cold drinks and cookies so be sure and bring lunch. Craig and I got to taking about scuba diving and he recommended *Bubbles Below*, run by Kenny and Linda Bail.

After spending an afternoon with Craig, I surely trust his judgment about Bubbles Below. So you see, we found a scuba center after all!

The good news is that the diving is really coming back after the disastrous hurricane of 1992. Kauai really was hit the hardest of all the islands.

Hanalei Sea Tours, Hanaiei, Kauai, Hawaii 96714 Tel: 800-733-7999

BUBBLES BELOW SOUTH SHORE DIVE SITES

South Shore diving means turtles. Big Hawaiian green sea turtles reaching 300 pounds. These large graceful reptiles socialize with their young giving us families of multiple generations to visit underwater. Through long term tagg-ing, studies have shown that there are only 750 adult female green turtles. In 1978, all turtles in Hawaii became protected under the Endangered Species Act. This Act has allowed the population to replenish themselves again, but turtles grow slowly, not reaching sexual maturity until 25 years. There are a dozen dive sites where divers can swim with the turtles and learn to distinguish between the males and females. Experience the turtles, the lava tubes, the thick black coral garden and the friendly fish of the South side.

Turtle Bluffs

The depth range is 45 ft. to 90 ft. Many female turtles live in this area, a great place to see sharks, eagle rays, eels and octopus. Some rare fish sightings can occur here. Often we drift from the Bluffs to Fishbowl.

Fishbowl

Depth range from 45 ft. to 80 ft. Schools of blue stripe snappers and other species fill the bowl to the brim so divers are immersed in swimming fish. There is also a resident white tip reef shark.

The General Store

Depth ranges from 55 ft. to 90 ft. This is a site of a 19th century shipwreck. Huge anchors encrusted with coral are amongst the rubble which was once a large metal hull. There are also three lava tubes here, full of life, many fish, turtles, and black coral.

Brennecke's Ledge

The top is 50 ft. with a beautiful lava overhang down to 90 ft. We dive it at 80 ft. Large black coral trees hang down from the ceiling inter-spersed with mauve cup coral. Long nose hawk fish and sponge crabs live as neighbors. Several resident sharks and turtles live here.

Pyrami Magic

Lava fingers is complimented with many, many reef fish. Excellent variety of species of fish as well as coral. We dive this site as an 80 ft. dive. The magic here is with the Pyramid butterflies. There are hundreds of them packed in formation. Excellent fish photo opportunities.

Kuai Rays by Craig Wall

Deep Pinnacle

The top is 90 ft., the bottom a re-motely visited 200 ft. This pinnacle becomes a market for activity, with pelagics frequently cruising by. There is a great covering of red sponge which makes photography colorful.

Sheraton Caverns

User-friendly at it's best! This is a series of lava tubes which produce beautiful images. Visit the lobster rookery which is also a turtle burial site. The top is 35 ft., the bottom is just 65 ft. Many tame, friendly eels, large schools of taape and quite a few turtles. If you've always wanted a picture of a lionfish, this is your chance.

Super Bowl Sunday

A shallower dive with much variety of life. It is a sloping drop to 50 ft. A good place for turtles, eels, octopus and the white cheeked surgeon fish.

Sculptured Reef

The lava has been sculptured giving relief from 20 ft. to 50 ft. An excellent site for octopus and schooling fish.

Fast Lanes and Beach House Arch

Do these separately or in combo at 90 ft, the top is 60 ft. Friendly eels, turtles, and occasional sharks visit these areas.

The Icebox

Lava fingers with encrusting corals, 50 ft. to 90 ft. Excellent fish life. This is a good location for macro photography.

Oasis Reef

A great second dive. The top is 2 ft., the bottom is 35 ft. Pennantfish (Honiochus) school here along with lots of other critters. Truly a mecca for reef fish as this pinnacle juts up in the middle of vast sandflats.

Hanalei Sea Tour along Waimea Canyon by Craig Wall

Tortugas

A very pretty place to visit with a large resident population of horned helmet shells. Appropriately named for large turtles that live here. Depth is 50 ft.

What you really come to Kauai to see is the marine life. Twenty-nine per-cent of the fish are endemic to the Hawaiian Islands. Which means you aren't going to see 1/3 of our fish anywhere else.

SCUBA AND SNORKELING FACILITIES QUESTIONNAIRE

NAME: **Bubbles Below Scuba Charters**
ADDRESS: **6251 Hauaala Road**
Kapaa, Kauai, Hawaii 96746
CONTACT: **Ken or Linda Bail**
TITLE: **Owner/Operators**
TELEPHONE: **808-822-3483 (DIVE)**   FAX

CAPITAL: **Honolulu**
POPULATION: **50,000**
CURRENCY: **US $**
AIRLINES: **United Airlines**
NEED VISA/PASSPORT?   YES   NO **x**

GOVERNMENT: **USA**
LANGUAGE: **English**
ELECTRICITY: **110v**
DEPARTURE TAX? **No**
PROOF OF CITIZENSHIP?   YES   NO **x**

YOUR FACILITY IS CLASSIFIED AS: SCUBA CENTER   RESORT
BUSINESS HOURS: **7 a.m. - 7 p.m. 7 days a week**
CERTIFYING AGENCIES: **PADI, NAUI**
LOG BOOK REQUIRED?   YES   NO **x**
EQUIPMENT: SALES **x**   RENTALS **x (Boat customers only)**   AIR FILLS
PRIMARY LINE OF EQUIPMENT: **Scubapro/Sherwood**
PHOTOGRAPHIC EQUIPMENT: SALES   RENTALS **x (Boat customers only)**   LAB

CHARTER/DIVE BOAT AVAILABLE?   YES **x**   NO   DIVER CAPACITY **6 per trip**
COAST GUARD APPROVED?   YES **x**   NO   CAPTAIN LICENSED?   YES **x**   NO
SHIP TO SHORE?   YES **x**   NO   GPS   YES **x**   NO   RADAR?   YES   NO **x**
DIVE MASTER/INSTRUCTOR ABOARD?   YES **x**   NO   BOTH **x**

DIVING & SNORKELING: SALT **x**   FRESH
TYPE OF DIVING/SNORKELING IN AREA: WALL **x**   BEACH   WRECK   REEF **x**   CAVE   ICE
DIVING/SNORKELING IN YOUR AREA IS BEST SUITED FOR: BEGINNER **x**   INTERMEDIATE **x**   ADVANCED **x**
BEST TIME OF YEAR FOR DIVING/SNORKELING: **Year round**
TEMPERATURE: **NOV-APRIL: 73 F**   **MAY-OCT: 76 F**
VISIBILITY: **DIVING: 70 FT**   **SNORKELING: 30 FT**

PACKAGES AVAILABLE: DIVE **x**   DIVE STAY   SNORKEL   SNORKEL-STAY
ACCOMMODATIONS NEARBY: HOTEL **x**   MOTEL   HOME RENTALS **x**
ACCOMMODATION RATES: EXPENSIVE **x**   MODERATE **x**   INEXPENSIVE **x**
RESTAURANTS NEARBY: EXPENSIVE   MODERATE **x**   INEXPENSIVE **x**
YOUR AREA IS: REMOTE   QUIET WITH ACTIVITIES **x**   LIVELY
LOCAL ACTIVITY/NIGHTLIFE: **Limited: Mostly at local hotels**
CAR NEEDED TO EXPLORE AREA?   YES **x**   NO
DUTY FREE SHOPPING?   YES **x**   NO

LOCAL EMERGENCY SERVICES
COASTGUARD: 246-0390
TELEPHONE: 911
CALLSIGNS: **HA 333CP**

NEAREST HYPERBARIC TREATMENT FACILITY
AUTHORITY: **Hyperbaric Treatment Center-Honolulu**
LOCATION: **Kauai Veterans Memorial Hospital, Waimea**
TELEPHONE: **338-6431**

LOCAL DIVING DOCTOR:
NAME: **Dr. Robert Overlock**
LOCATION: **Kauai Veterans Memorial Hospital**
TELEPHONE: **338-9431**

Divers are also enchanted with Kauai's large turtle population. The hurricane did not alter their numbers, it just gave them one heck of a ride. Tripod, a 300 lb. three legged female turtle who is a resident at Sheraton Caverns' dive site, is still around and doing great.

Maui

We docked at Kahului, Maui for the next two days.

My diving was scheduled with *Ocean Activities Centers* located in Kihei, Maui.

Senior Captain Allen Glaberson was on deck for me for the afternoon dive. An instructor for 18 years, he's lived on Maui for seven years after cruising and captaining yachts all over the world. He has many anecdotes of his world travel to regale you with as you drive through the countryside.

We reached the dock in Kihei where The No Ka Oi IV (meaning The Finest) is docked. My first encounter was with charming Olivier Navarre from Brittany ,instructor, guide and my buddy for the afternoon.

There is ample room aboard in the stern for equipment, and divers may sit in the shaded full cabin. There is a kitchen, head and shower aboard. Life rafts, life jackets, oxygen and first aid are also carried.

Captain Allen invites you to visit him up top where while you learn about Maui and its diving, you can also catch a little sun.

There is a maximum group of 12 divers with a ratio of one guide to six divers.

Our first site was *Inside Reef Molo-kini Crater*. The Molokini Crater is a Marine Park and so therefore nothing can be taken from the sea here. If one is lucky enough to find an exploded bullet shell, they may take that. In 1942, Kahoolawe Island, just behind Molokini, was used for target practice and so the ammunition floats over to the crater.

Usually, the afternoon winds bring swells and heavy sea. Most of the dive boats head for the crater in early morning. For some reason, this afternoon we had almost a dead calm. No one complained.

After a giant stride entry, we descended to 79 feet. The water was warm, 81 degrees Fahrenheit, and the visibility near 100 feet. There was a slight current as we reached bottom, but this served to bring out a myriad of fish. We saw beautiful peacock grouper, bluestripe butterfly fish, barred filefish, saddle wrasse, spotted yellow tang, trumpet-fish, orangeband sturgeonfish, a spotted moray eel, spotted pufferfish and both adult and juvenile bullethead parrotfish. As we delighted in the array, out of the corner of my eye I spotted a 4 foot white tip reef shark.

The current picked up and we took advantage of just letting it carry us along. I must confess, it almost carried me out to sea, I got so absorbed in the topography and fish life. It was a real struggle making it back to the boat. On every dive you learn something new. My lesson today was never become complacent or so involved in your surroundings that you lose sight of changing sea conditions!

Olivier found an exploded bullet shell and presented it to me.

Homeward bound, the sun began to set, the breezes were warm, the sea a wondrous color of changeable blues, the company genial, interesting and funny. Yes, I looked forward to tomorrow's dive even if we had to start out at 6 a.m. My only consolation was my husband would rise with me for he had opted for the water rafting, leaving at 6.

Allen was at the ship bright and early. When we reached the dock, other divers and snorkelers were already showing certification cards and filling out medical forms. Don't even think about fooling this crew with a letter or excuse you left your certification card at home. They are polite enough to fax the certifying agency with your name and address and year of certification to check, so you'd better be on the up and up!

As the *Na Ka Oi IV* pulled out of the harbor, we were given the same safety boat and dive briefing as before. We would dive at *Reefs End* again in *Molokini Crater*. We had both snorkelers and scuba divers aboard.

As we cruised out, we were pleasantly surprised that hot tea, coffee, juice and fresh blueberry cake were served. Allen and the crew really go out of their way to make the entire trip an enjoyable experience. When you add to this the highlevel of safety standards and professionalism, this is an outfit that's hard to beat!

The platform on the boat makes both entrance into the water and reboarding the boat easy and comfortable.

Our maximum depth would be 75 to 80 feet for 35 minutes with a safety stop at 15 feet for 3 minutes. We descended and there was a beautiful drop off with ledges jutting out at all levels. The visibility was 100 feet which enabled us to really investigate between the ledges for critters. Cauliflower coral covered almost the entire area of our dive. Yellow stripe goatfish, ornate butterfly fish, bright yellow tang, red lip parrotfish, forcefish, Hawaiian cleaner wrasse, pinktail durgeon and eye stripe surgeon fish were a handful of species we met along the dive.

Mid Reef was our next dive site. This was a shallow dive and we had ample time to check out the entire area.

Descending and making our way toward the reef, we came upon schools of moorish idol, Hawaiian squirrelfish, barred filefish, bluestripe butterflyfish, orange band surgeon fish, achilles tang, yellow tang, lei triggerfish, pinktail durgeon, and Hawaiian sergeants. We had 100 foot visibility for a perfect and pretty dive with varied sponges and coral, and a nice variety of fish.

As we ascended, we saw about 25 boats. We now realized why we had departed so early. It is tempting to wait until later, but Allen is right to start the group off early. His is usually the first boat. I don't know about you, but I don't like to dive in large groups so this operation would be my choice upon return!

Editor's Note
Allen can arrange a day's trip to Lanai providing there are six people in the party. The following is Captain Allen H. Claberson's interesting and informative contribution.

Maui has a well deserved reputation as a great place to take a diving vacation. In addition to having the best weather in the Hawaiian Islands, it also has a tre-mendous variety of activities and natural beauties to see when you are not diving. Whatever accommodations you pick, the best advice is to rent a car at the airport from one of the half dozen or so major rental agencies. Maui has NO public transportation, and while Ocean Activities Center does provide transportation to some trips, most other companies do not. Besides, many of the nicest parts of the island are only accessible by car, unless you want to tie yourself to a tour group.

Lahaina has historical sights from the time of the whalers and was the original capital of the Hawaiian Islands during the monarchy. There are a number of buildings of historical interest, forts and prisons, including the oldest lighthouse in the Pacific. In addition, Lahaina is full of shops, restaurants and art galleries. At night it offers a wide range of live music and entertainment.

Throughout the island are dozens of "micro climates", ranging from desert and lava fields through lush rain forest with roaring waterfalls and cool, clear pools of water in sculpted volcanic basins. The two mountains each provide numerous trails for hiking and on Haleakala the 10,000 foot elevation provides literally every kind of climate from desert to alpine along the 40 miles of highway leading to the summit.

In addition to hiking and scuba, there are 18 golf courses on the island as well as numerous tennis courts, submarine rides, horseback riding and helicopter tours. My favorite helicopter tour is on Blue Hawaiian, the West Maui, Molokai trip. Most people will not get to Molokai and this is an excellent way to see some of the highest sea cliffs in the world (3,000+ feet) and get an overview of the Islands at the same time. As the channels between the Islands are usually very rough, I recommend the helicopter as the smoothest and easiest way of taking a quick look.

Accommodations on Maui range from campgrounds close to Maalaea Harbor (windy, but close to the dive boats) through hundreds of condominiums available for vacation rental spread out all along the West (leeward/sunny) coast of the island to full service hotels and top (expensive) luxury resorts like Stouffers Wailea Beach, Grand Wailea (formerly Grand Hyatt) and the Kea Lani.

Unless money is literally no object, the rental condominiums offer a good value for the money. With kitchens included, they can help keep the high cost of eating out every night.

There is lots of expensive dining on Maui, some of it is also good. Food, in general, is much more expensive on Maui than on the mainland. Remember, everything has to come 2,250 miles on ship to get here. A $3.00 box of cereal is $6.00 in Maui. Still, the fish is fresh and there are a few great restaurants which compare favorably with mainland ones, both in quality and price. The Waterfront in Maalaea Harbor is excellent for dinner, with a great view of the harbor and Molokini Island. Maalaeais Buzz's Wharf is perfect for a Mahi Mahi burger and a beer after the morning dives.

Wrasse, Hawaiian National fish by Doug Hoffman

For those who want something simpler, or want to bring home some fresh fish to cook, the Fresh Island Fish Co. in Maalaea (across from the Coast Guard Station) sells a good selection caught by the local fishermen in the harbor. For a special treat, try their smoked Marlin sticks. Perfect for those fans of smoked, dried or other "jerky" kinds of finger food. Great for packing to the beach or that picnic on the trip to Hana.

Of course, the main reason a diver would come to Maui is to go diving. Maui offers lots of diving opportunities at all levels of experience.The best known location is Molokini Crater, a cindercone situated in mid-channel between Maui and the island of Kahoolawe. Nearly 3 miles off the Maui shoreline, Molokini rises from depths of 250 feet to 350 feet to form a half-moon islet with sheer cliffs going up nearly 200 feet above the ocean. Inside the crater is the largest hard coral concentration in the State of Hawaii. The rock ridges and coral reefs form a bowl-like inside with several coral ridges separated by sand channels which slope down to depths of 130 feet or more. Much of the inside, though, is less than 40 feet deep and filled with fish. Molokini is a major snorkeler location as well as a diving one. Like Hanauma Bay on Oahu (a similar formation), Molokini is a fish and bird preserve and no one is allowed on the islet or to take anything (including shells) from there.

Sea life is abundant and fairly used to divers' presence. There area number of semi-tame moray eels, a good population of docile white tip reef sharks, and often manta rays are seen when the plankton counts are high.

Visibility at Molokini is usually 100+ feet and 150-200 feet days are common. Water temperature varies from a low of 72 degrees Fahrenheit in mid-winter to 80 degrees Fahrenheit by mid-summer and stays warm through the end of October.

On the outside flanks of Molokini, erosion has cut the walls away to near vertical drops, with many ledges and overhangs dropping off to 300+ feet on the sides and 250 feet on the back (south) wall. Again, visibility is so good that it is often possible for divers to be at 80 feet or 90 feet and look down and see the bottom of the ocean. These "outside" dives are all done as drift dives and as there is effectively no bottom, they are usually considered a more advanced dive. Often when on these dives in the winter (whales season usually December through early April), divers are able to hear and sometimes see even Humpback whales as they cruise around the crater. The Humpbacks, especially the yearlings, seem to like the crater and can often be seen circuiting it during the day.

SCUBA AND SNORKELING FACILITIES QUESTIONNAIRE

NAME **Ocean Activities Center**
ADDRESS **1847 So. Kihei Road #203**
Kihei, Maui 96753
CONTACT **Captain Allen Glaberson**
TITLE **Senior Captain, No Ka Oi IV**
TELEPHONE **808-879-4781** FAX **808-879-7427**

CAPITAL: **Honolulu** GOVERNMENT: State of Hawaii
POPULATION: **90,000 (Maui)** LANGUAGE: English
CURRENCY: **US $** ELECTRICITY 110v
AIRLINES: **United, Delta, American** DEPARTURE TAX? No
NEED VISA/PASSPORT? YES NO **x** PROOF OF CITIZENSHIP? YES NO **x**

YOUR FACILITY IS CLASSIFIED AS: SCUBA CENTER RESORT
BUSINESS HOURS: **0600 -2100**
CERTIFYING AGENCIES: **PADI**
LOG BOOK REQUIRED? YES NO **x**
EQUIPMENT: SALES RENTALS AIR FILLS
PRIMARY LINE OF EQUIPMENT: **Scubapro**
PHOTOGRAPHIC EQUIPMENT: SALES RENTALS LAB

CHARTER/DIVE BOAT AVAILABLE? YES **x** NO DIVER CAPACITY **12 per trip**
COAST GUARD APPROVED? YES **x** NO CAPTAIN LICENSED? YES **x** NO
SHIP TO SHORE? YES **x** NO LORAN YES NO **x** RADAR? YES NO **x**
DIVE MASTER/INSTRUCTOR ABOARD? YES NO BOTH **x**

DIVING & SNORKELING: SALT **x** FRESH
TYPE OF DIVING/SNORKELING IN AREA: WALL **x** BEACH **x** WRECK REEF **x** CAVE **x** ICE
DIVING/SNORKELING IN YOUR AREA IS BEST SUITED FOR: BEGINNER INTERMEDIATE **x** ADVANCED
BEST TIME OF YEAR FOR DIVING/SNORKELING:
TEMPERATURE: NOV-APRIL: **75 F** MAY-OCT **80 F**
VISIBILITY: DIVING: **100 FT** SNORKELING: **50 FT**

PACKAGES AVAILABLE: DIVE DIVE STAY **x** SNORKEL SNORKEL-STAY **x**
ACCOMMODATIONS NEARBY: HOTEL **x** MOTEL HOME RENTALS **x**
ACCOMMODATION RATES: EXPENSIVE **x** MODERATE **x** INEXPENSIVE
RESTAURANTS NEARBY: EXPENSIVE MODERATE **x** INEXPENSIVE
YOUR AREA IS: REMOTE QUIET WITH ACTIVITIES **x** LIVELY
LOCAL ACTIVITY/NIGHTLIFE:
CAR NEEDED TO EXPLORE AREA? YES **x** NO
DUTY FREE SHOPPING? YES NO **x**

LOCAL EMERGENCY SERVICES NEAREST HYPERBARIC TREATMENT FACILITY

COASTGUARD: **Maalea Station** AUTHORITY: **University of Hawaii**
TELEPHONE: **244-5256** LOCATION: **Honolulu Kewalo Basin**
CALLSIGNS: **WTM 3510** TELEPHONE: **1-523-9155**

LOCAL DIVING DOCTOR:
NAME: **Dr. Norm Estin**
LOCATION: **Napili Tower, Suite 100, 200 Nohea Kai   Dr. Lahina**
TELEPHONE **667-7676**

Hilo

We arrived in Hilo early in the morning, anchoring at 8 a.m. There is no scuba diving on Hilo, so we opted for the Kenai Air Hawaii Helicopter ride.

Beginning their business 40 years ago in Alaska, Kenai has been operating helicopter rides in these islands since 1968.

We arrived at the air field and were given a briefing on the safety precautions of the flight and flight plan.

There were five of us and a pilot. You can choose between "Trail of Fire" or "Fire and Rain" flights."

We chose the "Trail of Fire", but our pilot was so obliging that my feeling was we got a combination of both.

As we climbed into the air, Hilo unfolded before us, the orchid farms, the small, bustling village, the sea and a complex of coves and crevices creating a portrait of the unique underwater landscapes and the mountains.

As we flew higher and closer to the mountain, we could see lava erupting-down the side and spilling her way towards the sea. As we got nearer, red hot lava appeared and when above, her belly was bright as a furnace, orange, red heat streaming from within. It was fascinating and terrifying.

Lava moves at a rate of 35 miles an hour.

We left the mountain and moved toward the sea. The only thing visible was black rock, evidence of the lava's destruction. When we reached the sea, we could see where the lava spills into it. The temperature of the water reaches 130 to 160 degrees Fahrenheit.

The pilot then circled around the area, showing us more of the shoreline and came upon a place where an entire village had been wiped out. Only a handful of houses remain. People still live in them, totally isolated with no road access, but still they survive.

Kona

Anchoring at Kona at 7:30 a.m., we were all prepared for a day's sail, dive and lunch on the *Fairwind*.

Picked up at the dock by a jolly Hawaiian driver, our group numbered about 20, both snorkelers and divers.

The Tradewinds is a very large catamaran staffed with a friendly and helpful crew.

Our destination for the day would be Kaavalava Cove. I had spent two days here before on a liveaboard because the seas outside were too high for us to navigate. The Cove is a Marine Park Sanctuary and the site where Captain Cook was massacred along with his crew. There is a beautiful-white marble statue in his honor right inside the cove. As I had done some 6 dives there before, I knew the cove well. It has good dive sites for both the beginner and advanced and some wonderful snorkeling.

Entry would be by giant stride. We swam to the front of the boat, giving the OK signal and then doing a free descent or went down the anchor line, meeting at the bottom at 20 feet.

Things did not go well at the onset. One lady's regulator was not functioning properly, mine was free flowing and another gentleman's tank had a leak. After we got the equipment problems sorted out, we all descended. The dive site was a gentle slope going to 90 feet with sandy bottom.

Our maximum depth was 60 feet with 40 minute maximum bottom time. We were to spend 10 minutes at 60 feet and then 25 to 30 minute sat shallower levels since 3/4 of the dive was very shallow. Anyway...when we all got our act together, we set off and began to delight in the underwater attractions.

Orangeband surgeonfish, Hawaiian squirrelfish, banded angel fish, flame angel fish, longnose butterfly fish, the ornate butterfly, nunu trumpet-fish, barred filefish, pufferfish, peacock grouper, yellow tang, crown of thorn starfish, turkey fish, bullethead parrotfish, moray eel, and moorish idol were all to be found.

All other divers returned to the boat and the divemaster and I buddied up. Our prize was an octopus, quite large, that we played with for about 10 minutes.

Bottom time up, we made a safety stop and reboarded.

I have suggested that *Tradewinds* make sure that every piece of their equipment is serviced and continue to be on a regular basis.

This was our last night aboard so when we returned we tended to packing as everyone is asked to disembark by 9 a.m.

Sailing during *Aloha Festival* gave us a real sense of being in and a part of Hawaii's history.

Early the next morning, we pulled into Oahu.

Editors Note: The U.S.S. Constitution and The U.S.S. Independence have been recently purchased by the Delta Queen Steamboat Co. of New Orleans.

Many of you are familiar with their fine standards of operation.

Cornel J. Martin, Vice President of Corporate Affairs for Delta Queen, sailed with us. During our time with him he assured us that the ships would undergo open heart surgery but nothing would be changed as to their character.

In fact, they have and will continue to consult with the world's authorities on Hawaii so that guests can expect to continue the same experience of the Hawaiian culture, and if I sense Cornel and his company's objectives as well as I think I do, passengers can be assured of even more of an authentic Hawaiian experience.

Simply, we say, "Maloha" to the entire crew of the S.S. Constitution for memories that will always remain warm and dear to us.

We had booked the Kahala Hilton and two days of diving with Jack Pappas before returning home. Please see Honeymoon and Anniversary section for Kahala Hilton.

Italy

Wendy Canning Church

POEM BY JOHN MASEFIELD

SEA-FEVER

> "I must down to the seas again, to the lonely sea and the sky,
> And all I ask is a tall ship and a star to steer her by,
> And the wheel kick and the wind's song and the white's sail's shaking,
> And a gray mist on the sea's face and a gray dawn breaking.
>
> I must down to the seas again, for the call of the running tide
> Is a wild call and a clear call that may not be denied;
> And all I ask is a windy day with the white clouds flying,
> And the flung spray and the blown spume, and the sea-gulls crying.
>
> I must down to the seas again, to the vagrant gypsy life, to the gull's way
> and the whale's way where the wind's like a whetted knife;
> And all I ask is a merry yarn from a laughing fellow-rover,
> and quiet sleep and a sweet dream when the long trick's over."

Quote Star Clipper Brochure

Sea-Fever Catch it Riding the Newest Greyhound of the Seas

No poem could more aptly describe the cruise that took us through a sampling of France and Italy's beautiful islands for our anniversary. It is this same spirit and love for the sea that enabled the ship's owner to build the newest, tallest and fastest "tall ship," the Star Clipper.

The Star Clipper plies the Mediterranean in the summer, and the Caribbean in the winter with her sister ship the Star Flyer. The Star Flyer sails the Caribbean year round.

Mikael Kraft, owner of both these ships, grew up in the port of Saltsjobaden on the Stockholm archipelago. Home to one of the finest shipyards in the world, the Plgms shipyard was just a few feet from his door.

Mikael's first job, at the age of six, was carrying varnish and mixing wood stain for the old-timers, who would tell him tales of the great sailing ships. The "Clippers," that had dominated the oceans in the late 19th century. These were named "the greyhounds of the seas" by historian Carl B. Cutler.

With the wondrous mixture of a young boy's dream and a passion for the sea, birth was given to these beautiful maidens, the Star Clipper and Star Flyer. Each 360 feet long, making them the largest clippers ever built. The S.P.V. Star Clipper was launched in May 1992 in Ghent, Belgium. Her registry is in Luxembourg. Classed by Lloyds 100A1+. She is the first clipper in this class since 1912.

Fashioned after the old Yankee Clipper Ships of the mid 19th century, she is a larger version of a four masted Barguentine. Her sail area is 36,000 square feet, length 360 feet, beam of 50 feet, mast height 213 feet, draft of 18 feet, gross tonnage 2298, speed under engine 12 knots, speed under sail 17 knots, and carries 180 passengers and a crew of 70. There are 90 air conditioned cabins most with private marble bathrooms, wall-to-wall carpeting, wall safe, multi-channel radio, television, telephone, reading lamps, dressing tables, mirror and wardrobe, 110 volt outlet and a hair dryer. Category 1 staterooms have refrigerators and whirlpool baths. While some staterooms are furnished with fixed double beds, most cabins in categories 1 to 5 are furnished with twin beds that convert to a double bed. Please advise your preference at the time of booking. Category 6 cabins are furnished with upper and lower berths, bathrooms are not in marble and the cabins do not have a television.

There is a dining saloon, piano lounge, bars, library and ample deck space for two swimming pools, deck chairs and stretch-out areas.

This is not a ship designed for children because of the rigging, nor does she have access for the handicapped.

We arrived in Nice at five o'clock in the afternoon which is the earliest that one is allowed to board the vessel. The Captain and First Mate were on hand to greet us.

The crew offered us a rum punch and a buffet table was set nearby. Mediterranean music played in the background. It was a warm and cheerful beginning. High standards of service, performed in a professional manner with genuine warmth and enthusiasm, prevailed throughout the entire sailing. Luggage is placed in your cabin by your steward, who is there for any service you may require during your sail.

We went topside and stowed our scuba gear in the lockers provided and met with the scuba director. While we were discussing the diving and our schedule, a charming and affable gentleman approached. "Hello, my name is Mikael Kraft, welcome aboard."

Mikael was to be seen everywhere that week. He takes a "hands on" approach with his guests, dining at a different table at each meal, checking on the beach activities, and he is a seasoned and enthusiastic diver, who believes a day without diving is like a day without sunshine.

Since we were not to set sail for Corsica until eleven o'clock, we decided to investigate the Nice waterfront. We walked the back streets and alleys and visited the little shops along the quay.

We dined at a superb restaurant called Les Pecheurs, 18 Quai Des Docks (93-89-59-61) which is closed on Wednesdays. They specialize in seafood. I had a Normandy lobster, with a sauce similar to a lobster bisque. My husband (and buddy) chose shrimp scampi and said he had never had better.

Restaurant prices were three times those in the USA. At the time we traveled, the exchange rate in both France and Italy was against the dollar. This is just one of the reasons we found our sailing to be priced right. The meals alone make it a bargain!

We boarded the ship and sipped a brandy on the outer deck as the Star Clipper slowly slipped out of Nice and sailed into the moonlight on a course for Corsica.

Each morning would begin with the Captains "story time" regarding the day's activities and our current destination.

The week long sailing encompasses stops at historic islands, tours of the islands, trips to the beach, with all sorts of grown-up water toys and wonderful snorkeling. There are Zodiac trips daily to caves and ocean marble quarries, as well as other spots of interest for sightseeing and picture-taking and of course scuba diving.

Scuba divers should not expect the kind of dive schedule that one would have on a liveaboard, where diving is unlimited. The ship usually sails at night, which limits night diving and because it arrives at different spots at different times, there cannot be a fixed diving schedule.

Cruising the Italian Riviera courtesy of Alan Bell Public Relations Director

What you can count on, however, is the incredible visibility, experiencing the thrill of diving in marble quarries, diving in small groups, exploring enchanted dive sites, and some of the most beautiful underwater topography I have ever seen. Schedules are dictated by the winds, which are always subject to change.

The itinerary is refreshing, because it lends itself to a balanced, yet unregimented, vacation, rather than having to be at a certain place each day at a designated time.

Our first port of call was the city of Calvi on the French island of Corsica. Calvi is an ancient fortified town.

In antiquity, the Romans appreciated the safety of its well sheltered harbor. They called it "Sinus Casiae" and "Sinus Casalvi" which is the origin of its current name.

Calvi has always been the capital of Balagne, one of the most prosperous regions on the island. Both the location of Calvi in the Mediterranean and its natural advantages, have made it the subject of political disputes. It has had to withstand at least seven sieges. During the siege of 1794, the town received 24,000 cannon balls, some of which are still visible in the ramparts. It was here that the future Admiral Horatio Nelson, then a young Captain, lost his eye. The city was forced to surrender and spent two years under British administration. It was not until 1797, after Bonaparte's victories in Italy, that Calvi was returned to France.

A half day excursion takes you to some typically old and picturesque villages. Leaving the harbor, we drove through Calvi along the main road and up towards Calenzana, then through the interior across Zila, Monte Grosso, and over the Salvi Pass with its splendid view overlooking the plains of Calvi. We continued on to Cateri for wine and cheese tasting then to Aregno and Vonvent, where the road narrows and climbs up to the fortified eagle's nest of San Antonio, Corsica's oldest village. Our last stop was Corbara, the birthplace of Queen Davia of Morocco, and the location of an old monastery. The views are extremely beautiful, as the road winds back down to the coast - the scattered islets of Ile Rousse, illuminated red by the setting sun and the coast back to Calvi. The excursion is on air-conditioned coaches with English- speaking guides.

We did our first dive that morning on the wreck of a World War II B17 bomber lying in 100 feet of water. The wings and cockpit are still intact but the tail has long since disappeared. It was quite interesting to swim into the plane from behind. There are an array of multicolored sponges on the aircraft. Nearby, in shallower water (60 feet), was a fascinating rock formations. Delightful soft corals, fans and unusual fish, such as the Scorpion, which the French call "Poisson Roscasse" called it home.

Our second dive of the day was at a small cave encircled by rocks. We entered the water and the visibility was fantastic! We dropped down to 50 feet and made our way out of the cave, heading toward the rock formations that surrounded it. The boulders were huge. We saw stingrays, schools of wrasse, a bright pink sponge and a number of orange sponges reaching towards us from the boulders. Purple and blue corals dotted the ocean floor, as well as blue sea urchins, which were a first for me. Schools of sea brean and oblade swam along with us.

Our second port of call was Bonifacio, Corsica. Bonifacio is situated in the extreme south of Corsica, in a narrow gully flanked by white chalk cliffs. From the top of these cliffs, legend has it Lestrygon giants hurled rocks and boulders down onto Ulysses and his fleet. It is a fascinating Genonese stronghold, with houses right on the cliffs' edge. Bonifacio is a most curious town that is divided into two areas: the marine or the harbor, and the upper town, boasting a Medieval city perched on a vast limestone plateau.

It is a charming place, with many fine boutiques and restaurants. There is a small aquarium, which we visited, that has an excellent sampling of Mediterranean sea life.

We bought a book in order to help us identify the fish life in these waters.

We dove late that afternoon at a group of rock formations well out to sea. Again, the visibility was superb. There were schools of oblade, which can be identified by their yellow stripes, and schools of castagnole, which are small black fish with gray dots. The topography was very interesting with many tunnels and caves, as well as mountainous terrain to investigate. The diving in general is quite good off Corsica. There are soft corals and a fair amount of marine life.

Our next port was Sardinia which was settled by the Phoenicians who endowed it with writing art and trade. Its independent thrifty people have subsisted for hundreds of years as fishermen and olive growers. It is the second largest island in the Mediterranean, but is largely unknown to tourists. It is blessed with a sun warmed climate and spectacular natural beauty, which is why Aga Khan developed the Costa Smeralda. Porto Cervo, on the rugged northeast coast, is one of the foremost yachting playgrounds in the world.

While anchored off Porto Cervo, we took one of the launches that the Star Clipper sends into the port. There are many boutiques filled with beautiful objects. Even if one does not buy, it is still fun to browse. We were always curious for news from the U.S., and a stop at port would send passengers scampering for one of the few available copies of the International Herald Tribune or U.S.A. Today.

We did a dive at dusk with Colin Hargrave, the dive leader for the day. We anchored well out of the harbor near two sheer cliffs (where the Guns of Navaronne was filmed). The fish that one sees diving in the daytime were preparing for bedtime and the nocturnal fish were preparing for their evening foray. We came upon a rather large octopus. Darkness had arrived when we discovered this amazing creature, so we shined our dive lights on it and watched as it changed colors.

We swam further out to sea and reached a stretch of sandy bottom where we found an abundance of crabs and bright red starfish. As we ventured further along the terrain, it turned into a high grassy area similar to the kelp forests of California. Hidden among these were tiny blue shrimp and a scorpaena scrofa, which looks like a hogfish.

Bottom time up, we ascended. The moon was shining brightly over the Mediterranean, a perfect exit to a perfect dive. The dive was followed by a hot shower, a delicious dinner and early bedtime.

We arrived at Elba at eleven o'clock the next day.

Elba is the third largest of the Italian islands. The population of 30,000 in the winter swells to 160,000 in the summer months.

We chose the perfect time of the year to travel, when the tourist season is almost over and life in these islands is quieter. At this time (September), you still get the advantage of beautiful weather. We had no rain and not even one cloudy day.

Elba is of historical importance as Napoleon was exiled there on May 3, 1814. Many people believe he chose it, not for the climate, but because of its proximity to mainland Italy, to which he would eventually escape. While he was on Elba, Napoleon made many contributions to the island. He improved the roads, planted olive and grape vineyards, upgraded the school system and organized the iron mines. In February 1815, he escaped and made his way back to Paris and his ultimate defeat at Waterloo. His next exile was to St. Helena from which there was no escape, and where he died.

We took the tour which covers practically the entire island. The landscape is a breathtaking succession of sea views and luxuriant, perfumed Mediterranean vegetation. Between Portoferraio and Procchio, there was a stop at Caponne, an enchanting spot in the beautiful green Bidola valley with a fine view across the lovely gulf of Procchio. After our stop in Caponne, the tour took us down to Marina di Campo and then stopped at Monumento on the gulf of Lacona before continuing on to Porto Azzuro. At Porto Azzuro there are many shops that sell minerals and crystals. Before going back in Portoferraio, we made a stop in Grotte to visit the remains of a Roman villa. We also stopped at a wine cellar for a wine tasting. The tour is on an air conditioned coach, with an English speaking guide.

When we returned, Colin had all the gear ready to make two night dives since the ship was not departing until eleven that evening. We took a twenty minute ride in the Zodiac to a spot near an isolated lighthouse.

It was quite dark when we went over the side and descended to 70 feet. We made our way along a rock wall directly beneath the lighthouse. We spotted a blue lobster hidden in a cluster of rocks that were decorated with beautifully colored coral and sponges. The Aetinia Rouge, a pink sponge is the most beautiful. On a stretch of sandy bottom, we saw hundreds of red starfish.

The first dive was a deep one, so with bottom time up, we ascended to change tanks and gas out.

Our second dive took us further out from the lighthouse to a stretch of sandy bottom. There, we came upon a small octopus and lobster. On the walls we found mustard, pink and orange sponges.

The beautiful lighthouse, high on the rocks, lit our way back to our floating home. We turned to see the lighthouse and all agreed how blissful it would be to live there, with its beauty and serenity, looking out to sea each day, and of course being able to dive the intriguing waters at its base.

After dinner we went on deck. A local band, hired for the evening, played romantic Italian music into the night. Champagne was indeed in order.

We set sail for Porto Venere which sits on the eastern side of the Italian Riviera, a favorite spot for the experienced traveler and yachtsman, but still natural and undiscovered by most. It was here that the ship would reprovision and we would have one of our most memorable dives.

The old section of Porto Venere is a maze of tiny alleyways that climb up the hillside. Most of the houses are jammed tightly side by side - often seven stories high and three yards wide. This is a fascinating town to explore, if you do not mind a lot of climbing, so wear comfortable shoes.

The castle above the church is worth seeing, if only for the spectacular view of the city and harbor. At the top portion of your climb, you will be charged an entrance fee. The view and small gallery is worth it.

Outside of the harbor and surrounding the cliffs are a number of marble grottoes. Marble is no longer mined in Porto Venere. We maneuvered the Zodiac into one of these grottoes and dropped anchor. Descending to 40 feet, we swam along oneside to the end, and then back along the other side, investigating the many shades of marble. As we began to ascend, we looked down and saw sheer walls of pure white marble. It was breathtaking. Ascending even further, we found different ledges, each blanketed with dazzling orange and mustard colored sponges. Sea snails were living in the crevices, along with sleeping crab. We spent the rest of the dive investigating these different ledges and playing with an octopus.

Portofino was our last port of call and the most beautiful.

One villa is more beautiful than the next, and they stretch high on the mountains and down to the sea. There is a sense of timelessness here as if nothing has changed or ever will.

Portofino dates from Roman times. It was a possession of the Benedictines and in 1414 was passed over to the Republic of Genoa. It saw invaders of many nationalities until, in 1815, it was included in the kingdom of Sardinia. At one time it was a quiet fishing village with tall and colorful houses facing the square and harbor. Now Portofino has become a world class resort

We dove in the late morning. Our Zodiac was filled with divers eager to get the last glimpse of the terrain and sea life underneath the clear and pristine waters.

(Please see Chapter Seven Underwater Wonders of the World.)

In the period of some two decades prior to 1860 the phrase "Clipper Ship" was the highest honor that could be bestowed on a vessel. Cutler wrote "a Clipper ship has lines clean, long and smooth as a smelt, sharp arching head, thin hollow bow, convex sides, light, round and graceful stern - in all they cried out "Speed and Grace'."

As Mikael was motoring the Zodiac after our last dive, the Star Clipper came into view. She was all of the above and more. She was the dream come true of a six year-old boy. I know this man still has dreams he will bring to fruition.

Once more the world can see these "greyhounds of the sea" ply the world's waters under the keen hands of Mikael Kraft.

We set sail for Nice that evening. Brandy was indeed in order as this beautiful lady of the sea set sail. We toasted to her crew and to our good fortune to have chosen such a perfect avenue to celebrate our very special anniversary.

For more information contact: Divers Exchange International, 37 West Cedar Street Boston, MA, 02114, (617) 723-7134 Fax: 617-227-8145.

Editor's Note: We strongly recommend flying British Airways to Nice. We flew from Boston stopping in Heathrow. The service is impeccable and they are by far the best choice. One should also consider joining the Executive Club for they offer a great deal of comfort to the weary traveler. They serve tea, coffee and offer other complimentary beverages, and snacks.

SCUBA AND SNORKELING FACILITIES QUESTIONNAIRE

NAME **Star Clipper**
ADDRESS **Based in Miami, Florida**
CONTACT **Wendy Church, DEI, 37 West Cedar Street, Boston, MA 02114**
TITLE **Booking Contact**
TELEPHONE **617-723-7134** FAX **617-227-8145**

CAPITAL: GOVERNMENT:
POPULATION: LANGUAGE:
CURRENCY: ELECTRICITY:
AIRLINES: DEPARTURE TAX?
NEED VISA/PASSPORT? YES NO **x** PROOF OF CITIZENSHIP? YES NO

YOUR FACILITY IS CLASSIFIED AS: SAILING SHIP **x** RESORT
BUSINESS HOURS: CERTIFYING AGENCIES:
LOG BOOK REQUIRED? YES **x** NO
EQUIPMENT: SALES RENTALS **x** AIR FILLS
PRIMARY LINE OF EQUIPMENT:
PHOTOGRAPHIC EQUIPMENT: SALES RENTALS LAB
CHARTER/DIVE BOAT AVAILABLE? YES NO DIVER CAPACITY
COAST GUARD APPROVED? YES **x** NO CAPTAIN LICENSED? YES **x** NO
SHIP TO SHORE? YES NO LORAN YES NO RADAR? YES NO
DIVE MASTER/INSTRUCTOR ABOARD? YES NO BOTH
DIVING & SNORKELING: SALT **x** FRESH

TYPE OF DIVING/SNORKELING IN AREA: WALL BEACH WRECK **x** REEF CAVE ICE
DIVING/SNORKELING IN YOUR AREA IS BEST SUITED FOR: BEGINNER **x** INTERMEDIATE **x** ADVANCED
BEST TIME OF YEAR FOR DIVING/SNORKELING:
TEMPERATURE: NOV-APRIL: F MAY-OCT: F
VISIBILITY: DIVING: FT SNORKELING: FT
PACKAGES AVAILABLE: DIVE DIVE STAY SNORKEL SNORKEL-STAY
ACCOMMODATIONS NEARBY: HOTEL MOTEL HOME RENTALS
ACCOMMODATION RATES: EXPENSIVE MODERATE INEXPENSIVE
RESTAURANTS NEARBY: EXPENSIVE MODERATE INEXPENSIVE
YOUR AREA IS: REMOTE QUIET WITH ACTIVITIES LIVELY **x**
LOCAL ACTIVITY/NIGHTLIFE:
CAR NEEDED TO EXPLORE AREA? YES NO DUTY FREE SHOPPING? YES NO

LOCAL EMERGENCY SERVICES NEAREST HYPERBARIC TREATMENT FACILITY
COASTGUARD: AUTHORITY:
TELEPHONE: LOCATION:
CALLSIGNS: TELEPHONE:

LOCAL DIVING DOCTOR:
NAME:
LOCATION:
TELEPHONE:

Jamaica (Xaymaca), West Indies

Jamaica lies 590 miles from Miami. It is the third largest Northern Caribbean island: 146miles long 51 miles wide - 4, 441 square miles in total. The topography is lush and green with mountain ranges reaching 7,000 feet that run down to the edge of the sea.

Jamaica's history is quite similar to that of the other islands. The Arawak Indians arrived in 600A.D. and established a settlement. They named their new home, Xaymaca, land of wood and water. The name was later changed to Jamaica.

The Spanish, under Christopher Columbus, landed in the 1600's and obliterated the Arwaks through means of murder, overwork, and the diseases they had brought with them. Pirates and buccaneers plied the Jamaican waters. The most notorious of these pirates was Henry Morgan, who plundered the Spanish ships. The Spanish lost interest in Jamaica due to its lack of silver and gold.

The English landed in 1665 and found the island to their liking. They established permanent settlements and laid the foundation for the lucrative sugar and rum trade. Slaves were brought from Africa to tend both the plantation houses and the fields. Many of these slaves rebelled (the Maroons) and went into the Blue Mountains to live an independent existence. The English granted slaves their freedom in 1838.

In 1865, Jamaica became a Crown colony. Independence was achieved in 1944, and Jamaica became a member of the Commonwealth of Nations in 1962.

Today, Jamaica's population of 2,300,000 is made up of a variety of different nationalities. Hence the motto: "Out of many one people." English is the official language, but you will hear the natives speak Patois, a combination of Creole and English.

Visitors to Jamaica will not find a sleepy little island where quaint customs abound. Rather, they will find a land of wood and water with a level of energy and comfort to fit any budget and taste -from the quiet of a fully-staffed private villa on its own beach, to the small guest house in a village where the sounds of Reggae and Bob Marley hang on the breeze.

Swept Away, Negril, Jamaica

"Everything is included, but the crowds" is the aphorism for Swept Away. They even include the cost of your wedding which includes a ministers fee, marriage license, tropical bouquets, wedding cake and champagne. The all inclusive vacation is becoming more of a rule than an exception for travelers.

Located on the northern most tip of Jamaica in Negril,which is 60 miles from the Montego Bay Airport (90 minutes by car). Swept Away is a 20 acre world of tranquillity and relaxation. Ten of these acres are beach front on Long Bay, the other ten across the street, allow the resort to possess the most comprehensive sports complex in the Caribbean.

This "couples only" hideaway has 134 air-conditioned suites, each with its own verandah. One can choose a view of the gardens, the atrium, or the beach. The large verandahs are a perfect place to have a continental breakfast, read or just lay back and take in the breathtaking views.

We chose a suite that overlooked the atrium, which put us close enough to the "action", yet far enough away to ensure peace and quiet. It was a delight to view the towering palms, sunsplashed in the early morning, reaching skyward from the center of our home away from home. In the evening as we climbed the stairs, the palms and surrounding plantings were illuminated by both spot lights and the stars overhead. After dinner, as we drifted off to sleep, the scent of these plantings would mix with that of the sea and were carried on a gentle breeze that filled our room.

Being scuba divers, we are early risers and on the way to breakfast each morning found that the only other people up were those in charge of maintainingthe grounds. They had already been up for hours raking the beach and tending the grounds. The same attention to detail applies to the entire staff at Swept Away. They are genuinely friendly and always eager to assist you in anyway they can. The complex as a whole has the feeling of a private estate rather than a public resort. The owner of this "private estate", Lee Issa, is frequently on the premises, making Swept Away a "hands on" establishment. He introduces himself to the guests and can be seen everywhere

One never needs to leave the compound with all there is to offer at Swept Away. The open air dining room serves breakfast, lunch and dinner. At night, this is where you will find the evening's entertainment presented by the resident staff. This is definitely where the "action" takes place after dark. Most nights they have a theme dinner and accompanying cabaret.

Above the dining room is an open air verandah where one can sit on very comfortable couches and chairs, read or play backgammon, checkers or billiards. There is also a television room as well as a piano bar. There are four full-service bars that also offer non-alcoholic fruit concoctions. Tea is served everyday at five.

The "veggie bar" located on the beach, serves fresh fruit and vegetable juice, sandwiches, fresh vegetables and other light snacks. Pizzas are made on request at the Sports Bar. "Feathers",Swept Away's gourmet restaurant, is located across the way at the Sports Complex. The cuisine is not only delicious, but also beautifully presented. Reservations are a must and please dress for the occasion.

I defy even the most athletic to be bored at the Sports Complex. There are ten tennis courts - five clay and five hard courts, all lighted for night play. There are squash and racquetball courts and a 1/2 mile running track. One will also find a basketball court and a lap pool. The gym has a variety of weights and exercise equipment along with aerobics classes, yoga classes, Jacuzzis, a sauna and steam baths.

Massages are offered at an extra charge - treat yourself to one. Be sure to request Oya Ozcan, a delightful, highly skilled woman. She has a degree in physical therapy and massage. You will also find a nurse on the premises at the Sports Complex. She is on duty from 9:00 a.m. until midnight. A doctor is on call 24 hours a day at an additional charge.

On the ocean side one can choose to splash in the freshwater pool or enjoy a ride in one of the glass bottom boats. They also offer sunfish sailing, water skiing, kayaking, windsurfing, snorkeling and scuba diving. Parasailing is available at an additional charge.

Below is a just a sample of the tours one can take if they wish to get off the premises and discover the rest of Jamaica (see the Tour Desk to arrange for all tours):

Great Eagle "Catamaran Cruise Party" - The most popular tour. Includes snorkeling at Negril's largest reef (all gear and life jackets on-board), scenic cruise up the West End along the caves and cliffs, open bar and snacks, live Reggae musicians, Limbo dancing, Bamboo dancing, and a stop at "Joseph's Cave" where the movie 2000 Leagues Under the Sea was filmed. Videos are taken of the entire cruise which can be viewed (and purchased) at the Tour Desk.

Black River Safari Boat Tour - A beautiful taxi ride takes you to this boat trip (1 and 1/2 hours long). You will see native and migratory birds, crocodiles basking in the sun, the longest river in Jamaica, and the gorgeous Mangrove swamps. A Jamaican lunch is included. After lunch the boat takes you to the fabulous YS Falls. Take a plunge into the cool waters or just marvel at the quiet charm of the YS countryside and the foliage. The tour finishes up with a tour along Bamboo Avenue, which you have probably seen in the "Come back to Jamaica" commercials.

Horseback Riding at Babo's Stable - Ride on some of Negril's best horses (not only in good condition, but these horses are loved.) Only a 10 minute drive from Swept Away (round-trip taxi included) takes you into the spectacular hills of Negril where the Rastafarian live. The guides are wonderful. This trip is a must for the experienced rider. For the beginners, the guides will take pictures of and for you - just ask.

Deep Sea Fishing - In Negril they catch Blue Marlin, Bonita, Barracuda, King Fish, Tuna, and Dolphin (not Porpoise). The trip is four hours long and the boats can take up to 7 people. Bar and snacks included as well as all bait and tackle.

Cuba - One day trip - Special visas are obtained, nothing is stamped in your passport. You will learn about the people, culture and history of this exciting and beautiful country. Visit the Morro Castle with its breath-taking vistas of the Sierra de Maestra Mountains and its Museum of Piracy. Tour the oldest rum distillery in the world - now called Caney - formerly Bacardi. Shop for world famous Cuban cigars, rum and souvenirs. Air-conditioned bus tour of Santiago de Cuba, the second largest city in Cuba. You get an English-speaking guide. Head downtown to Carlos de Caspedes Square and marvel at the gorgeous architecture of pre-Castro Cuba. Lunch at beautiful El Morro restaurant and much, much more. Cameras welcome.

Night-time glass bottom boat - Take a ride up the West End on the Sundowner and check out the sunset (comfortable sunset deck on-board). Includes open bar, snacks and Reggae music. Marvel at Negril's rocky cliffs and caves. Then, when the sun goes down and it's dark, they put the lights on the glass bottom. The marine life you will see in the evening is totally different from the daytime. Educational, comfortable, exciting, a knowledgeable crew - all the ingredients for a great time!

Swept Away Resort, Jamaica by Swept Away Resort

Belvedere Estate - A beautiful 1 hour drive through Jamaica's countryside brings you to the magnificent Belvedere Estate. The lush gardens possess a tremendous variety of flowers, plants, and trees. Taste pineapple and orange juice from their groves. Charming guides take you through this absolutely lovely Living Museum. They have reproduced a working Jamaican village from the 1800's. Lunch is served in the reproduction "Cook House". Visit the sugar mill and factory that actual works. See and taste the cane juice as it is made into white and brown sugar. Learn coffee, pimento and cocoa drying techniques. A Rastafarian Herbalist explains the use of a wide variety of tropical herbs and spices. View two gorgeous waterfalls and the Blacksmith, Bakery and the Village Souvenir Shop.

Mountain Valley Bamboo Rafting - Take a romantic ride through incredible countryside on your Bamboo Raft (comfortable and dry). Complimentary drink and lunch is included. Then onto "Rhea's World" for a tour of their Banana plantation and "zoo," where you will find a large variety of exquisite tropical birds, a Jamaican snake, beehives, rabbits, and a lovely liquor tasting of a number of different Jamaican drink delicacies.

Swept Away has the diving most able and safety conscious staff. They check your C Card and ask you to fill out a rather extensive medical form. Everyone, and I mean everyone, is checked out in the pool before they are allowed to dive. This might upset some of you experienced divers, but it is for your own protection and the safety of those diving with you. No one in Jamaica is allowed to get their tanks filled unless they are diving with a qualified guide.

The center itself is well maintained and caries an up to date list of equipment - no need to bring your own! Gear is set up for you before the dive and is broken down and rinsed after the dive.

Your inclusive package with Swept Away covers two one tank dives daily. There are a myriad of dive sites to explore - most of them only 10 to 20 minutes from shore. The boat can handle 23, but we never had more than 10. It is a spacious and comfortable boat that is run by Captain Hanes, who is a member of the Jamaican Olympic Boxing Team, and his assistant Junior. My only suggestion is that they add a canopy to the boat to protect you from the sun.

Advanced divers are scheduled for 9:00 a.m. and 1:30 p.m. beginners, resort courses or those taking a Discover Scuba introduction go out at 11:00 a.m. However, some days there was a combination of divers on the 11:00 a.m. trip. There are two shallow reefs and we quite enjoyed them; it gave us more bottom time as well. In addition, it is always a delight to see people experience their first dive; their faces filled with awe at the new and magical world they have discovered.

Following is a sample of the diving - most of which are drift dives. You ascend and descend with your buddy and there is always a lead guide and a trailer.

Shark's Club - Entry by giant stride. Requires safety stop at 15 feet for 3 minutes. A great first dive! Here you will discover many tunnels and arches along the reef. We did not sight any sharks, but we did spot a grouper that weighed nearly 100 lbs.. We also saw schools of blue cromis, creole wrasse, angelfish, and both white and spanish grunts. Water temperature was 82F. and the visibility was 150 feet.

Fish Pond - This is a shallow reef dive that is scheduled for Monday, Wednesday and Friday for the people taking the Resort Course and for the beginners. My buddy and I went each day we enjoyed it so much. One descends to the sandy bottom at 30 feet and then swims towards the reef where all types of reef fish abound: moray eels, trumpet fish, four eyed butterfly fish, yellow tail, snapper, and baby squid. I also spotted a puffer fish in a barrel sponge on my descent. He was obviously agitated because he had already swallowed 10 times its weight in water.

Deep Plane - This dive site is only 10 minutes from shore. Descending down to 80 feet one comes upon an airplane wreck along a healthy reef that is home to many a barracuda and trigger fish.

Discovery Reef - This dive is located some 50 minutes from shore. It is a reef dive with a maximum depth of 90 feet. Unfortunately, the Jamaican waters have been so fished out that they can hardly compare to the wonders of Australia and Belize, but the topography makes up for the lack of fish life. Hard and soft corals cover the reef in a rainbow of colors. The formations are very diverse and some unique to these waters. This is a truly beautiful dive.

The Throne Room - Only 15 minutes from shore, this dive was my favorite. The throne room is located in 38 feet of water. On the way down into the cavern you will

School of Squirrel fish surveying corals by Wendy Canning Church

pass along a reef covered with a multitude of soft and hard corals. Once through the tunnel you are free to sit on a giant orange sponge in the shape of a throne! It is quite a kick to see each diver take his turn sitting on the throne.

There is a special boat for snorkeling which takes guests to a number of sites. It is remarkable the variety of fish one sees. Not only will you see small reef fish, but larger ones a swell, such as stingrays. I suggest that even the scuba divers make at least one snorkeling trip.

The topography is breathtaking. The lace like purple and pink corals that one sees in the shapes of bowls and vases are simply magnificent. Jamaica is a perfect location for those who want to try scuba diving via a Resort Course. I would recommend it to anyone who wants to take the full course in order to receive their certification (this is offered at an extra charge). Many dive sites are perfect for those that have done their pool and classroom work at home and need only to complete their open water dives for certification.

I have been diving all over the world and to me the diving at Swept Away offered a relaxing and beautiful experience. I do not want to dive deep on every dive, nor do I need to see pelagics on every dive. The underwater world as a whole is a gift that I always enjoy.

You can get married 24 hours after arriving in Jamaica if you have applied for your marriage license and submitted proof of status. You will need proof of citizenship (certified copy of birth certificate, signed by a notary public, which includes your father's name); parent's written consent if under 21 years of age; proof of divorce if applicable (certified copy or original certificate of divorce); copy of death certificate for widow or widower. You do not need a blood test.

Many airline carriers serve the Montego Bay airport. We booked a charter flight from Boston through Sunburst Holidays that was operated by Capitol Air. We were quite pleased with the service we received from Sunburst Holidays. They operated on time and were on par with any other airline. They have offices in New York, Los Angeles, Baltimore, Atlanta, and Montego Bay. Sunburst Holidays has been in operation since 1973 and they are the "Jamaican Specialist." Departure taxes are included in your airfare. Your transfer to Swept Away is provided in the Swept Away package. You will need proof of citizenship.

Sunburst Holidays in the United States 1-800-666-8346
Outside of the United States write or fax: 212-942-9501
Sunburst Holidays, 4779 Broadway, New York 10034

SCUBA AND SNORKELING FACILITIES QUESTIONNAIRE

NAME **Resort Divers - Swept Away**
ADDRESS **P.O. Box 77, Negril, Shop #6**
Island Plaza, Ochio Rios, Jamaica
CONTACT **Angela Sham or Courtney Brown**
TITLE **OWSI, MSDI**
TELEPHONE **957-4061**   FAX **957-4060**

CAPITAL: **Kingston**   GOVERNMENT: **Democratic**
POPULATION: LANGUAGE: **English**
CURRENCY: **Jamaican Dollar**   ELECTRICITY: **110v/50 cycles**
AIRLINES: **American**   DEPARTURE TAX? **Yes**
NEED VISA/PASSPORT? YES **x** NO   PROOF OF CITIZENSHIP? YES NO **Passport**

YOUR FACILITY IS CLASSIFIED AS: SCUBA CENTER   RESORT **x**
BUSINESS HOURS: **8:30 a.m. to 4:00 p.m.**
CERTIFYING AGENCIES: **PADI**
LOG BOOK REQUIRED? YES **x**   NO
EQUIPMENT: SALES **x**   RENTALS **x**   AIR FILLS **x**
PRIMARY LINE OF EQUIPMENT: **Sherwood**
PHOTOGRAPHIC EQUIPMENT: SALES   RENTALS   LAB

CHARTER/DIVE BOAT AVAILABLE? YES **x** NO   DIVER CAPACITY **24**
COAST GUARD APPROVED? YES **x** NO   CAPTAIN LICENSED? YES **x**   NO
SHIP TO SHORE? YES **x** NO   LORAN YES NO   RADAR? YES **x**   NO
DIVE MASTER/INSTRUCTOR ABOARD?   YES   NO   BOTH **x**

DIVING & SNORKELING: SALT **x**   FRESH
TYPE OF DIVING/SNORKELING IN AREA: WALL   BEACH   WRECK **x**   REEF **x**   CAVE   ICE
DIVING/SNORKELING IN YOUR AREA IS BEST SUITED FOR: BEGINNER **x**   INTERMEDIATE **x**   ADVANCED **x**
BEST TIME OF YEAR FOR DIVING/SNORKELING:
TEMPERATURE: **NOV-APRIL:**   **73 F**   **MAY-OCT:**   **85 F**
VISIBILITY: DIVING: **100+ FT**   SNORKELING: **100+ FT**

PACKAGES AVAILABLE: **Included with stay at Swept Away x**   SNORKEL   SNORKEL-STAY
ACCOMMODATIONS NEARBY: **Located at Swept Away Resort x**   MOTEL   HOME RENTALS
ACCOMMODATION RATES: EXPENSIVE **x**   MODERATE **x**   INEXPENSIVE
RESTAURANTS NEARBY: EXPENSIVE **x**   MODERATE **x**   INEXPENSIVE **x**
YOUR AREA IS: REMOTE   QUIET WITH ACTIVITIES   LIVELY **x**
LOCAL ACTIVITY/NIGHTLIFE:
CAR NEEDED TO EXPLORE AREA?   YES **x**   NO
DUTY FREE SHOPPING?   YES **x**   NO

LOCAL EMERGENCY SERVICES   NEAREST HYPERBARIC TREATMENT FACILITY
COASTGUARD: AUTHORITY: **Peter Gayle**
TELEPHONE: LOCATION: **Discovery Bay Marine Lab**
CALLSIGNS: **Channel 16 Marine**   TELEPHONE: **973-2241**

LOCAL DIVING DOCTOR:
NAME: **Dr. Kellerman, Bruhn**
LOCATION: **Mile Clinic**
TELEPHONE: **57-4888**

St. John, U.S. Virgin Islands

Steve Simonsen

ABOUT THE PHOTOGRAPHER

In 1978, Steve Simonsen helped open the first dive shop in Boulder, Colorado. In 1979, he became a NAUI instructor. He first began using a Nikonos II in Cozumel, Mexico. Steve has traveled to exotic destinations such as Moorea in French Polynesia, the Red Sea in Egypt, Martinique in the French West Indies, Cancun and Playa Blanca in Mexico.

Steve and his new family moved half way around the world to Micronesia in the Western Pacific where he started his current business entitled Marine Scenes. Lured back to the natural beauty of St. John's National Park. Steve now bases operations at Low Key Watersports. He can be found most days on the colorful reefs surrounding St. John photographing divers and marine life.

Caneel Bay, Cinamon Beach, St. John, USVI by Steve Simonsem

A Rock Resort

Opened in 1955, and set on its own peninsula, bordered by the Atlantic and Caribbean Oceans, Caneel Bay has seven separate beaches, more than 500 species of wildly varied plant life and is located at the heart of the 5,000 acre Virgin Islands National Park. The Resort, located on the beautiful 19 square-mile island of St. John, U.S. Virgin Islands, was the first Rock Resort. The key to Caneel Bay is its solitude; it is a naturalist's wonderland where the landscape overshadows all that stands within it.

Laurance S. Rockefeller "discovered" Caneel Bay in 1952, on a Caribbean sailing trip. Eighty five percent of the island was jungle, the population was 400. Seeking to turn the untouched land into the type of resort he would choose for the perfect vacation, he purchased the old Caneel Bay Plantation. In 1955, Mr. Rockefeller began to develop theisland by building roads, establishing power plants and fresh water capabilities. He personally worked on the design and amenities of the resort. He then donated the property to Jackson Hole Preserve, a non-profit conservation oriented foundation supported by the Rockefeller family. The preserve later purchased 5,000 acres surrounding Caneel Bay and donated the land to the federal government, paving the way for the creation of the National Park, is made up.

The Hotels' staff is made up of 440 employees is of local citizens trained on the island.

Caneel Bay has 171 guest cottages and rooms. The guest rooms are airy and spacious, featuring rich Caribbean woods, hand-woven fabrics and simple, elegant furnishings. A plantation fan cools the air as gentle trade winds flow through your open windows. All rooms and cottages have spectacular views of one or more of Caneel Bay's seven beaches, beautiful gardens or tennis courts.

A sumptuous lunch buffet as well as an a la carte menu, is available at the Caneel Bay Beach Terrace. This open air dining room located just a few steps from the Caneel Bay shoreline, is also a popular spot for breakfast and the weekend Grand Buffet. All meals feature attentive service and delicious cuisine prepared with health and fitness in mind. After dinner, a Caribbean band serenades in the adjacent Caneel Bay Bar. Each Wednesday afternoon at the bar, guests are invited to join rum mixing and tasting seminars.

Freshly grilled lobster, fish, steaks and freshly made pasta are the hallmarks of the Sugar Mill, an enchanting dining experience set inside the flower covered ruins of an ancient sugar mill. The elevated restaurant overlooks Caneel Bay with the twinkling lights of St. Thomas in the distance. This was our favorite place to dine!

Parallel to the shore between the Beach Terrace dining room and the Caneel Bay Bar, the lower level Breezeway and upper level Starlight Terrace offer a great place for a cocktail.

The Turtle Bay Estate House is a romantic setting, reminiscent of the sugar plantations, that offers gourmet dining in its two-tiered open air dining room. In season, an a la carte breakfast and lunch buffet are also served. Afternoon tea and evening cocktails are served on the terrace overlooking the channel which offers picturesque views of the neighboring islands and the passing yachts.

The Activities Desk can arrange for sightseeing adventures by jeep, boat and taxi to a number of interesting destinations, from the 5,000 acre National Park to boat trips and shopping on St. Thomas. The nearby town of Cruz Bay features a variety of quaint shops and restaurants. Excursions are also available to Little Dix Bay, a sister Rock Resort and other destinations on the resort's cruisers, the Lady Caneel II, Caneel Bay Mary II and Calypso. Caneel Bay's kitchen will pack a picnic lunch for guests to enjoy at any number of destinations, including the storied Annaberg Plantation and the restored ruins of its famous sugar mill.

With over 500 varied species of plant life, Caneel Bay is a sightseers dream and there is no better way to experience its beauty than by foot. Hike among the many nature trails throughout the 5,000 acre Virgin Islands Natural Park. Caneel Bay also offers well marked and lighted pathways throughout its grounds to aid hikers, joggers and strollers.

Managed by the well-respected firm of Peter Burwash International, Caneel Bay's eleven all-weather tennis courts challenges players of all levels. Surrounded by tropical gardens, the elegant terraced Tennis Park offers complimentary clinics and private lessons at hourly and half hour rates. There is also an outstanding Tennis Pro Shop. Tennis packages are available.

Beaches ring the peninsula like a necklace. The seven famous beaches of Caneel Bay are: Honeymoon Beach, Caneel Beach, Little Caneel Beach, Paradise Beach, Scott Beach, Turtle Bay and Hawk's Nest. With these seven separate beaches, Caneel bay offers a wide variety of activities both in the water and out. Stop by the Caneel Bay Beach Hut and arrange to set sail on a sunfish or windsurfer. In addition, Caneel Bay and the surrounding area offer many aquatic activities, including a lap pool, boat rentals, deep sea fishing, snorkeling and scuba diving. The lady who conducts the snorkeling tours is a legend at Caneel Bay. She definitely knows her marine life and will make the tour both interesting and informative.

Pair of Grey Angel Fish by Steve Simonsen

Caneel Bay can be reached via San Juan, Puerto Rico, and via St. Thomas, U.S. Virgin Islands. Both are served by frequent flights from most major United States gateways. In addition, Caneel Bay's yachts operate between downtown St. Thomas and Caneel Bay several times each day. Caneel Bay also operates regular service three times each week to its sister resort, Little Dix Bay, on Virgin Gorda in the British Virgin Islands. Proof of citizenship is required when traveling between the United States and the British Virgin Islands.

SCUBA AND SNORKELING FACILITIES QUESTIONNAIRE

NAME **Low Key Watersports, Inc.**
ADDRESS **P.O. Box 431**
St. John, USVI 00831
CONTACT **Ann Marie Estes**
TITLE **Owner**
TELEPHONE **809-776-7048** FAX **809-776-6042**

CAPITAL: GOVERNMENT: **U.S.A.**
POPULATION: **4,000** LANGUAGE: **English**
CURRENCY: **US $** ELECTRICITY:
AIRLINES: **Delta, American** DEPARTURE TAX?
NEED VISA/PASSPORT? YES NO **x** PROOF OF CITIZENSHIP? YES NO **x**

YOUR FACILITY IS CLASSIFIED AS: SCUBA CENTER **x** RESORT
BUSINESS HOURS: **0800-1800 Mon-Sun**
CERTIFYING AGENCIES: **PADI**
LOG BOOK REQUIRED? YES **x** NO
EQUIPMENT: SALES **x** RENTALS **x** AIR FILLS **x**
PRIMARY LINE OF EQUIPMENT: **Sherwood, US Divers, Dacor**
PHOTOGRAPHIC EQUIPMENT: SALES **x** RENTALS **x** LAB **x**

CHARTER/DIVE BOAT AVAILABLE? YES **x** NO DIVER CAPACITY **6**
COAST GUARD APPROVED? YES NO CAPTAIN LICENSED? YES NO
SHIP TO SHORE? YES **x** NO LORAN YES NO RADAR? YES NO
DIVE MASTER/INSTRUCTOR ABOARD? YES **x** NO BOTH

DIVING & SNORKELING: SALT **x** FRESH
TYPE OF DIVING/SNORKELING IN AREA: WALL BEACH WRECK **x** REEF CAVE ICE
DIVING/SNORKELING IN YOUR AREA IS BEST SUITED FOR: BEGINNER **x** INTERMEDIATE **x** ADVANCED
BEST TIME OF YEAR FOR DIVING/SNORKELING: Summer - April - September
TEMPERATURE: **NOV-APRIL:** **78 F** **MAY-OCT:** **82 F**
VISIBILITY: **DIVING:** **70 FT** **SNORKELING:** **30 FT**

PACKAGES AVAILABLE: DIVE DIVE STAY SNORKEL SNORKEL-STAY
ACCOMMODATIONS NEARBY: HOTEL **x** MOTEL HOME RENTALS **x**
ACCOMMODATION RATES: EXPENSIVE **x** MODERATE **x** INEXPENSIVE **x**
RESTAURANTS NEARBY: EXPENSIVE MODERATE **x** INEXPENSIVE **x**
YOUR AREA IS: REMOTE QUIET WITH ACTIVITIES **x** LIVELY
LOCAL ACTIVITY/NIGHTLIFE:
CAR NEEDED TO EXPLORE AREA? YES NO **x**
DUTY FREE SHOPPING? YES **x** NO

LOCAL EMERGENCY SERVICES NEAREST HYPERBARIC TREATMENT FACILITY
COASTGUARD: **St. Thomas/Waterfront** AUTHORITY: **Dr. Boaz**
TELEPHONE: **809-776-3497** LOCATION: **St. Thomas, USVI**
CALLSIGNS: TELEPHONE:

LOCAL DIVING DOCTOR:
NAME: **Dr. Boaz**
LOCATION: **St. Thomas, USVI**
TELEPHONE: **809-776-4605**

APPENDIX

Environment – Divers and Reefs	*Glen Reem*
Safe Snorkeling	Forward by *Prince Charles* Forward by *Lionel F. Blandford*, Director and Founder, BSAC National Snorkelers Club Forward by *Mike Holbrook*, BSAC, National Diving Officer
How to Choose an Instructor	*Bill Vanderclock*
First Aid	*Joyce and Jon Huber*
How to Choose a Dive/Snorkeler Charter	*Jill and Mark Stanton*
Tips for Travelers	*Coleman F. Church 3rd*
Camp for Kids – Camp Marchand	*Smithy McIntosh*

DIVERS & REEFS:
Protecting Our Diving Environment
Glen Reem

Diving Experience: YMCA SCUBA course, Boston, 1959. Lobstering in Boston area to 1984.

Tropical diving: Cozumel, Andros with WHOI, Red Sea, Bonaire (many times). Member Boston Sea Rovers. Program Director, Boston Sea Rovers Annual Underwater Clnic 10 years; Member, Marine Careers Committee. Member, Board of Directors, Our World Underwater Scholarship Society. Retired.

Volunteer at: The Maritime Center, Norwalk, Connecticut; Spring Point Museum, South Portland, Maine. I dove near Boston for 25 years, always ending up with a lobster bag- and usually a few lobsters. Then I "gave my eldest (daughter) to my church" as co-owner of Sand Dollar Dive and Photo on Bonaire. And my 1/4 wet suit shrank around my middle. Since then my diving has been in Bonaire. Last year I went through the "old divers blues"- I hovered over the bottom and wondered why I was there.

Then I realized that for years I had been enjoying watching the animals. And I enjoyed telling people about the things I found interesting. I tried underwater photography on my next trip. But still photos can't show behavior in action. Ah, but video. So now underwater video has cured my "old diver's blues"!

All who dive should find such a solution.

As human beings, we must have concern for the whole earth environment. As SCUBA divers, and snorkelers, we must be particularly aware of the water environment. Whether the location is the untouched western Pacific or Lake Michigan at Chicago, a local lake or quarry or the Caribbean, the water is our diving life. All our diving is controlled by the water environment and it's quality. As divers we can help that environment both by the way we handle ourselves and by encouraging others to do their part wherever they can. I have used the term "reef" below- put yourself in your own environment.

Our own actions have their direct effects on the animals, plants and the substrate itself. Touching plants and coral, handling animals, taking shells or coral and spearfishing all can have adverse effects on a reef, especially in an area visited by many divers.

Buoyancy control is an important part of reef conservation, as well as diver safety. When you are in control of your buoyancy you can take positions in the water that keep you from touching living things on the reef. There is some controversy about how much damage is done when a diver touches living coral gently. There is no question that crashing into a brain coral or breaking staghorn harms it. Kicking fins onto a coral will tend to smother some of the animals. Practice hovering without moving. You have seen dive guides floating motionless with arms folded. I find that is a good way to watch the reef go by. The fish seem to be less alarmed if your arms and legs are not in constant motion. When you hover in one spot for a few minutes the fish will decide you are at part of the environment and simply swim around close to you doing their usual thing. If your dive operator gives Buoyancy Control or Photo Buoyancy Control courses, take them. They usually last only an hour or two including a dive to practice. Most people use much less weight from then on and enjoy diving more with their new found control and confidence.

Ask your dive guide/operation to let your group stay in one spot long enough to really look at it. Swimming rapidly up current to 1500 pounds of air pressure and then back to the boat is a small part of what any dive can be. Use your hovering ability to watch the animals. Slide down close to the anemones and sponges and look to the small shrimp and crabs that live inside. The closer you get to most things underwater the more you see of a tiny world that is invisible during a fast cruise down the reef. When you ease close to a grouper at a cleaning station watch for the parasites zipping around on his back and sides as well as for the cleaners. Watch how the goatfish burrow into the sand all the may to the back of their gill covers. Go up into the quiet, shallow water and see how many of the juvenile fish you can match with their adult coloring. Go out to the shallow under any anchored boat or ship tied up at a pier (check with the local harbor master for sailing times with ships. Propeller current can be deadly.). Baitfish often school there and will be visited by their predators like tarpon and jacks. Ask where else baitfish gather and swim with them.

Go diving in the late afternoon or at dusk to see very different behavior (and more animals!) than at 9 am or 2 pm. There is something fascinating to be seen everytime you stop and look. Dive around rock jetties and piers at night including right at the dive operation. Rock lobster and red night shrimp commonly come out to the edges of their rocky daytime hiding places. On Bonaire, large tarpon come in to fish by the lights of waterside restaurants. Dawn is also a different world on the reef as the guard changes from night fish to day.

Handling any animal stresses it: I certainly don't want to be handled by any elephant-sized creature I don't know. Passing seahorses from diver to diver, or frightening a puffer into inflating may be fun for the divers - but certainly not for the fish. Puffers tell you that by swimming away. Too often the seahorse just passes out, and likely into another fish when you let it go. If you do gently pick up a crab or shrimp or small sleeping fish, put it back just where you found it. Reclusive fish turned loose out in the open have a way of disappearing into a passing hogfish or the tarpon which has been looking over your shoulder on a night dive. And many shrimp live in mated pairs, so do unto them...

Some handled fish return the favor with teeth. Most moray eels really don't like to be touched- some do. Ask your local dive guide before trying. They usually know the fish in their area and can tell you which 7 foot green moray wants her back scratched. And, of course, there are those animals and plants that are poisonous or have spines that lodge in your flesh. Buy a good critter identification book and study it on the plane ride. Recognition of species will make all of your dives more fun.

There are many good books about reef animals. The book Pisces Guide toWatching Fishes: *Understanding Coral Reef Fish Behavior* by Roberta Wilson and *James Q. Wilson* (Pisces, 1992; originally Harper, Rowe, 1985) is the best I have seen about animals in their habitat. It is not an identification guide but rather describes what the reef is, the animals that live there and how they act and interact.Chapters include swimming, eating, senses, color, reproduction and much more. It's examples are taken from all around the globe. This one book has explained so much of what I have seen and given me so many more things to look for that I believe every fish-watching diver ought to have a copy close at hand.

My favorite identification books are *Divers and Snorkelers Guide to the Fishes and Sea Life of the Caribbean, Florida, Bahamas and Bermuda* by F. Joseph Stokes (The Academy of Natural Sciences of Philadelphia, 1984) and *Seashore Life of Florida and the Caribbean* by Gilbert L. Voss (Banyan Books, Inc., 1980). Stokes is a small sized book that uses color drawings to show all it's animals. It has many more different fish than any of the photo books and so is my choice for fish identification; it is quite sparse on other classes of life. Voss has line sketches of almost any plant and animal except fish. These three books make a very good foundation for enjoying underwater photography, video or just plain diving. My Caribbean diving bias shows in my choice of identification books: I know there are good guides to Pacific coast and Indo-Pacific life but I am not familiar with them. Examine the books at your dive shop and ask your tour operator and friends for their recommendations.

Ask before feeding fish. Many resorts actively discourage the feeding of any fish by divers. They do this both to protect the divers (yellowtail snappers can become obnoxious when they expect to be fed, moray eels have been known to come out and try sampling the nearest diver) and to avoid modifying the behavior of the fish in lesser ways. Also be careful how you feed. Even snappers can nip fingers. Moray eels (favorite bad guy in this article!) are notorious for their bad eyesight and love of fish pieces. It is wise to wear brightly colored gloves when feeding morays, and don't use fish. Hot dogs don't cause feeding frenzies, and Cheese Whiz has no place on any reef.

Spearfishing can be one of the most damaging activities on a reef. It always depletes a population faster then it can regenerate - it takes more than a year to grow a mature fish. And any fish taken causes the remainder to spread out to fill the available space. The smaller the habitat, the greater the effect per fish taken. A few jacks removed from a school of 2000 may not be a noticeable change. One grouper from a small reef area makes a difference. Personally I am against spearfishing in reef environments.

Many divers do not control the motion of their instrument consoles and other attachments; they dangle unseen and free over the coral. It is important to keep an octopus regulator from dragging on the bottom for safety purposes: a second stage filled with sand is a real surprise to an out-of-air diver. Console control is important to the reef. It is easy to break coral or gorgonians while freeing a caught gauge set. Or just by bouncing it along. Recently manufacturers have made specially curved assemblies that conform to the body to best slim the divers profile, but that really isn't necessary. BC's commonly include high pressure hose restraints that keep the console close to the divers body. Even a snorkel keeper can be used to hold the console hose just as it is used to keep an octopus in the "vital triangle". The main thing is to control your equipment.

A personal sidebar about consoles. I am a firm believer in wearing my important gauges on my arm, not in a console. The major reason is that I want my decompression computer (DC) to stay with me if I have an accident. Rescue courses teach divers to drop the weight belt and discard the BC of a victim - a DC in a console will likely be lost, or at least separated from the victim at the very time the receiving medical people will most need it's information. When my DC is on my arm, it comes out of the water with me and calmer minds can think to forward it on with me. It is easy to look at so I check it often. I also carry a backup depth gauge, a watch and small compass on the same arm. This system started before even submersible pressure gauges came along but I keep to it for the reasons above. One last excellent reason is that my lifeguard device stays under my gentle, careful control at all times. It is not liable to being stepped on the deck of the boat or being banged about by a careless dive guide or diver. This is a personal thing with me- but I do believe it worth consideration by all divers who use decompression computers.

Then there are the things we can influence. Both dive operations and resorts can have adverse influences on the water environment. As divers we can look critically at the way things are done and make known our opinions about harmful practices.

Most of the tropical resorts (and all liveaboards) we love to dive with are in remote areas away from any municipal sewage treatment such as we have in theUnited States. When local resort by resort treatment is done by leaching fields in a coral substrate, the resulting "gray water" is very rich in nutrients because it leaches so quickly into the sea through the grossly porous old coral substrate. This can be seen in some resort areas where plant and animal life diminishes and "green hair" algae flourish in the shallow water just offshore. Proper control of sewage (and food and cooking wastes) is more expensive and requires better management than simple leaching fields- but isn't that the core of all environmental affairs? Watch for this and let the resort know about things you don't like it, you anonymous reviewers for dive newsletters: check out all these areas and let us know who is "environmentally good" or "bad". Even writers with article bylines can tell their readers how each resort handles these matters. I believe it is an important part of an evaluation of any dive operation.

One of the actions that is most destructive of the reef environment is dive boat anchoring on reefs. Both the anchor and it's chain tear at the coral. In recent years Marine Parks have been established around several of the islands in the Caribbean and in Florida. Most of these Parks set aside areas where diving can be done as well as sections that are completely off limits. Most also prohibit spearfishing and the taking of even dead shells and coral from the water. Dive boats (and all others) are required to tie up at fixed moorings instead of anchoring on the reef. The moorings have almost eliminated the extensive reef damage caused by anchors dropped and dragged on the reefs. If your dive operators still drop anchors on the reef, talk to them and urge the placing of moorings, and support the Parks by following their rules. Some Parks charge each diver a fee that goes directly to support of the Park. Another $10 or $20 cost on a dive trip is a small price to pay to know that the reef will be just as good, or better, the next time we or our friends or children's children return.

There are so many divers in some places that the reefs have been significantly damaged. Less frequented areas are still relatively untouched. Whatever the present condition of the reef we are diving on, our actions make a difference for the future. Together we can give our water environment the best chance of "being the best it can be".

Safe Snorkeling

Foreword by Prince Charles

For many years The British Sub-Aqua Club's diving manual has been one of the world's recognized authorities on sports diving.

The BSAC is to be congratulated on the production of this fully updated edition.

It is a great pleasure for me to be asked to introduce this manual for what is a growing number of diving enthusiasts. I am sure it will continue to influence significantly the growth of this adventurous activity, and I am sure it will also provide me with extremely useful information on how to improve my own diving technique!

Charles

Foreword by Lionel F. Blandford

In snorkeling, as with most other sporting activities, a little knowledge can be a dangerous thing! So it was with this maxim in mind, in 1974, that the National Snorkelers Club was founded.

Specifically intended for children, the NSC went from strength to strength to become a very popular and rapidly growing organization. By December 1990, over 50,000 children in the 400-plus nationwide branches had successfully passed the meticulous training courses in safe and efficient snorkeling.

The vast expanses of water largely covering the Earth provide a great opportunity for the practice of sailing, wind-surfing, swimming, canoeing and many other exciting leisure activities. But none is more thrilling and enjoyable than snorkeling, with the ability to observe in a leisurely way the wonderful world beneath the sea.

The original *NSC Snorkeling Manual* has served its purpose very well over the years. But the increasing interest in this fascinating sport from young and old alike has resulted in the production of this considerably more comprehensive and informative manual.

Snorkeling for All is a complete guide to the sport, giving details of where to learn, equipment, training and techniques, along with information on underwater photography and many other related topics.

I am delighted to endorse this excellent book and can thoroughly recommend it as essential reading for all who are interested in the underwater world, regardless of age.

Study the book and train hard and I am sure you will have the years of pleasure that I, and many other enthusiasts, have enjoyed from this wonderful sport.

Lionel F. Blandford
Director and Founder, BSAC
National Snorkelers Club

As founder of the BSAC's National Snorkelers Club in 1974, Lionel Blandford has developed his tireless energy and enthusiasm towards the training of youngsters in the sport of underwater swimming. Although *Snorkeling for All* has been designed to encompass all age groups, it is unlikely that this manual could have been produced without his initial inspiration.

Mike Holbrook
BASC National Diving Officer

*Reprinted with the permission of the British Sub-Aqua Club, Snorkeling for All, published by Stanley Paul, London. BS-AC, Telford's Quay, Ellesmere Port, South Wirral, Cheshire L65 4FY. Telephone: (051) 357-1951.

Snorkeling for All is the latest manual from the British Sub-Aqua Club, supporting the Club's new snorkel training initiative. Kendall McDonald reviews this broadly aimed book, from which the illustrations on this page are taken.

SNORKEL GUIDE

Good books don't just happen. A great deal of thought goes into them before a single word is written, and it is clear that *Snorkeling for All* is no exception. A great deal of clear thinking was done before work started on this manual, the fifth in the BS-AC series of standard works about sport diving.

Two major decisions about the content of this manual were taken. The first was to treat snorkeling as a sport in its own right and not just something you did in the run-up to diving. The second decision was just as revolutionary. It was to accept that, as far as Britons are concerned, most snorkeling takes place in warm waters on holiday.

So when you buy your copy of the BS-AC's latest manual, you will very soon spot the results of those decisions in print. The title *Snorkeling for All* means exactly that - a sport for all the family. And as soon as you turn the pages you will see the weight that is given to the sea conditions abroad in which most British snorkelers will find themselves on holiday.

So appropriate is the new-style guide to snorkeling that I can see holiday companies offering the manual to their clients, or at least suggesting in their brochures that they read it.

Snorkeling for All is, in fact, the flagship of the BS-AC's totally new approach to the sport. Not only have the Club slashed the cost of snorkel membership to a mere three pounds, they've also completely revised the teaching of the snorkeling programme. This makes the heavily illustrated book vital to anyone who wants to snorkel.

But the manual does not suggest on every page that you must join the British Sub-Aqua Club. More emphasis is laid on the art of snorkeling and the enjoyment to be gained from it.

Mike Holbrook, the Club's National Diving Officer, believes that snorkeling should be a sport separate from diving.

"If any one of a family then becomes hooked on the underwater world and wants to go diving, the Club will be delighted," he says. "And if they've learned about snorkeling from us, it would be only natural for them to want to learn to dive in the same safe and sensible way.

"*Snorkeling for All*, packed with easy-to-follow coloured illustrations and stunning colour photographs, is safe and sensible throughout. Though they say that no-one can learn to dive from a book, I'm not so sure that this applies to snorkeling.

Certainly you would have no difficulty in equipping yourself properly from the excellent spreads devoted to masks, fins and snorkels, with the emphasis on what to look for in each category. And the chapters dealing with basic techniques are comprehensive enough to get the novice doing things the right way at once.

The use of life jackets is followed by compasses and other accessories, then correct signaling is followed by detailed advice on rescue skills.

Once all this has been mastered, the text flows smoothly into open water techniques and covers the use of protective clothing Lycra one-piece body suit for really warm waters, neoprene shorties and full wetsuits for colder climes.

Safety is stressed all the way through, particularly in the open water advanced techniques and coping with various sea conditions at home and abroad.

Other chapters deal with such things as octopus, aqualacrosse and mono-fin swimming. There's even a touch of photography, how to keep fit for snorkeling, holiday gear packing, expeditions, marine life and conservation.

For anyone going on a seaside holiday anywhere in the world, and who thinks it might be nice to do a bit of snorkeling in that lovely warm water, this book is essential reading.

And for more serious snorkel divers, it is the only book they need on their shelves!

Snorkeling for All is published for the British Sub-Aqua Club by Stanley Paul, London, at 10.99 pounds (8.99 pounds to BS-AC members). BS-AC, Telford's Quay, Ellesmere Port,. South Wirral, Cheshire L65 4FY (tel. 051-357 1951).

Editor's Note: Reprinted with permission from Diver Magazine, The Magazine of Sub-Aqua Diving, Undersea Exploration and Research, address: 55 High Street, Teddington, Middlesex, TW11 8HA, England.

How to Choose an Instructor

by Bill VanderClock

Bill Vander Clock is a Professor of Computer Science and has been a SCUBA instructor since 1984. He has taught SCUBA at Rochester Institute of Technology, The National Technical Institute for the Deaf and currently runs the SCUBA program at Bentley College in Waltham Massachusetts. Bill's travels have taken him diving throughout the USA including reef diving in Key Largo, Fla., giant kelp diving in Monterey, Ca., drift diving in the San Juan Islands, Washington, wreck diving in New Jersey, altitude diving in Lake Tahoe, Nevada, underground diving in Bonne Terre, Missouri, and archeological diving in Watkins Glenn, NY. His favorite dive sites are on the north shore of Massachusetts where you will find him year round with his students. When not diving Bill spends his time fighting computer viruses.

Anyone who decides to become a SCUBA diver usually starts the process by trying to find a training program that fits all the important criteria like location, time and cost. Invariably the potential diver runs into the "we are better" routine. Sometimes it's a dive shop saying that they are better than the other shop in town. Most often however it is war of letters that really don't mean much to the potential diver. Someone will say "Make sure that it is a NAUI course." or "Don't take it if it's not a PADI course." or "YMCA classes are the best." or "SSI is the only SCUBA program worthtaking.". This mumbo-jumbo of letters can get very confusing for someone who just wants to take a basic SCUBA class. It is my contention that the shop, the letters of the program and yes, even the cost are secondary considerations to the most important consideration in choosing a SCUBA training program. The instructor who is going to open the door to diving for you is far more important than any other consideration in choosing a diving program.

SCUBA training in the United States is self-regulated. There is no governmental agency that controls how people learn SCUBA or how they dive after they are trained. This is possible because of the non-government certification organizations that set standards for SCUBA training and the excellent safety record that has been maintained by the certification agencies. There are a dozen or so certification organizations that offer SCUBA courses. PADI (the Professional Association of SCUBA Instructors), NAUI (the National Association of Underwater Instructors), SSI (SCUBA Schools International), YMCA (Young Mens Christian Association), NASDS (National Association of SCUBA Diving Stores) are but a few of the various organizations that certify SCUBA divers. The particular organization associated with the certification card a student earns is more related to politics than program features and many instructors are certified to teach by more than one of the organizations. In fact, the training programs are so similar between different organizations that instructors will often offer their students a basic certification card from the organization of their choice.

The instructor who teaches the SCUBA course you take is more important than the shop, the agency, what is included in the course or what isn't included. This person is going to set the tone, teach the skills and give you the information that would take years to collect on your own. How you feel about the sport and, to a large degree, how you will feel about yourself will be determined by this person. Like any other group of people there are many different types of SCUBA instructors and there are some extremes. Fortunately, there are very few bad instructors and they don't last long in the industry. It requires a great deal of skill and dedication to teach SCUBA and most instructors do not earn enough to really compensate them for the time and energy invested in teaching.

The best way to pick a SCUBA course, and this applies to advanced as well as basic SCUBA, is to take the time to meet and compare the instructors who will be teaching the courses you are interested in. Many dive shops have a social night where perspective divers can meet and talk with the instructors. Sitting in on a classroom session that the instructor is teaching, regardless of what class it is, is another good way to get a feel for the instructors teaching style. Talking to people who have taken a course from the instructor is another possibility but you need to be careful. The right instructor for you is not necessarily the correct instructor for someone else. It is also helpful to have some idea of what you are looking for in teaching style. Every SCUBA instructor has to convince people that they are going to be all right breathing underwater. They have to get their students to complete skills that are required by the certifying agency although the students may not be interested in doing those skills. The personality of the instructor probably has more impact than anything else. Most instructors tend to be friendly, outgoing people who can get along with most people. Some people worry about experience and look for the instructor who has been teaching the longest. I find however that the newest instructors sometimes have the most enthusiasm and, having just been tested, are more familiar with the best and newest ways to teach. Since very few instructors actually teach for more than a couple years, old, worn out instructors are not very common. There are some excellent instructors who have been around forever and can be found by word of mouth because they have trained so many people.

In conclusion, take the time to check out your potential instructor, the time is well spent.

First Aid
Joyce & Jon Huber

Joyce and Jon have operated an advertising and photography service since 1971 in New Jersey. They began diving the Caribbean in 1975 and have since maintained a collection, both photographic and written, on different diving locations for themselves and diving buddies. In 1990 they updated the collection and created a guide with co-author Christopher Lofting, "Best Dives of the Western Hemisphere" published by Hunter Publishing, Edison, N.J.

Though intended as a helpful guide for new divers, the book has proven wide appeal to all experience levels and is currently being expanded into a series. The first of the series, "Best Dives of the Caribbean" came out Winter, 1994. For additional information, write to Hunter Publishing, 300 Raritan Center Parkway, Edison, NJ 08818. Phone: 908-225-1900 or FAX 201-945-6105.

First Aid Tips for Minor Diving-Related Injuries
Jon Huber, Joyce Huber & Christopher Lofting

Cuts and scrapes on coral reefs, jelly fish stings or first-day-out sunburns can ruin a diving vacation.

Follow up treatment by a physician is recommended. For serious cuts or injuries seek immediate medical assistance.

CORAL CUTS

Coral animals leave behind a hard skeleton, which is frequently razor sharp and capable of inflicting deep, painful wounds. Some living corals have stinging cells similar to those in a jellyfish and produce a sting which rapidly disappears, but may leave itchy welts and reddening.

The most delicate-appearing corals are often the most dangerous. Coral cuts, while usually fairly superficial, can take a long time to heal.

Prevention

Coral should not be handled with bare hands. Wetskins, made of lightweight lycra and ideal for warm water diving or snorkeling, offer a bit of protection. Many marine parks have outlawed wearing gloves to protect the coral. Divers should exercise extreme caution when exploring a reef formation which is subject to heavy surge and wave action or surface and bottom current. It is easy for the unprepared diver or snorkeler to be swept or tumbled across coral. Consequences can be serious. Be prepared.

First Aid

Control local bleeding. Cover with clean dressing. Treatment of stinging coral wounds: clean wound being sure to remove all foreign particles. A tetanus shot is recommended. Wash with soap and water since live coral is covered with bacteria. Or wash with a baking soda or weak ammonia solution, followed by soap and fresh water. When available, use a cortisone ointment or antihistamine cream. An application of meat tenderizer may speed up the healing process. The venom from stinging sea creatures is a protein, which the tenderizer destroys. Mix the tenderizer with water to make a paste. The wound should be covered with a sterile dressing to prevent infection. A commercial sea sting kit, available from dive shops, is useful for minor coral scrapes. Severe wounds must be treated by a doctor.

JELLYFISH STINGS

Many marine animals sting, including jellyfish, stinging corals and sea anemones. Most sting injuries are minor and will clear up quickly. The most common are caused by jellyfish. When you come in contact with a jellyfish, you are exposed to literally thousands of minute stinging organs in the tentacles, yet the stinging results only in painful local skin irritation. The Portuguese Man-of-War is an exception and its sting has in rare cases resulted in death.

Prevention
1. Do not handle jellyfish. Even beached or apparently dead specimens may sting.
2. Tentacles of some species may dangle as much as 165 ft. Stay away to prevent contact
3. Wet suits or protective clothing should be worn when diving in waters where jellyfish are abundant

First Aid
1. If you're stung, remove any tentacles and attempt to prevent untriggered nematocysts from discharging additional toxins by applying vinegar (acetic acid), 10 percent formalin solution, sodium bicarbonate, boric acid, or xylocaine spray. Vinegar appears to be the most effective in reducing additional nematocyst discharge. DO NOT USE FRESH WATER OR RUB SAND ON THE AREA - you may cause additional nematocyst discharge.
2. Antihistamines or analgesics have been useful in relieving itching and redness. Meat tenderizer may also be useful in relieving the pain.
3. A commercial sea sting kit, available at dive shops, is recommended for jellyfish stings.

SEA URCHIN PUNCTURES
Sea urchins are radial in shape with long spines. They are widespread in the Western Hemisphere. Penetration by the sea urchin spine can cause intense local pain. The spines can go through wetsuits, booties and tennis shoes.

First Aid
1. Large spine fragments may be gently removed but be careful not to break them into smaller fragments that might remain in the wound.
2. Alternately soaking the injured extremity in hot then cold water may help dissolve small fragments.
3. Get medical attention for severe or deep punctures.

Treatment
1. Clean wound.
2. Remove as much of the spine as possible, try first removing those spines which can be grasped with tweezers. Spines which have broken off flush with the skin are nearly impossible to remove and probing around with a needle will only break the spines into little pieces. Most of the spines will be dissolved by the body within a week. Others may fester and can then be removed with tweezers. Some forms have small venomous pinchers which should be removed, and the wound should then re-absorb. Some divers have found the use of a drawing salve helpful.

In severe cases surgical removal may be required when spines are near nerves and joints.

X-rays may be required. Spines can form granulomas months later. Spines may regulate to other sites.

STONEFISH, ZEBRAFISH AND SCORPIONFISH STINGS
Stings by these fish have been known to cause fatalities. Divers and snorkelers should avoid handling them or any venomous fish.

Venomous fish are often found in holes or crevices or lying well camouflaged on rocky bottoms. Divers should be alert for their presence and should take care to avoid them at all times.

First Aid
1. Get victim out of water.
2. Lay patient down.
3. Observe for shock.
4. Wash wound with salt water (cold) or sterile saline solution.

5. Soak wound in hot water for 30 to 90 minutes (not hotter than 50 degrees centigrade or 120 degrees Fahrenheit. Use hot compresses if wound is on the face.
6. Get immediate medical assistance.

SUNBURN
Prevention
Some of the most severe sunburns can be received on cloudy days when the sun is not visible. Snorkelers spending a great deal of time floating face down on top of the water are frequent victims of badly sunburned backs and legs. Long-sleeved shirts and long pants are recommended for snorkelers. At the very least a tee shirt should be worn.

Treatment
A variety of sunburn ointments and sprays are commercially available and should be carried in every dive bag. If no special ointment is available, bandages soaked in tannic acid, boric acid, or vinegar will provide some relief. The victim should avoid further exposure until the condition has passed.

SEA LIONS
Sea Lions are normally harmless. However, during the breeding season, large bull sea lions may be irritated and nip divers. Attempts to handle the animal may result in bites. Bites are similar to dog bites and are rarely severe.

Prevention
Look, but don't touch.

DIVERS ALERT NETWORK
This diving accident network (DAN) was formed in 1981 to assist in the treatment of underwater diving accidents by providing a 24-hour telephone emergency number (919) 684-8111. This number, which may be called collect in emergencies, is received at the national DAN headquarters located at Duke University Medical Center. For medical problems, the caller is connected with a physician experienced in diving medicine. The physicians will assist with diagnosis and initial treatment of an injured diver and supervise referral to appropriate decompression chambers while working with regional coordinators throughout the nation.

DAN does not maintain any treatment facility and does not directly provide any form of treatment, but is a service which complements existing medical systems.

DAN support comes from membership and contributions from the diving industry. It is a not-for-profit, tax-exempt, public service organization.

Members of DAN receive a comprehensive emergency first aid book along with membership card and several decals displaying the emergency phone number. At this writing, membership costs $15 ($20 non U.S. address). Mail should be addressed to: DIVERS ALERT NETWORK Box 3823, Duke University Medical Center, Durham, NC 27710.

DAN now offers medical insurance which, for $25 per year, covers decompression-chamber and air ambulance costs for diving related accidents. Write to DAN for additional information.

Reprinted with permission from Best Dives of the Western Hemisphere, Jon Huber, Joyce Huber & Christopher Loftin & Hunter Publishing Inc., 300 Raritan Center Parkway, Edison, NJ 08818.

How to Choose A Dive/Snorkel Charter?

MARK STANTON
    An avid sport diver since 1978, Mark now makes his living producing the DIVERS DOWN TELEVISION SERIES. In 1986 he began his television career by producing the first 26 episodes which aired on <u>New England Sports Network</u> (NESN). Mark shoots all the underwater footage for the program and is also the on-camera host.

JILL STANTON
    Co-producer of DIVERS DOWN TELEVISION SERIES since its' inception Jill shoots topside camera, scores music, and directs. Her talent at "capturing the unique" on tape helps round out the programs' visual effect. Jill's love for the sea shows through the beautiful footage.

DIVERS DOWN
    Over 85 half hour episodes have been produced to date and the program is now seen in over 60 million homes on regional cable sports networks around the United States. Programs have been shot from Nova Scotia to Bahamas and as far west as California. Divers Down now offers Come-Along Travel for viewers who want to combine a vacation trip with the unique opportunity of being on television.

THE FINER POINTS OF BOAT SELECTION

From the day one completes the final check-out dive in their certification course the quest is on to find the best dive sites. Most times the search begins by literally stepping off from some sandy beach or rocky promontory to explore the depths along the shore. Such strategy brings the diver to the intertidal zones and depths usually not exceeding forty feet. Although the attractions are varied and often spectacular the experience seems somehow incomplete. There is a certain feeling, a sort of magic if you will, of diving from a boat at a site far from shore. It is as if we have been granted the priviledge of visiting a piece of the planet that was never meant for us to see.

Boat diving is generally accepted as the preferred method when compared to beach diving. The chores associated with transporting heavy dive equipment over often rugged terrain, surface snorkel swimming against 'longshore currents, and getting sand or dirt in every possible nook and cranny of one's dive gear are not the greatest motivating factors. Diving from a boat covers a wide spectrum of concepts starting with a one man kayak to a one hundred foot plus liveaboard diveboat. From the smallest to the largest there are common concepts and ultimate benefits. A boat is not only a means of transportation to the dive site but a means for the diver to instill added safety to the act of self immersion.

Unless you have grown up on the water and had the privilege of owning a boat, the sudden need for a vessel can be overwhelming. Boating is an activity which must be handled with as much seriousness as learning to dive. Far too often people jump right in to purchase a boat and end up having major regrets because they were not educated enough to make the proper choice. One of the best ways to avoid this entire scenario is to spend at least a couple of seasons diving from commercial charter boats. You will find that like in any other business there are good and bad operators. Over time you will learn not only who runs a good charter boat, but what specifically allows that boat to be able to offer you an enjoyable day at sea.

Everyone knows that heavily traveled areas like the Caribbean are loaded with dive charter outfits. What is often overlooked, but with less frequency these days, is the rapidly growing domestic charter fleets. With sport diving expansion in the neighborhood of 10 % annually it is not surprising that more and more captains have turned their wheels and set a course for the reefs and wrecks instead of the fishing grounds. What one must be on the lookout for is the operators who have not properly educated themselves to make such a transition. It is rare, but an occasion one might run into a situation where a boat will run with only the bottom line in mind. Minimal effort might be spent on the comfort and safety of the paying customer provided the Coast Guard regulations are met. Obviously one wants to avoid this scenario at all cost, the way to do it ? As with anything in life - RESEARCH !

Word of mouth is perhaps the best advertising any business can have. Charter boats are no exception. If a group spends a day at sea and fulfills their expectations in a safe and comfortable manner at a reasonable price then the word will get out that this is a boat and crew to do business with. Ask other divers for such information and you will find there is a wonderful resource all around you. Once the search is narrowed down to perhaps two or three vessels one should implement a more thorough inspection of the operator. Begin by making phone contact. Remember that you are the customer and pay attention to how you are treated. If possible speak directly with the captain and try to get a feel for his personality. If feasible visit the boat at the dock before making your, decision. An unannounced visit to the marina may be very revealing. Make mental notes for yourself as to how ship shape the vessel appears to be. Make your arrival around the time she pulls in at the end of a charter and observe the behavior of the disembarking passengers. Does it look and sound asif they had a terrific day ? Don't be shy either, ask a few of them what they thought of the trip. Once the off loading is complete, introduce yourself to the captain and divemaster, strike up a conversation about their operation. Ask what dive sites are typically visited. Are there any special services offered ? What is the cost of a charter ? How many passengers are typically on board ? One can save a lot of time and money by doing some basic research.

The way to make any boat trip enjoyable is to offer passengers an interesting trip on a comfortable vessel at a fair price. It is directly up to you as the paying customer as to what is interesting and when the price is reasonable. Conversely it is directly up to the captain and crew as to how comfortable the vessel is. Comfort does not mean plush seating or the like when choosing a dive boat. Instead one should be concerned with the ratio between boat size and complement of passengers. Is there proper attention paid to equipment storage ? Can one climb back aboard easily ? Is there an area where one can get out of the sun ? These and many other factors determine the checks and balances of what makes a good charter boat. Personnel aboard the vessel are as important to your satisfaction as the equipment. Does the dive master properly brief the group on what to expect ? Is the divemaster helpful with dive equipment needs ? Does your in-water experience have a level of comfort and control generated by the understanding of your needs by the divemaster ? If not you may have made the wrong choice.

The performance and skill level of captain and crew can be explored ahead of time, but until one has made direct personal interaction as a paying customer the final determination cannot be made. Regarding the boat and its' amenities however one can easily run down a check list before the boat ever weighs anchor. Some of the things that make a charter boat a professional operation are as follows:

1. AMPLE SECURE SCUBA TANK STORAGE - Whether gunwale mounted racks or below decks bunks, no tank should make the trip rolling around the deck.
2. AMPLE GEAR STORAGE - An accessible area on the main deck of reasonable size should be set aside for each passenger to "work from". Often times a raised motorbox is ideal for this purpose.
3. SEATING - Bench style seating along the gunwale is adequate - provided it does not interfere with rollover entries.
4. FRESH WATER DUNK TANK - Used for initial rinse of camera gear and other sensitive equipment.
5. DRY STORAGE - For clothing, towels, tools, film and other related items. Usually found below decks.
6. HEAD - A clean, comfortable and private facility with proper usage instructions
7. SUN PROTECTION - Some form of overhead canopy is extremely important to avoid heat stroke, sunburn, and other maladies.

8. DIVE PLATFORM - For giant stride entries and easy exits.
9. LONG STURDY LADDER - Style and designs vary as much as the underwater terrain.
10. SCOOT LINE - Runs underwater from stern to anchor rode to assist diver swimming to bow after entry at stern.
11. TAG-LINE - 100' or more of floating line with large float trailing from stern in case a diver misses the anchor line on ascent.
12. HANG-BAR - For multiple divers to hold on during decompression or safety stops. Typically hung from stern area - use a connector line to anchor rode if diving in areas with reduced visibility.
13. HANG-LINES WITH CLIPS AND RINGS - Hung from the boat to safety stop depths to allow divers to "clip" camera gear or tool bags so as not to tire during hang time.
14. UNDERWATER STROBE - Attached to anchor rode 10' off bottom as a beacon for returning at the end of the dive.
15. HANG-TANK - Minimum of 50 cubic foot tank with regulator and octopus hung at 20' depth in case of emergency.
16. COOLER WITH SOFT DRINKS AND FRESH POTABLE WATER - To avoid fluid loss and heatstroke.
17. REDUNDANT ELECTRONIC NAVIGATION & COMMUNICATIONS SYSTEMS - In the event of unit failure or emergency the vessel should not be at a disadvantage to either finding a dive site or communicating to other stations.
18. PROPER DISPLAY OF DIVE AND ALPHA FLAG WHEN APPROPRIATE - Large flags should be waving at a height well above sea level for proper visibility.
19. ANCHOR SYSTEM QUICK-RELEASE WITH MARKER BUOY - In the event that the vessel must leave the dive site due to some emergency such a system would allow divers to hang and wait until the boat returns.
20. PROPER GROUND TACKLE FOR EXPECTED CONDITIONS - Various anchor types, grapnel hook or mooring set ups will all contribute to the ease and access of certain dive sites.

All points considered boat diving and snorkeling is a serious endeavor that demands great respect. To know the sea one has to spend many years with her, then one only knows her. No one controls her. If she is treated gently and her warnings are heeded she will offer unbelievable rewards, measured in visions of the mind's eye as one sits by the fire on a cold snowy eve, memories of wonderful days spent offshore underwater.

Tips for Traveling

Coleman F. Church 3rd

TRAVEL ADVISORY

Check with your State Department or embassy before traveling to another country to see if there is a travel advisory, warning, or any caution that they have posted for your benefit. U.S. State Department Travel Advisory (202) 647-5226.

When you arrive in a politically unsettled country check in with your embassy and leave them a copy of your itinerary.

DOCUMENTS

Call the embassy of the country you are planning to visit and check what papers or visas are required to enter the country. You should also check on their passport requirements. For example: to enter Kenya your passport must have a expiration date that is at least six months after the date of your planned departure from Kenya.

Also check to see if you are required to have any shots or vaccinations before or after your trip (i.e. Malaria). Carry the record of your inoculations with you.

HEALTH

Be sure to bring a sufficient supply of all prescription drugs that you need or feel you may need on your trip. Ask your doctor for copies of your prescriptions and bring them with you in case of loss or theft.

If you wear prescription glasses, be sure to pack an extra pair.

PACKING YOUR SCUBA GEAR

The first thing to pack is your certification card(s) and your log book(s). It is also wise to get a letter from your doctor stating that you are healthy enough to dive.

Always have your gear serviced before a trip.

Pack your gear in the order of suiting up, i.e. your wet suit should go in your bag last since it is the first thing you will put on and your fins and mask first since you will put them on last. Bring along a spare mask and a re-dive kit with extra 0-rings, toothpaste to clean your mask, extra batteries for your lights, an extra head strap for your mask, etc.

Make sure you have a whistle for your BC and take along a small mirror. This way if there is a great deal of boat traffic, you will be able to reflect the sun off the mirror so that someone who is unable to hear you can at least spot you. A small magnifying glass is nice to take along tucked into the pocket of your BC so that you can investigate the little things under water.

Always bring two lights (one as a backup).

Take along plenty of suntan oil, a long sleeve shirt and a hat - many boats do not offer protection from the sun.

Bring as much film as you think you will need -then double that amount. You inevitably run out of film, and it can be very expensive and sometimes difficult to find. Do not let them run it through the x-ray machine at the airport, as it can ruin the quality. Carry it in a separate bag so that it is easy to both find and remove from your carry on luggage and you can hand it to the inspector at the airport. In addition, you should carry all of your expensive camera equipment with you. Cameras have a tendency to disappear from luggage that is checked.

If possible, it is wise to carry your regulator separately for the same reason. Mares sells a great little regulator bag that doubles as a cooler when you arrive at your destination.

MONEY

Make a duplicate list of your travelers check numbers and leave it with a trusted friend or in a safety deposit box in your room or at the front desk of your hotel. Make a list of your credit cards that you are taking with you and do the same as with the travelers checks.

The best rate of exchange is usually at a bank in the foreign country you are visiting. Never carry a great deal of cash on your person, but do always have a few U.S. dollars -they can perform miracles worldwide.

DRESS CODE

Take along a change of clothes in your carry on luggage if possible so that if your luggage is lost you will have something to wear until it arrives.

Leave all expensive jewelry etc. at home. Traveling with it is only an invitation for trouble.

Do dress accordingly when you travel and respect the dress code of other countries.

AIRPORT

Try to arrive two hours ahead of your scheduled time of departure for international flights and flights to small islands on lesser known airlines. It is a real bore, but you just might find yourself bumped from a flight or miss your flight because of long lines at the airport (This happened to us in the Dominican Republic and in Greece).

Take along a large bottle of water (i.e. one of those large Evian or Poland Spring plastic bottles) and drink it throughout your flight. Rule of thumb is for every hour in the air a passenger should consume one 8 ounce glass of water. This will help with jet lag and help you adjust to any increases in elevation at your destination. Remember, drinking alcohol on the plane only dehydrates you. The effects from alcohol are greater in the air than on the land, so be careful of the amount you drink, you will get intoxicated quicker than you realize.

Never take pictures at the airport. Many officials will take your film and occasionally your camera, and in critical instances you and your camera.

Last, but not least, NEVER DIVE OR SNORKEL ALONE.

Please share your traveling tips with us. We are here to help and assist you. If you have any questions or comments, please contact: Divers Exchange International, Inc., 37 West Cedar Street, Boston, MA, 02114. Telephone: (617) 723-7134; Fax (617) 227-8145.

Camps for Kids – France

Smithy McIntosh

I, Smithy McIntosh, am the Director of Camp Marchand along with my mother Rosalie Tallman. When I turned twelve, my family moved to rural France to renovate a typical Perigourdine farmhouse and establish a summer camp for young Americans. I lived year round in the village of Monsac for seven years and spent the last twelve summers being a part of our program. Today, our goal as directors is to constantly improve the camp.

Diving with Camp Marchand in Rural France

Camp Marchand is like no other camp in the world. It's the only residential camp for Americans in all of France. Our program is based at an 18th century farm in the Dordogne region. We offer numerous classes, excursions, social events, and more recently, scuba diving.

Camp Marchand's goal has always been to offer children a wealth of educational opportunities, as well as lots good old fashioned fun. Today, the camp offers two four-week sessions per Summer to 45 children ages 11-16. Each participant in the program takes four classes, each meeting six hours per week.

One of these classes must be a French class. Our French program is unique due to our native French instructors, as well as its hands on approach. Aside from the classroom situation, the students venture into markets, cafes, cheese makers, local vineyards, in order to practice their newly acquired language skills. Participants are taught how to speak the everyday language and live the everyday life of the Perigord region. To top it off, half of every camp meal is conducted entirely in French, so table talk is definitely a strong point.

Besides French, campers choose three of our class offerings; French cooking, Tennis, Photography, Creations, and Rock Climbing / Mountain Biking. Each of these classes enables students to benefit from certain aspects of the region.

Last, but definitely not least, is the recently added Scuba class. We offered this class for the first time in the Summer of 1992, and it was a great success! We certified 19 campers and three staff members as PADI Open Water Divers. Our English instructor held classes in the large pool at Marchand, as well as in the classroom with the aid of his slides and videos.

At the end of each session, the entire camp heads to the Mediterranean coast, the Loire valley, and Paris. During the Mediterranean stay, the dive students head to the village of Cerbere, where they stay in a campground, and perform their checkout dives from the shore. I fortunately found these dive sites thanks to some great French divers that I met in the nearby city of Narbonne. We have performed about 15 dives together in this area and still stay in touch. The diving in this area offers a wealth of underwater sites, especially for new divers. The rock formations are imposing and offer great opportunities for the campers to see numerous octopus, reef fish, beautiful red starfish, and much more. For more experienced divers, magnificent deep dives and night dives are a must!

The great aspect of this location is the sense of responsibility and camaraderie gained here by the young divers. The detachment from the bulk of the camp, accompanied by the three divers/counselors, is a great advantage. The young divers camp together, cook together, wash gear together, and generally help each other through the hardships of their first ocean dives. I feel that every member of each group leaves the village a better and stronger person.

We at Camp Marchand are definitely planning on offering this unique Mediterranean experience to divers over the age of sixteen. Aside from the diving, the beautiful fishing villages, towering hills, vineyards, and of course, wonderful cuisine should be explored by all.

For more information on Camp Marchand contact Divers Exchange International, 37 West Cedar Street, Boston, MA, 02114. Telephone: (617) 723-7134 Fax: (617) 227-8145.